WINDOWS 3
SECRETS

By Brian Livingston
InfoWorld Windows Columnist

Foreword by Cheryl Currid
Founder and President, Currid & Company

IDG Books Worldwide, Inc.
An International Data Group Company
San Mateo, California 94402

Windows 3 Secrets

Published by
IDG Books Worldwide, Inc.
An International Data Group Company
155 Bovet Road, Suite 730
San Mateo, CA 94402
415-358-1250

Library of Congress Catalog Card No.: 91-72756

ISBN 1-878058-23-1

Printed in the United States of America

10 9 8 7 6 5 4 3 2 1

Project Manager: Janna Custer, Senior Editor
Editor-in-Chief: Michael E. McCarthy
Production Manager: Lana Olson
Technical review by Dan Willis, Senior Analyst, 3M Corp.
Text preparation and proofreading by Shirley E. Coe
Indexing by Ty Koontz
Interior design by Peppy White and Francette Ytsma
Production by University Graphics, Palo Alto, California

Distributed in the United States by IDG Books Worldwide Inc.
Distributed in Canada by Macmillan of Canada, a Division of Canada Publishing Corporation.

For information on translations and availability in other countries, contact Marc Mikulich, Foreign Rights Manager, at IDG Books Worldwide. Fax 415-358-1260.

For sales inquiries and special prices for bulk quantities, write to the address above or call IDG Books Worldwide at 415-358-1250.

Dedication

This book is dedicated to my wife, Margie.

Acknowledgement

The publisher would like to give special thanks to Bill Murphy, without whom this book would not have been possible.

About the Author

Brian Livingston, *InfoWorld* Windows columnist, is the president of Windows Consulting in New York City, which specializes in converting companies from character-based to graphical-based applications.

Mr. Livingston has been involved with computers since 1968, when he first learned programming in Fortran IV on the IBM 360 mainframe series.

After working in mainframe environments, Mr. Livingston moved to the DEC VAX architecture. In this setting, he concentrated on developing minicomputer database applications for a variety of companies. He was responsible for the development of early electronic funds transfer software, and accomplished one of the first successful merge-purge operations to combine voter-registration lists with 1980 U.S. Census data.

Most recently, Mr. Livingston has been responsible for projects using the Windows and Macintosh environments across networks. He has helped companies convert from DOS to a complete suite of Windows applications, and move from copper-based to fiber-optic networks.

Mr. Livingston is a member of the InfoWorld Review Board and PC World's User Advisory Board, and is a Contributing Editor to *Systems Integration* magazine and The Cobb Group's computer newsletters. He was a member of the Board of Directors of the Microcomputer Managers Association from 1987 to 1991, and chaired the Micro Standards Committee, sponsored by the MMA and others, for two years. Mr. Livingston frequently speaks at such events as Comdex, PC Expo, the Windows & OS/2 Conference, Unix Expo, and other industry conferences.

About IDG Books Worldwide

Welcome to the world of IDG Books Worldwide.

International Data Group (IDG) is the world's leading publisher of computer periodicals, with more than 150 weekly and monthly newpapers and magazines reaching 25 million readers in more than 40 countries. If you use personal computers, IDG Books is committed to publishing quality books that meet your needs. We rely on our extensive network of publications — including such leading periodicals as *Computerworld, InfoWorld, Macworld, PC World, Portable Computing, Publish, Network World, SunWorld, AmigaWorld,* and *GamePro* — to help us make informed and timely decisions in creating useful computer books that meet your needs.

With every IDG book we strive to bring extra value and skill-building instruction to the reader. Our books are written by experts, with the backing of IDG periodicals, and with careful thought devoted to issues such as audience, interior design, use of icons, and illustrations. Our editorial staff is a careful mix of high-tech journalists and experienced book people. Our close contact with the makers of computer products helps ensure accuracy and thorough coverage. Our heavy use of personal computers at every step in production means we can deliver books in the most timely manner.

We are delivering books of high quality at competitive prices, on topics customers want. At IDG, we believe in quality, and we have been delivering quality for 25 years. You'll find no better book on a subject than an IDG book.

Jonathan Sacks
President
IDG Books Worldwide, Inc.

International Data Group's publications include: ARGENTINA'S Computerworld Argentina; ASIA'S Computerworld Hong Kong. Computerworld Southeast Asia, Computerworld Malaysia. Computerworld Singapore, Infoworld Hong Kong, Infoworld SE Asia; AUSTRALIA'S Computerworld Australia, PC World, Macworld, Lotus, Publish; AUSTRIA'S Computerwelt Oesterreich; BRAZIL'S DataNews, PC Mundo, Automacao & Industria; BULGARIA'S Computer Magazine Bulgaria, Computerworld Bulgaria; CANADA'S ComputerData, Direct Access, Graduate CW, Macworld; CHILE'S Informatica, Computacion Personal; COLUMBIA'S Computerworld Columbia; CZECHOSLOVAKIA'S Computerworld Czechoslovakia, PC World; DENMARK'S CAD/CAM WORLD, Computerworld Danmark, PC World, Macworld, UnixWorld, PC LAN World, Communications World; FINLAND'S Mikro PC, Tietoviikko; FRANCE'S Le Mond Informatique, Distributique, InfoPC, Telecoms International; GERMANY'S AmigaWelt, Computerwoche, Information Management, PC Woche, PC Welt, Unix Welt, Macwelt RD; GREECE'S Computerworld, PC World, Macworld; HUNGARY'S Computerworld SZT, Mikrovilag; INDIA'S Computers & Communications; ISRAEL'S People & Computers; ITALY'S Computerworld Italia, PC World Italia; JAPAN'S Computerworld Japan, Macworld, SunWorld Journal; KOREA'S Computerworld, PC World; MEXICO'S Computerworld Mexico, PC Journal; THE NETHERLAND'S Computerworld Netherlands, PC World, AmigaWorld; NEW ZEALAND'S Computerworld New Zealand, PC World New Zealand; NIGERIA'S PC World Africa; NORWAY'S Conputerworld Norge, PC World Norge CAD/CAM, Macworld Norge; PEOPLE'S REPUBLIC OF CHINA'S China Computerworld, China Computerworld Monthly; PHILLIPPINE'S Computerworld Phillippines, PC Digest/PC World; POLAND'S Komputers Magazine, Computerworld; ROMANIA'S Infoclub; SPAIN'S CIM World, Communicaciones World, Computerworld Espana, PC World, AmigaWorld; SWEDEN'S ComputerSweden, PC/Nyhetherna, Mikrodatorn, PC World, Macworld; SWITZERLAND'S Computerworld Schweiz, Macworld; TAIWAN'S Computerworld Taiwan, PC World, Publish; THAILAND'S Computerworld; TURKEY'S Computerworld Monitor, PC World/Turkiye; UNITED KINGDOM'S Graduate Computerworld, PC Business World, ICL Today, Lotus UK, Macworld UK; UNITED STATES' AmigaWorld, A+, CIO, Computerworld, Digital News, Federal Computer Week, GamePro, InfoWorld, Lotus, Macworld, Network World, NextWorld, PC Games, PC World, Portable Office, PC Letter, Publish, Run, SunWorld Journal; USSR'S MIR PC, Computerworld, Computer Express, Network, Manager Magazine; VENEZUELA'S Computerworld Venezuela, Micro Computerworld; YUGOSLAVIA'S Moj Mikro

Contents

Tables and Reference Charts

Foreword

by Cheryl Currid
President, Currid & Company

Brian Livingston has earned his stripes on his way to becoming one of the country's preeminent Windows gurus. He's completed exhaustive research and study into the inner workings of one of America's favorite software programs. Through these several hundred pages, you'll see his special techniques and secrets unfold. Brian has carefully and painstakingly documented everything you always wanted to know about Windows but were afraid (or didn't know enough) to ask.

Windows 3.0 has taken corporate and personal computing by storm. From its May 1990 introduction, Windows has taken a place in computer history as one of the most significant software products to be introduced.

But installing and maintaining Windows 3.0 is often no small feat. Because Windows will run on just about any combination of personal computer hardware and software, it can be a challenge to maintain. The challenge comes with many subtleties that lie just below the level of many users' understanding.

In this book, *Windows 3 Secrets*, Brian gives you his experience and warns you about the tricks and traps of getting Windows installed, optimized, and working on any number of computer configurations. His work can save you thousands of hours in fine-tuning the Windows configuration and setup.

Brian's work is geared to both the novice and the expert. In each section he provides enough information and background to take the reader through the steps and the learning process. This book could save readers thousands of dollars of support charges!

Chapter 1
Read This First

Reading this chapter will help you get the most information from this book in the least possible time.

Windows 3 Secrets is designed to give you power over the complexity of Windows. While Windows' cute icons give it an easy-to-use look, anyone who has used Windows for a while has found there's a lot going on underneath the surface that is not explained in the manual.

If you are already experienced in Windows, I believe *Windows 3 Secrets* will give you control over the optimization of Windows in ways you may not have known. If you are a beginner to Windows, this book can help make you an expert.

How to Use This Book

If you have not yet installed Windows:
You should turn immediately to section C, "Configuring Your System," and start reading from Chapter 15. Then turn back to Chapter 2 and continue from there.

If you are a new PC user:
You should also read Chapter 15, especially the box entitled "The Least You Need to Know About DOS" then turn to Chapter 2.

If you are experienced in DOS and Windows:
Continue from here right on to Chapter 2.

Who This Book Is For

I truly believe that whether you are an expert or a beginner, you can learn things in this book that you might otherwise never know about Windows. I've researched and written *Windows 3 Secrets* to give you access to Windows' *undocumented features, unexpected anomalies,* and some much-needed *workarounds*. This book is a road map (with some overview to help novices learn the lay of the land) leading to many details for Windows pros to explore. But there are a few things this book is *not.*

This book is not an "introduction to Windows." Most computer software books today are like this — mainly a rewrite of a software program's manual, but in a more conversational, readable style. Such books usually explain each of the menu items in a piece of software and describe the choices in a more organized way than the manual, but don't really give you anything you couldn't find in the manual itself.

You wouldn't think Windows would need many introductory books of this kind, because all its menus are in plain sight and are explained by Windows' built-in Help system (simply press F1). Therefore, if a topic is described adequately in the official Windows manual, I haven't included it here. But if you need help pulling down Windows' menus and figuring out what they do, you should first peruse the Windows manual or obtain a book for Windows beginners such as *Windows 3 Companion*, by Lori Lorenz & R. Michael O'Mara (Microsoft Press, 1990), or *Windows 3 Power Tools,* by The LeBlond Group (Bantam Books, 1991).

On the other side of the coin, this is not a book for programmers who develop Windows applications in the C language. Many of the undocumented features described in this book will be helpful to programmers using Windows, but this is not a programming book. If you program in C, an excellent book on Windows coding techniques is *Peter Norton's Windows 3.0 Power Programming Techniques,* by Peter Norton and Paul Yao (Bantam Books, 1990).

This book is for everyone in the middle — if you've learned how to pull down the menus, but you're not interested in rewriting Windows yourself, *Windows 3 Secrets* will show you what you need to make Windows work for you.

How Commands Are Explained

Although Windows makes many things possible at the click of a mouse, there are times when it is faster to type a command at the keyboard. When I show such a command in this book, for clarity it's on a separate line or lines, or is in a different typestyle when embedded in the text of a paragraph.

Sometimes, you must type a command exactly as shown. In other cases, you may substitute some parts of the command with a name that is specific to your particular PC. All commands in this book indicate the differences among these parts of commands by the following rules:

1. Parts you must type exactly as shown appear in ALL CAPITALS.

2. Parts you may substitute appear in "lowercase" letters.

3. Parts that are optional appear in curly braces {like this}.

For example, the following command typed at a DOS prompt shows you a directory listing of all files that match the filenames you specified (and, if you wish, pauses when the screen fills up):

```
DIR filename {/P}
```

When such a command appears embedded in the text of a paragraph, it appears in SMALL CAPITALS and *italics,* such as DIR *filename* {/P}. One exception to this rule is batch files, which appear with most commands in uppercase.

Whenever you see the term *filename,* you can substitute any full-length filename specification. In the command above, instead of *filename* you could type MYFILE.DOC, C:\WINDOWS*.DOC, or anything that DOS recognizes as the complete specification for one or more filenames.

Special keys on the keyboard are indicated by an initial capital letter, such as Enter, Tab, Backspace, Shift, Alt, Ctrl (control), and Esc (escape). These keys are not indicated by a special typographic convention (because you know not to type "e-n-t-e-r" when I say "press Enter"). In a few cases where there might be some confusion, these keys are surrounded by square brackets to indicate that they should be pressed, not typed, as in

```
[Tab][Tab]Sincerely yours...
```

If one of the shift keys (Shift, Alt, or Ctrl) should be *held down* at the same time that you also press another key, the two keys are shown together, separated by a plus sign. "Ctrl+A" means *hold down the Ctrl key, then press the A key, then release both.* "Ctrl+Shift+A" means hold down both Ctrl and Shift while you press A, and so on.

If you are supposed to *let up* on a key *before* pressing another one, those keys are separated by commas. In Windows, pressing and releasing the Alt key activates the main menu. In order to pull down File on the main menu and choose the Open command, I might say "press Alt+F, O to run File Open." As you can see in this paragraph, menus you can pull down from the keyboard with the Alt key have an underscore beneath the letter you press.

Windows Terms

You probably already know that Windows operates in one of three different modes on your particular computer system. These are called *real mode, standard mode,* and *386 enhanced mode.* In this book, I use the following terms for standard mode interchangeably: *standard mode, 286 protected mode,* WIN /S, and WIN /2. Similarly, the terms *386 enhanced mode, 386 mode, enhanced mode, 386 protected mode,* and WIN /3 are all interchangeable. Both standard mode and 386 mode use the "protected mode" of Intel's 286 and 386 processors. So if I say that Windows is in *protected mode* this means either standard mode or 386 mode.

In cases where I have described concepts that are relevant to word processing or spreadsheet applications, I have used Word for Windows and Excel as examples of such applications. Market studies consistently show that these are the applications most often used in Windows computing. But this does not imply any recommendation of these products over others that may be better suited to your needs, such as word processors like Amí Professional and WordPerfect for Windows, or spreadsheets like Wingz and 1-2-3/W.

How to Find the Good Parts

I have organized this book so you can sit down and read it straight through, from Chapter 1 to the end, like a mystery novel. But to help you quickly jump to the information you need for your particular PC configuration, there are some features of this book you should know about: the icons that point to helpful items in the text, and the book's overall structure.

The Icons

The following icons in the margin indicate a nearby paragraph or para-graphs of particular interest.

Undocumented Features are items that are not explained in the Windows manual, or are described inadequately (if at all) in the README.TXT file that comes with Windows. These features may have been left out of the manual either because they were added after the manual was written or because they were "too powerful" for end users.

Workarounds are procedures or temporary fixes that can help you solve a problem or add functionality to your configuration. In many cases, you are given more than one alternative to get around a particular situation. It is your choice whether to implement one of these alternatives or wait until the situation changes in a future release of Windows or a related product.

Error Messages Decoded are explanations of dialog boxes that Windows displays when problems occur. Sometimes the correct response to these problems is not well described by these dialog boxes, or the correct re-sponse is actually the exact opposite of what the dialog box suggests. There is no complete list of messages, but this is a guide to the most misunder-stood ones.

The Book's Overall Structure

Windows 3 Secrets is organized into four sections:

Section A: Optimizing Your Software discusses Windows and software applications that run under it (both Windows and non-Windows).

Section B: Exploiting Your Hardware covers hardware that Windows runs on, including all PCs and PC peripheral devices.

Section C: Configuring Your System describes how to configure your software and hardware to optimize Windows.

Section D: Excellence in Windows Shareware explains each of the Windows shareware programs on the diskettes that accompany this book.

Within these sections, the chapters may be summarized as follows:

Chapter 1: Read This First (this chapter) contains important information about the book as a whole.

Section A: Optimizing Your Software

Chapter 2: Customizing Your Windows Start-Up describes undocumented features of Windows that allow you to change the logo it displays, define a start-up routine that executes automatically, and set up the File Manager so it runs fast.

Chapter 3: Secrets of the Windows Applets explains features of the "bundled" mini-applications — the Control Panel, Executive, Paintbrush, and others — that you may not be aware of.

Chapter 4: Secrets of Windows Applications delves into little-known aspects of running graphical applications such as Word for Windows, Adobe Type Manager, Intermission, and others.

Chapter 5: Secrets of DOS Under Windows describes methods to get the most out of non-Windows applications, including multitasking and sharing data.

Chapter 6: Programming in WordBasic explains several aspects of the Basic language, which eventually will appear in all major Windows applications, including several undocumented key codes that can be used in Word for Windows and other programs.

Section B: Exploiting Your Hardware

Chapter 7: Computers explains the real differences between various brands of PCs, including information on BIOS incompatibilities, differences in extended memory handling, and quirks in specific models of machines.

Chapter 8: Disk Drives includes detailed information on problems under Windows that have caused the total loss of information on hard disks larger than 32MB in size, as well as configuration secrets of CD-ROM players, Bernoulli drives, floppy drives, and other media.

Chapter 9: Keyboards defines the entire character set available from the keyboard under Windows, in addition to several anomalies of 84-key and 101-key keyboards in general and various keyboard brands in specific.

Chapter 10: Mice and Pointing Devices examines the differences in configuration among Logitech, Mouse Systems, and Microsoft-compatible mice and trackballs, and describes some of the conflicts that can make these sensitive little rodents stop working.

Chapter 11: Modems and Communications unveils the mysterious world of electronic communications under Windows, including undocumented settings that must be added for Windows to work with certain modems and communication ports.

Chapter 12: Networks describes ways to set up Windows on a network that can give you greater ease-of-use and power than on a stand-alone PC (not necessarily the "official" way to set it up).

Chapter 13: Printers covers several differences among Windows' handling of LaserJet, PostScript, dot-matrix, and other printing devices.

Chapter 14: Video Boards and Monitors explains the little-understood overlap between the areas of memory above 640K that video boards use and the same areas of memory that Windows tries to use.

Section C: Configuring Your System

Chapter 15: Installing and Configuring Windows should be the first chapter in this book that Windows beginners should read, and the first chapter that Windows experts should turn to for some important facts about your CONFIG.SYS and AUTOEXEC.BAT files.

Chapter 16: Using Memory Managers details ways to get the most out of your memory by using Windows' HIMEM.SYS, Quarterdeck Office Systems' QEMM386, and Qualitas's 386Max — including what to do when things go wrong.

Chapter 17: Configuring DOS 5 for Windows adds even more ways to utilize memory with this important upgrade.

Chapter 18: WIN.INI AND SYSTEM.INI Reference provides you with quick reference charts describing every command in these two files.

Section D: Excellence in Windows Shareware

How to Use This Windows Shareware describes the products that have been determined the best shareware for Windows, followed by separate chapters on the various programs.

Giving You the Best Explanation Possible _____

Since there is no technical support hotline available for books, I've tried to include in one place everything you might need to know on each particular subject. For this reason, I may describe a procedure in one chapter that is also touched on in another chapter on a related subject. This minor repetition should make it much easier for you to follow each discussion, rather than making you flip from chapter to chapter to follow a step-by-step explanation. If you run across a detail that you learned previously, simply skip to the next topic.

One of the worst offenses that a computer book can commit is to resort to a phrase like, "It is important to do *XYZ;* you can find a description of how to do this in your DOS manual." In most cases, it would have been just as brief for the author to state the exact syntax that the reader should use — and it certainly would be more helpful. In this book, therefore, I have included this precise information wherever appropriate in each chapter. If you already know the syntax of a DOS or Windows command, you can skip the line that defines it, but it doesn't hurt to have this information at your fingertips in *Windows 3 Secrets*.

The *ultimate* crime by authors is to describe some important configuration information, then say, "Experiment until you find the correct values." Such an author has condemned hundreds or thousands of readers to boring trial-and-error. He or she could have spared readers this effort by performing the experiments in the first place and describing a general rule of thumb for people to follow. Wherever possible, I have tried to give you this kind of formula, instead of teasing you with some optimization trick but forcing you to do all the work.

As Windows Evolves _____

No software company remains successful for long without upgrading its products, and Microsoft is no exception. Windows is certain to expand its capabilities and change its features through the years. As it does, certain secrets and tricks may change as well. In fact, you may never know exactly *when* Windows has changed. Microsoft and many other companies are known to make changes to their software products without announcing the differences or (in some cases) even changing the version numbers. Prior to Windows 3.0, Windows/286 was sold in versions numbered 2.1, 2.1a, 2.1b,

2.1c, and 2.1d — but none of these changes was announced, even though most of the revisions kept one or more Windows applications from working the same way as before. (These applications were "broken" until patches could be distributed.)

Additionally, some of the features of Windows may or may not work the same way on your particular configuration as they do on other people's configurations. I have tried to describe as many of these anomalies as possible, but there is no way to define every eventuality. Make sure that you test any novel features of Windows on dummy data files before trying them on the only copy of, say, your name-and-address database.

Further, I've listed contact phone numbers for dozens of sources of information throughout this book. But we all know that these numbers change over time. For this reason, I've included as many different addresses, 800 numbers, fax numbers, and other contact methods as were available for each source, in the hope that at least *one* of these would stay the same through most moves. And since Microsoft and many other Windows vendors are located in the United States, but their 800 numbers do not work outside the U.S., I've included direct-dial numbers too so you can call that number from wherever you are in the world (if you can't reach representatives of these companies in the country where you are located). For Windows technical support, call Microsoft at 206-637-7098; see Appendix A for more support numbers.

Why I'm Telling You All This

Reading page after page of Windows anomalies, secrets, and incompatibilities in this book, you might say, "Why the description of all these problems? Don't you like Windows?"

I *love* Windows. Having used Macintosh networks and Sun workstations, I keep coming back to Windows. I can use its clicky icons, or I can race through a string of commands at a DOS prompt under Windows, if I please. Its familiarity and its compatibility with all kinds of relatively inexpensive hardware from a variety of vendors in a free, competitive market is a joy.

I strongly believe that revealing all possible information about how Windows works — when it works well and when it doesn't — will cause Windows to sell more copies than if this information were unavailable.

Companies that are interested in converting to Windows are far more likely to do so if all the information about it is widely available — the devil you know is far less fearsome than the one you don't. Once you have precise information on a product's behavior in a wide variety of circumstances, you can live within those limits (until the next release). If Windows' behavior seems erratic for no reason, the reaction of an individual or a company is likely to be postponement of a conversion, not acceptance.

As more facts about Windows become available, Windows' adoption becomes far more possible for people who otherwise might not have had all the information they needed.

Where Are the Acknowledgements?

Most authors place the names of helpful people in tiny type around the "legal matter" section of their books. This ensures that few readers will find these names. I have chosen, instead, to acknowledge people who provided information — to me or to the computer-users community in general — within the body of the text where it is likely that you will actually notice them.

Much of the information in this book originated in documents created by people who were not personally identified. This includes Microsoft internal documents and bulletin-board systems, PC manufacturer's technical notices, and anonymous E-mail messages. (I haven't included any anomalies I could not confirm with either Microsoft or another authoritative source.) I am grateful to the people who created these technical papers.

Beyond the people who provided individual facts, however, I want to thank the people who provided this book with background and context on Windows. This includes Cheryl Currid (an inspiration to us all), Dan Willis (a better manager than I'll ever be), Ed Robbins, Harlan Lax, Jorge Torres, Nancy Blagman, and Willi Martinez (true Windows professionals), David and Sharon Dean, and everyone at the Windows & OS/2 Conference, the Association of Shareware Professionals, the Windows & Presentation Manager Association, Windows Users Group Network, InfoWorld, IDG Books Worldwide, Quarterdeck FaxPress, Lotus Prompt, and my friends at Microsoft OnLine — many of whom must remain nameless here so they can stay in their jobs and continue providing invaluable information on Windows to the world.

Thank you all, and I certainly hope you enjoy the book!

SECTION A

OPTIMIZING YOUR SOFTWARE

Chapter 2
Customizing Your Windows Start-Up

In this chapter...

I'll help you customize your Windows start-up by discussing:

▶ Undocumented features that allow you to start Windows without it displaying the Windows advertising screen that normally appears.

▶ Ways to trick Windows into displaying *your* favorite logo screen instead of merely suppressing the display of the Windows logo.

▶ How to compress bitmap graphics files so they take up less space on your hard disk, but still work to display your favorite graphic as a logo screen.

▶ How to configure the Windows Program Manager so it uses less memory when you start Windows.

▶ Undocumented features of the Recorder that allow you to command Windows to start up in a certain way or with a certain configuration, just as the AUTOEXEC.BAT file commands DOS to configure itself in a certain way.

▶ How to use the Recorder to operate on the Windows File Manager, dramatically speeding up its performance.

▶ Methods you can use to define icons in the Program Manager to run almost *any* series of Windows tasks automatically, not just start up a single application.

▶ Alternative programs, some of which are included on the diskettes that accompany this book, that offer you even more control over start-up configuration and behavior.

Do you remember the first day you saw Windows 3.0 running? I do. It was such an improvement over the look and feel of DOS — and, if you used Windows 2.*x,* such an improvement over *that* — that you were probably drawn into a period of exploration and experimentation of Windows to see what this new, colorful environment could do.

I'd like to encourage that sense of exploration of Windows. And what better place to start exploring Windows than to examine the ways, documented and undocumented, that Windows starts itself. When we know the secrets behind the way Windows starts itself and looks around for commands that we've ordered it to carry out, we gain a great deal of power and control over Windows that we wouldn't have without this knowledge.

This chapter is not an "introduction" for beginners — although beginners will profit from the techniques unveiled here — but a key into the very inner workings of Windows. I use the techniques described in this chapter every day when I start Windows, and I hope you'll find some of them useful as well.

If you haven't yet installed Windows on your personal computer, turn directly to the chapters in the section "Configuring Your System" and start there; then return to this chapter so you can see for yourself how these techniques work.

WIN.COM

Undocumented Ways to Start Windows

Almost every Windows user learns that WIN.COM is the program that starts Windows. The very first section of the Windows manual explains that you must type WIN at a DOS prompt to begin.

But most people don't know how WIN.COM works when it starts Windows, and how to make this start-up program work to customize your computer system.

Windows, as you are probably aware, runs in one of three different modes, depending on the capabilities of the PC it is running on. You can force Windows to start up in any one of these three modes (if your system is capable of the mode you want) if you start WIN.COM with the following "switches":

WIN /R	starts Windows in real mode
WIN /S or WIN /2	starts Windows in standard mode
WIN /3	starts Windows in 386 enhanced mode

Real Mode is for PCs that are limited to 640 kilobytes (K) of memory. This mode is also the only mode that Windows can run in on an XT-class computer — but other limitations (as described in the Computers chapter) make it unlikely that many people will want to run Windows on an XT.

Standard Mode requires a 286-class computer or higher, and at least 1 megabyte (MB) of memory (actually, 640K of conventional memory plus 256K of extended memory on top of that, for a total of 896K).

386 Enhanced Mode requires at least a 386-class computer, and at least 2MB of RAM (actually, 640K plus 1024K of extended RAM). Additionally, although it doesn't say this anywhere in the Windows manual, you must have 5 to 6MB of free hard disk space in order to run 386 enhanced mode reliably on a machine with as little as 2MB of RAM. Without this much free disk space for Windows to write its "temporary files," large print jobs may abort, and it may not be possible to start one or more DOS sessions under Windows. For these reasons, 3 or 4MB of RAM is a preferable minimum requirement to run enhanced mode on a 386-based system. For more information on this, see the 386 section in Chapter 7.

A peek at the WIN.COM program reveals that it is a tiny thing — under 4,000 bytes in size. How does this miniscule program display the elaborate Windows graphical user interface?

It doesn't. WIN.COM is simply a *loader* of the programs that do the real work of Windows. WIN.COM inspects your PC's configuration — the amount of memory and the type of processor your system has — and turns control over to one of several programs that run Windows in real mode, standard mode, or enhanced mode. WIN.COM doesn't turn control over to the successor program, however, until the WIN loader has first: (1) switched your PC monitor into whatever graphics mode it is capable of, and (2) displayed the Microsoft Windows logo. It is at this exact point that we can customize WIN.COM to our own needs — dispensing with the Windows logo and displaying instead any graphic you please, even your own logo!

First, let's examine some of the simpler customizations of WIN.COM, and then move on to the more complex.

It is widely known that if you want to start Windows without watching the Windows logo come up every time, you can type a program name after the

WIN command, as a parameter to WIN.COM itself. For example, you might call for the Windows Calculator when you start Windows by typing:

WIN CALC

This method does start Windows without displaying the Windows logo, and the Calculator does appear on-screen automatically, ready for your use. (The Calculator program, of course, must be located on your DOS Path or you must specify the full name of the program, such as C:\UTIL\CALC, for this to work.)

But the disadvantage is that if you are using a Windows program like the Program Manager as the command center for Windows (the *shell*), running a parameter like CALC after WIN reduces the Program Manager to an icon instead of leaving it open on-screen, where you could select programs from it after you are through using the Calculator. This is a minor inconvenience — you can double-click on the Program Manager icon and restore it to its open, unfolded position on the screen — but there is a better way.

An undocumented feature of WIN.COM is that it starts Windows without displaying the Windows advertising logo, *if* you add a space and a colon (:) after the command WIN. It looks like this:

WIN :

The colon after the command WIN has the effect of starting Windows without switching into graphics mode and displaying the usual advertising screen. Starting Windows in this way also has the beneficial effect of not minimizing whatever shell program, such as the Program Manager, you are using. Another way to get the same effect is to type WIN and a space, followed by pressing the F7 key, then Enter. On the command line this looks like WIN ^@. Since this "Ctrl+At sign" after WIN does the same as a colon after WIN, the remainder of this discussion will use only the colon method in all examples.

(Windows 2.*x* users may recall that the undocumented method to start that version of Windows without displaying the advertising logo was to type WIN followed by a space and the Enter key. That no longer works with Windows 3.*x*. Additionally, Windows 2.*x* experts knew that they could start an application such as Excel without also starting Windows' MS-DOS Executive — thereby saving valuable memory — by typing WIN:EXCEL, with no spaces between WIN, the colon, and EXCEL. This, too, no longer works.)

Using a colon on the WIN command line introduces a few complications. For one thing, any switches such as /R, /S, or /3 must come *before* the colon or any program names that you want Windows to load. These command lines would be correct:

```
WIN /S :

WIN /3 EXCEL MYSHEET.XLS
```

But these command lines would not:

```
WIN : /S

WIN : EXCEL
```

The rule for the use of WIN.COM can be expressed in this way:

```
WIN {modes} {program name} {parameters}
```

where *modes* can be /R, /S, /2, or /3; *program name* can be a colon or any executable program; and *parameters* are any filenames or other parameters the program supports.

These rules are a little complicated to remember, when all you want to do is get rid of the advertising screen when you start Windows. One way to cope with this is to use a text editor to write a small batch file that starts Windows without its logo screen, whether or not you type in any program parameters to WIN.COM. The batch file shown in Figure 2-1, which I call W to make running it shorter than typing WIN, allows you to type in any parameters to WIN.COM (as long as the mode switches come first). But if you just type W with *no* parameters after it, Windows is forced to start without its advertising screen, just as though you'd remembered to add the trailing colon.

W.BAT starts Windows without its logo screen by checking to see whether any parameters that you typed when starting the batch file could be a program name. If so, that program will prevent Windows from displaying its logo screen. If not, the batch file automatically adds a colon to the WIN command, so you don't have to remember to. The statement

```
if "%1"=="" set LOGO=:
```

tests whether the first parameter to the batch file is blank. If so, then *all* the parameters must be blank, and the batch file sets up a variable called LOGO containing the necessary colon for WIN.COM.

```
@echo off
c:
cd \win
set LOGO=
if "%1"=="" set LOGO=:
for %%P in (R r S s 2 3) do if %1==/%%P if "%2"=="" set
LOGO=:
win %1 %2 %3 %4 %5 %6 %7 %8 %9 %LOGO%
set LOGO=
cd \
```

Figure 2-1: A batch file that starts Windows without its logo. This batch file, W.BAT, adds a colon after the WIN command unless a program name (something other than a Windows mode switch) is the first or second parameter to the batch file. The C: drive is used for example purposes — use whatever drive you've installed Windows on.

The next statement tests whether or not the first parameter to the batch file is one of the mode switches (/R, /S, /2, or /3). If it is, and there is a second parameter, then that second parameter must contain a program name, and the colon on the WIN command line must be left out. But if the first parameter is a mode switch followed by nothing else, then it is appropriate to tack on the colon. The following statement does this:

    for %%P in (R r S s 2 3) do if %1==/%%P if "%2"=="" set LOGO=:

The batch file then starts Windows, including anything that was added as a parameter to the batch file, plus a colon to suppress the advertising screen if appropriate, with the following statement:

    WIN %1 %2 %3 %4 %5 %6 %7 %8 %9 %LOGO%

If there are no parameters, then variables %1 through %9 will be blank. It makes no difference when WIN.COM is run whether there are a few extra blank spaces between the command WIN and the colon symbol.

W.BAT always, therefore, runs Windows without its advertising screen, regardless of whatever modes or additional programs you specify to run.

You may wonder if there isn't an easier way to get rid of the advertising screen than writing a batch file. There is, but it requires making changes to WIN.COM itself. These changes are harmless, though, and exploring this alternative method gets us closer to our final goal — replacing the Windows logo with one of our own.

The Ingredients Inside WIN.COM

A look inside WIN.COM gives us the information we need to customize it to our heart's desire. WIN.COM is actually three programs in one. As you recall, when you run WIN.COM, it performs three functions:

♦ It determines whether to start Windows in real, standard, or enhanced mode.

♦ It switches your PC into a graphics mode that your video board supports.

♦ It displays the Windows advertising logo.

If you've looked at the filenames on your original Windows diskettes, though, you may have noticed that no program named WIN.COM appears on those diskettes. The WIN.COM file is actually created on-the-fly by the Windows Setup program when you first install Windows. Setup forms WIN.COM by adding together three files:

♦ The first file, called WIN.CNF, is a small executable file which detects the configuration of your PC.

♦ The second file is another executable file, and switches your PC into the appropriate graphics mode for your display hardware. Setup chooses this file after it determines what video board you have, as follows:

VGALOGO.LGO	for VGA, Super VGA, or 8514/A displays
EGALOGO.LGO	for EGA color displays
EGAMONO.LGO	for EGA monochrome displays
CGALOGO.LGO	for CGA, EGA B&W (64K) and Plasma displays
HERCLOGO.LGO	for Hercules Monochrome Graphics displays

♦ The third file, the bitmapped graphic advertisement that Windows displays, is in a compressed format called Run Length Encoded (RLE):

VGALOGO.RLE	for VGA, Super VGA, or 8514/A displays
EGALOGO.RLE	for EGA color displays
EGAMONO.RLE	for EGA monochrome displays
CGALOGO.RLE	for CGA, EGA B&W (64K), and Plasma displays
HERCLOGO.RLE	for Hercules Monochrome Graphics displays

Setup simply locates these files on the Windows diskettes, combines them into a single file, names the resulting file WIN.COM, and places it in your Windows directory. The original three files — whichever ones are appropriate for your system's display hardware — are placed in the \WIN\SYSTEM subdirectory, where they remain in case you rerun Setup and it needs to recreate your WIN.COM file. (I call the directory that my Windows files are in the C:\WIN directory. But your Windows directory may be called C:\WINDOWS or any name you chose when you ran Windows Setup.)

You can use these files for your own customization needs. But before you do anything with these files, you must protect WIN.COM and the other files just listed from any changes. Switch to your Windows directory and make the WIN.COM file and its component files in the System subdirectory into read-only files, by using the DOS ATTRIB command:

```
c:
CD \win
ATTRIB +R WIN.COM
CD SYSTEM
ATTRIB +R *.CNF
ATTRIB +R *.LGO
ATTRIB +R *.RLE
```

Now that your existing WIN.COM is protected from any accidents, we can take the remaining steps to customize your Windows start-up routine. Nothing we do in the following paragraphs will change the WIN.COM file the Windows Setup program originally installed for you.

First, make a copy of the WIN.CNF file from the \WIN\SYSTEM subdirectory to the \WIN directory. Name the copy WI.COM so it is shorter than WIN.COM (indicating that something is missing) and so it won't interfere with WIN.COM (which is now write-protected and cannot be copied over or deleted anyway). The following commands accomplish this and run WI so you can see the result:

```
COPY c:\win\system\win.cnf c:\win\wi.com
CD \win
wi
```

When you run WI.COM, it contains only the program code that examines your configuration and starts Windows in real, standard, or enhanced mode. Since the code that displays the advertising screen has been left out, Windows launches immediately into the Program Manager or whatever other Windows programs you normally see after you start Windows. In this case, you don't need to append a colon after WI (the new command to start Windows) to keep the advertising screen from displaying. The Windows logo isn't present in the file at all.

Making Windows Display Your Own Logo

Eliminating the advertising screen from the Windows start-up routine, unfortunately, doesn't provide much of a time savings. Depending on the speed of your system and hard disk, skipping the logo loading and displaying period cuts only a second or so off the time you spend waiting for Windows to become fully operational after you issue the initial command.

Since this is the case, you might as well enjoy the opportunity to display your *own* logo — or any other graphic you like — while waiting for Windows to finish loading its various files and device drivers.

As we saw a few paragraphs ago, the Windows logo is contained in a file with a name like VGALOGO.RLE. It isn't important what the name of the file is — you can make a graphic file with any name, containing almost any bitmap image that Windows can display. The secret is putting this bitmap file together with the other components of WIN.COM in a way that works when Windows looks for such a file upon start-up.

First, you should know what an RLE file is. It was previously mentioned that the Windows logo is contained in a run-length encoded format. This RLE format is just an ordinary bitmap file (like the bitmap files included with Windows that are provided as "wallpaper," such as RIBBONS.BMP and PARTY.BMP) after it has been compressed.

Monochrome bitmap files, before compression, contain one bit of data for every pixel displayed on the screen — perhaps the first bit is black, the second bit is black, the third bit is white, and so on. Sixteen-color bitmaps require *four* bits of data to represent every pixel, since each pixel could be one of 16 (or 2^4) possible colors.

When a bitmap file, however, is converted to an RLE file, it takes less space on disk. The RLE file contains information such as, "2 pixels of black, 12 pixels of white, 20 pixels of blue," and so on. The file stores the number of pixels (the run length) of each color, instead of storing the meaning of each individual pixel.

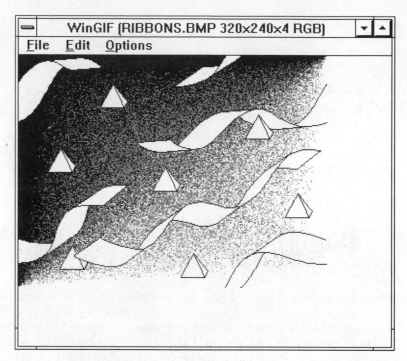

Figure 2-2: WinGif with the RIBBONS.BMP bitmap file.

You can convert any bitmap file that is in Windows' proprietary .BMP format to an RLE file by using a graphics program that can read and write both formats. WinGif, a program included on the shareware diskettes with this book, is perfectly suited to do just that. (The name WinGif derives from the fact that the program can convert graphics files between Windows' formats and CompuServe's Graphics Interchange File format.)

If you have a bitmap file all ready to go, you can use it in the procedure that follows. But in this example, I'll use the file RIBBONS.BMP, as shown loaded into the WinGif program in Figure 2-2. This file is ready to use, and won't require additional preparation other than compressing it into the RLE format. The RIBBONS.BMP file was installed in your Windows directory when you first ran Windows Setup. This procedure shouldn't hurt the file in any way. (If you use a file of your own, you should know that there is a limit of about 55K on the size of the compressed file that will work in this procedure. You'll need to use a graphic that compresses well in order to fit it into WIN.COM's limitations. A graphic with a solid background is ideal, since the solid area can easily be described by the run-length method as a long run of a single color. Microsoft's VGALOGO.RLE file, since it consists mostly of a blue background, is compressed down to less than 15K in size.)

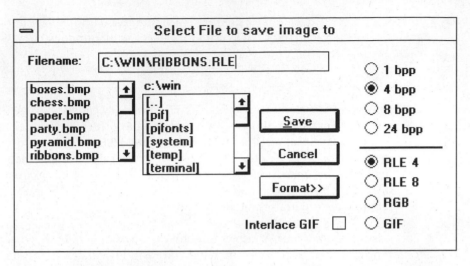

Figure 2-3: File formats supported by WinGif.

STEPS:

Making Windows display RIBBONS.BMP

Step 1. Install the WinGif program, if necessary, and run it inside Windows by double-clicking its icon or pulling down the File Run menu and typing WINGIF.EXE. Pull down WinGif's File menu and Open the file RIBBONS.BMP from your Windows directory. Enlarge the WinGif window so you can see the whole image, if need be, by dragging one of the corners of the window. Your screen should look like Figure 2-2.

Step 2. Open the File Save dialog box. Click the button labeled Format to see the formats you can save the file in. Click the radio button marked RLE4. This means the file will be saved in a 4-bit-per-pixel (4bpp) RLE file — the format used to display the Windows start-up logo. Change the filename so it says C:\WIN\RIBBONS.RLE (not BMP). Your screen should look like Figure 2-3. Click OK to save the file.

Step 3. Open a DOS session in Windows, or exit Windows so you can get a DOS prompt. Our next step is a DOS COPY command that, as yet, has no equivalent in Windows. Change to the \WIN\SYSTEM directory, where the files WIN.CNF and VGALOGO.LGO should be located. The following COPY command will combine together (concatenate) the three files that make up WIN.COM into a single file in the C:\WIN directory — let's call our new file MYWIN.COM:

```
copy /b win.cnf+vgalogo.lgo+c:\win\ribbons.rle c:\win\mywin.com
```

Now you have a new file in your C:\WIN directory called MYWIN.COM. The plus signs (+) in the above COPY command have the effect of making DOS add the three files WIN.CNF, VGALOGO.LGO, and RIBBONS.RLE one after another into the single MYWIN.COM file. The /b switch in this COPY command forces a full bit-for-bit binary copy operation. Without this switch, COPY would ordinarily treat this operation as the addition of simple ASCII text files, and might leave out important information.

Assuming that your Windows directory is on your DOS Path, you can now type MYWIN at the DOS prompt and start Windows. Early in the start-up sequence, Windows displays RIBBONS.RLE — not the normal advertising screen! You may notice that the Ribbons bitmap displays in a corner of the screen, not the full screen. This is because the RIBBONS.BMP file that we started with is only a portion of the size of a full VGA screen. When you make your own logo file, be sure to make it 640 × 480 in size if you have a VGA display. (If you have a Super VGA, 8514/A, or other display with higher-than-VGA resolution, use the VGA resolution for your start-up graphic anyway — Microsoft doesn't provide a *.LGO file to switch into any higher-resolution mode than VGA.)

If you have an EGA display, create a graphic that is 640 × 350 in size, and for a CGA display, 640 × 200 monochrome. Be sure to use the appropriate *.LGO file, as described above, for the display you are using.

And remember the 55K limitation on the RLE files that can be used in this procedure. If you look at the size of RIBBONS.BMP vs. RIBBONS.RLE, you'll see that the original file is 38,518 bytes long while the compressed file is down to 33,262 bytes. That isn't much compression — less than 15 percent — because the RIBBONS.BMP file is composed of almost random splotches of color, which are not as susceptible to run-length encoding. The VGA-resolution Microsoft Windows logo, by contrast, is only 14,782 bytes long even though it occupies four times as much screen area as RIBBONS.RLE. The Windows logo screen compresses much better because of its large solid color areas.

RLE files have another significant use. All the wallpaper bitmap files provided with Windows require a healthy chunk of hard disk space — CHESS.BMP, the largest bitmap, is 153,718 bytes long. But if you compress them to RLE4-format files, *they still work as wallpaper in their compressed*

form! You can install them in the Control Panel under the Desktop icon, and they are decompressed on-the-fly as Windows needs them. More on this topic can be found in the discussion of the Control Panel in the next chapter.

You can, as stated earlier, call the MYWIN.COM file that results from the COPY concatenation procedure any name you like. I wouldn't call it WIN.COM, because you may want to go back to the original configuration as created by Setup if you have any problems with this method.

The ability to customize your start-up screen is a nice feature of the Macintosh, and it's great to have the same ability under Windows, too. But since Microsoft doesn't provide information about the start-up screen, you want to be able to go back to your unedited WIN.COM for trouble-shooting or for when you are contacting software vendors about incompatibilities in their products. You don't want to be using an unusual WIN.COM when you're trying to track down an elusive quirk that pops up in your system.

Several people contributed publicly or anonymously to the process of determining this exact start-up sequence under Windows. University student Mike Mezaros published a lengthy description of this procedure in a bulletin board message, and author Kevin Bachus printed an explanation and built a batch file around the process in *InfoNet Monthly* (an electronic publication available from 107 S. Holliston Ave., Suite #307, Pasadena, CA 91106). My method is a little different from theirs, but I offer thanks to them and many other people who worked toward this solution.

Program Manager

Working with Program Manager as the Windows Shell

Once you've got Windows started, with the options and start-up screen the way you want them, you will probably be confronted with Windows' Program Manager. The Setup program automatically installs the Program Manager as your primary command center, or *shell,* unless you specify a different shell in the SYSTEM.INI file that comes with Windows. If you open that file with Notepad, a few lines from the top you'll see the line

```
shell=progman.exe
```

The main distinction of a shell program is that when you exit the shell, you are exiting Windows, too. Program Manager is the default shell, although many people use the File Manager or the much faster (and older) MS-DOS Executive as the shell instead. One strike against using the File Manager as the shell, though, is that when exiting, the File Manager first asks if you *really* want to exit the File Manager, and *then* asks if you want to exit Windows.

Actually, almost any Windows program, such as Microsoft Excel, can be used as the shell. When you exit *that* shell application, you exit Windows, just as you do when the File Manager is the shell. It doesn't make much sense, however, to use as a shell a program that doesn't have the ability to launch other programs. The only reason would be to develop a computer system designed to run only one program and no other, such as a terminal in a public place that displays a map or similar information. If a mischievous user exited the application, a batch file could start the application right up again, and it would be impossible for the user to get down to the Program Manager and start other programs (such as Solitaire!), because no copy of the Program Manager would be running or present on the hard disk.

Even in this case, it might be possible for the designer of such a system to find a way to launch *one* other application, as needed. Excel was distributed some time ago with a database query add-on called Q&E. This was in the days of Windows 2.*x* and, to get the largest available memory space, the Excel user was instructed to start Excel *without* the MS-DOS Executive (Windows 2.*x*'s shell). Since Q&E was a separate but necessary program, the dilemma for the Excel developers was how to start it running under Excel without the program-launching features of the Executive. The solution was to change the filename of the Q&E program to CONTROL.EXE. Then, you could pull down Excel's File Run menu and click on the Control Panel button. Windows thought it was starting the Control Panel program, but it actually ran *any* program named CONTROL.EXE. This trick still works if you need access to a subsidiary program under a shell that is a major app, such as Word for Windows or Excel.

Unless you choose another shell program explicitly, however, what you get is the Program Manager. When Windows is first installed, the Program Manager looks like a hodge-podge of subwindows of various sizes, and it is sometimes difficult to find exactly the program icon you need in all the confusion. Power users quickly rearrange this setup so that the windows are organized in a way to make as many functions as possible immediately visible. One of the ways that I can tell how long someone has been using Windows is that novices still have the default window arrangement inside Program Manager and frequently mutter things like, "Now where is that Notepad icon?" More-experienced users have at least clicked once on the Window Tile command to force the Program Manager to set all the

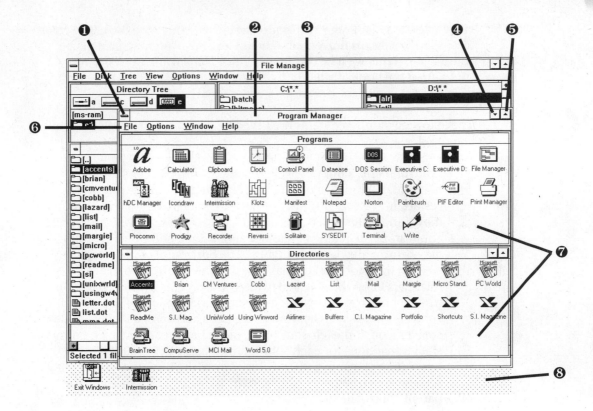

Figure 2-4: Program Manager after reorganization.

subwindows side-by-side instead of on top of one another. And heavy users have gone further and reduced the total number of subwindows, while making each icon do as much work as possible.

An example of a slimmed-down, reorganized Program Manager is shown in Figure 2-4. This figure shows a Program Manager that has been set up into only two subwindows. All of the icons in each window are visible at all times, not hidden by other subwindows. The top subwindow, called the Programs group window, contains icons only for those programs that create no files or just a few files that can be kept in a single directory — Control Panel, Recorder, Notepad, etc. The lower subwindow, called the Directories group window, contains icons for programs that create so many files that you must separate them into directories in order to find them efficiently. These icons automatically change into the proper subdirectory when double-clicked, and launch the appropriate application ready to open the file you want. There is a bit of a trick to setting up icons that act in this way, since Windows displays an error message when you try to do it. The error message is easily circumvented — but before I explain that, let's define some of the terms we'll be discussing. Since I'll be using these terms throughout the book, it's better if we agree in advance what the anatomically correct names for the parts of Windows are.

The following numbered items are keyed to the screen items pictured in Figure 2-4.

❶ **Control menu icon:** When clicked once, this icon, depicted as a horizontal bar, drops down the Control menu for the window it resides in. This menu always contains options to minimize, maximize, move, and otherwise resize the affected window, as well as closing the application, switching to another application, and other functions that may be provided by the program. The horizontal bar is meant to suggest the shortcut key that accesses the Control menu, which is Alt+Spacebar. When clicked twice, this icon closes the application (asking first to save any open documents). Applications that open subwindows — such as word processors and spreadsheets — show a smaller icon at the left edge of the menu bar (item ❻) which performs similar functions for each subwindow. That icon is called the Document Control menu, and is accessed from the keyboard by pressing Alt+Hyphen, or by pressing the right-arrow key after opening the parent control menu.

❷ **Title bar:** A title bar almost always appears in a full window or a partial-screen window. The title bar contains the application name (its title). It is widely known that placing the mouse on the title bar and dragging it is the easiest way to move a restored window around the screen. But the fact that *double-clicking* the title bar maximizes the window (or restores it if it is already maximized) is an *undocumented feature.* The fact that this works makes the maximize/restore button described below in item 5 totally unnecessary, since the title bar is so much larger and easier to hit with a mouse. Perhaps this feature isn't in the Windows manual because of some incompatibility. But it's worked on every PC configuration I've tried.

❸ **Title:** The title is the name of the Windows application plus the name of the current document, for those apps that display that name. When the app is minimized, the entire title bar (including any document name) is displayed below the minimized icon on the icon line (defined below in item 8). If your icon line is too cluttered, try "restoring" any document in the application before minimizing that application. Restoring the document to a portion of the application's screen area usually causes the app to remove the document's name from the title bar.

❹**Minimize button:** Turns the window into an icon on the icon line. The keyboard shortcut is Alt+Spacebar, N.

❺**Maximize/Restore button:** Maximizes the application to occupy the full screen, or restores it to its former area on a portion of the screen (if already maximized). This button is completely unnecessary, since the much larger title bar (above) does the exact same thing. But the keyboard shortcut is Alt+Spacebar, X or R, respectively.

❻**Menu bar:** The menu bar contains drop-down menus. Most people learn new applications just by pulling these down and examining all the choices. If you write down the keyboard shortcuts that appear on these drop-down menus in an application, sometimes you wind up with a better quick-reference card for yourself than what comes in the package with the app.

❼**Child windows:** Child windows, or subwindows, can only exist within the "parent window" that created them. When they are the "active window" (the one that currently has the focus of the keyboard if you type something) they have their own document control menu, as described above, and have their own rules and logic, governed by Microsoft's Multiple Document Interface (MDI) specification. You can switch among them in a round-robin fashion by pressing Ctrl+Tab or Ctrl+Shift+Tab (to go around in reverse order). Note that some applications, such as Word for Windows, use Ctrl+Tab for other functions.

❽**Icon line and the Desktop:** This is where icons appear for applications that have been minimized. After this line is filled from left to right, a second line above the first is created. So if you can't find an icon and the Desktop is crowded, perhaps the icon is hidden behind a window that is obscuring a second line of icons. The Desktop is an interesting "hot button" of its own. Double-clicking anywhere on an unoccupied section of the Desktop brings up the Windows Task List, showing every application that is currently running. Ctrl+Esc does the same thing. This is very handy when you can't find an icon or window that you *know* is under there somewhere.

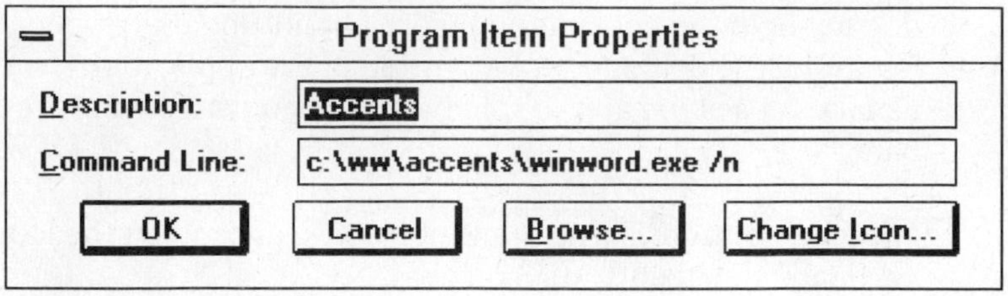

```
┌─────────────────────────────────────────────────────────┐
│ ━        │        Program Item Properties                │
├──────────┴──────────────────────────────────────────────┤
│ Description:    │Accents│                                 │
│                                                           │
│ Command Line:   c:\ww\accents\winword.exe /n             │
│                                                           │
│   ┌────────┐  ┌────────┐  ┌──────────┐ ┌──────────────┐  │
│   │   OK   │  │ Cancel │  │ Browse...│ │ Change Icon...│  │
│   └────────┘  └────────┘  └──────────┘ └──────────────┘  │
└─────────────────────────────────────────────────────────┘
```

Figure 2-5: The Program Item dialog box.

Organizing the Program Manager Group Windows

Now that the parts of the Program Manager (and most other windows) are defined, it's fairly easy to discuss the reorganization of the Program Manager as your Windows shell.

In Figure 2-4, the icons in the top child window, called the Programs group window, have straightforward meanings. The icons that the Windows Setup program did not define for you when you installed Windows can be quickly added by clicking File on the menu bar, then clicking New and Program Item. When you click OK, a dialog box similar to Figure 2-5 appears. You type the title for the icon in one text box (a title such as Clock), and the command that you want Windows to run in the other (in this case, CLOCK.EXE or just CLOCK, since Windows doesn't need the .EXE extension). If you don't specifically change the icon file that will be used for that application, Windows automatically displays the icon that is contained within the application itself (all Windows apps are supposed to contain one or more icons internally).

But the icons in the lower child window in Figure 2-4, called the Directories group window, are a little more involved. The Directories group contains several Winword icons, each of which starts Winword in a different subdirectory on the C: drive. Because there is one Winword icon for every subdirectory, a separate Winword icon does not even need to appear in the Programs group window. And if a new directory is needed as the number of files grows, a new icon that starts Winword in *that* directory can easily be created. (To create a duplicate of an existing icon in the Program Manager, hold down the Ctrl key while you drag the original icon to a new location with a mouse. This Ctrl+Drag procedure causes a duplicate icon, with identical properties, to be made instead of simply moving the original icon. Once you have the duplicate icon placed where you want it, pull down the File Properties menu and change the icon's properties to those of your new definition.)

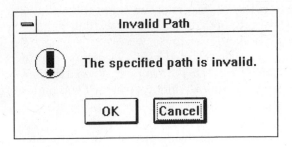

Figure 2-6: The Invalid Path dialog box.

The properties of the Accents icon, which starts Winword in a directory where I store information on the international characters available under Windows (see Chapter 9), are shown in Figure 2-5. This example, for the icon titled Accents, opens Winword in the directory C:\WW\ACCENTS. The /N switch is an undocumented feature that tells Winword not to open a new Document1. For more information, see Chapter 6, "Programming in WordBasic." The dialog box in this figure is for Windows 3.0; Windows 3.1 has a text box in its Program Item Properties dialog box to define start-up directories for applications, and the following procedure is less necessary.

The trick to making Windows start an application in a directory other than the one the application is located in is to place the directory *of the data files* in front of the application name, in this case WINWORD.EXE, instead of the directory where the application is actually located. In this case, the Word for Windows program files are on a completely different drive, in the directory D:\WW.

The anomaly with defining an icon's properties in this way under Windows 3.0 is that whenever you specify that an application should start in a directory other than the directory in which the application itself is located, Windows 3.0 displays the confusing message in Figure 2-6. The correct response is "OK." This problem is fixed in Windows 3.1.

Another anomaly: because Windows automatically uses the icon inside the file you've specified on the Command Line in the Properties dialog box, when you specify a data start-up directory, Windows can't find the icon for the application. Therefore, you must start the Properties dialog box again and change the icon file manually to the right one, with the correct path, and click OK without changing the command line this time. As mentioned above, Windows 3.1 handles this correctly, so you won't have to run through these steps so often.

When the Accents icon that we've defined is double-clicked, Windows reads the command line property of that icon. Windows then changes to the C:\WW\ACCENTS directory and tries to run WINWORD.EXE. Since the Word for Windows program files are not located in that directory, Windows then looks in each directory on the DOS Path in turn. When it finds WINWORD.EXE in D:\WW, Windows runs Word for Windows just as if you had told it the actual location of Word for Windows in the icon's properties.

For this to work, every application with an icon that starts in a directory other than the one containing the application's program files must be included in the DOS Path statement in your AUTOEXEC.BAT file. Since the Directories group window contains icons that start up in data directories for Word for Windows, Excel, and Word for DOS, your Path statement in AUTOEXEC.BAT would look as follows (including directories that contain COMMAND.COM, batch files, DOS, and Windows itself):

```
PATH=c:\;c:\bat;d:\dos;d:\win;d:\ww;d:\xl;d:\word
```

On the other hand, you can also define an icon with a command line that loads a single data file, such as a Word for DOS document. In that case, you can start the application in a directory that the application isn't located in, without placing that application on the Path. This is accomplished by editing the [Extensions] section in your WIN.INI file. By placing the application's full path in front of the application's name in the [Extensions] section, you can force Windows to find and start that application, as follows:

```
[Extensions]
doc=d:\word\word.exe ^.doc
```

The properties of your icon in Program Manager would look as follows:

```
Description:      Annual Report

Command Line:     c:\worddocs\annual.doc
```

This icon, when double-clicked, starts Microsoft Word in your D:\WORD directory (because that is the setting for Word in the [Extensions] section of WIN.INI), then opens the file ANNUAL.DOC from the C:\WORDDOCS directory.

This method works only if the application does not need to use the DOS Path to locate additional files of its own, such as overlay files. And, of course, the application must be able to load a file that is listed as a parameter on its command line, such as WORD ANNUAL.DOC.

A word about directories in the Path statement: You can easily add a new directory to the Path whenever you install a new program. But DOS imposes a limit of 127 characters on the Path statement, as it does with most DOS commands. So it's important to use short, two- or three-letter names for directories that will go into your Path, or you will run out of room sooner than you might like.

Additionally, you shouldn't install new Windows applications into the Windows directory itself, or into a subdirectory under Windows. If a new version of Windows is released with a filename that is the same as a filename for an application you have installed into the Windows directory, you could wipe out that file when you install the new Windows.

The bad habit of installing Windows applications directly into the Windows directory started in the old Windows 2.*x* days, when you couldn't run a program from the Windows Executive shell without actually seeing the filename in the window to double-click on it. Now that the Program Manager and the File Manager both allow a program to be started without actually being in that directory, the practice of installing applications into the Windows directory or a subdirectory has no purpose and can be very harmful to your programs or data. Yet software vendors *still* tell buyers of their products to install their software in the Windows directory, and Microsoft encourages software vendors to promote this — just because they don't think you can handle editing your Path statement!

For the record, all it takes to edit your Path statement is to open C:\AUTOEXEC.BAT in Notepad, add the new directory (and a semicolon) to the PATH= line, save the file and reboot your PC. How hard can that be? I know that some people can't find the "Any" key when confronted with the message, "Strike any key to continue," but I think it's in error to install various software programs into or below the Windows directory just to keep from having to edit the Path.

Now a word about data directories: All of the previous comments about keeping directories that must be in your Path down to two- or three-letter names should be ignored when it comes to directories that contain data files. These directories should be as long and descriptive as possible. Since Windows applications allow you to move from one directory to a sub-directory (and back) by simply clicking a mouse, there is no longer any excuse for cryptic, abbreviated, two-letter directory names for data. In fact, since icons like the Accents icon described above allow you to start up in any directory, no matter how far down it is in the "tree" of directories, you should be able to set up Windows so there is very little clicking around from one directory to another.

This might be a good time to mention the fact that DOS is not limited to 8-letter filenames. (Another myth exploded!) Under DOS, a filename can be up to 127 characters long, but every *ninth* character must be a backslash. I know that this is an unorthodox way to describe DOS filenames. But if you look at filenames this way, and take advantage of Windows features for quickly switching among your data directories, you should be able to make up much more descriptive names for files than people who think only in terms of that 8-letter straight-jacket. A perfectly good filename for an annual report might be C:\1992\ANNUAL\REPORT. (Since directory names can contain a period and a 3-letter extension as well as an 8-letter name — for a total of 12 characters — it's actually true that only every *thirteenth* character in a long name must be a backslash. But I find extensions in directory names to be confusing, and don't recommend it.)

On a more serious note about long filenames, it's absolutely true that there is no good reason for either DOS or Windows applications to limit their users to 8-letter filenames. The DOS file system is purely a convenience for applications, which can and should display to their users any name the user wants. The long filenames that users prefer can then be mapped by the application onto cryptic 8-letter DOS filenames, but there is no reason for us users to ever encounter the abbreviated form.

A popular DOS database program called DataEase, reportedly the second largest-selling database program in the world after dBase, is one of several programs that works exactly this way. When you create a database form or printed report in DataEase, you may type in any name you want, up to 20 characters, including spaces. DataEase itself then creates a DOS file to contain this information, using the 8-letter restriction. If you want to see which 20-letter forms correspond to which DOS filenames, you simply choose an option on the menu and DataEase displays the information both ways. But there is no need to do this except curiosity.

All Windows applications should work this way, with long names typed in and translated on-the-fly to short DOS names. All dialog boxes should display the long names (with the short names as an option). Ask for this feature when you're buying software. (When DOS can support 32-character filenames, all Windows applications will have to support long filenames.)

Using the Program Manager to Tune Your Memory

Once you've started Windows, one of the first things you should do is pull down the Help menu and click on About Program Manager. This choice has nothing to do with "help," but displays a valuable box showing the mode

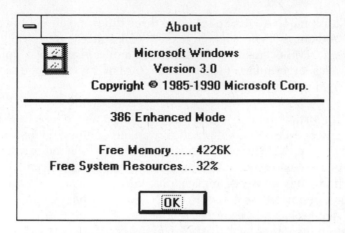

Figure 2-7: The Help About Program Manager dialog box.

that Windows started in (real, standard, or 386 enhanced), the amount of free RAM you have, and the percentage of "System Resources" you have left. This box is shown in Figure 2-7.

You should open this dialog box after you first install Windows, and occasionally after that. In the first place, you want to make sure that Windows started in the mode that you thought it would (real, standard, or enhanced). If Windows does not find enough memory to start in a given mode, it automatically starts in one of its lower modes, without necessarily telling you about it. The Help About box is the best way to make sure that something about your memory configuration hasn't gotten the better of Windows.

The amount of free RAM displayed is also an important indicator. You should make sure that Windows is accessing approximately the amount of memory you think should be available to it. In real mode, this number will include both conventional and expanded memory. In standard mode, the number includes only conventional and *extended* memory (that memory located above the 1MB line on 286 computers and higher).

In 386 enhanced mode, the number includes not only conventional and extended memory, but also any hard disk space that Windows can use to swap programs into when it runs out of real memory. The amount of hard disk space that Windows can use in this way is dependent on the amount of available RAM and the total amount of free disk space (Windows won't claim all disk space — it sets an upper limit for itself based on the percentage of the disk that is free). Windows can use up to 16MB of RAM, *and* can manage additional hard disk space up to three times the amount of actual, physical RAM chips. If enough memory and disk space is free, Windows could access 64MB of "memory" in enhanced mode. In any case, you will probably see a larger number for available RAM in 386 enhanced mode than you will see in real or standard mode.

The most important information in the Help About dialog box, however, is the System Resources number, practically an undocumented feature — it doesn't appear in the Windows manual glossary, and the index sends you to a nonexistent cross-reference — although it's the most significant element in determining the number of applications you can run as well as their stability and performance. A note in the Readme file that accompanies Windows defines system resources as follows: "This number is the percentage of system resources available." You could contact Microsoft's Department of Redundancy Department to find out what *that* means — but allow me to explain.

System resources is an area of memory that is managed by the Windows input manager, which is the program USER.EXE, and by the Windows Graphic Display Interface manager, GDI.EXE. These two programs are loaded by Windows when it starts. They are essential for keeping track of all the windows that have been created by applications system-wide, and for managing the drawing of objects on the screen, respectively.

Each of these two programs are limited to a data area 64K in size to manage all of the windows, objects, lines, and so on. The system resources percentage reports to you the percentage of memory left in either of these areas, whichever one is smaller.

The 64K areas are *segments* of memory that are dependent on the real mode of the Intel family of processors. Even if Windows is operating in standard or enhanced mode, the system resources area is limited to 64K segments. This was a decision made to improve Windows' overall performance, because accessing data objects that are located in a known 64K area is faster than calling for them across a larger area.

The system resources percentage available never rises to 100 percent, because Windows modules use up some of this memory just to display the Desktop, the Program Manager, and so on. If you start the Program Manager with only one child window, and nothing else on the Desktop, you should be able to get free system resources of 80 percent or more. And here is the real significance of system resources for the allocation of memory in your computer.

Each child window that you create in the Program Manager takes up about 2 percent of system resources. I have seen cases where people have created 10, 15, or more group windows under Program Manager, and then don't know why their system resources are down under 50 percent. Once you have displayed a group window in the Program Manager, even iconizing or closing that group window doesn't restore the system resources — Program Manager has permanently claimed that memory (in version 3.0). This is one of the best arguments for limiting the number of icons and group windows in the Program Manager. If you start Windows with few child windows, resources for the entire system are freed up.

This 2 percent figure also applies to any child windows that *any* applications create, not just Program Manager. In this case, a child window refers to almost any rectangular area that an application can open, move, or close. In Word for Windows, for example, 2 percent of system resources (approximately) are consumed by each of the windows described as the Ruler, the Ribbon, and the Status Line. In Excel, child windows include every spreadsheet window and every chart window that is open.

Applications themselves are major consumers of system resources. You can check Program Manager's Help About box, then open one application at a time to see the impact on your memory. Each application, such as the File Manager, Paintbrush, etc., consumes from 2 to 8 percent of the system resources just by sitting there in memory. Opening further child windows under these applications just adds to the demands.

Nothing would be wrong with this, except that the manner in which applications handle this shared resource is crucial to the stability of Windows as a whole. Loading the Print Manager, for example, nominally requires only about 2 percent of System Resources. But when Print Manager is spooling a large print job, 20 to 50 percent of system resources can be dedicated to it. Worse, if you are printing a job to a disk file (as opposed to a printer), and the print job aborts because your disk fills up, this 20 to 50 percent can become "stuck" and won't be released by the Print Manager (under version 3.0).

And when you fall below about 15 percent of free system resources, Windows won't allow you to open *any* additional windows, no matter how much free RAM you may have. For this reason, opening applications that occupy about 4M of RAM may be about the maximum possible under Windows 3.0, given the limits of system resources. (More than this amount of *data* may not have much impact on system resources, however, unless the data file contains graphic elements.) Conversely, if you have only 2M of RAM installed, you'll probably run out of RAM when opening applications, before you run out of system resources.

Fortunately, most Windows applications are modular and don't require their entire bulk to be loaded into memory at all times, so 4M represents a lot of open applications. Every system is different — you'll have to open your own program and data files to see how these limitations may affect you. For now, just remember that the fewer child windows you create in applications such as Program Manager and File Manager, the farther you'll be able to go with your other applications.

More Program Manager Secrets

The look and feel of the Program Manager is a refreshing change from the look of DOS, and even from the text-only look of the Executive shell (the only shell available for Windows 2.*x*). But this pleasant appearance can still be frustrating when those cute icons won't do what you want. To make your life easier, I've collected a few workarounds for common Program Manager complaints.

One of the biggest frustrations you can encounter when arranging the Program Manager icons the way you want them is that the Program Manager doesn't necessarily *save* your clever arrangement. You can drag your icons into the position you want with a mouse, then pull down the Window menu and click Arrange Icons to order them into compact rows. But when you exit Windows and start it up again, you'll find that all your icons are back in their old positions unless you checked the "Save Changes" box when you exited. Strangely, most individual Windows applications, such as Excel and Winword, are now astute enough to ask you, "Do you want to save file XXX?" when they receive a request from Program Manager to exit before you've saved your changes — but the Program Manager doesn't give you this courtesy itself.

But you *can* save the position of your icons in the Program Manager without exiting Windows entirely, and the workaround for this is pretty easy.

After you've moved your icons and clicked Arrange Icons, open any DOS application or session. Hold down the Shift key while double-clicking the DOS icon. The Shift key forces Windows to load (rather than run) the DOS session, and it appears minimized on the icon line instead of starting up full-screen.

Now double-click the Program Manager Control bar to exit Windows. Turn "Save Changes" *on,* then click OK to exit. The Program Manager writes the position of all your icons into the group-window files that it maintains in its text file PROGMAN.INI. But then Program Manager notices that a DOS application is open. Depending on the application, canceling the exit at this point brings you right back into the Program Manager, and you've forced it to save the position of all your icons!

Another way to do something similar, if you're moving icons pixel by pixel with a mouse, instead of letting the Arrange Icons menu command do it for you, is to trick Program Manager into writing the position of an individual icon. If you move an icon from one spot to another within the same group window, Program Manager doesn't record the new position until you Save Changes when exiting Windows. But if you drag and drop the icon into a window where you don't want it, then drag it into position in the window where you do want it, the position is saved. Program Manager writes the position of new icons that are moved *into* a group window, but ignores moves *within* a window.

Last, but not least, if ultimate catastrophe strikes and the files that Program Manager uses to store your laboriously created group windows become scrambled or erased, you can get back the Main, Accessory, and Games windows that Windows created when you first installed it. Pull down the File menu, click Run, and in the Run text box type SETUP /P. This rebuilds your Program Manager default groups. Then back up any files in your Windows directory with a .GRP (group) extension. You can't read these text files with an editor, but you can see a list of them in the PROGMAN.INI file, which you can open in Notepad or any plain text editor.

Recorder

Undocumented Features for Making an Autoexec for Windows

By this point, you've started Windows the way you want it, you've organized your shell, and you're ready for work. But you might notice that something is missing. Windows is supposed to be an improvement over DOS, but Windows seems to lack anything like the DOS AUTOEXEC.BAT file that sets up your programs as you like.

You can gain a powerful, Autoexec-like feature by using an undocumented feature of a small Windows applet that goes almost unnoticed by most people — the Windows Recorder.

—	Program Item Properties

Description: | Progman Min |

Command Line: | recorder.exe -H ^+F16 c:\recorder\macros. |

[OK] [Cancel] [Browse...] [Change Icon...]

Figure 2-8: The properties behind an icon that runs Recorder.

The Recorder, a utility that records actions and plays them back on command, has been roundly criticized by users because it requires that you start macros manually (by opening Recorder and choosing a key combination such as Ctrl+Shift+A). Nothing in the Windows manual suggests that Recorder can be made to run a macro automatically every time Windows starts, like AUTOEXEC.BAT. Nor does it explain that you can define an icon to run a whole series of tasks under Windows, not just run a single application.

But you can use undocumented features of the Recorder to do both of these things. Every time Windows starts you might, for example, want to use the Recorder to resize or reposition the applications that are open. Or you might want to create an icon that, when double-clicked, opens several related windows and positions them conveniently for your use. The properties of this icon would appear as in Figure 2-8. See "Making an Icon Run a Macro" later in this chapter.

The Recorder supports the following command-line syntax:

RECORDER -H *hotkey filename*

The "-H" switch tells the Recorder to run the macro in the specified file that has been defined on the specified hotkey. (The "-H" switch sometimes works better as an uppercase letter than as a lowercase letter, as we shall see below.) This hotkey can be any one of several printable keys on the keyboard (A-Z, 0-9, punctuation), as well as function keys (F1 through F16 are supported, even if your keyboard does not have that many function keys) and other special-purpose keys. (These keys include Backspace, Caps Lock, Del, Down, End, Enter, Esc, Home, Insert, Left, Num Lock, Page Down, Page Up, Right, Scroll Lock, Space, Tab, and Up.)

The hotkey designation can and should include the Ctrl, Shift, and Alt keys in any combination. The following table shows the symbols that are used to represent these keys:

```
Ctrl    ^
Shift   +
Alt     %
```

A macro defined as Ctrl+Shift+F10 in the file C:\RECORDER\MAINFILE.REC, therefore, would be started from the DOS prompt by starting Windows with the following instruction (Recorder assumes the extension .REC if no extension is given):

```
WIN RECORDER.EXE -H ^+F10 c:\recorder\mainfile
```

This method of starting macros automatically adds an infinite number of functions that can be set up to run themselves under Windows. The Recorder can even be used to fix the biggest complaints about the Windows File Manager: that it can't display the directory trees of two different drives at the same time, and that it is too slow reading the directories when switching to a new drive.

Normally when the File Manager starts up, it displays only one window showing the current drive (usually drive C:) as shown in Figure 2-9. At this point, it takes some waiting time if you want to open a window displaying another drive, such as D:. Let's fix the behavior of the File Manager so it displays the directories of *all* drives, as an example illustrating the hidden power of the Recorder.

This example will make more sense if you have Windows running on your PC and you actually type in all the instructions while reading this. And, if you do this, at the end of the demonstration you'll have a working Autoarrange macro for Windows, much like the AUTOEXEC batch file that executes automatically after DOS starts up. This macro displays the File Manager in the background, arranges the directory-tree windows of all your drives, and makes File Manager switch almost instantly between drives. The Program Manager runs in the foreground, so you can click an object there or just as easily switch to File Manager to click on one of its objects. (The following example assumes that you have two hard drives named C: and D:. If you don't have two hard drives, substitute A: for D: in step 11 below, and place a formatted floppy drive in drive A: before starting this process.)

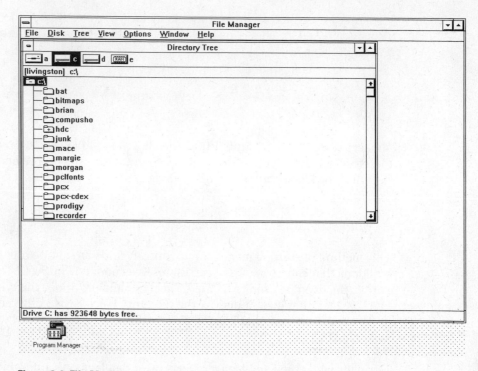

Figure 2-9: File Manager before running a macro to configure it.

STEPS:

Changing File Manager to Display the Directories of All Drives

Step 1. Edit WIN.INI. To run this example, you must change your WIN.INI file so that the File Manager (WINFILE.EXE) runs when Windows starts. Use Notepad to edit the [windows] section that begins your WIN.INI file, so it looks like the following lines (if you have several items on the RUN= line, make WINFILE.EXE the *last* item so it has the keyboard focus when Windows finishes loading):

```
[windows]
load=
run=winfile.exe
```

Step 2. Edit SYSTEM.INI. Make sure that the SHELL= line in the [boot] section of your SYSTEM.INI file starts the Program Manager

(PROGMAN.EXE). Open SYSTEM.INI with Notepad to make sure the line looks as follows:

```
[boot]
shell=progman.exe
```

Step 3. **Exit Windows completely.** Quit out of Windows. Change to your C: drive and create a directory called C:\RECORDER to store the macro you are about to record. (This way it won't be stored automatically in the Windows directory, which is cluttered enough already and may change the next time you upgrade.) Use the following commands:

```
c:
CD \
MD recorder
```

Step 4. **Restart Windows.** When you start Windows, any items on the LOAD= line in your WIN.INI file should appear as minimized icons at the bottom of the screen. File Manager should load and work for a few seconds creating a picture of the directories on your C: drive. Because the File Manager is running, Program Manager loads only as a minimized icon, not as an open window of its own. Leave this setup as it is until we've finished recording the macro.

Step 5. **Run the Recorder from the File Manager.** To do this, pull down File Manager's File menu and choose Run (Alt+F, R). This opens File Manager's Run dialog box. At this point, simply type RECORDER.EXE in the dialog box and click OK. This starts Recorder (if it is in your Windows directory and the Windows directory is on your DOS Path).

Step 6. **Set the options in Recorder.** Pull down the Options menu, and make sure that all of the following options are *on*: Ctrl+Break Checking, Shortcut Keys, and Minimize On Use, as shown in Figure 2-10. If any of these options do *not* have a check mark beside them, select them to turn them on.

Step 7. **Define the macro name and shortcut keys.** Pull down the Macro menu and choose Record. A Record Macro dialog box appears, as shown in Figure 2-11. Type in the macro name: Auto-arrange. (The name "Auto-arrange" helps to distinguish the macro from the AUTOEXEC.BAT file that is used by DOS.)

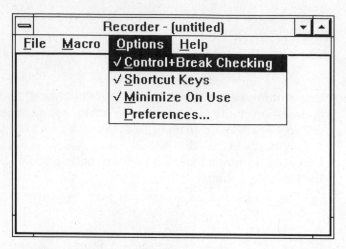

Figure 2-10: The Recorder and its Options menu.

Click the mouse in the Shortcut <u>K</u>ey box and type F16. Your keyboard probably doesn't have a function key higher than F12. (Wyse terminals and some others do include 16 function keys, which is why Windows supports them.) But even if your keyboard doesn't have an F16 key, Recorder still recognizes such "imaginary" function keys as F13 through F16. This makes these function keys good choices for macros that you will always run automatically (from a batch file), leaving your *real* function keys

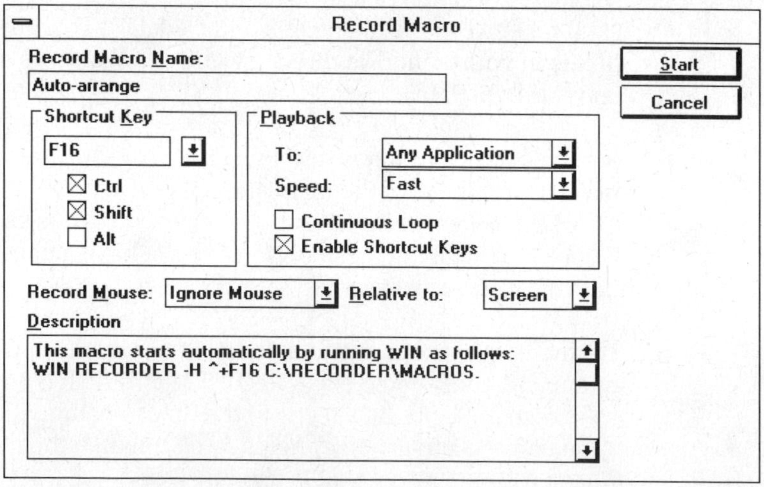

Figure 2-11: The Record Macro dialog box.

for macros you want to start manually (from the keyboard in Windows).

Click Ctrl *on* and Shift *on* but leave Alt *off.* This sets the Auto-arrange macro to playback on Ctrl+Shift+F16. Because Windows applications use many Alt- and Ctrl-key combinations, all your individual macros should be placed on Ctrl+Shift key combinations, which Windows apps almost never use.

Step 8. Define the macro Playback Options. Make sure the Playback Options box is set as follows:

Playback To:	Any Application
Playback Speed:	Fast
Record Mouse:	Ignore Mouse
Relative To:	Screen

Step 9. Define the macro description. Click once in the Description box and type the following (make sure *not* to press the Enter key to end the first line in the description box):

```
This macro starts automatically by running WIN as follows:
WIN RECORDER -H ^+F16 C:\RECORDER\MACROS.
```

Pressing the Enter key makes the macro-recording process start immediately. The description box has word wrap, so just keep typing until the first line wraps around by itself to start a second line. (Recorder doesn't allow a Shift+Enter combination in wraparound text boxes, as other Windows applications do, so you can't circumvent this with Shift+Enter.)

Step 10. Start the macro. When the Record Macro dialog box is exactly the way you want it, press Enter to accept the settings. The Recorder window reduces itself to an icon and anything you do now becomes part of the macro itself. For this reason, you must perform each of the following actions *from the keyboard only.* Put the mouse aside and don't touch it.

Step 11. Record the 11 keystrokes of the macro. Press the key combinations shown in the left column of the following list. These 11 keystrokes are the entire macro. Don't type the comments in the right column; they're for your information only.

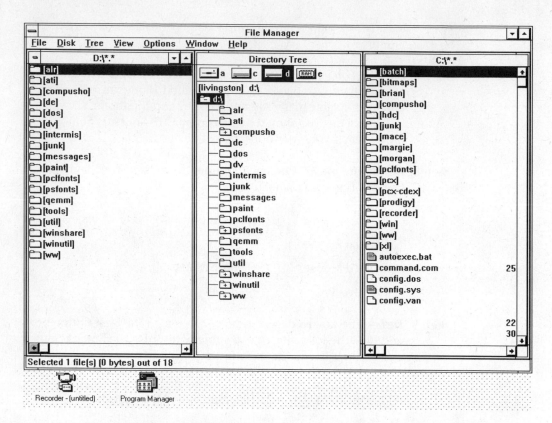

Figure 2-12: The File Manager after Shift+F4. After "tiling" the File Manager display into "child windows," all the directories on each drive are visible. Changing from one drive to another by clicking on the title bar of each window is almost instantaneous. The Directory Tree child window can now be used to display the contents of a floppy disk, RAM drive, or any other drive.

Press:	Comments *(Don't Type These)*
Enter	creates a child window for the C: drive
Ctrl+Tab	switches back to the Directory Tree child window
Ctrl+D	displays the D: drive directories
Enter	creates a child window for the D: drive
Shift+F4	tiles all child windows (see Figure 2-12)
Ctrl+Esc	brings up the Windows Task List (see Figure 2-13)

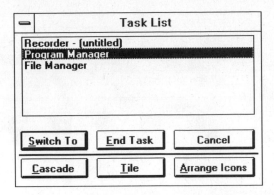

Figure 2-13: The Task List. Pressing Ctrl+Esc displays this list of all running applications. Pressing the letter P and Enter switches the Program Manager into the foreground.

Press:	**Comments** *(Don't Type These)*
P	the letter P selects the Program Manager
Alt+S	switches to Program Manager (see Figure 2-14)
Ctrl+Break	stops recording the macro
Alt+S	selects Save Macro
Enter	confirms Save Macro

Step 12. Save the file containing the macro. At this point, the Recorder is still minimized as an icon at the bottom of the screen. Using the mouse, double-click it to bring Recorder to the foreground (or press Ctrl+Esc and switch to Recorder using the Task List). Pull down the File menu and select Save As. Type in the following as the filename:

        c:\recorder\macros.

Important: Be sure to type a period after the word "MACROS." We are saving this macro in a file with no extension (for reasons we shall see shortly), and the period is necessary for Recorder to find the "MACROS." file without adding a ".REC" extension. Click OK and the file is saved, with your macro included within it.

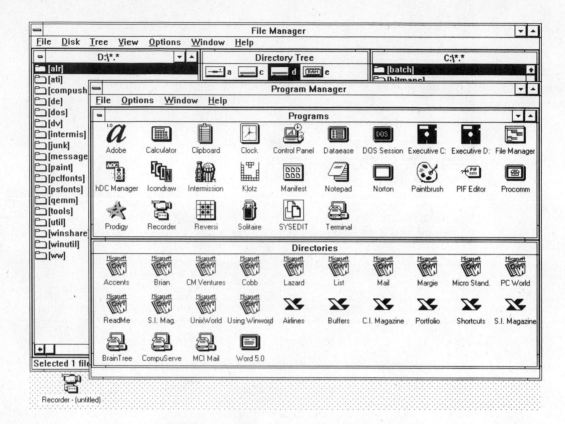

Figure 2-14: The final result of the Recorder Auto-arrange Macro. This is what your screen might look like at the end of the macro. The Program Manager is displayed in the foreground, where any application may be run. But a single click of the mouse on the File Manager makes it the foreground, where every file is now accessible.

Step 13. Exit Windows. Open the Program Manager and exit Windows completely. It doesn't matter whether or not you "save changes" in response to Program Manager's dialog box — we haven't changed anything that hasn't already been saved.

Step 14. Edit the batch file that starts Windows. Open the batch file that starts Windows and edit with a text editor the line that contains the command WIN to make it the same as the line below. If you don't have a batch file that starts Windows, use a text editor or Notepad to make one called W.BAT (and save it in a directory on your DOS Path) that contains this line (don't forget the period after "macros":

```
WIN RECORDER -H ^+F16 c:\recorder\macros.
```

Save this batch file and exit the text editor.

Step 15. Start Windows and watch your Auto-arrange macro work. As Windows starts, it runs the File Manager (because it's on the RUN= line in your WIN.INI file), starts the Recorder macro (because it's on the WIN command line that started Windows), and loads the Program Manager (because it's on the SHELL= line in your SYSTEM.INI file). Program Manager loads itself as an icon, in this case, because it minimizes itself whenever other programs are starting in Windows' start-up sequence. Any other applications listed on the LOAD= line in your WIN.INI also show up on the icon line. At this point, Windows would normally stop, making you do the work to arrange these icons and windows as you like. But here, the Auto-arrange macro takes over, transforming the File Manager into the form that you devised.

By first opening drive C:, then drive D: (or whatever drives you included in your macro), File Manager ends up with a separate window for the directory tree of each drive. Click the mouse on the title bar of the drive C: window, then the drive D: window. The switch from one drive to another is responsive, almost immediate. File Manager still requires the same amount of time to open a drive window for the first time. But by getting this opening delay out of the way at the very beginning of the Windows session, you never have to go through it again until you turn off and restart Windows on the next occasion. You can simply leave File Manager running in the background all day and switch among drives and subdirectories as necessary in the course of your work.

You'll notice that the Recorder icon is still present on the bottom of the screen, ready for you to press any other hotkey you may have defined. It's all right to leave it there throughout your Windows session (it closes itself when you exit Windows). One good use for it would be to define hotkeys that allow you to switch instantly to other running applications — perhaps Ctrl+Shift+E for Excel, Ctrl+Shift+W for Word for Windows, and so on. (These applications must be running in the background for these hotkeys to work, unless you define a macro that actually starts these apps.) In any case, the Recorder icon displays beneath itself the message, "Recorder - Macros." The reason we didn't add an extension to the MACROS file earlier is to get this simple display. A three-letter extension would just add to the clutter and make the icon's title less understandable.

Once you've run through the macro creation process, creating another macro can take less than a minute. The Windows Recorder doesn't give you the ability to edit the text of a macro — to change the macro, you need to record it again. But this should be fairly quick, and there are even ways around this limitation.

First, a Recorder macro can include a shortcut key that starts *another* macro. You can make the last keystroke of your Auto-arrange macro something like Ctrl+Shift+Z. Then, if you want to add more actions to your macro after it is finished, just define a macro in the same MACROS file with Ctrl+Shift+Z as the key assignment. Recorder will run whatever is in the Ctrl+Shift+Z macro after finishing with the Auto-arrange macro.

Second, you could make the entire Auto-arrange macro consist of a series of hotkeys — Ctrl+Shift+1, Ctrl+Shift+2, Ctrl+Shift+3, and so on — and leave the meaning of each hotkey undefined until you decide on the functions you want to perform in sequence. If you define, say, three actions and then want to insert another action in between the second and the third, it's easy enough with the Macro Properties menu choice in Recorder to redefine one action from Ctrl+Shift+F3 to Ctrl+Shift+F4, making room for a new Ctrl+Shift+F3 submacro. You can combine up to five macros into a single macro in this way.

Seeing the Events You've Recorded

One criticism of the Recorder is that you can't see the text of the macros you record. While it's true that you can't edit a Recorder macro without buying a separate product to do so, you *can* use an undocumented feature of the Recorder to see the events you've recorded. This can be useful if the macro you're trying to perfect has a little problem, and seeing what sequence of events is actually inside the macro would help you find that problem.

To use this undocumented feature, open the Recorder window with a macro file loaded. Highlight the name of the macro you wish to examine. At this point, if you pull down the Macro menu and click Properties, you ordinarily see a dialog box with the settings for that macro: the hotkey combination it uses, whether it includes mouse events or not, and so on.

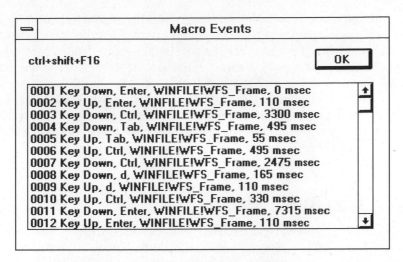

Figure 2-15: The undocumented Macro Events dialog box.

But if you hold down the Shift key while clicking Macro Properties, a completely different dialog box opens up, as shown in Figure 2-15. This is the Macro Events dialog box, which lists every keyboard and mouse event contained in the macro.

This list includes every key-up and key-down action, and the name of the program in which these actions took place. Additionally, the list includes the amount of time between each keystroke. (This timing information is not used when the macro is played back unless you specify "Playback Speed: As Recorded.")

If you find an error in your macro, you will still have to rerecord the sequence, but this hidden feature of the Recorder may make finding such an error a lot quicker.

Macros Won't Run Automatically from WIN.INI

One thing that won't work when you try to run a Recorder macro automatically every time you start Windows is placing the Recorder command in the LOAD= or RUN= lines in your WIN.INI file. If you wanted to start Recorder and run the macro defined as Ctrl+Shift+A in the C:\RECORDER\MACROS. file, for example, the following line in WIN.INI would *not* work:

```
RUN=RECORDER.EXE -H ^+a c:\recorder\macros.
```

This line would not have the desired effect because Windows interprets each item (separated by spaces) in the LOAD= and RUN= lines in the WIN.INI file as individual commands. The "-H" hotkey switch, for instance, would not be loaded by Windows as a switch to the RECORDER.EXE program. Instead, Windows would look on the DOS Path for an executable program called -H.COM or -H.EXE. Finding no such program, Windows displays an "Application Execution Error" message instead of feeding the switch into Recorder. You must place programs with parameters like this in the batch file that starts Windows (after the WIN command), not in WIN.INI.

Making an Icon Run a Macro

To make an icon run a macro that you've created with the Recorder, you need two things: a macro saved in a file and named with a shortcut key combination, and a new icon for this purpose.

With the Program Manager on the screen, we can define the simplest of macros for testing purposes: a macro that simply minimizes the Program Manager to an icon. Of course, we could simply accomplish this by clicking on the "minimize" button in Program Manager. But let's create this macro just to demonstrate the use of icons to run Recorder actions.

STEPS:

Making an Icon Run a Macro

Step 1. Open Recorder with the MACROS file loaded (if it isn't already). Pull down the Macro menu and click Record. In the Record Macro dialog box, change "Any Application" to "Same Application" in the Playback Options box. Name the macro "Program Manager Minimize," define the shortcut key as Ctrl+Shift+F15, and type in "reduces Program Manager to an icon" as a description. (Again, function keys F13 through F16 are good choices on which to define macros that you only plan to run from an icon and not by pressing a hotkey combination from the keyboard.) Click OK to start recording the macro.

Step 2. Remember not to use the mouse, even in this short macro. Press Alt+Spacebar to pull down the Control menu, then N to Minimize. Press Ctrl+Break to stop recording the macro. Press Alt+S to select Save Macro and Enter to confirm.

Step 3. Double-click the minimized Recorder icon to open its window. Pull down the File menu and click Save. This preserves the Ctrl+Shift+F15 macro in the file for future use. Then close the Recorder.

To create an icon for this macro, hold down the Ctrl key and drag the Recorder icon to an unoccupied position in the Program Manager window. Holding down the Ctrl key while dragging the icon makes a duplicate of the Recorder icon, leaving the original in place. We will just change the properties of the new icon to run the Recorder macro.

Make sure the new Recorder icon is highlighted (click it once if it isn't, so the title underneath the icon changes color). Pull down the File menu in Program Manager, then click Properties. Change the Description of the icon to Minimize Macro. Change the Command Line to read:

```
RECORDER.EXE -H ^+F15 c:\recorder\macros.
```

Again, it's important to remember the period after the word "macros," since this allows Recorder to find the right file, which has no extension. Additionally, the letter "H" should be capitalized because of the noticeable difference between the behavior of the icon when the "H" is uppercase or lowercase (which will be described in a moment). Click OK to save the meaning of this icon.

Now double-click on the icon. Program Manager should collapse into the minimized state and appear as an icon on the bottom of the monitor screen. Your icon works. You can now place almost any series of actions, simple or complex, behind a single icon.

Working Around Macro Recording Limitations

With all of the above features, Windows Recorder is still an extremely limited macro program. One of its anomalies is that the Recorder must *not* be running (in a window or as an icon) when an icon that starts a macro is double-clicked to run it. You can test this yourself. Restore the Program Manager to a window (instead of an icon, if you ran the previous macro). Start Recorder, load the MACROS file, and minimize Recorder. Make sure the command line of the "Minimize Macro" icon is using an uppercase "-H" switch. Then double-click this icon to run the macro. The Recorder opens up into a window, but it only highlights the macro you wanted and does not actually run it. At this point, you would have to double-click on the name of the macro to run it, which is an extra step.

Minimize the Recorder window without running the macro. Change the File Properties of the Minimize Macro icon so the "-H" switch is now lowercase ("-h"). Click OK to save this change, then double-click on the icon to run the macro. This time, when Recorder comes up, it not only does not run the macro, but also displays an error message. This message says that the proper syntax is "recorder.exe -h hotkey filename" — with the "-h" switch in lowercase! Clicking OK gets rid of this message, and then it is again possible to double-click on the macro name to start it. But it is curious that an error message should be generated by something so simple as one of the switches being in upper- or lowercase — and that the help text would mistakenly encourage the use of the wrong case!

In addition to this, only one copy (instance) of the Recorder can be running at any one time. You cannot run two instances of the Recorder in the background, one with a certain set of macros you use, and the other with an alternate set you also want access to. Only one Recorder can run in memory — if you need to load another macro file and start to run Recorder again to do this, the first instance of Recorder simply unloads its existing macro file and loads the new one itself. (You can define icons to load different macro files automatically. Just include the filename after the command RECORDER.EXE, with no -H switch or hotkey in between.)

You will also run into trouble if you define a hotkey combination that is the same as a hotkey defined in another Windows application. You wouldn't assign a Recorder macro to the letter "A," naturally, because then you couldn't use the letter A in your word processor or text editor. But you might think you could get away with defining a macro on Ctrl+A or Alt+A. I wouldn't recommend this, because many Windows applications use almost all Ctrl and Alt combinations. If you *do* define a hotkey that is the same as a hotkey macro in a running Windows application, the Recorder will take precedence over the macro in your application. And if you specified that the Recorder macro should play back only into the "Same Application" that you recorded it in, Recorder will try to switch away from your foreground Windows app and then play back into its "home" app (displaying an error message if that app isn't running). For this reason, I always recommend the use of Ctrl+Shift combinations, which most Windows apps leave alone, for all user-defined macros.

Recorder may have trouble, too, with certain specific hotkey combinations or keystrokes in particular applications. Every hotkey that should be legal in Recorder did not necessarily start a macro properly in my testing. In some cases, it was necessary to change a hotkey from a Ctrl+Alt combination to Ctrl+Shift before it would work. In other cases, the order in which the symbols for Ctrl (^), Shift (+), and Alt (%) were placed on the command line made a difference in whether or not macros would run automatically.

One particular Windows application — Windows Write, a basic-level word processor — may exhibit problems if you record Tab keystrokes. Try recording and playing back the following macro in Write:

    [Tab][Tab]January 1, 1999[Enter]

    [Enter]

    [Tab][Tab]My dear friend:[Enter]

The Tab keystrokes may not be inserted properly when the macro is played back, and the Enter keys may appear in Write as page breaks instead of carriage returns. If this problem presents itself, Microsoft suggests using Shift+Tab and Shift+Enter instead of the usual Tab and Enter keys when recording a macro in Write.

All DOS applications running under Windows have a more serious problem with the Recorder. No keystrokes recorded while in a DOS application are saved in the Recorder macro. Of course, these keystrokes don't playback when the macro is run, either. Recorder has the ability to start any application, whether the program is a Windows app or a DOS app, but it can capture keystrokes only in Windows apps. If you try to record keystrokes in a DOS application, you may receive the error message "No events recorded." Recorder macros consist only of Windows "message" packets, which are understood by Windows applications but not DOS applications. If you need to start a DOS app with a macro, and then make that program do something such as load a file, it may be possible to work around this limitation in one of the two following ways:

1. Include the file you want the DOS application to load as a parameter after the name of the DOS program itself, on the command line or in a PIF file that runs the program. Using the File Run command to start the DOS Edlin editor, for example, you could enter the command EDLIN MYFILE.TXT instead of just starting Edlin and trying to use Recorder to play back Edlin instructions.

2. Write a batch file that runs the sequence of character-based commands you want to run in the DOS session. Then define a PIF file that runs this batch file, and have Recorder start that PIF file.

Finally, a significant anomaly of the Recorder is that the first key combination in a macro cannot be any of the combinations that include the Ctrl key. This prevents the first action of a macro from being Ctrl+Esc, which is needed to bring up the Windows Task List to select an application. To work around this limitation, you must include at least one other keystroke before performing the action that requires the Ctrl key. Pressing Alt+Spacebar to bring up the Recorder Control menu, then restoring and immediately minimizing the window again (or just pressing Esc to close the Control menu), may be enough to allow you to include the remaining keystrokes that you wish.

Recording Actions with the Keyboard Instead of a Mouse

Since mouse actions are unreliable in a macro (because the window into which the macro is playing back might be a different size or in a different location, etc.), most or all macro actions should be performed with the keyboard alone. Windows makes almost all actions available from the keyboard as well as the mouse. Choosing items from a menu by pressing Alt and the first letter of the command, for example, is almost universal across Windows applications. The most natural actions to perform with a mouse, however, are those that may be the hardest to remember how to perform from the keyboard: moving and sizing windows.

These actions can be handled from the keyboard by following these steps, which work in virtually every commercial Windows program:

Moving a window. Press Alt+Spacebar, then M for move. Then use the cursor-arrow keys to move the window left, right, up, or down. Press Enter to accept the new position.

Sizing a window. Press Alt+Spacebar, then S for size. Press one of the cursor-arrow keys to indicate which one of the four sides of the window you want to expand or contract (top, bottom, left, or right). Then use the cursor-arrow keys to make the window larger or smaller. Press Enter to accept the new size. Repeat these steps to expand or contract other sides of the window.

In addition, you will find many shortcut-key actions that make the mouse unnecessary for most actions in the File Manager, Program Manager, and many other applications. These shortcut keys may be seen by pulling down each of the menus from the menu bar in each application.

Alternatives to the Recorder

There are more powerful programs than the Recorder, by far, for automating the start-up and other routines you need under Windows. You may find that the Recorder offers you just the functionality you need, or you may want to use the Recorder because it comes free with Windows and you don't want to pay for extra programs. But if you want more flexibility, the following programs certainly offer you a superset of the Recorder's capabilities.

RecRun, a shareware program on the diskettes included with this book, resolves some of the problems using the Recorder. When you use RecRun, a separate executable Windows program, to start a Recorder macro, RecRun automatically retrieves the macro from its file on disk and tricks Recorder into carrying it out, whether or not Recorder was running originally. RecRun uses a slightly different syntax on its command line than Recorder — see the "Excellence in Windows Shareware" section for details.

Bridge Batch is a Windows batch language from the same company that created the Recorder for Microsoft: Softbridge, Inc. Bridge Batch can open and move Windows and record keyboard and mouse actions. Utilities include a dialog box editor and a way to set hotkeys on the keyboard. The program lists for under $200 at this writing. And a big brother is available, Bridge Tool Kit, with all the capabilities of Bridge Batch plus DDE communications between programs and message-passing across networks, for about $700 plus the cost of runtime modules per user. Softbridge, Inc., 125 Cambridge Park Dr., Cambridge, MA 02140, 800-955-9190 or 617-576-2257.

PubTech BatchWorks is a batch language with macros that provide an easy way to create simple dialogs with a user, such as its ASKYESNO function that displays a box and acts on the resulting button-press. BatchWorks lists for under $100, and is a commercial version of WinBatch. Publishing Technologies, Inc., 7719 Wood Hollow Dr., Suite 260, Austin, TX 78731, 800-PUBTECH or 512-346-2835.

WinBatch, on the diskettes included with this book, is perhaps the best solution for Windows automation. With over 100 functions, WinBatch gives you the ability to handle almost anything you can think of under Windows. WinBatch has a small registration fee and offers a discount on top of that to anyone who bought a copy of Bridge Batch or BatchWorks. It's by the same company that developed the noted Command Post menu enhancement under Windows 2.*x:* Wilson WindowWare, 2701 California Ave. SW #212, Seattle, WA 98116, 206-937-9335. See the "Excellence in Windows Shareware" section for more information.

Summary

In this chapter, I have described features of Windows, some obvious and some not so obvious, that you can use to gain control over the Windows start-up sequence and loading of programs.

▶ How the WIN.COM file is made up, and how to take it apart so you can disable Windows' logo screen or substitute a logo screen of your own.

▶ Ways in which the Program Manager and its group windows use up your PC's System Resources, and how to minimize their impact.

▶ Undocumented features of the Recorder that allow you to add AUTOEXEC.BAT-like features to Windows, or define almost any actions you want onto a particular icon.

▶ How to set up Windows' File Manager to improve its performance in switching among drives and directories, using some of the tricks of Recorder macros.

Chapter 3
Secrets of the Windows Applets

In this chapter...

I discuss undocumented features of many of the free utilities you get with Windows:

▶ Adding abilities to the File Manager that were left out in the original implementation of that disk utility.

▶ Uses for three undocumented utilities automatically installed on your disk by Windows Setup but which don't appear as an icon in your Program Manager: the Executive, System Editor, and WINHELP.EXE.

▶ How to view the secret "gang screens" that pop up inside your favorite Windows applications — if you know the passwords.

▶ Exploiting hidden features of the Calculator, Control Panel, and Paintbrush.

▶ The pros and cons of upgrading to versions of Windows higher than 3.0 to get fixes for problems that you may not know existed.

W indows includes a variety of small utility programs that provide simple functions such as editing text files (Notepad) and adding numbers (Calculator).

On the surface, many of these utilities seem weak at best. Most can't even be configured to start up occupying the full screen, since they don't save settings in WIN.INI, like other Windows programs do. (This is true of the following applets: Calculator, Calendar, Cardfile, Clipboard, Clock, Control Panel, File Manager, Notepad, Paintbrush, Recorder, Reversi, the PIF Editor, Print Manager, Setup, Solitaire, Terminal, and Write.) The Program Manager is the only applet bundled with Windows that saves your preferred position for it into its own configuration file, PROGMAN.INI. The rest require that you start them with a utility such as RunProg (on the diskettes included with this book) to size them.

But some useful features of these applets, which are not so obvious from the Windows documentation, can turn these bundled toys into valuable workers on your desktop.

File Manager

In the preceding chapter, Customizing Your Windows Start-Up, I discussed some procedures in the Recorder section for speeding up the File Manager and making it more usable. In this chapter I cover other behaviors of the File Manager, providing functions that this disk utility should have shipped with.

Printing Directories From File Manager

It was a tremendous oversight in version 3.0 of the File Manager that you could *look* at your disk directories, but could not *print* those directories on your printer.

Printing a directory under DOS is as easy as giving the command DIR > *LPT1* (where LPT1 may be replaced with any printer port you are using). The greater-than symbol (>) redirects the output of the DIR command (or any DOS command) to the device you name, such as the printer on Line Printer porT 1. It is pretty painful to lose this redirection feature under Windows. The File Manager's File Run dialog box in version 3.0 not only doesn't allow the use of redirection symbols in commands, but also doesn't allow *any* internal DOS commands, such as DIR, COPY, or DEL. (These commands are internal to the COMMAND.COM file and do not correspond to "external" DOS files on your hard disk.)

 To try to recover some printing functions in the File Manager that we take for granted under DOS, Microsoft prepared a technical note suggesting that you write a batch file named D.BAT containing just the line DIR %1 > *LPT1*. Then, you could pull down File Manager's File Run dialog box and run the command D.Bat *directory,* which would run the batch file and print whatever directory you specified. But there's a much easier way.

In the File Manager, pull down the File Run dialog box and type:

```
COMMAND.COM /C DIR > lpt1
```

This starts a copy of COMMAND.COM and orders it to run a directory listing, redirecting the printout to LPT1. If File Manager is not currently in the directory you want, you can specify any directory, as follows:

```
COMMAND.COM /C DIR directory > lpt1
```

One quirk of this undocumented workaround is that it won't necessarily work if you have a PIF file named COMMAND.PIF. If you do, Windows will run that PIF file and not look for any parameters on the command line, only those that are specified in the PIF file. To get around this (so that I can run COMMAND.COM /C with parameters if I want), the PIF file that I use to start a DOS session is called DOS.PIF rather than COMMAND.PIF. Windows looks for PIF files with the same name as the DOS applications you try to run under Windows; if it doesn't find one, it starts the DOS application with the settings in its _DEFAULT.PIF file. You should open the _DEFAULT.PIF file with the PIF Editor to make sure its default settings are appropriate for your system. See Chapter 5 for more information about these settings.

Another benefit of the COMMAND /C workaround in File Manager's File Run dialog box is that it gives you access to all the other internal DOS commands. Your screen wavers while Windows switches modes from graphics to text to accomodate DOS, so you don't want to use this capability a lot. But it's there when you need it.

Associating Files with *Any* Number of Extensions

One of File Manager's most useful features is its capability to associate an executable program with files that have certain extensions. Windows installs itself with several associations already written into the WIN.INI file. .TXT files, for example, are associated with the Notepad. When you double-click on a file associated with an application in File Manager, it launches that application and places the name of the file on its command line as a parameter, loading that document automatically (in this case, loading a text file into Notepad for editing). Files with such specified extensions appear in File Manager with little document icons, while files with no associations have only plain icons.

This associative system falls down, however, with applications like Notepad because text files can have almost *any* extension, as in README.TXT, README.DOC, README.1ST, READ.ME, etc. There are too many possibilities to associate them all. In addition, File Manager has no way to associate with particular applications those files that have *no* extensions. This is actually a limitation of the WIN.INI file, where the associations are stored under a section headed [Extensions].

To give File Manager the ability to launch Notepad (or whatever text editor you like) and load *any* file that you highlight in a directory window, you can create a simple macro with the Recorder. A good place to save this macro would be in the MACROS file that you created in the previous chapter.

With the Recorder loaded as an icon, and with the file MACROS loaded (but not yet recording), switch to the File Manager. Highlight any text file in a directory window. Double-click the Recorder icon to open its window. Pull down Recorder's Macro menu and click Record. Name the macro LaunchEditor and set the hotkey to Ctrl+Shift+N for Notepad (or another letter if you use a different editor). The other settings can be the same as the Auto-arrange macro described in the previous chapter. Click OK to start recording. You should be returned to the File Manager, where your filename is still highlighted.

The next step is to copy this filename to the Clipboard. One way to do this is to pull down File Manager's File menu and click Print. The Print dialog box appears, with the name of your file highlighted in a text box. Press Ctrl+Insert, which transfers that highlighted name to the Clipboard. Then press the Tab key twice to move to the dialog box's Cancel button, and press Enter to cancel the printing.

Finally, pull down the File menu and click Run. In the Run dialog box, fill the command line with NOTEPAD and a space. Then press Shift+Insert to paste your filename from the Clipboard into the dialog box after NOTEPAD. Press Enter to start running this command line, and watch Notepad load your file.

Now press Ctrl+Break to end recording, and save the macro when asked to do so. Close the Notepad window by pressing Alt+F4. You now have a way to open any text file that you highlight in File Manager. Highlight a text file different from the one you just used. Press Ctrl+Shift+N and watch Notepad open up, with your new text file loaded automatically. When Recorder plays back your macro, it carries out the *actions* that you specified — it doesn't open the exact same file you loaded into Notepad during the recording session.

This method can be used to make any application accept files with any extension. Simply define macros using different hotkeys than the one that starts Notepad.

Avoiding Problems That Make Directory Windows Unstable

The File Manager gives you the ability to rename directories by highlighting the directory and choosing Rename from the File menu. If that directory is already open in a child window when you do this, however, File Manager version 3.0 neglects to rename the child window displaying that directory. But since the directory now has a new name on your disk, any attempt to access files in the child window results in a "File Not Found" error message.

Additionally, if you close a directory in a child window that has been reduced to an icon at the bottom of File Manager's display, that window takes with it File Manager's ability to use the keyboard to move to another directory. You can demonstrate this for yourself. Highlight a directory folder and double-click it (or press Enter) to open that directory in a child window. Make sure there is enough room at the bottom of the File Manager display for an icon. Minimize the child window to an icon by pressing Alt+Hyphen, then N (or clicking the Minimize button with a mouse). Press Ctrl+Tab until the title beneath this icon is highlighted, then press Ctrl+F4 to close it. Notice that you now cannot move up and down the list of directories with the cursor-arrow keys in the original window. To unstick the cursor, run a function such as Help About by pressing Alt+H, then A. When you click OK to close the Help About dialog box, the cursors will work again to move among directories in the File Manager.

Another action that can cause more serious problems, including freezing Windows entirely, is using File Manager's Search function incorrectly. Search is a handy feature that allows you to find any file or set of files in a directory or anywhere on an entire disk. After performing the requested search, for *.COM, say, the Search function displays a "search results window" listing the full path location for every file that matches the request. An invalid search request, such as .COM (with no wild card at the beginning of the file specification), leads to an unstable memory condition that can only be cured by using Alt+Tab to switch to the program you are using as the Windows shell, and running File Exit to exit and restart Windows.

The search results window has other anomalies as well. You can move files from the search window to another location by dragging them with the mouse. When you do this, the window updates itself to show that this file has moved. Performing this operation from the keyboard (pulling down the File menu and choosing Move) does *not* update the display correctly. File Delete and File Rename have similar behavior. Watch this window carefully if you often require these features.

Regardless of any actions you perform manually in File Manager, though, you should be aware of the updating of *all* directories in child windows. When an application (other than File Manager) creates, deletes, moves, or renames files, these changes will refresh the child window display only if one of the following two conditions apply:

1. The application manipulating these files is a Windows application (using standard Windows functions).

2. You are running a DOS application under Windows in 386 enhanced mode, and there is a line in the [386Enh] section of your SYSTEM.INI file that states FileSysChange=Yes. This statement forces Windows to monitor all disk activity by DOS applications, so changes to files can be sent to the File Manager in a Windows message. Since this monitoring slows down the performance of DOS applications running under Windows, you may decide to leave this statement set to No and accept that the File Manager directory displays may not reflect the latest changes made by DOS applications.

To ensure that a child window in the File Manager is updated with the most recent information, simply press F5 while that window is the active window. The F5 key causes File Manager to reread the directory and display it in its current form.

Using File Manager's Folder Icons

One of the conveniences of the File Manager is the way it allows you to move, copy, or delete whole directories of files all at one time. In the File Manager's Directory Tree window, each directory is represented by an icon in the shape of a folder, followed by the name of the directory. Directories that have subdirectories are indicated by a folder containing a plus sign (+), while directories that are currently displaying all their subdirectories are indicated by a folder containing a minus sign (-). This is shown in Figure 3-1. Clicking once on a folder with a plus sign makes that directory display all its subdirectories, while clicking on a folder with a minus sign makes the directory display only its own name.

This system works fine until you start using another feature of the Directory Tree window: double-clicking on the directory icons to actually open a listing of the files in that directory. In File Manager version 3.0, if you double-click on a directory icon that contains a plus or minus sign, that directory

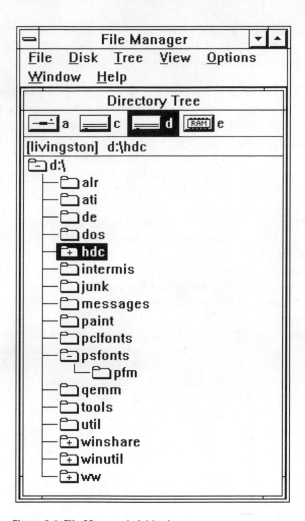

Figure 3-1: File Manager's folder icons.

doesn't immediately open a directory window. It first opens or closes its subdirectory display (which may not be what you wanted), and *then* opens a directory window that lists its files. Windows, which controls all mouse messages, does not send applications a different message when a mouse is double-clicked inside their window instead of simply single-clicked. Windows expects applications to wait the amount of time that you specified in the Control Panel for mouse double-clicks, and then determine for themselves whether two mouse clicks in a row are a double-click or two different single-clicks. File Manager 3.0 does not wait for the second click on a folder icon before acting on the first, but opens or closes the subdirectory display whether or not you really intended to double-click the icon.

This behavior changes in a later version of Windows, but if you face this situation in your copy of Windows, a way around it is to recognize that each directory in File Manager's Directory Tree window is actually represented by two different "hot spots." The first is the folder icon, while the second is the text name for the directory. Double-clicking on the text name, instead of the folder icon, always opens the corresponding directory window, without changing File Manager's display of subdirectories.

 Another topic related to these folder icons is the undocumented way to control their color. When Windows is installed, these folder icons are displayed as a drab grey color, which makes the File Manager window look heavy and clunky, in my opinion. These colors cannot be changed with the Control Panel, but you can change them by manually editing your WIN.INI file using the undocumented settings BUTTONFACE and BUTTONSHADOW.

The BUTTONFACE setting controls the color of push-buttons such as OK and Cancel in most dialog boxes, and also controls the color of File Manager's folder icons. A BUTTONFACE=255 255 255 setting makes these push-buttons and folders white on the inside. Any other color setting for BUTTONFACE returns the folder icons back to their original grey color. I find the white color a lot easier to look at, and it reproduces better when I print a File Manager screen to a laser printer for record-keeping purposes. A BUTTONSHADOW=0 0 0 setting makes the lower-right of most dialog buttons black (my preference), but has no effect on File Manager icons.

I make sure that WIN.INI files in systems I work with contain the following two lines in the [Colors] section to implement these preferences:

```
[Colors]
ButtonFace=255 255 255
ButtonShadow=0 0 0
```

Each setting, of course, uses the same *red green blue* numbering system as all other entries in the [Colors] section. Upper- and lowercase is not important in these settings.

The Undocumented Way to Show All Directories

You probably already know how to display a different drive and its list of directories in the File Manager's Directory Tree window — you click the icon for the drive you want to display or press Ctrl+C (for drive C:, etc.) with the keyboard. Then, if you want to show all subdirectories below the top level of directories, you click Tree Show-All on the menu or press Ctrl+*. But there is an easier and faster way to accomplish the same thing.

Although it isn't explained in the Windows manual or the File Manager's help system, if you hold down the Shift key while clicking a drive icon, File Manager displays all levels of the directory tree for that drive. This saves you a few keystrokes or mouse clicks every time you need this feature.

A Quick Reference for File Manager

Now that some of the lesser-known functions of the File Manager have been discussed, this topic might best be concluded with a tool that is seriously needed to get the most out of the File Manager — a quick reference chart to major mouse and keyboard shortcuts. This chart appears in Figure 3-2.

This chart is not an exhaustive list, by any means. A complete list of all keyboard and mouse actions in the File Manager would have to include many well-known functions, such as holding down the Shift key and pressing cursor-arrow keys to highlight several filenames in a row. Many of these generic shortcuts, which work in almost all Windows applications, are listed in Chapter 9. You can list other shortcuts by accessing File Manager's Help Keyboard menu item.

The Windows Executive _____

Using the MS-DOS Executive as a Second Shell

Since both this chapter and Chapter 2 have gone into detail on two of the shells provided with Windows — the Program Manager and the File Manager — some space should be given as well to three totally undocumented programs that come with Windows, one of which is a shell itself. That program is the MS-DOS Executive. The others are SysEdit, an editor for CONFIG.SYS and similar files; and WinHelp, a hypertext reader. These programs are discussed in the next section.

Keyboard Action	Result
Ctrl+Slash (/)	Selects all files in the current directory window.
Ctrl+Backslash (\)	Deselects all files in the current directory window.
Ctrl+Asterisk (*)	Shows all subdirectories (in the Directory Tree window).
Ctrl+Tab	Cycles through all directory windows, even if they're not visible.
Ctrl+*letter*	Changes to the specified drive (in the Directory Tree window).
Shift+F4	Tiles all open directory windows.
Shift+F5	Cascades all open directory windows.
F5	Refreshes listings (if the contents of a window have changed).
F7	Moves the selected files (after you type a destination directory).
F8	Copies the selected files (after you type a destination directory).
Del	Deletes the selected files (after you confirm).
Enter	Opens the selected directory or runs the selected application. Same as double-clicking the mouse.

(continued)

Figure 3-2: File Manager shortcuts reference chart.

Mouse Action	Result
Mouse Drag	*Moves* the selected files (if the destination directory is on the same drive as the source directory) or *copies* the selected files (if the destination directory is on a different drive than the source directory).
Ctrl+Drag	Forces File Manager to *copy* the selected files instead of moving them.
Alt+Drag	Forces File Manager to *move* the selected files instead of copying them.
Mouse Click	Selects a file and deselects any previously selected files.
Shift+Click	Selects a group of files between the one clicked and one that was previously clicked.
Ctrl+Click	Selects a file *without* deselecting any previously selected files.
Ctrl+Shift+Click	Selects a group of files between the one clicked and one that was previously Ctrl+Clicked, without deselecting any previously selected groups of files.
Shift+Click	(on a drive icon) Changes the Directory Tree window to the selected drive and forces the tree to display all subdirectories. *(Undocumented feature.)*

Figure 3-2: File Manager shortcuts reference chart *(continued).*

No mention of the Executive, SysEdit, or WinHelp applications appears in the Windows manual. Nor does an icon for these applications appear in a group window in the Program Manager when Setup installs Windows for you. But they are installed on your disk, lying dormant in your main Windows directory until you run across them yourself.

The Executive, of course, was the only shell provided with Windows 2.*x* and fell into some disrepute because it displayed only filenames — no icons — and didn't live up to the promise of the graphical user interface that

Windows offered. Microsoft obviously doesn't want the crude, fast Executive reflecting on the new, "cool" Windows, which is why there's no mention of it. It appears on the disk only for the sake of compatibility in companies that have built front-ends around the pull-down menus of the Executive.

Yet the Executive has some advantages of its own that Windows users deserve to know about. (Why it was called the *MS-DOS* Executive I'll never know, since it's a true Windows app, not a DOS program.) Some of these advantages are:

1. The Executive has many of the same capabilities as the newer File Manager but is much faster. The Executive can display directories, launch applications by double-clicking on the name of a program, load files into applications by double-clicking on a file with an extension that matches an association set up in WIN.INI, and move and copy files from the keyboard (but not drag them with a mouse).

2. The Executive has the ability to support multiple instances of itself. Unlike the File Manager, which refuses to start another copy of itself, you can run two copies of the Executive in order to compare two directories or drives side-by-side. (Be careful, if you do this, not to move or copy any files that might become "lost" in the confusion between the two Executives.)

3. You can start the Executive with it displaying a certain drive by preceding its filename on the command line with that drive. For example, defining an icon's properties with the Command Line D:\MSDOS.EXE starts the Executive and makes it display the current directory of the D: drive.

4. You can fully customize the Executive's menu structure to perform a wide variety of tasks automatically, by using an add-on utility like WinBatch from Wilson WindowWare. (See the WinBatch chapter in the "Excellence in Windows Shareware" section for an address and order form for.)

5. Most interestingly, the Executive is the only Windows application that, when placed in the LOAD= line of WIN.INI, doesn't just load itself but runs itself almost full-screen, as though you had placed it on the RUN= line instead. Because the Program Manager (or any shell program) minimizes itself when you place any program on the RUN= line of WIN.INI, this is a valuable feature of the Executive. Because it RUNs when you only told it to LOAD, the Program Manager is fooled and comes up as an almost-full-screen app itself, *not* minimized. This is

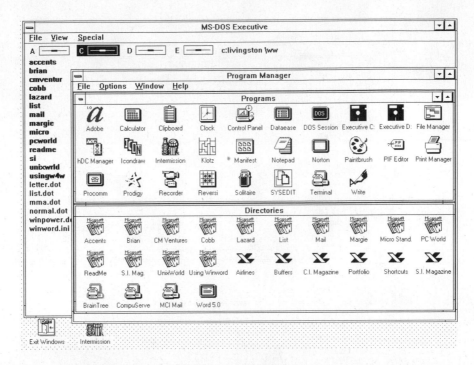

Figure 3-3: The Executive loads behind Program Manager.

the only way to get two shells to start up automatically — one, in the front, being the Program Manager, while the other, waiting in the background if you need a quick peek at your directories, is the Executive. See Figure 3-3: with the Executive on your LOAD= line and Program Manager on the SHELL= line in your SYSTEM.INI file, both programs start up as shown automatically — no Recorder tricks are necessary to make both shells appear on-screen, as was discussed in the previous chapter in the File Manager section.

I have frequently used the Executive's load vs. run behavior to start up both Program Manager and the Executive when working on projects that required a lot of file viewing. When the File Manager was just not fast enough for the job, the Executive was a refreshing change of pace. It's not very fancy — Microsoft was so intent on *not* upgrading it for the release of Windows 3.0 that they didn't make it display artsy 3-D drive icons like the File Manager, or even give it a Help system — but speed is sometimes its own reward.

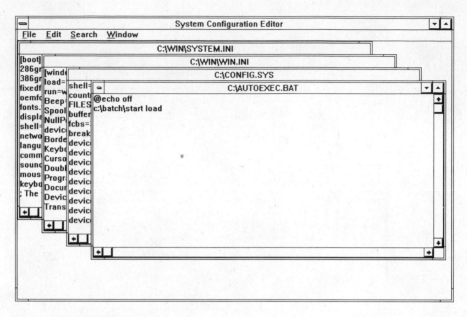

Figure 3-4: The SysEdit window.

SysEdit

Another undocumented program in your Windows directory, besides the Executive, is a funny little editor called SysEdit. This text editor opens only four files — CONFIG.SYS and AUTOEXEC.BAT from the C: drive, and WIN.INI and SYSTEM.INI files from the Windows directory. This is shown in Figure 3-4.

When Windows 3.0 was in beta testing in the months before the commercial version was released, SysEdit was always installed by Windows Setup in one of the Program Manager groups. As soon as the commercial version started shipping, however, SysEdit disappeared from the Program Manager (presumably because it was "too powerful" for end users) and became just another file buried in the dozens of other files in your Windows directory. This almost guaranteed that it would become a "hot tip" for industry pundits. Every PC magazine on the newsstand raved about how great this hidden editor was.

I can't say that I share these feelings about little SysEdit. It can't edit other files that are important to Windows, like PROGMAN.INI. It only finds your CONFIG.SYS and AUTOEXEC.BAT files if they are in the root directory of drive C: — not much use if you're on a network and these files aren't in that location. And if you use SysEdit while Windows is running under the DOS "compatibility box" of OS/2 (not something I recommend), SysEdit doesn't find DOS's

CONFIG.SYS and AUTOEXEC.BAT, but instead finds *OS/2's* CONFIG.SYS and AUTOEXEC.BAT, which are *very* different files and not suited for casual editing.

Anyway, it's rare that you would need to make a change simultaneously to all four of the files that SysEdit opens. A much better way to accomplish the kind of tasks you would want to do with SysEdit is to define both .INI and .SYS as extensions that automatically launch Notepad. This way, you can pull down the File Run command in either Program Manager or File Manager and type CONFIG.SYS — or just double-click on the file CONFIG.SYS — to start Notepad with CONFIG.SYS already loaded. Because you can't actually run a .SYS file like a .COM file, you might as well treat .SYS as an extension that brings up Notepad, in order to gain fast editing access to your CONFIG.SYS. And since Notepad allows multiple instances of itself, you can use this method to start two or three Notepads and compare the text of different files side by side, if you ever need to.

To accomplish this association, open your WIN.INI file in Notepad and make sure that the [Extensions] section includes the following entries:

```
[Extensions]
ini=notepad^.ini
sys=notepad^.sys
```

Some people add BAT=NOTEPAD^.BAT to the [Extensions] section also, so that Notepad automatically brings up for editing any batch file they double-click on. People who do this also make sure that all batch files under Windows are actually run from PIF files (a good idea, in order to test each of your batch files for compatibility with Windows). For this to work, the PROGRAMS= line in WIN.INI must be edited to delete BAT as an extension that Windows assumes will start programs. After this edit, your PROGRAMS= line should look as follows (where [bat] indicates that the extension BAT has been edited out):

```
Programs=exe com pif [bat]
```

Finally, if you need to edit the four configuration files quite often, you can define icons in the Program Manager that bring up CONFIG.SYS, AUTOEXEC.BAT, and so on inside Notepad anytime you double-click the icon. Simply create new icons by clicking File New Program-Item from the Program Manager menu, then define the command line for those items similar to the following:

```
NOTEPAD autoexec.bat
```

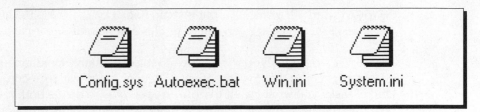

Figure 3-5: Fast access to your configuration files.

This method of specifying a different Notepad icon for each of your configuration files — CONFIG.SYS, AUTOEXEC.BAT, WIN.INI, and SYSTEM.INI — results in a row of four icons in a Program Manager window that looks like Figure 3-5.

WinHelp

Your Free Hypertext Applet

The third and final undocumented Windows application discussed in this chapter is WINHELP.EXE. Everyone who uses Windows for more than a few minutes, of course, knows that pressing the F1 key or clicking Help Index in most applications displays a Help window. But fewer people know much about the free-standing WinHelp application itself.

WinHelp is a full Windows program in its own right. If you pull down File Run in Program Manager or File Manager, and type WINHELP, the WinHelp application opens its own window, ready for you to use File Open to examine any file you may have that is in Windows .HLP format. This is shown in Figure 3-6.

In addition to providing help screens for commercial Windows applications, WinHelp can serve as a basic hypertext reader for *any* document file you care to build in Windows .HLP format. WinHelp has the ability to jump to any other portion of a document based on "hot words" that are clicked, and to display pop-up windows defining terms that appear in different colors. .HLP files can display fonts in a variety of sizes, for ease of reading in many different applications. WinHelp could be used to create documentation for internally developed company software, a graphical parts catalog for a supply company (updated monthly or weekly), a jobs bank complete with printable application forms, and on and on.

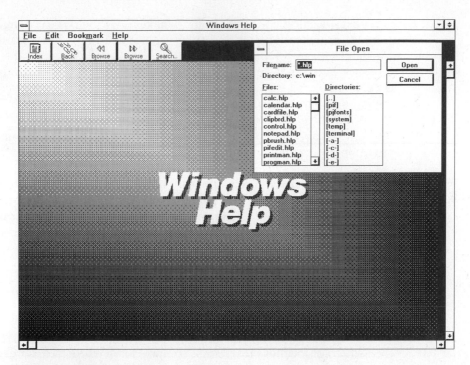

Figure 3-6: The WinHelp reader window.

The only way to prepare text files in .HLP format (at the time that Windows 3.0 was released) was by using the Windows Software Developer's Kit (SDK). But enterprising, independent programmers have worked to create stand-alone utilities that can compile your documents into this format at will. None of these products were ready for prime time at this writing, but should be advertised publicly by the time you read this.

WinHelp's ability to load independent .HLP files will allow you to define an association for these files in the [Extensions] section of your WIN.INI file. Then you can simply click on any .HLP file and open it automatically. Your [Extensions] section will look like this:

```
[Extensions]
hlp=winhelp^.hlp
```

You should do this with caution, however. Not all Windows 3.0-compatible applications use WinHelp to display their help windows. In particular, applications that load their own help engine, such as Excel, 2.1's EXCELHLP.HLP, won't work properly if the .HLP extension is hard-coded to WinHelp in your WIN.INI.

One customization you might want to make to WinHelp is to change the colors the application uses to display its "hot words" — Jump words that, when clicked, switch the reader to other sections of a document, and Glossary words that pop up a definition window when the left mouse button is held down over the word. On certain displays, such as laptop screens or monochrome monitors, the default green color that WinHelp uses for these words may be difficult or impossible to see. Or you might just prefer that these words appear in red or some other assertive color that demands attention.

Naturally, since the WinHelp application itself isn't documented in the Windows manual, there's no mention of how to change these colors, either. The following are the undocumented settings you can use in your WIN.INI file to determine these colors. Create a [Windows Help] section (if one doesn't already exist in your WIN.INI) and insert lines like these:

```
[Windows Help]
Jumpcolor=red green blue
Popupcolor=red green blue
```

The variables *red, green,* and *blue* are numbers from 0 to 255 that represent the RGB color for these text items. To make jump words red, for example, you would specify JUMPCOLOR=255 0 0. Case is not important in the keyword in WIN.INI.

Other Applets _____

The remainder of this chapter will discuss undocumented features and workarounds for other Windows applets such as the Control Panel, Calculator, and Paintbrush. But before launching into those topics, I need to explain a couple of undocumented features that really don't fit in anywhere except under "other."

One of the funniest hidden Windows features is the "gang" screen that documents the Microsoft people who worked on the Windows 3.0 project, as shown in Figure 3-7. This screen takes over as a kind of wallpaper, listing everyone from "the magicians" (developers) to "moms and dads" (including chairman Bill Gates, v.p. Steve Ballmer, etc.), with their e-mail handles — first name and last initial.

```
THE MAGICIANS:
aaronr amitc arthurc bobgu chipa chrisc chrisg clarkc craigc davidds davidw earleh fernandd georgep glenns gunterz
jaywant jimmat kens kensy lalithar marcw mikecole mikedr peterbe philba ralphl richp rong sankar toddla tonyg
THE TESTERS:
bertm camp chrissh chriswil davidti dougr erich jeffst johnen johns korys lyndahi mattl randyg richsa rong stephenb stuart
terrib timg tycar
USER ED:
betsyt chrisbr chrisdo chrish danbr danda davee garyb joank jimgr jimro kathypf laurak laurap lindah lindas loriw marcsm
marionj michaelm niklas pauli peggy petrar robertaw rosem scottmc sharot shelleym stevenwa tonye
PROGRAM MANAGEMENT:
davidcol ericst greglo jodys lisacr markwa melissmo timmcc
MARKETING:
celesteb danbo jonro richab sherryr tomja
SCENERY:
alig tandyt virginia susank
SPECIAL THANKS TO:
bobm chrisla donha kaikal lins neilk scottlu stevewo MSFT
MOMS:
chrisga julieg lorisi maryho sarahh
DADS:
billg russw steveb
```

Exit Windows   Intermission   Paintbrush   Microsoft Word   Program Manager

Figure 3-7: The Windows 3.0 Gang screen.

To see this screen on your PC, first minimize all your applications. Then hold down the F3 key while typing WIN3, and then release F3. Press the Backspace key, and the Microsoft Gang appears. Clicking once on the Desktop gets rid of it again.

This same type of screen appears under Windows 2.*x* if you type F1 F5 F9 F4 Backspace. Neither version's trick works in the other version.

Some of the Windows applets contain gang screens, too. Windows Write, a little executive word processor, has one, although since Write had only one primary developer this screen is more like a "gang of one." To see it, open Write (double-click its icon, or File Run WRITE.EXE) without loading a document. Hold down the Ctrl key while you click the right mouse button on the "Page 1" area at the bottom of the screen. Then pull down the Help menu and select About Write. The subsequent dialog box fills up with a "party" scene consisting of random colored balloons. The animation finishes with the message "Latest by PaulT," a reference to Paul Travis, the developer of Write. An interesting feature of this animation is that it will not appear after you have loaded a document into Write. Performing any such action in Write has the effect of overwriting the area of memory occupied by the code for the animation — a nice design touch that frees up Write memory for more serious uses.

An even more impressive gang screen appears in Word for Windows 1.x. Pull down the Format menu and click Define Styles. Click the Options button. Choose to Define Style Name NORMAL and set it to be Based On NORMAL. You will see a message that you cannot define a style based on itself. Click OK to accept this message, then click Cancel to get out of the Define Styles dialog box. Pull down the Help menu and click About. Once you see the About dialog box, put CapsLock *on,* then hold down the keys O, P, U, and S. The dialog box turns into a fireworks display, with the names of Winword's development gang rolling through the box like movie credits. Press Esc to get rid of the effect.

Since all these credits are taking up space in the program file on disk anyway, I don't know why there can't just be a choice on the Help menu that displays these names without having to follow all the stage directions. I guess part of the fun is knowing that only the "in-crowd" is aware of these tricks. Well, welcome to the club.

Calculator

The Case of the Missing "Advanced" Features

The Windows Calculator is a much-appreciated utility, especially since it now converts numbers among the decimal, binary, and hexadecimal numbering system for those of us who have to figure out the manuals that come with some of our system-integration applications these days.

Calculator, however, has one odd quirk. You can switch between its Standard mode, which is a simple, four-function calculator, and its Scientific mode, which offers a far wider variety of algebraic and statistical choices. But the square-root button, which appears in the Standard view, disappears from the Calculator in Scientific view, where it is needed the most!

There is a fairly simple way to get the square-root function back, without toggling back and forth between Scientific and Standard modes.

Any number, raised to the power of $\frac{1}{2}$, produces its own square root (as in $81^{0.5}=9$). Place the original number, such as 81, in the Calculator's window, as shown in Figure 3-8. Then press the Calculator's "x to the power of y" button. Type in the number .5, then press the equal sign ($=$) or whatever the next operation will be, such as addition or subtraction. You have taken the square root of 81, and the number 9 appears in the window.

```
┌─────────────────────────────────────────────────────────────┐
│ ─              Calculator                                  ▼ │
├─────────────────────────────────────────────────────────────┤
│ Edit  View  Help                                             │
│      ┌──────────────┐                                        │
│      │ √ Scientific │                                        │
│      │   Standard   │  ┌──────────────────────────────┐ 81.  │
│      └──────────────┘  └──────────────────────────────┘      │
│                                                              │
│  ○ Hex  ◉ Dec  ○ Oct  ○ Bin   │ ◉ Deg   ○ Rad   ○ Grad │    │
│                                                              │
│  [  C  ] [ CE ] [ Back ]  □ Inv    □ Hyp    [   ] [   ] [   ]│
│                                                              │
│  [ Sta ] [ F-E ] [ ( ] [ ] ] [ MC ] [ 7 ] [ 8 ] [ 9 ] [ / ] [ Mod ] [ And ]│
│                                                              │
│  [ Ave ] [ dms ] [ Exp ] [ ln ] [ MR ] [ 4 ] [ 5 ] [ 6 ] [ * ] [ Or ] [ Xor ]│
│                                                              │
│  [ Sum ] [ sin ] [ x^y ] [ log ] [ MS ] [ 1 ] [ 2 ] [ 3 ] [ - ] [ Lsh ] [ Not ]│
│                                                              │
│  [  s  ] [ cos ] [ x^3 ] [ n! ] [ M+ ] [ 0 ] [ +/- ] [ . ] [ + ] [ = ] [ Int ]│
│                                                              │
│  [ Dat ] [ tan ] [ x^2 ] [ 1/x ] [ PI ] [ A ] [ B ] [ C ] [ D ] [ E ] [ F ]│
└─────────────────────────────────────────────────────────────┘
```

Figure 3-8. In the Calculator's Scientific mode, the "x to the power of y" button can substitute for the missing square-root button.

Control Panel

Shrinking Your Wallpaper

The Windows Control Panel is the nerve center for an amazing array of settings, defaults, and preferences. It's not important to list them all here — most of these functions are adequately described in the Windows manual. But I'd like to start this discussion of Control Panel secrets with a topic that many people will find directly useful: how to shrink your "wallpaper" bitmap files down to a smaller size on your hard disk, but still enjoy the use of them.

I haven't included much information about wallpaper in this book or the accompanying diskettes, because I find that the use of wallpaper — any bitmap image other than a seamless, colored background — hurts Windows' performance. Specifically, whenever wallpaper is displayed and a portion of it is visible on the Desktop, Windows must constantly rewrite the bitmapped image every time an object is moved. And regardless of whether the wallpapered Desktop is visible or not, it's an object that Windows must keep track of in memory. A 16-color VGA wallpaper image is more than 150K in size.

But adding, selecting, and customizing wallpaper is one of the little joys of using Windows rather than DOS. So if you're going to use it, you might as well be able to claim back some of the hard disk space you lost when the wallpaper .BMP files that come with Windows were installed.

I touched on this subject in the previous chapter when I described the fact that the Windows logo, which Windows displays every time it loads, is not a bitmap, but is a Run Length Encoded (RLE) file — a compressed file. Windows bitmaps are fairly inefficient ways to store graphical data. The Windows bitmap format describes each pixel in the image, whether it is white, black, red, blue, or whatever. The Paintbrush .PCX format, by contrast, has a certain amount of compression built in. You can see this for yourself simply by opening a .BMP file in Paintbrush, then immediately saving it as a .PCX file. The .PCX file will take up fewer bytes.

RLE files are yet another way to save space when dealing with complex graphics files. In an .RLE file, a graphic is described as "20 pixels of red, 30 pixels of white," and so on, instead of every pixel being described.

It turns out, although this is undocumented, that Windows has the capabilities to display a bitmap file, whether it is in .BMP format *or* .RLE format. Try this for yourself: open the Control Panel and double-click on the Desktop icon. Every Windows installation includes at least one .RLE file — the Windows logo. Specify this file as your wallpaper; if you have a VGA system, the file is called VGALOGO.RLE, if you have an EGA system, EGALOGO.RLE, and so on. You'll need to specify the full path, since the Control Panel can't find files in directories other than the Windows directory. The logo file will be in the System subdirectory under Windows, so type something similar to C:\WINDOWS\SYSTEM\VGALOGO.RLE (whatever is appropriate for your configuration). See Figure 3-9.

Click OK to make the change take effect. You should see the Windows logo appear as wallpaper on your Desktop.

There are a few minor caveats to this procedure. First, unlike most Windows list boxes in which you specify filenames, you can't type *.RLE in the Control Panel Desktop dialog box and expect it to show you a list of all filenames that match that description in the current directory. Control Panel is limited to showing filenames in the Windows directory, so you'll have to know in advance the name of the file you want to specify.

Second, there are a variety of reasons why your Desktop wallpaper might not change immediately when you do this. If Windows is in real mode, and an application (including Windows) is using expanded memory, you must quit and restart Windows before the new file is loaded as wallpaper.

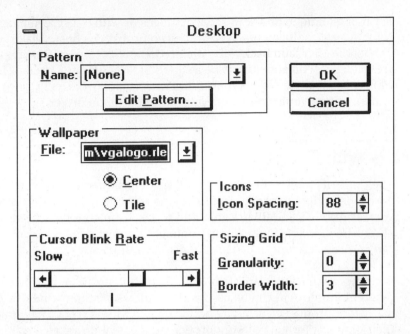

Figure 3-9: Specifying an .RLE file as Desktop wallpaper.

Third, you may not see any immediate effect if you toggle between the Centered setting for the wallpaper image and the Tiled setting. Changing the bitmap filename at the same time as changing the Center/Tile option usually works to "unstick" Control Panel so that restarting Windows is not necessary to set the change in your wallpaper.

Finally, you must have enough memory left to display the image. If you receive the message, "Unable to use *xyz.ext* as a Bitmap," then you may not have enough memory available to handle the file.

With the above concerns taken care of, though, you can use the Control Panel support for .RLE files to significantly reduce the disk space consumed by your wallpaper files. You need a program to convert bitmap files to the RLE4 format, and both WinGif and Paint Shop, shareware programs on the diskettes that accompany this book, work well for this purpose. After converting, you may find that the compressed files take up 10 to 50 percent less disk space.

Just as with the .RLE files contained in the Windows logo screen (discussed in the previous chapter), however, there may be a size limitation on .RLE files that the Control Panel can display. The limit on the logo screen is about 55K for an .RLE file — a size that can easily be exceeded by a complex image.

Try this technique first with smaller images or with full-screen images that contain large, solid areas of color: they compress the best. (Make sure not to confuse Microsoft's .RLE format with CompuServe's RLE format— they are different. You should also be aware that RLE4 files are 16-color files, while RLE8 files are 256-color files, and won't display correctly on your system unless you have a 256-color video board and driver.)

Difficulties with Fonts

The Control Panel is the most important means to add and remove Windows screen fonts, through its Fonts icon and dialog box. Other programs, such as Adobe's and Bitstream's, add screen fonts, but these fonts should always be viewable in the Control Panel by choosing the Fonts icon and clicking on each typeface in turn to display samples.

Windows 3.0 brings new possibilities and problems to fonts, however. A different font format can be used with Windows 3.0 than Windows 2.*x*, and many font products (including Adobe's Type 1 fonts) require upgrades from their older 2.*x* formats to work properly under Windows 3.0. Additionally, even when fonts are added with the Control Panel, all Windows applications may not immediately recognize them. Word for Windows, for example, does not list new fonts in its pull-down typeface menu until you click Printer Setup and then OK. This rebuilds Winword's printer-capabilities list, which is maintained in the machine-readable WINWORD.INI file. Other Windows word processors, such as Windows Write, always recognize all fonts in the Control Panel without requiring any separate steps.

Another difference is that Windows 2.*x* displayed an error message if fonts installed by the Control Panel (and listed in the [fonts] section of the WIN.INI file) were not actually present on the disk, having been deleted or corrupted, perhaps. Windows 3.0 does not display any such message. If you experience a problem with fonts, always check the font files on disk and ensure that they match the files listed in WIN.INI.

Other actions that you can take through the Control Panel may affect your system in a negative way. If you want to install a new set of screen fonts, and use the Control Panel to delete all the existing fonts, the Add Fonts button in Control Panel becomes useless and your PC may even freeze. In this situation, you must run Setup, which reinstalls the fonts. Then add the fonts you want *before* deleting the others. Make sure you always have a valid Helvetica font (or Helv or other, similar name), since Windows uses this sans-serif typeface to display its dialog boxes and error messages.

Similarly, adding the same screen font twice may paralyze Control Panels ability to add and remove fonts (and conflict with other functions). You must change the WIN.INI file manually in this case to remove any lines that contain the same typeface information.

Additionally, deleting one of the screen fonts that comes with Windows (Helv, Tms Rmn, Courier, and Symbol) in order to see the effect of a third-party font may make it impossible for you to add back the original screen font (even after removing the third-party font). If you remove the resident Tms Rmn typeface, for example, and then attempt to add it back, Windows displays its "hourglass" pointer as though it were taking some action, but nothing happens — even though no error message appears. To fix this situation, you must exit and restart Windows. This restores your ability to reinstall one of Windows' screen fonts.

Colors and Patterns May Be "Stuck" if Control File Is Lost

Control Panel functions such as Colors and Desktop Patterns, which are used to change Windows' appearance, are stored in the CONTROL.INI file (usually located in the Windows directory or, on a network, in each user's personal directory). If you make a change to Colors or Desktop Patterns, but these changes never become effective, it may be necessary to check CONTROL.INI. If this file is corrupted or marked read-only (as it might be if the only copy is on a network drive), the Control Panel cannot write changes into this file and doesn't display an error message. CONTROL.INI is a plain text file that can be opened and viewed with Notepad or any text editor. Confirm that it is writeable and not scrambled or otherwise damaged. In case CONTROL.INI is corrupted or missing, it may be necessary to copy a vanilla copy of CONTROL.INI from another Windows installation, or rerun Setup to obtain a fresh copy. Once the new copy is in the Windows directory (or a writeable directory on the Path), subsequent changes to it should store and display correctly.

Timeslicing May Allow Incorrect Values

The Control Panel acts as the primary means to control the amount of time that foreground and background applications receive when Windows is running in 386 enhanced mode. You can change the values (timeslices) for applications by choosing the "386" icon in the Control Panel. Applications may be set to receive between 1 and 10000 timeslices, relative to other applications (which also receive their allotted slices of time). Microsoft technical support representatives sometimes suggest that specifying a

Foreground setting of 10000 is a way to ensure that whatever DOS application is in the foreground will get all the available timeslices if it is not idle, regardless of the value set for applications in the background. Another way to achieve a similar result (and get the fastest possible performance for a DOS application running under Windows) is to make a PIF file for the application, with the Exclusive box marked Yes. This application then has exclusive use of all the timeslices while it is running full-screen. Notice, however, that this can interfere with other applications that *should* get a little time in the background — perhaps electronic mail messages or fax reception.

In any event, *never* set the maximum value to anything higher than 10000. The Control Panel doesn't check to see whether the number you enter is valid or not, and doesn't display any error message if you type, say, 10001. But this can lead to erratic behavior and is difficult to trouble-shoot.

Notepad

Determining Notepad's Maximum File Size

The Windows Notepad is a handy plain-text editor for making changes to configuration files like WIN.INI, as noted earlier in this chapter. But Notepad version 3.0 has one serious drawback — it can't edit files that grow larger than a certain size.

The Windows manual states that the maximum size for a Notepad file is "approximately 50,000 characters," but the actual limitation depends on what you are doing with the file you currently have open.

If you just want to *look* at a text file, you can open a file as large as 54K in Notepad. To *edit* in Notepad, however, the file cannot be larger than 45K. If you add material to a file in Notepad and receive the message, "Insufficient memory to complete this operation," you've probably run into this limitation. You may still be able to save and load the file again at this point, even if you can't edit it.

A far more subtle limitation to Notepad is its Word Wrap feature. When you click Edit Word Wrap, you can type paragraphs in Notepad without your text floating off into space at the right edge of the window. This is fine until you try to *print* such a file. Notepad doesn't word wrap when it's printing, so all those paragraphs tend to print as long lines disappearing off the right edge of the paper. I can't tell you how many text files I've received from other people, on bulletin boards or mailed to me on diskettes, that were saved with Word Wrap *on* in Notepad and which can't be successfully printed by Notepad or by copying them to the printer! At this point, it's necessary to load the files into Windows Write or some serious word processor, set margins manually, and print the file again.

For all these reasons, you'll probably find it easier to use the WinEdit program from the diskettes included with this book. Set the [Extensions] section in your WIN.INI file so WinEdit starts up when you double-click files with extensions like .TXT, .DOC, and so on, as shown:

```
[Extensions]
txt=c:\winedit\winedit.exe  ^.txt
doc=c:\winedit\winedit.exe ^.doc
```

Paintbrush

16-Color vs. 256-Color Bitmaps

The Windows Paintbrush represents a leap in capabilities over the paint program included with Windows 2.*x* — Microsoft Paint. For one thing, Paintbrush is capable of editing graphic files in 16 colors with the standard VGA video driver, or 256 colors if you have enough memory on your video board to support a 256-color driver.

This versatility can cause some confusion, however, if you aren't careful. Although it doesn't say so in the Windows manual, if you load a 256-color graphics file in Paintbrush 3.0 while you are actually using a 16-color video driver, and you then save the file, you *permanently truncate* the 256-color file down to a 16-color image. This occurs even if you choose the 256-color format in the File Save dialog box.

Replacing the PrintScreen Function

A hidden capability of the Paintbrush is that it provides you with one of the few ways to restore a basic DOS capability that somehow was left out of Windows 3.*x* — the ability to press the PrintScreen key and make the current screen print on your printer.

You can restore DOS's PrintScreen capability under Windows if you use either, SnagIt or Utility Pak on the diskettes included with this book. SnagIt, for example, turns your Ctrl+Shift+P key combination into a PrintScreen function that you can configure as you like, automatically printing the screen, or saving it to a file, or a number of other options.

But you should also know the procedure to perform the PrintScreen operation under Windows Paintbrush. You might, after all, someday use a PC that isn't equipped with a copy of SnagIt. Or the Paintbrush procedure may be useful when you need to modify a quick screen shot.

Under Windows, pressing the PrintScreen key does not send the screen to the printer, even if you have a graphics printer such as a LaserJet, PostScript, or dot-matrix printer. Instead, the PrintScreen key sends a copy of the screen to the Windows Clipboard. (The Alt+PrintScreen key combination, by contrast, sends only the *active* window, which may not necessarily include the entire screen, to the Clipboard.) Since the Clipboard cannot print files, you might think that you are stuck without a way to print whatever it is on the screen that you wish to document.

The Paintbrush can help you out of this situation, although it takes more steps than the PrintScreen function in DOS. Just do the following (it helps if Paintbrush is already loaded as an icon at the bottom of your screen while you step through this example):

STEPS:

Printing Your Screen in Windows

Step 1. Capture the screen. Position on the screen whatever it is you want to print. Press the PrintScreen key to capture the entire screen, or Alt+PrintScreen to capture just the active window.

Step 2. Maximize Paintbrush. Activate Paintbrush and maximize it to occupy the full screen.

Step 3. Create a large, blank slate. If you captured the full screen, pull down the Options menu in Paintbrush and click Image Attributes. Change the measurements of the image to "pixels" instead of "inches" or "centimeters." Edit the number of pixels so that the image will have about 10 percent more pixels in both width and height than your actual screen driver. For example, if you are using a Super VGA driver with a resolution of 800×600, set the image attributes for 880×660 pixels. (This allows a little "white space" around the screen capture that you are about to import into the Paintbrush, in case you need to move or crop the image.) Click OK. Make sure the background color is white (or whatever color you want the background of your screen-capture to be). Then pull down the File menu and click New to create a blank area the correct size for your screen capture.

Step 4. Zoom out. Pull down the View menu and click Zoom Out. This forces the entire area of your image to be displayed inside the rectangular "viewport" in which Paintbrush displays your image file. (The Windows manual calls this viewport the "drawing area.") Then press Shift+Insert to paste your screen capture from the Clipboard into the viewport. After a few seconds, you see a grey, shaded area the size of your screen capture. Your screen should look like Figure 3-10. Use the mouse to drag this image away from the edge of the viewport (again, so you have some white space in which to move or crop the image later). Then click on any of the tools at the left edge of the Paintbrush window, such as the brush or eraser. Paintbrush beeps once, then changes the grey, shaded area to a small representation of your captured screen.

Step 5. Print or Save. Now pull down the View menu and click Zoom In. At this point, you can save the file as a bitmap (.BMP) or Paintbrush (.PCX) file, or print the image by choosing File Print. You usually get the best results when printing a screen shot to a laser printer when you click the Use Printer Resolution box *on*, and specify a scale of 200%. See Figure 3-11. (Printers with a resolution other than 300 dots-per-inch will require a different setting.) If you want to print only a *portion* of the screen, Paintbrush offers a "Print Window Partial" radio button that allows you to drag the mouse over the part of the image you want to print.

This method is a lot faster to *do* than it is to *describe*. Although it's a lot more cumbersome than just pressing the PrintScreen key and automatically getting a screen dump on your printer, you do have a lot more control over what portion of the screen is printed, and what size it appears, than with the DOS PrintScreen function. And it doesn't hurt to know this method — this is how I produced all the screenshots in this book.

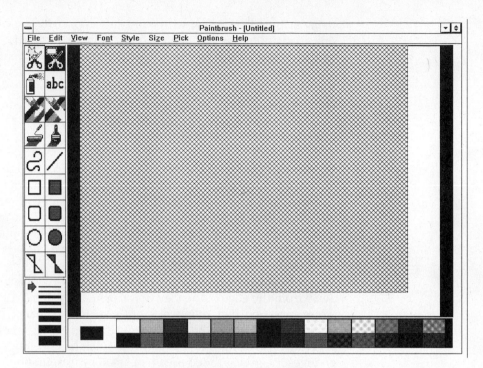

Figure 3-10: A Print Screen image after pasting into Paintbrush.

Windows — Upgrade Information

Version 3.0a Upgrade

Microsoft began shipping Windows version 3.0a in December 1990, after having shipped over one million copies of version 3.0 during the previous seven months. Version 3.0a corrects the following problems:

SmartDrive and larger-than-32MB hard disks. The SmartDrive disk-caching program included with Windows 3.0a now detects the presence of (and prevents itself from accessing) nonstandard hard disk partitions that are larger than 32 megabytes. The original 3.0 version of SmartDrive corrupted hard disks that were partitioned this way with disk utilities such as Ontrack Computer Systems' Disk Manager, Priam Systems' InnerSpace, Storage Dimensions' SpeedStor, and Golden Bow Systems' Vfeatures Deluxe. See Chapter 8 for more information.

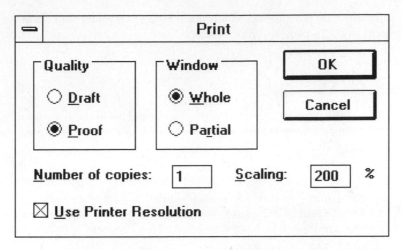

Figure 3-11: The Paintbrush Print dialog box.

SHARE command in DOS 4.01. An incompatibility between Windows and DOS 4.01's SHARE command (a program that is required to prevent some hard disk conflicts) has been resolved.

Corrections to standard mode. Windows 3.0a includes an updated DOSX.EXE file, a DOS extender used by Windows in standard mode (286 protected mode). The extender provides a link between DOS applications running under Windows in protected mode and DOS routines that require real mode.

New Network NetBIOS driver. A new, corrected version of NetBIOS, which is required by some applications to communicate over a network, is included. This will improve the stability of DOS 3270 terminal-emulation programs and other network-specific programs.

New printer drivers. Several printer drivers that were not available when Windows 3.0 was shipped are now included with version 3.0a. One of the most significant additions is a new driver for the HP LaserJet III, which adds Resolution Enhancement capabilities to grey-scale printing and is said to improve overall performance. Other drivers include a new PostScript driver that supports more models and clears up some problems printing graphics files larger than 64K in size. Extended ANSI characters (characters like the copyright symbol, which are not on the keyboard) can now be printed with improved drivers for HP's DeskJet printer and IBM Graphics Printers.

The upgrade package also includes a 20-page booklet that responds to the most commonly asked questions on Microsoft's telephone support lines.

Version 3.0b Upgrade

Microsoft began shipping Windows version 3.0b in the second quarter of 1991. This revision includes all the changes in version 3.0a, plus the following:

DDE fixes. The Windows kernel was patched in order to enable some DDE links that were not possible under Windows 3.0. For example, certain DDEInitiate and DDEExecute statements between Word for Windows and Excel will not work without this patch. This problem is described in the Dynamic Data Exchange section of Chapter 4.

UAE fixes. Version 3.0b and version 3.0a both include patches that eliminate a few rare causes of "Unrecoverable Application Error" messages. However, this affects only certain cases, and offers no improvement for Windows applications, such as Word for Windows, that cause UAE messages when they write to a memory segment without checking that the memory is actually free.

Correct PIF installation in WIN.INI. If you install Windows 3.0 into the same directory as Windows 2.x, you may receive the error message, "No association exists" when you try to run a PIF file. This is because the Windows 3.0 Setup program does not write the letters PIF into your WIN.INI file in the PROGRAMS= line. You must add this extension manually, if it is not already present, before Windows will recognize PIF files as files that it can run. Version 3.0b fixes this, and always writes the extension PIF into the PRO-GRAMS= line if it is needed.

Version 3.1 Upgrade

At this writing, Microsoft was preparing a release of Windows version 3.1. The following is a list of some of the additions in this version:

TrueType. Windows 3.1 includes TrueType, a program that displays fonts on-screen and prints them to printers that do not have internal fonts. The TrueType proportional fonts included with Windows 3.1, however, are limited to Times Roman and Helvetica, and therefore do not add much functionality to PostScript printers, or LaserJet printers that already have a Times/Helvetica cartridge.

File Manager improvements. Windows 3.1 includes a File Manager that reads directories much faster than the File Manager in Windows 3.0, and has other enhancements. This corrects some of the major complaints regarding this Windows shell.

Miscellaneous fixes. Windows 3.1 has a number of other fixes, including an expansion of the 64K System Resources memory segment, which prevents this area from becoming exhausted so quickly when you open applications that use many icons, such as the Program Manager, the Tool Bar in Word for Windows and Excel, etc.

How to Upgrade

You do not need any of the upgrades described above unless you use one of the features listed. Microsoft charges varying amounts for each upgrade, ranging from a standard list price for upgrades that increment a version number (such as version 3.0 to 3.1), to as little as $10 for upgrades that increment a letter (such as 3.0 to 3.0a). Some of the upgraded files (such as printer drivers) are also available by downloading them from CompuServe's MSWIN area. For more information, call Microsoft at 206-637-7098.

Summary

In this chapter, some of the secrets of the Windows applets have been examined. You should be able to use this information to:

▶ Print directories from the File Manager and use other shortcuts to make this utility faster and more productive.

▶ Take advantage of the Executive, SysEdit, and WinHelp when these applets are the best-suited utilities for your particular task.

▶ Display the "gang screens" that are built into many of the most popular Windows applications, including Windows itself.

▶ Work around various Windows limitations using undocumented features of the Calculator, Control Panel, and Paintbrush.

▶ Determine for yourself whether or not you need to upgrade from Windows 3.0 to higher numbered versions to solve various device incompatibilities.

Chapter 4
Secrets of Windows Applications

In this chapter...

I explain several of the factors that can affect the performance, predictability, and pleasure you can expect out of Windows applications:

▶ Installing Windows applications to give yourself the greatest flexibility and ease of upgrading in the future.

▶ Running Windows applications from shells like the Program Manager and File Manager, or through alternative (and perhaps quicker) means.

▶ Protecting Windows applications (and your data) from accidental or intentional corruption by other PC users.

▶ Optimizing Windows for the best performance of the graphical environment itself, and of Windows applications under that environment.

▶ Taking advantage of screen fonts — the ones that came with Windows and those you add from third-party packages — in such a way that you minimize the impact of these fonts on your overall performance.

▶ Customizing and configuring the most popular Windows programs, Word for Windows and Excel, as examples of little-understood and undocumented features that affect these and other applications.

▶ Examples of Dynamic Data Exchange (DDE) between applications such as Word for Windows and Excel, and some of the anomalies that can occur in software versions prior to the development of the newer Object Linking and Embedding (OLÉ) specification.

The primary purpose for running the Windows environment is, of course, to run Windows applications. And, for the most part, Windows applications, whether running simultaneously or separately, behave well. This contrasts with DOS applications running under Windows, which may never be quite as trouble-free as one would like (see Chapter 5, "Secrets of DOS Under Windows").

But Windows applications, too, have their share of quirks and tricks. And the common installation approach of "just stick the disk in drive A: and type SETUP" may not result in the best configuration of Windows applications to take advantage of your particular hardware — even as Windows-based install routines get smarter.

Installing Windows Applications

Don't Install Windows Apps Into the Windows Directory

A bad habit has taken hold among some Windows applications — they recommend or *require* that you install them into exactly the same directory that contains all your Windows files.

This habit has its origins in Windows 2.*x*. In those days, the only way to select a file or start an application with a mouse in the MS-DOS Executive shell was to physically switch into the directory containing the file or application. All this switching led to the practice of installing major Windows applications (such as Excel) into subdirectories under the main Windows directory — or into the Windows directory itself — where it was easy to click on the application you wanted to start (for example, EXCEL.EXE).

Windows 3.*x* makes these conventions obsolete. You can define an icon that always starts an application, regardless of the actual directory containing that application.

Yet the habit of installing applications into the main Windows directory persists. Even modern applications such as Adobe Type Manager insist on locating themselves in the main Windows directory. ATM gives you a choice of directory names for its font files, but not for the executable files themselves.

This is dangerous because it is not always easy to tell, after the fact, which files belong to which applications. Windows installs over 120 different files when you install it — and that doesn't count additional drivers you might add later. Pouring more files into this soup is bound to get you into trouble as soon as you need to upgrade. Here's why:

When a new version of a Windows application is released, you may wish to install this version on your computer system. Drivers from different versions of Windows and Windows applications, however, should not be mixed in the same directory. Almost every past revision of Windows (from Windows 2.0 to 2.1, and *definitely* from Windows 2.1 to 3.0) has required some changes to applications that run under Windows. But, if you install an upgrade to Windows (or one of its applications) into the same directory as the former copy, how can you be sure that *every* file is now compatible with the current version?

The only solution is to install every Windows application into its own, separate directory. This way, when a new version is released, you can easily install the new version and determine that the older version is completely deleted. I realize that this goes contrary to the installation instructions of many Windows packages, and that it seems like a little more work. But you will avoid *hours* or *days* of confusion a little way down the road, when a new installation won't exactly work and you have to find out what each little file does (or is supposed to do).

How to Separate an App from the Windows Directory

I'll use Adobe Type Manager as an example to show you how an application that has forced itself to be installed in the Windows directory can be moved safely to its own directory. ATM is a widely used utility for generating on-the-fly screen fonts. It's no better or worse than other Windows utilities — I use it as an example since many people are already familiar with it.

While installing ATM, you can observe that it copies a handful of executable files to your hard disk, and makes one important change to your SYSTEM.INI file — all of which is described in the ATM manual.

Aside from the font outlines that Adobe Type Manager copies to your hard disk when you install it (which you can place into any directory you specify), ATM copies to your hard disk the following files:

Filenames:	**What They Are:**
c:\windows\ATM.INI	the ATM initialization settings
c:\windows\ATMCNTRL.EXE	ATM's Control Panel
c:\windows\system\ATM.DLL	ATM's Dynamic Link Library
c:\windows\system\ATMSYS.DRV	ATM's System Driver

As you may know, .INI files must be located on the DOS Path for Windows applications to find them. Adobe Type Manager, furthermore, requires that its ATM.INI file be located in the same directory as your WIN.COM. So *that* file needs to stay put, but the others can be located almost anywhere we like.

I prefer to move these files into a separate directory called C:\ATM. To do this, first make sure that Adobe Type Manager is turned off (you run ATMCNTRL.EXE to do this). Then, using Windows' File Manager (or whatever utility you prefer), create the directory C:\ATM, and drag these three files into it — ATMCNTRL.EXE from the \WINDOWS directory, and ATM.DLL and ATMSYS.DRV from the \WINDOWS\SYSTEM directory.

Next, you must edit the one significant change that ATM made to your SYSTEM.INI file. When you installed Adobe Type Manager, it replaced Windows' own computer system driver file (SYSTEM.DRV) with its own system driver (ATMSYS.DRV). After this change, ATM's driver intercepts all requests that Windows applications make to Windows' system driver. If these requests involve displaying a new font on the screen, ATM services the request by providing the application with the desired screen font characters. If not, ATM's driver passes the request on to the original Windows system driver.

To accomplish this revision to the chain of command, the Adobe Type Manager installation changed a line in the [boot] section of your SYSTEM.INI file from this:

```
[boot]
system.drv=system.drv
```

to this:

```
[boot]
system.drv=atmsys.drv
atm.system.drv=system.drv
```

Since we just moved ATM's ATMSYS.DRV file into its own directory, we need to make sure that our SYSTEM.INI file accurately reflects this new location. Windows' SYSTEM.INI file assumes that any driver without a directory name in front of it must be located in the directory \WINDOWS\SYSTEM. In reality, any driver file mentioned in SYSTEM.INI may be located in *any* directory, if you insert the directory name in front of the filename. This assists you in moving non-Microsoft drivers out of the Windows directories. To reflect our move of ATM's system driver, for example, simply insert the correct directory name in front of ATMSYS.DRV so the SYSTEM.INI file looks like this:

```
[boot]
system.drv=c:\atm\atmsys.drv
atm.system.drv=system.drv
```

The next time you start Windows, Windows will load the ATMSYS.DRV driver from your C:\ATM directory. If you use the ATM Control Panel to turn ATM *on,* the Adobe logo appears briefly in the lower-left corner of your screen when you start Windows. If ATM is *off,* its driver still loads, but the Adobe logo appears crossed out to indicate that the driver is handing all control over to Windows' own system driver.

Finally, we must also place the C:\ATM directory on the DOS Path. This enables ATMSYS.DRV to find its library file ATM.DLL. It also enables the Program Manager icon that starts Adobe Type Manager's Control Panel to find the file C:\ATM\ATMCNTRL.EXE.

This procedure is much easier to *do* than it is to describe here in print. It goes very quickly, and will save you time a little way down the road. How? Someday, an upgrade to Adobe Type Manager will appear. If ATM is already located in a separate directory, you can easily manage the upgrade. I describe this procedure in the following topic.

Upgrading a Windows Application

Continuing with Adobe Type Manager as an example, let's examine this upgrade process.

1. Knowing that you want to upgrade (but that the upgraded version may not be trouble-free, and you might have to go back to the older version), you first rename the Adobe Type Manager directory from C:\ATM to a different name, perhaps with the version number in it, such as C:\ATM1. (Both Windows' File Manager and DOS 5.*x* can rename directories.)

2. Next, you install the new Adobe Type Manager, just as though it were a totally new install. Adobe Type Manager finds your ATM.INI file (since it is located in the same directory as your WIN.COM file) and preserves

any settings you may have customized. But the new ATM does *not* copy itself over your older system and driver files (which would have the effect of wiping them out), because you have moved them. This is exactly what we want.

3. If the newer version of ATM conflicts with some other software (or fails to meet your needs in whatever way), you can simply delete the new ATM, identifying and removing the files using the same procedure we used to separate ATM from Windows in the first place. Then, to put the older, tested version of ATM back in place, rename the directory C:\ATM1 back to C:\ATM. When you restart Windows, everything should be back to normal.

If you had installed the newer version of ATM over the older version, the newer version would have permanently copied over some of its earlier files. This would make a rollback to the older version (which is quite frequently necessary with new software) difficult — impossible, in fact, if the original diskettes from the older version aren't available at your fingertips. ("Where are those diskettes we installed two years ago...") This problem is compounded if the application is mixed into the main Windows directory, making the identification of the app's individual files much more difficult.

Many Windows applications have problems when you mix files from different versions into the application's *own* directory. Installing Word for Windows 1.1a over version 1.0, for example, in many cases didn't successfully update some of the "graphics import filters" that come with Winword. This caused some hard-to-diagnose errors.

A separate directory for each application, and a separate directory for each version of an application, is the best general rule. To implement this, don't put version numbers in the directory names that you use for the current versions of applications. (Install Windows into a directory named C:\WIN instead of C:\WIN3, for example.) Use a version number in a directory name only for directories that contain an old, obsolete version of a program — which you plan to delete as soon as the new version has proved itself compatible with all your other software. For example, when it comes time to upgrade an application such as Excel from Excel 2.1 to Excel 3.0, move Excel 2.1 from C:\EXCEL into a C:\EXCEL21 directory. Then the new version can use the same C:\EXCEL directory name that the old version did. This way, all your icons, batch files, etc. will continue to work without time-consuming edits to change their references to the directory name.

Upgrading to New Versions of Windows

The preceding advice to keep different versions of the same application in different directories until you are sure you can delete the old copy applies *double* to Windows itself.

Far too many people have come to grief because they made the mistake of installing Windows 3.*x* into the same directory where Windows 2.*x* resided. Windows 3.0 did not always destroy copies of old device drivers that were located in the Windows 2.*x* directory. Then these old drivers crashed Windows 3.0, garbled Windows print jobs, and caused many other headaches that were difficult to diagnose and correct. Additionally, Windows 3.0 sometimes didn't add some lines that were needed to the WIN.INI file — because a WIN.INI file already existed in the Windows 2.*x* directory and the Windows installation was programmed to preserve whatever preferences were already in this file.

These problems can be avoided by renaming the C:\WINDOWS directory to something like C:\WIN-OLD (making sure it's not on your Path), and then installing the new Windows diskettes into a new, empty C:\WINDOWS directory. In this case, you are guaranteed that all of the drivers in your C:\WINDOWS directory are compatible with the new version of Windows. And you ensure that every change that Windows needs to make during a complete install actually does take place.

This method requires a little more work initially than the method of just installing all applications into the same gigantic directory and hoping that everything continues to work. It requires that you make sure all applications and data are kept separate from each other. And it requires that any third-party driver files that crept into the *old* \WINDOWS\SYSTEM directory get moved into the *new* \WINDOWS\SYSTEM directory — or, better still, into their own directory (with directory-name references in SYSTEM.INI, as we did earlier in the example with the ATM drivers) so you won't have to move them ever again.

Don't assume future versions of Windows won't have these installation problems when you install into the same directory over and over, no matter how intuitive the Windows installation program gets. Here's an example to illustrate why:

Windows does not copy all the drivers from its distribution diskettes to your hard drive when you run Setup. Far from it — this would litter your drive with hundreds of files. Instead, Windows copies only a minimum set of drivers needed for your particular system. The other drivers you have to install on an as-needed basis, to support peripherals such as printers, scanners, external drives, and so forth.

For example, if you add a CD-ROM player to your system (which will become common as these devices plummet in cost), Windows requires that you install from its distribution diskettes a driver called LANMAN10.386 to support it in 386 mode. (This is explained in detail in Chapter 8.)

When you upgrade to version *X.x* of the newest, greatest Windows, however, the new version may not know that you customized your system with this driver. (And Windows can't copy this CD-ROM driver to everyone's computer just in case they need it.) The result is that you are left with an *old* CD-ROM driver in your *updated* Windows directory. When the new Windows program tries to run the old driver, your system will probably crash or have other problems.

As absurd as it sounds, this is exactly the type of incompatibility that can take you hours of hair-pulling to isolate and correct. If you install the new version of Windows into its own directory, of course, you must also remember to install the new CD-ROM driver. But you would have to take this one additional step to install the new driver file anyway. And installing it into a new directory is far better than dealing with hard-to-find device conflicts that could crop up in an old, mixed-version directory.

The differences between device drivers for Windows 2.*x* and Windows 3.*x* illustrate the problems you can have. If you still have drivers for some older devices that only offer Windows 2.*x* versions, and you keep these drivers in your Windows 3.*x* directory, *you can only use Windows in real mode.* If you use standard or enhanced modes, problems are highly likely.

Running Windows Applications

How Shall I Start Thee? Let Me Count the Ways

You probably already know two of the ways to start Windows applications in the Windows environment. You can double-click an icon in the Program Manager, or double-click the filename of the application in the File Manager (such as double-clicking EXCEL.EXE to start Excel).

Other ways to start Windows applications are not as well understood, however. For example, you might want to start an application, but run it in

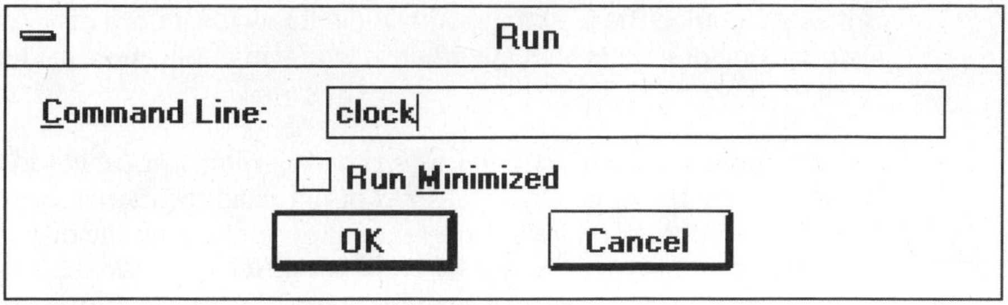

```
┌──────────────────────────────────────────────────────────┐
│ ═                        Run                               │
├──────────────────────────────────────────────────────────┤
│                                                            │
│  Command Line:   ┌──────────────────────────────────────┐ │
│                  │clock                                 │ │
│                  └──────────────────────────────────────┘ │
│                    ☐ Run Minimized                         │
│                 ┌─────────────┐   ┌─────────────┐          │
│                 │     OK      │   │   Cancel    │          │
│                 └─────────────┘   └─────────────┘          │
└──────────────────────────────────────────────────────────┘
```

Figure 4-1: The File Run dialog box. You can run any application that is on the Path by typing its name and pressing Enter.

the background as an icon, not as a foreground process with its own window, in order for another application to get information from it by using Dynamic Data Exchange. Word for Windows might have to obtain updated chart information from Excel, for example, but you don't actually need to *see* Excel.

To accomplish this, hold down the Shift key when you double-click the application's icon in the Program Manager or its name in the File Manager. The application loads as usual, but only the application's icon appears — minimized on the icon line at the bottom of the Desktop area.

To try this, hold down Shift while double-clicking the Windows Clock icon. You get a tiny display of the time of day on your icon line, without the Clock coming up in a window and taking up valuable screen space.

The Fastest Ways to Start Windows Applications

If you don't want to take the time to locate the Program Manager (it might be under several other windows on your Desktop) or to open several windows in the File Manager to find the directory that contains an application you want to open, you can start a Windows application from your keyboard.

If the application is on your DOS Path, such as the Windows Clock, you can run it from either the Program Manager or the File Manager by typing Alt+F, R *clock* (substitute any application name for *clock*). Pressing the Alt key activates the main menu, pressing F pulls down the File menu, and pressing R chooses Run. Windows' File Run dialog box appears, into which you type *clock* and press Enter, as shown in Figure 4-1. If you check the box that says "Run Minimized," Windows runs the program in the background, displaying it as an icon on the Desktop instead of in its own window. (This is the same as holding down the Shift key when starting an application, as described earlier.)

If the application you want to run *isn't* on your Path, you can run it anyway by inserting the directory name in front of the application name. To start the WinEdit application (a Windows text editor, located on the diskettes that accompany this book), you could type Alt+F, R C:\EDIT\WINEDIT (assuming that WinEdit is in a directory named C:\EDIT). You must be sure that the applications you start in this way do not need to be in your Path statement in order to find other files, such as help files or .DLL files.

The undeniably fastest way to start an application *and* load one of its document files is to simply type the document filename in the File Run dialog box. This eliminates the time required to start the application, access its File Open dialog box, click on the proper directory, and then click on the document name.

For this to work, Windows must know that when you want to "run" a document, such as a text file named MYFILE.TXT, you actually want to load an application that opens such files. The application is said to be *associated* with the file, and this association is determined by the file's extension (the .TXT in MYFILE.TXT). All these associations are stored in the [Extensions] section of your WIN.INI file.

When you install Windows, it automatically writes several of these associations into your WIN.INI file. Text files (with a .TXT extension) are already associated with Notepad, as shown by this line in the [Extensions] section:

```
[Extensions]
txt=notepad.exe ^.txt
```

This line indicates that "running" a file such as MYFILE.TXT actually causes Windows to run the command following the equals sign (=). In this case, Windows executes the command NOTEPAD.EXE MYFILE.TXT, which opens Notepad with your file already loaded. The term "^.txt" in this example tells Windows to substitute whatever filename you indicated, in place of the caret character (^).

(Since Windows automatically associates the extension .INI with Notepad, the fastest way to see the contents of WIN.INI is to type Alt+F, R WIN.INI. This shortcut applies to SYSTEM.INI, PROGMAN.INI, and other initialization text files, as well.)

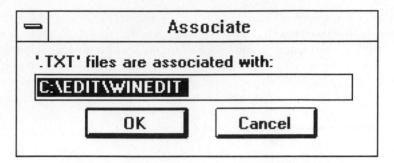

Figure 4-2: The File Associate dialog box. This association causes WinEdit to be run in the C:\EDIT directory, and load any .TXT file you specify.

If you want to change your Windows editor from Notepad to, say, WinEdit, you can change the association in your WIN.INI file. One way to do this is to highlight a file with the extension .TXT in the File Manager. Then click File Associate. This produces the File Associate dialog box, as shown in Figure 4-2.

If WinEdit is on your Path, simply type WINEDIT and click OK. This causes the [Extensions] section of WIN.INI to look as follows:

```
[Extensions]
txt=winedit ^.txt
```

If WinEdit is not on your Path, insert the directory name in front of WinEdit, such as C:\EDIT\WINEDIT. This looks like the following in WIN.INI:

```
[Extensions]
txt=c:\edit\winedit ^.txt
```

It isn't necessary to include WinEdit's "executable" extension (.EXE) in this line — or in *any* line in your WIN.INI file. When you give the command WINEDIT, Windows automatically tries to run WINEDIT.EXE. Typical Windows applications always have an .EXE extension, which Windows assumes. So you can make this section of your WIN.INI easier to read by eliminating the unnecessary .EXE terminology.

These redundant extensions also clutter up the LOAD= and RUN= lines at the beginning of the WIN.INI file. Since there is a 127-character limit to each of these lines, you can avoid potential trouble in the future by leaving out the characters .EXE in this section as well as the [Extensions] section.

Another feature you can add to the [Extensions] section is to automatically invoke any switches that a particular application is supposed to run. You might have a document editor, for example, that creates a backup copy before opening a file, if you include a switch such as /B on the command line. You could force the editor to do this every time you double-clicked a text file, by adding a line such as this:

```
[Extensions]
doc=myeditor ^.doc /B
```

In special cases, you might want to dispense with loading a file at all, and instead send some other command line to an application. For instance, you can start Microsoft Word for DOS with a switch that loads the last document you worked on (whatever it was). To take advantage of this, associate Word with a "dummy" extension and force Word to load the last file, not the dummy file, by making the following entry in the [Extensions] section:

```
[Extensions]
dum=word /L
```

When you type something like A.DUM into a File Run dialog box, two things happen: (1) Windows runs WORD.EXE, which starts Word for DOS; (2) Windows then passes the remainder of your command line to Word. Your command line, in this case, does not contain a filename — only the /L switch. Word interprets this command line to mean that it should load the last document you edited. Word keeps track of which document this is in a separate initialization file it stores on your disk. (This may be a bad example, since you should always run Word for DOS from a PIF file, but I directly run Word here simply to illustrate the point.)

You don't even need a file named A.DUM anywhere on your hard disk for this to work. Windows doesn't look for the actual file when you "run" A.DUM. It simply executes whatever line you've associated with the dummy extension in your WIN.INI file, and lets the application worry about what's on the rest of the command line.

Launching Without Program Manager or File Manager

An even quicker way to start Windows applications (and DOS applications as well) doesn't require either Program Manager *or* File Manager. You can use an alternative launcher to start applications. One such launcher is named (what else) Launch, which is a shareware program you will find on the diskettes included with this book.

When Launch is running, anytime you press and hold the left mouse button on an unoccupied section of your Desktop (Windows' colored or patterned background), Launch pops up a text box listing all your applications. (You must first define these applications in a file named LAUNCH.INI on your Path. You can also launch applications and simultaneously load an associated file by "running" a file with an association in your WIN.INI file.)

When you point to an application name in Launch's pop-up text box and let go of the mouse button, that application starts. This method of launching applications doesn't require any screen area, unlike the Program Manager, which must be running in a window before it can start an application. Any point on the Desktop is enough for Launch.

See Section D, "Excellence in Windows Shareware," for more information on Launch.

Running Windows 2.x Apps Under Windows 3.x

One of the Windows applications you might want to run under Windows 3.x is an older copy of Windows itself, such as Windows/286 version 2.x. You would do this if you had an older Windows application that you installed with a run-time version of Windows (which is limited to running only that one application), and if that application is not available in a Windows 3.x version.

Instead of running Windows 2.x under Windows 3.x, you could define a PIF file to run Windows 3.x in *real* mode (using the command WIN /R), and then run that PIF under Windows 3.x in *enhanced* mode. (PIF files are thoroughly discussed in Chapter 5, "Secrets of DOS Under Windows.") In real mode, after all, Windows 3.x is just like any other DOS application that runs in graphics mode — it doesn't use extended memory or play any "protected mode" tricks.

This never works well, however. When an instance of Windows 3.x in real mode starts under Windows 3.x in enhanced mode, the new copy of Windows looks for the same WIN.INI and SYSTEM.INI files that the original copy of Windows did when it first loaded. This quickly causes sharing conflicts, which usually abort what you're trying to do.

Starting a run-time version of Windows/286 version 2.x under Windows 3.x should fare better — if it is installed in a separate directory, and if you stay in that directory so the run-time instance of Windows doesn't look for the

WIN.INI file that belongs to Windows 3.*x* (which, of course, Windows 2.*x* could accidentally load from your DOS search path).

But again, so many things can go wrong — even if you can get it to work grudgingly on your system — that you really should quit Windows 3.*x* before starting the run-time version of the Windows 2.*x* application. (Best of all, upgrades to Windows 3.*x* versions of most software packages are now available, usually inexpensively, so you won't need the older run-time versions.)

Even if you run the two versions of Windows totally separately, there are some rules you should be aware of, which are described next.

Running Windows 3.*x* and 2.*x* on the Same Computer

If you have copies of both Windows 3.*x* and Windows 2.*x* installed on the same hard drive, you should make sure to take the following steps:

STEPS:

Running Windows 3.*x* and 2.*x* Simultaneously

Step 1. Include the directory that contains Windows 3.*x* in the PATH= statement in your AUTOEXEC.BAT file, but not the directory that contains Windows 2.*x*.

Step 2. When you start applications under Windows 3.*x* or use a device driver (including a print command, which loads a printer driver), make sure that the current directory is not the directory that contains Windows 2.*x*'s drivers. Windows (all versions) searches the current directory for files before looking in directories on the Path.

Step 3. The version of Windows' HIMEM.SYS memory manager in your CONFIG.SYS file must be the version that comes with Windows 3.*x*, not the one that came with Windows 2.*x*. The 3.*x* version can support both releases of Windows, but not vice versa.

Step 4. If the copy of Windows 2.*x* you are using is the 386-specific version (Windows/386 2.*x*), however, you must use the versions of Windows' SmartDrive and RamDrive programs that came with Windows 2.*x*. The versions of SmartDrive and RamDrive that come with Windows 3.*x* will not support Windows/386 2.*x*.

Protecting Windows Applications_____

The Best Add-Ins

The ease of use of Windows' graphical interface poses a threat as well as a benefit to the integrity of your Windows applications and data files. If you leave your PC for a few minutes or longer, Windows makes it all too easy for someone — intentionally or unintentionally — to corrupt or delete your files.

By turning off all the Confirmation Options in the File Manager, for example, then highlighting your C: drive icon and pressing two keys, someone can easily delete every file in every subdirectory on your hard disk. (To make sure that *you* don't do this accidentally, whenever you delete files in the File Manager, be sure to *read* what it says it is about to delete before you click OK. If the dialog box says, "Current directory is C:\ — Delete: C:\," click Cancel and identify what you *really* want to delete. I have seen people make this error.)

Sometimes coworkers, meaning to be funny, cause damage that is almost as devastating. In one office, an associate of mine had printed a long status report about projects for various department heads. Only minutes before copies of the report were to be distributed to each of the VPs involved, she noticed that someone (while she was away from her computer for a few minutes) had changed the names of all the company officers from, say, Bob Jackson to Boob Jerkhead. While the result was an amusing document, this was definitely *not* funny at the time. It took her far longer to proofread and correct the entire report than it took someone to highlight and change the names it contained.

For these reasons, the most important application you can add to Windows is a screen saver. A screen saver? Yes — for the security of your PC, your best defense is a program that automatically blanks your screen after a few minutes of inactivity and displays a small, animated image until you return and type in a password. This type of application is much more likely to be used than a "keyboard locking" program, which requires you to remember to press a certain hotkey combination every time you walk away. It is exactly when you think you will "only be away for a second" that you'll be delayed and someone may take the opportunity to experiment with your mouse. Furthermore, a keyboard-locking program that simply blanks the screen (without displaying a moving image) may suggest that you have gone home, prompting someone to turn off your machine. This power-down, of course, wipes out any changes to files that you were working on but had not yet saved to disk.

Many simple screen-savers are available for Windows — some of the best shareware savers appear on the diskettes that accompany this book. But a screen-saver is a surprisingly difficult application to write for Windows 3.*x,* and to find one with all the features and screen-saver effects you want may require that you turn to commercial software. A sophisticated screen saver, for example, must deal correctly with all three Windows modes; must correctly detect when you are working in a full-screen DOS session under Windows (this is difficult, since Windows isn't handling the DOS application's keyboard); and must correctly detect attempts to circumvent its password protection, such as someone rebooting your PC.

After evaluating several shareware and commercial screen savers, I found one that offered all these features — it's a Windows application called Intermission. This program is one of the few that can detect if you are working in a DOS session under Windows. (Other savers either blank the screen after a few minutes — even if you are typing furiously into a DOS app — or, at the other extreme, refuse to blank the screen if a DOS session is running.) The only limitation to this support for DOS sessions is that you must be running in Windows' 386 enhanced mode for Intermission to take over from a DOS app and blank the Windows screen. Under real or standard modes, taking control from a DOS program could have disastrous effects. If the application was writing to disk or communicating with a remote computer, shutting down the DOS process could lose data in the disk file or from the remote host. Windows in real or standard modes doesn't provide a way to adjust to and prevent these incidents, so no screen saver can be allowed to take control in these cases.

Further, the author of Intermission, Anthony Andersen (who built up the product as shareware before developing the more powerful version that became a commercial application), found a way to guard against people simply rebooting your PC and starting Windows. If your machine is rebooted while the Intermission password protection is in effect, Intermission's driver remembers this when Windows is restarted and immediately blanks the screen and requires your password, just as before. This is not ironclad protection, but it's as good as you can get without installing "hardware key" adapter boards and the like.

Intermission's dialog box, showing many of its configuration options and some of the dozens of screen-saver effects that are included with it, appears in Figure 4-3. Intermission costs less than $50 (with a generous site-license policy for companies), and is available from ICOM Simulations, 648 South Wheeling Road, Wheeling, IL 60090, 708-520-4440.

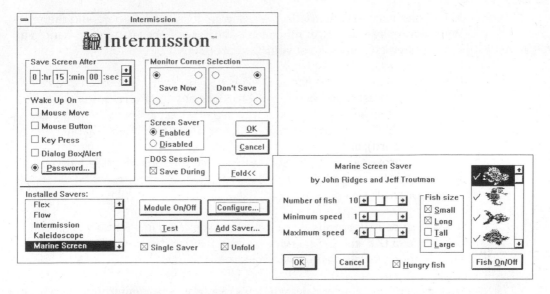

Figure 4-3: Configuring the Intermission Screen Saver. You can blank the screen immediately by moving a mouse into the "Save Now" corner, or by leaving the system inactive for the specified period of time.

Optimizing Windows Applications

Improving Windows' Performance

Because Windows' graphics mode places so many more demands on PCs than character-mode applications do, it's natural that most people ask if there is any way to speed up the execution of programs under Windows. When people ask this question, they usually mean, "on my present hardware."

Aside from upgrading the speed of the computer on which you run Windows, I'm afraid that I'll have to give you the bad news first:

> *If Program Manager's Help About box reports that at least 1MB of real RAM is presently available, and you are using a disk cache, Windows is probably running as fast as it will ever run on your particular hardware.*

Unfortunately for those who have seen the headlines in PC magazines ("Make Windows Soar on a 286" screamed one on its cover), Windows is almost entirely dependent on the speed of your CPU, graphics adapter board, and hard disk (in that order). Beyond a few tweaks here and there, Windows really doesn't get much faster unless you make an investment in a faster system, for the sake of your own productivity.

How fast a system is "fast enough"? This question will be debated endlessly by Windows users, and I'm not going to make any friends by wading in with my answer. But, since I've worked with Windows on just about every class of PC, I feel compelled to give as definitive a prescription as possible.

First, since the question is one of performance, we must define what you mean by "adequate performance." Adequate performance must be determined for two different types of PC users.

The first type of user runs Windows at home or only incidentally in an office, using it to check an E-mail service occasionally, write one-page text files with Notepad, or play games like Solitaire.

The second type of user runs Windows in a production environment, where there is constant pressure to produce documents, presentations, and other tangibles. If this PC user is a touch typist, he or she probably learned to type on a machine that provided an immediate response every time a key was pressed. Studies have shown that even small lags in response time seriously reduce the number of words a typist can produce. One reason that the old IBM Selectric typewriter was such a runaway success was its immediacy (compared with other electrics of the era). Adequate performance under Windows for a production worker must be measured against this standard.

These two types of PC users obviously have different criteria for what is adequate for their needs.

To summarize my recommendations for these two types of users:

"Adequate Performance" for Notepad and Solitaire users: A 16-MHz 386SX (or a fast 286) with 2MB of RAM.

"Adequate Performance" for production office workers: A 25-MHz or better 386DX with 4MB to 8MB of RAM.

At first glance, my distinction between incidental users and production users may strike you as excessive. Unfortunately, many people who have evaluated Windows for their companies have loaded a single application on a 386SX, typed some text, and decided, "This is fast enough." What is missing from this evaluation is the use of Windows over a longer period of time, under the demands that emerge in a working office.

In the course of a typical business day, people may have to work on documents that are 20 pages long instead of one page. That cuts the performance of Windows word processors right off the bat. Then, if you add a single graphic or a table with graphic gridlines, you have perhaps doubled the size of the file or halved the response time of screen updates, respectively. If there are any DDE links to other applications, you may find the response time halved again. This is the true performance that must be tested — not a brief session at the keyboard, but a real day in a high-production environment.

In my experience, you need a new PC that is about twice as fast as your old one to get the same perceived performance from a Windows application that you were used to from a character-based application. If you are upgrading a 10-MHz 286, that means a 20-MHz 386; if a 16-MHz 386SX, then a 33-MHz 386DX. (I know it's pure heresy to say this, but it's true to my subjective experience.)

Don't misunderstand me. You may be perfectly satisfied with the performance of Windows on your existing desktop machine. If so — great! You should by all means continue using your particular configuration.

But if you are *dissatisfied,* especially in an office environment, you should easily be able to make a case for an investment in faster hardware to run Windows. The reason? Businesses pay people money to work at a job, and a faster machine almost always costs far less than the amount of money the company would pay each person in time wasted on an inadequate machine.

How much do computer upgrades cost? Most businesses are required to compute the cost of computer equipment over a period of three years or more — you cannot compute the cost as a one-time, lump-sum payment. Thinking like a business, you should calculate the cost of a new PC investment as a certain amount of dollars per month or per day, not as a single bite.

To illustrate: a skilled clerical worker may make $20,000 per year in a major U.S. city. When you add the cost of the required insurance, taxes, and office space for each employee, the true cost of this staff person quickly adds up to $25,000 per year or more. With about 250 working days in a calendar year, this means that this single clerical employee costs the company $100 per day.

The cost of a $3,000 386DX computer, however, spread over the working days in a three-year period of time, is only $4 per day. If this investment is financed, interest charges add slightly to this figure. But the point is that, if the business scrimps and buys only a 386SX for this employee, it will be saving only about $1 per day. Meanwhile, the company is wasting whatever percentage of the $100 per day they are paying that staff person while he or she waits for the slower machine to do its processing. Most businesses cannot afford to waste this much of their staff time in attempting to save a dollar a day.

In my own personal use, merely working on the chapters of this book under Windows forced me to upgrade from a 386/16 to a 386/33 in order to finish within deadline. But since both of the computer systems were financed, rather than purchased outright, I ended up paying the same amount per month (over the next 36 months) for the 386/33 as I had been for the 386/16.

Aside from my own use, I am familiar with several businesses that buy only *486*-based PCs for their clerical workers who use Windows. Since these companies plan to use these machines for several years, it does not make economic sense for them to buy less than the fastest systems currently available. These machines must be adequate to run the software that will be prevalent two years from now (which will be even more demanding than the Windows of today) or this business is throwing its money away.

Again, if you are completely happy with Windows on your present configuration, don't misinterpret me as saying you must trade it in. (No letters, please!) But simple mathematics indicates that, if you are paying people by the hour — or your time is valuable in some other way — getting a faster computer to run Windows usually pays for itself in very short order.

Performance Tuning

If you have already upgraded your hardware for Windows, or you cannot change the hardware but want to gain better performance, you should check the following list of recommendations. No list can be 100 percent complete — this entire book contains performance recommendations in various chapters. But these are some of the major candidates you should examine for possible Windows performance improvements.

Install at least 4MB of RAM. Windows itself occupies about 1MB, and major applications such as Word for Windows and Amí claim another megabyte or so. Due to the hard-disk accesses necessary to read data when memory is depleted, a PC with 2MB of RAM or less may run applications twice as slowly as one with 4MB. This is the single biggest improvement you can make in Windows' overall performance.

Use standard mode. On a 386, standard mode is almost always at least 10 percent faster than enhanced mode (although you lose some abilities when running DOS sessions). See Chapter 7 for the differences between standard and enhanced modes.

Use disk caching and RAM drives. Install Windows' SmartDrive, or one of the faster, third-party disk caching programs, as well as the Windows RAM drive program, if you have enough memory. These options are described in Chapter 8.

Avoid background DOS sessions. If you are running a DOS session in the background while using a Windows application in the foreground (on a 386 machine), make sure the PIF for the DOS application is not set to a high background priority level that could steal time from your main task. PIF files are described in Chapter 5.

Close a few windows. Some Windows applications can also steal time from your main task, because you cannot control the percentage of processor time that each running window claims. Time some of your Windows applications with Word for Windows running in the background, then without it. Even the Intermission screen-saver's effects slow down if Winword is in the background, supposedly idle.

Use draft mode. If your Windows applications have the ability to switch to a plain-text draft mode, which uses the fast, Windows "system" font instead of several bitmapped fonts, use this mode to type and edit until working on a layout is required.

Avoid screen font scalers. Programs that generate screen fonts on-the-fly, such as Adobe Type Manager and True Type (in Windows 3.1) always degrade performance while they create characters for you. Turn these effects off until you need them for layout, or read the discussion later in this chapter on how to get the best trade-off between bitmapped screen fonts and on-the-fly scaling.

Maximize your window. When several window frames are visible on your screen, Windows must expend a few CPU cycles to keep track of which one the mouse cursor is over, so it can change the cursor shape, and so on. This effect is minimal — maximizing your current window may not make any difference that you can perceive.

Beyond these limited performance enhancements lie the true Windows upgrades — faster processors, faster video graphics adapters, and faster disk drives. For more information on the latter two upgrades, see Chapters 8 and 14.

Optimizing Your Screen Fonts

Using Font-Scaling Programs

Screen fonts can degrade performance under Windows, especially if you are using an on-the-fly font-scaling program such as Adobe Type Manager or TrueType. In this section, I discuss how to get the best performance possible by making a trade-off between bitmapped screen fonts and scaled-on-demand fonts. But a complete discussion of Windows fonts is beyond the scope of this chapter. An entire book could be written on this subject — and, in fact, one has been. See Daniel Will-Harris's *TypeStyle: How to Choose and Use Type on a Personal Computer* (Peachpit Press, 1990) for a complete treatment. (Also, some incidental information on screen fonts is contained later in *Windows 3 Secrets* in Chapter 14, and on printer fonts in Chapter 13.)

Windows installs itself with a limited selection of screen fonts. Included is one fixed-pitch typeface, Courier, in which all the letters are the same width. Also included are two proportional typefaces: Tms Rmn and Helv (curiously titled so as to avoid legal problems with companies that invented and have trademarks on the typeface names Times Roman and Helvetica). These screen fonts are used to represent all the text typefaces you might use in a document. Additionally, Windows installs a Symbol screen font, with various math and Greek characters. All PostScript printers can print these Symbol characters. LaserJet printers can also print them if you install a LaserJet Symbol printer font, which is bundled with applications such as Word for Windows. (To install this printer font, you insert in a floppy drive the Word for Windows diskette that contains a directory named \SYMBOL.W3, then run the Control Panel's Fonts installer.)

Besides these *bitmapped* font files, which contain an actual bitmap for every letter of each typeface in each supported size, Windows installs three *stroke* fonts, called Roman, Modern, and Script. These fonts do not contain bitmaps of certain type sizes, but instead contain instructions used by Windows to draw lines that manufacture characters of any size. These stroke fonts are used to draw letters on the screen and on printing devices that have little or no selection of fonts, such as dot-matrix printers.

In publishing terminology, a *typeface* refers to a set of characters with common features: Times Roman is a different face than Helvetica. A *font,* in its original meaning, was a specific *size* and *weight* of a typeface. Therefore, Times Roman 10-point bold is a different *font* of Times Roman than Times Roman 12-point italic.

The advent of desktop publishing, however, permanently confused these terms. Word for Windows' type selection ribbon across the top of the screen, for example, uses the term *font* to mean what used to be a *face,* and *points* to mean what used to be a *font.* Since it is hopeless to expect this to be corrected, I will use the terms *typeface* and *font* interchangeably, as Windows itself does.

The screen fonts installed in your Windows configuration always appear in the [fonts] section of your WIN.INI file. Assuming that you have all of Windows' screen fonts installed, and you are using a VGA or Super VGA display, your [fonts] section looks as follows:

```
[fonts]
Symbol 8,10,12,14,18,24 (VGA res)=SYMBOLE.FON
Tms Rmn 8,10,12,14,18,24 (VGA res)=TMSRE.FON
Courier 10,12,15 (VGA res)=COURE.FON
Helv 8,10,12,14,18,24 (VGA res)=HELVE.FON
Modern (All res)=MODERN.FON
Roman (All res)=ROMAN.FON
Script (All res)=SCRIPT.FON
```

Since the font files listed are all located in the \WINDOWS\SYSTEM directory, no directory name is included in front of these filenames. But if you want to install third-party screen fonts with Control Panel and then move them out of your Windows directories (to keep them safe in case some Microsoft files bear the same filenames in the future), simply insert the correct directory name in WIN.INI after the move.

Windows 3.0 has a [fonts] section anomaly that you should know about, however. Under Windows 2.*x,* if one of the fonts listed in WIN.INI couldn't be found on your hard disk, you received an error message so warning you. Windows 3.0 doesn't check these files to see if they're readable or not. So if you're missing a screen font that you know you installed, check your spelling in this section.

If you have a laser printer and don't use stroke fonts, you can save a small amount of memory (about 5K) under Windows by removing the stroke fonts Roman, Modern, and Script. You do this by running Control Panel's Fonts program, highlighting each of these three font names and clicking Remove.

This doesn't improve performance noticeably, but it does make the list of fonts shorter (therefore easier to use) when you select fonts in an application. The Fonts program doesn't delete these font files from your disk (it only removes them from WIN.INI), so you can always reinstall them from your \WINDOWS\SYSTEM directory if desired.

Because the Windows fonts are supplied only in the even-numbered point sizes from 8 to 24 pt. (point), and only for two proportional typefaces (Tms Rmn and Helv), products such as Adobe Type Manager, Bitstream Facelift, and SuperPrint became popular. ATM, for example, installs *font outline* files on your hard disk, and uses these outlines to create bitmaps of any size on your screen when you use a font of that size and style in an application. These applications can also create bitmaps to print these typefaces on printers that do not ordinarily support many fonts (including LaserJet, dot-matrix, and ink-jet printers). In Windows 3.1, Microsoft introduces its own font-scaling technology, TrueType. But the proportional typefaces included with TrueType remain limited to Tms Rmn and Helv, creating a continued demand for type products with a wider selection of faces.

Balancing Screen Fonts and Scaled Fonts

A problem with performance arises when these type scalers are running under Windows. Scaling a screen font from an outline on a disk can never be faster than using screen fonts that have already been loaded into memory by Windows. Even on a 33-MHz 386, a touch typist notices the increased time that is required to generate screen fonts and display them while a document is being typed. This slowdown occurs until all the characters that will be used in a document have been scaled — then there is less of a drag on performance.

Additionally, sending a bitmap of a page to a printer (in order to produce fonts that the printer does not initially support) is always slower than using fonts internal to that printer.

There is a way to improve the performance of custom screen fonts, which involves a change to the configuration of the particular type scaler program you use. In this discussion, I use Adobe Type Manager as an example for these programs.

When you install ATM, it creates a file called ATM.INI, which makes certain assumptions about the way you want it to work. One of these assumptions is that you want ATM to take over from Windows and generate screen fonts for all characters in a document that are 9-pt. size or larger. Therefore, when you type 10- or 12-pt. Tms Rmn (the most widely used sizes in business documents), ATM generates the bitmap pattern for each character, instead of using the 10- and 12-pt. screen fonts that Windows already has loaded (and would ordinarily display). This results in a noticeable slowdown, until every character you will use in the current document has been generated and is resident in memory used by your application.

One solution to this problem is to generate and install bitmapped screen fonts for all sizes from 8 to 14 pt. Then, you configure Adobe Type Manager to generate on-the-fly fonts only for type that is 15 pt. or larger. Since 95 percent of the text and subheads in most documents is 14 pt. or smaller, this results in almost immediate response time while typing text matter. Only when generating a headline does ATM require a momentary delay, and in business correspondence such headlines are usually few in number.

These installable screen fonts can be generated by Adobe's Font Foundry, a program that is included free with every Adobe Type Library package. Font Foundry also comes with the ATM Plus Pack, which contains the 22 "extra" (non-Times and -Helvetica) faces found in PostScript printers. (Unfortunately, the Font Foundry is not bundled with the basic ATM package itself.) After generation, these screen font files can be installed with the Control Panel's Fonts program and used immediately.

Configuring ATM to scale type only above 14 pt. (or above 12 pt., or any size you choose) requires a manual change to the ATM.INI file located in your Windows directory. Open this file with Notepad and locate the SYNONYMPSBEGIN= line in the [Settings] section. (This line determines the point size at which PostScript scaling begins for typefaces named in the [Synonym] section of the file.) By default, this line specifies scaling at 9 pt. and higher, as shown:

```
[Settings]
SynonymPSBegin=9
```

Change this value to 15 (or the value you choose) so it looks as follows:

```
[Settings]
SynonymPSBegin=15
```

The next time you start ATM, it will use only the screen fonts that are already installed and loaded into memory, except for those characters larger than the value you specified.

When you generate screen fonts using the Font Foundry, creating them only up to about 14 pt. saves memory, since the larger point sizes take up much more room in memory than the smaller ones do. If you especially want to save memory, don't generate different screen fonts for the bold, italic, and bold-italic weights of each typeface. If a screen font does not contain these attributes, Windows simulates them with double-width and slanting effects. (None of the screen fonts that are bundled with Windows include these attributes.) Type purists, though, will not be impressed with the look of this.

You should plan to generate during this process some uneven point sizes, especially 9 pt. and 11 pt. These sizes take up little additional memory but add a great deal to the versatility of your documents. At the relatively coarse resolution of a laser printer (compared to the resolution of type in a glossy magazine), 12-pt. type is too bulky for business correspondence, but 10-pt. type is too hard to read. You might find 11-pt. type to be the best compromise, using 9 pt. for headings and footnotes.

Optimizing Word for Windows

If you have taken the steps described earlier in this chapter to improve Windows' performance, there are few other ways to achieve comparable speed gains from applications such as Word for Windows. The topics in the remainder of this chapter are designed to help you take advantage of subtle configuration settings and undocumented features that increase response time or help you to be more productive in other ways.

Using the Correct Printer Definition

One thing that can definitely affect the speed of Word for Windows screen redraws is its use of printer definition files. Word for Windows attempts to display the spacing of words in each line the way your printer will print them. This is determined by the width that each character will occupy when printed — not the width of the screen font in Windows. (This assumes that you have turned *on* Winword's "Display As Printed" option in the View Preferences dialog box. If not, Winword uses the widths of screen fonts for each line and doesn't show you where word wrap will occur when printed.)

Word for Windows uses a description of each character's width that it gets from the printer driver corresponding to the current default printer in Windows' Control Panel. But when you change printers in the Control Panel,

Word for Windows does not automatically adjust to the change. It may continue to use fonts and character widths that are designed for some other printer. Using a font in Winword that is not part of the current printer definition causes a noticeable slowdown in drawing typed characters on the screen.

The cure for this problem is simple, but is seldom understood by Word for Windows users. Winword maintains a list of fonts available for the current printer within its own initialization file, WINWORD.INI. When you change printers, Winword ignores printer information from Windows and continues using the old information stored in WINWORD.INI. To update this information, pull down the File menu, and click Printer Setup. When a dialog box appears that shows the available printers, click OK and Winword rebuilds the WINWORD.INI file with the correct printer information.

Setting Other Options for Performance

A few other configuration steps can be taken in the View Preferences dialog box that affect Winword's performance. Turning *off* the display of Pictures can dramatically improve Winword's screen redraw speed — if your document includes any bitmapped graphics. If you have imported a graphic from Paintbrush or the Clipboard, Winword will display this graphic as a plain rectangle, which is much faster than drawing a representation of the actual image, if the Pictures setting is *off*. Winword will *print* the graphic normally in either case.

You can also improve performance somewhat by turning *off* Table Gridlines (if your document contains tables) and Text Boundaries (if you work in View Page mode).

An even greater improvement in performance may be gained by turning off View Page mode entirely. In Page mode, Winword displays not only the running text of your document, but also the exact placement of headers, footers, and columns. This is significantly slower than Galley mode, which is in effect if all the special modes under the View menu (Page, Outline, and Draft) are *off*. Unfortunately, there is no choice on the View menu for Galley mode. You must simply be aware that you switch into that mode by switching all other modes *off*.

Draft mode, of course, is the fastest of all. In this mode, however, Winword does not show the difference on the screen between bold, italic, and underlined text. Instead, Winword uses a single system font for all text (with underlining indicating all types of emphasis). This makes Draft mode most suitable for typing rough copy for a document, switching into one of the other modes only when formatting or layout are necessary.

Using the Customize Settings

Two other settings that can affect performance appear in Winword's Customize dialog box, accessed through the Utilities menu. The first setting, Background Pagination, recalculates the display of page breaks whenever you add new material to a document. Turning off background pagination probably won't result in a noticeable improvement in performance, except perhaps in Page mode.

The other setting, AutoSave Frequency, keeps track of the amount of time since you last saved the document and periodically asks if you want to save the file to your disk (you set how frequently this occurs). This setting shouldn't affect Winword's performance perceptibly enough that you should turn it off unless absolutely necessary, however.

Undocumented Feature to Control Winword's Memory Use

On some occasions, you may not be as concerned with Word for Windows' overall performance as you are with getting it to start *at all.* In tight memory situations under Windows' real or standard modes, the approximately 750K of RAM that Winword requires just to load itself may be too much for your system.

 If you are in this situation, you may be aided by an undocumented feature that allows you to restrict the amount of memory that Winword claims when it first loads. Insert this setting, called EMMLIMIT=, into the [Microsoft Word] section of your WIN.INI file. To restrict Winword to 512K of RAM (a good minimum starting point), the line would look as follows:

```
[Microsoft Word]
EMMLimit=512
```

This line is not case sensitive. Since restricting Winword's memory in this way may slow the performance of some operations (while Winword reads the necessary segments from your hard disk), this should be invoked only if absolutely necessary to load Winword or other applications simultaneously.

Interchanging Documents

After considering some of the configuration settings that can affect Winword's performance, let's turn our attention to some of Winword's undocumented features that enhance its capabilities.

One of the facts of life when you start using Word for Windows is that you will, sooner or later, have to open a document that was originally created in another word processing program. For example, you might receive documents from users of DisplayWrite or Microsoft Works. More commonly, your company may be upgrading to Word for Windows from Microsoft Word for DOS or Word for the Macintosh, with hundreds or thousands of documents already stored in these older Word formats.

This would not, at first glance, be a problem. Winword includes "import filters" that allow you to open documents from all these formats, converting them on-the-fly into Winword's format.

As soon as you open, say, a Word for DOS or Word for Mac document, however, you may notice a serious difference. Any document that is over one or two pages long requires *more* pages to print out from Winword than it did originally. Financial statements that used to fit on one page are now somehow expanded so that the last several lines print at the top of the next page.

This is because Winword uses a different form of spacing between lines than Word for DOS or the Mac. In DOS Word or Mac Word, you can specify a Line Spacing value of "auto," and Word automatically line-spaces each line an amount equal to the size of the largest font on that line: 12-pt. type gets 12-pt. line spacing, 14-pt. gets 14-pt. and so on. Printers refer to type that is set this way as "set solid," because there is no extra space between lines.

The "auto" setting is convenient for typists, since automatic line spacing makes it unnecessary to change spacing every time you start a paragraph that uses a larger or smaller type size than the one before. (You may also hear "line spacing" called "leading," which is pronounced "ledding," after the small strips of lead that printers used to insert between lines when setting metal type. I use the terms *leading* and *line spacing* interchangeably in the remainder of this chapter.)

Winword, unlike Word for DOS and Mac, adds an arbitrary amount of extra spacing to every line. For example, Winword spaces 10-pt. type with an extra 2 points between every line. This makes a huge difference: a document in 10-pt. type, imported into Word for Windows, would print with 12 lines at the bottom of each page pushed onto the *next* page. These extra lines add up quickly, making every such document 20 percent longer! This major anomaly threatens the whole idea of interchanging documents among DOS, Windows, and Mac-based word processors. But it isn't a bug — it's actually a design feature.

Different versions of Word for Windows handle this "expanding" function differently. In Winword 1.0, the expansion of paragraphs followed this rule:

6-pt. to 18-pt. type	2.0 points added per line
20-pt. to 24-pt. type	2.5 points added per line
etc.	

In Winword 1.1, however, the rule changed to the following:

8-pt. type	1.5 points added per line
10-pt. type	2.0 points added per line
12-pt. type	2.5 points added per line
14-pt. type	3.0 points added per line
18-pt. type	3.5 points added per line
etc.	

Whoever tried to "help" us by adding this anomaly to Word for Windows created a dilemma instead. This extra line spacing doesn't follow any known industry standard. People in the publishing industry learn that line spacing should not be adjusted according to the point size of the type, but according to the *length of the line.* Longer lines require more line spacing between them than shorter lines, so your eye can swing from the end of one line to the beginning of the next without losing your place. Smaller sizes of type, when set in wide columns, require *more* line spacing, not less. And larger headlines, instead of requiring more line spacing proportional to their size, require *less*, since headlines are already easily readable and look better set solid.

Fortunately, an undocumented feature of Word for Windows partially corrects this dilemma and facilitates the interchange of documents.

To illustrate this, let's say that you have paragraphs marked in Word for DOS with "1 li" spacing (this equals "1 line," which means 1/6th of an inch in Word). When this document is brought into Word for Windows, Winword interprets this "1 li" spacing to mean "1 line plus 2.5 points" if the paragraph uses 12-pt. text.

To fix these paragraphs, simply insert a minus sign (–) in front of the Line Spacing value, using the Format Paragraph command. This makes "1 li" look like "–1 li." Contrary to what you might assume, this does not mean that each line will move backwards one line when printed. The minus sign enables you to convert the *relative* line spacing used by Winword into *absolute* line spacing. As soon as you make this change, Winword will print the document using exactly 1 line space per line (1/6th of one inch), just as Word for DOS and the Macintosh do.

This feature works whether you specify line spacing in lines (li), inches (in), centimeters (cm), picas (pi), or points (pt). You can type an absolute value using any of these units (by placing a minus sign in front of the value), and Winword uses your specified spacing instead of expanding the spacing.

Absolute line spacing gives Word for Windows another important capability. If you specify an absolute line spacing value *smaller* than the size of the type, you get *negative leading* on your printout. This is a highly desirable feature for desktop publishers, who often want to set lines of headlines fairly close to each other. This isn't possible in versions of Word for DOS or the Macintosh — they simply refuse to accept a line spacing value less than the size of the type. If you do this in Winword, Windows "cuts off" the tops and bottoms of letters when displaying them on-screen. But they print just fine, if you don't push the lines too closely together.

Unfortunately, absolute line spacing doesn't work to fix the "auto" setting. You can't type "–auto" and get back the same spacing you had in a Word for DOS or Mac document. If the author of the original document used paragraph "styles" to define the size and spacing of text, you can change the style definition from "auto" to "–12 pt." or whatever the correct setting would be. If not, you have to change each group of text individually.

Absolute line spacing has a few side effects you should know how to correct. When a paragraph is formatted with *relative* line spacing, it expands to accommodate the largest text or graphic on each line. If you specify "–1 li" to get *absolute* line spacing, however, a line that you import a graphic into does not expand, so you see only one line's worth of the graphic. This also affects the rows of tables — if you type more than one line of text into a row of a table, only one line appears.

These problems are corrected by simply clicking on the "one-line spacing" icon that appears in Winword's Ruler bar at the top of the screen. Clicking this icon changes the selected paragraph's line spacing from whatever setting you originally had, to "1 li" spacing, which accommodates any size graphic or table row.

Someday, hopefully, a lot of corporate word processing users will be pleased to find that line spacing has been corrected in a new release of Word for Windows. This includes: (1) a way to configure Winword so that "auto" spacing reverts to its original meaning of *absolute* line spacing; (2) a way to specify line spacing as "solid," "solid+1 pt." or "solid+10%"; and (3) a way to specify line spacing that is correctly determined by line width, such as "solid+loose," "solid+medium," or "solid+tight."

Correcting Other Import Anomalies

If you have many documents that were created in Word for DOS or the Macintosh, and your company has one or more PostScript printers (or a LaserJet printer with a font cartridge), you may have formatted text in one of the typefaces built into those printers. When you upgrade to Word for Windows and use those older Word documents, you naturally want Winword to use the same typefaces that Word did.

Winword, however, does not use the same method to specify typefaces that Word for DOS does. To translate these typefaces when you import a Word document, Winword looks in a file named PCW-RTF.DAT (which means "PC Word to Rich Text Format data file"). This plain text file contains a list of numbers that Word for DOS uses to specify typefaces and the names of the typefaces that Winword uses.

When you install Winword 1.*x,* this file contains the following two lines:

```
0;courier,modern
16;tms rmn,roman
```

There are two problems with this file: (1) it translates only Courier and Times Roman, but you may have specified other typefaces in your documents; and (2) "16" is not the correct number for Times Roman. This error causes strange printouts of DOS Word documents imported into Word for Windows. For example, text that was specified in DOS Word as Times Roman Italic prints out from Winword as Zapf Chancery Italic (since that is the closest match the confused PostScript printer can find).

These problems can be avoided by renaming PCW-RTF.DAT to PCW-RTF.OLD; typing the following lines in a text editor; and saving the result as PCW-RTF.DAT in your Winword directory:

```
# PCW-RTF.DAT
# Lines beginning with number signs (#) are comments.
0;Courier,modern
7;Courier,modern
8;Helv,modern
9;AvantGarde,modern
10;Helvetica-Narrow,modern
16;Bookman,roman
24;Tms Rmn,roman
25;NewCenturySchlbk,roman
26;Palatino,roman
50;ZapfChancery,decor
56;Symbol,symbol
60;ZapfDingbats,symbol
```

This file correctly converts any PostScript or LaserJet cartridge fonts you specified in DOS Word to the same typefaces in Winword. Each line contains the typeface number that DOS Word uses to represent text; the name that Winword uses for the same face (case is ignored) and the type *family* that the printer should use if the exact typeface requested is not available.

Some remarks about this "font-mapping" definition file are necessary. In case you want to add any other typefaces, lines in the PCW-RTF.DAT file must appear in alphabetical order (a to z, 0 to 9). The first typeface mentioned, number 0, is the default font for the printer. It must be a fixed-pitch font, either 10 or 12 pitch.

In case you need to convert documents from Word for Windows *back* to Word for DOS (and preserve the typefaces you specified), a similar file named RTF-PCW.DAT must be created. This file must contain the Word for Windows font names first, followed by Word for DOS font numbers (no font families). Other font-mapping files for DisplayWrite and Microsoft Works can also be created using similar methods.

Information on this process appears in the appendix "Translating Fonts" in the *Microsoft Word for Windows Technical Reference* (Microsoft Press). The Microsoft Word font numbers are described in the booklet *Printer Information for Microsoft Word,* included with Word for DOS.

Converting Merge Fields and Styles

Winword includes two WIN.INI settings that control how DOS Word's "merge fields" and style sheets are converted when imported into Winword. The first setting is described only in the CONVINFO.DOC file, one of several sample documents in your Winword directory; the second is undocumented.

Word for DOS merge fields, such as DATA and NEXT, are used to show where addresses (and the like) are inserted from a data file into a form letter. These fields are always surrounded by chevrons (« and »). Winword assumes that chevrons indicate merge fields, but European languages use these characters as open and closed quotation marks. To force Winword to import chevrons as literal text (not as field markers), insert the following two lines in your WIN.INI file after the [Microsoft Word] section:

```
[PCWordConv]
ConvertMerge=no
```

Word for DOS style sheets incorporate all the information about text in documents that you have marked with styles. When Winword imports a Word for DOS document, the style sheet information is lost if Winword doesn't know where the corresponding style sheet file is (in this case, all paragraphs become directly formatted). Before Winword discards this information, however, it displays a dialog box asking where the style sheet is. If directly formatting all the text in DOS Word documents you import is OK with you, you can prevent this dialog box from appearing every time by adding the following to the [PCWordConv] section of WIN.INI:

```
[PCWordConv]
StyleDialog=no
```

Setting Up a Default WIN.INI for Winword

Since all the settings for the [Microsoft Word] section of WIN.INI (which configures Microsoft Word for Windows) are not located in one single place in Winword's documentation, you might want to add all the possible settings to your WIN.INI now, fixed to their default values. This makes it easier to edit them later if you want to change one of them, without having to look in manuals for the exact place the setting is documented.

Shown below is a typical default setting for the sections of WIN.INI that configure Winword. I have added one comment line for each line of code (a good practice anytime you add anything to WIN.INI):

```
[Microsoft Word]
; Set Conversion to No to import nonnative formats as plain Text.
Conversion=Yes
; The following line is set equal to the number of text import filters.
CONVNUM=1
; All your installed text import filters will be listed here.
CONV1="Word for DOS" D:\WW\CONV-WRD.DLL ^.DOC
; You can set the default extension to "WRD" or whatever you like.
doc-extension=doc
; Tell Winword the directory containing your document templates.
dot-path=c:\winword
; Tell Winword the directory containing your WINWORD.INI file.
ini-path=c:\winword
; Tell Winword the directory containing LEX-AM.* spelling files.
util-path=c:\winword
; Set Winword's insert-date format (or it uses the Control Panel's).
dateformat=MMMM d, yyyy
; Set Winword's insert-time format.
timeformat=h:mm am/pm

; Set NewLook to "0" for 2-D instead of 3-D buttons (Winword 1.1).
NewLook=1
; Don't use this line unless Winword hasn't enough RAM to load.
; EMMLimit=512

[WWFilters]
; All installed graphic filters will be listed here. Important: labels to
; left of the "=" must not exceed 330 characters total in this section.
Paintbrush PCX=PCXIMP.FLT,PCX

[PCWordConv]
; Set ConvertMerge to No to convert chevrons as plain text.
ConvertMerge=Yes
; Set StyleDialog to No to directly format imported DOS Word files.
StyleDialog=Yes
```

Shading Paragraphs and Tables

Word for Windows does not include a feature to add shading to paragraphs or cells of tables. However, there are several ways to work around this limitation.

If you have a PostScript printer, you can open the EXAMPLES.DOC file that is included with Winword, and click "Install" to add a PostScript Shading macro to your main menu that will provide shading to paragraphs and tables.

If you do not have this macro, shading may also be added to paragraphs *manually* by inserting a {Print} field at the beginning of a paragraph. Press Ctrl+F9 to insert a field (two special braces appear). Then type within the braces:

```
{Print \p para "wp$box .97 setgray fill."}
```

The \p switch sends the subsequent PostScript commands directly to the printer without interpretation by Winword. In this case, the text after "\p" commands the printer to fill the relevant paragraph with a grey shade of a certain value. The fraction in this field (.97) is the percentage of *white* in the shading; decrease this number to darken the shade.

Laser printers with 300 dpi resolution print a darker grey than the number suggests. A setting of .97 (3 percent black) prints on a laser printer about the same as a 10 percent black tint would in a glossy magazine. A change in the darkness of the shade on a laser printer occurs about every .03 change in the fraction. That is, shading values of 1, 2, and 3 percent all look the same on a laser printer, because the printer's 300-dpi resolution does not allow it to create a different shade for each different percentage setting. Shading values of 4, 5, and 6 percent all print the same, but a little darker than 3 percent, and so on. Figure 4-4 shows the printed appearance of these values.

To shade an individual cell in a table instead of a whole paragraph, insert the {Print} field shown above at the beginning of the cell, but change the term *para* to *cell.* To shade a table row, use the term *row.*

The PostScript Shading macro mentioned earlier defaults to a shading value of 30 percent. This is much too dark a tint to place over most text. You can change this default value by editing the PostScript Shading macro and changing the line that says *30%* to *3%.* A 3 percent value allows you to print a grey tint over even the smallest text and keep it legible. (Chapter 6 explains how to edit a macro.)

Winword will not display the shading of a paragraph or a table on the screen or in Print Preview, but it will print. Be aware, however, that subsequently moving such a table with Winword's Format Position command may cause a

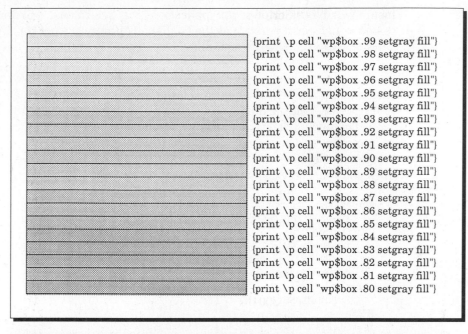

Figure 4-4: **Winword PostScript grey tint codes.** The darkness of the tint changes only every 3 percentage points on laser printers due to their relatively coarse resolution.

{Print} field in the table to mistakenly shade the whole table, rather than the cell or row indicated. In fact, this anomaly of PostScript printers may be the only way for you to shade an entire table in Word for Windows.

If you do not have a PostScript printer, you may *still* be able to add shading to cells in a Winword table. First, open Excel. Format a spreadsheet cell as Shaded, then highlight the cell. Hold down the Shift key while clicking Edit Copy Picture on the menu. Then, in Word for Windows, place the insertion point in a cell and click Edit Paste to paste the bitmap into the cell. This is a crude method, but has the effect of shading a cell in your Winword table by sending a shaded area as a graphic to your printer.

FastSave Confuses Some Applications

Word for Windows sometimes performs a "fast save." This feature improves performance by saving text changes as an addendum to the original file, instead of rewriting the entire file. The new file looks normal when you are inside Word for Windows, but applications that scan Word for Windows documents for errors (such as the Grammatik grammar checker) may not work as expected with these files.

You can correct such problems by simply disabling the FastSave feature. To do this, open the Winword file NORMAL.DOT, which is your Normal document template file. Edit the FileSaveAs macro by pulling down the Macro menu, then clicking Edit. In the dialog box that appears, make sure that the Show All box is *on,* and select the Global level of macros. Scroll through the list of Winword macros, and open FileSaveAs. Change the macro to the following; lines you must add appear in **bold**:

```
Sub MAIN
    Dim dlg As FileSaveAs
    GetCurValues dlg
    On Error Goto BYE
REM "0" disables FastSaves
    dlg.FastSave = 0
    Dialog dlg
    Super FileSaveAs dlg
BYE:
End Sub
```

Click on File Close to close the macro window. Click OK when asked if you want to save the FileSaveAs macro as you have modified it. The new macro will immediately take effect. From now on, files will be saved in a fully written-out version when you save them with File Save-As (or press F12), although not necessarily when you use Winword's File Save command.

When you exit Winword, answer OK when asked whether you want to save global glossary and command changes. This makes the change permanent, instead of merely for the current session. More information on editing macros is contained in Chapter 6.

Glossary Entries Cannot Be 10 Point

Like Word for DOS, Word for Windows allows you to define sequences of keystrokes that you can "play back" by typing an abbreviation, then pressing F3.

Due to a bug in Winword 1.0 and 1.1, however, it is not possible to insert such a glossary entry into a document if the entry is defined as 10 points in size, but the Normal style in your Normal template is defined as any size *other* than 10-pt. If your Normal text style, for example, is 12-pt. Times Roman, but you insert a glossary entry that is formatted as 10-pt. Avant Garde, that entry will print as 12-pt. Avant Garde.

Actually, the glossary entry will *look* correct when you insert it. But the next time you start Word for Windows, the entry has mysteriously changed to 12-pt. — making this problem particularly difficult to diagnose.

 The workaround is to leave the Normal style defined as a 10-pt. font in your Normal template, and use another template — with a different name, such as Letter — as the *real* template for your documents. A macro that automates this switch for you is described in Chapter 6 and provided on the diskettes that accompany this book.

Another anomaly that affects such Winword glossaries is that, if you format a glossary entry as **bold,** that entry should retain its bold attribute whenever it is pasted into a line of text. The entry loses its bold attribute, however, if it is pasted into a line that is *already* bold. These anomalies are fixed in later releases of Winword.

Additional Word for Windows Information

If you or your company rely on Word for Windows, new and detailed information that is not found in the manuals is contained in several files mixed in with sample documents in your Winword directory. You should open and print out the files in this directory named CONVINFO, ISV, KEYCAPS, README, and TECHREF (all with a .DOC extension) and a file named README.TXT.

Optimizing Microsoft Excel

Since Excel has been on the market longer than Word for Windows, its configuration options are better understood and documented. But some of Excel's WIN.INI settings are worth reviewing, because many of them have performance implications for spreadsheet users who might not know of them. Since I described Word for Windows' documented and undocumented WIN.INI settings earlier in this chapter, for comparison Excel's settings are described here.

If you included every Excel setting in the [Microsoft Excel] section of your WIN.INI file, and they were set to their default values, this section might look like the following. The meaning of each command line is explained further. Each of these settings requires Excel 2.0 or higher, unless otherwise stated in a comment line:

```
[Microsoft Excel]
Options=119
Open=filename
Font=Tms Rmn,10
Maximized=1
Entermove=0
EMMReserved=128
ExtendedMemory=1
Randomize=0
; The following lines require Excel 2.01 or higher.
Block=
Autodec=0
Menukey=
; The following line requires Excel 2.1 or higher.
Swapsize=128
; The following line requires Excel 2.1c or higher.
NewLook=1
```

The **OPTIONS=** line (none of these lines is case sensitive) is evaluated by adding together the values of six settings that control configuration aspects of Excel, as follows:

1	Turns on Scroll Bars
2	Turns on Formula Bar
4	Turns on Status Bar
16	Cells are referred to as A1 (not R1C1 as in "row 1, column 1")
32	Turns Short Menus *on* (turns Full Menus *off*)
64	Excel accepts DDE requests (Ignore Remote Requests is *off*)
119	Total for OPTIONS= line

The **OPEN=** line causes Excel to open the spreadsheet file you name (the complete directory name must be included for Excel to find the file). This file can be a hidden Excel macro file (.XLM file) with an "Auto_open" macro that configures Excel for you.

The **FONT=** line sets the default typeface and size used for new worksheets. I like using 8-pt. Helvetica Condensed for spreadsheets, which is easy to set with the statement FONT=HELVETICA-NARROW,8 (if you have that font).

MAXIMIZED=1 forces Excel to start full-screen, whereas 0 starts it in a partial-screen window.

ENTERMOVE=1 causes the Enter key to move the active cell pointer *down* one cell. A value of 0 causes Enter to simply end a formula without moving the pointer.

The **EMMRESERVED=** line sets aside a certain amount of memory for Excel's Macro Translation Assistant, if necessary.

Setting **EXTENDEDMEMORY=1** indicates that it is OK for Excel to move some program code into extended memory if necessary. You would change this to 0 only if extended memory on your system is not reliable if used in this way.

If you set **RANDOMIZE=1**, Excel uses your PC's clock to obtain a different result every time you use the function RAND( ) to generate a random number. The default value of 0 causes Excel to always start randomizing using 0.5, which may not create the randomness you wish.

If Excel is using expanded memory (as in Windows **3.x** real mode), you can set **BLOCK=2** to force Excel to treat groups of 8 rows as blocks. These 8-row blocks fit easily into 16K expanded memory pages, since blocks like this cannot themselves be larger than 12K. This saves conventional memory, but hurts performance. Excel normally treats groups of 16 rows as blocks when using expanded memory, and groups of 32 rows as blocks when using extended memory (as in Windows **3.x** standard and enhanced modes). This is more efficient and should not be changed unless you are running out of conventional memory in Windows real mode.

The setting **AUTODEC=1** forces Excel to use the Fixed Decimal number format. The default value of 0 does not set Fixed Decimal format.

You can set any key to activate the menu by specifying it on the **MENUKEY=** line. By default, Excel activates its menu bar if you press Alt, F10, or the slash key (/). Specifying a MENUKEY frees the slash key to become the first character in a cell, instead of activating the menu bar.

The **SWAPSIZE=128** line can be used to set a value lower than 128K for the memory Excel uses as a swap area. This setting should not be used unless Excel does not even have enough memory to load when it tries to allocate 128K as a swap area.

Like Word for Windows, Excel has a **NEWLOOK=1** setting that forces its menu bar to display grey, 3D-looking buttons. Specifying NEWLOOK=0 substitutes larger, black-and-white buttons (as in earlier versions of Excel).

Additional Excel Information

If you are a serious user of Excel, new information not found in Excel's manuals is contained in the file named README.TXT that comes with Excel. You can open and print this file by using Notepad.

Dynamic Data Exchange

DDE Between Excel and Word for Windows

Both Excel and Word for Windows support Dynamic Data Exchange (DDE) — the ability to send and receive messages that cause one application to carry out another's requests. Since the introduction of Winword, a popular thought has been to use DDE to send a table of figures from a document into Excel, cause Excel to create a chart with those figures, and import the chart back into Winword. This would provide better consistency between tables of figures and imported graphics that illustrate them, because when the numbers in the document change, the charts could change, too, instead of becoming outdated.

We have seen earlier in the section on Excel's WIN.INI settings that DDE requests from other applications can be turned off (subtract 64 from the value of the OPTIONS= line, or set this in Options Workspace). This can interfere with any "hot links" that might be set up to Excel from within other applications like Winword. But many other quirks can interfere with a DDE link.

A discussion of DDE is beyond the scope of this book. A good source of information on DDE is contained in Charles Petzold's *Programming Windows, 2nd Edition* (Microsoft Press, 1990). But a few points about DDE should be mentioned here.

Most Windows users are familiar with simple forms of DDE — cutting and pasting between programs. Highlighting a line of text, pressing Shift+Del to cut it out of one program, and then Shift+Insert to paste it into another, is a kind of simple data exchange and it almost always works.

More complicated forms of DDE, which involve programming in Winword's WordBasic language, however, can hang your PC on certain instructions in some cases. Microsoft technical support reports that an error can occur when a macro in Word for Windows uses the DDEExecute statement to open communications with Microsoft Excel. Using this statement can cause the message "Unrecoverable Application Error" (UAE), and it is then necessary to reboot. The following Word for Windows macro illustrates this behavior:

```
rem  Establish DDE to Excel and load the "annual" file.
channel1=DDEInitiate("excel", "ANNUAL.XLS")
rem  Send the command FILE SAVE-AS ANNUAL2.
DDEExecute channel1, "%faANNUAL2{enter}"
```

When you start the macro, the Excel border flashes. Clicking on the Excel window causes the UAE and the system hangs. This has been confirmed as a problem in the Windows 3.0 kernel that is serious enough to make DDE unusable in such cases.

Additionally, the DDEInitiate statement in a Word for Windows macro can cause a "Cannot Initiate Link" message. This can happen when a full path is given for the application, as in the following statement (where EXCEL.EXE is installed in an \XL subdirectory below the \WINDOWS directory):

```
rem  Establish DDE to Excel and load the SHEET1 spreadsheet.
channel1=DDEInitiate("C:\WINDOWS\XL\EXCEL", "SHEET1.XLS")
```

Strangely enough, the link occurs correctly, despite the error message. If this message occurs, click OK and check to ensure that your macro did, in fact, operate as expected. Then try to eliminate the error message by (1) making sure the affected application is on the DOS Path, and (2) removing from the DDEInitiate statement the pathname ("C:\WINDOWS\XL\" in the example above), leaving only the application name ("EXCEL").

These problems were corrected in later versions of Windows, Winword, and Excel. Probably the best workaround is to upgrade to Excel 3.0 or higher and other applications that support Object Linking and Embedding (OLÉ). OLÉ is proving to be a more sophisticated and stable version of the dynamic data exchange that DDE was invented for. In its best form, OLÉ allows one application to obtain services from another application, without you having to make sure that both applications are running, and so on. Most major Windows applications are expected to support some form of OLÉ within the next few months or years.

Summary

In this chapter, configuration secrets affecting Windows applications exclusively have been explained. This includes:

▶ The installation of Windows applications so that upgrades do not pose insurmountable problems when switching from one version to another (and perhaps back).

▶ Alternative ways to launch Windows applications, encompassing the fastest means to do this within and without the Program Manager and File Manager.

▶ Using screen savers with password protection to safeguard your Windows-based PC from casual passers-by.

▶ Optimizing the performance of Windows itself and some of the applications you are likely to run under Windows.

▶ Making changes in the way that screen font scalers such as Adobe Type Manager are configured, in order to achieve the best balance between the speed of installed screen fonts and the accurate display of larger type sizes.

▶ Configuration secrets affecting Word for Windows and Excel — two Windows applications that the majority of Windows users run.

▶ Some anomalies regarding Dynamic Data Exchange (DDE).

Chapter 5
Secrets of DOS Under Windows

In this chapter. . .

I explain many of the little-known settings and workarounds required to run DOS applications under Windows, and cover the following topics:

▶ Some reasons to run or not run DOS applications under Windows in one of its "DOS sessions."

▶ Descriptions of several DOS commands and applications that must *never* be run under Windows.

▶ Secrets of starting COMMAND.COM running under Windows, and setting up the DOS session environment the way you want it.

▶ Ways to get back the features of the Clipboard and the PrintScreen key that you may otherwise lose when running a DOS application under Windows.

▶ How to give DOS applications under Windows *more* than 640K of conventional memory.

▶ Techniques to run DOS apps alongside Windows apps to give both environments more power.

▶ Gaining the maximum performance from DOS applications that you've switched from full-screen mode into a "small window."

▶ Difficulties that you may run into when you run *two or more* DOS sessions simultaneously, as opposed to only one.

▶ How to optimize the performance and features of your DOS programs in exclusive-use or multitasking modes.

▶ Decoding DOS-specific error messages that Windows displays from time to time.

▶ Gaining proficiency over the mysterious PIF Editor, so you know how to control your own configuration choices.

▶ Some specific PIF considerations regarding a variety of DOS applications under Windows.

DOS Under Windows

Don't Use Windows as a DOS Menu System

One of the beauties of Windows is the attractive environment it provides from which to start applications. Unfortunately, although the Program Manager makes it easy to start *Windows* applications, using it as a pretty menu system to start *DOS* applications is probably more trouble than it's worth.

Windows applications are designed to run under Windows. DOS applications, on the other hand, all too often reveal incompatibilities when started under Windows. Even DOS applications that are fully compatible with Windows should be started from a special Windows file called a Program Information File (PIF) in order to give them the best performance, and these PIF files take time to set up properly. (The procedure is explained later in this chapter.)

If all you really want is an attractive, graphical menu system for character-based DOS apps, you should evaluate simple, graphical front-ends such as the DOS Shell program provided with DOS 5, which virtually removes itself from memory when a DOS application is started and doesn't impact performance.

Or, if your primary goal is to multitask two or more DOS applications, you should try Quarterdeck Office Systems' DESQview environment. DESQview handles both character-based and graphical DOS applications well, and multitasks them on any XT, AT, or 386. (Windows multitasks DOS applications only on a 386.) If you want the fastest multitasking performance for Windows and DOS apps together, you can run Windows in standard mode under one DESQview session (Windows apps achieve maximum speed under standard mode, as explained in Chapter 7), and run your DOS programs in separate DESQview sessions — switching among them at the touch of a key.

But most Windows aficionados — myself included — want *everything* running under Windows. If this is your preference, then this chapter is for you.

DOS Commands You Shouldn't Run Under Windows

Before we proceed, let's make sure to cover a few DOS commands and applications that must *never* be run while Windows is also running.

Whether you are in Windows' real mode, standard mode, or enhanced mode, it is easy to start a DOS session by double-clicking the DOS icon from the Program Manager. Once this DOS session is running full-screen, it looks and feels pretty much like DOS always has — you get a C> prompt, most of the commands still work, and so on. (In this book, *DOS session* always means *a DOS session under Windows,* as opposed to being at the *DOS prompt* itself, without Windows running.)

It's easy to forget that Windows is still running somewhere behind this black-and-white DOS face. Even if Windows isn't actually *running,* but is suspended (as in real and standard modes), it still has files open and in use, such as the Windows kernel and any documents that Windows applications may have loaded. These open files are ripe for destruction by a variety of DOS commands and processes.

In general, any DOS application that "fixes" information that may be damaged on your hard disk *should not* be run in a DOS session. An application that looks for and corrects "cross-linked files," for example, may think that open Windows files are cross-linked (this means two files claiming space in the same cluster on the disk, an indication that one of the files is in error). If this application "fixes" the problem, your open Windows files will be rewritten into several smaller files, each the size of one cluster, waiting for you to put them back together.

Warning: Specifically, you *should not run* the following DOS applications in a DOS session:

DOS commands that reorganize your disk, which includes CHKDSK /F (but CHKDSK without its /F "fix-it" parameter is all right), FDISK, RECOVER, SELECT, and FORMAT C:, of course (but FORMAT A: and FORMAT B: are fine).

Disk optimization programs that rearrange files so you can access them faster or reset your hard disk interleave so the drive transfers data faster. These programs include the optimization routines in Mace Utilities, PC Tools, Vopt, and Norton Disk Doctor (NDD.EXE) and SpeedDisk (SD.EXE); and interleave adjusters such as Gibson Research's SpinRite. (Many new versions of utilities, such as Norton Utilities version 5.*x,* check to see whether you are trying to do something dangerous under Windows, and warn you — but you shouldn't take this for granted.)

Disk cache programs such as PC-Kwik, HyperDisk, Vcache, Power Cache, Flash, etc. Disk caches like these should always be started *before* Windows, not in a DOS session — and if you use a cache program other than Windows' SMARTDRV.SYS, you must also make sure it is compatible with all Windows modes (see the "Alternative Disk Caches" topic in Chapter 8).

File undelete utilities which appear in many utility packages under a variety of names. These utilities can misinterpret Windows' use of the File Allocation Table (FAT), which is a crucial listing of your directories and files.

Character-based backup programs. For performance, third-party DOS "fast backup" programs often read and write files directly, using Direct Memory Access (DMA). This can interfere with Windows (especially in enhanced mode) or any other multitasking software that is running simultaneously. Perform DOS-based backups without any other programs running, or obtain a Windows-based backup package (which can run in the background, saving you time).

All of the above types of programs can be run safely *before* starting Windows or *after exiting* Windows (assuming that they are compatible with your system in the first place). And some changes made in DOS commands in version 5.0 and higher make them more safe. But *don't count on it* — the DOS 5.0 manual warns you not to run CHKDSK /F in a DOS session (CHKDSK still doesn't test whether Windows is running before acting on its /F parameter).

The following types of programs may merely confuse Windows, causing error messages, for example, without doing serious damage:

DOS commands that redefine drive letters and directory names, including APPEND, ASSIGN, JOIN, and SUBST; and DOS commands that "extend" COMMAND.COM to provide access to drives, including SHARE and FASTOPEN (DOS 3.3 and higher).

DOS applications that must be the foreground application to prevent crashing (like Microsoft Flight Simulator — literally and figuratively); and applications that try to switch your computer into protected mode when it is already *in* protected mode (some versions of Oracle and other "DOS extender" applications).

Memory-resident programs that load into memory and then vanish until you press a "hotkey" combination. Many of these "terminate-and-stay-resident" (TSR) programs work well under Windows, but there are so many different TSRs in existence that you should confirm each program's compatibility under Windows with its maker before you experiment with it.

Many of these programs will work fine in a DOS session — but it's better to be safe than sorry. If in doubt, *don't run it under Windows.* Find out for sure from the publisher of the program, or exit Windows completely to run such applications.

To protect against programs that might damage your data if run in a DOS session, the registered version of WinSafe (a shareware program located on the diskettes that accompany this book) can be configured for a variety of situations. The shareware version protects against CHKDSK /F — one of the biggest problems. See Section D, "Excellence in Windows Shareware," for more information.

To give you practical details on the rules governing some of the DOS commands just listed, the commands CHKDSK, SHARE, and SUBST and their effects under Windows are described in the paragraphs that follow.

CHKDSK.COM

The CHKDSK (Check Disk) program is an old fossil from DOS 1.0. People often use it just to find out how much DOS conventional memory is free, since it displays this total after checking the current hard disk for errors. As described earlier, CHKDSK can interpret open Windows application files as "cross-linked" files — files that erroneously claim the same space on the hard disk. (CHKDSK calls these *lost chains.*) If CHKDSK finds files like this, it reports them and asks if you want them fixed (converted to separate files). Whether you say Yes or No, however, doesn't matter. CHKDSK *doesn't* fix them unless you remembered to start CHKDSK with its /F parameter (Fix errors).

If you *did* run CHKDSK /F, it deletes any files that are "cross-linked," whether you answer Yes or No to its question "Convert lost chains to files?" Answering No deletes the files completely. Answering Yes deletes the files after rewriting them into separate, new files named FILE0000.CHK, FILE0001.CHK, etc. Each of these files is only the size of one cluster on your hard disk —

usually 2,048 bytes (or some other multiple of 512). It is then your job to examine each of these files, figure out what order they were originally in, and paste them back together using commands like COPY FILE1+FILE2 FILE3. This is probably not what you had on your list of things to do today.

To keep CHKDSK /F from doing this to your files, prevent CHKDSK /F from running in a DOS session by using the WinSafe program, located on the diskettes that accompany this book.

If you cannot use WinSafe, or are using a computer where this program is not available, you can prevent CHKDSK /F from running in a DOS session by renaming CHKDSK.COM to CHKDSK!.COM and typing in the following lines as a batch file named CHKDSK.BAT. You must also have the program ISWIN.COM, which sets the DOS errorlevel variable to 1 or higher if any mode of Windows is running. This program is explained later in this chapter under the topic "Detecting That Windows Is Running."

```
ECHO OFF
IF "%1"=="" GOTO :OK
    ISWIN
    IF NOT ERRORLEVEL 1 GOTO :OK
        ECHO.
        ECHO You can't use CHKDSK options under Windows.
        ECHO.
        GOTO :END
:OK
    CHKDSK! %1 %2 %3 %4 %5 %6 %7 %8 %9
:END
```

This batch file checks to see whether you have typed any parameters after CHKDSK. If not, it's OK to run CHKDSK under Windows.

If you *did* type any parameters, the batch file checks to see whether Windows is running. If not, again it's OK, and the batch file runs CHKDSK with any parameters you typed (%1, %2, etc.).

Only if Windows *is* running do you receive an error message that you can't use parameters to CHKDSK under Windows. This filters out parameters that may be harmless under Windows (such as CHKDSK /V, the "verbose" option that displays all filenames while they are being checked). But this small inconvenience is worth it to protect yourself against having to put your Windows files back together like a jigsaw puzzle. (Even without parameters, CHKDSK.COM won't operate on a network drive, so you don't have to test for this.)

For this batch file to work, you must rename CHKDSK, by using the following command in your DOS directory:

```
REN CHKDSK.COM CHKDSK!.COM
```

I use an exclamation point (!) on the end of DOS files that need renaming. This "point" character is a legitimate DOS filename character, and it allows me to run the original command itself, if there is ever any need to do so. For example, to run the original CHKDSK.COM program after renaming it, you would type CHKDSK! at a DOS prompt. The exclamation point acts as a reminder that you are doing something unusual.

Finally, as in any batch file, you must type a space between CHKDSK and /F for the batch file to realize that there is a parameter. If you omit the space, the batch file runs CHKDSK without any parameters, which is harmless. You can simply run the command again with the space, if you forget.

SHARE.EXE

It is essential that you run SHARE in your AUTOEXEC.BAT before starting Windows. This prevents two processes (two applications under Windows, two windows in the File Manager, and so on) from corrupting files by trying to write to them simultaneously. This can happen in the most innocent circumstances. Microsoft advises you to run SHARE in the README.TXT file that comes with Windows — but far too few ever read this file.

Using SHARE (which goes back to DOS 3.0) is explained in Chapter 15. (If you are using a network, see also the discussion of SHARE.EXE in Chapter 12.) To summarize, you should place the following in your AUTOEXEC.BAT file before starting Windows:

```
SHARE /F:2048 /L:20
```

If you try to run SHARE in a DOS session, you receive the error message, "SHARE has already been loaded," whether or not you previously loaded it. Windows is causing this message in order to discourage you from loading SHARE under windows.

SUBST.EXE

The SUBST command, available since DOS 3.1, makes a whole subdirectory look like the root directory of a drive letter. When you issue the command

```
SUBST x: c:\long\path\name
```

from that point on, whatever you do to drive *x:* is actually being done to the directory *c:\long\path\name*. (You must use the statement LASTDRIVE=*X* in your CONFIG.SYS — notice there is no colon — if *x:* is higher than E:.)

This trick has been used by countless PC managers to make several directory names fit into a single PATH= statement, which usually is limited to 127 characters. It is also handy with older DOS programs that can change to any drive letter, but cannot change directories. (I know of programs still in use that have this limitation.)

The SUBST command is unreliable when the following DOS commands are used: ASSIGN, BACKUP, CHKDSK, DISKCOMP, DISKCOPY, FASTOPEN, FDISK, FORMAT, JOIN, LABEL, RECOVER, RESTORE, or SYS. And it doesn't work on networked drives.

The Windows Setup program is particularly sensitive to the SUBST command. When you run Setup to install Windows, it inspects the files on all your drives, looking for programs to install in Program Manager. When it encounters a drive letter created with SUBST, Setup tends to choke up ungracefully.

For this reason, Microsoft advises that you remove the SUBST command from your system if you run Windows. Several people I know, however, only remove SUBST to run Windows Setup. After Setup is done, they replace the SUBST statement they need, and Windows seems to work fine.

Since there are many ways this can go wrong (in the File Manager, for example), I don't recommend that you use SUBST if there's any way to avoid it. If you have a SUBST statement in your AUTOEXEC.BAT, remove the line that loads it, or eliminate all SUBST commands before starting Windows by running

```
SUBST x: /D
```

where *x:* is any drive with a SUBST in effect. The switch /D disconnects any previous SUBST commands on that drive letter. To see any drive letters that the SUBST command may have been used on, type SUBST at a DOS prompt without any parameters.

If you need a longer PATH= statement (and you can't simply shorten some directory names), obtain a package called Batutil. This set of utilities allows you to insert up to 255 characters into the DOS Path. Over 100 other extensions to the DOS batch language are included, including Stackey, which feeds keystrokes into DOS applications to automate their start-up. The combined set of programs was less than $50 at this writing. Contact Support Group, Inc., P.O. Box 130, McHenry, MD 21541, 800-872-4768 or 301-387-4500, or by fax at 301-387-7322.

COMMAND.COM Under Windows

O Say Can You C>

After reading the preceding section about the problems with DOS commands in a DOS session under Windows, you may feel daunted. If you are responsible for Windows running on several PCs in a company, you might think, "I'll keep people out of trouble — I'll delete the DOS session icon from Program Manager."

That isn't a good idea. Anyone who wants to get a DOS prompt can simply quit Windows (cursing you the while), or learn to use Alt+F, R command to pull down the File Run menu in Program Manager and start COMMAND.COM.

There are good reasons to run a DOS session under Windows, in fact. There are still many things you can do at a DOS prompt that aren't possible in Windows.

Just look at a simple example such as copying files and ensuring that the copies are exact duplicates of the originals. Many people — myself included — always run the DOS COMP command to compare the originals with the duplicates. I have a small batch file that does this for me every time I copy files. (In some non-IBM versions of DOS, this function is performed by the command FC, for File Compare.) Even in the File Manager, Windows has no capability like this.

If you think it's unnecessary to make sure the files were copied accurately, remember that floppy diskettes and hard disks don't always write exactly what they're told, if the truth be known. And the good old COPY command isn't perfect, either.

For example, you might want to move all your old *.DOC files out of one directory and into an empty directory — perhaps if you're planning to review them later and delete some. If you change to the old directory and issue the command

```
COPY *.DOC \SAVE
```

the COPY command eventually reports "*nn* files copied," and everything looks normal. Now you can DEL *.DOC to erase these files from the old directory, right? Wrong.

If you made a mistake, and there *was* no \SAVE directory, the COPY command you issued merely copied all your *.DOC files over and over onto a single file named SAVE in the root directory. Deleting all the *.DOC files from your old directory means that all your documents (except one) are *gone*.

This error would immediately have been detected by following the COPY command with a COMP command, such as:

```
COMP *.DOC \SAVE
```

But Windows has no such "compare" feature when it copies files. You are left to *assume* that all the copies are exactly the same — but with PC drives, that isn't a good assumption. DOS has a VERIFY ON option, but it only verifies that some kind of file was written, not that the copy is an exact duplicate.

In any event, there are many valid reasons to work at a bare DOS prompt now and then. So the best course of action is simply to make sure that DOS sessions under Windows are configured well for your system.

Setting the Prompt for DOS Sessions

Ironically, one of the programs that you must make sure *not* to run in a DOS session under Windows is WIN.COM itself. The bare, stark display of the C> prompt against an expanse of black screen makes this an easy mistake. After working at a DOS prompt for a while, it's natural to want to start Windows again by typing WIN, or W if you start Windows from a W.BAT batch file. If Windows is already running (as it is if you got to the DOS prompt by clicking the DOS Session icon), this can result in anything from an error message to hanging your system.

You might think that you could *remind* yourself that you're running a DOS session under Windows by starting a batch file from the Program Manager that changes your DOS prompt from something like C> to TYPE EXIT TO QUIT DOS — C>. You then try to start a batch file, such as:

```
ECHO OFF
PROMPT=Type EXIT to quit DOS — $P$G
```

In this batch file, the PROMPT command *should* change what you see in the DOS session to include your "exit" message, followed by the full pathname of the current directory ($P) and a greater-than sign ($G).

But you quickly find that your PROMPT command *fails,* with the error message "Out of environment space." And then your DOS session closes by itself, throwing you right back to Windows.

What happened? There's nothing in the Windows manual about this. Can't you run a batch file from Windows?

Sure you can. To explain this mystery and a workaround for it, I'll first describe a fix for the environment space, then how to make a DOS session that was started from a batch file "stick."

Preserving the Environment

The DOS "environment" is an area of memory used to store the PATH= and PROMPT= statements in your AUTOEXEC.BAT files. You can also put any other kind of information there, then read this area of memory later in batch files. Whatever is presently stored in the environment is displayed when you type SET at a DOS prompt. If you issue the command SET LABEL=1234, then type SET by itself, you see that LABEL=1234 is part of the environment, along with your Path and Prompt statements. These text strings that you set in the environment are called *environmental variables*.

DOS sets the maximum size for this environment area when it runs your CONFIG.SYS file. Unless you specify otherwise, this memory area is limited to 160 bytes. This is usually not enough, so I recommend that you always specify at least 512 bytes by making the first line of your CONFIG.SYS say the following:

```
SHELL=c:\command.com /E:512 /P
```

The specification *c:\command.com* must state the exact location of your copy of COMMAND.COM. The */E:nnn* parameter sets the environment size in bytes. (If you use DOS 3.0 or 3.1, the number after /E: represents blocks of 16 bytes, so to get 512 bytes of environment space you specify /E:32, which is 512 divided by 16.) The parameter /P is required and makes COMMAND.COM load itself permanently (instead of immediately exiting).

If your environment was previously limited to only 160 bytes, however, this was *not* the cause of the "Out of environment space" error message you got when trying to set a different prompt in a DOS session. The environment is even more limited than this under Windows, unless you know how to correct it.

When Windows (or any DOS application) starts, it receives from DOS a copy of whatever is in the environment at that moment. To give the application as much memory as possible, DOS doesn't hand it the entire 160-byte environment space (or whatever you set the value to). It only gives the application that part of the environment that has some text values in it, *plus* a few extra bytes that round it up to an exact multiple of 16 bytes. If there are 60 characters currently in the environment, DOS adds 4 blank bytes to give each application 64 bytes — a multiple of 16.

When you start Windows, it receives this part of the environment, like any DOS application. And when you start a DOS session under Windows, your DOS session has only that same environment size to work with — 64 bytes or whatever. Therefore, it can never have more than 15 bytes free in which to set environmental variables, and usually fewer.

You could fix the DOS prompt under Windows by starting Windows from a batch file (call it W.BAT) and, *before Windows loads,* setting the prompt that you want to display in DOS sessions. The following batch file would make any DOS session display the "exit" message discussed earlier:

```
ECHO OFF
PROMPT=Type EXIT to quit DOS — $P$G
WIN
PROMPT $P$G
```

The first prompt statement sets the prompt used under Windows. The second one (which runs after you have exited Windows) sets the prompt back to the normal style you want to use in DOS when Windows *isn't* running. There are several more-elegant ways to set the prompt in a DOS session, which I discuss after this topic.

Fixing the prompt *still* doesn't relieve the environment space problem in a DOS session. Say you wanted to run a batch file from Windows that does the following: (1) sets an environmental variable, then (2) starts an application which *reads* that variable to configure itself. Your batch file's SET LABEL=WHATEVER command would fail, just as the prompt did in the first example.

The answer for this might be called the "environmental preservation" act. To create an environment space in a DOS session that is large enough to support the addition of environmental variables, you must run COMMAND.COM from Windows with a switch like one used in the SHELL= command described earlier.

Specifically, to start a DOS session with an environment size of 512 bytes, pull down Program Manager's File Run menu, then type:

    COMMAND /E:512

In this line, there is no /P parameter. You are not starting an original, permanent instance of COMMAND.COM. You want this copy to go away when you type EXIT to quit the DOS session and return to Windows. Hence, it is temporary. (If you are using DOS 3.0 or 3.1, the number after /E: is not the number of *bytes,* but the number of *16-byte chunks* as described earlier, and you should change this number accordingly.)

When you run this line from Windows' File Run dialog box, a DOS session starts and you get a black screen with whatever C> prompt was in effect before Windows loaded. But now, you have an environment space in which to work. Type SET JUNK=ABCDEFGHIJKLMNOP (or any 16 letters), then type SET by itself. All the letters you typed are now in the environment. Type SET JUNK= with nothing after the equals sign, then SET again. You have eliminated the variable JUNK from the environment, and the space it formerly used is available again for other variables.

Instead of typing this into the File Run dialog box every time you want a DOS session, you should put this command line into a Program Information File (PIF) and run that instead. By defining a DOS Session icon that runs this PIF, your environment space will always be large enough to meet your needs.

Using the PIF Editor to create this PIF file (call it DOS.PIF) is fairly simple. All you need to know to make this PIF is the following settings:

    Command Line: C:\COMMAND.COM
    Window Title: DOS Session
    Optional Parameters: /E:512

The rest of the details of creating PIFs are described fully in "Mysteries of the PIF Editor," later in this chapter.

Another way to provide yourself with some workable environment space in DOS sessions is to "pack" the environment with nonsense characters. These characters can then be deleted by any batch file that wishes to use environment space. To use this method, you would start Windows from a W.BAT batch file that looks as follows:

```
ECHO OFF
SET HOLDER=XXXXXXXXXXXXXXXXXXXXXXXXXXXXXX
WIN
```

When you subsequently run a batch file in a DOS session, the first few lines of the batch file would look like this:

```
ECHO OFF
SET HOLDER=
SET REALONE=whatever
{remainder of batch file commands go here}
```

This batch file uses the SET HOLDER= command (with nothing after the equals sign) to eliminate the nonsense variable from the environment. This frees up that amount of environment space, which the batch file can use to establish real, useful variables.

This method is an ugly kludge, however, and I don't recommend it. You must remember to do all these commands every time, and it doesn't help DOS applications that may need to add to the environment for some reason. It's much better to start all DOS sessions with a command like COMMAND /E:512, as described earlier.

Survival of Batch Files Under Windows

Now that you understand the procedures for setting prompts and starting a DOS session with a large enough environment space, you can start a batch file that *configures* that environment. As you recall, when you originally tried to run a batch file under Windows to set the prompt and then leave you at that DOS prompt to work, your batch file was immediately terminated and you were thrown back to Windows.

This happened because after the last line of your batch file was executed, Windows assumed (correctly) that batch processing was finished and reclaimed the memory used by that session.

The secret to making this batch file survive, giving you that Zen-black screen in which to work at a DOS prompt, is to make the last line of the batch file the equivalent of the COMMAND instruction. The best way to do this is to use an environmental variable that you may already have seen when you ran the SET command: the COMSPEC variable.

When you turn your PC on, DOS itself sets an environmental variable named COMSPEC equal to the path specification in which COMMAND.COM may be found. This usually looks like:

```
COMSPEC=C:\COMMAND.COM
```

Many things can change the location of the COMMAND.COM file that you execute — especially networks. But no matter where COMMAND.COM is located for you, the COMSPEC variable identifies that location.

Therefore, to make a batch file survive, make the last line equal to the environmental variable COMSPEC, as shown:

```
ECHO OFF
PROMPT Type EXIT to quit DOS — $P$G
%COMSPEC%
```

When this batch file runs, DOS interprets any item between percent signs (%) as an environmental variable, and inserts the value of that variable. If your COMSPEC is equal to C:\COMMAND.COM, this batch file is translated by DOS into:

```
ECHO OFF
PROMPT Type EXIT to quit DOS — $P$G
C:\COMMAND.COM
```

Using %COMSPEC% at the end of a batch file is a safer method to use than hard-coding the word COMMAND into the batch file, since the environmental variable works in all cases and in all PC configurations. Notice that there is no need to use parameters after %COMSPEC% or COMMAND — the word itself is all you need.

Since this batch file adds to the DOS environment (because it makes the Prompt longer), you must start this batch file from a copy of COMMAND.COM that increases the environment, just as we did earlier when we ran COMMAND.COM from the File Run dialog box. To run this batch file (or any such batch file), add the name of the batch file onto the *end* of the parameters when you run COMMAND.COM. If this batch file is named MYPROMPT.BAT and is located in a directory on your Path, the command line you would use in File Run would look as follows:

```
COMMAND /E:512 /C MYPROMPT
```

In a PIF file, the same command would be specified as:

```
Command Line:        C:\COMMAND.COM
Window Title:        DOS Session
Optional Parameters: /E:512 /C MYPROMPT
```

You can place any DOS program (.COM, .EXE, or .BAT) after the /C in this command line. That program will load with its own enlarged environment space. If this environment space isn't needed, simply run the DOS program directly from its own PIF, without starting a secondary copy of COMMAND.COM first.

A Colorful Banner Prompt Under Windows

The wording "Type EXIT to quit DOS" certainly reminds you not to try running WIN.COM again while you're in a DOS session. But this black-and-white prompt is tiresome, especially as you watch it repeated over and over again, every time you type a command.

You might prefer a reminder that is more appealing and, at the same time, more graphical in keeping with the spirit of Windows.

If so, you can replace boring DOS prompts with the colorful prompt described below. To utilize a prompt like this, you need the DOS screen-and-keyboard driver ANSI.SYS loaded in your CONFIG.SYS file. (ANSI.SYS requires approximately 4K of memory when loaded, but this bite is well worth it when you see what ANSI can do.) Add this line anywhere in CONFIG.SYS:

```
DEVICE=c:\dos\ANSI.SYS
```

If you have a third-party replacement for ANSI.SYS with a slightly different name (such as FANSI.SYS), or if your DOS directory is not named C:\DOS, change the DEVICE= line to reflect the name and location of your version of this driver. If you've just added this line to CONFIG.SYS, you must reboot to make the change take effect.

```
ECHO OFF
PROMPT ESC[sESC[fESC[0;30;46mESC[K DOS Session Under WindowsESC[15CAlt+Tab to
  switch; type EXIT to close.$_ESC[0;37;40;1mESC[KESC[uESC[B$P$G
WIN
PROMPT $P$G
```

Figure 5-1: A batch file that starts Windows with a banner DOS Session prompt.

Next, you must add a line to your W.BAT batch file that starts Windows. If
you don't have a W.BAT file, create one now with a text editor. The prompt
you are about to create is one long line, in the terse jargon of ANSI.SYS, but
once it's finished you may find it's worth the effort.

Your W.BAT file should look as shown in Figure 5-1. In the PROMPT= line, the
word ESC stands for the "escape" character (ASCII character number 27). If
your text editor doesn't give you a way to place the actual Escape character
in a file, just type the letters E-S-C; I'll explain how to convert this sequence
of letters into an escape character. (Because of the difficulty in entering the
Escape character in most editors, I am including this batch file on the disks
that accompany this book.) The PROMPT= statement must be typed with
uppercase and lowercase letters exactly as shown, and all on one line,
although it will wrap around on your screen (I know it looks like garbage,
but it'll be clear shortly).

If your text editor does not allow you to place the "escape" character
directly into a file (Notepad doesn't, for example), and you typed the letters
E-S-C into this batch file, you can quickly convert all the instances of E-S-C to
the actual Escape character. This is done with the DOS line editor, Edlin. It
only takes three commands, so you can spend a minimum amount of time in
Edlin if you (like most people) hate it.

To convert the letters E-S-C to the actual Escape character, do the following
steps.

STEPS:

Converting E-S-C to the Escape Character

> **Step 1.** At a DOS prompt, in the directory containing W.BAT, give the
> command EDLIN W.BAT. Edlin loads the batch file into memory
> and displays the message, "End of input file." This is good — it
> means there was plenty of memory to read the entire file to
> the end.

```
┌─────────────────────────────────────────────────────────────────┐
│ DOS Session Under Windows            Alt+Tab to switch; type EXIT to close.│
│ Microsoft(R) MS-DOS(R)   Version X.X                              │
│          (C)Copyright Microsoft Corp 19nn-19nn                    │
│                                                                   │
│                                                                   │
│ C:\>_                                                             │
│                                                                   │
│                                                                   │
│                                                                   │
│                                                                   │
│                                                                   │
│                                                                   │
└─────────────────────────────────────────────────────────────────┘
```

Figure 5-2: A DOS Session with the top-line banner prompt you created.

Step 2. You should see an asterisk (*) at the left edge of the screen. This means that Edlin is running. Type the following after the asterisk: the number 1, a comma, a number sign (#), the letter r, the uppercase letters ESC, Ctrl+Z, Ctrl+V, and a left square bracket ([ ). If the line on-screen looks as follows, press Enter:

   *1,# rESC^Z^V[

Step 3. The line you just typed, in Edlin jargon, means "From line 1 to the last line in the file, replace the letters ESC with an Escape character." After pressing Enter, several lines should roll by and show that the line containing your Prompt statement was converted. You should again have Edlin's asterisk prompt at the left edge of your screen. Type E to end your editing session, then press Enter. This saves the file W.BAT as you edited it.

Step 4. If any of the previous steps did *not* work, press the letter Q at Edlin's asterisk prompt, then press Enter. This quits without writing any changes to your W.BAT file. When Edlin asks if you want to "Abort edit? (Y/N)," press Y to answer Yes.

Once you have edited W.BAT, you can use it to start Windows. Once Windows loads, start a DOS session. You should see a banner across the top of the screen, and a regular DOS C> prompt, as shown in Figure 5-2. The top line on-screen is a light blue color; in this black-and-white illustration, light blue is represented by a background of small black dots.

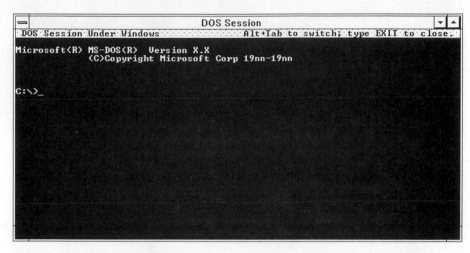

Figure 5-3: A DOS Session with the banner prompt after you press Alt+Enter to run it in a Window.

This prompt is an improvement over the plain C> prompt in many ways. First of all, it's all on the top line, so it isn't repeated on every line down the side of the screen as you type commands. And instead of listing EXIT as the only command to return to Windows, it gives you the alternative of Alt+Tab, which returns you to the Program Manager or whatever shell you launched the DOS session from. You can, in fact, *hold down* the Alt key and press Tab repeatedly to see a listing, one after another, of all other running applications that you can switch to. Release the Alt key, and that application becomes the foreground. (In case you have a BIOS that doesn't support Alt+Tab, use Alt+Esc instead.)

If you are running Windows in 386 enhanced mode, and your DOS session started as a full-screen window, you can press Alt+Enter to reduce it to a small-screen window, as shown in Figure 5-3. This DOS Session window appears in front of the other windows on your Desktop, and can be moved around with the mouse. You can even use a mouse, at this point, to highlight a block of text to copy to the Clipboard. (You can't, however, resize the DOS Session window with a mouse, since its size is fixed at 80×25 characters.)

In either case, full-screen or in a small window, you have given your DOS session its own sort of "title bar." There aren't any pull-down menus, of course, but your banner prompt does make it easier for you (and anyone else who uses your PC) to remember that you're running under Windows, and what the keystrokes are to switch between DOS and Windows.

The banner line is redrawn every time the C> prompt appears. But if you're in the midst of a long DOS command, such as a DIR /P command that lists a directory longer than one screen page, the banner conveniently disappears until another C> prompt is available.

If your system has a fast video ROM BIOS, or this ROM is copied into fast "shadow RAM" by your PC, this redrawing of the banner shouldn't notice-ably affect the performance of your DOS session. If your video ROM *is* too slow, you'll have to decide whether the impact is enough to deter you from using this type of banner. If you regularly use "windowed DOS apps" in 386 mode, you can increase the speed of all such windows by inserting a line similar to

```
WINDOWUPDATETIME=200
```

in the [386Enh] section of your SYSTEM.INI file (this is explained later in this chapter in the "Windowed DOS Apps" topic).

And you should be aware of one interesting point when using ANSI se-quences like this one in your DOS prompt. If you type SET inside your DOS session, you see all the variables in your environment — *except* the full text of your PROMPT= statement. That's because ANSI.SYS is actually intercepting and executing these instructions every time they're written to the screen. Your SET command simply executed your Prompt again, instead of display-ing its text. Nothing to be concerned about.

Making Your Own Prompt with ANSI.SYS

If you want to design your *own* banner prompt (or a prompt that shows up in any location you like), you'll need to know how to change the PROMPT= statement that creates this type of banner. First, let me explain what each element of the ANSI.SYS statement that creates the banner does. In the following discussion, the letters E-S-C mean the actual "escape" character, ASCII number 27.

Taking apart the PROMPT= statement item by item, each element (shown on the left) does the following (explained on the right):

Command:	Action:
PROMPT=	Sets the DOS Prompt equal to the following
ESC[s	Saves the present cursor location

ESC[f	Moves the cursor to row 1, column 1; the setting ESC[2;3f would move it to row 2, column 3
ESC[0;30;46m	Resets colors to 0, then sets them to cyan and black; the number for each color is explained below
ESC[K	Erases line from the current cursor position to end
DOS Session Under Windows	Writes this text string to the screen
ESC[15C	Moves cursor 15 spaces to the right
Alt+Tab to switch; *etc.*	Writes this text string to the screen
$_	The Prompt command to start a new line
ESC[0;37;40;1m	Sets colors to black and white, intensified
ESC[K	Erases the line immediately beneath the banner
ESC[u	Restores the cursor to its original location
ESC[B	Moves cursor 1 line down (for a new C> prompt)
PG	The Prompt command to display Path and ">" sign

The preceding explains almost all the ANSI.SYS commands available. However, if you are designing your own prompt, you might also need the following commands:

Command:	Action:
ESC[nA	Moves the cursor up n rows
ESC[nB	Moves the cursor down n rows
ESC[nC	Moves the cursor right n columns
ESC[nD	Moves the cursor left n columns
ESC[2J	Clears the screen with current colors and moves the cursor to the Home position: row 1, column 1

And if you want to design your own colors, you need the following chart of numbers that stand for each available color:

Color Attribute:	Action:
0	Resets all attributes to light grey on black
1	Intensifies the foreground (text) color

4	Underlines text (on monochrome systems)
5	Makes the foreground text blink
7	Reverse video on
8	Canceled (invisible) text; black on black
30	Black foreground
31	Red foreground
32	Green foreground
33	Yellow foreground
34	Blue foreground (underlined on mono)
35	Magenta foreground
36	Cyan foreground
37	White foreground
40	Black background
41	Red background

Color Attribute:	Action:
42	Green background
43	Yellow background
44	Blue background
45	Magenta background
46	Cyan background
47	White background

All the above colors are set using the command

```
ESC[color1;color2;...;colorNm
```

where *color1* is one of the numbers in the list of Color Attributes. You may have as many of these attributes in the same command as you need. They must be separated by semicolons (;) and the command must end with a lowercase "m."

You usually begin a color command with a zero (0) to reset everything — turn blinking off, for example — then continue with the numbers for foreground color (the text color) and background color. If you use the number "1" as one of the attributes, the text color is made brighter (intensified). Intensified colors are not always what you would expect. Intensified yellow is yellow, but "unintensified" yellow is actually brown.

You could set all your DOS sessions to black text on a light grey background (similar to the Windows black-on-white color scheme) by using the following in your PROMPT= statement:

```
ESC[0;30;47m
```

If you set your prompt to this color, don't then forget to clear the entire screen to this color scheme. This requires the DOS command CLS in batch files you start from Windows. Using white on black in DOS sessions is easier.

Detecting That Windows Is Running

Using the WINDIR Variable

In the previous discussion, I covered ways to start DOS sessions and configure COMMAND.COM for your preferred method of operation under Windows. Once your DOS session is running, you may have several different batch files that your system offers. However, you want to make sure that none of these batch files run dangerous DOS applications (such as CHKDSK /F) if the batch file happens to be in a DOS session at the time. How can a batch file detect this?

If you ran the SET command in a DOS session during one of the experiments earlier in this chapter, you may have noticed a curious string in the environment — one you didn't place there. This variable probably looked like this (the capitalization is exactly as you would see it on-screen):

```
windir=C:\WINDOWS
```

When Windows is running, it places this variable in your DOS environment automatically. The variable "windir" is set to the directory that contains WIN.COM. This is usually the directory that contains *all* your Windows files. But if you, like many people, have moved WIN.COM and all *.INI and *.GRP files to *another* directory in order to keep writable data files out of the Windows program directory (and then placed that directory on your Path in front of the main Windows directory), the "windir" variable will be set equal to *that* directory.

With this knowledge, you might think that a batch file could test whether or not it was running in a DOS session under Windows by checking for the existence of a variable named "windir," as follows:

```
ECHO OFF
IF NOT "%windir%"=="" GOTO :ERROR
    {perform dangerous DOS tasks here}
    GOTO :END
:ERROR
    ECHO You cannot use this batch file while Windows is running.
:END
```

In this batch file, the IF NOT statement tests whether the variable *%windir%* is equal to nothing (in other words, does not exist). The percent signs (%) are necessary in a batch file to identify "windir" as an environmental variable. The quote marks (") are necessary so that the batch file has something on both sides of the double equal signs, in case *%windir%* is blank.

This batch file, however, will fail to detect the "windir" environmental variable, even if Windows is running. This is due to the fact that Windows 3.0 sets the "windir" variable using *lowercase* letters. In DOS, environmental variables are always converted to UPPERCASE. Therefore, your batch file is testing for the string "WINDIR," not "windir," and there is no match.

If you are an experienced DOS user (and your version of Windows is prior to the one that was fixed), you could force Windows to place this variable into the environment in all capital letters. You would do this by making a copy of WIN.COM called MYWIN.COM. With the DOS DEBUG program or any bit editor, you would then edit MYWIN.COM, changing the string "windir" to "WINDIR." In some versions of WIN.COM, this string was located around 02E5. By running MYWIN.COM instead of WIN.COM, your batch files could successfully test for the environmental variable "WINDIR."

Don't do this if you are the least bit (no pun intended) unfamiliar with DEBUG or program editors in general. I am not going to explain this procedure any further here (DOS programmers can easily proceed, using the information I've given), because there's a much easier and safer way to test for Windows.

```
N ISWIN.COM
A 100
MOV      AX,4680
INT      2F
XOR      AL,80
MOV      CL,AL
MOV      AX,1600
INT      2F
AND      AL,7F
OR       AL,CL
CMP      AL,80
JZ       011A
MOV      AH,4C
INT      21
MOV      AX,1605
XOR      BX,BX
MOV      ES,BX
XOR      SI,SI
MOV      DS,SI
XOR      CX,CX
MOV      DX,0001
MOV      DI,0300
INT      2F
CMP      CX,+00
JNZ      0139
MOV      AX,1606
INT      2F
MOV      AL,80
OR       AL,CL
MOV      AH,4C
INT      21

R CX
41
W
Q
```

Figure 5-4: A debug script, ISWIN.DEB, that creates ISWIN.COM to test for Windows.

Using ISWIN.COM

You can create a simple program called ISWIN.COM by typing into a text editor the lines shown in Figure 5-4. Make sure you leave a blank line after the INT 21 instruction, and that you press Enter after the Q in the last line (instead of closing the file without finishing this line). Save the file into a directory on your DOS Path, naming it ISWIN.DEB.

After saving this file, give the command DEBUG<ISWIN.DEB at a DOS prompt. The Debug program reads your file and creates the program ISWIN.COM. This

program is a reliable method for determining whether you are in a DOS session under Windows. It can even tell you which mode and version of Windows is running.

When you run ISWIN.COM, it sets a variable known as the DOS *Errorlevel*. This variable is normally set by DOS programs and other applications. It may be equal to any value from 0 to 255, inclusive. Programs usually set the Errorlevel equal to 0 if their routines completed normally, and equal to 1 or other numbers if errors were encountered.

ISWIN.COM sets the Errorlevel according to the following table:

Errorlevel:	Meaning:
0	Windows is not running
1	Windows/386 2.*x* is running
3	Windows 3.*x* is running 386 enhanced mode
4	Windows 4.*x* is running 386 enhanced mode
127	Windows/386 2.*x* is running
128	Windows 3.*x* is running real mode
255	Windows 3.*x* is running standard mode

Since all these Errorlevels are set to 1 or more if any version of Windows is running, you could jump out of a batch file, if necessary, by running ISWIN.COM and testing the result with a single command:

```
ECHO OFF
ISWIN
IF ERRORLEVEL 1 GOTO :ERROR
    {place your "dangerous" DOS commands here}
GOTO :END
:ERROR
    echo You can't use this batch file while Windows is running.
:END
```

In this batch file, the statement IF ERRORLEVEL 1 means "if the Errorlevel is 1 or more, carry out the rest of this line."

Testing the Errorlevel in a batch file doesn't clear the value. It remains valid until another DOS program sets it again. Therefore, if you needed to be specific about *which* mode or version of Windows was running, you could test the Errorlevel several times in a batch file and branch to different

```
N ISSHARE.COM
A 100
MOV      AX,1000
INT      2F
MOV      AH,4C
INT      21

R CX
9
W
Q
```

Figure 5-5: A Debug Script to Test for SHARE.EXE.

commands. The command IF ERRORLEVEL 3 IF NOT ERRORLEVEL 4 DOTHIS, for example, would run the program DOTHIS only if the Errorlevel was equal to 3 (indicating Windows 3.x in enhanced mode).

While you're testing for Windows, you should also test whether SHARE.EXE was loaded before Windows. As you'll recall from the discussion of the SHARE command earlier in this chapter, SHARE must be loaded in your AUTOEXEC.BAT file to prevent the corruption of your files if two or more applications are running (see the SHARE.EXE topic in Chapter 15 for some exceptions to this rule).

You can test for the presence of SHARE.EXE by using an even simpler program than ISWIN.COM. Use a text editor to type in the Debug script shown in Figure 5-5 — it's only 11 lines long. Save the file in a directory on your DOS Path, calling it ISSHARE.DEB.

Once you've saved this file, run the command DEBUG<ISSHARE.DEB. Running the resulting ISSHARE.COM program sets the DOS Errorlevel to 1 (yes) if SHARE is loaded and 0 (no) if it is not.

Now you can use ISSHARE.COM in your W.BAT batch file that starts Windows. The following W.BAT checks to see whether SHARE.EXE is loaded before starting Windows. If SHARE has *not* been loaded, the IF statement loads it:

```
ECHO OFF
ISSHARE
IF NOT ERRORLEVEL 1 SHARE /F:2048 /L:20
WIN
```

I would like to thank Fran Finnegan for his development of these tests. Fran is chairman of Finnegan O'Malley & Company Inc., a Windows consulting and contract programming firm and developer of E-Mail Manager, a Windows electronic-mail application. The firm may be contacted at 1945 Washington Street, 7th Floor, San Francisco, CA 94109-2967, 415-929-7386.

These programs appeared in Fran's column in *Microsoft Systems Journal* (in a slightly different form), March 1991, and as such represent Microsoft's official way to test for the presence of Windows. Additionally, methods to test for Windows and SHARE.EXE from C-language programs were set forth. Subscriptions to *Microsoft Systems Journal* are available by writing to 666 Third Avenue, New York, NY 10017.

Using the Clipboard in DOS Sessions

Making DOS Apps Recognize the Clipboard

The Windows Clipboard is an extremely useful area of memory for Windows applications. Unfortunately, it doesn't work perfectly with DOS sessions.

In Windows applications, highlighting text and pressing Ctrl+Insert copies the text into the Clipboard. Pressing Shift+Delete has the effect of *deleting* the text from the application while moving it to the Clipboard. In either case, moving the cursor to another location or another application, then pressing Shift+Insert, pastes the text into the new location. These same actions can be accomplished with a mouse by clicking Edit Copy, Edit Cut, and Edit Paste — choices that appear on the main menu of almost all Windows applications. After performing any of these actions, you can view the contents of the Clipboard memory area by running the CLIPBRD.EXE program included with Windows. This program is actually a *viewer* of the Clipboard, not the Clipboard itself. The Clipboard memory area can contain many types of data other than text — bitmap graphics, Windows metafile graphics, and so on.

DOS applications, however, vary widely in their support for the Windows Clipboard. Many DOS apps are totally oblivious to the existence of the Clipboard (or, for that matter, of Windows). But other programs, such as Microsoft Word for DOS versions 4.*x* and 5.*x*, have choices right on their menus for copying to and pasting from the Clipboard. (This assumes that Windows is running and, therefore, a Clipboard exists.)

These menu choices fail if Windows is running in real mode or standard mode. Windows 2.*x* (either the 286 or the 386 version) always made pasting from the Clipboard available to DOS applications; but Windows 3.0 "lost" this ability, except in 386 enhanced mode. If you know the secret, though, you can get the Clipboard back — even in old DOS apps that are unaware such a thing as the Clipboard *exists.*

Under all three Windows 3.*x* modes, you can copy text *from* a DOS application *into* the Clipboard — simply press the PrintScreen key. (You have lost the ability to use PrintScreen to send the DOS app's screen to the printer under Windows 3.0 in real and standard modes — see "PrintScreen in DOS Sessions" immediately after this topic.)

But to paste text *from* the Clipboard *into* a DOS application under real or standard modes, you must use the following workaround:

STEPS:

Pasting from the Clipboard into a DOS Application

Step 1. Place the cursor in your DOS application at the point where you want text from the Clipboard to be inserted.

Step 2. Switch to the Windows application that contains the text you want to transfer, using Alt+Tab+Tab to see a list of your currently running applications. (*Hold down* the Alt key, press the Tab key repeatedly, then release the Alt key when the name of the desired application appears. If your BIOS does not support Alt+Tab, use Alt+Esc.)

Step 3. In the Windows application, highlight the text you want to transfer and press Ctrl+Insert to copy it to the Clipboard.

Step 4. Find the "DOS" icon representing your DOS session. This icon is now minimized on the icon line at the bottom of your Windows Desktop, since you previously switched away from your DOS session.

Step 5. Click once on the DOS icon to pop up its Control menu. Click the <u>P</u>aste choice on the menu. (If you haven't copied anything to the Clipboard first, <u>P</u>aste won't appear as a valid choice on this menu, which is why most people don't know it's there.)

Step 6. Double-click the DOS icon to restore it to its previous full-screen, foreground status. *Voilà!* Your selected text has been inserted into your DOS application, exactly as if you had typed it yourself. If your highlighted text ends with a carriage return, you can even feed complicated DOS commands to a C> prompt in this way.

If you are running Windows in 386 enhanced mode, Paste will appear on the menu of DOS icons as Edit Paste. Additionally, in 386 mode, your DOS application might be running in a window instead of full-screen. In that case, you don't have to minimize the DOS application to an icon to use this method. Instead, click once on the Control Bar in the upper-left corner of the sizeable window. Then choose Edit Paste on the drop-down menu that appears.

Also in 386 mode: If the text that appeared in your DOS application is missing a few characters, the program may not be able to receive keystrokes as fast as the Clipboard is capable of sending them. In this case, you need to run this application from a PIF file that has the Allow Fast Paste option turned *off.* (Editing PIF files is described later in this chapter.)

End Runs Around the Clipboard

If you have major problems making a DOS application accept material from the Windows Clipboard (and you've tried the method explained above), there may be a formatting conflict. All three applications involved in a cut-and-paste — the source of the material, the Clipboard, and the recipient of the material — must have *some* format in common in order for the transfer to work.

To get around this, you might have to first save the material into a file on your hard disk. You can then merge this file into your DOS application to transfer the material. It's commonly known that you can save text into a plain text file on disk using the Windows Notepad. But to save textual material that has *formatting* you don't want to lose, such as bold and italic type or different type sizes, try saving it with Windows Write as a "Microsoft Word format" file. Many DOS programs can import Microsoft Word files, complete with formatting.

A possibility for graphics is to save the graphic in a .PCX or .BMP format on disk using Windows Paintbrush. Then try to open this file in your DOS application.

Finally, if you already have an object in the Clipboard, you can use the Clipboard's menu to save it to a file in a format called .CLP. At this writing, few applications (other than the Clipboard itself) can open or do anything with files in this format. One exception is a special utility that you can obtain from Microsoft, which converts .CLP files into a format usable by Microsoft Word for DOS. This utility, called CLIPSAVE, is available through Microsoft Product Support Services at 206-454-2030; ask for the "Windows Clipboard Save Utility."

Can't Start a DOS App? Delete the Clipboard

If you can't start a DOS session because of low memory, the Clipboard may, surprisingly, be the cause. Windows 3.0 removed the limitation that previously kept the Clipboard from handling the cutting-and-pasting of objects larger than 64K (such as whole documents or large graphics). Now that the Clipboard can handle almost anything, though, any large objects that you copy stay in memory until you copy something else.

One solution to this problem would be to start the Clipboard application, then click Edit Delete. This displays a dialog box asking you to confirm (by clicking OK) the clearing of whatever is taking up memory in the Clipboard. But there's a better way.

If you are in a low-memory situation, simply copy *a single character* into the Clipboard from any application. This erases whatever was previously in the Clipboard and releases the corresponding amount of memory, except what's needed for the one character. You needn't leave your current application or answer any dialog boxes. *Now* try to run whatever program would not start earlier due to lack of memory. I have freed over 200K of memory at times by using this method. (You can check this for yourself. Press the PrintScreen key in any Windows application to copy the entire screen into the Clipboard as a graphic. Run Program Manager's Help About box to see your available memory. Then copy a single character and run Help About again. The difference is the memory you freed. In 386 mode, the difference includes virtual memory.)

Using the PrintScreen Key in DOS Sessions

What to Do When PrintScreen Won't Work

From the beginning of time (starting with the IBM PC-1), the PrintScreen key has been used to print a copy of your screen on your primary printer.

When you run a DOS application under Windows, you'll probably find this function *gone.*

While Windows is running, pressing the PrintScreen key causes a copy of your screen to be sent to the Windows Clipboard. Pressing Alt+PrintScreen sends a copy of the currently active (foreground) window to the Clipboard. Since Clipboard has no way to print, you must first paste the information into another application that *does* have a print function.

Since the key combinations PrintScreen and Alt+PrintScreen both do the same thing in a full-screen DOS session (copy the contents to the Clipboard), you would think Windows would leave the PrintScreen function alone in DOS applications. But both key combinations are initially reserved by Windows for itself.

To revert to the normal function of the PrintScreen key in DOS sessions, start a DOS application from a PIF file and turn *on* the PIF's Reserve Shortcut Key box labeled "PrtSc." (Leave the Alt+PrtSc box *off,* so you can still use this key combination in case you *do* want a DOS screen sent to the Clipboard.) However, this only works in DOS sessions under Windows 386 enhanced mode. Under real and standard modes, the "PrtSc" and "Alt+PrtSc" boxes in PIF files are "broken" in Windows 3.0 — no matter how you set them, Windows continues to monopolize these key combinations.

Until this problem is corrected, you can recover the PrintScreen function in a DOS session under real and standard modes by commanding DOS itself to print the screen on your printer. You can create a tiny, 3-byte file that does exactly this, by typing into a text editor the lines shown in Figure 5-6. Be sure to leave a blank line after the RET instruction. Save this file in a directory on your DOS Path, and call it PRSCREEN.DEB.

Once this file is saved, give the command DEBUG<PRSCREEN.DEB at a DOS prompt. The Debug program creates PRSCREEN.COM in the current directory. When run at a DOS prompt (or from within a DOS application), PRSCREEN

```
A100
INT 05
RET

RCX
3
N PRSCREEN.COM
W
Q
```

Figure 5-6: A 3-byte program, PRSCREEN.DEB, that enables the PrintScreen function under real and standard modes.

sends the PrintScreen instruction directly to your ROM BIOS, whether Windows is running or not.

The three bytes in this new utility consist of three instructions that: (1) tell DOS to execute an interrupt; (2) specify interrupt 5; and (3) exit. Interrupt number 5 (or 05 hex, as programmers know it) is used on all PCs, of course, to start the PrintScreen routine.

To use this utility, start a DOS session from Windows. At the DOS prompt, type DIR or some other command that puts a few lines of text on the screen. Then give the command:

PRSCREEN

You will see that your printer prints the lines that were displayed on your screen.

If you have a laser printer, the printer's "Form Feed" light probably went on, indicating that something was received, but no paper emerged from the printer. This is because most laser printers wait until a full page is filled before ejecting a printed sheet. At this point, you could go over to the printer, turn *off* its "On Line" button, press its "Form Feed" button to eject the page, and turn the "On Line" button back *on*. But it would be much easier to send the printer a form-feed instruction from the keyboard. To do this at the DOS prompt, type

ECHO ^L>LPT1

where the "^L" means Ctrl+L (not a caret character [^] followed by the letter "L").

If you need to do this frequently, you can place these short commands in a batch file and run *that* when you need a PrintScreen.

Of course, this procedure works best when you need a PrintScreen of a plain DOS session — one at the bare C> prompt, not with a DOS application running. Inside a DOS application, you may be able to use a COMMAND option on the menu to run the PRSCREEN.COM utility and print a copy of your application's screen. But this may not be possible within your particular DOS applications.

As an alternative, some applications offer a PrintScreen command on their main menus. If these commands directly send out an Interrupt 5 to the BIOS, they too will circumvent Windows' monopolization of the PrintScreen key. But not all DOS applications give you this capability. Until Windows makes the PrintScreen key available to all DOS sessions in all Windows modes, getting printed copies of your DOS applications' screens is a hit-and-miss proposition.

Giving DOS Sessions More Than 640K

Quarterdeck's VIDRAM Utility

Conventional memory, that portion of your computer's RAM from 0 to 640K, is often a factor in the performance of DOS applications. The more memory they have, the faster they run (because they can load more program code or data files from your hard disk into RAM).

You can give a DOS session *more* than 640K of conventional memory under Windows, in any mode. In fact, you may be able to add enough conventional memory for the DOS CHKDSK program to report 736K as your total RAM — an addition of 96K.

The special tool that allows you to work this bit of magic is a utility from Quarterdeck Office Systems called VIDRAM.COM. This utility is free with the purchase of QEMM386, Quarterdeck's memory-manager for Windows and other 386 applications. (See Chapter 16 for more information on QEMM386 and Quarterdeck.)

When you start a DOS session, CHKDSK reports that 640K is the total count of RAM, with a substantial chunk of this amount taken up by COMMAND.COM and other programs and device drivers. To increase this total up to 736K, you run the command VIDRAM ON, which loads VIDRAM.COM and enables it to remap the 96K of RAM just above the 640K line. At this point, any DOS application you start, which has its own way to report on the amount of memory available, will report that about 90K of RAM is free that was not previously seen.

Several conditions are required in order for you to gain this memory. First, DOS must be in text mode, and you must use only applications that run in text mode until you disable VIDRAM. Second, you must be using an EGA, VGA, or higher-resolution adapter (with VGA downward-compatibility). Third, you will only be able to gain 64K — not 96K — if you have a monochrome video adapter in your system and you are in monochrome mode.

EGA and VGA adapters normally use the 64K area immediately above the 640K line for their graphics memory chips. Monochrome video boards, and some VGA boards in monochrome modes, use another 32K area of memory immediately above *that*. (See Chapter 14 for a diagram of these areas of memory.)

If you are not using a graphics mode on your EGA or VGA system, but are in text mode, your EGA or VGA board is operating in yet another 32K area, which is immediately above the monochrome area. This means that the entire 96K area between the 640K line and your text-mode memory is sitting idle. From VIDRAM's point of view, this area is being *wasted*.

The VIDRAM.COM program simply moves the DOS 640K line upwards. It moves the line up 64K or 96K, depending on the presence of EGA/VGA/monochrome boards in your system. This memory area, of course, is already occupied by the memory chips on your EGA or VGA memory board — which now become available to your DOS applications *as conventional memory!* If you don't have enough memory in this area, or it is unsuitable, VIDRAM uses the services of QEMM386 to convert some extended memory into conventional memory in this area. The VIDRAM.COM program then takes up a few kilobytes for itself, primarily to ensure that no application is allowed to switch from text mode into graphics mode. If you try, VIDRAM writes a message on the screen informing you that you must use text mode until VIDRAM is disabled.

To take advantage of this memory under Windows, you can start a DOS session in the normal way, then run VIDRAM from the DOS prompt, followed by the program name of your application. A better way is to write a small batch file that loads both VIDRAM and your application, and start the batch file from a PIF. In the PIF file, you define the amount of conventional memory desired as "-1," which gives the application all available memory, instead of "640K," the normal maximum setting.

I have run Lotus 1-2-3 and many other DOS applications in this larger 736K memory space, and they work fine. The only problem occurs with applications that normally run in text mode, but *test* for the presence of a graphics board. Lotus 1-2-3 is a perfect example — it tests for an EGA or VGA if you've configured it to be able to switch into that mode to view charts. The solution is to reconfigure such applications to run only in text mode — 1-2-3 can be set up with a "Graph Display" choice of "None," for example. In 1-2-3's Setup routine, you could save this configuration with a name, such as TEXTONLY. You would then start 1-2-3 with this as a parameter on the command line, like this:

```
123 TEXTONLY
```

When you want to use 1-2-3 normally, without the extra memory provided by VIDRAM.COM, simply start 1-2-3 without the trailing parameter.

Running DOS and Windows Apps Together _____

Windows makes it convenient to start your favorite Windows applications and DOS applications, all at the same time, when you run Windows. Once each of these applications has loaded, you can switch among them using Alt+Tab+Tab or Alt+Esc, or by pressing Ctrl+Esc to select from the running applications listed in Windows' Task List dialog box.

This approach can reduce the performance of your Windows and DOS applications, however, if you have not set PIF files for the DOS applications to keep them from absorbing time slices from Windows applications. (This is explained later in the section on the PIF Editor.)

Some other anomalies affect the use of DOS and Windows applications together, as well. For example, if you commonly switch between Word for DOS to view older documents and Word for Windows to try to import such documents, you might find it convenient to make Windows run both applications every time you start Windows. To do this, you would change the RUN= line in your WIN.INI to run your PIF file for Word, then run Word for Windows, as follows:

```
RUN=word.pif winword
```

If you use Windows 386 enhanced mode, you might define your WORD.PIF so it starts Word for DOS in a sizeable window on your Desktop, instead of full-screen. However, when Windows runs first a "windowed" DOS application, then a Windows application on the RUN= line, it may not switch the "keyboard focus" away from the DOS window and into the Windows application. This means that, when you start typing, your keystrokes (in this example) go into the Word for DOS window, not the Winword window.

The cure for this (if Windows behaves this way on your system) is to click your mouse on any noncritical area of the Windows application. This always gives it the keyboard focus. Without a mouse, you can switch to this window by pressing Alt+Esc or Alt+Tab+Tab.

Launching Batch Files from Macro Languages

In other cases, you might want to start a DOS batch file from within a Windows application. For example, you could command a Windows application to start a batch file in order to send a listing of the current directory to your printer — a common task that almost no Windows application can perform.

To do this, you would create a macro within your Win app, assuming it has something like Winword's WordBasic or Excel's macro language. In Excel, a macro to start a batch file named MYBATCH.BAT (from a PIF) would look like the following:

```
RunMyBatch
=EXEC("mybatch.pif")
=RETURN()
```

In WordBasic, this same action would appear something like this:

```
SUB MAIN
SHELL "mybatch.pif", 3
END SUB
```

These examples illustrate a good reason why you should define PIF files to run all your batch files (or define a single, master PIF file that you rename over and over for each of your batch files). Unless the PIF for a batch file you run from a Windows macro language specifies Background: Off, Windows (in 386 mode) may switch away from the batch file before it is finished carrying out its tasks. This would return control to the Windows application that launched the batch file *prior to the batch file's completion*. This could lead to errors that might be hard to diagnose.

Windowed DOS Applications

One of the Luxuries of 386 Mode

Under Windows 386 enhanced mode, you can define a PIF file for a DOS application that makes that app start in a portion of the screen area, instead of occupying the full screen. This way, you can see the DOS application, but also see corners of your Windows applications running behind it, which makes switching among them easier. If a DOS text-mode application started full-screen, you can place it in a small window instead by pressing Alt+Enter.

If you never run Windows in 386 mode — because standard mode is faster, or because you have a 286-class PC — you don't need to read this section, or the following section on "Running Two or More DOS Sessions." These capabilities are 386-dependent.

Windowing a Graphical DOS Application

One of the frustrations of "windowed" DOS sessions is trying to start in a small window a DOS application that uses graphics (or switching such a program from full-screen to windowed by pressing Alt+Enter).

If you launch such a DOS program, you'll probably receive the following Windows error message:

"You cannot run this application while other high-resolution applications are running full-screen. The application will be suspended until a low-resolution or text application is running full-screen. Check the PIF settings to ensure they are correct."

You might be confused by this message — because all three of its statements are incorrect:

1. The "other high-resolution applications running full-screen" that the message is talking about is Windows itself, and there's nothing you can do to it that will help you run your graphics application in a window. You need to press Alt+Enter to make the *DOS application* full-screen.

2. Running "a low-resolution or text application full-screen" also will not help. You must run the *high-resolution* application full-screen.

3. There is nothing you can do with "the PIF settings" that will change this. You cannot run a DOS high-resolution graphics application in a window under any circumstances.

By "high-resolution" Windows almost always means EGA or VGA resolution. When Windows says "low-resolution," it means CGA resolution. Windows is not capable of running a DOS program using EGA or VGA graphics mode, unless that program occupies the entire screen. (If you need to run two or more DOS applications in graphics mode and see parts of each application simultaneously in small windows, the DESQview environment from Quarterdeck Office Systems has this capability on a 386.)

You might also see the "You cannot run this application..." message if you try to start in a small window a DOS application that you feel certain uses only text mode. The problem in this case is probably that the DOS program is displaying some kind of corporate logo in a graphics mode, before switching into text mode for its normal operations.

Lotus 1-2-3 Release 3.1 does this kind of thing, but you can make the start-up logo use text mode instead of graphics mode by starting this release of 1-2-3 with the parameter -M (as in text Mode). Other programs may have different parameters you can use to disable their initial graphics logo screen, so you can start them in a window instead of full-screen. If you cannot disable the logo, you must define the PIF file to start the application full-screen, then use Alt+Enter to manually switch it into a window after it has entered text mode.

Another type of problem results from DOS apps that can be configured to use a 28-line or 43-line mode on an EGA or VGA display, instead of the usual 25-line text mode. Microsoft Word and many other DOS programs have this capability. Windows usually won't allow these applications to be windowed.

Any application that offers a "print preview" feature almost certainly switches into graphics mode to display this reduced image of the page. If you are running one of these DOS apps windowed, you must press Alt+Enter to switch it to full-screen before starting its print-preview mode.

The only way to run a graphics-capable DOS application in a window is to install the app's video driver for CGA resolution. This is not as bad as you might think. 1-2-3 Release 3.1 comes with a driver entitled "CGA for Windows," which is specially tailored to allow you to display Lotus graphs in a small window under Windows 3.*x.* You first prepare a spreadsheet in 1-2-3 text mode, then switch to graphics mode to see how the corresponding graph looks. The CGA driver, of course, displays lines that are more jagged than an EGA or VGA driver would. But the graph still looks much the same, either way, and of course the graph *prints* exactly alike no matter what video driver is installed.

Optimizing Windowed DOS Performance

You may find that the screen refresh rate of your text-mode DOS applications is slower when windowed than when running full-screen. Some little-known settings can correct this.

You should insert a line into the [386Enh] section of your WIN.INI file, similar to the following:

```
[386Enh]

WindowUpdateTime=200
```

This setting controls the speed at which Windows updates the display of non-Windows applications running in small windows. Without this setting, Windows defaults to a value of 50. The SYSINI3.TXT file that comes with Windows 3.0 says that this is the number of milliseconds that Windows takes for its own needs, in-between updates of the windowed DOS display. This is exactly the opposite of the correct information. In fact, the WINDOWUPDATETIME= setting is the *priority* given to updating the windowed DOS display — as opposed to any other tasks that Windows may need to do in the background, such as updating its timers, etc. Increasing the value of WINDOWUPDATETIME= has the effect of giving *more* time, not *less,* to the windowed DOS display — probably what you want.

I have tried various numbers for this setting on different systems — every multiple of 100 between 200 and 900, then down to 25 as well. Specifying a value of 200 seems to give as good a performance as setting it to 900, so I now use 200 as my preferred setting. You can perform a simple test to find the correct value for your system, however.

To run this test, you need a command that does nothing but write text to the screen. Unless you have a commercial benchmark program that you prefer, the DIR command will do. Create a batch file called something like TESTDIR.BAT. This file should contain ten DIR commands in a row; you don't even need an ECHO OFF statement, so you can see the DIR commands working. This batch file would look as follows:

```
DIR
DIR
DIR
DIR
etc.
```

Run this batch file at a DOS prompt within a windowed DOS session, using SYSTEM.INI's default setting, timing it from the moment you gave the command to the moment the last DIR finished. After the first DIR command, DOS should get this directory information from its buffer memory, so disk performance is not as important as screen-write performance. Then change to WINDOWUPDATETIME=200, restart Windows, and run the batch file again. Continue by changing this value to 900. (The maximum value allowed is 1000.) If you get no additional benefit, set it back to 200. If it *does* make a difference, try a setting in the middle. Fix this value at whatever is the lowest setting that gives you the same performance as higher settings.

Additionally, you should read the topics under the "Optimizing DOS Performance Under Windows" section later in this chapter. This section contains information that can improve the performance of *all* DOS applications under Windows, not just windowed DOS applications.

Changing Screen Fonts for "Windowed DOS"

Certain screen fonts are used when you run a DOS application under Windows, which were installed when you ran Setup. You can change the proportion of the DOS window that appears — to make it taller and more legible, or shorter and more compact — by installing different fonts from your original Windows diskettes. The procedure for this is described in Chapter 14.

Mice in Windowed DOS Apps

Although it is possible to use a mouse in a DOS session (by installing MOUSE.SYS in your CONFIG.SYS file, as described in Chapter 10), when the session is windowed, you lose mouse functions.

In a windowed DOS session, the mouse becomes a tool for *all* windows that are on the Windows Desktop. You can no longer use the mouse to move objects in your DOS application or click items on the application's menu.

You *gain* one capability in this mode, however. Once the DOS application is windowed, you can drag the mouse over a rectangular area of text to select it for copying to the Clipboard. This is true even if the DOS application has *no support whatsoever for mice.*

To do this, drag the mouse over the portion of the windowed DOS session you want to copy. The area changes to the "highlight" color. Then pull down the session's Control menu (by clicking the grey bar in the upper-left corner of the window frame) and click Edit Copy. This places the text in the Clipboard. You can then paste it into any application that supports text.

While you do this, the title bar of the application changes from a name like "DOS Session" to "Select DOS Session," indicating that you are presently highlighting (selecting) an area. During this time, keyboard input to the DOS session is suspended. Windows itself is performing the selection, which is why it works even in mouse-unaware DOS applications. If you need to abort the selection before finishing it, simply press the Esc key. The application returns to normal and the title bar reverts to saying "DOS Session."

Running Two or More DOS Sessions

Problems When You Start or Exit a Second App

If you use Windows 386 enhanced mode to run two or more DOS sessions simultaneously, different conditions apply than when you run only one.

The first DOS application you start, for example, may make some change to your computer hardware that prevents another DOS application from loading. Or you may find that the two applications work together just fine, until you try to exit one or the other. Then your machine hangs, spontaneously reboots, or your monitor displays garbage instead of what you expect.

These problems may be corrected by adding to the [386Enh] section of your SYSTEM.INI the following line:

    local=EGA$

Unlike most lines in *.INI files, the value after the equals sign (=) in this line is *case sensitive,* and should be typed exactly as shown. The word "EGA" must be in all capitals, and must be followed by a dollar sign ($). Notice that a line saying LOCAL=CON probably already exists in your [386Enh] section. Do not delete this line when adding the LOCAL=EGA$ line.

The LOCAL= statement determines whether a particular computer resource will be shared among all running DOS sessions. The statement LOCAL=EGA$ indicates that certain video-mode functions that are performed in one DOS session should not affect any mode information in other sessions. The statement LOCAL=CON indicates that the PC console (the DOS term for the keyboard and display) must be kept separate for each DOS session. If this statement were removed, and the console became a *global* resource, using the keyboard in one DOS session could fill the keyboard buffer in other DOS sessions.

DOS always converts its internal representation of reserved device names, such as CON, LPT1, COM1, etc., to uppercase. For this reason, the names of devices after the equals sign in the LOCAL= statement must be capitalized or DOS will not recognize them.

Starting Multiple DOS Applications

If you need to open many DOS sessions simultaneously under Windows in 386 mode — three, four, five, or more — try opening these sessions *before* opening Windows-based applications. In low memory situations, you may be able to open more DOS applications (and still open a required Windows application) than if you open them in the reverse order. This is due to the way that Windows applications manage and discard portions of their own code, as needed, depending on available memory. If you regularly run Windows under memory-starved conditions, of course, you will experience poorer performance than you could obtain by adding sufficient RAM.

Optimizing DOS Performance Under Windows

Turning the Monitor Ports Setting Off

You should make sure that the PIF file starting your application has the Monitor Ports settings turned *off*. The Monitor Ports settings are only needed in case the application changes the display in such an unorthodox way (usually in EGA mode) that Windows can't possibly tell what is going on. In such cases, Windows must install a memory-resident "monitor" program that handles all video writes and reports the current status of the video display to Windows. This seriously hurts DOS performance. Yet when you create a PIF, or use Windows' standard _DEFAULT.PIF, the Monitor Ports setting defaults to *on* for high-resolution (EGA and VGA) modes unless you specifically turn it *off*.

Turning the FileSysChange= Setting Off

DOS applications may write to your hard drive more slowly under Windows in enhanced mode than they normally do, unless you make sure the setting FILESYSCHANGE=OFF appears in the [386Enh] section of your SYSTEM.INI file.

This setting determines whether Windows will monitor disk-write activity by DOS sessions and update the directory windows in the File Manager whenever a file is written, renamed, or deleted. Such monitoring slows DOS applications.

If there is no FILESYSCHANGE= line in your SYSTEM.INI, this setting defaults to *on*. The Setup program, however, usually writes the FILESYSCHANGE=OFF statement automatically when you install Windows. This is worth checking if you use DOS sessions under enhanced mode.

If this setting is *off,* and File Manager (or a similar utility) was running when you started a DOS session, any directory windows that are open when you return will not show changes the application made to your files. But you can quickly update such a window by pressing the F5 key, which forces File Manager to reread the directory and display its current status.

Don't Use a DOS App's Shell Command in a DOS Session

Many applications give you the ability to "shell out" to a DOS prompt without exiting the application. The application halts while this prompt is displayed, until you type EXIT to return to the application. This is usually implemented by a "Shell" or "System" command on the application's main menu.

Under Windows, however, shelling to DOS from an application and then returning can seriously slow down that application's performance. This has been reported with versions of Lotus 1-2-3 as well as WordPerfect. When you use the DOS prompt, something may be left in memory that is not freed when you type EXIT, and this drags down the application's normal functions.

A better way to get a C> prompt while using an application in a DOS session is to return to Windows by pressing Alt+Tab; you can then start another DOS session from the Program Manager.

Changing the Minimum Timeslice

Windows ships with certain default settings in effect for operation in 386 enhanced mode. One of these settings is the *minimum timeslice* value. This number determines the number of milliseconds (thousandths of a second) that a DOS session can have for its own use, before Windows may switch away to other processes. Windows probably configured itself for a value of 20 milliseconds when you installed it. This means that Windows can switch to another process no more often, theoretically, than every 1/50th of a second.

This value was determined in order to make Windows run without problems on even the slowest 16-MHz 386 imaginable. Even on a 16-MHz machine, though, this value might be quite high for your system. At a CPU cycle rate of 16,000,000 cycles per second (16 MHz), your CPU could process 320,000 cycles before Windows would move on to the next process (with a minimum timeslice value of 20).

I have obtained better performance for DOS sessions by changing this value from 20 to 5. And, just for curiosity's sake, I have run 33-MHz 386 systems at a minimum timeslice value of 1 for days on end, with no ill effects. Smaller timeslice values make DOS displays (and some Windows functions, in fact) perceptibly smoother and less jerky.

Microsoft technical support reports that a low value can be counter-productive. As you give each process in a multitasking system a smaller and smaller timeslice, the amount of time the multitasker (Windows) must spend in the switching process itself becomes a larger and larger percentage of the total CPU cycles available. At some point, you must increase the minimum timeslice so that each process can do enough meaningful work while it has the CPU to offer you good perceived performance.

The minimum timeslice value is specified in your SYSTEM.INI file under the [386Enh] section. The format is MINTIMESLICE=20, where *20* is the number of milliseconds allowed for each DOS session. The easiest way to change this setting is to use the Control Panel to open the 386 Enhanced dialog box. (This choice is only available if you are in 386 mode.)

Multitasking DOS and Windows Applications

The issue of multitasking is one of the most puzzling aspects of Windows computing. In 386 mode, Windows can keep DOS applications running even while they are in the background. And Windows can run two or more DOS sessions, each of which can be running in the background — sending data to a printer, receiving files over a communication line, and so on. But the exact settings that provide the best performance for these applications are difficult to determine.

First, let me define some differences between multitasking Windows applications vs. DOS applications:

1. Windows multitasks all Windows applications, whether it is in real mode, standard mode, or 386 mode. You can demonstrate this by starting Windows in real mode and opening two copies of the Clock utility side by side. Both clocks keep up with the time — even the one in the background.

2. Windows multitasks DOS applications only in 386 enhanced mode. In real mode or standard mode, a DOS application you started under Windows is "suspended" when you switch away from the DOS session and back to Windows. (If you need to run two DOS applications simultaneously, you can use Quarterdeck's DESQview or several other environments that can multitask whether running on a 386, a 286, or an XT.)

To control the amount of time that each running application is given by Windows, several settings are provided.

In SYSTEM.INI, in the [386Enh] section, setting WINTIMESLICE=100,50 controls how much time Windows itself gets when it is in the foreground (100) and the background (50). This setting is most easily changed through the 386 Enhanced dialog box in the Control Panel. There is only one setting for Windows, not for individual Windows applications. You cannot specify the relative amount of time that different running Windows applications receive — they decide themselves when to give up control and let Windows give time to other Windows applications.

In the PIF Editor, by contrast, timeslices may be specified differently for each DOS application run from a PIF. Windows defaults to a value of 100 for DOS applications in the foreground and 50 in the background, unless you change these values in the PIF itself.

What do these numbers, 100 and 50, mean? Are they percentages? No — setting a foreground value to 100 does not mean that that application will get 100 percent of the CPU's time when in the foreground. Are they timer ticks? (The DOS internal timer is set to tick about every 1/18th of a second.) No — there is no way in Windows to specify a certain number of timer ticks for each application. Are they, then, milliseconds (thousandths of a second)? Again, no. They do not quantify any exact measurement of time.

I prefer to think of these settings as giving each application a few *moments* of the CPU's time. One application under Windows might get 50 moments, then another one gets 100 moments, and so on around the circle. How long are these moments? It varies from system to system. Since the term *moments* is as vague as possible, it is a useful way to visualize the effect of multitasking under Windows.

Allow me to clarify this by using the following two diagrams.

When Windows is in 386 mode, and any Windows application currently has the keyboard focus, Windows itself is in the foreground. If you are also running two DOS sessions, both of these sessions are in the background. With the default settings, Windows gives itself 100 moments of the CPU's time. Each DOS session in the background receives 50 moments. This is illustrated as follows:

All Windows Applications 100 moments	**DOS #1** 50 moments	**DOS #2** 50 moments

If you switch to DOS Session number 1, then *it* becomes the foreground and receives 100 moments of the CPU's time. DOS Session #2 is still in the background, so it still receives 50 moments. And no Windows application is in the foreground, so *all* Windows apps (including Windows itself) are in the background and are supposed to share 50 moments among themselves. This is illustrated as follows:

DOS Session #1	DOS #2	All Win Apps
100 moments	50 moments	50 moments

This is the *theory* of Windows multitasking. But the *reality* is much different.

In theory, each DOS session that is running receives a minimum timeslice of the CPU; then, *all* Windows applications share one timeslice among themselves. But if all of your running Windows applications are idle, they are supposed to "release" their timeslice so Windows can switch more quickly to the next application in turn. This could result in Windows giving a foreground DOS session more time than its PIF settings would imply.

In addition to this, Windows' exhibits an extremely strong bias toward whatever DOS session is in the foreground — regardless of your timeslice values or PIF settings. This foreground bias is designed to allow your current DOS session to respond to your keystrokes in a more timely manner than might otherwise be the case, so using a DOS application under Windows seems less sluggish.

I performed some experiments, running two DOS sessions under Windows in 386 mode on a 33-MHz 386. All applications were run with the Windows default settings of 100 for applications in the foreground, and 50 for applications in the background. Therefore, the foreground DOS session was given a foreground priority of 100, the background DOS session was given a background priority of 50, and Windows was given a background priority of 50.

The two running DOS applications simply wrote the time of day to different hard disk files, in loops that repeated over and over again (so that variations in performance would average out). One of the applications, obviously, was in the foreground, while the other was in the background. But both applications were displayed in small windows, one above the other, on a large 8514/A display, in order to view their progress.

Since both the applications wrote messages to the screen occasionally, Windows interpreted this as a user activity at the console (the screen and keyboard). This warranted Windows giving the foreground DOS application a much larger slice of time than the background DOS app, to provide better perceived response time to the user.

The foreground DOS application, in this experiment, received *18 times* the amount of time that the background DOS application did. This was despite the fact that the foreground application was supposed to get only twice as many "moments" of the CPU's time as the background app.

This relationship would be illustrated as follows (since no Windows applications were running, the time given to Windows itself was not measured):

DOS Session #1	**#2**	**Win**
100 moments	5	(?)

Specifically, it took the application in DOS Session #1 only 1.6 seconds to carry out each loop. But it took DOS Session #2 30 seconds to carry out each loop — 18 times longer.

To test the effect of the MINTIMESLICE= setting in SYSTEM.INI (described earlier in this chapter), I ran these applications again. I first changed the minimum timeslice value from 20 to 10. On another round of tests, I changed the value to 5. In each case, I rebooted the machine in case anything might interfere with Windows putting these settings into effect.

The results, surprisingly, were almost exactly the same using shorter timeslicing intervals for each application. The foreground DOS session still required only about 1.6 seconds to perform each of its loops. With timeslicing set at 10, however, the background DOS session *improved* its time from 30 seconds per loop to about 29.6, and at a setting of 5, improved again to 28.3 seconds.

I do not claim that these are exhaustive tests of Windows performance. I don't consider them to be true benchmarks at all. I simply use them to illustrate the considerations that you must examine if your requirements dictate running one or more DOS applications under Windows, and you need some idea of their relative performance.

There is, at this writing, no widely available software utility that can test for you the interaction between the various multitasking settings of Windows. You should be able to run such a utility, and receive a report recommending that *this* setting should be *x,* while *that* one should be *y.* Without such a utility, you must change these settings manually and run your DOS apps to see if you can perceive any difference.

If you need detailed statistics, however, on how your DOS applications run under Windows, you should obtain a copy of Personal Measure, a background task analyzer. You load Personal Measure before starting the application you wish to inspect. After exiting that application, Personal Measure gives you a report on the use of the CPU, disk, and other resources in your system.

Since version 1.5, Personal Measure has been compatible with all three Windows modes. It also works with networks. You could load it in two DOS sessions and draw your own conclusions, using your own hardware and software configuration — the only configuration that truly gives you meaningful information. Personal Measure is priced a little over $100 and is available by contacting Spirit of Performance, Inc., 73 Westcott Road, Harvard, MA 01451, 508-456-3889.

Decoding DOS-Specific Messages

Standard and Enhanced Mode Kernel Errors

You may receive the following error message when you try to start a DOS application under Windows:

Application Execution Error: Unexpected DOS Error #11

This message does not really indicate a DOS error. Instead, it suggests that the Windows "kernel" executable — KERNEL.EXE, KRNL286.EXE, or KRNL386.EXE — has found something wrong with a file in the Windows \SYSTEM subdirectory. This could be a corrupted or missing "grabber" file, such as VGA.GR3 (so called because it grabs control of the video display), or the files WINOA286.MOD or WINOA386.MOD, which run DOS sessions (Old Apps) in 286 or 386 modes.

You may be able to use Windows' EXPAND.EXE program to expand the original copies of these files off the Windows distribution diskettes and replace the corrupted versions. To do this, copy EXPAND.EXE from Windows Disk #2 into your Windows subdirectory. Then find the diskette with the replacement file you need, and give the command:

EXPAND a:\filename c:\windows\SYSTEM

If this does not correct the problem, Microsoft recommends reinstalling Windows.

Family-Mode Apps Won't Run Directly

The File Manager and Program Manager provide several ways to run DOS applications. You can double-click a filename in the File Manager, for example, or you can pull down the File menu, choose Run, and then type in the program name under either File Manager or Program Manager.

If you use these methods to try to run a DOS-based application that can also run under OS/2 (called a "bound" or "family-mode" application), however, you find that the program will not start. Windows displays the message "Insufficient Memory." But memory is not the problem.

Although these family-mode applications can start themselves under either DOS or character-based OS/2, the executable .EXE file that makes this dual identity possible is in a new format that Windows cannot run directly. You can fix the error by creating a PIF file that starts the family-mode program. Run the PIF instead of running the program directly.

Increasing Files in CONFIG.SYS vs. SYSTEM.INI

All applications open files when they run. DOS provides a method to set aside enough memory to keep track of the various files that applications may need to read and leave open. This memory area is set aside by a statement in the CONFIG.SYS file, such as FILES=30. This allows DOS to reserve memory for the names that applications use to manipulate files, which are called "file handles."

When you use Windows in 386 mode to start a DOS application that uses a lot of open files, you may see the following error message:

    Insufficient File Handles, Increase Files in Config.sys

This message is in error, and changing the FILES= statement in your CONFIG.SYS will not make it go away. Instead, the message should advise as follows:

    Add "PerVMFiles=15" to the [386Enh] section of SYSTEM.INI.
    If 15 is not enough file handles, increase the number to 20.

The number of file handles specified in the CONFIG.SYS file relates to the number of file handles that are available to applications running under DOS (including Windows, which runs on top of DOS). The PERVMFILES= statement in SYSTEM.INI refers to the number of file handles that can be open per virtual machine under Windows. (A *virtual machine* is a DOS session that is running under Windows in 386 enhanced mode.) Without any PERVMFILES= statement in SYSTEM.INI, Windows defaults to only ten file handles allowed within a DOS session. This may not be enough for some DOS applications.

Microsoft recommends 30 file handles in CONFIG.SYS. You should change the file handles per virtual machine in SYSTEM.INI only if you receive an error message. Each file handle requires a very small amount of memory — only a few bytes under DOS.

The number of handles specified by the FILES= line in CONFIG.SYS and PERVMFILES= in SYSTEM.INI combined cannot be greater than 255 (although it is unlikely anyone would need to approach this limit).

PIF Files Require Change to WIN.INI

If you receive the message "No association exists for this data file" when trying to run a PIF file, you may need to edit your WIN.INI file to specifically include PIFs. When Windows 3.0 is installed into the same directory as an older Windows 2.x installation, it may not edit your WIN.INI to include PIFs as a recognized program type. (Windows/386 didn't require the specific inclusion of PIFs in order to run them.) Edit the PROGRAMS= line in your WIN.INI to look as follows:

```
Programs=com exe bat pif
```

When you restart Windows, it will run PIFs when you double-click on them in the File Manager or invoke them from icons.

The Mysterious PIF Editor

The Windows PIF Editor is used to make Program Information Files that run DOS applications under Windows. If you plan to run any DOS sessions, it will definitely pay for you to learn what these PIFs are doing to your applications' performance.

Probably no other Windows applet inspires so much fear, uncertainty, and doubt as the PIF Editor. This is because it seems to have *so many* settings, and there's no way to know for sure whether you have chosen the optimum settings for any particular DOS application. The PIF Editor uses strange, jargon terms that no one understands (like XMS Memory), instead of familiar, jargon terms that a few people might understand (like Extended Memory, which XMS Memory stands for). And the PIF Editor provides no way to place comments into PIF files so that you and those who come after you can remember *why* you set certain options the way you did.

But nothing can do more for the performance of your DOS applications under Windows than perfecting your knowledge of these options in the PIF Editor. And it isn't that hard, once you decode this little dialog box.

The PIF Editor is actually one of the best examples of *context-sensitive help* in Windows. When you don't understand one of the PIF Editor's options, simply place your blinking cursor inside the relevant box and press F1. A help screen appears and explains *that particular option*. This help text is often better than the explanation you find in the Windows manual itself.

Since this help information is so easily accessible, I have not merely re-peated in this chapter the same, documented explanation of each PIF setting. Instead, I describe in the following pages the implications and side effects of many of these settings. Additionally, I provide a one-page refer-ence chart to each of the PIF Editor's screens (one for its standard mode, another for its enhanced mode). You can use these charts as a memory aid to the PIF Editor's options, and resort to the F1 key, the Windows manual, or my explanations in this chapter only when you need further elaboration.

Figure 5-7 shows Windows' factory-set defaults for the PIF Editor, in both standard and enhanced modes.

Figure 5-8 is my recommended standard-mode settings for a DOS Session, and is accompanied by a reference chart for the PIF Editor in its standard mode.

Figure 5-9 shows the enhanced mode's "basic" settings, while Figure 5-10 is for the enhanced mode's "advanced" settings.

In addition, I offer you a way to set your "default" PIF in order to optimize *all* your DOS sessions for *your* particular system. This can also save you a great deal of time by acting as a quick starting point for other PIF files you make.

Figure 5-11 is accompanied by an overall chart and reference guide to the recommendations for this default PIF.

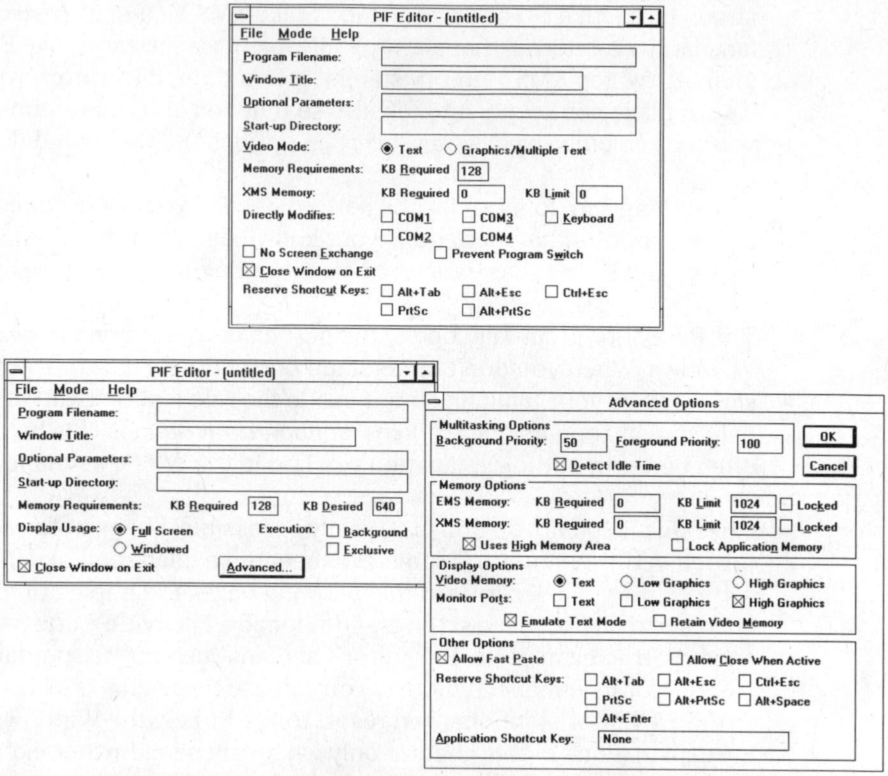

Figure 5-7: The default settings when you start the PIF Editor — don't use these defaults. The PIF Editor's standard mode is shown above, enhanced mode (basic and advanced dialog boxes) under that.

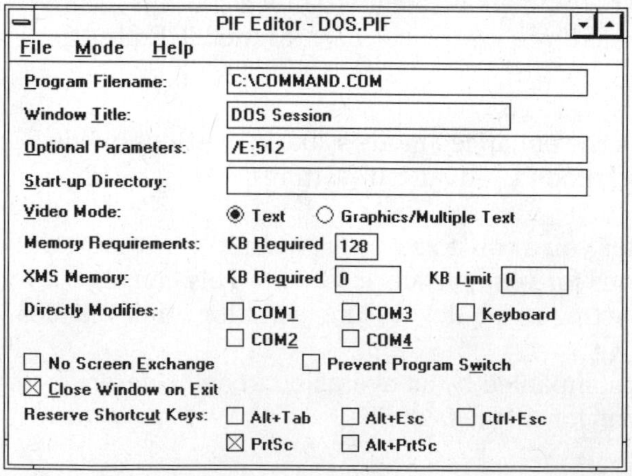

Figure 5-8: Recommended standard-mode settings for a DOS Session.

PIF Editor Reference Chart

Standard Mode (also Real Mode)

Program Filename	Full path of executable name; for example, C:\COMMAND.COM.
Window Title	Descriptive title, used below icon when application is minimized.
Optional Parameters	Any parameters loaded after application, such as the file to open. Use "?" to prompt you for parameters. *Different parameters may be used in enhanced mode than in standard mode.*
Start-up Directory	Drive and directory Windows makes current, e.g., C:\. Anything here may prevent you from associating file extensions.

Video Mode:
  Text
  Graphics/Multiple Text
	A different video mode may be set for enhanced mode.
	Initially reserves enough memory for text (1 video page).
	Reserves more memory for graphics, or 8 video text pages.

Memory Requirements:
  KB Required
  XMS Memory
    KB Required
    KB Limit
	Different memory requirements may be set for enhanced mode.
	The PIF won't start without this much conventional memory.
	
	The PIF won't start without this much extended memory.
	Allows the app to claim up to this much extended memory. Set to -1 to give the app all extended memory.

Directly Modifies:
  COM Ports
  Keyboard
	Selecting these options prevents switching away from the app:
	If on, Windows allocates the port to only one app at a time.
	If on, Windows needn't save the app's current state or display.

No Screen Exchange	If on, disables PrtSc copies to Clipboard; saves a little memory.
Prevent Program Switch	Disables shortcut keys; prevents switching away from app.
Close Window on Exit	If off, a DOS prompt remains in window when the app is exited.

Reserve Shortcut Keys:
 	
  Alt+Esc
  Alt+PrtSc
  Alt+Tab
  Ctrl+Esc
  PrtSc
	Gives the application the exclusive use of the following keys.
	A different set of keys may be reserved in enhanced mode.
	(Windows ordinarily uses these combinations as shown):
	Switches from one app to the next, in round-robin fashion.
	Copies the active window to the Clipboard.
	Switches between current and previous application.
	Displays the Windows Task List.
	Copies the full screen to the Clipboard.

Figure 5-8a: Use in connection with Figure 5-8.

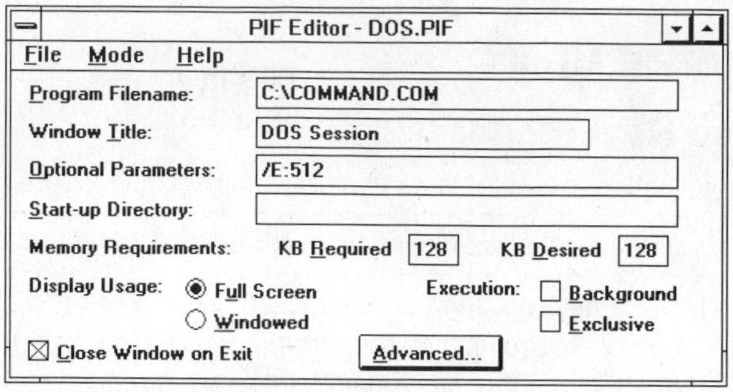

Figure 5-9: Recommended enhanced-mode "Basic" settings for a DOS Session. Increase the value of KB Desired if you want to do more in this DOS session than run small commands like DIR.

PIF Editor Reference Chart

Enhanced Mode — Basic Options

Program Filename	Full path of executable name; for example, C:\COMMAND.COM.
Window Title	Descriptive title, used below icon when application is minimized.
Optional Parameters	Any parameters loaded after application, such as the file to open. Use "?" to prompt you for parameters. *Different parameters may be used in standard mode than in enhanced mode.*
Start-up Directory	Drive and directory Windows makes current, for example, C:\. Anything here may prevent you from associating file extensions.
Memory Requirements:	*Different memory requirements may be set for standard mode.*
KB Required	The PIF won't start without this much conventional memory. Set to -1 to give the app all Windows-discardable memory.
KB Desired	Allows the app to claim up to this much conventional memory. Set to -1 to give the app all Windows-discardable memory.
Display Usage:	
Full Screen	Starts app full-screen; toggle to windowed with Alt+Enter.
Windowed	Starts in window; takes more memory; toggle with Alt+Enter.
Execution:	
Background	Allows app to run in background, using its Background Priority. (Windows overrides this if WINEXCLUSIVE=YES in SYSTEM.INI.) If off, Background Priority in the Advanced options is ignored.
Exclusive	Allows app to run exclusively when running in the full screen; even Windows is suspended until the app is exited or windowed.
Close Window on Exit	If off, a DOS prompt remains in window when the app is exited.

Figure 5-9a: Use in connection with Figure 5-9.

The following material provides as much detail as possible on some of the PIF Editor's settings — detail which you may *not* find when you read the Windows manual. First, I describe aspects of PIFs in general. After this are sections on quirks of the PIF Editor in both its standard mode (which is also used in real mode) and its enhanced mode.

Don't Use Windows Default Settings

The settings that automatically appear every time you start the PIF Editor are designed for the worst possible case — an ill-behaved EGA graphics application that might (in 386 mode) use both extended *and* expanded memory. These settings will almost certainly harm the performance of your DOS programs under Windows. Additionally, the "default" PIF file that comes with Windows, named _DEFAULT.PIF (the first character of the filename is an underscore), uses these worst-case settings for *every* DOS application that you start (unless you define a PIF that overrides these settings). Later in this chapter, I describe how to change your _DEFAULT.PIF file to optimize performance on your system. But even after you do this, the PIF Editor defaults to the original settings — not the ones you choose in your _DEFAULT.PIF. So beware of saving a PIF file with one of these performance-harming settings, as described below. (And I'll show you how to make the PIF Editor come up with the defaults that *you* want.)

Make a Separate Directory for Your PIF Files

Once you start generating PIFs, and you get good at it, you will accumulate a surprising number of these little files. You may find you want two or more PIFs for certain DOS applications, to configure them differently or assign them more or less memory in certain circumstances. And you should have PIFs for running batch files you need under Windows.

For this reason, I recommend that you create a separate directory, such as C:\PIF, and move all your PIF files into that directory. This allows you to easily see and manage these files. Those with computer management backgrounds will recognize that this separates a program's code (the Windows executable files) and its data files (PIFs), and so prevents writing new data into the same directory that contains the program itself.

When you move your PIFs into C:\PIF, you must place the C:\PIF directory in your AUTOEXEC.BAT's PATH= statement, prior to the C:\WINDOWS directory. This enables Windows to find them. You must reboot (to rerun AUTOEXEC.BAT) for this change to take effect.

PIF Editor Reference Chart

Enhanced Mode — Advanced Options

Multitasking Options:	*Background Priority is ignored if the Background option is off.*
Background Priority	Relative time the app gets in background; range: 0 to 10000.
Foreground Priority	Relative time the app gets in foreground; range: 0 to 10000.
Detect Idle Time	If on, Windows stops giving time to the app if it seems idle.
EMS Memory:	
KB Required	The PIF won't start without this much expanded memory. Some apps won't get any EMS unless some is required here.
KB Limit	Allows the app to claim up to this much expanded memory. Set to -1 to give the app all expanded memory.
Locked	If on, Windows will not swap the app's EMS memory to disk. This speeds switching but may keep other apps from loading.
XMS Memory:	*Different requirements may be set for XMS in standard mode.*
KB Required	The PIF won't start without this much extended memory.
KB Limit	Allows the app to claim up to this much extended memory. Set to -1 to give the app all expanded memory.
Locked	If on, Windows will not swap the app's XMS memory to disk. This speeds switching but may keep other apps from loading.
Uses High Memory Area	Allows HMA-aware apps to share the first 64K of extended.
Lock Application Memory	If on, Windows will not swap the app's conventional memory. This speeds switching but may keep other apps from loading.
Video Memory:	*A different video mode may be set for standard mode.*
Text	Initially reserves enough memory for text mode (about 16K); Windows can adjust this later if the app switches modes.
Low Graphics	Initially reserves about 32K for CGA-resolution graphics.
High Graphics	Initially reserves 128K for EGA- or VGA-res graphics; this takes memory from the pool, leaving less for other apps.
Monitor Ports:	
Text	Required only if app writes to screen unusually in text mode.
Low Graphics	Required only if CGA display is garbled when you switch back.
High Graphics	Required in EGA modes so Windows can monitor operations.

(continued)

Figure 5-10a: Use in connection with Figure 5-10.

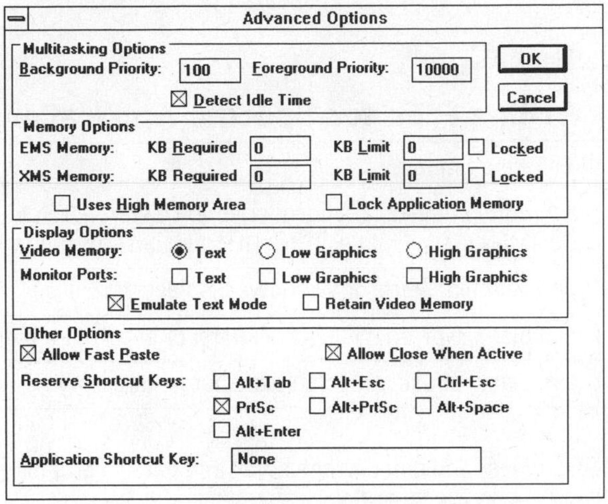

Figure 5-10: Recommended enhanced-mode "Advanced" settings for a DOS Session.

Emulate Text Mode	If on, increases the application's speed displaying text. Turn off if text or cursor is garbled when you switch back to app.
Retain Video Memory	If on, locks app's unused video memory. If off, the app may not be able to switch modes if another app has taken available memory.
Allow Fast Paste	Turn off only if app can't take text as fast as Clipboard pastes it.
Allow Close When Active	Turn on only if app uses standard DOS file handles and does not leave files open.
Reserve Shortcut Keys:	Gives the application the exclusive use of the following keys. *A different set of keys may be reserved in standard mode.* (Windows ordinarily uses these combinations as shown).
Alt+Enter	Toggles between full-screen and windowed (if possible).
Alt+Esc	Switches from one app to the next, in round-robin fashion.
Alt+PrtSc	Copies the active window to the Clipboard.
Alt+Spacebar	Pulls down the Control Menu of the active window.
Alt+Tab	Switches between current and previous application.
Ctrl+Esc	Displays the Windows Task List.
PrtSc	Copies the full screen to the Clipboard.
Application Shortcut Key	Specifies a combination that brings app to foreground, if running.

Figure 5-10a: Use in connection with Figure 5-10 (cont'd.).

PIF Editor Reference Chart

Rules of Thumb on Writing PIFs for Specific Applications

Settings in Both Standard and Enhanced Modes:

Program Filename	Full directory and application filename. To start batch files, use C:\COMMAND.COM (with /E:512 /C FILENAME.BAT as a parameter).
Window Title	Type something here, or Windows displays the PIF's filename.
Optional Parameters	Leave blank, type specific parameters, or use "?" for a dialog box.
Start-up Directory	Leave blank, or use a batch file to change directory.

Settings in Standard Mode:

Video Mode	Text, unless you can't switch away and back in graphics mode.
Memory KB Required	128; setting a higher requirement doesn't provide more memory.
XMS Memory	0, unless the app can use HIMEM.SYS-type extended memory.
COM Ports	Off, unless the app is a serial communications-type program.
Keyboard	Off, unless the app takes direct control of the keyboard.
No Screen Exchange	Off, unless a few bytes of memory would help the app load.
Prevent Program Switch	Off, unless the application crashes when you switch away from it.
Close Window on Exit	On, unless you need to read text on-screen after exiting the app.
Reserve Shortcut Keys:	PrtSc on. Others off, unless needed specifically by the application.

Settings in Enhanced Mode:

Memory Requirements	Required: 128. Desired: -1, unless other apps need some memory.
Display Usage	Full-screen, unless the app runs well in a small window.
Execution: Background	Off, unless the app does something useful in the background.
Execution: Exclusive	Off; use Foreground: 10000 unless you want Windows halted.
Close Window on Exit	On, unless you need to read the screen after exiting the app.
Multitasking Options:	*If Execution: Background is off, Background Priority is ignored.*
Background Priority	100, unless the app needs more time in background.
Foreground Priority	10000, unless background apps can't wait until this app is idle.
Detect Idle Time	On, unless the app quietly runs timers or is Windows-aware.
EMS KB Required	0, unless the app uses expanded; then require 256 or more.
EMS KB Limit	0; if needed, setting a limit runs faster than specifying -1 (all).
EMS Locked	Off, unless the app crashes without instant access to expanded.

(continued)

Figure 5-11a: Use in connection with Figure 5-11.

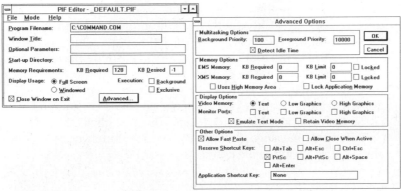

Figure 5-11: Recommended settings for your _DEFAULT.PIF file. Use this default PIF as the starting point for PIFs you create for specific applications, using the rules of thumb shown opposite this page.

XMS KB Required	0, unless the app uses HIMEM.SYS-type extended memory.
XMS KB Limit	0; if needed, setting a limit runs faster than specifying -1 (all).
XMS Locked	Off, unless the app crashes without instant access to extended.
Uses High Memory Area	Off, unless the app actually uses HMA memory access.
Lock Application Memory	Off, unless the app crashes if swapped from conventional to disk.
Video Memory	Text, unless you can't switch away and back in graphics mode.
Monitor Ports	All off, unless using EGA, or if the app's screen is garbled.
Emulate Text Mode	Off, unless text or cursor is garbled when you switch back to app.
Retain Video Memory	Off, unless you run out of memory switching to graphics mode.
Allow Fast Paste	On, unless the app can't take text as fast as Clipboard pastes it.
Allow Close When Active	Off, for apps that write files. On, for plain, C> prompt sessions.
Reserve Shortcut Keys	PrtSc on. Others off, unless needed specifically by the application.
Application Shortcut Key	"None." Use Ctrl+Esc or Alt+Tab+Tab to switch applications.

Figure 5-11a: Use in connection with Figure 5-11 (cont'd.).

Additionally, you should change the Program Manager icon that starts the PIF Editor, so that the Command Line of this icon reads C:\PIF\PIFEDIT.EXE instead of just PIFEDIT.EXE. This makes the PIF Editor change to the C:\PIF directory, where it is easy for you to click File Open and choose from a complete list of your PIF files.

(To make this change, click once on the PIF Editor icon to highlight it. Then click File Properties on the Program Manager menu. In the dialog box that appears, change PIFEDIT.EXE to C:\PIF\PIFEDIT.EXE. When you click OK, you may receive the message "The specified Path is invalid!" Click OK to get rid of this message — it means that Windows didn't find the file PIFEDIT.EXE in the directory C:\PIF. In case the PIF Editor icon has changed to a plain, default icon, you must click File Properties again. This time, instead of changing the Command Line, click the Change Icon button in the dialog box. Specify PIFEDIT.EXE as the location of the icon, click Next Icon to make this take effect, then click OK twice to get entirely out of the dialog box. Windows 3.0 does not allow you to change an icon's Command Line and its Icon File in the same session. Once again, you must click OK to deal with the "invalid Path" message. But now that you're done, your PIF Editor will always start up in the file containing your PIFs.)

A Batch File Can Start a PIF File

When run under Windows, a DOS batch file gains one capability that it doesn't have outside Windows — it can run PIF files from within itself.

This is one way to set certain environmental variables for a DOS application before you run it. Alternatively, you can load terminate-and-stay-resident (TSR) programs in a batch file, before the PIF that starts your primary DOS application. You can then access the TSR from within that DOS app — without using up memory in every DOS session by loading that TSR prior to starting Windows.

To do this, simply place the name of the PIF file in a line of the batch file, just as you would run any other program. Windows detects that you have run a PIF and sends the proper commands to DOS, just as you have specified them when you set up the PIF in the first place. For example, to load a memory-resident program called RESIDENT.EXE, and then load MYAPP.EXE from a PIF, your batch file might look like this:

```
ECHO OFF
c:\path\resident
c:\path\myapp.pif
```

In this case, when you exit MYAPP, Windows reclaims the memory that the DOS session used, terminating the TSR and releasing its memory as well.

Delete the [pif] Section from WIN.INI

If you installed Windows 3.*x* into the same directory as a previous installation of Windows (including limited run-time versions), the 3.*x* Setup program probably did not remove a section headed [pif] in your WIN.INI. This section was required by PIFs in earlier versions of Windows, but can have negative effects under Windows 3.*x*. Specifically, there may be an entry in the [pif] section that limits COMMAND.COM to a certain amount of memory. This would limit every DOS session you start with COMMAND.COM. Delete this section entirely (or, if you're hesitant to delete it, comment it out by putting semicolons [;] in front of each line, including the line that contains the heading "pif" in square brackets).

You Must Specify Both Standard and Enhanced Options

The PIF Editor saves two different sets of options for each PIF you create: one set is used if Windows is in real or standard mode, the other if Windows is in 386 enhanced mode. Options that exist in both modes (such as the switches that you use on the command line to start a program) are *not necessarily saved* for both modes. If you created a PIF while you were in enhanced mode, but you happened to be in standard mode when you ran the PIF, any command-line switches that you defined for the program in enhanced mode would not be found. You must switch the PIF Editor from one mode to the other in order to define these options for your programs.

The settings that both standard mode and enhanced mode have in common (and whether PIF settings you make in one mode are automatically effective in the other mode) are shown in the following table:

Setting:	Effective in both standard and enhanced modes:
Program Filename	Yes
Window Title	Yes
Optional Parameters (Switches)	No
Start-up Directory	Yes
Video Mode (Text or Graphics)	No
Memory Requirements	No
XMS (Extended) Memory	No
Close Window on Exit	Yes
Reserve Shortcut Keys	No

When you specify in one mode of the PIF Editor any of the settings marked "No" in the above table, you must switch into the other mode and specify them again (then save the PIF file). This feature of the PIF Editor, of course, also allows you to specify *different* parameters for a program, depending on whether you launch it under Windows in real or standard modes, or in 386 enhanced mode.

When you switch the PIF Editor into its enhanced mode to make these settings — but Windows is running in standard mode — the PIF Editor displays the discouraging message, "The PIF information you enter may not be appropriate." Ignore this message; if you *don't* enter information for both standard and enhanced modes in your PIFs, they may be inappropriate for your needs.

Standard and Enhanced Mode Settings

The following options exist in both the standard-mode and the 386 enhanced-mode settings of the PIF Editor. See the following sections, "Standard Mode Settings" and "Enhanced Mode Settings" for options that exist only in one or the other of those two modes.

Program Filename

There are advantages to naming a PIF file with the same 8-letter filename you enter into the Program Filename box. If you start an application by running it from the Program Manager or File Manager — with a command such as File Run MYAPP.EXE — Windows automatically uses the settings in any PIF file with the same 8-letter filename as the application, such as MYAPP.PIF. (The PIF file must be located on the Path for this to work.) If Windows finds no such PIF, it uses the settings in the _DEFAULT.PIF file.

If you run a PIF file by its own name, however (for example, with a command such as File Run DOTHIS.PIF), the PIF may have a different 8-letter filename than the application it starts.

In any case, you *must* enter a valid filename in this box. Otherwise, the PIF Editor won't save your PIF. This is true even when you are editing your _DEFAULT.PIF file, which totally ignores what's entered in the Program Filename box (as described in the topic "Editing Your Default PIF").

Window Title

The text you type in the Window Title box appears as the application's icon title when the DOS session is minimized. In 386 mode, this title also appears in the application's title bar when you run it in a small window. But if you leave this box blank, Windows then displays the filename of the PIF (without the extension .PIF).

Optional Parameters

You can type into this box whatever switches your DOS application needs when it starts up. But any parameters you type after the PIF name (when you run a PIF from the Program Manager or File Manager) *override* the parameters that you specified in the PIF itself. For example, commanding File Run MYAPP.PIF /ABC forces your app to use the parameter /ABC instead of whatever you defined in the PIF. Thus you can use one set of switches to start the application most of the time and use a different set occasionally.

Another technique is available; you can place a question mark (?) in the Optional Parameters box, which makes Windows display a dialog box asking what parameters (such as a document name to load) should be fed into the program.

This option, however, may not work for batch files started from a PIF. The question mark option works as expected with executable .COM and .EXE files, but not with .BAT files, due to a bug in Windows 3.0. One workaround would be to write a batch file that asks the user for a variable before starting the program, instead of starting the program directly. The ability to ask for a variable is not available through standard DOS batch commands, however; this capability requires that you obtain a third-party utility such as Batutil (described earlier in the section on SUBST.EXE), which can be run within the batch file itself.

Start-up Directory

You are encouraged by the Windows 3.0 manual to specify a start-up directory to change to before loading your DOS application. However, an undocumented feature of the Start-up Directory box is that, if you specify *any* directory in this box, it may prevent the PIF file from loading any document that you may have associated with that PIF.

For example, say you create a WORD.PIF file to start Microsoft Word for DOS. You then create the association DOC=WORD.PIF ^.DOC in the [Extensions] section of WIN.INI. This association should load into Word for DOS any .DOC file that you double-click in File Manager (or specify in a File Run dialog box). But if any directory is specified in the PIF's Start-up Directory box, it prevents this document name from being passed to Word.

This may be corrected in a later release of Windows. But in any case, if your application *must* be located in a certain directory for it to work, it's better to make the PIF start a batch file that changes the directory prior to loading the application.

Video Mode: Text or Graphics

You can actually start a DOS program that uses EGA or VGA graphics from a PIF in which you have set the video mode to Text. Setting this option to Text provides some additional memory for the application. However, when the application switches to graphics mode (upon start-up or subsequently), you may not be able to switch away from the application until you exit it completely. Or, if you *do* manage to switch to Windows and start another application, Windows may "give away" your DOS application's "extra" video memory, preventing you from switching back to the DOS application in graphics mode. The "Text" option, therefore, is best suited for DOS applications that use graphics mode, but which you never intend to switch away from.

The term "multiple text" in the label for the Graphics/Multiple Text button in standard mode means "applications that use more than one page of text memory." In this case, "page" stands for one screen-full of text. An application normally needs only 4K of video memory to display one screen of text. (80 columns times 25 lines equals 2,000 bytes — plus one "attribute" byte per character, which contains each letter's color — for a total of 4,000 bytes.)

If an application uses multiple video-memory "pages" — up to eight are available on a PC, requiring as much as 32,000 bytes — it may need the Graphics/Multiple Text button checked in its PIF, even if it displays only text. Applications may use multiple text pages as a way to switch instantaneously from, say, the top to the bottom of a document (both parts of the document are already in video memory).

In 386 enhanced mode, the PIF Editor contains an additional option in this section that can prevent Windows from "giving away" your application's unused video memory. This is the Retain Video Memory check box. If you leave this setting *off,* you may not be able to switch back to a DOS application after leaving it and starting a Windows application. If you turn it *on,* you may not be able to leave a DOS application and start a Windows application (if Windows is memory-starved).

Memory Requirements

Under standard mode, DOS sessions you start receive all available conventional memory from Windows. This is because only one DOS session is possible in standard mode, and all Windows applications are suspended while the DOS session is in the foreground. Setting the KB Required box to a number higher than 128 doesn't provide your application with any more conventional memory.

Under enhanced mode, however, if you fill the KB Required box with the value "-1" instead of a number representing a DOS application's minimum memory requirement, your application *may* get more conventional memory. This is because the "-1" setting forces any running Windows applications to release any discardable memory objects they presently have in conventional memory.

This also works in the KB Desired box (which appears in the PIF Editor only in enhanced mode). But if your application doesn't *require* or make any use of more than a certain amount of memory, filling this box with a smaller number makes the application load faster, and leaves more memory for other applications. You should create a separate PIF, for example, for "small" DOS sessions in which you plan to run only DOS commands such as DIR, DEL, and so on. Settings of 128K for KB Required and KB Desired would be adequate for these tasks.

XMS Memory (Extended Memory)

In case your DOS application makes use of extended memory in a way that would be compatible with running under Windows, the XMS Memory settings allow you to specify minimum and maximum limits for this application. The limits are specified in the XMS: KB Required and XMS: KB Limit boxes, respectively.

Lotus 1-2-3 Release 3.1 was one of the first DOS applications to use extended memory under Windows in this way. In technical terms, 1-2-3 Release 3.1 was one of the first applications to use the "DOS Protected Mode Interface" (DPMI) specification, which Microsoft prescribes as the correct way to access extended memory under a multitasking environment. (DPMI applications obtain extended memory through HIMEM.SYS or other "XMS managers" such as Quarterdeck's QEMM386.SYS.)

However, if your application *doesn't* use extended memory, don't allow any values other than 0 (zero) into these boxes. If Windows does not have to allow for the possibility that the application *might* request some extended memory, it frees some conventional memory for your app.

You will note that there is no setting for *expanded* memory in the PIF Editor's standard mode, unlike its enhanced mode. This is because Windows in standard mode and real mode allows a DOS session to use *all* expanded memory. An add-in board with expanded memory must be present in your system, and an expanded memory manager (typically identified with a name ending in EMM.SYS) must have been loaded in your CONFIG.SYS before starting Windows.

In Windows' enhanced mode, Windows itself provides expanded memory for DOS sessions. A variety of third-party memory managers are also available that provide expanded memory for DOS applications when Windows is *not* running. (See Chapter 16 for details.)

Standard Mode Settings

The PIF Editor dialog box in standard mode has far fewer options than in enhanced mode (described later in this section). The following items explain some quirks about these options that might not be obvious.

Directly Modifies

If your application takes direct control of the keyboard or uses COM ports (such as a communications program), you must check one or more of the boxes in this section. The COM port check boxes also prevent you from starting this PIF if a Windows application is already using one of the COM ports. Selecting *any* of the boxes in the Directly Modifies section has the same effect as selecting the Prevent Program Switch box described below —

you cannot switch back to Windows until you exit your DOS application completely. But it doesn't hurt to turn on the Prevent Program Switch box as well.

No Screen Exchange

If the setting No Screen Exchange is *on,* the use of the key combinations PrintScreen and Alt+PrintScreen to copy the DOS session's screen to the Clipboard are disabled. This saves a little memory, which the DOS application can use. The No Screen Exchange option has the same effect as reserving both of these key combinations for the application in the Reserve Shortcut Keys section, described below. You should be aware that Windows is not capable of sending a *graphics* screen from a DOS application to the Clipboard in real or standard modes, no matter how these key combinations are set. Windows can only send *text* screens to the Clipboard under these modes.

Prevent Program Switch

If you never want to switch from your DOS application back to Windows without first exiting the application completely, you should mark this box *on.* This frees a little more conventional memory for the application (which Windows would otherwise use to check for application-switching key combinations). See also "Directly Modifies," above, and "Reserve Shortcut Keys," next.

Reserve Shortcut Keys

The boxes you mark in this section have the same effect as the Prevent Program Switch box — but only if you mark *all* the boxes Alt+Tab, Alt+Esc, and Ctrl+Esc. Again, it doesn't hurt to check both sets of boxes, even if they appear to have the same effect.

As mentioned earlier in this chapter, checking the boxes to reserve the PrtSc and Alt+PrtSc key combinations for your application *doesn't work* in real and standard modes under Windows 3.0. These boxes are only functional in DOS sessions under enhanced mode. Some suggestions for getting these keys back are described under the earlier section "Using the PrintScreen Key in DOS Sessions."

Enhanced Mode Settings

The following section describes features that exist only in the enhanced mode settings of the PIF Editor. Note that the options that exist in both standard and enhanced modes were described earlier in the section "Standard and Enhanced Mode Settings." See that section for descriptions of the following settings:

> Program Filename
> Window Title
> Optional Parameters
> Start-up Directory
> Video Mode
> Memory Requirements
> XMS Memory

Display Usage: Full-Screen or Windowed

Starting a DOS session in a small window takes slightly more memory than starting it full-screen. So if your application won't start in a window, try flipping this setting to full-screen. But another reason the application might not be starting in a window is that a company logo is programmed to run in graphics mode before switching the session to text mode. This causes an error message if you start the app "windowed." See "Windowed DOS Applications" earlier in this chapter for more information on this problem.

Execution: Background and Exclusive

If the Execution: <u>B</u>ackground check box is *off,* whatever number you specify in the <u>B</u>ackground Priority box for this application is ignored. This is because the application will never be allowed to run in the background at all.

According to Lotus Corp., Lotus 1-2-3 Release 3.1 does not run correctly in the background. If your application has no such limitation, you should turn the <u>B</u>ackground setting *on.*

Even with Execution: <u>B</u>ackground *on,* however, your app won't get any time when it's in the background if one of the following is true:

1. Another PIF is running with Execution: <u>E</u>xclusive *on;*

2. Another PIF is running with Foreground Priority: 10000, and that application is currently busy doing something; or

3. The line WINEXCLUSIVE=TRUE appears in the [386Enh] section of your SYSTEM.INI file. This gives Windows 100 percent of the CPU cycles when any Windows application is in the foreground (in 386 mode). The easiest way to check or edit this setting is to open the 386 Enhanced dialog box in the Control Panel (which only appears in 386 mode, of course).

The Execution: Exclusive setting for a PIF, in addition to halting all other running DOS sessions, may interfere with Windows background tasks that need to receive timeslices (perhaps a Windows screen-saver utility or a scheduler that reminds you of appointments).

A better way to get fast performance for a DOS application might be to leave the Exclusive check box *off,* but specify a Foreground Priority of 10000. This particular setting gives the application all available CPU cycles, unless the application has completed all its processing and is waiting for you to press a key (in other words, is idle).

The Exclusive setting, in any case, loses some of its power when you switch a DOS application from full-screen to windowed. Even if you checked the Exclusive box, a windowed DOS application will still give some time back to Windows. (Windows must be able do things like change the shape of the cursor arrow when you move it over parts of different visible windows.)

Multitasking Options

See the section "Multitasking DOS and Windows Applications" earlier in this chapter for detailed information on setting these options.

The "Advanced Options" Button

If you click the Advanced button in the PIF Editor, and no Advanced Options dialog box opens, you are probably in a memory-starved situation — Windows cannot make room in memory for the dialog box to appear. In this case, closing other windows to free up memory won't help (although this works with other low-memory problems). You must first close the PIF Editor and then close other windows, before starting it again.

Detect Idle Time

This setting, when turned *on,* enables Windows to stop giving DOS applications any timeslices if Windows determines that the application is doing nothing but waiting for you to press a key. This cut-off can make foreground Windows applications run faster when a DOS session that needs no timeslices is running in the background.

Whether Windows *correctly* determines that a DOS application is idle, however, varies from application to application. One company I work with uses a DOS calendar-and-scheduling program, which their users leave open in a small window in 386 mode while using other applications. The program features a text-mode time-of-day display that updates itself once a second. Users can set appointment reminders in the program, and the program beeps and displays a notification message at the specified time.

The problem with this application was that if a 386 running Windows was idle for one or two hours, the time-of-day display would eventually get "stuck" at a random point in time. The program had been cut off from timeslices by Windows, which didn't see any activity when it checked the program.

The users were able to work around this problem by moving the mouse, which woke the scheduler up and caused it to display the correct time again and regain all its functions. The proper fix was much more effective — we turned the PIF's Detect Idle Time check box *off* so Windows couldn't shut down this little app.

This scheduler is an example of an older, Windows-unaware DOS application. Newer DOS apps, however, can detect when they are running under Windows and send it a message whenever they are merely waiting for a keystroke. This makes your whole system run faster, since Windows doesn't have to give timeslices to that application until you start using it again.

Ironically, the Detect Idle Time option is intended for the older kind of DOS app. The rules for its use with the newer kind of program are not intuitive. You should set this option according to one of the following three rules:

RULES:

Using Detect Idle Time with DOS Apps

Rule 1. If the application is an older one, and does not do *anything* in the background that is important, turn Detect Idle Time *on.*

Rule 2. If the application does something once a second, or intermittently when a certain event occurs (such as midnight), turn Detect Idle Time *off.*

Rule 3. If the application is a newer, Windows-aware type, turn Detect Idle Time *off.* Your applications will all run a little faster if Windows gets the "idle" message directly from these applications and does not have to test for it.

Unfortunately, it is difficult to determine whether a particular DOS application does or does not send this "idle" message to Windows. If the documentation doesn't mention this feature, you have to assume that it hasn't been added to the program yet. (If it's not in the manual, ask a technical person at the software company whether the program, when idle, *loads the AX register with the value 1680 hex and calls interrupt 2F.* Any C programmer will know what you're talking about. If the program *doesn't* do this, it's so easy to add that this feature should be included in the next minor upgrade to the application.)

EMS Memory (Expanded Memory)

The EMS Memory options (which provide access to Windows' Expanded Memory Specification manager) include two settings for the minimum and maximum amounts of expanded memory that this application should be allowed. These boxes are labeled KB Required and KB Limit. The effects of these settings may not be what you think, however.

Say you have an application that doesn't require expanded memory, but uses it if it is available. You might think you should specify KB Required: 0 and KB Limit: 1024 (one megabyte).

Many DOS applications, however, do not "see" any expanded memory unless you *require* Windows to provide some. This is because Windows is not making any expanded memory available to the application until the app makes a specific request. If the application checks to see how much expanded memory exists, before explicitly requesting any, it finds none and may conclude that none can be created for it. Lotus 1-2-3 Release 2.01 is an example of this type of application.

The "Beyond PIFs" section later in this chapter includes a discussion of this problem, using Lotus 1-2-3 as an illustration of how to configure this type of application; configuring other DOS programs that may be partly or completely incompatible with DOS sessions under Windows is also discussed.

Lock EMS, XMS, or Application Memory

Although there are three separate check boxes for EMS Memory Locked, XMS Memory Locked, and Lock Application Memory, I treat them in the same topic here for simplicity. All these settings do very much the same thing.

Since few people have ever heard of "locking" memory (before Windows), this concept causes some confusion. It's actually simple: if part of an application's memory is "locked," Windows is prohibited from swapping (writing) that memory to your hard disk if you switch away from that application.

"Locking" memory means that switching away from and back to a DOS session may be faster, since you have precluded any possible disk writes. But you may not be able to open other Windows or DOS applications, because the memory that Windows would ordinarily free (by swapping background applications to disk) will be totally unavailable.

Note that despite the name of the "Lock Application Memory" option, this check box does not lock all the memory that your application is using — only the *conventional* memory it uses. You must also check the boxes for expanded memory (EMS) and extended memory (XMS) to lock these types of memory, if your application uses them.

You should generally leave these "locking" options *off,* unless your application uses conventional, expanded, or extended memory continuously (even in the background) and swapping that memory to disk would paralyze the application.

Uses High Memory Area

The high memory area (HMA) is the first 64K of extended memory. It is the only part of extended memory that an application running under DOS can access while still in real mode. Very few DOS applications currently use this memory area. This is unfortunate, because otherwise they would have almost 64K more conventional memory available to them. The Windows memory manager, HIMEM.SYS, and all other compatible memory managers make this 64K area available to Windows or any program that requests it.

The rule for the Uses <u>H</u>igh Memory Area check box is: if you start two PIFs under Windows — both of which use the HMA — Windows will switch this memory between them, so they can both benefit from using it.

If you turn *off* this HMA check box, an application started from that PIF cannot access any of the HMA from within Windows, even if it would otherwise be capable of doing so.

If a DOS application, however, claims the HMA *before* you start Windows, then no Windows application or PIF can use it.

DOS applications that can use the HMA generally make this fact well known in their publicity and documentation. You can leave this check box *on,* unless you know that two applications in particular would conflict if using it simultaneously. In that case, turn it off for the application that requires less memory.

Monitor Ports

It is essential that you turn all Monitor Ports settings *off,* unless you are running a DOS application that absolutely needs this setting. This is the most important step you can take to improve the performance of some applications under Windows. Unfortunately, Windows defaults to leaving one of the Monitor Ports settings *on* unless you specifically create PIF files (and change your _DEFAULT.PIF) to turn it off.

If a Monitor Ports setting is enabled, Windows installs a memory-resident program that grabs access to your video hardware before starting your DOS application. This resident program (which "monitors" your video board) significantly slows down your application's screen writes.

This monitoring program is only necessary if the application writes to video memory in such a way that Windows cannot detect mode changes. For example, a video board may have a hardware-based screen cursor. An application, however, can change the shape of this cursor through software commands. When you switch away from this application, and then switch back, Windows tries to restore the display to the condition it was in when you left it. If Windows is unaware of the change to the hardware, your display could be garbled or blank. This mostly affects EGA displays and should not be a problem with VGA modes.

The Monitor Ports section of the PIF Editor has three settings: Monitor Text, Monitor Low Graphics, and Monitor High Graphics. Text modes rarely require any monitoring. The same is true for "low-resolution graphics," meaning CGA. You may need to leave the Monitor High Graphics (meaning EGA and VGA) setting *on,* however, if you run programs that use EGA graphics.

Turn all these settings *off* in your PIF files unless an application displays garbage when you switch away from it and then back to it.

Emulate Text Mode

Applications that display text run faster if the Emulate Text Mode setting is *on.* This allows Windows to use faster routines if the application uses standard ROM BIOS calls to write text to the screen. You must turn the setting off if garbage appears on the application's screen or you lose control of its mouse when you run it under Windows.

Retain Video Memory

The Retain Video Memory option is very similar to "locking" an application's conventional, expanded, or extended memory (described earlier).

If you turn Retain Video Memory *off,* when you switch away from a DOS application and start a Windows application, then switch back to the DOS application and try to change to its graphics mode, there might not be enough memory available. If this is the case, your application will hang or your screen will go black or display garbage.

If you turn Retain Video Memory *on,* when you switch away from your DOS application Windows will not release any of this memory to start Windows applications. If memory is low, this may prevent you from starting additional programs until you exit the previously started DOS session.

Allow Fast Paste

The Allow Fast Paste option, when turned *on,* allows Windows to transfer information from the Clipboard into a DOS session as fast as the Clipboard can send it. Turn this setting off only if your DOS application loses characters when text is pasted into it from the Clipboard (or nothing happens when you click Paste on the DOS session's Control menu).

Allow Close When Active

If the Allow Close When Active option is *on,* you can get rid of an iconized DOS session by clicking the icon once, then clicking Close on its Control menu. If the session is windowed, you can do the same thing by double-clicking its Control Bar. In either case, Windows displays a dialog box and asks you to click OK to confirm your decision to close the app. This is usually faster than choosing Exit on the application's own menu, or typing EXIT at a DOS session's C> prompt — the steps you have to take if the Allow Close option is *off.*

But it's very important to turn this option off for applications that open and write files. If Windows closes one of these applications while it is writing to a file, that file may become garbled.

It's *possible* that you might be able to close a DOS application, even if it has files open, without ill effects on those files, *if* the application uses DOS file handles correctly. But some applications still use a much older DOS method, called *file control blocks,* which Windows can't close. Programs that use file control blocks to refer to filenames can often be recognized because these programs can only open files in the current directory. This is primarily true of earlier versions of popular applications, including DataEase 2.1 and WordStar 3.3 (or before).

For safety, it's better to close *all* file-handling applications by using their Exit menu, instead of Windows' quick-and-dirty Close method.

DOS sessions that have no open files and are merely waiting for you to type a command, however, may certainly have the Allow Close option *on.* For example, it's always all right to close a session that is doing nothing but displaying a C> prompt.

Reserve Shortcut Keys

The Reserve Shortcut Keys section of the PIF Editor includes settings for the following key combinations (each of these combinations is discussed more fully in Chapter 9):

Key Combination:	Action in Windows:
Alt+Enter	toggles full-screen apps to windowed
Alt+Esc	switches to each application in turn
Alt+PrtSc	copies the active window to Clipboard
Alt+Spacebar	displays a window's Control menu
Alt+Tab (or Alt+Tab+Tab)	switches among applications
Ctrl+Esc	displays the Windows Task List
PrtSc	copies the whole screen to Clipboard

Unless you change the PIF settings, Windows diverts the PrintScreen key's function, sending the screen to the Clipboard instead of to your printer. I believe that PIFs for DOS sessions should always turn the PrintScreen option *on* to restore the PrintScreen key's normal printing role. If you ever need to send a copy of the DOS screen to the Clipboard instead of the printer, press Alt+PrintScreen. This way, you don't need to give up the traditional use of your PrintScreen key in order to access the Clipboard.

One option that Windows *doesn't* allow you in a PIF is reserving the use of the Alt key itself. Some DOS applications use a press and release of the Alt key to perform certain functions. Reserving this key would avoid any conflicts between such applications and the role of this key in Windows (to "activate" its main menus). You would lose the ability to switch from the session back to Windows, until exiting the application, but this might be acceptable to you.

If you are a situation where a DOS session has "grabbed" the Alt key, and you can't use it in Windows, there may be a way for you to recover. Windows and virtually every Windows application also defines the F10 key the same as the Alt key. Press the F10 key, then the letter of your menu choice.

Application Shortcut Key

The Application Shortcut Key box allows you to specify a key combination that will bring the DOS session to the foreground if it is already running. This combination must include either the Alt or the Ctrl key, plus a function key or printable key. You can include the Shift key in the combination, but not the keys Backspace, Enter, Esc, PrintScreen, Spacebar, or Tab.

This Shortcut Key option has two major drawbacks: (1) it doesn't work if the application *isn't* running, and (2) you can only define shortcuts for *DOS* applications, not *Windows* applications, which seems strange.

Another problem is that many Windows applications already use almost all the available Alt and Ctrl combinations. You risk conflict with a Windows application function by defining a shortcut key for a PIF.

A better way to perform the Application Shortcut Key task is to define "hotkeys" in a macro file that you load with Recorder every time you start Windows. (This is explained in Chapter 2.) You can easily define one hotkey that switches to each of the applications you use and, if the application isn't running, an alternative hotkey that *starts* the application for you (something a PIF Shortcut Key can't do).

If you just want to switch to running applications, an easier way to do this is to press Ctrl+Esc to display the Task List. This allows you to switch to any running application, DOS *or* Windows. (Double-clicking your mouse on an unoccupied area of the Windows Desktop also brings up the Task List.)

Whether you use the Recorder or the PIF Editor to define hotkeys, always use Ctrl+Shift combinations, which most Windows applications leave untouched so you can assign them to macros.

If you happened to set a Shortcut Key for a PIF, and you later want to get rid of it, you can't just delete the key combination from this box and save the PIF. The previous key assignment isn't actually deleted unless you succeed in entering "None" in the box. And you can't just type the word — you must place your cursor in the box and press Shift+Backspace to specify "None."

Editing Your Default PIF

Setting your default PIF file correctly can add substantial performance gains to DOS applications that do not have their own customized PIF files. Once you perfect your default PIF, this file can save you time when defining a new PIF.

Additionally, the existence of a properly configured default PIF provides you with a way to configure the PIF Editor itself. You can make the PIF Editor come up with the defaults *you* want, instead of coming up with its factory-set defaults.

My recommendations for a default PIF are shown earlier in this chapter in Figure 5-11. Since these settings are dependent on the configuration of your own system, the comments in the accompanying chart indicate rules of thumb that you should follow to determine the correct values. The most important subjects are expanded on in the following paragraphs.

Loading the _DEFAULT.PIF File

To edit your _DEFAULT.PIF file, pull down the File menu in Program Manager or File Manager and click Run. In the File Run dialog box that appears, type:

```
PIFEDIT _DEFAULT
```

The PIF Editor comes up automatically, with the contents of the _DEFAULT.PIF file already loaded. The PIF Editor assumes a .PIF extension if you do not type it as part of the filename.

In case you edit your _DEFAULT.PIF file, then want to go back to the settings as they originally were, simply open the PIF Editor with no parameters. It automatically starts with all the standard defaults. Click File Save-As, give the name _DEFAULT.PIF, and overwrite your edited version. This produces a _DEFAULT.PIF exactly like the original.

You can determine the appropriate settings for your system by using the _DEFAULT.PIF reference card that accompanies Figure 5-11. Some settings that may benefit from additional explanation are described in following sections.

Program Filename

When you start a DOS application that does not have a PIF of its own, Windows uses the settings in the _DEFAULT.PIF. Windows substitutes the DOS application's name for whatever you typed in the _DEFAULT.PIF's Program Filename box. The PIF Editor, however, will not let you save the _DEFAULT.PIF file without an actual, valid filename in this box. Therefore, I enter C:\COMMAND.COM here as a placeholder.

386 Multitasking Options

Most people who run DOS applications under Windows want those applications to run at full speed and not slowed by Windows. Few people consistently run several applications, each app printing, communicating, and calculating at once. For this reason, the _DEFAULT.PIF I recommend gives DOS applications a Foreground Priority of 10000 (the maximum setting). In this PIF, the Exclusive check box is *off,* even though it might seem that the Exclusive option would give you better DOS performance. But the Exclusive option can interfere with some Windows background applications, such as screen savers and schedulers. Foreground Priority: 10000 gives your DOS app the maximum possible performance, but gives other apps a little time when your foreground app becomes idle.

Similarly, since most people want the fastest performance from Windows when they are using their *Windows* applications, I show the PIF's Background check box *off.* This allows the maximum time for Windows applications when they are in the foreground.

Of course, if you need to run several background processes in real-time, change these settings to fit your situation.

Saving Your Default PIF

When your options are set to your liking, pull down the PIF Editor's File menu and click Save. Or, double-click the Control Bar to exit the PIF Editor, and click Yes when it asks if you want to save your changes to _DEFAULT.PIF.

You don't have to close the PIF Editor first. Once you click File Save, you can immediately try any PIF you write. If you don't like the way your PIF works, the PIF Editor is still open and you can edit and save the PIF and try it again.

Changing Defaults While a Program Is Running

If you need to change the Multitasking Options (Background or Foreground Priority) for a DOS session that you've started in 386 enhanced mode, you can do so without exiting the session, editing its PIF, and starting it again. To do this, make sure the application is in text mode, then press Alt+Spacebar. This switches the session into a small window and pulls down the window's Control menu. Click Settings on the menu. A dialog box appears, in which you can change the Background and Foreground Priority for the session, as well as change the settings for Exclusive and/or Background Operation. When you click OK, your new settings are in effect until you exit the session.

One additional button allows you to terminate the session entirely. But this isn't recommended — there's no guarantee that simply kicking the application out of memory will undo any changes it made to your computer, such as setting interrupts. This option should be reserved strictly for occasions when a DOS session hangs and you can't get out of it — but Alt+Spacebar somehow still gets you back into Windows. Even in this unlikely event, you should reboot after terminating a rogue DOS session, or your Windows environment may be unreliable.

Making the PIF Editor Use Your Defaults

One of the little frustrations of Windows is that, once you've edited your _DEFAULT.PIF with the correct settings for your system, opening the PIF Editor always displays the worst-case defaults that come with Windows — not your new preferences. But there's a way to fix this.

Click the PIF Editor icon in the Program Manager once to highlight it, then click File Properties. Change the Command Line that starts the PIF Editor so it looks like the following:

    c:\pif\PIFEDIT _DEFAULT

When the PIF Editor starts with this parameter, all your customized defaults are displayed. This is a much faster way to make new PIFs for applications than starting from scratch. Simply change whatever settings you need, then click File Save As to save the file to a new name.

In order to prevent accidentally overwriting your _DEFAULT.PIF file, make it read-only by entering the following command in the File Run dialog box of Program Manager or File Manager (or use your favorite utility):

```
ATTRIB +R c:\windows\_DEFAULT.PIF
```

If you need to edit your _DEFAULT.PIF file after doing this, you can remove its read-only attribute with the reverse command:

```
ATTRIB -R c:\windows\_DEFAULT.PIF
```

Beyond PIFs—Making Applications Recognize Expanded Memory

As discussed earlier in the topic "Enhanced Mode Settings — EMS Memory," some DOS applications may not recognize expanded memory in a Windows 386-mode DOS session unless their PIF *requires* some expanded memory (instead of simply *allowing* it to have some).

Lotus 1-2-3 Release 2.01 is this type of DOS application. (More than 80 percent of 1-2-3 users in Fortune 2000 companies and U.S. government agencies were still using Release 2.01, according to a 1990 study — and 3 percent were using Release 1A, which Lotus discontinued in 1986! — so in most companies this isn't merely an academic point.)

One company I worked with found that 1-2-3 Release 2.01 reported that it didn't have any expanded memory under Windows in enhanced mode — on a 386 with 4MB of RAM — until KB Required was set to 256. During these tests, the KB Limit was set to "-1" to allow 1-2-3 every bit of expanded memory available.

An application under Windows may not get as much expanded memory as you would expect, even when you hand over all EMS. There are different *kinds* of expanded memory. When Lotus, Intel, and Microsoft years ago came up with expanded memory — so that spreadsheets could be created using more than 640K of RAM — all expanded memory was required to be located above the 640K line. This was called LIM EMS version 3.2.

Since LIM 3.2 was too limiting, AST Research, Ashton-Tate, Quadram, and other companies came up with an Expanded Memory Specification that allowed expanded memory to be located above *or below* the 640K line, giving DOS applications access to larger quantities of this memory. Their spec was called *enhanced* EMS, or EEMS.

Finally, Lotus, Intel, and Microsoft agreed that this was better and upgraded their specification so it could do the same. The upgraded specification is virtually identical to EEMS, and is called LIM EMS version 4.0, or simply LIM 4.0.

Windows 3.*x* provides expanded memory to DOS applications according to the LIM 4.0 specification. Some 16K "pages" of expanded memory may be placed *above* the 640K line, while others may be placed *below*.

Applications such as 1-2-3 Release 2.01, however, access expanded memory using only the LIM 3.2 specification. They cannot "see" expanded memory pages that are located below the 640K line — and therefore cannot use this expanded memory, even though it exists.

On a 386 with 4MB, running Lotus 1-2-3 Release 2.01 from a PIF with KB Required set to 816, and KB Limit set to -1 (all expanded memory), Lotus's Worksheet Status screen reports that the memory available to 1-2-3 is 273,040 bytes of conventional memory — but only 376,648 bytes of expanded memory, not 816K. About 440K of expanded memory is "lost" to 1-2-3 Release 2.01 because it can't see this memory.

This experimental 1-2-3 PIF was initially designed to accommodate another DOS application loaded from WIN.INI: a network E-Mail application that was not available in a Windows version at that time. By eliminating this other DOS app, it was possible to define a PIF for 1-2-3 Release 2.01 that set KB Required to 1280 instead of 816. (KB Limit remained at -1.) This resulted in 1-2-3 reporting 851,552 bytes of expanded memory — a notable gain, but still missing about 440K.

Lotus 1-2-3 Release 3.1 posed another series of problems; it runs under Windows in all modes — but it comes with a ready-made PIF and instructions stating that only 64K of Windows extended memory can actually be used by 1-2-3 in enhanced mode. The remainder of 1-2-3's memory comes from virtual memory (very slow hard disk space) and from "bypassing some of the Windows conventions when it requests memory." If you use 1-2-3 Release 3.*x* under Windows, you should request from Lotus the technical paper "Product Technical Marketing — Spreadsheet Application Series: 1-2-3 Release 3.1 Does Windows." Contact Lotus Customer Support at 55 Cambridge Parkway, Cambridge, MA 02142, 617-253-9150.

The company that performed these tests concluded that Lotus 1-2-3 — all versions, even after upgrading to 1-2-3 Releases 2.2 and 3.1 — was "barely compatible" with Windows. The solution to these problems was to define an icon that exits Windows, loads the application from a plain DOS prompt, and then (after the application is exited) *automatically restarts Windows.* As far as the user is concerned, he or she has double-clicked an icon to run, say, 1-2-3 Release 3.1, and that application appears to have run under the Windows environment like any other. Only a few momentary changes in video mode betray the difference.

How can a Windows icon start and stop a DOS application, even after Windows is no longer running? The answer is explained in the next topic.

Running Totally Incompatible Apps Under Windows

If you determine that a certain application is totally incompatible with Windows and will not run in a DOS session no matter what you do, you can still define an icon that starts that application from within Windows. You might even want to do this for some DOS apps, as just discussed, that *will* run under Windows but seem like just too much trouble.

 If this is the case, here is a workaround to let you define an icon that runs these applications without disturbing the look of the Program Manager or making you exit and restart Windows manually throughout the day:

1. Define an icon that starts a Windows macro. To do this requires the WinBatch language (which is located on the diskettes that accompany this book) or any other third-party Windows macro facility, such as PubTech BatchWorks or Bridge Batch (see Chapter 2). The macro simply writes on your hard disk a small file that is used later. You might write a line like, "Hello, incompatible app," and save it in a file named INCOMPAT.RUN.

2. The next and final action of this macro is to exit Windows. The macro language may have its own "exit Windows" command. If not, make the macro run WINEXIT.EXE, a public-domain program (included on the *Windows 3 Secrets* diskettes) that exits Windows without requiring a response to any dialog boxes. (If a running application has documents open that you must first save, you will see dialog boxes in that case, of course.)

3. For this to work, Windows must be started from a batch file such as W.BAT. This batch file looks for files with names like INCOMPAT.RUN. If such a file exists, it acts like a "flag" to the batch file, indicating that the

batch file should run a particular application. Your W.BAT batch file would look something like the following:

```
ECHO OFF
IF EXIST c:\temp\incompat.run DEL c:\temp\incompat.run
WIN
IF EXIST c:\temp\incompat.run c:\bat\incompat.bat
```

This batch file first deletes any old "flag" files that remain from previous usage of your Program Manager icon. It then starts Windows, and — after you exit Windows — looks again for your "flag" file, INCOMPAT.RUN. If such a file exists in a certain directory, the IF EXIST statement executes INCOMPAT.BAT, which starts your incompatible DOS application. The batch file INCOMPAT.BAT would look like this:

```
ECHO OFF
cd \directory
incompat.exe
IF EXIST c:\temp\incompat.run w.bat
```

After running the incompatible application, this restarts Windows *if the application was started from a Windows icon in the first place.* Your INCOMPAT.BAT batch file, of course, determines this by checking whether your "flag" file exists. W.BAT, in turn, deletes this flag, so the DOS application doesn't run again the next time you exit Windows, unless you request it.

Notice that none of the batch files we started from within other batch files in this example use DOS tricks such as COMMAND /C *filename.bat.* Tricks like this force the second batch file to *return* to the original batch file, at the same line from which it was invoked. In this case, we don't *want* the secondary batch file to ever return to its parent. Once the secondary batch file starts, the first batch file is terminated.

I certainly don't claim that this is an elegant or particularly smooth way to run applications that are incompatible with Windows. In an ideal world, all applications would be compatible with each other, and every DOS application would have a Windows version. But if you have real-world applications and have to make them run with Windows, this may be one of your few hopes to get everything working — and it's better than having to do the same steps manually every time. Hopefully, as DOS apps improve their Windows-awareness, we won't need this type of workaround much longer.

TSRs Under Windows

In the character-mode DOS environment, you may have become used to loading terminate-and-stay-resident (TSR) programs. The most famous TSR is probably Borland's Sidekick. Such a TSR stays in memory after you load it, but runs invisibly until you press its hotkey combination.

Windows eliminates much of the usefulness of these TSRs, because it takes direct control of the keyboard. When you load a TSR, then start Windows, pressing the TSRs hotkey combination does not "wake up" the TSR. The key combination is not passed along to programs that were loaded before Windows.

Under Windows 2.*x*, the undocumented key combination Ctrl+NumLock disabled Windows' control over the keyboard for the duration of *one keystroke*. In other words, after you pressed Ctrl+NumLock, the next key combination you pressed was actually passed "through" Windows to any TSR that might be looking for that combination. The Pause key did the same thing as Ctrl+NumLock — this feature could be viewed as "pausing" Windows' control over the keyboard.

The Pause feature was correctly used by third-party disk cache programs that were compatible and could be loaded before Windows. These caches could use certain key combinations to reconfigure themselves — to "flush" the contents of their cache to disk on command, for example.

But other TSRs, few of which were Windows-aware, would try to pop-up in text mode, seemingly freezing the Windows graphical display. The TSR gained control, but its menu was not displayed and therefore it could not be exited.

The Ctrl+NumLock feature disappeared from Windows 3.0 — its passing as undocumented as its existence — so this method of sending commands back to TSRs is no longer available.

Clever programmers, however, will continue to find ways to add value to both the DOS and Windows environments with TSRs.

Many TSR programs will work just fine if you define a PIF for them and start them in their own window under Windows. This is especially true of TSRs that can be started with a "nonmemory-resident" switch on their command line. There is no reason for a TSR to disappear from sight when you load it under Windows; it can stay right on-screen, where you can use it or minimize it into an icon sitting on the icon line of your Desktop. By placing this PIF in the LOAD= line of your WIN.INI file (for example, LOAD=MYTSR.PIF), such an icon can be waiting for you every time you start Windows. It's important to create a PIF for TSRs, since you want to limit the amount of memory they get to the minimum required — not 640K.

TSR programmers can do far more with their utilities than this, however. Whenever Windows loads or exits, it issues an interrupt 2F, "broadcasting" its action to all TSRs and device drivers running in a system. Any TSR that is "looking" for this event can take advantage of it.

For example, a TSR can use this interrupt to detect that Windows is starting (and what version and mode it's loading). The TSR can respond to this information by disabling its hotkeys (since they won't work under Windows, anyway) and freeing up any extra memory, especially expanded memory that might conflict with Windows. (This is exactly the method that the SmartDrive disk cache uses to give back its memory when Windows loads.) Before Windows actually starts, the TSR could insert its own PIF file into the LOAD= line of WIN.INI, so a Windows-compatible version of the TSR would be available on the icon line the minute Windows finished setting itself up!

Naturally, it would be nice if the TSR's documentation *informed* people that all this was going to take place (so they could circumvent it if desired). But think how convenient it would be to have the same utility under Windows that you relied on under DOS — or, better yet, a genuine Windows version of that utility.

I'd like to thank Jeff Roberts of RAD Software for this idea, which he described at length in the February/March 1991 issue of *PC Techniques* magazine.

Using DOS Extenders Under Windows

"DOS extender" programs are DOS applications that break the 640K memory barrier by accessing extended memory on 286-based systems and higher. The term "DOS extender" also refers to programming tools that *enable* such programs to be written. These tools were developed in the late 1980's by companies such as Phar Lap Software, Rational Systems, and Eclipse Computer Solutions — all of Cambridge, Massachusetts.

Many programs that require more than 640K of RAM were developed using these tools. Some of these programs are well known, including:

Autocad 386
FoxBase 386
IBM Interleaf Publisher
Lotus 1-2-3 Release 3.*x*
Mathematica 386
Oracle Corp.'s Oracle
Paradox 386
SmallTalk-80 386

Memory managers that support and provide memory for these programs include:

Compaq Computer's CEMM.SYS
Intel Corp.'s ILIM386.SYS
Qualitas, Inc.'s 386MAX.SYS
Quarterdeck Office Systems' QEMM386.SYS

Multiuser software that was developed using DOS-extender tools includes:

Digital Research's Concurrent DOS
The Software Link's PC-MOS
Intelligent Graphics Corp.'s VM/386

In 1988, early in the development of DOS extenders, these and other companies formalized a standard, under which these software products could run in the same machine without conflicts. This standard was called the Virtual Control Program Interface, or VCPI. Programs using this means to communicate (interface) with each other could run simultaneously, and users could switch from one to the other under multitasking software such as Quarterdeck's DESQview environment.

Windows 3.*x* may have difficulty running many of these programs. Saying that the VCPI specification did not allow Windows to multitask in a graphical environment, Microsoft developed its own extended-memory specification and built it into Windows 3.0. This specification is called the DOS Protected Mode Interface, or DPMI. Intel brought the affected companies together at a meeting in early 1990, and changes were made to the DPMI spec that all parties agreed would ease the development of DPMI-compliant programs. For the foreseeable future, programs written to access extended memory will increasingly use DPMI standards.

Many DOS extender programs have already been updated to the new specification. Quarterdeck's QEMM386 memory-manager, for example, currently supports programs that request any form of above-640K memory — expanded memory (LIM EMS 3.2, LIM EMS 4.0, or EEMS), VCPI, or DPMI. Lotus 1-2-3 Release 3.1, as a DPMI-compliant program, runs under Windows in all three modes, even though this was not possible for 1-2-3 Release 3.0.

Windows 3.*x*, particularly in its 386 mode, may be unable to run those DOS extenders that have not yet been converted. Under its real and standard modes, though, Windows may be able to run many of these programs. You must verify the capabilities of Windows with these programs by asking each vendor individually.

If you run a VCPI-compliant program under Windows, and it uses compatible methods when Windows is in 386 mode, you can turn off the warning message that Windows displays when applications request VCPI memory, by inserting the following line into the [386Enh] section of your SYSTEM.INI file:

```
[386Enh]
VCPIWarning=false
```

Information on the DPMI specification can be obtained free of charge by contacting Intel Literature Sales, P.O. Box 58130, Santa Clara, CA 95052, 800-548-4725, or from Intel representatives in other countries.

The VCPI specification can be obtained from Phar Lap Software, 60 Aberdeen Avenue, Cambridge, MA 02138, 617-661-1510.

OS/2 Anomalies

Applications that are capable of running under both DOS and OS/2 are called "bound" or "family-mode" applications. These programs cannot be run directly under Windows 3.*x*. They must be started from their own PIF files, as previously discussed in the PIF Editor section of this chapter. If you try to run a family-mode app directly, Windows displays the message, "Insufficient Memory." But memory is not the problem — you need to define a PIF for this app.

Other problems occur if you attempt to run Windows 3.*x* under OS/2, as of version 1.3. When Windows is in real mode under OS/2, you cannot start any non-Windows applications. Instead, Windows displays the message, "Windows cannot run non-Windows applications under OS/2."

Additionally, certain key combinations that Windows uses may actually be reserved by OS/2 when Windows is running under OS/2. For example, the combination Ctrl+Esc — which usually displays the Windows Task List — displays OS/2's Task List instead. To work around this behavior, press Alt+Spacebar in any Windows window. From the Control menu that appears, click Switch To. You can then use the Task List to switch to another application.

DOS Anomalies

The remainder of this chapter describes configuration issues that you may need to consider when using specific DOS applications in conjunction with Windows. These applications are listed alphabetically by company name or category (not necessarily the name of the software product itself).

Borland Reflex

Slow Performance May Relate to Hard Drives

Borland Reflex may slow considerably under Windows in enhanced mode. This problem, which relates to the application's method of enhancing hard-disk performance, may be corrected by making sure the following line appears in your SYSTEM.INI under the [386Enh] section:

```
[386Enh]
VirtualHDIrq=false
```

Borland Paradox

Use of Expanded Memory

Paradox versions 3.0a and 3.01 use expanded memory in a way that may conflict with other applications under Windows 3.*x*. Paradox does not check to see whether the 64K expanded-memory page frame is composed of four contiguous 16K pages before trying to allocate expanded memory for itself. Because it is possible to configure the page frame under Windows as four *noncontiguous* 16K areas, Paradox may hang. To avoid this, make sure the page frame consists of one unbroken 64K area. Test this by inserting a line in the [386enh] section of the SYSTEM.INI file such as:

```
[386Enh]
PageFrame=E000
```

where E000 is the beginning of an area that you believe is free for the page frame. In 386 enhanced mode, if this area is *not* free, no DOS applications will have access to expanded memory.

Alternatively, in 386 enhanced mode you can eliminate Paradox's use of expanded memory by running Paradox from a PIF with both EMS Required and EMS Limit set to 0. (If you are using Windows in real mode or standard mode, removing the expanded memory manager from your CONFIG.SYS is the only way to prevent Paradox from accessing expanded memory.)

Additionally, Paradox does not allow other programs to use expanded memory simultaneously. You must prevent other such programs from running while Paradox is using expanded memory.

Games and Other Graphics Programs

May Run Faster with Second COMMAND.COM Loaded

DOS games such as AdLib, and other programs that use graphics, may run faster if you start them from a PIF that loads them *as a parameter* to COMMAND.COM. To do this, your PIF would look like this:

```
Command Line:          C:\COMMAND.COM
Optional Parameters:   /C PROGRAM.EXE
```

This starts a secondary copy of COMMAND.COM, which loads the program it finds following the switch /C (for Copy). Although this takes a little extra memory, it may be more efficient for the loaded program's performance.

Games may also run better when started (in 386 mode) by setting Video Memory to High Graphics, but disabling the settings Monitor Ports, Detect Idle Time, Uses High Memory Area, and Allow Fast Paste. If your screen displays garbage with these settings, it may be necessary to reenable the Monitor Ports settings for the program's particular graphics mode — CGA (Low Graphics) or EGA/VGA (High Graphics). I would like to thank Dan Thomas for this idea.

Microsoft Flight Simulator

Must Not Be Run in Background

Microsoft Flight Simulator should not be switched to the background, since its operation (when it doesn't have the keyboard focus) can be unpredictable. Run Flight Simulator from a PIF and reserve all Shortcut Keys that allow switching away from the application (Alt+Enter, Alt+Esc, Alt+Spacebar, Alt+Tab, Ctrl+Esc).

Microsoft Multiplan

Incompatible with Enhanced Mode

Microsoft Multiplan is an older spreadsheet that has a small market in the U.S., but is popular in other countries, particularly Japan where it was at one time that country's largest-selling spreadsheet application. As of version 4.2, Multiplan runs correctly under Windows 3.x's real and standard modes, but not under 386 enhanced mode. You may receive the following Windows error message:

> This application has violated system integrity and will be terminated — close all applications, exit Windows, and reboot your computer.

In other cases, copying a formula or inserting or deleting a group of rows or columns may simply hang your machine, without displaying any error message. There is no workaround for this version of Multiplan.

Microsoft Word

Requires Upgrade to Use Alt Combinations

Under Microsoft Word for DOS 5.0, the key combinations Alt+Tab and Alt+Spacebar may act strangely under Windows 3.x. You may also have difficulty when you attempt to copy information into Windows' Clipboard.

You may be able to work around one of these behaviors by pressing Alt+X, then the Spacebar — an alternate way of specifying the Alt+Spacebar command, which formats characters for normal text in Word for DOS. A better solution is to obtain at least version 5.0a, an unadvertised upgrade to Microsoft Word, which has a special keyboard driver to support these key combinations under Windows.

Won't Run Windowed When in 43- or 50-Line Mode

If you have configured Word for DOS to use 43- or 50-line text modes on an EGA or VGA video adapter, these modes will run full-screen under Windows, but will freeze if you try to switch Word into a small window under Windows' enhanced mode. You will receive the Windows error message:

You cannot run this application while other high-resolution applications are running full-screen.

The "other high-resolution applications" that Windows is talking about is Windows itself, running in EGA or VGA mode (or higher). At this point, you will not be able to quit Word for DOS.

Instead, press Alt+Enter to return Word to full-screen mode, or pull down the Control menu, click Settings, then click Full Screen. This will restore your access to Word for DOS' menu.

Intuit Quicken

Identified as Borland Quattro by Windows Setup

Intuit's Quicken program is a top-selling personal finance program. When you run Setup to install Windows, it incorrectly identifies Quicken as Borland Quattro. The result is an icon in your Program Manager labeled "Quattro," with settings for Quattro, although it actually starts Quicken.

This occurs because both Quattro and Quicken are programs named Q.EXE. Setup identifies programs on your hard disk by their executable name. It then copies a PIF file for Q.EXE from the SETUP.INF text file that controls the Windows installation routine.

If this is the case on your system, you can open the Q.PIF file in the PIF Editor and change its settings to those Microsoft recommends for Quicken. These include:

```
Program Filename:       c:\quicken\Q.EXE
Window Title:           Quicken
Optional Parameters:    {none}
Start-up Directory:     c:\quicken
KB Required:            128
KB Desired:             640
Display Usage (386)     Full screen (or Windowed, your preference)
Execution (386)         (Background or Exclusive, your preference)
Close Window on Exit    On
```

Microsoft recommends that you not load "bill minder"-type TSRs included with Quicken, such as BILLMIND, prior to starting Windows. Load these in a batch file under Windows before starting Quicken.

WordPerfect

Floppy Drive Writes May Be Erratic in Enhanced Mode

Running WordPerfect 5.1 under Windows in enhanced mode may lead to difficulties in saving files to floppy drives with F10, WordPerfect's File Save key. WordPerfect displays a message that it cannot read the floppy, but it may have been able to do so earlier in the session. The problem may come and go. Exiting and restarting Windows, then running WordPerfect again may correct the problem for a while.

This problem may occur if drivers such as SMARTDRV.SYS are loaded in your CONFIG.SYS file *prior* to the line that loads HIMEM.SYS.

If this is not the case, and the floppy disk you are using is correctly format-ted (and not write-protected), you can work around this problem by defin-ing a "block" for the entire document using WordPerfect's Alt+F4 key combination. Then press the F10 key to write this "block name" to drive A: or B:.

Alternately, you can circumvent this problem if you use WordPerfect's F7 (Save and Exit) key.

Use of Expanded Memory May Require Upgrade

If Windows freezes when you try to start WordPerfect 5.1, the application's use of expanded memory may be the cause of the problem. Releases of WordPerfect 5.1 dated 11/06/89 have a problem accessing expanded memory. WordPerfect ships a free upgrade to users with program files of this date. You may find the date by using a DIR command on the WordPerfect directory, or by pressing WordPerfect's F3 (Help) key — the date appears in the upper-right corner.

If you can work without expanded memory temporarily, starting WordPerfect with the parameter /NE eliminates its use of expanded memory and should fix the problem. Additionally, starting releases of WordPerfect dated *after* 11/06/89 with the parameter /32 forces the program to use EMS version 3.2 specifications. This can correct expanded memory problems under Windows and also eliminates screen-display problems that occur on some configurations.

Upgrades in the U.S. may be obtained by calling WordPerfect at 800-321-4566. In other countries, contact the WordPerfect representative in your area.

Repeat Performance May Cause Insufficient Memory

If you receive the error message "Insufficient Memory" when you try to start DOS applications under Windows, the option for Keyboard Enhancement offered by WordPerfect's Repeat Performance driver may be the cause.

If you installed this option, your CONFIG.SYS file will contain a line like the following:

```
DEVICE=c:\RP.SYS=ON repeat=70 delay=20 {etc.}
```

This entry may occupy enough conventional memory to prevent other DOS applications from loading under Windows. Delete or comment-out this line in CONFIG.SYS to see if this frees enough memory to start a DOS session.

WordPerfect Office May Require Upgrade

If WordPerfect Office is started under Windows, but its Notify option is not functioning, you may need an upgrade to a later version. Contact WordPerfect technical support at 800-321-3253. Outside the U.S., contact the WordPerfect representative in your area.

Set "Detect Idle Time" *Off*

You may find that starting WordPerfect from a PIF file with the "Detect Idle Time" setting *on* slows some WordPerfect operations as much as 100 percent. For example, an operation such as mail merge may appear to Windows as no activity over a substantial period of time.

XyWrite

Alt+Tab Must Be Reserved in XyWrite PIF

The XyWrite word processor (a DOS application) uses one of the key combinations that is meaningful to Windows. Specifically, the Alt+Tab combination displays a tab table in XyWrite, but switches to Windows if this combination is left unchanged in the PIF that starts XyWrite.

You can restore XyWrite's original use of this combination by marking the Alt+Tab box *on* in the Reserve Shortcut Keys section of the PIF you use to start XyWrite. When you do this, switch the PIF Editor from enhanced mode to standard mode (or vice versa) and make sure that the PIF you save has the change recorded in *both* modes.

Summary

In this chapter, I have explained in detail the challenges you may encounter when running DOS applications in conjunction with Windows. This includes:

▶ DOS commands that you should *never* run in a DOS session under Windows.

▶ Running COMMAND.COM under Windows, and how to configure a basic DOS session, including customizing the DOS prompt.

▶ Recovering functions of the PrintScreen key and the Windows Clipboard that might otherwise be lost in DOS sessions.

▶ Gaining up to 736K of conventional memory, instead of only 640K, for text-mode DOS applications under Windows, using the VIDRAM.COM utility.

▶ How to gain the maximum performance for DOS applications while Windows is running, including DOS applications running "windowed" instead of full-screen.

▶ Problems you may encounter when running two or more DOS applications simultaneously under Windows, as opposed to running only one DOS application.

▶ Understanding the vagaries of Windows' multitasking options while running DOS sessions from PIF files while other Windows applications are also running.

▶ Learning the meaning of several nonobvious, DOS-specific error messages that Windows may display.

▶ Mastering the PIF Editor, and creating a default PIF that is tuned to the needs of your specific PC system.

▶ Working around problems with certain DOS applications that may behave differently under Windows than they do otherwise.

Chapter 6
Programming in WordBasic

In this chapter...

The topics I cover in this chapter include:

▶ Changing Word for Windows' behavior with macros.

▶ Fixing a Winword bug with a simple, one-instruction macro.

▶ Assigning your macros to hotkey combinations, even undocumented ones.

▶ Making Winword display all the filenames in a directory when you run File Open or Insert File, instead of only files matching Winword's *.DOC default.

▶ Using AutoExec macros to make Winword start up the way you want (running the File Open dialog box automatically, in this case).

▶ Adding functions Winword is missing, such as the ability to print the current page upon a single command.

▶ Inserting new items into the menus that come with Winword.

▶ Separating Winword's features into global and template levels so that new global macros can be distributed easily on a network.

▶ Adding the ability to type accented and special characters easily from U.S. keyboards that lack keys for these features.

Word for Windows is part of a new generation of Windows applications — programs with their own programming language. Along with such heavy-weight Windows applications as Excel and Amí Professional, Word for Windows can be programmed to perform an enormous variety of tasks. This includes searching and replacing text, printing selected pages of documents, combining parts of documents into others, and so on *ad infinitum*. Any of these new functions, once programmed, can be configured to start upon the press of a single key, or placed on one of Word for Windows' pull-down menus where it can be started by the click of a mouse.

This programmability is exploited through the WordBasic language, an extension of Microsoft's Basic language. These extensions allow a person proficient in WordBasic to do things to text that are far beyond the abilities of Basic itself — specify the size and style of text, change the formatting of paragraphs, even insert different phrases into a document based on certain key words that already exist in the prose.

Because there are few printed resources on using the WordBasic language — which will become a feature of every major Windows application in a few years — I have devoted this chapter to some practical examples that can help you work around some irritating problems. These examples should apply to applications other than Word for Windows as new releases of Windows software incorporate this handy and capable language.

If you have never programmed in Basic, don't avoid this chapter out of fear — the examples will lead you step by step through a series of macros that you can type in and start using immediately to improve your control over Word for Windows. And if you use the NORMAL.DOT and LETTER.DOT files included on the diskettes that accompany this book, all the macros described in this chapter become immediately available to you and to the other templates you use with Word for Windows.

Word for Windows Macros

Starting and Editing a Macro

Macros are controlled through the Macro pull-down menu on Winword's main menu bar. Clicking the Macro item on this menu pulls down the options shown in Figure 6-1.

These options, in the order they appear on the Macro menu, are:

Record a macro: When this option is chosen, Winword watches the actions you perform next (opening a file, searching and replacing text, etc.) and translates them into WordBasic commands that are saved into a file. While you are recording a macro in this way, this option changes into a **Stop Recorder** choice. When you are through recording a macro, click Stop Recorder.

Run a macro: After you record a macro, choosing Run presents you with a list of those macros that are available. Double-clicking on one of them runs the macro with that name.

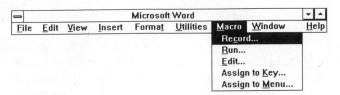

Figure 6-1:The Macro menu.

Edit a macro: Choosing this option presents you with a list of macros that are available. Selecting one of them displays the full text of the macro in a macro editing window, where you can manually edit the macro and add commands that cannot be recorded from the keyboard.

Assign to key: This option enables you to make the macro run whenever you press a certain key combination that you define. This method only allows you to place macros on key combinations that include the Ctrl and Alt keys (such as Ctrl+F10). Shortly, I'll show you a method (which isn't in the Word for Windows *User's Reference* manual) for assigning a macro to *any* key or key combination, allowing you to redefine punctuation marks or any other printable keys on the keyboard.

Assign to menu: This option enables you to make a macro name appear underneath one of the main menu items, as though it were a part of Word for Windows from the beginning. This menu option only allows you to append your macro to the bottom of existing pull-down menus, but it *is* possible to change the order of the items on these menus and even alter the words listed on the main menu line (as we shall see).

Creating Your Own Macros

NewPageDown — The Simplest Possible Macro

The best way to learn about Word for Windows macros is to create one for yourself. We'll start with the most basic macro possible — it consists of only one line of instruction — but this simple program has the important purpose of fixing an irritating bug in Word for Windows.

You may have seen the error message "Unrecoverable Application Error" while running Winword. This message means that Winword has used some memory that didn't belong to it, probably because the program attempted some action in an improper way. Once you receive this message and click

OK, Windows usually takes over and kicks Winword out of memory entirely, aborting any document you might have been working on.

Microsoft technical support reports that this situation can occur in Word for Windows versions 1.0 and 1.1 when you take such an innocent action as pressing the Page Down key (or clicking downward on the scroll bar with a mouse). Due to a flaw in the internal Winword programming for the Page Down key, merely moving down one screen-page can hit Winword at a particular point in its processing cycle when that action causes an unrecoverable error.

The NewPageDown macro redefines the Page Down key and avoids the piece of internal Winword code that sometimes causes this error. When you make Winword run this macro every time you press the Page Down key, instead of running its own internal code for handling Page Down, you force Winword to skip the part of its code that contains the programming error. Running your macro causes Winword to execute code that runs correctly.

Follow the directions in the remainder of this chapter by typing the actual steps at your PC with Word for Windows running.

Before adding any macros to your Word for Windows application, however:

> **SAVE A BACKUP COPY OF YOUR NORMAL TEMPLATE.**

Since additions to your macros actually write a new copy of your NORMAL.DOT document template file, you must save a copy of this file in case an accident occurs (and accidents *always* occur). Use the File Manager or DOS to make a copy of NORMAL.DOT to another file named NORMAL.SAV or NORMAL.ORI ("ORI" for "original"). Winword ignores templates with extensions other than .DOT, so this file will remain untouched unless you need it to recover from a mistake in the future. After you add a macro, make *another* copy of NORMAL.DOT to *another* backup name so you have several versions from which you can recover.

Recording a Macro

Close all documents, then open the file NORMAL.DOT. Next, pull down the Macro menu and click Record. This summons up a dialog box in which you are asked to provide a name and description for the macro you are about to record. Type "NewPageDown" as the name and "fixes intermittent UAE on

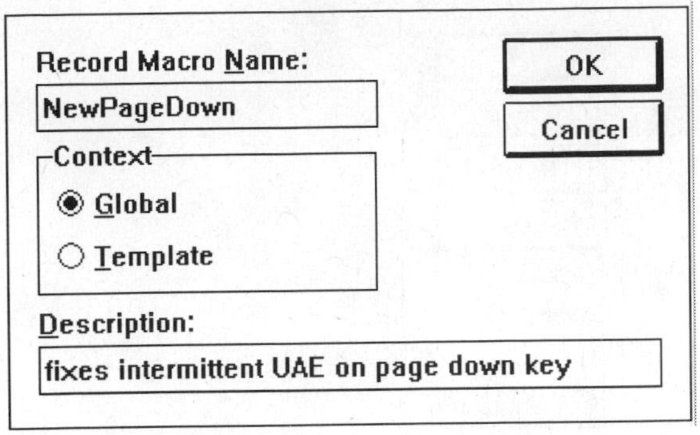

Figure 6-2: Starting the NewPageDown macro.

page down key" as the description. Make sure the context button is set to "Global" and click OK. The dialog box should look like Figure 6-2.

Winword starts recording the macro the instant you click OK. No message is displayed — any actions you now perform will become part of the macro.

For the NewPageDown macro, you will record only one keystroke. Press the Page Down key on your keyboard. Then pull down the Macro menu and click Stop Recorder. Winword instantly writes the contents of your actions into a text file named NewPageDown. This macro has not yet been assigned to a key, nor has it been assigned to any menu. The only way to run the NewPageDown macro at this point would be to click Macro Run and select the macro name from a list that Winword displays.

The first thing you should do after recording a macro is edit it. Pull down the Macro menu and click Edit. Winword displays a list of macro names. If you haven't added any other macros yet, the only name Winword displays is "NewPageDown." The dialog box look like Figure 6-3; make sure the Show All box is clicked *off* to see only those macros you have added. With Show All *on,* Winword displays macro names for every function that Winword is capable of.

Highlight the NewPageDown macro name and click OK to edit it. Winword displays the full text of the NewPageDown macro in a macro editing window, as shown in Figure 6-4.

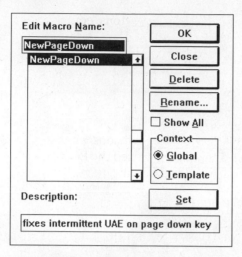

Figure 6-3: Macro Edit dialog box for NewPageDown macro.

The macro editing window includes several buttons that perform various tasks — Start, Step, Trace, and so on. Ignore these buttons for now. They will not be used in the macros in this chapter. For information on these buttons, and an explanation of all the functions available in Winword macros, you should print the TECHREF.DOC file located in your Winword directory. This file includes a short description of the WordBasic commands. A much better explanation than this, however, is available by purchasing a copy of the *Microsoft Word for Windows and OS/2 Technical Reference* from Microsoft Press (Redmond, Wash.: 1990).

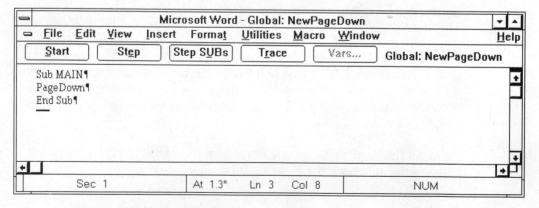

Figure 6-4: The Macro editing window.

Instead of puzzling over the macro editing buttons, concentrate on the wording that Winword has placed in this window. The entire macro consists of only three lines:

```
Sub MAIN
PageDown
End Sub
```

The line in the middle — PAGEDOWN — was obviously inserted by the Word for Windows macro recorder when you pressed the Page Down key. The other two lines — SUB MAIN and END SUB — indicate the beginning and ending of the macro, and are inserted by the macro recorder into every macro automatically.

A Winword macro, then, is built with the following structure, regardless of the content of the macro itself:

```
Sub MAIN
  {your commands go here}
End Sub
```

The entire macro is considered a *subroutine*. In Basic, a subroutine is a coherent set of instructions that accomplish a task. One subroutine may start another subroutine, or the entire subroutine may be self-contained, as in the NewPageDown macro. Every macro must have one MAIN subroutine, which is the purpose of the SUB MAIN statement that declares the name of this subroutine. And every subroutine must have an end point, which is the purpose of the END SUB statement.

The NewPageDown macro, in its present state, would run perfectly well from the Macro Run menu. But we need to make two more changes:

1. Edit the macro to conform to rules as described below.
2. Assign the macro to the actual Page Down key.

Macro Rules

Like everything else, macros have rules that make them easier to manage — if the rules are followed. These rules help you read the macro and help you and others understand the macro weeks or months later, long after the original purpose of the macro is forgotten.

RULES:

Rules for Managing Macros

Rule 1. Use comment lines to name and describe the macro. Winword ignores any line that begins with "REM" and anything after an apostrophe ('). In addition, Winword ignores any line that consists of a carriage return only. You can use these features to add comments to your macros. The minimum comments you need are a line telling readers the macro name, the date it was edited, and who edited it, and a second line that describes the purpose of the macro. You should also add a comment to the end of any line that might be unclear later (which is true of most lines). When you print the macro (in order to save a copy for future reference) and try to read it in the future, these comment lines will prove themselves invaluable.

Rule 2. Break the macro into sections and start each with a comment line. Since Winword allows blank lines (carriage returns) in macros, it is simple to add blank lines to break a macro into smaller chunks that are easier to understand. A remark at the beginning of each chunk describes the flow of the macro when you are reading through it at a later time.

Rule 3. Indent sections that represent loops or branches. Winword ignores any Tab characters in macros, so these too can be used to add clarity. Insert a Tab in front of each line after a statement that sets several other statements in motion. An IF statement that you use to run different branches of a macro, for example, might look like this:

```
If a=b Then
    run this command
    and this one
Else
    run some other command
End If
```

Rule 4. Use upper- and lowercase to identify commands and variables. Winword automatically changes the case of any commands in the WordBasic language into proper case when you save the macro — the statements *if, then,* and *else,* for example, are changed to *If, Then,* and *Else.* Labels in your macros should be easy to find when editing, and thus are usually typed in ALL CAPS. This leaves only the lowercase style for variables, both numeric and text-string, to distinguish them from commands and labels.

Rule 5. Specify ways the macro should handle errors. Every macro that displays a dialog box or performs other input/output actions should correctly handle errors, such as the user canceling out of the dialog box or requesting a filename that doesn't exist. WordBasic provides an ON ERROR statement that lets you specify what should happen in these cases. I'll discuss the use of this statement in several of the examples that follow.

Using the Macro Rules with the NewPageDown Macro

In order to make the NewPageDown macro more readable, add two comment lines to it, as suggested by the Macro Rules. The macro editing window allows you to use the keyboard or the mouse to move the cursor around the window, and you can insert and delete text as you would with any text editor. After adding the title of the macro, the date it was last edited, the person who edited it, and a description, the NewPageDown macro should look like Figure 6-5.

With the addition of the appropriate remarks, you are ready to print the macro and save the printed copy for future reference. Pull down the File menu and click Print.

While doing this, you may notice that many of the choices listed on the File pull-down menu are "greyed-out" by Winword since they are unavailable in the macro editing window. The Print Preview choice is greyed, for example, because you cannot preview a macro — it always prints as straight text. Additionally, several functions such as Format Character and Format Paragraph are unavailable in a macro editing window. Macros always appear and print as 10-point Times Roman text. If you want to print a macro in a different font, you must highlight the whole macro, copy it to the Clipboard with Ctrl+Insert, then paste it into a regular Word for Windows document with Shift+Insert.

Once the macro is printed, you can save it by double-clicking the document control icon in the upper-left corner of the macro editing window (the one immediately to the left of the word "File," *not* the control bar icon on Winword's own title bar). Since you added text to the macro, Winword asks you, "Keep changes to Global: NewPageDown?" Click Yes to save your

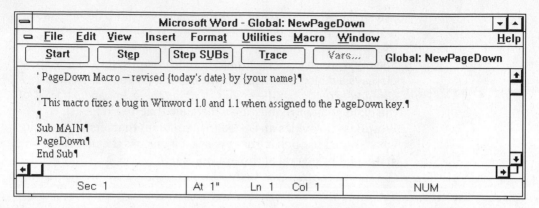

Figure 6-5: The Macro editing window after changes to the NewPageDown macro.

changes. Later, when you exit Winword entirely, it will ask, "Save global glossary and command changes?" This message is really asking whether you want to permanently save your new macros in the NORMAL.DOT document template file. Answer Yes, and Winword rewrites your entire Normal template, adding the macros you created. The process of rewriting this file may take one or two minutes.

Additional Macros

The remainder of the macros in this chapter will be described and illustrated without showing the macro editor itself. The process of creating the remaining macros in this chapter is similar to the creation of the NewPage-Down macro described above.

Assigning Macros to Any Key

Once you have edited a macro, you probably want to assign it to a key combination. When pressed, this key combination runs the macro without your having to pull down the Macro menu and clicking Run to start a particular macro.

As mentioned above, the Assign to Key command on Winword's Macro menu allows you to assign macros only to key combinations that include the Alt and Ctrl keys. But we want to assign the NewPageDown macro to the

Page Down key itself, so the page down action always executes the macro instead of Winword's internal PageDown routine. How can a plain, unshifted key be redefined?

Although it isn't explained in Winword's *User's Reference* manual, there is a command called MacroAssignToKey in the macro language itself that can be used to redefine *any* key, not just those combinations that start with Alt or Ctrl.

We could write a short macro that simply assigned the NewPageDown macro to the Page Down key. But this macro would be limited to assigning only that one macro to that one key assignment. Instead, the next macro in this chapter is written as a general-purpose routine to allow you to assign any macro to any key. This will be useful for many of the macros included in this chapter.

AutoAssignToKey Macro

To record the AutoAssignToKey macro, pull down the Macro menu and click Edit. When the Edit Macro dialog box appears, type AutoAssignToKey as the name, type "automatically assigns macro to key" as the description, make sure the context button Global is checked, and click OK. In this case, instead of recording a macro, Winword immediately opens the macro editing window and displays a bare-bones macro that consists of only three lines:

```
Sub MAIN
{blank line}
End Sub
```

The first and last lines are the beginning and ending points of the macro. Move the cursor to the beginning of the statement SUB MAIN and add the title and description of the macro. Then add the remainder of the macro between the two beginning and ending statements, so the macro looks like Figure 6-6.

The AutoAssignToKey macro is much longer than the NewPageDown macro. But this is still a relatively simple macro. It demonstrates two features of Winword's macro language: error trapping and displaying dialog boxes.

```
' AutoAssignToKey Macro — 1991 Brian Livingston

' This macro requests the name of a macro and the key to assign it to at the global level.

Sub MAIN
    On Error Goto BYE
    name$ = InputBox$("Type the name of the macro you want to assign to a key")
    number$ = InputBox$("Type the number of the key from the Winword Technical Reference")
    num = Val(number$)
    If num < 8 Or num > 1919 Then
        Beep 1
        MsgBox "Number of the key must be 8 to 1919."
    Else
        MacroAssignToKey name$, num, 0       ' assign macro to key at global (0) level
    End If
BYE:
End Sub
```

Figure 6-6: AutoAssignToKey macro.

The first line of the macro, after SUB MAIN, says ON ERROR GOTO BYE. This statement is necessary so the macro ends gracefully if the user clicks Cancel or presses the Escape key to cancel one of the dialog boxes displayed by the macro. Canceling out of a dialog box has the effect of sending an error message to Winword that can be detected by the ON ERROR statement. "On Error Goto BYE" simply means that if this condition occurs, the macro should branch to the macro label "BYE:" instead of executing the next statement in turn. As you can see, the BYE: label is placed just before the END SUB statement, so no other commands execute after the macro has gone to the BYE: label.

The other primary feature of this macro is its use of dialog boxes to obtain information from the user. For this purpose, Winword provides the INPUTBOX$ statement (which is pronounced "input box string"). The dollar sign ($) at the end of INPUTBOX$ indicates that this is a *string* function, which provides Winword with a variable that contains text instead of a number.

Functions such as this make it incredibly easy for your macros to display professional-looking dialog boxes without tedious C-language programming. Normally in a C Windows program, you have to specify the exact position of every object in a Windows dialog box, down to the exact number of pixels in each button and box. In WordBasic, however, the INPUTBOX$ statement

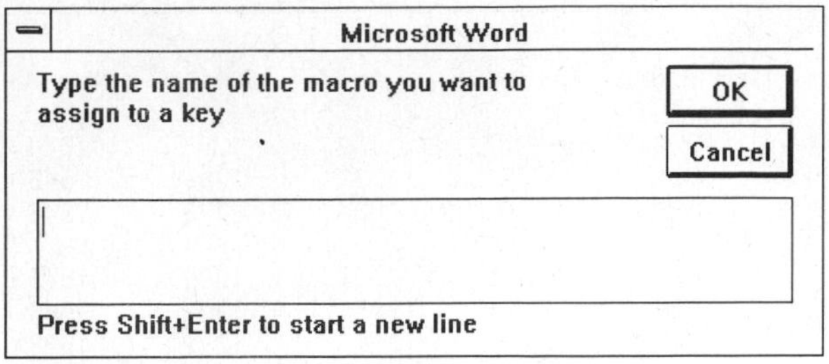

Figure 6-7: AutoAssignToKey dialog box.

automatically creates a dialog box like the one shown in Figure 6-7, complete with a title bar and OK and Cancel buttons. (The MSGBOX statement in the same macro displays a message and an OK button but allows no input.) But all these items are specified by the following single statement in the macro, which also places the contents of the user's input into a string variable called NAME$:

```
name$ = InputBox$("Type the name of the macro you want to assign to a
key")
```

The remainder of the macro obtains the number of the key that the macro should be assigned to, and uses the resulting variables to run Winword's MacroAssignToKey command, making the assignment effective.

Before this macro can be used, you need to know the number that Winword uses to refer to all the keys on the keyboard (and all key combinations). It would be preferable for the macro to simply ask for the name of the desired key combination itself (such as Ctrl+Shift+A), but Winword requires a number called a Key Code instead. These numbers are not included in the Winword *User's Reference*, but are described in the *Microsoft Word for Windows and OS/2 Technical Reference.* I have created a table listing these Key Codes in Figure 6-8. In addition, several Key Codes are undocumented, and I have listed these in Figure 6-9.

Looking at Figure 6-8, you may see patterns in the numbering of the key combinations. Each key is given a numerical Key Code by Word for Windows. When a key is pressed while the Ctrl key is held down, the value of the Key Code is increased by 256. Therefore, the Backspace key, which is normally Key Code 8, is numbered 264 when it is a Ctrl+Backspace (8+256 = 264). Similarly, the Shift key adds 512 to the value of a key, and Alt adds

Key	Key Code	Ctrl	Shift	Ctrl+Shift	Alt	Ctrl+Alt	Shift+Alt	Ctrl+ Shift+Alt
Backspace	8	264	520	776	1032	1288	1544	1800
Tab	9	265	521	777	1033	1289	1545	1801
Keypad 5 (NumLock off)	12	268	524	780	1036	1292	1548	1804
Enter	13	269	525	781	1037	1293	1549	1805
Esc	27	283	539	795	1051	1307	1563	1819
Space	32	288	544	800	1056	1312	1568	1824
PgUp	33	289	545	801	1057	1313	1569	1825
PgDn	34	290	546	802	1058	1314	1570	1826
End	35	291	547	803	1059	1315	1571	1827
Home	36	292	548	804	1060	1316	1572	1828
Ins	45	301	557	813	1069	1325	1581	1837
Del	46	302	558	814	1070	1326	1582	1838
0	48	304	560	816	1072	1328	1584	1840
1	49	305	561	817	1073	1329	1585	1841
2	50	306	562	818	1074	1330	1586	1842
3	51	307	563	819	1075	1331	1587	1843
4	52	308	564	820	1076	1332	1588	1844
5	53	309	565	821	1077	1333	1589	1845
6	54	310	566	822	1078	1334	1590	1846
7	55	311	567	823	1079	1335	1591	1847
8	56	312	568	824	1080	1336	1592	1848
9	57	313	569	825	1081	1337	1593	1849
a	65	321	577	833	1089	1345	1601	1857
b	66	322	578	834	1090	1346	1602	1858
c	67	323	579	835	1091	1347	1603	1859
d	68	324	580	836	1092	1348	1604	1860
e	69	325	581	837	1093	1349	1605	1861
f	70	326	582	838	1094	1350	1606	1862
g	71	327	583	839	1095	1351	1607	1863
h	72	328	584	840	1096	1352	1608	1864
i	73	329	585	841	1097	1353	1609	1865
j	74	330	586	842	1098	1354	1610	1866
k	75	331	587	843	1099	1355	1611	1867
l	76	332	588	844	1100	1356	1612	1868
m	77	333	589	845	1101	1357	1613	1869
n	78	334	590	846	1102	1358	1614	1870
o	79	335	591	847	1103	1359	1615	1871
p	80	336	592	848	1104	1360	1616	1872

(Continued next page)

Figure 6-8: Values of key combinations in Winword.

Key	Key Code	Ctrl	Shift	Ctrl+Shift	Alt	Ctrl+Alt	Shift+Alt	Ctrl+ Shift+Alt
q	81	337	593	849	1105	1361	1617	1873
r	82	338	594	850	1106	1362	1618	1874
s	83	339	595	851	1107	1363	1619	1875
t	84	340	596	852	1108	1364	1620	1876
u	85	341	597	853	1109	1365	1621	1877
v	86	342	598	854	1110	1366	1622	1878
w	87	343	599	855	1111	1367	1623	1879
x	88	344	600	856	1112	1368	1624	1880
y	89	345	601	857	1113	1369	1625	1881
z	90	346	602	858	1114	1370	1626	1882
Keypad 0	96	352	608	864	1120	1376	1632	1888
Keypad 1	97	353	609	865	1121	1377	1633	1889
Keypad 2	98	354	610	866	1122	1378	1634	1890
Keypad 3	99	355	611	867	1123	1379	1635	1891
Keypad 4	100	356	612	868	1124	1380	1636	1892
Keypad 5	101	357	613	869	1125	1381	1637	1893
Keypad 6	102	358	614	870	1126	1382	1638	1894
Keypad 7	103	359	615	871	1127	1383	1639	1895
Keypad 8	104	360	616	872	1128	1384	1640	1896
Keypad 9	105	361	617	873	1129	1385	1641	1897
Keypad *	106	362	618	874	1130	1386	1642	1898
Keypad +	107	363	619	875	1131	1387	1643	1899
Keypad ,	108	364	620	876	1132	1388	1644	1900
Keypad -	109	365	621	877	1133	1389	1645	1901
Keypad .	110	366	622	878	1134	1390	1646	1902
Keypad /	111	367	623	879	1135	1391	1647	1903
F1*	112	368	624	880	1136	1392	1648	1904
F2*	113	369	625	881	1137	1393	1649	1905
F3	114	370	626	882	1138	1394	1650	1906
F4	115	371	627	883	1139	1395	1651	1907
F5	116	372	628	884	1140	1396	1652	1908
F6	117	373	629	885	1141	1397	1653	1909
F7	118	374	630	886	1142	1398	1654	1910
F8	119	375	631	887	1143	1399	1655	1911
F9	120	376	632	888	1144	1400	1656	1912
F10	121	377	633	889	1145	1401	1657	1913
F11*	122	378	634	890	1146	1402	1658	1914
F12*	123	379	635	891	1147	1403	1659	1915
F13*	124	380	636	892	1148	1404	1660	1916
F14*	125	381	637	893	1149	1405	1661	1917
F15*	126	382	638	894	1150	1406	1662	1918
F16*	127	383	639	895	1151	1407	1663	1919

* For F1-F2 and F11-F16, Windows uses Alt+F1 and Alt+F2 to simulate F11 and F12 for older keyboards without F11 and F12 keys. Because of this feature, Windows forces Alt+F11 through Alt+F16 to have the same meaning as Alt+F1 through Alt+F6. This may interfere with your ability to redefine these function keys plus the Alt key and Alt+Shift.

Figure 6-8: (continued).

Key	Key Code	Ctrl	Shift	Ctrl+Shift	Alt	Ctrl+Alt	Shift+Alt	Ctrl+Shift+Alt
Pause	19	275	531	787	1043	1299	1555	1811
Scroll Lock	145	401	657	913	1169	1425	1681	1937
; (semicolon)	186	442	698	954	1210	1466	1722	1978
= (equals sign)	187	443	699	955	1211	1467	1723	1979
, (comma)	188	444	700	956	1212	1468	1724	1980
- (hyphen)	189	445	701	957	1213	1469	1725	1981
. (period)	190	446	702	958	1214	1470	1726	1982
/ (slash)	191	447	703	959	1215	1471	1727	1983
' (backquote)	192	448	704	960	1216	1472	1728	1984
[(left bracket)	219	475	731	987	1243	1499	1755	2011
\ (backslash)	220	476	732	988	1244	1500	1756	2012
] (right bracket)	221	477	733	989	1245	1501	1757	2013
' (apostrophe)	222	478	734	990	1246	1502	1758	2014

Figure 6-9: Undocumented key combinations in Winword. These numbers correspond with 13 keys on the keyboard which are useful as user-defined key combinations but do not appear in the Word for Windows *Technical Reference* manual.

1024. These values add together when more than one shift key is held down while a key is pressed. Ctrl+Shift+Alt+Backspace, therefore, has a value of 1800 (256+512+1024+8 = 1800).

You may notice gaps in the numbering system in Figure 6-8. Key Codes 37-44, 47, 58-64, 91-95, and 128-255 do not appear on the chart, for example. Some of these codes correspond to punctuation marks in Figure 6-9, including the comma, period, brackets, slashes, and quote marks.

These punctuation marks are convenient to use for hotkey combinations. The quickest hotkeys for macros are those that require you to press only two keys simultaneously, such as Ctrl+A or Ctrl+Z. But Winword has already claimed for its own accelerator keys virtually every combination of the Ctrl key with every letter of the alphabet and the 12 function keys. Since Winword does not use punctuation marks as hotkeys, we can place macros on such quick key combinations as Ctrl+/ (control-slash) and Ctrl+] (control-right bracket).

(The exceptions to this rule are the hyphen and equal sign. Winword already uses Ctrl and Ctrl+Shift with the hyphen to insert optional and nonbreaking hyphens, and with the equal sign to make subscripts and superscripts.)

Microsoft has not documented the Key Codes for these punctuation keys in Winword. But they work (some of them on U.S. keyboards only), and it's a shame they didn't show up in the first or second revision of the Word for Windows *Technical Reference.* Some of these combinations may not be available on computers with older BIOS chips. If you need these keys as accelerator keys for macros, be sure to carefully test the operation of your newly defined key combination, in case certain combinations won't work with your configuration.

And, of course, don't redefine a printable character like the period unless you really intend to eliminate the use of the period key as a regular usable character. There are cases, though, when this may be exactly what you intend. Microsoft provides a macro in the EXAMPLES.DOC file (included in your Word for Windows directory) that redefines the apostrophe (') and double-quote (") keys so they produce "smart quotes." These quote marks are "smart" because, when you press the key for a single quote or double quote in your document, Winword automatically determines whether the quote mark should be an open or a closed quote mark (like this: " and "). This type of quote marks are used in magazines and books, and they look better than the straight-down quote marks (like this: ' and ") that most computers produce.

You can learn more about the process of redefining printable keys by opening the EXAMPLES.DOC file and clicking Macro Edit to read the EnableSmartQuotes and DisableSmartQuotes macros included there. This file also provides an easy way to install these macros in your copy of Word for Windows by clicking a button in the document marked "Install."

Another case where you might want to redefine printable keys is with an infrequently used key on the keyboard. One that comes to mind is the backquote key (`), also known as a *grave* accent. This character is usually located on the same key as the *tilde* (~). These keys could be useful for adding accents to words such as crème de menthe and piñata. But Microsoft has provided no way for these keys to be pressed and automatically add the accent they represent to a basic letter. So you might decide to use these conveniently located keys (as well as some shifted keys, such as @ and ^) for some other purpose. If you do redefine a printable key (such as the backquote), give yourself a way to type the key using its old meaning (perhaps by defining a macro that inserts a backquote when you press Ctrl+backquote).

When redefining the keyboard, the overall best strategy for hotkey combinations is to use Ctrl+Shift plus A through Z and 0 through 9. Winword, along with most other Windows applications (including Windows itself), uses none of the keys A–Z or 0–9 with Ctrl+Shift, so these are good combinations to allow end users to redefine. (The one exception to this rule is Ctrl+Shift+8, which toggles Show All on and off in Winword.)

In addition, Winword does not use any Ctrl+Alt combinations, so these make good macro key combinations also. (There are two exceptions: Winword uses Ctrl+Alt+F1 for Lock Field and Ctrl+Alt+F2 for File Open, the same commands as Ctrl+F11 and Ctrl+F12.) Ctrl+Alt combinations should be employed only by experienced users, however, since holding down Ctrl+Alt makes it possible to accidentally hit Ctrl+Alt+Del, which reboots the computer.

Certain key combinations are difficult or impossible to redefine. Windows uses the Alt key with F1 and F2 to simulate the F11 and F12 keys for older keyboards without F11 and F12 keys. Alt+F1 always means the same thing as F11, for example, and Alt+Shift+F1 always means the same thing as Shift+F11. For this reason, Winword resists efforts to redefine these F1-F2 and F11-F12 key combinations. I've tried it and haven't had any success at all.

The hotkeys for Edit Undo and Edit Repeat, in addition, are locked in by Winword and cannot be altered. The meanings of Edit Undo and Edit Repeat constantly change, depending on the last operation you performed. Such functions are best left alone.

Assigning NewPageDown to the Page Down Key

Now that the Key Codes have been charted, it is possible to assign the NewPageDown macro to the Page Down key itself. To do this, pull down the Macro menu and click Run. Select AutoAssignToKey and click OK (or simply double-click the name AutoAssignToKey and it starts running).

When the AutoAssignToKey macro displays a dialog box asking for the name of the macro to assign, type NewPageDown and click OK. Another dialog box appears, asking for the key number from the Winword *Technical Reference* manual for the key you want to redefine. The Page Down key has a Key Code of 34 in Figure 6-8. Type this number and click OK. Winword now begins using the macro when the Page Down key is pressed, instead of its own internal code. Both routines are equally fast, so there is no performance penalty for redefining the key in this way. And it avoids some Unrecoverable Application Errors that might otherwise be generated.

Since the AutoAssignToKey macro redefines each key on a *global* level, Winword stores this change in your NORMAL.DOT document template file.

The change is stored in memory until you exit Word for Windows. At that point, Winword asks, "Save global glossary and command changes?" This means that Winword wants your confirmation to write the macro permanently into your NORMAL.DOT file. Answer "Yes." Saving the NORMAL.DOT file may take one or two minutes if this template already contains several other macros and glossary entries that need to be saved.

Unassigning a Key Definition

Now that you have a way to redefine any key, you also need a way to *reverse* that definition. If you make a mistake or just change your mind, you'll be glad that you added a macro to automate the reversal of a key assignment.

I've found myself in this situation more than once as my macro needs have changed. And experimentation always leads to its share of blunders, which must be cleaned up. I once accidentally redefined the Alt key itself, and as soon as the change took effect, it seemed that nothing else worked — not even the Ctrl key was working correctly! I had tried to define a macro on the value 1024 (which represents the Alt key) plus a value for a printable key. Somehow, the two values never got added together, and my macro wound up redefining just key 1024, which made the Alt key (and apparently a lot of other functions) virtually useless. All I could do to recover was to exit Winword without saving any changes. I was fortunate to have recently saved the other changes I was working on, or the blunder would have required a new Normal template to be constructed from scratch.

The AutoUnassignToKey macro shown in Figure 6-10 performs the function of removing or unassigning a key redefinition you have associated with a macro. A macro name isn't required to unassign a key definition. The Key Code of the redefined key is all that is necessary. The AutoUnassignToKey macro runs WordBasic's Unassign command twice — the first time removes the relationship between the former macro and the key combination, and the second reestablishes the original meaning (if any) that that key combination had under Winword.

Editing an Existing Winword Function — File Open

So far, we have created a simple, one-instruction macro (NewPageDown), and created an entirely new macro from scratch (AutoAssignToKey). Now we can turn our attention to modifying an existing function of the Word for Windows main menu — the File Open function.

```
' AutoUnassignToKey Macro — 1991 Brian Livingston

Sub MAIN
    On Error Goto BYE
    number$ = \
    InputBox$("Type the number from the Winword Technical Reference of the key to unassign")
    num = Val(number$)
    If num < 8 Or num > 2014 Then
        Beep 1
        MsgBox "Number of the key must be 8 to 2014."
    Else
        MacroAssignToKey "", num, 0, .UnAssign          ' unassigns key at global (0) level
        MacroAssignToKey "", num, 0, .UnAssign          ' resets key to original meaning

BYE:
End Sub
```

Figure 6-10: AutoUnassignToKey macro. The backslash at the end of the third line of the macro indicates a statement that continues on the following line.

The ability to redefine actions that appear on the main menu is the real strength of Winword's WordBasic language. Since it was impossible to anticipate every function that Word for Windows users would need, Microsoft made it possible for functions to be added or created by modifying the original functions themselves.

The File Open function is a perfect example of how easy this can be. File Open itself is controlled by a macro of sorts, as are all the other menu items in Word for Windows. To see this, pull down the Macro menu and click Edit. When the dialog box shown earlier in Figure 6-3 appears, click the Show All box *on.* This displays in the list box all the Word for Windows functions — those that are built in as well as the macros you define.

Select File Open in this list and click OK. Winword displays in the macro editing window the wording of a macro that runs every time you choose the File Open command from the main menu. Before you make any changes to this macro, it looks like Figure 6-11.

The FileOpen macro is not stored in the NORMAL.DOT document template file — it is part of the internal code of Word for Windows. When you view the FileOpen macro in the macro editing window before it has been customized, you are actually viewing a description of what the FileOpen macro would

```
Sub MAIN
Dim dlg As FileOpen
GetCurValues dlg
Dialog dlg
Super FileOpen dlg
End Sub
```

Figure 6-11: File Open macro before editing.

look like if it *were* a separate macro. As soon as you edit the FileOpen macro, it becomes a specific text file that is stored in your NORMAL.DOT file (the next time you exit Word for Windows and save all changes).

You may notice that the unedited FileOpen macro shown in Figure 6-11 does not include any error-trapping statements such as ON ERROR GOTO BYE. This is because Winword automatically handles error conditions, such as users canceling out of dialog boxes or requesting nonexistent filenames, with internal code. As soon as you make a single edit, however, this internal error-handling code is disabled in deference to whatever error trapping you specify in your macro. If you don't specify any, a simple press of the Esc key during your macro can trigger a confusing Basic-language error message. This is why almost every customized macro should include an ON ERROR statement.

Because Word for Windows uses its own functions unless you have changed them, it is easy to modify menu functions and then restore them back to their original meaning. Any change you make to the function as shown in Winword's macro editing window becomes part of the behavior of the function. But if you make a mistake or just want the function to return to its original behavior, simply pull down the Macro menu, click Edit, select the macro name, and delete it. Once the customized macro is deleted, the Word for Windows function with that same name reverts to its internally stored behavior.

One aspect of Word for Windows that most users say they would like to change is the filenames that are displayed in the File Open dialog box. Word for Windows displays only those filenames that match the three-letter extension that Word tacks onto files it saves. (Winword uses .DOC by default, but this can be changed to .WRD or any other extension by adding the line DOC-EXTENSION=WRD to the [Microsoft Word] section of your WIN.INI file.)

```
' FileOpen Macro — 1991 Brian Livingston

' This macro changes the File Open dialog box to show all filename extensions.

Sub MAIN
        Dim dlg As FileOpen
        GetCurValues dlg
        On Error Goto BYE              ' if user presses Escape, exit macro
        dlg.Name = "*.*"               ' show filenames with all extensions
        Dialog dlg
        Super FileOpen dlg
BYE:
End Sub
```

Figure 6-12: File Open Macro after editing.

To change this behavior so Winword displays *all* extensions, such as documents produced by other word processors or text editors, make the changes that are indicated by **boldface** type in the FileOpen macro, as shown in Figure 6-12.

The text in boldface demonstrates two WordBasic features: error trapping and redefining dialog boxes. Before we examine the new lines, though, let's first follow the meaning of the macro before it was edited.

The macro before editing performs the following actions:

1. It *dimensions* or sets up a variable called DLG, which is actually a dialog box with all the attributes of the dialog box that appears when you choose File Open from the main menu.

2. It gets the current values for a dialog box of that type and fills the variable DLG with those values.

3. It displays the dialog box (with the DIALOG DLG statement).

4. When the user clicks OK in the displayed dialog box, Winword runs its internal code for the File Open function (obeying the SUPER FILEOPEN statement), using whatever values the user typed in when presented with the dialog box. The "super" level of commands is internal to Word for Windows and cannot be altered by a macro.

The super level is one of three levels of hierarchy that Winword uses to determine which macro to run when macros in different templates have the same name.

Below the super level is the global level. Macros on the global level are stored in the NORMAL.DOT file and are loaded automatically by every new document.

Below the global level is the template level. Macros on the template level are available only to documents that were created with the File New command and were based on that particular template.

Winword has an internal function called FileOpen (this is a macro on the super level), and when this procedure is completed we will also have a macro on the global level called FileOpen. Therefore, Winword will choose to run the global macro named FileOpen when you choose File Open from the main menu. Within the global macro, the statement SUPER FILEOPEN is supposed to force Winword to turn processing at that point over to its internal FileOpen code rather than running another copy of the global FileOpen macro.

(In fact, Winword's *Technical Reference* manual is inaccurate concerning the SUPER command — it does not force Winword to use the higher-level [internal] macro. Winword always uses an internal function when a macro with the same name is referred to within a macro. The use of the command SUPER is simply a visual reminder to us that the macro is going to use an internal function called FileOpen, not the global macro called FileOpen. In a similar way, WordBasic's LET command, as in LET VARIABLE=0, is unnecessary: VARIABLE=0 does exactly the same thing, but is less clear. If you want to have one macro run another macro, you must use the command MACRORUN *macroname* instead of simply naming the macro as a command.)

The lines in boldface in Figure 6-12 change the behavior of the File Open function in the following ways:

1. Word for Windows is instructed to go to the end of the macro in case the user cancels out of the dialog box that is displayed, or if any other error occurs (this is achieved by the line ON ERROR GOTO BYE:);

2. Instead of using *.DOC as the filename to be displayed in the File Open dialog box, the default Name field is changed to *.*, displaying all filenames (this is achieved by the line DLG.NAME="*.*").

```
' InsertFile Macro — 1991 Brian Livingston

' This macro makes the Insert File function display all filename extensions.

Sub MAIN
        Dim dlg As InsertFile
        GetCurValues dlg
        On Error Goto BYE               ' if user presses Escape, exit macro
        dlg.Name = "*.*"                ' show all filename extensions
        Dialog dlg
        Super InsertFile dlg
BYE:
End Sub
```

Figure 6-13: The InsertFile macro after editing.

Once you have made these edits, close the macro editing window and reply "Yes" when asked if you wish to save changes to the global: FileOpen macro. Choose File Open from the main menu and verify that Winword correctly displays all filenames in the File Open dialog box, just as you programmed it to do.

InsertFile Macro

After modifying the FileOpen macro, you might assume that all filenames will now appear in every dialog box that opens files. A quick examination of Winword's main menu reveals, however, that a similar modification needs to be carried out on the InsertFile function, since it too displays only files with Winword's default extension unless told otherwise.

Pull down the Macro menu, click Edit, and open the InsertFile macro. Edit it to appear as in Figure 6-13, then save it.

By now, you should see a pattern in these edited macros. Even without the *Technical Reference* manual, Winword's macros have a certain logic that makes its fairly easy to modify them as you wish.

This completes the process of redefining the File Open and Insert File functions. These macros are simple, but illustrate some of the basic procedures that make WordBasic so powerful.

At this point, a more difficult task is called for — and one that may provide an even more useful function than any of the preceding macros.

Automatically Running FileOpen When Winword Starts

In order to examine the capabilities of WordBasic in more depth, let's try to change a feature of Word for Windows that happens automatically, not when we press an accelerator key. It turns out that we can gain control over the start-up procedures that Word for Windows follows every time it is loaded.

When Winword loads for the first time, it normally displays an empty document — a veritable blank sheet of paper known as "Document1." Often, however, when people start Word for Windows they want to work with an existing document, not a blank document.

An AutoExec macro is required to change Winword's behavior so that instead of opening a blank document, it displays the File Open dialog box and displays a list of filenames for you to choose from. Then you may double-click any filename to load it, or press Esc to cancel the dialog box and open a blank document as before.

Winword's AutoExec macro is similar in concept to the AUTOEXEC.BAT file that DOS loads every time you turn on your PC. If DOS finds a file named AUTOEXEC.BAT, it runs the commands in that file. If not, DOS simply displays a prompt and waits for a command.

Winword's AutoExec supports many more commands than DOS's AUTOEXEC.BAT — the entire WordBasic language. If Winword finds a macro called AutoExec (in the global template NORMAL.DOT, or in a separate template file that is being loaded), it runs the commands in that file.

Winword provides options for several other macros that run automatically under certain conditions. These macros have the following special names:

AutoExec	runs when you start Winword.
AutoOpen	runs when you open a file containing this macro.
AutoNew	runs on new files based on templates with this macro.
AutoClose	runs when you close a file containing this macro.
AutoExit	runs when you exit Winword.

The AutoExec macro has the features that we are looking for. It can control the behavior of Word for Windows when it first starts up. The AutoExec macro, it would appear, can tell whether or not Winword is already loading a file and, if not, it can summon up a File Open dialog box to allow a choice of filenames.

This task turned out to be quite a complex program to perfect. But once finished, the program itself is simple to type in and use.

To control Winword's start-up behavior, we must know each of the ways that the program can load itself. Winword may be started up in two ways besides double-clicking its icon in Windows' Program Manager: (1) it can be started from the Windows File Manager by double-clicking a document icon with an extension that Winword recognizes; or (2) it may be started from the DOS command line along with Windows by typing a command such as:

```
WIN WINWORD c:\dir\filename
```

In either of these cases, the AutoExec macro should detect that Winword has already loaded a file and refrain from displaying the File Open dialog box.

Things are not this simple, unfortunately. The AutoExec macro executes *after* Winword has started to load, but *before* Winword actually opens any file specified on its command line. Therefore, the AutoExec macro cannot determine whether Winword is opening a file, because when AutoExec runs, Winword has not yet loaded the blank "Document1" or any other document.

For this reason, I developed two macros — an AutoExec macro and another macro that is *called* by AutoExec. The second macro runs after Winword has loaded any file previously specified. Therefore, the second macro can tell whether such a file was loaded and display the File Open dialog box or not, as appropriate.

These two macros, AutoExec and AutoFileOpen, take advantage of an obscure command in the WordBasic language — the ONTIME statement. The ONTIME statement can be used in a macro to run another macro at a certain time — 12:00 noon, say. But in this case, we will use the ability of the ONTIME statement to run another macro, not at a particular time, but as soon as Winword becomes idle (indicating that it has completed loading and opening any file that was specified on the command line).

```
' AutoExec Macro — 1991 Brian Livingston

' This macro runs every time Winword is opened. It starts a macro that opens the File Open dialog box.

Sub MAIN
        On Error Goto BYE                       ' if user holds down Escape, don't run
        OnTime Time$(), "AutoFileOpen", 0       ' after Winword loads (wait indefinitely), run macro
BYE:
End Sub
```

Figure 6-14: The AutoExec macro. The function "TIME$()" provides the macro with the current time. In this case, it allows the "ONTIME" statement to start running the AutoFileOpen macro immediately after Winword becomes idle, instead of waiting for a certain time of day. The number 0 indicates that the ONTIME statement should wait indefinitely for Winword to become idle, instead of waiting a certain number of seconds and then aborting.

To create the macros shown in Figures 6-14 and 6-15, run Macro Edit, name the macro, then type the text of the macros. Neither AutoExec nor AutoFileOpen are macros that already exist, so they must be edited and the statements typed in from scratch.

The AutoExec and AutoFileOpen macros work regardless of whether Winword was started with a filename or without. These macros will work slightly faster, however, if you use an undocumented feature of Winword to start the program without loading its blank Document1 every time.

In the Program Manager, highlight the Winword icon by clicking it once. Pull down the File menu and click Properties. In the dialog box that appears, place the switch /N after WINWORD.EXE on the Command Line. This switch instructs Winword to start with "No Document1." Preventing this blank document from loading saves time when the AutoExec and AutoFileOpen macros are waiting for Winword to become idle so they can open the File Open dialog box.

Additionally, there are two ways to keep the AutoExec macro from running, in case you want to circumvent it and start a blank Document1 using the Normal template.

First, the AutoExec macro is constructed so that the user can press the Esc key before the macro has executed; this sends the macro to the BYE: label, effectively ending it. To make Winword detect this Esc keypress, wait until

```
' AutoFileOpen Macro — 1991 Brian Livingston

' AutoFileOpen is run by the AutoExec macro. It displays a File Open dialog box, unless the user has
' already loaded a file by double-clicking on it in the File Manager. If the user presses Escape or cancels
' out of the dialog box, the macro opens a new, blank document instead of opening a file.

Sub MAIN
    Select Case FileName$(0)         ' evaluate the name of the current file
    Case ""                          ' in this case (no name), the user ran "winword /n"
        USERBOX                      ' run the File Open subroutine shown below
    Case "Document1"                 ' the user ran "winword" with no parameter
        FileClose 2                  ' first close empty Document1, and don't save it
        USERBOX                      ' then run the File Open subroutine shown below
    Case Else
        REM if name is not blank or Document1, it was loaded from File Manager, do nothing
    End Select
End Sub
'
Sub USERBOX
    Dim box As FileOpen              ' dimension a dialog box
    GetCurValues box                 ' fill the box's fields with defaults
    box.Name = "*.*"                 ' show filenames with all extensions
    On Error Goto NEWDOC             ' if user presses Escape, run FileNew
    Dialog box                       ' accept user's filename selection
    Super FileOpen box               ' if it exists, open the requested file
    Goto BYE                         ' skip the FileNew statement below
NEWDOC:
    FileNew 0, "NORMAL"              ' open new document based on Normal template
BYE:
End Sub
```

Figure 6-15: The AutoFileOpen macro. This macro determines which of three conditions Winword is in: (1) Winword was started with no document, using its /N switch; (2) Winword was started with a blank Document1; or (3) Winword loaded an existing file. In either of the first two cases, the macro runs the subroutine named USERBOX, shown in the bottom half of the macro.

the Microsoft copyright notice appears on Winword's screen, then hold down the Esc key for a few seconds until you hear a beep. When you let the Esc key up, Winword displays a blank document just as it would have without the AutoExec macro.

Even without the macro's added Esc feature, Winword supports another switch that disables AutoExec in every case. Starting Winword with an /M switch avoids running AutoExec entirely. Think of this as the macro-over-ride switch.

The other Auto macros — AutoOpen, AutoNew, AutoClose, and AutoExit — can be prevented from running by holding down the Shift key while performing the command that would normally execute the macro. To disable the AutoExit macro, for example, hold down the Shift key while clicking File Exit.

This example introduces two major new concepts: the CASE statement, which chooses different instructions to run based on its evaluation, and the main routine running a subroutine, which is called USERBOX.

The SELECT CASE statement is used, in this macro, to determine whether or not Winword has already loaded a file that was specified on the command line. It does this by comparing the filename shown in Winword's title bar (this is called FILENAME$(0)) against (1) the name "Document1" and (2) a blank name (shown in the macro as two quote marks with nothing between them). If the filename is blank, the first CASE statement moves directly into the USERBOX subroutine and displays the File Open dialog box. If the filename is Document1, the macro closes this blank document (to save memory) and *then* starts the USERBOX subroutine. If the filename is anything else, the macro simply ends since a file is already loaded and nothing else needs to be done.

The subroutine USERBOX appears in the lower half of the AutoFileOpen macro. A comment line consisting of several hyphens separates it from the upper half of the macro simply for ease of reading. The subroutine dimensions a File Open dialog box and displays it, much like the FileOpen macro we just modified previously in Figure 6-12. The difference is that, in the AutoFileOpen macro, canceling out of the dialog box macro does not just end the macro, but instead runs the File New command to start a blank document.

The subroutine is used — instead of placing all the instructions in the MAIN routine — because the macro needs to display the USERBOX under two different sets of circumstances (two different CASE statements). Placing all the dialog box statements in one subroutine makes the macro shorter and easier to change later.

This concludes the discussion of the AutoExec and AutoFileOpen macros. Now let's move on to a macro that takes up almost a full page to write down — a macro, appropriately, that prints a single page on demand.

Printing the Current Page — The PrintThisPage Macro

Sometimes a problem bothers you so much that it stays with you until you fix it. That was the case with me regarding Word for Windows' lack of a simple keystroke to print the current page. WordPerfect and many other word processing software packages provide a function key combination that prints only the page you are working on, without you having to know the page's number or the exact location of the top or bottom of the page.

Winword, of course, does provide in its File Print dialog box a method to print from page X to page Y, and you can specify the same page number for the beginning and end of the print job in order to print the current page. Winword's status line at the bottom of the screen reports what page number the cursor is on. But ironically, this status line is replaced when the File Print dialog box is on the screen by the irrelevant message, "For Help, press F1," which wipes out the page number information you need to know.

In addition, if the document you are working on is formatted to begin numbering pages with a number other than 1 (as it might be if you are working on a separate chapter file in a multichapter document), the status line indication of the current page number is wrong. If the document begins numbering with, say, page 20, the status line indicates that you are on page 1 — not page 20 — when the cursor is on the first page of the document. But if you instruct the File Print dialog box to print page 1, you get nothing — File Print wants to be told to print page 20!

Frustrated by the lack of a simple function key that would enable me to print the current page without knowing its exact number, I spent a great deal of time mulling over the best way to add this feature to Word for Windows. I would like to thank David Goodhand of Microsoft's New York office for suggesting the approach that resulted in the macro that appears in Figure 6-16.

The PrintThisPage macro prints the page the insertion point is on — which is *not* necessarily the page currently on the screen. The macro inserts a {Page} field, reads the page number, then inserts that number into the File Print dialog box as the page to be printed.

This macro is fairly slow because it must repaginate the document in order to know what page the {Page} field is on. (An opened document may not be paginated correctly, and having Background Pagination ON does not immediately correct this.) After the macro repaginates the document, the File Print menu command repaginates again from page 1 to the page that is

```
' PrintThisPage Macro — 1991 Brian Livingston & David Goodhand

' This macro prints the page the insertion point is on — NOT necessarily the page currently on-screen.

Sub MAIN
On Error Goto BYE
REM test for macro editing window
    If InStr(WindowName$(), ": ") <> 0 Then
        MsgBox "This command is not available in a macro editing window -- use File Print"
        Goto BYE
    End If

REM save location of insertion point (first delete any bookmark from a previously-interrupted macro)
    If ExistingBookmark("cursor_was_here") Then InsertBookmark "cursor_was_here", .Delete
    InsertBookmark "cursor_was_here"

REM save current preferences, then display field codes as results
    fieldstate = ViewFieldCodes()       ' save the user's setting for viewing field codes
    Dim prefbox As ViewPreferences      ' dimension a variable based on View Preferences dialog box
    GetCurValues prefbox                ' fill the variable with the current default values
    showstate = prefbox.ShowAll         ' save the current state of the Show All setting
    StartOfLine                         ' this prevents deleting any selection, and avoids specifying
                                          the wrong page when cursor is at end of last line of a page
    ViewFieldCodes 0                    ' show the numeric value of the Page field instead of text
    ShowAll 0                           ' turn Show All off to show numeric value of Page field

REM insert a page field and put its value in File Print
    UtilRepaginateNow                   ' calculate page breaks in the document
    InsertField "page"                  ' insert the actual page field
    CharLeft 1, 1                       ' move the cursor over the Page field and select it
    Dim printbox As FilePrint           ' dimension a variable based on File Print dialog box
    GetCurValues printbox               ' fill the variable with the current default values
    printbox.Range = 2                  ' tell the dialog box to print range From and To, not All
    printbox.From = Selection$()        ' place the number in the Print From box
    printbox.To = Selection$()          ' place the number in the Print To box
    EditClear                           ' delete the Page field without harming the clipboard

REM restore original cursor location, delete bookmark, and restore user's view
    If ExistingBookmark("cursor_was_here") Then
        EditGoTo "cursor_was_here"
        InsertBookmark "cursor_was_here", .Delete
    End If
    ViewFieldCodes fieldstate           ' restore the user's settings for viewing field codes
    ShowAll showstate                   ' restore the Show All setting to its original state
    SendKeys "{enter}"                  ' click OK for the user — parameters are already set
    Dialog printbox                     ' display and execute the revised Print dialog box
    FilePrint printbox                  ' run the File Print command using the revised settings
BYE:
End Sub
```

Figure 6-16: The PrintThisPage macro.

being printed. This second repagination is forced because the PrintThisPage macro makes a (temporary) change to the document that File Print interprets as a change that requires repagination. This second repagination is not affected by turning *off* the document's SETDIRTY flag. There currently is no way to avoid this. ("Dirty" is a programming term for a file that has been changed but has not yet been saved to disk. Winword uses this concept to set an internal code that displays a dialog box reminding you that a "dirty" document should be saved before it is closed)

Some of the problems that had to be solved to perfect this macro included making sure that the {Page} field that determines what page to print would, in fact, obtain the correct page number. The cursor, for example, might be located at the end of the last line of a page when the macro is run (as it would be if you had just added a great deal of text and wanted to print just that page). In that case, the {Page} field would often wrap around to the *next* page when inserted, thus printing the page *after* the one you really wanted. This anomaly was corrected by making the macro move the cursor to the *beginning* of whatever line it happened to be on (it couldn't wrap to the next page then, no matter how much or how little text was on that line). Including this change, however, meant that the macro had to include routines to save and then restore the user's original cursor position. A macro should always return the user's screen to the exact condition that existed when the macro was started.

A completely different method that I tried (and then abandoned) to accomplish the PrintThisPage function was as follows: moving to the top of the current page, selecting the text on that page, and printing the resulting selection. This method, however, cannot be used because of a bug in Winword 1.0 and 1.1. Any footnote within a selection prints the correct number in the text, but incorrectly prints "1" at the bottom of the page. This behavior cannot be corrected by a macro. And, in any case, a macro using this method will still be required to repaginate the document in order to determine the correct beginning and ending points of the page. So there is no performance advantage in attempting to perfect this alternate method for demand page printing.

Assigning the PrintThisPage Macro to the File Menu

Use the following procedure to add the PrintThisPage macro to the File menu. Pull down the Macro menu and run MacroAssignToMenu. In the dialog box that appears (see Figure 6-17), click Assign to assign a separator between the last command on the File menu (Exit) and the command you

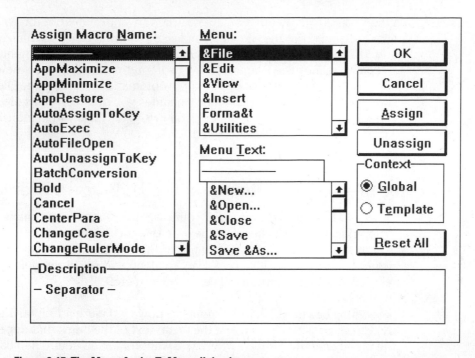

Figure 6-17: The MacroAssignToMenu dialog box.

are going to add. This inserts some neutral space between Print This Page and Exit, the command immediately above the new location of the Print This Page command. Then highlight the PrintThisPage macro in the Name list box.

When Print This Page appears in the menu text window, notice that Word for Windows has automatically added space between each of the words that begins with a capital letter. (Macro names must be all one word, but items on a menu look better as separate words.) Move the ampersand (&) that appears in the window from the P in Print to just in front of the T in This. Doing this is necessary to make the letter T underscored on the menu so the macro can be run from the keyboard. Since the choice Print already appears on the File menu, we cannot use P as the letter that selects the Print This File menu choice. (And because Close is already used, we cannot title the macro PrintCurrentPage and use the letter C.) Asymetrix Toolbook also uses T as the hotkey for their Print This Page menu command, and hopefully this will become a standard key sequence among all Windows applications that support "pages." Click Assign to add PrintThisFile to the File menu. Click OK to close the Assign To Menu dialog box.

When you complete this, you are returned to a normal Word for Windows window; pull down the File menu and see that Print This Page has been added at the end of the menu (separated from the critical Exit menu item by a separator line). See Figure 6-18. Winword automatically places new macros assigned to menus at the bottom of the command list. Below the File menu shown will be a list of the last four filenames you opened — this file listing cannot be removed or altered. Click on Print This Page with a mouse or type Alt+F, T with the keyboard to run the macro.

Changing the Order of Items on the Pull-Down Menus

Once you have added a macro of your own, you may want to change the order in which those choices appear on the pull-down menus. There is no way to simply drag the items into place with a mouse, as convenient as that would be. Instead, run Macro Assign To Menu and select the pull-down menu you wish to rearrange (File, Edit, View, etc.).

The dialog box in which this is done is shown in Figure 6-17. You must use the Unassign button to remove the menu text of the items that appear on the menu *after* the position where you want to add an item. Then use the Assign button to add your item(s), and add back those existing menu items that you removed.

Make sure that the correct letters are underscored in the items you add back. The underscore character indicates the hotkey that is used when selecting menu items using the keyboard. To underscore a character in a menu item, insert an ampersand (&) before the character, as shown in Figure 6-17.

And be sure to insert separator lines (by using the Assign key on the first item in the Macro Name list, which is a horizontal line) between those menu items that represent different categories of commands, or that might be dangerous if clicked accidentally.

One of these "dangerous" commands is the Exit menu item. This is why the menu item Exit is separated from the commands above and below it on the pull-down menu by separator lines. The Exit command does not respond well to the Assign and Unassign buttons in the Macro Assign To Menu dialog box. So I recommend that this command be left alone, as we did when we assigned the PrintThisPage macro to the File menu after the Exit command earlier in this chapter.

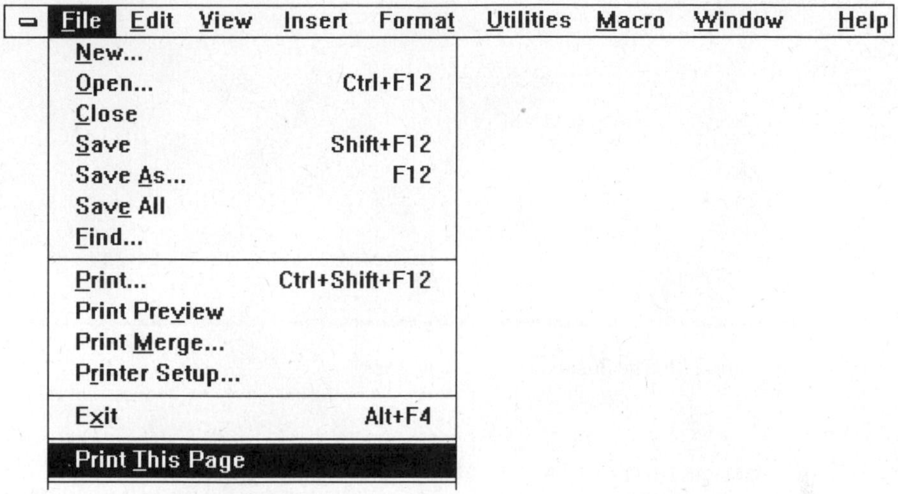

```
 □  File  Edit  View   Insert  Format   Utilities  Macro  Window      Help
    New...
    Open...                 Ctrl+F12
    Close
    Save                   Shift+F12
    Save As...                   F12
    Save All
    Find...

    Print...          Ctrl+Shift+F12
    Print Preview
    Print Merge...
    Printer Setup...

    Exit                      Alt+F4
    Print This Page
```

Figure 6-18: The File menu after the PrintThisPage macro has been assigned to it.

Changing the Wording of the Main Menu

It is even possible with macros to change the words that appear on Winword's main menu line. (It is not possible at this time to add an entirely new item to the main menu line in Winword, however.)

It has always bothered me, for example, that one of the choices on Word for Windows' main menu (Format) cannot be selected from the keyboard by pressing Alt and the first letter of the command (F). Because the first letter of the File pull-down menu is underscored, someone at Microsoft decided to leave the word Format as it was but underscore the *last* letter (Format).

I have never been able to figure out why the Format main menu choice was not called Tools or, even better, Typography. All of the selections under the Format pull-down menu affect the character, paragraph, and document typography and positioning. With the Format menu item renamed to Typography, the letter T can still be used to select the pull-down menu (making this change compatible with anyone who has learned to access the menu this way). And all the main menu choices become consistent in using the first letter of their name as a keyboard hotkey.

Figure 6-19 shows the text of a macro that uses Winword's RenameMenu command to change the Format menu item to Typography. The

```
' RenameFormatMenu Macro — 1991 Brian Livingston

' This macro changes the Format menu item to Typography.

Sub MAIN
    RenameMenu 4, "&Typography"
End Sub
```

Figure 6-19: The RenameFormatMenu macro.

RenameMenu command must be followed by a number (0 through 7) to indicate which item is being renamed:

File	0
Edit	1
View	2
Insert	3
Format	4
Utilities	5
Macro	6
Window	7

Additionally, the RenameMenu command must be followed by a word or words in quotes that indicates the new text to appear in place of the old menu item name. Like all other items on pull-down menus, one of the letters of the new text must be preceded by an ampersand (&) to indicate that that letter will be underscored on the menu and will act as the keyboard hotkey to select that choice.

Notice that changing the name of the menu item from Format to Typography does not change the workings of any macros that use WordBasic commands such as FormatCharacter and FormatParagraph. They work the same way as before. See Figure 6-20, a renamed main menu.

Macros on a Network

One problem administrators of a network face is how to distribute new macros that have been written by programmers to all Winword users on the network. Macros (even in Basic) can be very complicated, as we have seen,

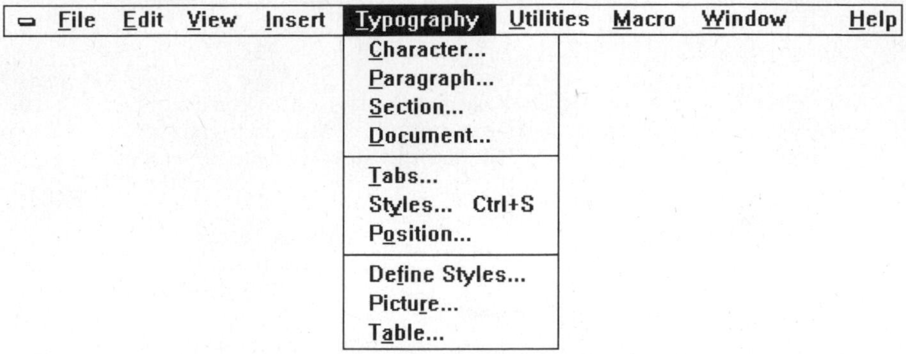

⚬	File	Edit	View	Insert	Typography	Utilities	Macro	Window	Help

Character...
Paragraph...
Section...
Document...

Tabs...
Styles...   Ctrl+S
Position...

Define Styles...
Picture...
Table...

Figure 6-20: The renamed main menu.

and once a macro is written all users should be able to benefit from it without having to type it in themselves.

Macros, however, are all stored in Winword's standard document template, which is a file called NORMAL.DOT. If this file is kept in the Winword directory and is made read-only, individual users on the network cannot save changes to their preferred character and paragraph formats. If each user is given a separate copy, on the other hand, and allowed to customize it at will, you cannot copy updated versions of NORMAL.DOT (with newly written macros and key assignments) into users' directories without eliminating the old file containing users' own formatting preferences.

The best solution to this dilemma is to make a copy of the NORMAL.DOT document template (and other templates) for each user in his or her personal directory. The NORMAL.DOT file is then made read-only (with the DOS ATTRIB command), and a generic template called LETTER.DOT is created. An AutoExec macro must be written which Winword executes every time it starts. The AutoExec macro instructs Winword to use the character and paragraph formatting preferences contained in LETTER.DOT instead of NORMAL.DOT.

The Letter document template (and all other templates in the same directory) inherit all the macros and key assignments contained in NORMAL.DOT. In this way, users may use the Letter template to set any default typeface, size, etc., which they need for their everyday documents. But whenever the computer staff develops new macro functions (or places additional functions on key combinations like Ctrl+Alt+F10), simply copying a new version of NORMAL.DOT to all users' personal directories immediately distributes the changes to them (the next time they start Winword).

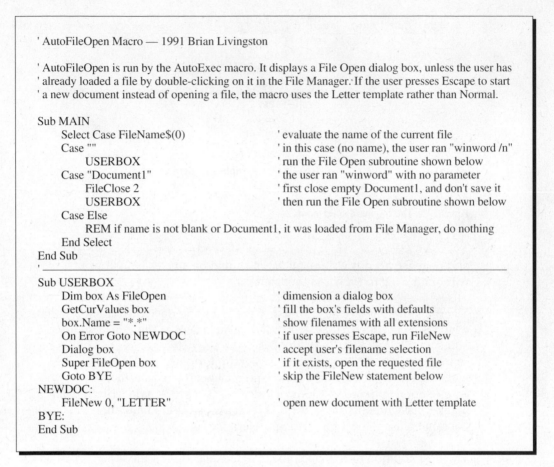

```
' AutoFileOpen Macro — 1991 Brian Livingston

' AutoFileOpen is run by the AutoExec macro. It displays a File Open dialog box, unless the user has
' already loaded a file by double-clicking on it in the File Manager. If the user presses Escape to start
' a new document instead of opening a file, the macro uses the Letter template rather than Normal.

Sub MAIN
      Select Case FileName$(0)              ' evaluate the name of the current file
      Case ""                               ' in this case (no name), the user ran "winword /n"
            USERBOX                         ' run the File Open subroutine shown below
      Case "Document1"                      ' the user ran "winword" with no parameter
            FileClose 2                     ' first close empty Document1, and don't save it
            USERBOX                         ' then run the File Open subroutine shown below
      Case Else
            REM if name is not blank or Document1, it was loaded from File Manager, do nothing
      End Select
End Sub
'_____
Sub USERBOX
      Dim box As FileOpen                   ' dimension a dialog box
      GetCurValues box                      ' fill the box's fields with defaults
      box.Name = "*.*"                      ' show filenames with all extensions
      On Error Goto NEWDOC                  ' if user presses Escape, run FileNew
      Dialog box                            ' accept user's filename selection
      Super FileOpen box                    ' if it exists, open the requested file
      Goto BYE                              ' skip the FileNew statement below
NEWDOC:
      FileNew 0, "LETTER"                   ' open new document with Letter template
BYE:
End Sub
```

Figure 6-21: The AutoFileOpen macro for networks.

This network strategy uses the same AutoExec macro previously shown in Figure 6-14, but requires changes to the AutoFileOpen macro that was shown in Figure 6-15. The most basic change is that the AutoFileOpen macro must open a new document based on the Letter document template instead of the Normal template when the user starts a new document. This is accomplished by simply changing the name of the template that the File New statement opens at the end of the AutoFileOpen macro from NORMAL to LETTER, as shown in Figure 6-21.

For this macro to succeed, of course, a template named LETTER.DOT must already exist in the directory set up for each user's templates. This Letter template can be created simply by copying NORMAL.DOT to a file named

```
' FileNew Macro — 1991 Brian Livingston

' The FileNew dialog box in Winword 1.0 and 1.1 has a bug which disables the "Cancel" button.
' Clicking Cancel while a macro is running does not cancel the macro, but starts a new file anyway.
' There is no way to work around this at present. Running FileNew always starts a new file.

Sub MAIN
        Dim dlg As FileNew
        GetCurValues dlg
        On Error Goto BYE               ' if user presses Escape, exit macro
        dlg.Template = "LETTER"         ' show Letter template as default
        Dialog dlg
        Super FileNew dlg
BYE:
End Sub
```

Figure 6-22: The FileNew macro after editing for network use.

LETTER.DOT. Before this is done, however, any global macros and glossary entries in the Normal template should be removed and the Normal template saved to write the changes to the file. Without this step, all global macros and glossaries in NORMAL.DOT will become useless when copied to LETTER.DOT (since a template named anything but Normal cannot hold global entries). They will continue to take up space in the LETTER.DOT file, however, and the Letter template will take longer to save when changes are made to it in the future.

To carry out the network strategy, the File New function must also be amended so that choosing File New always defaults to opening a new document based on the Letter template. (The user may still select another template from the list in the File New dialog box.)

And finally, the Edit Glossary function must be changed so that new glossary entries that users add are always saved in the template, not the global, level. After the Normal template is made read-only, trying to save glossaries to the global level merely results in a frustrating error message.

These two changes are shown in Figures 6-22 and 6-23. The lines you add are shown in boldface. The comment lines at the beginning of the macro explain a harmless bug in Winword 1.x that prevents the Cancel button in Winword's FileNew dialog box from actually averting the opening of a new file. This is corrected in a future Winword version.

```
' EditGlossary Macro — 1991 Brian Livingston

' This macro causes the Edit Glossary dialog box to default to the Template level rather than
' Global. This is necessary when users automatically use the Letter template rather than Normal,
' and want to define their own glossary entries.

Sub MAIN
     Dim dlg As EditGlossary
     GetCurValues dlg
     On Error Goto BYE
     SendKeys "%T%N"                    ' sets level to Template and opens Name box
     Dialog dlg
     Super EditGlossary dlg
BYE:
End Sub
```

Figure 6-23: The EditGlossary macro after editing for network use.

Since all users on the network have the ability to modify and save their own templates, each user must have a personal set of templates in a directory on the network to which they have read-and-write access. The following two lines must be inserted in WIN.INI under the [Microsoft Word] section for Winword to find document templates in a directory other than its own main directory:

```
[Microsoft Word]
; Sets the directory for NORMAL.DOT and other document templates.
dot-path=c:\template
```

Accessing Special Characters

Adding Bullets and Other Characters to Your Keyboard

Windows gives you the ability to insert a large number of special characters into your documents, in addition to the keys that appear on your keyboard. If you have an English-language keyboard, your keyboard of course is limited to those letters that appear in the English alphabet (A through Z). But even if you have a keyboard for French, German, or some other language that includes keys for accented letters (such as á), you can access a great many other characters as well.

Windows uses a character set with up to 256 different letters or symbols per typeface. The first 32, numbered 0 through 31, are usually nonprintable control characters. The characters numbered 32 through 127 normally correspond with keys on English-language keyboards. That leaves about 128 more characters that do not appear on your keyboard — regardless of your language.

The layout of these characters is shown in a chart in Chapter 9, so it is not duplicated here. But many of these characters are extremely useful. The copyright symbol (©) is character number 169, for example — a symbol that cannot be printed with the IBM "PC-8" character set in use when you are at the DOS prompt.

It is usually easy to write macros that place these special characters on certain key combinations. You could, for example, define a macro to type the copyright symbol that would consist of only three lines:

```
Sub MAIN
Insert Chr$(169)
End Sub
```

If you want to access special characters in typefaces other than common ones like Times Roman and Helvetica, however, it's a little more complicated. Most PostScript printers include a Symbol font, for example, and Word for Windows bundles an installable Symbol font that makes these characters available for LaserJets as well. (You install this font using the Control Panel's Printers icon, reading the Symbol file from the \SYMBOL.W3 directory on the Word for Windows disks.) Many PostScript printers and others also come with a Dingbats font, which includes many more symbols, particularly arrows, ballot boxes, and numbered bullets. But writing a macro that inserts these characters requires that you save the name of the typeface that is already in use in the document, so you can change to the typeface that has the special character and change back to continue typing normally.

Figure 6-24 illustrates a macro that handles this switching process to insert a bullet (•) from the Symbol font into your text. You may know that the Word for Windows *User's Reference* lists character number 149 as the bullet character in Times Roman and other text typefaces. This is only true, however, if you are printing to a genuine Adobe PostScript printer. Other printer drivers, including the LaserJet and Epson drivers, among others, implement this character as a plain letter "o" — not a very good substitute for a bullet. All printer drivers that support the Symbol font implement the

```
AddEnBullet Macro — 1991 Brian Livingston

' This macro inserts a bullet, and requires a printer with the Symbol font. All PostScript printers
' have this font, and Word for Windows comes with an installable Symbol font for LaserJets.
' Place this macro on Alt+F3, near the "@" symbol (which resembles a bullet) on 101-key keyboards.

Sub MAIN
On Error Goto BYE
If InStr(WindowName$(), ": ") <> 0 Then        ' test for macro editing window
     Beep 1
     Print "This character cannot be inserted in a macro editing window"
Else
     If SelType() = 2 Then EditClear           ' if text is selected, delete it because you cannot find
     userface$ = Font$()                       ' what typeface is in use (from a selection)
     Font "Symbol"                             ' change to Symbol font
     Insert Chr$(183)                          ' insert the bullet character
     Font userface$                            ' restore current typeface
End If

BYE:
End Sub
```

Figure 6-24: The AddEnBullet macro.

bullet character correctly at position 183, so it is much more reliable to insert this character so that a document containing a bullet can be printed correctly on a variety of printers.

The macro in Figure 6-24 also tests whether you are trying to insert a bullet into a macro in Winword's macro editing window. The macro will exit with a warning message if this is the case. The macro editing window does not allow changing to any typeface other than Times Roman, and therefore will not support any characters from the Symbol or Dingbats fonts.

I place this macro on the Alt+F3 key combination. On 101-key keyboards, the F3 key is directly above the "at" sign (@), which resembles a bullet and helps me remember this key assignment. This bullet character is called an "en" bullet because it is about the size of the letter "n," as opposed to a large "em" bullet, which is character 108 in the Dingbats font. This macro can be used as a model to insert any character that must come from a typeface other than the normal text face.

Typing Accented Characters

A serious limitation of English-language keyboards is that they do not include any keys that add accents to make letters such as é and ñ. These accents are important, for typing people's proper names, for example, but especially because I don't want to spell "résumé" wrong when I'm submitting a job application!

These characters and the need to deal with them are treated at more length in Chapter 9. In this chapter, I include the code for five macros that make it possible to type almost any special character on English-language keyboards with no more than two key strokes.

The special-character chart presented in Chapter 9 may seem like a hodgepodge of random alphabets upon first glance. But there is actually a simple structure underlying these characters in Windows' ANSI character set. The fact is that almost all characters numbered 161 to 255 in the ANSI sequence fall into the following five categories.

1. **Letters with an acute accent**. These six vowels have corresponding characters with acute accents:

A	E	I	O	U	Y	a	e	i	o	u	y
Á	É	Í	Ó	Ú	Ý	á	é	í	ó	ú	ý

2. **Letters with a grave accent**. These five vowels have corresponding characters with grave accents (pronounced to rhyme with "Slav" or "slave"):

A	E	I	O	U	a	e	i	o	u
À	È	Ì	Ò	Ù	à	è	ì	ò	ù

3. **Letters with a circumflex**. These five vowels have corresponding characters with a circumflex (or "hat"):

A	E	I	O	U	a	e	i	o	u
Â	Ê	Î	Ô	Û	â	ê	î	ô	û

4. **Letters with an umlaut**. These five vowels (plus the lowercase "y") have corresponding characters with an umlaut (or "dieresis"):

A	E	I	O	U	a	e	i	o	u
Ä	Ë	Ï	Ö	Ü	ä	ë	ï	ö	ü

5. Letters with a tilde, and other symbols. This category includes letters used in Spanish and Portuguese such as ã and ñ, and other letters and symbols that can be combined into a single macro. This macro covers most of the special characters you might want to type into a document, but you can use the macro as a guide to redefine new or additional characters as you like. To print certain characters in the following list — the bulleted numerals and the ballot box — requires a printer with the Zapf Dingbats font:

A	C	D	E	L	N	O	Q	R	S	T	X	Y
Ã	Ç	Đ	Æ	Ł	Ñ	Õ	Ø	®	§	ä	×	¥

a	c	d	e	f	l	m	n	o	q	r	s	t	x	y
ã	ç	δ	æ	ª	Ł	º	ñ	õ	ø	®	ß	ä	×	¥

!	@	#	$	&	-	_	=	+	<	>	?	/
¡	©	❏	¢	¶	–	—	å	Å	«	»	¿	Ø

1	2	3	4	5	6	7	8	9	0
①	②	③	④	⑤	⑥	⑦	⑧	⑨	⓪

I have developed five macros, shown in Figures 6-25 through 6-29 at the end of this chapter, that allow users of English-language keyboards to type any of the letters on the keyboard, then press a single key combination to convert that letter to its alternate form.

The method I recommend is to type the unaccented form of the letter on your keyboard, then follow that letter with a Ctrl+key that indicates what accent should be added to the letter. The keystrokes I use are as follows:

To add an acute accent:	Press Ctrl+´	a becomes á
To add a grave accent:	Press Ctrl+`	a becomes à
To add a circumflex:	Press Ctrl+^	a becomes â
To add an umlaut:	Press Ctrl+:	a becomes ä
For other conversions:	Press Ctrl+]	a becomes ã

By defining macros that work when you press Ctrl plus the key that most suggests the accent to be added, it is no longer necessary to remember long number combinations to insert special characters in your documents. To type "café," simply type the word on the keyboard, then press Ctrl+Apostrophe to add the accent. You no longer have to look up Alt+0233 to type an "é."

In cases where the symbol that looks like the accent falls on the shifted part of a key (for example, the circumflex is represented by the caret (^) on top of the 6 key), the following macros allow the key to add an accent whether the key is shifted or not (for example, Ctrl+6 works as well as Ctrl+Shift+6 to add ^ to a letter).

Placing these macros on key combinations such as Ctrl+Backquote (`) requires the use of undocumented Word for Windows Key Codes, which are described earlier in this chapter. These Key Codes are numbered as shown in the following macros only on U.S. keyboards, and may differ on other national-language keyboards. But since U.S. keyboards, with their limited character set, are the main problem, these macros are designed to work around that specific problem.

One final comment: in many of these macros I have deliberately sacrificed brevity in order to improve the readability and clarity of what the macro is doing. This is designed to make the macros easier for you to examine and alter to fit your own needs, if you desire. In the AddOtherAccent macro, for example, I include several tests to determine whether the macro is running inside a macro editing window or a real document. These tests only run in those cases in the macro where such a condition would make a difference. And including these tests only in those cases, and not making a single test at the beginning of the macro (which would be unnecessary in most cases), actually speeds up the macro slightly.

```
' AddAcuteAccent Macro — 1991 Brian Livingston

' This macro adds an acute accent ( ´ ) to the character before the insertion point, if appropriate.
' Place this macro on Ctrl+Apostrophe ('), Key Code 478 on U.S. keyboards.

Sub MAIN
On Error Goto BYE
If SelType() = 2 Then Goto TOOLONG            ' exit if multiple characters are selected
If Not(CharLeft(1, 1)) Then Goto NOCHAR       ' exit if macro cannot select the character to the left
Select Case Selection$()                      ' get the value of the selected character
      Case "A"
            Insert "Á"
      Case "E"
            Insert "É"
      Case "I"
            Insert "Í"
      Case "O"
            Insert "Ó"
      Case "U"
            Insert "Ú"
      Case "Y"
            Insert "Ý"
      Case "a"
            Insert "á"
      Case "e"
            Insert "é"
      Case "i"
            Insert "í"
      Case "o"
            Insert "ó"
      Case "u"
            Insert "ú"
      Case "y"
            Insert "ý"
      Case Else
      Beep 1
      Print "You can only add an acute accent ( ´ ) to the letters A, E, I, O, U, Y, a, e, i, o, u, y"
      CharRight 1
End Select
Goto BYE

TOOLONG:
      Beep 1
      Print "You can only accent a character to the left of the insertion point, not a selection."
      Goto BYE

NOCHAR:
      Beep 1
      Print "The character to be accented must be to the left of the insertion point."

BYE:
End Sub
```

Figure 6-25: The AddAcuteAccent macro.

```
' AddGraveAccent Macro — 1991 Brian Livingston

' This macro adds a grave accent ( ` ) to the character before the insertion point, if appropriate.
' Place this macro on Ctrl+Backquote ( ` ), Key Code 448 on U.S. keyboards.

Sub MAIN
On Error Goto BYE
If SelType() = 2 Then Goto TOOLONG            ' exit if multiple characters are selected
If Not(CharLeft(1, 1)) Then Goto NOCHAR       ' exit if macro cannot select the character to the left
Select Case Selection$()                      ' get the value of the selected character
      Case "A"
            Insert "À"
      Case "E"
            Insert "È"
      Case "I"
            Insert "Ì"
      Case "O"
            Insert "Ò"
      Case "U"
            Insert "Ù"
      Case "a"
            Insert "à"
      Case "e"
            Insert "è"
      Case "i"
            Insert "ì"
      Case "o"
            Insert "ò"
      Case "u"
            Insert "ù"
      Case Else
      Beep 1
      Print "You can only add a grave accent ( ` ) to the letters A, E, I, O, U, a, e, i, o, u"
      CharRight 1
End Select
Goto BYE

TOOLONG:
      Beep 1
      Print "You can only accent a character to the left of the insertion point, not a selection."
      Goto BYE

NOCHAR:
      Beep 1
      Print "The character to be accented must be to the left of the insertion point."

BYE:
End Sub
```

Figure 6-26: The AddGraveAccent macro.

```
' AddCircumflex Macro — 1991 Brian Livingston

' This macro adds a circumflex ( ^ ) to the character before the insertion point, if appropriate.
' Place this macro on Ctrl+Circumflex (Ctrl+Shift+6), Key Code 822, and Ctrl+6, Key Code 310.

Sub MAIN
On Error Goto BYE
If SelType() = 2 Then Goto TOOLONG              ' exit if multiple characters are selected
If Not(CharLeft(1, 1)) Then Goto NOCHAR         ' exit if macro cannot select the character to the left
Select Case Selection$()                        ' get the value of the selected character
      Case "A"
            Insert "Â"
      Case "E"
            Insert "Ê"
      Case "I"
            Insert "Î"
      Case "O"
            Insert "Ô"
      Case "U"
            Insert "Û"
      Case "a"
            Insert "â"
      Case "e"
            Insert "ê"
      Case "i"
            Insert "î"
      Case "o"
            Insert "ô"
      Case "u"
            Insert "û"
      Case Else
      Beep 1
      Print "You can only add a circumflex ( ^ ) to the letters A, E, I, O, U, a, e, i, o, u"
      CharRight 1
End Select
Goto BYE

TOOLONG:
      Beep 1
      Print "You can only accent a character to the left of the insertion point, not a selection."
      Goto BYE

NOCHAR:
      Beep 1
      Print "The character to be accented must be to the left of the insertion point."

BYE:
End Sub
```

Figure 6-27: The AddCircumflex macro.

```
' AddUmlaut Macro — 1991 Brian Livingston

' This macro adds an umlaut ( ¨ ) to the character before the insertion point, if appropriate. Place this
' macro on Ctrl+Semicolon (;), Key Code 442, and Ctrl+Colon (:), Key Code 954 on U.S. keyboards.

Sub MAIN
On Error Goto BYE
If SelType() = 2 Then Goto TOOLONG            ' exit if multiple characters are selected
If Not(CharLeft(1, 1)) Then Goto NOCHAR       ' exit if macro cannot select the character to the left
Select Case Selection$()                       ' get the value of the selected character
      Case "A"
            Insert "Ä"
      Case "E"
            Insert "Ë"
      Case "I"
            Insert "Ï"
      Case "O"
            Insert "Ö"
      Case "U"
            Insert "Ü"
      Case "a"
            Insert "ä"
      Case "e"
            Insert "ë"
      Case "i"
            Insert "ï"
      Case "o"
            Insert "ö"
      Case "u"
            Insert "ü"
      Case "y"
            Insert "ÿ"
      Case Else
      Beep 1
      Print "You can only add an umlaut ( ¨ ) to the letters A, E, I, O, U, a, e, i, o, u, y"
      CharRight 1
End Select
Goto BYE

TOOLONG:
      Beep 1
      Print "You can only accent a character to the left of the insertion point, not a selection."
      Goto BYE

NOCHAR:
      Beep 1
      Print "The character to be accented must be to the left of the insertion point."

BYE:
End Sub
```

Figure 6-28: The AddUmlaut macro.

```
' AddOtherAccent Macro — 1991 Brian Livingston

' This macro transforms the character before the insertion point into a misc. alternate
' form. Place this macro on Ctrl+Right-Bracket ( ] ), Key Code 477, and on
' Ctrl+Tilde ( ~ ), same as Ctrl+Shift+Backquote, Key Code 960 on U.S. keyboards.

Sub MAIN
On Error Goto BYE
If SelType() = 2 Then Goto TOOLONG          ' exit if multiple characters are selected
If Not(CharLeft(1, 1)) Then Goto NOCHAR     ' exit if macro cannot select the character to the left
Select Case Selection$()                     ' get the value of the selected character
    Case "A"
        Insert "Ã"                           ' Portuguese uppercase A-tilde
    Case "C"
        Insert "Ç"                           ' Uppercase C-cedilla
    Case "D"
        Insert "Ð"                           ' Icelandic uppercase Eth
    Case "E"
        Insert "Æ"                           ' uppercase AE ligature
    Case "L"
        Insert "£"                           ' U.K. Pound Sterling currency mark
    Case "N"
        Insert "Ñ"                           ' Spanish uppercase Nya
    Case "O"
        Insert "Õ"                           ' Portuguese uppercase O-tilde
    Case "Q"
        Insert "Ø"                           ' Scandinavian uppercase O-slash
    Case "R"
    If InStr(WindowName$(), ": ") = 0 Then   ' test for macro editing window
        Let usersize = FontSize()            ' save current size in order to restore it
        Let userscript = SuperScript()       ' save superscript state
        Insert "®"                           ' Registered trademark symbol
        CharLeft 1, 1                        ' select the symbol
        ShrinkFont                           ' reduce it to the next available size
        ShrinkFont                           ' reduce it again
        FormatCharacter .Position = 5        ' superscript it 2.5 points (5 half-points)
        CharRight 1, 0                       ' move insertion point back to start
        FontSize usersize                    ' restore size previously in use
        SuperScript userscript               ' restore superscript state
    Else
            Goto INMACRO                     ' cannot use Format commands in macro window
    End If
    Case "S"
        Insert "§"                           ' Legal section symbol
```

(continued next page)

Figure 6-29: The AddOtherAccent macro. If your printer does not have the Zapf Dingbats font, you must comment out those Case statements that change to the Dingbats character set, specifically Case "0" through "9," and Case "#".

```
Case "T"
     If InStr(WindowName$(), ": ") = 0 Then' test for macro editing window
          Let userface$ = Font$()              ' save current typeface in order to restore it
     Font "Symbol"
     Insert Chr$(228)                          ' Trademark symbol
     Font userface$
     Else
               Goto INMACRO                    ' cannot use Format commands in macro window
     End If
Case "X"
     Insert "×"                                ' Math multiplication symbol
Case "Y"
     Insert "¥"                                ' Japanese Yen currency mark
Case "a"
     Insert "ã"                                ' Portuguese lowercase a-tilde
Case "c"
     Insert "ç"                                ' lowercase cedilla
Case "e"
     Insert "æ"                                ' lowercase ae ligature
Case "f"
     Insert "ª"                                ' Portuguese ordinal feminine
Case "l"
     Insert "£"                                ' U.K. Pound currency mark
Case "m"
     Insert "º"                                ' Portuguese ordinal masculine
Case "n"
     Insert "ñ"                                ' Spanish lowercase nya
Case "o"
     Insert "õ"                                ' Portuguese lowercase o-tilde
Case "q"
     Insert "ø"                                ' Scandinavian lowercase o-slash
Case "r"
If InStr(WindowName$(), ": ") = 0 Then        ' test for macro editing window
     Let usersize = FontSize()                ' save current size in order to restore it
     Let userscript = SuperScript()           ' save superscript state
     Insert "®"                               ' Registered trademark symbol
     CharLeft 1, 1                            ' select the symbol
     ShrinkFont                               ' reduce it to the next available size
     ShrinkFont                               ' reduce it again
     FormatCharacter .Position = 5            ' superscript it 2.5 points (5 half-points)
     CharRight 1, 0                           ' move insertion point back to start
     FontSize usersize                        ' restore size previously in use
     SuperScript userscript                   ' restore superscript state
     Else
```

(continued next page)

```
            Goto INMACRO                      ' cannot use Format commands in macro window
        End If
Case "s"
    Insert "ß"                                ' German lowercase double-s
Case "t"
If InStr(WindowName$(), ": ") = 0 Then        ' test for macro editing window
    Let userface$ = Font$()                   ' save current typeface in order to restore it
    Font "Symbol"
    Insert Chr$(228)                          ' Trademark symbol
    Font userface$
    Else
            Goto INMACRO                      ' cannot use Font commands in macro window
        End If
Case "x"
    Insert "×"                                ' Math multiplication symbol
Case "y"
    Insert "¥"                                ' Japanese Yen currency mark
Case "1"
If InStr(WindowName$(), ": ") = 0 Then        ' test for macro editing window
    Let userface$ = Font$()                   ' save current typeface in order to restore it
    Font "ZapfDingbats"
    Insert Chr$(192)                          ' Circled numeral 1
    Font userface$
    Else
            Goto INMACRO                      ' cannot use Font commands in macro window
        End If
Case "2"
If InStr(WindowName$(), ": ") = 0 Then        ' test for macro editing window
    Let userface$ = Font$()                   ' save current typeface in order to restore it
    Font "ZapfDingbats"
    Insert Chr$(193)                          ' Circled numeral 2
    Font userface$
    Else
            Goto INMACRO                      ' cannot use Font commands in macro window
        End If
Case "3"
If InStr(WindowName$(), ": ") = 0 Then        ' test for macro editing window
    Let userface$ = Font$()                   ' save current typeface in order to restore it
    Font "ZapfDingbats"
    Insert Chr$(194)                          ' Circled numeral 3
    Font userface$
    Else
            Goto INMACRO                      ' cannot use Font commands in macro window
        End If
Case "4"
If InStr(WindowName$(), ": ") = 0 Then        ' test for macro editing window
```

(continued next page)

```
        Let userface$ = Font$()              ' save current typeface in order to restore it
        Font "ZapfDingbats"
        Insert Chr$(195)                     ' Circled numeral 4
        Font userface$
        Else
            Goto INMACRO                     ' cannot use Font commands in macro window
        End If
Case "5"
If InStr(WindowName$(), ": ") = 0 Then       ' test for macro editing window
        Let userface$ = Font$()              ' save current typeface in order to restore it
        Font "ZapfDingbats"
        Insert Chr$(196)                     ' Circled numeral 5
        Font userface$
        Else
            Goto INMACRO                     ' cannot use Font commands in macro window
        End If
Case "6"
If InStr(WindowName$(), ": ") = 0 Then       ' test for macro editing window
        Let userface$ = Font$()              ' save current typeface in order to restore it
        Font "ZapfDingbats"
        Insert Chr$(197)                     ' Circled numeral 6
        Font userface$
        Else
            Goto INMACRO                     ' cannot use Font commands in macro window
        End If
Case "7"
If InStr(WindowName$(), ": ") = 0 Then       ' test for macro editing window
        Let userface$ = Font$()              ' save current typeface in order to restore it
        Font "ZapfDingbats"
        Insert Chr$(198)                     ' Circled numeral 7
        Font userface$
        Else
            Goto INMACRO                     ' cannot use Font commands in macro window
        End If
Case "8"
If InStr(WindowName$(), ": ") = 0 Then       ' test for macro editing window
        Let userface$ = Font$()              ' save current typeface in order to restore it
        Font "ZapfDingbats"
        Insert Chr$(199)                     ' Circled numeral 8
        Font userface$
        Else
            Goto INMACRO                     ' cannot use Font commands in macro window
        End If
Case "9"
If InStr(WindowName$(), ": ") = 0 Then       ' test for macro editing window
```

(continued next page)

```
            Let userface$ = Font$()              ' save current typeface in order to restore it
            Font "ZapfDingbats"
            Insert Chr$(200)                     ' Circled numeral 9
            Font userface$
            Else
                    Goto INMACRO                 ' cannot use Font commands in macro window
            End If
    Case "0"
    If InStr(WindowName$(), ": ") = 0 Then       ' test for macro editing window
            Let userface$ = Font$()              ' save current typeface in order to restore it
            Font "ZapfDingbats"
            Insert Chr$(201)                     ' Circled numeral 10
            Font userface$
            Else
                    Goto INMACRO                 ' cannot use Font commands in macro window
            End If
    Case "!"
            Insert "¡"                           ' Spanish exclamation point
    Case "@"
            Insert "©"                           ' Copyright symbol
    Case "#"
    If InStr(WindowName$(), ": ") = 0 Then       ' test for macro editing window
            Let userface$ = Font$()              ' save current typeface in order to restore it
            Font "ZapfDingbats"
            Insert Chr$(111)                     ' open shaded ballot box
            Font userface$
            Else
                    Goto INMACRO                 ' cannot use Font commands in macro window
            End If
    Case "$"
            Insert "¢"                           ' Cent sign
    Case "&"
            Insert "¶"                           ' Legal paragraph mark
    Case "-"
            Insert "–"                           ' En dash
    Case "_"
            Insert "—"                           ' Em dash
    Case "="
            Insert "å"                           ' Scandinavian lowercase a-ring
    Case "+"
            Insert "Å"                           ' Scandinavian uppercase A-ring
    Case "<"
            Insert "«"                           ' European open quote mark
    Case ">"
            Insert "»"                           ' European close quote mark
```

(continued next page)

```
            Case "?"
                    Insert "¿"                          ' Spanish question mark
            Case "/"
                    REM InsertFieldChars does not replace the selection; a space is necessary
                    Insert " "                          ' insert space character
                    CharLeft(1, 1)                      ' select the space character
                    InsertFieldChars                    ' prepare field for overstrike equation
                    Insert "eq"                         ' insert first part of equation
                    CharRight(1, 0)                     ' move past space character
                    Insert "\o(0,/)"                    ' produces numeral 0 overstruck with slash
                    CharRight 1, 0
            Case Else
            Beep 1
            Print \
    "Must be A C D E L N O P Q R S T X Y (upper or lower), f m ! @ # $ & - _ = + < > / ?, or 0-9"
            CharRight 1
    End Select
    Goto BYE

    TOOLONG:
            Beep 1
            Print "You can only accent a character to the left of the insertion point, not a selection."
            Goto BYE

    NOCHAR:
            Beep 1
            Print "The character to be accented must be to the left of the insertion point."
            Goto BYE

    INMACRO:
            Beep 1
            Print "This character cannot be accented or transformed in a macro editing window."
            CharRight 1

    BYE:
    End Sub
```

Summary

In this chapter, I've covered the following topics:

▶ How you can create and edit your own macros.

▶ How to control Winword's behavior when it starts, opens files, and exits.

▶ How to change the dialog boxes that appear when you click File Open and other commands from the main menu.

▶ How to add to, and move items on, the menu itself.

▶ How to control the meaning of each key and key combination on your keyboard, even if these combinations are undocumented.

▶ How to run Winword on a network in such a way that word processing users have control over the styles in their templates, while programming staff members retain the ability to customize global macros in users' Normal template.

▶ How to access special characters in Windows' ANSI characters set from U.S. keyboards that don't have corresponding keys.

The information in this chapter only scratches the surface of Winword's customization capabilities. Far more information is available in the *Microsoft Word for Windows and OS/2 Technical Reference,* but this chapter has described many features and benefits of Winword's macro language that are not found in such reference books. As more and more Windows applications follow the lead that has been set by Winword, Excel, and Amí, the possibilities for using Windows applications as programming front-ends to other tasks will truly be limited only by your imagination.

SECTION
B

EXPLOITING YOUR HARDWARE

Chapter 7
Computers

In this chapter. . .

Topics I'll cover include:

▶ What "100% compatibility" means.

▶ The three classes of PCs that Windows supports, and what capabilities you can take advantage of within each class.

▶ Differences in various versions of DOS that can affect the compatibility of your machine and its performance under Windows.

▶ Variations in the basic input/output system (BIOS) of particular computer manufacturers, and how these can affect the functioning of Windows on your system.

▶ The eight incompatible methods PCs use to access extended memory, and how Windows' HIMEM.SYS memory manager adjusts to these methods.

▶ The meaning of the mysterious "asterisks" on Microsoft's Windows Hardware Compatibility List.

▶ Specific anomalies that you may encounter on brand-name computer systems, arranged alphabetically by vendor name.

Windows reveals the strengths and weaknesses of your personal computer more than almost any other program. To get the best possible performance in a graphical environment (which requires much more information to be written to the screen than a character-based program does), Windows takes direct control of devices such as video graphics adapters, keyboard controllers, and other components in your computer system. Instead of using slower means of driving these components, Windows writes directly to these devices, assuming that they follow a certain method of handling this data. If your computer system uses a different method than the one Windows expects to find, you must either upgrade your system for compatibility or reconfigure Windows using one of over 125 settings in the SYSTEM.INI file that controls how Windows uses your hardware.

This chapter explains, in as clear and complete detail as possible, ways to achieve compatibility with Windows on a wide variety of specific and brand-name PC configurations.

Windows Compatibility

The Search for 100% Compatibility

Myths and Realities

From the beginning of the IBM PC standard, which began in 1981 when the market success of the IBM PC created a single dominant yardstick that various other manufacturers had to comply with, personal computers have been sold with the claim of "100% IBM compatibility."

However, it has been very difficult to test and certify that a machine from vendor A is in fact 100 percent compatible with one from vendor B. You might think it would be possible to simply test everything that a program can do on both machines. But the number of possible routines that a software program can perform on a PC makes this impossible. There just is not enough time to try billions or trillions of algorithms to see which ones work and which ones don't.

Instead, the compatibility of most PCs (including IBM) has been tested by running the most popular software packages of the day. If all the packages worked, the machine was declared compatible.

Years ago, running Microsoft Flight Simulator (which writes directly to video memory and plays other tricks) was considered the stiffest test of an unknown PC's compatibility. Today, Windows 3.*x* pushes computers even harder, with its use of the "protected" modes of 286 and 386 hardware, which few popular programs before Windows ever did. Microsoft may actually be performing a service for the entire PC industry by disseminating complete personal-computer compatibility suites disguised as airplane games and cute graphical environments.

What About IBM Compatibility?

Purchasing only IBM-brand PC hardware and software has been no guarantee of compatibility through the years, contrary to popular belief. Successive models of IBM PCs have suffered numerous bouts of incompatibility with each other and with third-party hardware that previously established industry standards.

Examples of incompatibilities in early IBMs abound, such as a bug in BIOS implementations of early IBM ATs that causes them to lose a day when left running over a weekend (a common occurrence in companies that must run their equipment 24 hours a day). And the incompatibilities between newer IBM memory boards and those that had become standard in the PC industry became clear only with the disastrous introduction of DOS 4.0, the first version of DOS written by IBM rather than Microsoft. DOS 4.0 worked only with IBM-brand expanded memory boards, not those from much more common brands such as AST and Intel. (Microsoft later accommodated both types of boards by releasing MS-DOS 4.01.)

With the introduction of its Micro Channel Architecture in 1987, differences among IBM models became far more pronounced — aside from even the obvious incompatibilities between MCA boards and boards that had been developed for the original Industry Standard Architecture (ISA).

Differences among the 16-MHz, 20-MHz, and 25-MHz versions of the IBM PS/2 Model 70 (a 386-based desktop machine) cause these systems to be compatible with certain MCA adapters and not with others. The Intel AboveBoard/ MCA, for instance, is one of the most popular ways to add RAM to PS/2s. But due to the different timing of memory-caching features in the PS/2 Model 70 at 25 MHz, the original Intel AboveBoard/MCA won't work in these machines. Neither will the Micro Channel adapter for the Bernoulli Box, a popular removable disk drive by the Iomega Corp. Both the AboveBoard and the Bernoulli adapters were redesigned by their respective companies to accommodate incompatibilities introduced to the MCA specification by the Model 70 386/25.

Incompatibilities in the BIOS implementation in IBM's PS/2 Model 55SX (a 16 MHz 386SX machine) trip up programs that utilize extended memory, such as Lotus 1-2-3 Release 3.0. Although these programs work well on other PS/2s, on the Model 55SX their use of extended memory shifts the keyboard into an all-capitals state. Pressing the slash (/) key to access the menu in 1-2-3 just produces a question mark, for example. (Lotus and other companies have produced software patches that allow their software to accommodate the differences in these PS/2s.)

More recently, developers of MCA adapters that utilize the "bus master" features of Micro Channel machines found that several releases of IBM's PS/2 Model 80 don't support bus-mastering at all. (Bus master boards, such as network adapter boards, can transfer data by communicating directly to other devices without slowing down the CPU.) These machines, purchased by thousands of companies and promoted by IBM from 1987 on for their implementation of advanced MCA features, actually require the replacement of their motherboards to make them compatible with bus-mastering.

IBM acknowledged this problem when the Model 80s would not run IBM's new 16/4 Token-Ring Adapter, introduced in 1991. But the problem also affects IBM's Wizard coprocessor board, Northern Telecom's Lanstar/MC network adapter, Proteon's Pronet-4 Busmaster, Racore's 4X16 Token-Ring Adapter, and several other boards — all of which adhere to the MCA spec. The incompatibility only affects Model 80s that run at 20 MHz. If you use one of these machines, request IBM's Engineering Change Authorization (ECA) 048-8580 (12/90), which describes the problem and its fix.

Since the above incompatibilities are generic to IBM machines (and affect many applications, not just Windows) I have not included these anomalies under "IBM" in the alphabetical section later in this chapter on vendor-specific configurations for Windows. I mention these problems here simply to illustrate that even IBM cannot perfectly test its computers for 100 percent compatibility with its own specifications. It is too much to expect that other manufacturers can do a better job of testing their own PCs for the thousands of little things that future versions of programs like Windows can try to do. Constant evolution toward better and better compatibility is all that can be hoped for.

What to Do to Achieve Compatibility

As one of Microsoft's Windows development managers has put it, "In a nutshell, compatibility is a myth." The development of Windows revealed so many differences between PCs in the market (especially after IBM quit marketing the classic PC/AT as a common denominator for the industry) that Windows simply had to be able to accommodate itself to all those differences.

This is what led to the 125-odd settings in Windows' SYSTEM.INI file, which adjusts Windows for various hardware quirks, and the eight different modes that HIMEM.SYS uses to access extended memory on a variety of machines (as described later in this chapter).

What is important is that Windows does a remarkable job of adapting itself to the computer hardware you try to run it on, thanks to the flexibility the Windows development team built into its code. To save yourself a lot of time (especially if you are responsible for more than one computer that uses Windows), it's best not to pretend that these differences in hardware don't exist, but to acknowledge them and learn the basic rules that govern these systems.

Understanding these rules requires a description of the three classes of PCs that Windows recognizes, the variations in OEM versions of DOS, the differences in the BIOS implementations that various computer manufacturers use, and the variations in extended memory implementations that HIMEM.SYS adapts itself to.

The Three Classes of PCs

It may seem obvious that Windows runs differently on three classes of PCs — XT-class systems (with 8088 and 8086 processors), AT-class systems (with 80286 processors), and 80386-class systems and higher (386, 486, 586, etc.). But there are some not-so-obvious implications to these various classes.

386-Class Systems

Systems based on 386 or higher processors (including the 386SX chip) can run Windows in all of its three *modes* — real mode, standard mode, and 386 enhanced mode. The 386 enhanced mode, by its very description, sounds like it would be the highest-performance mode. Many people are unaware, however, that Windows applications (running on a 386) almost always run faster when Windows is in standard mode than in enhanced mode.

The difference in performance ranges from slight to dramatic. I have timed some Windows processes (memory-to-memory transfers) that took more than twice as long in enhanced mode as in standard mode, on a 16-MHz 386DX. Since Windows applications use many types of processes, not just the same process over and over (as a benchmark test does), actual apps tend to mask this difference, and typically run only 10 to 15 percent slower in enhanced mode than in standard mode. But some applications, of which Asymetrix Toolbook is one, run up to 50 percent faster in standard mode.

The only rule is that you must try your own applications to judge the difference for yourself. You might time the following series of tasks, once in standard mode, then in enhanced mode, to obtain results for yourself. (Reboot the computer between tests for "clean" comparisons.) Start your word processor and open a document that contains many type styles and sizes. Run the Print Preview function. Close the document and open it again, to measure the effect of disk caching. Start your spreadsheet and load your largest file. Recalculate the formulas. Close and open the file again to measure disk caching. Generate a chart from some of the figures. Open Paintbrush and load Windows' CHESS.BMP graphic (or some other large graphic file you have). Record the time necessary to View Zoom In, then to View Zoom Out. Set Paintbrush's Options Image Attributes to the size of a 7" × 10" graphic on a laser printer (2100 pixels wide by 3000 pixels high), then record the time necessary to initialize this huge memory object when you click File New.

The 386 enhanced mode does provide a number of 386-specific features that may make this mode worthwhile to you, despite its slight overhead.

In enhanced mode, DOS applications that you start under Windows continue to run, even when they are in the background. (Standard mode halts such background DOS apps until you return them to the foreground.) You can switch a character-based DOS application from running full-screen to running in a small portion of the Windows screen area by pressing Alt+Enter. You can display two running DOS applications side by side in partial screen areas this way (if you have enough screen area).

On a 386, the Windows Clipboard gains the capability to send to DOS apps both text and bitmap graphics; in other modes, only text can be sent. And, in 386 enhanced mode, you are less likely to totally run out of memory for applications, since Windows can utilize hard disk space in addition to RAM (although this is much slower than real RAM).

Additionally, 386 enhanced mode may read from and write to hard disks somewhat faster than standard mode. Enhanced mode can take advantage of faster switching between protected mode and real mode, which is necessary to access hard drives under DOS. (This effect may be offset by SmartDrive's slower performance in enhanced mode, which is described in Chapter 8. Test your particular configuration to measure the net result.)

You must weigh the benefits of 386 enhanced mode, versus the improved performance of standard mode, based on the tasks you expect Windows to carry out.

286-Class Systems

IBM ATs and other machines with 80286 processors are limited to running Windows in its real and standard modes. As we have just seen, standard mode usually provides slightly better performance to Windows applications than enhanced mode. But the slower speed of 286 machines in general usually makes them less desirable for Windows' use than full 386-based systems.

XT-Class Systems

XT-class systems may be equipped with Intel's 8088 (the heart of the original IBM PC-1, with 16-bit processing power but a data path that can address only 8-bit memory) or 8086 (same as the 8088 but can address 16-bit memory). Additionally, some XT-class computers utilize Intel-compatible chips from NEC, the V20 and V30 (which correspond with the 8088 and 8086, respectively).

The slowness of XTs makes them a poor platform on which to run Windows. About the only purpose for running Windows on an XT would be to display a graphic or chart that changes slowly or not at all during the day (the high and low of today's stock averages, for example).

But even this display would be limited. Most people don't realize it, but it is not possible to display color on an XT-class system running Windows. Windows' EGA and VGA color drivers use 16-bit instructions for performance reasons, and these instructions require a 286 processor or better. If you configure Windows Setup for these drivers on an XT, the machine hangs as soon as Windows switches to graphics mode.

On an XT, you must run Windows Setup configured for "CGA" (which is really CGA's black-and-white 640×200 mode), "EGA black-and-white," "EGA monochrome," or "VGA with monochrome display." (You must, of course, actually have the hardware to display your selected mode, such as a VGA monochrome monitor.) In Windows Setup, the two EGA options indicate "(286 only)," which means these choices cannot be run in 386 enhanced mode, not that they won't run on an XT.

386 PCs with 2MB Also Require 5MB Disk Space

Although the minimum Microsoft-recommended system to run Windows is described as a 286-based PC with 1 megabyte of memory, this configuration is an *absolute* minimum that may not be adequate to complete some Windows operations. This is particularly true in the case of a 386 running Windows' 386 enhanced mode, in which Windows must load memory management software and establish temporary space on a hard disk to enable its virtual memory scheme.

A minimum of 2MB of RAM is required to run 386 mode. Even then, Microsoft has written in a technical support memo that such PCs require an additional 5 to 6MB of free hard disk space to function reliably. Without this hard disk space, functions such as print jobs may abort due to "out-of-swap-space" problems, as Windows attempts to manage print jobs by saving all or part of them to disk. Additionally, DOS applications started under Windows may report that they lack enough RAM to load or continue running. This is especially the case running applications (both Windows-based and DOS-based) that open temporary files while editing, sorting, or saving documents.

Once Windows runs out of both RAM and free disk space available for swapping, it may become impossible to open additional DOS sessions without closing others. Additionally, out-of-memory conditions sometimes cause applications to become confused or freeze (there are a large number of conditions that can cause out-of-memory errors). The only solution, if this problem affects your system, is to free up disk space that Windows can use as extra, swappable memory, or add RAM (up to at least 4MB of RAM) to increase the memory Windows can allocate to applications.

Running the Right DOS

Use the DOS Provided by Your Hardware Vendor

One essential step in ensuring compatibility with Windows is to make sure that your PC is running the version of DOS that is specified by the manufacturer of your computer.

For IBM PCs and PS/2s, this version of DOS is referred to as PC-DOS and is sold through IBM dealers. Versions of DOS provided by Microsoft to other computer manufacturers are referred to collectively as MS-DOS, and are sometimes called "generic" DOS. But all MS-DOS implementations do not operate flawlessly on all PCs.

In particular, it is important to run the DOS that is sold by the manufacturer of your PC (Compaq, Hewlett-Packard, AT&T, Olivetti, and Zenith, to name a few). These particular vendors have built performance enhancements into their computers that may require features in, say, HP-DOS. In addition, some PCs, such as those from Advanced Logic Research (ALR) and others, are designed to work with genuine IBM PC-DOS and you should obtain PC-DOS, not MS-DOS, from these vendors.

Perhaps you thought that all DOS versions, such as 3.3, were alike? Compaq DOS 3.31, developed by Compaq in cooperation with Microsoft to access hard disk partitions larger than 32MB, is up to revision G (starting from A), and Compaq DOS 4.01 is up to revision D.

BIOS Implementations

The Primary BIOS Sources

After the class of your computer system (XT, AT, or 386 and higher), the most important consideration when running Windows is the compatibility of its BIOS implementation.

Every PC includes a ROM BIOS — Read-Only Memory chips that contain the Basic Input/Output System for that specific computer. The read-only memory contains instructions that application programs can depend on to carry out certain functions, no matter how the specific hardware of that machine may be designed. For example, programs commonly request that the BIOS send information out the first parallel printer port, or write information to the first hard drive in a system. The program does not need to know the different characteristics of every computer manufacturer's parallel port or every disk manufacturer's drives. The BIOS is capable of translating the program's requests into commands for the specific devices used in that particular computer.

Since compatibility with IBM PCs and PS/2s is an important goal for other computer manufacturers, the quality of the BIOS implementation is an essential element of their overall development strategy. It is illegal for these manufacturers to simply duplicate the copyrighted programs in an IBM ROM BIOS. And IBM does not license its BIOS to PC-compatible makers. So the currently available ROM BIOS implementations from non-IBM sources were developed by engineers who knew what the BIOS was supposed to do, but had no access to the actual code that IBM had written. This is called working in a "clean room" environment.

Many of the oldest and largest PC-compatible manufacturers, such as Compaq, Hewlett-Packard, and Zenith, developed compatible BIOSs using their own in-house resources. Other vendors, including Dell, Everex, NEC, Northgate, Toshiba, and Texas Instruments, licensed BIOS implementations written by companies that specialized in clean-room development. The largest of these BIOS-chip sources are Phoenix Technologies, American Megatrends Inc. (AMI), and Award Software. A table listing computer manufacturers using BIOS chips from these and other sources is shown in Figure 7-1.

This chart cannot be a complete guide to BIOS implementations in different computer manufacturers' systems, because these manufacturers may have used BIOSs from two or more companies over the years. In addition, there is a great deal of overlap and cross-fertilization among BIOS implementations. Whereas Wang Computer is shown in the chart as developing its own BIOS, for instance, recent Wang PCs contain BIOSs that are actually licensed derivations of Phoenix BIOS revision 1.10M3.

As we have seen earlier in this chapter, it is difficult to ensure that one PC is 100 percent compatible with another, and BIOS implementations have definitely evolved toward greater compatibility over the years. As programs

AMI
Acma
AGI
Amax
American Research Corp.
Arche
Argo
Arima Computer Corp.
Automated Computer Technology
Bitwise
Blackship
Blue Star
Boss
Brain Computer Corp.
BSI
Bus Computer Systems Inc.
C2 Microsystems
CAF Technology Inc.
Citus
Clone Computers
Club American
CompuAdd
Computer Market Place Inc.
Destiny
Diamond
Dolch
Dyna
Dynamic Decisions
EasyData
Eltech
EPS Technologies Inc.
Everest Computer Corp.
Everex
Express Micro
Fora
Fortron
Fountain
Gateway
HiQuality Systems Inc.
Hyundai
II Blue Max
Insight Distribution Network
Micro Express
Micro Telesis
Mitsuba
MultiMicro Inc.
National Micro Systems
Network PC
Northgate
Novacor
Panther
PC Craft
PC Pros
Peregrine
Polywell
Premier
Proteus
Quill Corp.

SAI
Standard Microsystems
Systems Integration Associates
Tangent
Televideo
Transource
Tri-Star
Wedge

Award
Acma
Amax
Blackship
C2 Saber
Computer Market Place Inc.
Core International
CSR Inc.
Destiny
Dyna Micro
FastMicro
Hi-Q
Memorex Telex
Netis
Panther
Precision
Psion
Toshiba
Veridata
Wedge
Zeos

Chips & Technology
Reply Corp.

DTK (Datatech)
Computer Market Place Inc.
Tenex
Thoroughbred
Treasure Chest

Microid Research
PC Brand

Phoenix
Advanced Logic Research
Apricot
AT&T
Bitwise Designs Inc.
Blackship
Bus
Commax
CompuAdd
Core International
CSS Laboratories
Data General
Dataworld
Dell
Diamond

Digital Equipment Corp.
Dyna
Fortron
Gateway
Grid
Hertz
Master Computer Inc.
Matrix
Memorex Telex
Micro Express
Micro Telesis
Mitac
Mitsuba
National Micro Systems Inc.
NCR
NEC
Ogivar
Pan United Corp.
Panther
Precision Systems Group Inc.
Premier
SAI
Sanyo
Sharp
Swan
Syntrex
Tandy
Tangent
Tatung
Texas Instruments
Texas Micro Systems Inc.
Transource Computers
Twinhead
Unisys
USA Flex
Zeos

Quadtel
Austin
Coté Computers
Impulse
ITC

A ROM of One's Own
Acer
AST
Compaq
DTK
Epson
Hewlett-Packard
IBM
NCR
Olivetti
Osicom
Tandon
Tandy
Toshiba
Wang
Zenith

Figure 7-1: ROM BIOS sources for computer manufacturers. This is not a complete list by any means, but includes a sampling of the BIOS implementations used in 286, 386, and 486 PCs released during the last year. Note that some manufacturers used BIOS chips from more than one source for various PC models in their line.

have emerged with greater and greater capabilities, BIOS developers have had to ensure that these programs will run the same way on all PCs. This goal has been a moving target. Microsoft technical support estimates that as many as 50 percent of the 286-class computers sold before 1988 will not run Windows in standard mode without upgrades to their BIOS. Before that time, PCs for the most part did not have to deal with programs that addressed extended memory and switched rapidly between real mode and protected mode. There were few, if any, such programs to test these PCs against.

The pace of technology has accelerated so rapidly that BIOS implementations of only a few years ago now seem almost unbelievably limited. The first AT-class BIOS introduced by IBM was dated January 10, 1984. It drove the IBM AT at a 6-MHz rate and supported only an 84-key keyboard and a 20MB hard disk. Not until almost two years later, in a BIOS dated November 15, 1985, did IBM introduce support for 101-key keyboards and 30MB hard disks.

Unfortunately, purchasing a PC from IBM did not ensure future upgradability and customer support. IBM stopped supplying replacement BIOS chips for their PC and XT systems long before buyers of these machines stopped needing upgrades. These upgrades are particularly important in cases where the original BIOS does not support such peripherals as 3.5" floppy drives, 101-key keyboards, and common hard drive types. If you need an upgraded BIOS for IBM-brand computers, contact Komputerwerk of Virginia Inc., 8133 Forest Hill Avenue, Richmond, VA 23235, 804-320-8835.

In most cases, upgrading a BIOS implementation is as simple as removing and replacing a few chips located in sockets on the PC motherboard. Finding the correct replacement BIOS for your particular computer can be frustrating, however. Microsoft recently commissioned a study of PC upgrades and found that only about 10 percent of PC owners who obtained a version of DOS when they originally bought their computer had ever upgraded that version — and upgrading the BIOS chip is certainly even less common. Many telephone-support personnel in PC companies are not familiar with the differences among BIOS revisions. And variations that cause incompatibilities between different BIOSs are one of the most closely held secrets of the PC industry.

To shed some light on this subject, I have included the following descriptions of BIOS upgrades required to bring older PCs into compatibility with Windows 3.*x*. These comments, which apply to AMI, Award, and Phoenix BIOS implementations, are in addition to the specific descriptions that apply to PC vendors listed in alphabetical order in the Computer Anomalies section later in this chapter.

If you find that you need a BIOS upgrade, and it isn't possible to obtain it directly from the manufacturer of your PC, at least one source carries chips from all of the "big three" (AMI, Award, and Phoenix). This company is called Upgrades, Etc., and may be contacted at 15822 N.E. 165th St., Woodinville, WA 98072, 800-541-1943, or by fax at 206-881-8294. Other sources for BIOS upgrades are described in the following discussion of these three companies' chips.

AMI (American Megatrends, Inc.)

AMI BIOS implementations are used in popular direct-sales PCs from Hyundai, Everex, Northgate, and many others. While the latest revisions of this BIOS seem to work well under Windows, the company recommends that you use an AMI BIOS dated no earlier than September 1988. At this writing, the currently available 386-class implementation has a 1990 date.

AMI also states that you should use a keyboard controller revision referred to as "K8" when using a computer with an AMI-designed motherboard. For non-AMI motherboards with an AMI BIOS, you can use version K8 or K0 (K zero).

To find the version of AMI BIOS and keyboard controller implementation you have, write down the numbers that appear when you turn your PC off and back on. You should see a 16-digit number that has the following form:

abbb-nnn-mmddyy-Kx

The "mmddyy" represents the month, day and year of the BIOS revision. The "x" is the keyboard controller version.

If you do not use a recommended version of the AMI BIOS, Windows may hang your PC when you run Setup, or random keystrokes and other problems may occur when you use the keyboard in Windows.

Furthermore, AMI BIOS implementations dated prior to December 15, 1989 may have difficulties with IDE or ESDI hard drives (these drive types are described in Chapter 8). When running Windows in enhanced mode, these drives (such as Conner IDE drives) may momentarily "freeze" Windows for a period lasting five to ten seconds. This is long enough to abort Windows or non-Windows applications that may be running.

In addition to Upgrades, Etc. (listed earlier in this section), you may obtain AMI BIOS revisions by contacting AMI at 1346 Oakbrook Drive, Suite 120, Norcross, GA 30093, 404-263-8181 if you cannot order one directly from your computer maker.

Award Software

An Award BIOS is used in popular desktop and laptop computers by such names as Memorex Telex, Toshiba, Zeos, and others. Award BIOS implementations of 3.1 and higher have been fully tested and are compatible with Windows 3.*x*. If you have a lower revision number and it is working under Windows 3.*x,* there is no need to replace it. Award has tested revisions 3.04c, 3.04d, and 3.05 and found them to work properly.

Because Award uses the "hundredths place" in their decimal version number to indicate machine-specific revisions for particular PC makers, note that an Award BIOS numbered "3.15," for example, is not necessarily improved over one numbered "3.14." The 5 and 4 in these examples simply refer to BIOS chips used by different PC manufacturers.

Sources for upgraded Award BIOSs include:

In the western U.S. — Pinnacle Sales, 408-249-7400.

In the central U.S. — Komputerwerk, Inc., 851 Parkview Boulevard, Pittsburgh, PA 15215, 800-423-3400 or 412-782-0384.

In the eastern U.S. — Northeast Computers, 508-686-6468. Also, Unicore Software, 599 Canal St., Lawrence, MA 01840, 800-800-2467 or by fax at 508-683-1630.

If you cannot obtain an upgraded BIOS from the maker of your computer or one of the above sources, contact Award Software at 130 Knowles Dr., Los Gatos, CA 95030, 408-370-7979.

Phoenix Technologies

Phoenix was one of the first companies to develop BIOS implementations independent of IBM. Phoenix BIOSs are used in numerous PC compatibles, including Dell, Gateway, NEC, Swan, and many others.

Phoenix states that their BIOS implementations for 386-class systems have been tested and work with Windows 3.*x.* Phoenix 286-class chips should be upgraded to version 3.1 or later, even if Windows acts normally.

Like most BIOSs, the version number of Phoenix BIOS chips displays on screen when you turn your PC off and then back on. If you need to know the release date of the BIOS version, however, you need to display this information manually, using the DOS DEBUG.COM utility.

To do this, exit Windows and close all other programs. The Debug program should be located in your DOS directory and therefore is probably already in your Path. At a DOS prompt, type

    DEBUG

and press Enter. You should see a single hyphen (-) which indicates that Debug is running. At this point, type

    D F000:FFF0

which means "dump to the screen the 16 bytes of memory beginning at location FFFF0." (All of the "0" characters in this line are zeros, not the letter "o.") A line similar to the following appears on your monitor:

F000:FFF0 EA EB E0 00 F0 30 31 2F-31 35 2F 38 38 FF FC E0 .[...01/15/88...

The sixteen two-letter codes are hexadecimal numbers representing the contents of memory. The sixteen digits on the right edge of the screen include the release date of the BIOS revision, usually in a month/day/year format. (Upper-ASCII characters are indicated by periods [.] in the right-hand display.)

The next line on your screen should be a single hyphen, indicating that Debug is still running. You must quit Debug and return to the DOS prompt by pressing Q and then pressing Enter. When you see the DOS prompt, you can restart Windows or any other program.

Phoenix states that because there are so many different implementations of their BIOS chips for various manufacturers, you must contact the vendor who sold you your PC to obtain suitable upgrades. If this is not possible, contact Komputerwerk of Virginia, Inc., 8133 Forest Hill Avenue, Richmond, VA 23235, 804-320-8835. Phoenix Technologies may be contacted at 846 University Avenue, Norwood, MA 02062, 617-551-4000.

Other BIOS Implementations

If your BIOS is not from one of the preceding sources, you may contact one of the following companies.

Chips & Technologies, 3050 Zanker Road, San Jose, CA 95134, 408-434-0600.

DTK Computer, Inc., 15711 E. Valley Blvd., City of Industry, CA 91744, 818-333-7533.

Quadtel Corp., 3190J Airport Loop, Costa Mesa, CA 92630, 714-754-4422.

If your computer manufacturer is listed in Figure 7-1 as producing its own BIOS, you must contact that manufacturer directly, of course.

Variations in Extended Memory

The IBM AT was the first popular PC that could access more than 640K of RAM. The AT supported up to 16MB of RAM, of which the first 640K is referred to as *conventional* memory, and the remainder as *extended* memory. Extended memory should not be confused with *expanded* memory, which is usually provided on a separate add-in board.

You can usually tell how much conventional and extended memory is installed in a 286 or higher system, because the power-on self test (POST) that the machine runs counts each bank of memory and displays the total on the monitor. Conventional, extended, and expanded memory are described in more detail in Chapter 16. This count-up includes only conventional and extended memory, and on most machines does not include expanded memory.

DOS programs cannot ordinarily take advantage of extended memory unless they switch the CPU from real mode into protected mode. In protected mode, all the memory addresses up to 16MB are available, and applications are theoretically "protected" against other applications that might try to claim the same segments of memory that are already in use.

Because few DOS programs accessed extended memory until the introduction of Windows and "DOS extender" programs such as Lotus 1-2-3 Release 3.0, computer manufacturers had little to guide them in implementing this new memory technology. Therefore, Windows and its memory-manager program, HIMEM.SYS, must accommodate eight different ways that PC manufacturers provide entry to extended memory — including two different ways that IBM does it.

Usually, when HIMEM.SYS is loaded by your CONFIG.SYS file, it automatically detects the method used in your PC to address extended memory, and it configures itself accordingly. In other cases, the Windows Setup program may detect these variations when installing Windows, and it places a parameter at the end of the line that loads HIMEM.SYS in order to force it to use one of the eight methods. Finally, in cases where neither of the above approaches works, you must type this parameter into the HIMEM.SYS line in your CONFIG.SYS.

It is important to note that you should not type in one of these parameters unless the method that HIMEM.SYS is already using does not work on your computer. Switching from one parameter to another incorrect parameter could corrupt information on a hard disk or have other unexpected consequences.

The eight possible settings for HIMEM.SYS are as follows:

This Type Computer:	Uses This Parameter:	Or:
IBM AT or 100% compatible	/M:AT	/M:1
IBM PS/2	/M:PS2	/M:2
Phoenix Cascade BIOS	/M:PTLCASCADE	/M:3
HP Vectras (A and A+)	/M:HPVECTRA	/M:4
AT&T 6300 Plus (not 6300)	/M:ATT6300PLUS	/M:5
Acer 1100	/M:ACER1100	/M:6
Toshiba 1600 and 1200XE	/M:TOSHIBA	/M:7
Wyse 286s at 12.5 MHz	/M:WYSE	/M:8

If you have a PS/2-compatible computer with Micro Channel Architecture, but HIMEM.SYS does not recognize this machine as a PS/2-type, for instance, you would make the HIMEM.SYS line in your CONFIG.SYS look like this example:

```
DEVICE=c:\windows\HIMEM.SYS /M:PS2
```

You could also use the parameter /M:2, which does the same thing. But I recommend that you always spell out the parameter so its meaning is clearer later on when you or others read this CONFIG.SYS.

As mentioned earlier, you should not experiment, forcing HIMEM.SYS to use parameters that are not correct for your machine. But if HIMEM.SYS will not load, and you cannot determine from your PC vendor what parameter should be used, the parameter /M:PTLCASCADE provides the widest compatibility with the greatest number of "near-compatibles."

Microsoft's Compatibility List

Examining the PCs on the Hardware Compatibility List

With every package of Windows 3.*x,* Microsoft includes a printed document called the Microsoft Windows Hardware Compatibility List. This document lists PC components such as computer systems, video display adapters, printers, networks, mice, and keyboards that have been tested under Windows by Microsoft and found to work. (In the original distribution of Windows 3.0, this list was entitled the "Microsoft Windows Certified Hardware List," but Microsoft is backing away a bit from "certifying" other companies' hardware.)

The items found on this list include several computer systems that are preceded by an asterisk (*). This asterisk indicates that you must perform one extra step when you run Windows Setup on one of these systems. Windows cannot tell that the computer model in question is being used for Setup, so you must specify this model when Setup asks you to confirm on what configuration you are installing Windows.

At this writing, the computer systems (and one network operating system) that require this step are:

AST Bravo/386SX
AST Premium 286, 386/SX, 386/25, 386/33, 386C, 486/25 and 486/33
Everex Step 386/25
NCR PC386SX
NCR PC925
NEC PowerMate SX Plus
NEC ProSpeed 386
Toshiba T1600 Portable
Zenith Z-386/16, Z-386/20, Z-386/25, and Z-386/33
Microsoft LAN Manager Network, version 1.0

These computers are neither "bad" nor "incompatible." Windows simply cannot detect the use of memory areas higher than 640K by certain high-performance enhancements in these machines, such as video adapters and ROM BIOS shadowing.

When you tell the Windows Setup program that the machine you are installing Windows on is one of these, Setup uses settings in a text file called SETUP.INF on the Windows diskettes to write special parameters into your SYSTEM.INI file. This SETUP.INF (Setup information) file is also copied to your \WINDOWS\SYSTEM directory in case you run Setup again. It is interesting to display or print out this file to see some of the configuration details that Windows uses for different machines.

When installing for an "asterisked" machine, Setup reads the section of SETUP.INF headed with a [machine] label. If you examine the part of this section entitled "All 80386- and 80486-based AST machines," you find the following lines (I have added the comments after the semicolons to explain what these lines mean):

```
[machine]
"All 80386- and 80486-based AST machines","10"
system                      ; copy the standard SYSTEM.DRV file
kbd                         ; use the standard keyboard handler
t4s0enha                    ; type 4, subtype 0 enhanced keyboard
nomouse                     ; use this driver if no mouse exists
egahires                    ; use EGA unless otherwise specified
sound                       ; copy the standard SOUND.DRV file
comm                        ; copy the standard COMM.DRV file
nohimemswitch               ; no parameters needed for HIMEM.SYS
"emmexclude=E000-EFFF"      ; write this to the SYSTEM.INI file
```

In every case, these lines make Setup copy and use standard Windows files, just as it does for all other computers — except for the last line, which writes one statement into the [386Enh] section of the SYSTEM.INI file. This statement, which excludes the memory area E000-EFFF from use by Windows' expanded memory manager, is necessary because Windows cannot detect AST's use of this memory to improve the performance of the ROM BIOS chip.

That's not so bad, is it? You might think, from the asterisk, that something major was wrong, but in each case some small change like this is all that is required. Actually, all AST 386 and 486 machines don't even require this change, just earlier ones. Later models have adapted to accomodate Windows. Contact your AST dealer (or your dealer for the other computer manufacturers described above) for exact models that might or might not require special handling. To obtain the latest revision of the Hardware Compatibility List, contact Microsoft Product Support Services at 206-454-2030.

Computer Anomalies

This section includes items that require special attention if you use particular computer systems, CPUs, motherboards, and accelerator boards. The information is arranged alphabetically by computer vendor.

Advanced Logic Research (ALR)

Powerflex Models May Confuse Mice

If a serial mouse on your ALR Powerflex computer moves the cursor erratically or drags objects around the screen without the left mouse button being held down, you may need a motherboard revision to your CPU. To determine whether this is the case, turn the computer off, remove the cover, and look for a white revision-number sticker at the edge of the motherboard. A revision number such as "C-N" should appear on the sticker. If there is a bold period or bullet in the number (such as "C-N.OP" or "C-N."), then you do not need an upgrade. If not, contact an ALR dealer for an upgrade to your motherboard that could solve the mouse problem. Call ALR at 800-444-4257 for the location of the nearest dealer.

486 VEISA Floppy Drives Hang

The ALR 486 VEISA can hang when accessing floppy drives within the File Manager. Upgrading the Phoenix ROM BIOS PLUS chip to version 1.10.02 or higher fixes this problem. Call ALR product support at 714-581-6770.

All ChargeCard

The All ChargeCard, from All Computers, Inc., is a small, add-in board for 286-class computers that gives them some of the memory-management functions of a 386, without actually upgrading to a 386 processor. For example, a 286 with an All ChargeCard (which typically plugs directly into the 286 processor socket) enables memory-management software to convert extended memory into expanded memory on demand — a feat usually limited to 386 systems.

When running an All ChargeCard under 3Com network software, you may not be able to run Windows 3.*x* in protected mode. If this is the case, you may have to remove the line DEVICE=ALLEMM4.SYS from CONFIG.SYS. Alternately, Windows 3.*x* will run in real mode, and you can start Windows by using the command line WIN /R.

Contact All Computers at 1220 Yonge St., 2nd Floor, Toronto, ONT, Canada M4T 1W1, 416-960-0111.

Amstrad

Upgrade to Motherboard Revision "J"

Amstrad Computers are manufactured in Europe and are found more commonly in the U.K. and other European countries than in the U.S. Installation of Windows 3.x may cause Amstrad 286s and 386s to lock up during Windows Setup, requiring a cold reboot. If this is the case, you should upgrade the motherboard to the "J" revision or later.

Apricot

Requires ANSI.SYS and Special Drivers

Windows 3.x enhanced mode, running under Apricot DOS version 3.3, requires a device driver for the keyboard and display such as ANSI.SYS or a compatible program. Without ANSI support, the use of the Ctrl+Break key combination can close the wrong program.

ANSI support for these machines can be implemented by adding the line to the CONFIG.SYS file:

```
DEVICE=c:\dos\ANSI.SYS
```

Special drivers for other peripherals must also be used to run Windows in 386 enhanced mode. Obtain these from Apricot dealers.

AST Research

Keyboard Upgrade Required for Premium/286

You must upgrade the AST keyboard BIOS chip (which is not the same as the system ROM BIOS) in certain models of AST's Premium/286 computers if the machine hangs as soon as you press a key in Windows 3.x's protected mode.

The replacement keyboard BIOS is part number 500729-001 and is available from AST dealers. Windows is not the source of this particular anomaly. This upgrade is also required to run other applications that access extended memory, including Lotus 1-2-3 Release 3.0.

AST Rampage Memory Boards and PS/2s

The RAMTYPE.SYS driver for AST Rampage memory boards, which was current when Windows 3.0 was shipped, needs to be upgraded to a newer version if you are using a PS/2 or other Micro Channel-compatible computer *and* the Rampage board is providing both expanded and extended memory.

The version of RAMTYPE.SYS must be 1.20 or later to be compatible with HIMEM.SYS and other memory managers that allocate extended memory. For this reason, the Windows Setup program deletes the line DEVICE=RAM-TYPE.SYS from your CONFIG.SYS file. This causes other programs, which may be reliant on the RAMTYPE.SYS driver, to fail or act unpredictably.

You must obtain the new version of RAMTYPE.SYS from your AST dealer. Then, use a text editor to examine the file C:\CONFIG.OLD, which is an exact copy of your CONFIG.SYS before Windows changed it. Copy the syntax of the RAMTYPE.SYS line from this file into your new CONFIG.SYS.

The AST Fastboard and BIOS Implementations

The AST Fastboard is an accelerator board that upgrades 286-class PCs to a 386 processor. If you have problems running Windows 3.*x* on this board in standard or enhanced modes, you should take the following steps, in this order, to see if one of them is the cause of the problem:

STEPS:

For Problems with the AST Fastboard

Step 1. Remove or comment-out the line DEVICE=ASTEMM.SYS from your CONFIG.SYS file and reboot the machine to make the change take effect. If this causes Windows to operate normally, you may need a new version of this expanded memory driver. (While the driver is commented out, of course, no applications that depended on it to provide expanded memory will function as expected.)

Step 2. When rebooting the machine, write down the BIOS name, date, and version number that appears on the screen. If the display shows an AMI BIOS, you need a BIOS chip dated September 1988 or later for reliable operation. If you have a Phoenix BIOS, problems with this implementation and the Fastboard may be corrected with a newer chip, but the exact number of the required version was still uncertain at this writing.

> **Step 3.** If neither of the above steps solves the problem, you should install a new programmable array logic chip (PAL chip) for the Fastboard. This upgrade is available from AST.

Contact AST Research at 16215 Alton Parkway, Irvine, CA 92713, 714-727-9630 for more information on the proper configurations.

AT&T

386 Computers and Phoenix BIOS Implementations

If you have problems running DOS applications in a window on an AT&T 386 under Windows 3.*x* in enhanced mode, write down the BIOS copyright, version, and date that appears on screen the next time you reboot your PC. If the copyright notice indicates a Phoenix ROM version 1.10.14 or lower, take the following steps to see if they fix the problem.

Insert the AT&T Customer Test disk that came with the PC into drive A:. Reboot the PC and run the AT&T Setup utility. Disable the settings REDIRECT TO COM1 and REDIRECT TO COM2. Exit the Setup utility, being sure to save your changes. This should enable DOS applications to run in small windows in enhanced mode.

AT&T 60386/25 and Phoenix BIOS FB12

If the copyright notice that appears when you reboot your AT&T 60386/25 system includes the Phoenix ROM revision "FB12," you may not be able to display DOS applications under Windows. Contact AT&T for an upgrade to revision FB15 or higher.

AT&T 6300 and 6300 Plus PCs

The AT&T 6300 is one of the earliest PCs that AT&T introduced to the computer market. If HIMEM.SYS does not work on these PCs, it is not a problem with HIMEM.SYS; although it may not be apparent, the AT&T 6300 is actually an XT-class computer, and HIMEM.SYS requires a 286, 386, or higher processor. You cannot run HIMEM.SYS on an AT&T 6300, nor can you run Windows 3.*x* on these machines except in real mode.

For Windows 3.*x,* AT&T recommends upgrading AT&T 6300s to BIOS version 1.43 or higher. This upgrade is available through AT&T's National Parts Center by calling 800-222-7278 or 303-291-4525.

The AT&T 6300 Plus, which is often confused with the AT&T 6300, is a 286-class system and should be able to run HIMEM.SYS. However, HIMEM.SYS requires a special parameter to work with extended memory on the AT&T 6300 Plus. The HIMEM.SYS line in your CONFIG.SYS should look as follows:

```
DEVICE=c:\windows\HIMEM.SYS /M:ATT6300PLUS
```

The /M switch shown in the line above does the same thing as /M:5 but is clearer as to its meaning, so I recommend using the spelled-out version of the switch.

In addition, the AT&T 6300 Plus may require modifications when using an Intel Above Board, in order to be compatible with the RAMDRIVE.SYS driver. Contact AT&T at 800-922-0354 for information regarding this configuration.

See the Compaq section later in this chapter, under the topic: "286, 386, 486 Compaqs with 1MB May Not Run HIMEM.SYS."

Austin Computers

Serial Mice and PS/2-Style Mouse Ports

If you have a Microsoft-compatible mouse connected to an Austin Computer bus mouse port (similar to the mouse port on IBM PS/2s), you may be able to use the mouse in Windows 3.*x* real mode but not standard or enhanced mode.

This problem is related to the motherboard in certain Austin models. You can work around this problem by attaching the mouse to a serial port and configuring Windows to use a serial mouse. If this is not possible, you may be able to upgrade the motherboard to a later revision. For information, contact Micro City Computers at 2431 W. Airport Freeway, Irving, TX 75062, 214-570-7999.

Club American

Configure Club 486s as Everex 386/25

When installing Windows on a Club American 486, Setup identifies it as an "MS-DOS or PC-DOS system," and it does not appear on the Hardware Compatibility List that ships in the Windows distribution box. But Club recommends that their 486 systems be installed for Windows as Everex Step 386/25-type computers.

Even when configured as a Step/25, however, early models of the Club 486 may spontaneously reboot when running Windows. This is a timing problem in these models that may be corrected by an upgrade from Club American. Contact their technical support department at 3401 W. Warren Ave., Fremont, CA 94539, 415-683-6580.

Compaq

286, 386, 486 Compaqs with 1MB May Not Run HIMEM.SYS

Although some Compaq 286, 386, and 486 models ship with 1MB of RAM, it may not be possible for HIMEM.SYS to load on these machines. The extra 386K above the conventional 640K is not located at the 1MB line, but at a higher location (specifically, 0FA0000 hex). Some AT&T and Olivetti 386 computers are also set up this way. HIMEM.SYS requires the use of 64K of extended memory exactly at the 1MB line. Without HIMEM, it is not possible to run Windows in standard or enhanced mode. The solution is to add more user-addressable extended memory. Many computers, however, including some models from Compaq, AT&T, and Olivetti, locate extended memory so the extra 386K of the first 1MB is user-addressable, and therefore usable by HIMEM. The capability of these machines to run HIMEM.SYS must be determined on a model-by-model basis.

Compaqs May Require HIMEM.EXE to Fix HIMEM.SYS

Some models of Compaq PCs may have problems with the HIMEM.SYS file that Windows requires to run in standard and enhanced modes. Symptoms of this include uncontrolled reboots when the computer is powered on, and possible corruption of hard disk files. These problems may be resolved by using the HIMEM.EXE file, which is shipped on the Compaq User Programs diskette, versions 7.02 or later. For more information, request Document #264 from the Compaq Technical Index through your Compaq dealer.

Keyboard Utilities May Conflict with Mouse

If your mouse does not operate in Windows when connected to a Compaq computer's PS/2-style mouse port, this may be due to Compaq's extended keyboard utility programs KEYBP.COM and KEYBOARD.SYS. Versions 6.01 and 7.00 of these programs conflict with Windows 3.*x* while running early releases of Compaq DOS 3.31 and 4.01.

If this is your situation, you can reverse the conflict in one of two ways:

1. Delete or comment-out of your CONFIG.SYS and AUTOEXEC.BAT files the lines that load KEYBOARD.SYS and KEYBP.COM; or

2. Upgrade the version of DOS you are running to Compaq DOS 3.31 release G, or Compaq DOS 4.01 release D or higher.

The two keyboard utilities do not have any effect on Windows 2.*x,* but do affect version 4.01 of the Logitech Mouse driver, if you are using that driver.

SLT/286 Requires 84-Key Configuration

The Compaq SLT/286 laptop computer is equipped with an 84-key keyboard, but an option is available to purchase a separate, plug-in 101-key keyboard for use when the SLT is situated on a desk. This setup, however, still requires that Windows be configured for a "PC-XT type 84-key keyboard," because the SLT's keyboard controller chip is not equipped for the extra keys. This limits Windows' use of key combinations that are unique to 101-key keyboards, including F11, F12, Ctrl+Arrow keys, etc.

CompuAdd

316 SL Laptop Requires Supplemental Driver

If the display screen on your CompuAdd 316 SL laptop computer appears to "split" into separate areas when you exit a DOS application under Windows in enhanced mode, and the machine then hangs, you may need a special device driver in your SYSTEM.INI file.

Newer models of the 316 SL are shipped with Windows already installed; the virtual device driver VDDDRAG.386 has also been copied to the \WINDOWS\SYSTEM directory and loaded in SYSTEM.INI. Older models of this laptop included the device driver on a separate, supplemental diskette, but it may not have been installed.

If this driver is installed, it will exist in the SYSTEM directory, and the following line will appear in the [386Enh] section of the SYSTEM.INI file:

```
[386Enh]
DEVICE=VDDDRAG.386
```

If you do not have this driver, you can download it from CompuAdd's bulletin board system by dialing 512-250-3226 with your modem, or calling technical support at 800-999-9901. The downloadable file is named 316SLDRV.ZIP. This file, in turn, must be decompressed using a utility like PKUNZIP (on the diskettes included with this book).

Additionally, the 316 SL ships with a screen saver that relies on information from the keyboard and is not compatible with Windows. You must press Ctrl+Left-Shift+L from a DOS prompt, which toggles this saver off and on.

Dell

286-Based PCs Require HIMEM.SYS Switch

Older models of 286-based Dell PCs require the following HIMEM.SYS command-line switch in the CONFIG.SYS file:

```
DEVICE=c:\windows\HIMEM.SYS /M:7
```

The /M:7 switch indicates that the older Dell 286s handle extended memory in a way similar to the Toshiba 1600, which also requires this switch. Without this switch, HIMEM.SYS may not allow these PCs to boot up properly.

386 SX and Laptop Computers Require Exclude Statements

The Dell computers 316LT, 316SX, and 320LT require statements in SYSTEM.INI to allow Windows to run in 386 enhanced mode. These computers use memory areas for video-board RAM and BIOS shadowing that may not be detected by Windows; this can cause the display to appear scrambled or hang the machine.

The following lines should appear in the [386Enh] section of the SYSTEM.INI file:

```
[386Enh]
EMMExclude=C000-C7FF
EMMExclude=E000-FFFF
```

In addition, it may be necessary to access Dell's setup menu by pressing Ctrl+Alt+Enter at a DOS prompt in order to configure the BIOS shadowing. Contact Dell technical support at 800-624-9896 or 800-426-5150 for more information.

Epson

386 Portables Require Exclude Statements

Epson 386 portables contain ROM BIOS chips at an adapter-segment memory location that Windows cannot detect, causing it to hang or display other unexpected behavior in 386 enhanced mode. This can be corrected by including the following in your SYSTEM.INI file:

```
[386Enh]
EMMExclude=E000-EFFF
```

The IBM PS/2 series also contains ROM chips at this location, but Windows assumes that this position is occupied on Micro Channel machines and avoids using this area for memory management. Since the Epson 386 portables have industry-standard buses, Windows does not make this assumption and requires that these memory addresses be explicitly excluded in SYSTEM.INI.

Disabling Screen Savers in Epson Computers

Many Epson computers ship with screen-saver utilities included. These screen savers assume that no activity is occurring if they do not detect keypresses from the keyboard. When Windows is in operation, these screen savers do not receive keyboard interrupts, and can blank your screen even though you are actively using Windows.

If this occurs, you can regain control by using the keyboard to exit whatever Windows applications you were using, and then exit Windows. (Alt+F4 usually exits any Windows application, including Windows itself. Of course, you will not see anything on the screen until you have returned to DOS.) You can then disable the Epson screen saver before restarting Windows.

Everex

Everex 386/25 Requires Settings in SYSTEM.INI

Everex Step 386/25 computers include a front-panel LED display that shows hard-disk access and other information. This display is disabled when Windows enters 386 enhanced mode, unless you add the following lines to your SYSTEM.INI file. These commands are undocumented in the Windows manual or the SYSINI.TXT file that is included with Windows:

```
[386Enh]
8042ReadCmd=A2,1,F
8042ReadCmd=A3,1,F
8042WriteCmd=B3,8,F
```

These settings affect control codes that are sent to the Everex 8042 keyboard controller. Everex uses these codes to update the front-panel display. Without these settings enabled in your SYSTEM.INI file, Windows ignores and does not pass along any codes that are not part of the recognized keyboard controller command set.

Additionally, if you use Windows' 386 expanded memory manager EMM386.SYS on an Everex 386/25, you must exclude from use the adapter-segment memory area C600-C7FF. To do this, include the following "X=" statement at the end of the line in your CONFIG.SYS that loads EMM386.SYS:

```
DEVICE=c:\windows\EMM386.SYS  X=C600-C7FF
```

Gateway

Motherboard Revisions for Gateway 2000 386s

386-class Gateway 2000 systems may have problems running Windows in standard and enhanced modes because they are incapable of loading the HIMEM.SYS driver that Windows requires, despite any of the configuration parameters described earlier in this chapter.

These problems only occur on Gene II and Hawk motherboards installed in older versions of these computers. An upgrade to replacement motherboards by Bristol Technology Corp. (BTC) corrects this.

Some versions of Gateway 2000 computers also shipped with a memory manager from Micronics, which is incompatible with the Windows Setup program and causes it to hang if the driver is running when you try to install Windows. See the section on Micronics later in this chapter.

Contact Gateway at 610 Gateway Drive, North Sioux City, SD 57049, 800-523-2000 or 605-232-2000.

Head Start

Windows Setup on a Head Start LX-CD Computer

The Head Start LX-CD is an 8088-based computer equipped with a built-in VGA adapter. However, since Windows does not support color displays on 8088- or 8086-based systems (as described earlier in this chapter), you cannot install Windows for a VGA display on this machine.

Instead, install for CGA, Hercules monochrome, EGA black-and-white, or EGA monochrome. (The two EGA noncolor options only appear when Windows Setup is running on an XT- or 286-class system, not a 386.) For information on Head Start computers, contact the Phillips Service Company at 800-722-6224 or 213-217-1300.

Hewlett-Packard

Using HP-DOS Instead of PC-DOS or MS-DOS

On Hewlett-Packard PCs, even more than most computer brands, it is particularly important that you run the OEM version of DOS that is specific to your make of computer. In Hewlett-Packard's case, that is HP-DOS. You should not use IBM's PC-DOS or a generic version of Microsoft's MS-DOS.

If you try to run Windows in enhanced mode on an HP Vectra with generic MS-DOS, you may receive the message "Unsupported DOS Version." Other PC software may run as expected, however. This message indicates the possibility that you have the wrong DOS for your machine. This situation is complicated by the fact that some vendors selling HP computers packaged them with generic copies of DOS, leaving you without documentation of the correct version required.

To find the exact version of DOS on an HP computer, type COMMAND at a DOS prompt. Only the Microsoft copyright notice appears on-screen if it is generic MS-DOS. If it is specific HP-DOS, both HP and Microsoft copyright notices appear. You must obtain a copy of HP-DOS from an HP dealer if a generic DOS was installed when you purchased the machine.

IBM

Using Expanded Memory on PS/2 286s

IBM 286-based PS/2s use a device driver called XMA2EMS.SYS to provide expanded memory. Running Windows Setup, and allowing Setup to modify your CONFIG.SYS file, deletes this line. To provide expanded memory to DOS applications outside Windows, you must reinsert this line with a text editor. Find the file C:\CONFIG.OLD, which is an exact copy of your CONFIG.SYS file before Windows changed it, and place into your CONFIG.SYS file a line like the following, with whatever syntax was originally installed:

```
DEVICE=XMA2EMS.SYS
```

The PS/1 and Windows

The IBM PS/1, a 286-class machine, comes with a start-up routine that gives you a choice among different DOS shells and a CONFIG.SYS in ROM (built-in) or one on disk. You must configure this start-up program to use the CONFIG.SYS on disk, or the changes that Windows Setup makes to the CONFIG.SYS will never be read and HIMEM.SYS (which is necessary for Windows to run in standard mode) will never be loaded.

After running the start-up program, the command SHELL STB gets you back to the PS/1's normal shell.

Intel

The Inboard 386/PC XT Windows Version

The Intel InBoard 386/PC XT is an accelerator board that adds a 386 processor to a PC or XT computer (allowing it to run some but not all 386-specific software). Intel also makes the InBoard 386/AT, which upgrades 286-class computers to 386s.

The standard distribution of Windows 3.x does not run on an InBoard 386/PC XT except in real mode. You need to obtain an Intel OEM version of Windows for this accelerator board. Windows/386 version 2.1 also had a special release for the InBoard 386/PC XT. This situation does not affect the InBoard 386/AT, which runs Windows in all modes.

Contact Intel at 800-538-3373 for more information on their specific versions of Windows.

Micronics

Memory Manager Conflicts with Windows Setup

Windows Setup will hang when you install Windows if a driver for the Micronics Memory Manager is loaded in your CONFIG.SYS file. This driver may be named MICEMM4D.EXE, MICEMM4F.EXE, MICEMM4G.EXE, or similar. (These filenames are abbreviations for MICronics Expanded Memory Manager and have nothing to do with mice drivers.)

These memory manager files shipped with PCs that contain a Micronics motherboard and with some versions of Gateway 2000 computers and others. You must delete or comment-out the line in your CONFIG.SYS that contains these device drivers (and reboot your PC for the changes to take effect) before installing Windows. After installing Windows, you may or may not be able to use these drivers, depending on your version of the driver and your configuration.

Many other drivers besides Micronics interfere with Windows Setup. See Chapter 15 for information on removing these conflicts before installing Windows.

Microsoft

Updating the Mach 20 Accelerator Card

Around the time that OS/2 1.0 was introduced, Microsoft began shipping the Mach 20 board, an accelerator card that added a 286 processor to XT-class machines. The concept was that IBM XT users would install Mach 20 cards to run OS/2.

Several of the drivers that shipped with the Mach 20 cards must be upgraded to allow these boards to run Windows 3.*x*. Contact Microsoft's Product Support Services department at 206-454-2030 to obtain these drivers.

NCR

486 Internal Cache Conflicts with Windows Setup

Running Windows Setup on an NCR 486/25 causes the system to hang during the second installation diskette. Unless some other problem is evident (such as an incompatible video board), this may be due to the 8K internal memory cache present in the i486 processor (and implemented by NCR).

This problem can be eliminated, and Windows installed, by running the CMOS setup routine for the NCR machine and turning off this internal cache. If Windows installs successfully, it may be possible to reenable the cache and run Windows normally. (The 8K cache improves the performance of some programs.)

NCR 925 Requires Settings for EMM386.SYS

If you are using the Windows driver EMM386.SYS to provide expanded memory for DOS applications outside Windows, you must exclude some memory in the adapter-segment area on NCR 925 computers. This is accomplished by adding the following "X=" parameter to the EMM386.SYS line in your CONFIG.SYS:

```
DEVICE=c:\windows\EMM386.SYS X=E000-EFFF
```

NEC

Multispeed 286 Laptop Requires MODE Command

The NEC Multispeed 286 is a laptop with a CGA adapter driving a liquid crystal display screen. This requires that you configure Windows Setup for a CGA display. However, the display may be poorer quality than expected unless you run the following command prior to starting Windows:

```
MODE C080
```

This command sets the display to an 80-column color output and establishes the best mode to launch Windows. The file MODE.COM should be one of the files in your C:\DOS directory, and therefore will probably already be on your DOS Path when you give this command. (You can add it to your AUTOEXEC.BAT file to run it automatically when you start the Multispeed, but it doesn't hurt if you run it more than once.)

Northgate

Elegance 386 and Video Settings for Windows

If you encounter "garbage" on the screen when starting Windows in 386 enhanced mode on a Northgate Elegance 386, it may be necessary to change a setting on the video adapter. You must turn *off* the "video buffering" on the video board. Video boards normally shipped with the Northgate Elegance achieve this by switching *off* DIP switch number 4. As shipped, the video board attempts to buffer video signals when the Elegance 386 is in turbo mode. Windows requires the ability to write directly to video memory and will not allow these boards to buffer the signal.

Northgate 286 with AMI BIOS Require Switch

Northgate 286-class computers with a BIOS implementation by AMI require the "/M:8" parameter after HIMEM.SYS in the CONFIG.SYS file, as follows:

```
DEVICE=c:\windows\HIMEM.SYS /M:8
```

If this parameter is not specified, you may experience symptoms such as spontaneous hangs when using Windows in standard or enhanced mode, or when you boot the computer. The Windows Setup program incorrectly installs HIMEM.SYS on these machines as though it should use the "machine type 1" parameter.

To determine if your Northgate 286 has an AMI BIOS, write down any copyright notice that appears when you turn the computer's power on. AMI BIOS chips display an AMI notice.

Olivetti

Refer to the Compaq section earlier in this chapter, and the topic: "286, 386, 486 Compaqs with 1MB May Not Run HIMEM.SYS."

Packard Bell

Legend and Victory Models and Mouse Ports

The Legend and Victory computers by Packard Bell include both a PS/2-style mouse port and a serial port that a mouse can be connected to. A Microsoft-compatible mouse attached to the PS/2 mouse port responds to movements in Windows more quickly than the same mouse attached to a serial port. This is part of the system design for these computers and there is no workaround for the behavior.

Additionally, if your mouse "freezes" while in Windows in standard or enhanced mode, you may need an upgrade to the motherboard's keyboard controller. Contact Packard Bell at 800-733-4411.

Sun Tech

Memory Card Driver Can Corrupt Installed Files

If you receive messages such as "Trying to run in protected mode" when running Windows applets like Solitaire, some of your Windows files may have been corrupted (altered) when they were installed by Windows Setup. This can be caused by installing Windows while a driver for the Sun Tech memory card, RMS.SYS, is loaded in your CONFIG.SYS file.

If this is the case, you must delete all files from the Windows and SYSTEM directories, delete or comment-out the line in CONFIG.SYS that invokes RMS.SYS, reboot the machine, and reinstall Windows. After Windows has been installed, it should be possible to include the memory driver in your configuration again.

Tandy

BIOS Revision Required for Tandy 3000

The Tandy 3000, a 286-class system, requires a Phoenix ROM BIOS version 1.03.02 or later to run Windows in standard mode. Earlier versions do not allow protected mode on the processor. The Phoenix implementation on the Tandy line does not follow the same numbering system as other manufacturers, so direct comparisons between version numbers on different machines are not relevant in determining if a BIOS upgrade is needed.

2500 XL Requires Setup Change

Tandy's Model 2500 XL PC does not automatically read changes that the Windows Setup program makes to the CONFIG.SYS and AUTOEXEC.BAT files. This is because the 2500 XL has a version of DOS that is executed from a ROM chip, not from RAM. Windows may not run properly if the correct statements are not loaded from CONFIG.SYS and AUTOEXEC.BAT before running Windows. To correct this, simply start the Tandy SETUPXL program that is provided with the 2500 XL and make sure that the settings "Check for CONFIG.SYS" and "Check for AUTOEXEC.BAT" are *on*. It may also be necessary to change the default settings for files and buffers from 10 to a higher number. (Microsoft usually recommends FILES=30 and BUFFERS=20.)

Tandy 1000 Display Type for Windows Setup

The Tandy 1000, an older XT-class portable, is not supported by Microsoft and doesn't appear in the Hardware Compatibility List included in the Windows distribution box. Although Windows will run in real mode on the Tandy 1000, it's so slow that it's hardly worth considering. However, for Win 3 fanatics with lots of patience, Windows Setup can be run on Tandy 1000s, but Setup incorrectly detects the built-in EGA-resolution screen as a Hercules monochrome adapter. This must be changed to a CGA display for Windows to install properly.

For more information on these Tandy products, contact a Tandy Computer Center or call Tandy product support at 817-878-6875.

Toshiba

Toshiba is one of the world's most successful manufacturers of portable and laptop computers, and also distributes a line of desktop computers. While their desktop machines are similar in appearance to other PC compatibles, Toshiba's portables are distinguished by the vivid, bright orange displays on many of their best models. These brilliant displays make Windows an enticing environment on these portables (compared to portables with dim and "ghosty" LCD displays). But since most of the Toshiba portables were designed before Windows 3.0 made its tidal-wave impact on the software market, these units enjoy their share of incompatibilities and upgrade paths dictated by Windows' protected modes of operation. Because of the popularity of Toshiba's portables, and the attractiveness and growth of portable computing as a trend, I have made an effort to describe as fully as possible the Windows-specific conditions that apply to these machines. If you own a Toshiba, read carefully the following sections.

Older Laptop BIOS May Corrupt Hard Drive During Setup

The BIOS implementation in several earlier versions of Toshiba laptops may require upgrades to the more current version in order to avoid serious problems when using Windows, or simply running the Windows Setup program.

The following models of Toshiba computers have been tested with Windows 3.0 and found to be compatible *if they have the currently shipping BIOS version:*

> T1000XE
> T1200XE
> T1600
> T3100/20
> T3100e
> T3100SX
> T3200SX
> T5100
> T5200
> T8500

With earlier BIOS chips than the current version, however, these models can cause unforeseen consequences. For example, the Toshiba T3100/20 and T3100e can conflict with Windows Setup, causing it to write information over track zero (0) of your hard drive. This can alter the File Allocation Table (FAT) and make all the information on that drive unrecoverable.

This will not occur if these models are equipped with BIOS version 4.20 or later. In addition, models of Toshiba portables not on the above list shouldn't have this type of problem no matter what level their BIOS is.

For more information on these upgrades, contact Toshiba product support, 9740 Irvine Blvd., Irvine, CA 92718, 800-999-4273, extension 3, or 714-583-3000.

File Copy Error when Installing Windows

If you receive the message "Unknown File Copy Error" when installing Windows on a Toshiba laptop, you may have encountered an intermittent incompatibility between the floppy drives in these units and the kind of diskettes produced by mass-duplication machines. These machines, which operate at a faster production rate than is possible with ordinary floppy drives, create diskettes with a slightly weaker signal than floppies created in a PC's drive. Toshiba confirms that reading these diskettes may occasionally fail in their laptops.

Assuming that you have already checked the usual suspects in a Windows Setup failure (you switched to a plain-vanilla CONFIG.SYS and AUTOEXEC.BAT before installing, you have enough free disk space, etc.), you can take the following steps to install to a Toshiba laptop:

STEPS:

Installing Windows on a Toshiba Laptop

Step 1. Write-protect each of the original Windows distribution diskettes.

Step 2. Place Windows Disk 1 in a floppy drive and change to that drive with the A: or B: command.

Step 3. Type the command DISKCOPY and press Enter. When you give the DISKCOPY command with no parameters, it forces DOS to make an exact copy of the diskette in the current drive to another diskette in the same drive. DOS asks you to change diskettes at the appropriate times. You need the same number of blank diskettes as Windows distribution diskettes, and the format of these diskettes must be the same (1.2MB or 720K). The DISKCOPY command formats the new diskettes as it copies the files, so you don't have to format them first. Repeat this process for each of the Windows diskettes.

Step 4. After making these copies, use the command CHKDSK *a:* on each one. If this reports any "bad sectors" on the diskette, discard it and use another one. The DISKCOPY command may have copied a Windows file onto that bad sector, since it makes an exact image of the original diskette.

Step 5. Insert the first backup diskette you made, and type SETUP to start installing Windows, just as you would using the original distribution diskettes. Since these backup diskettes have a stronger signal (having been made with your own floppy drive), the complex Windows Setup routine should proceed with fewer floppy-read problems. After Windows is successfully installed, you can erase the files from the backup diskettes and use them for something else, or store them.

386-Mode Incompatibilities with Toshiba DOS 3.2

If you receive the error message "Unsupported DOS Version" when starting Windows in 386 mode under Toshiba DOS 3.2, it will be necessary for you to upgrade to Toshiba DOS 3.21 or higher. Several revisions of Toshiba DOS 3.20 were released, and some of these revisions are not compatible with Windows enhanced mode, so running WIN /3 won't work without Toshiba DOS 3.21 or later.

Reconfiguring Plasma Displays for Windows

Toshiba's brightest portable computer displays are referred to as "plasma" displays due to the method they use to create a bright orange image. While these displays are excellent for Windows (for a monochrome display), Toshiba's VGA-resolution displays automatically dim to a lower intensity when 50 percent of the screen or more is displaying a "white" area. This protects these units against overheating, but obviously makes it difficult to read a Windows window, since an all-white background is often used in applications.

To correct this situation and make white areas stay bright and readable, you must copy two files to your Windows directory, add two lines to your batch file that starts Windows, and change some colors in the Control Panel. These steps are as follows:

STEPS:

Reconfiguring Toshiba Plasma Displays

Step 1. Place your Toshiba diagnostics and supplemental diskette in a floppy drive. Copy Toshiba's video-change-display program VCHAD.EXE to your Windows directory with a command similar to:

```
COPY a:\VCHAD.EXE c:\windows
```

If you wish to keep unrelated files out of your Windows directory, it should be possible to copy this utility to any directory on your DOS Path.

Step 2. Place the Windows Disk 2 in a floppy drive and copy the file TOSHWIN.VCD to your Windows directory (or the same directory as VCHAD.EXE):

```
COPY a:\TOSHWIN.VCD c:\windows
```

This file is not in a compressed format, so it's not necessary to use Windows' EXPAND.EXE utility, as with other files on the Windows diskettes.

Step 3. With a plain text editor, open whatever batch file you use to start Windows (such as W.BAT). Make sure that the lines immediately before and after the WIN command that starts Windows look like the following:

```
c:
CD \win
VCHAD /R:TOSHWIN.VCD
WIN
VCHAD /C:1
```

These extra lines change the video display on the Toshiba to settings appropriate for the Windows environment (before you start Windows) and appropriate for DOS applications (after you exit Windows). If you copied the files VCHAD.EXE and TOSHWIN.VCD to a directory other than your Windows directory, alter the CD \WIN statement in this batch file to refer to that directory instead. Save this batch file and use it when you start Windows.

Step 4. If you can run Windows normally at this point, use the Color dialog box in the Control Panel to make the changes described in steps 5, 6, and 7. If not, you can use a text editor to directly change these settings in your WIN.INI file (as explained in step 8).

Step 5. In the Control Panel, double-click the Color icon. Pull down the Color Scheme listing and click the Fluorescent option.

Step 6. Click the Color Pallette button. Select the following screen elements and click on the color indicated:

Screen Element	Color
Window Background	5th column from the left, 5th color down
Window Text	White (bottom right-hand color)
Application Workspace	Last column on the right, 2nd color down

Step 7. The Color dialog box should look similar to Figure 7-2. Click the Save Scheme button, then click OK to store these changes. Click OK to close the Color dialog box. Windows should use these colors from now on, and you can stop here.

Step 8. If it was not possible for you to run Windows and accomplish steps 5, 6, and 7 through the Control Panel, perform this step instead. Copy the file WIN.INI in your Windows directory to a backup file. Then open WIN.INI with a plain text editor and change the [colors] section so the settings match the numbers shown here:

```
[colors]
Background=0 0 0
AppWorkspace=255 0 255
Window=0 0 128
WindowText=255 255 255
Menu=0 255 0
MenuText=0 0 0
ActiveTitle=255 0 255
InactiveTitle=192 192 192
TitleText=0 0 0
ActiveBorder=128 255 0
InactiveBorder=192 192 192
WindowFrame=0 0 0
Scrollbar=192 192 192
```

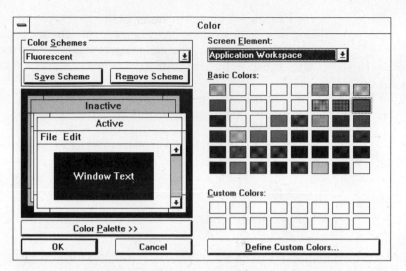

Figure 7-2: Setting the Color dialog box for plasma displays. This is a black-and-white approximation — the dialog box will look differently on your display.

Save these changes and close the text editor. When Windows starts, it should use these colors from now on.

386 Mode and Toshiba 5200 with VGA

If Windows runs in real mode and standard mode on your VGA-equipped Toshiba 5200, but hangs in 386 enhanced mode, it may be necessary to include the following line in the [386enh] section of your SYSTEM.INI file:

```
EMMExclude=A000-C7FF
```

The above line is not case sensitive. This line excludes Windows expanded memory management in an area that may be used by the Toshiba 5200's VGA adapter, but is not detected by Windows.

Enabling the Select Keys on a Toshiba T5100

The T5100 is a 386-based laptop with the compact keyboard layout typical of portable computers. If you set up Windows for an 84-key keyboard, however, the T5100 loses the ability to select blocks of text by holding down the Shift key and pressing direction keys (Shift+Arrow, Shift+PageUp, etc.).

To enable these selection key combinations, place the Toshiba Diagnostics diskette in a floppy drive and run the program TEST3.EXE. Press 0 (zero) to run the Setup option and configure the keyboard for 101-key instead of 84-key operation. Save the changes when you exit the program.

Next, run the Windows Setup program and define the keyboard as "Enhanced 101- or 102-key U.S. and non-U.S. keyboards." You can do this while installing Windows or, if you have already installed it, by running Setup from within the Program Manager. You can double-click the Setup icon or, if no Setup icon appears in your Program Manager, click File Run, type SETUP and press Enter.

DOS Application Errors on Toshiba T5100s

If you see the message "This Application Violated System Integrity" or "Parity Error 2" when running a DOS application under Windows protected modes on a Toshiba T5100, you may have encountered an incompatibility with the "Fast ROM" option on these machines. This problem may also be related to situations in which switching away from a DOS application and then switching back, using the Alt+Tab combination, causes the DOS window to be black or garbled.

If this is the case, try disabling the Fast ROM option by running the TEST3.EXE program on the Toshiba diagnostics diskette. Press 0 (zero) to run the Setup option, and indicate "negative" as your choice for Fast ROM. Save your changes when you exit the program.

For more information on these situations, contact Toshiba at 800-999-4273.

Windows Setup on a Toshiba T1600

The Toshiba T1600 portable requires that you switch *on* the automatic grey-scaling mode and internal EGA mode before running Windows Setup. If these settings are not enabled, Setup blanks the screen and freezes as soon as it switches to graphics mode during the install. Turning on these modes is performed by pressing combinations on the T1600 keyboard. The combination for your particular model is listed in the T1600 manual.

T1600 and the Logitech Series 9 Mouse

While Windows is compatible with the Logitech Series 9 mouse, the Toshiba T1600 may exaggerate the movements of this particular mouse so much under Windows that even small movements "fly" the mouse pointer all the way off the screen. Running the Mouse dialog box in the Control Panel and setting the mouse's scaling speed to its lowest possible setting usually corrects this problem.

Model T1200 XE Requires HIMEM.SYS Switch

Running Windows in standard mode on the Toshiba T1200 XE requires the switch /M:TOSHIBA to be added to the HIMEM.SYS line in the CONFIG.SYS file, as follows:

```
DEVICE=c:\windows\HIMEM.SYS  /M:TOSHIBA
```

If you are running Windows Setup on a T1200 XE, you should select "Toshiba 1600" as the PC type, rather than "MS-DOS or PC-DOS System." Setup will then insert the above line for you. Note that this procedure is not necessary for the Toshiba Model T1200 (with no XE), which operates correctly when specified to Setup as an "MS-DOS or PC-DOS System."

If you run Setup and specify CGA as the display adapter on the T1200 XE, Setup may not be able to correctly display the hardware options that it has detected. Specifically, the detected display line may appear blank, or you may not be able to see the line that is highlighted as you move from line to line with the cursor. To fix this, run Setup with the following parameter:

```
SETUP /I
```

The /I switch allows Setup to run without trying to automatically detect the type of hardware. Then select "Compaq Portable Plasma" as the display type, and "Toshiba 1600" as the PC type. Setup can then proceed, and Windows will work normally after Setup.

Zenith

Custom Version of Windows and Swapfile

Zenith-brand PCs must use the special Zenith OEM (original equipment manufacturer) edition of Windows 3.0, which is available from Zenith dealers. In particular, the Windows utility SWAPFILE.EXE, which creates a permanent hard disk swap file on 386-based systems, will not run correctly on Zeniths. If you run SWAPFILE.EXE on a Zenith computer, you may see the error message:

```
Swapfile could not find any drives suitable for creating a swapfile.
```

This is because many Zenith computers do not use the standard 512-byte hard disk sectors that are common on other PCs. Zenith's customized version of Windows operates correctly with these drives, and should be used instead of the generic version of Windows.

It is also important to run the current version of Zenith DOS, not IBM PC-DOS or a generic Microsoft MS-DOS, on Zenith machines when installing Zenith's version of Windows.

Zenith TurboSport BIOS and Double-Scan CGA

The BIOS in the Zenith TurboSport must be upgraded to version 2.4D or higher to run Windows. The currently available BIOS is several revisions higher than this and may be ordered as chip number 44465103. You can obtain information on this part by contacting Zenith product support at 213-695-0721.

Additionally, if you try to run DOS applications under Windows enhanced mode on a TurboSport, you may get the error message, "386 System Display Type Mismatch." This is because the Windows CGA driver can't handle the TurboSport double-scan CGA display (which fills in the gaps between the horizontal lines of a CGA screen, making it easier to read) in 386 enhanced mode. These DOS applications run normally in real and standard modes.

For more information on a possible fix for the double-scan CGA situation, contact Zenith Data Systems sales and service at 800-842-9000.

Zenith 386/16 Requires BIOS Revision

The BIOS in Zenith 386/16 PCs must be upgraded to version 2.6E or higher to run Windows. Upgrades may be ordered from Zenith by calling 616-982-3538.

SupersPort SX Floppy Drives in 386 Mode

If the screen fills up with random characters on your Zenith SupersPort SX after reading from or writing to a floppy drive, you may have encountered an incompatibility with Windows in 386 enhanced mode. This was fixed in a later release. It may not be possible if you have Windows version 3.0 to access the SupersPort SX floppy drive under Windows in enhanced mode.

Zenith 286s and 84-Key Keyboards

If the 84-key keyboard on your Zenith 286 desktop PC misses or duplicates keystrokes in Windows protected modes, this is because of an old scan controller chip in the keyboard itself. Since this part is not removable, the keyboard cannot be upgraded. Fixing this problem requires a different 84-key keyboard, or a 101-key keyboard from Zenith or other vendors (you must ensure that the BIOS in the PC will support a 101-key keyboard if you purchase one).

Summary

This chapter described many special configuration needs for particular computer manufacturers' PC systems. This covers:

▶ Problems in defining and achieving "100% compatibility" in the ever-changing PC market, and how to achieve the best compatibility possible with the various elements of a PC system.

▶ How Windows works on each of the three classes of PCs it supports, and what functions do and do not work within those classes.

▶ What versions of DOS work with which computer systems from various vendors and how this can affect your system's compatibility with Windows.

▶ Which BIOS implementations different computer manufacturers use in various models of their PCs, and how these implementations can affect your Windows applications.

▶ Ways in which HIMEM.SYS interacts with the eight different methods 286 and higher systems use to access extended memory.

▶ How to determine exactly what changes Windows is making to your SYSTEM.INI file when you tell Setup that you are installing on one of the systems marked with an asterisk in Microsoft's Windows Hardware Compatibility List.

▶ An alphabetical listing of several computer manufacturers and anomalies associated with Windows on their particular machines.

Chapter 8
Disk Drives

In this chapter. . .

I'll cover the following topics:

▶ The different hard drive types that Windows supports, and how certain types require special treatment.

▶ Making Windows work with some nonstandard hard disk types.

▶ Adding or deleting DOS commands in CONFIG.SYS and AUTOEXEC.BAT to take advantage of special drive features or to prevent problems during Windows installation or operation.

▶ Getting the most out of the SmartDrive disk cache program included with Windows (including some undocumented features that can enhance SmartDrive's performance on 386-based systems).

▶ Problems that have caused total data loss on some hard drives larger than 32MB when used with SmartDrive.

▶ Alternative disk caches that are faster and smarter than SmartDrive.

▶ Distinguishing between *permanent swap files, temporary swap files, temporary files,* and *application swap files,* and forcing Windows to use the fastest methods to write all these files.

▶ Benefiting from the fastest of all possible drives — a RAM drive.

▶ Realizing the potential benefits of high-performance SCSI drives while avoiding potential problems when using them with Windows.

▶ The anomalies of a wide variety of brand-name disk and drive manufacturers' products running under Windows.

Where would Windows be without hard disks? Since Windows 3.*x* requires a hard disk, and won't even run on a floppy-drive-only PC, we have all thankfully been spared from computer magazine "tips" like "How to optimize Windows on your two-floppy system!" But the wide variety of other kinds of disks that Windows can work with — hard drives, RAM disks, CD-ROMs, Bernoullis, and so on — *does* give you a great many opportunities to optimize your system to take advantage of the largest data files available and the best performance possible.

Hard Disks

A variety of hard disk types have evolved in the PC industry over the years, and Windows does its best to work with them all. Some of the drive standards that you may encounter are:

ST506. These drives, originally used with Seagate and other drives in IBM XT, AT, and some PS/2 computers, became the most common interface type among all PC manufacturers in the early years of the industry. ST506 drives use a digital recording method known as Modified Frequency Modulation, and are thus referred to as MFM drives. These drives require a separate controller, which in early XTs typically resided on a separate board such as Western Digital's WD1003-WA2 interface (now called the WD1003V-MM2), which supported two hard drives and two floppy drives.

ESDI. Enhanced Small Device Interface drives, commonly used in the Compaq Deskpro 386 and newer computer systems, upgrade the ST506 standard by allowing a typical data transfer rate of 10 million bits-per-second, compared to the 5 million specified for the ST506 interface. ESDI disks spin at the same rate as ST506 disks, but store data on tracks at twice the density, thereby doubling the theoretical speed of data retrieval. Both ST506 and ESDI drives are considered *device-level interfaces* because they communicate directly with the interface board in the computer system.

SCSI. The Small Computer System Interface is a *system-level interface,* because SCSI drives and other devices use, in effect, their own expansion bus to communicate with the computer system. This "bus" is typically a cable, connected to an interface in the PC, to which several different SCSI devices (disk drives, CD-ROM players, tape drives, etc.) may be attached. SCSI drives are often larger, high-performance devices, with drives larger than 1 gigabyte (1,000 megabytes) now available. The newest IBM PS/2s include support for SCSI devices.

IDE. Integrated Drive Electronics drives are a hybrid, containing all the controller circuitry necessary for communications with the computer system right on the drive itself. Since this requires less circuitry inside the PC, IDE drives are commonly seen in newer and smaller PCs and portables.

Many other types of drives exist, but these are the ones you will most likely find yourself working with in the PC-compatible market.

How Windows Works with Hard Drives

Windows ships with a "Certified Hardware List" in its distribution box, and supports the common drive types used as the standard configurations for the computer manufacturers just listed. This includes support for all four types listed above: ST506, ESDI, SCSI, and IDE. But Windows' method of accommodating these drives varies according to the mode of operation (real, standard, or 386 enhanced mode) and whether the drive uses a device-level or a system-level interface.

Windows in real and standard modes reads and writes to hard drives in much the same way ordinary DOS applications do. If Windows is in standard mode, and therefore is utilizing a 286 or 386 processor's protected mode of operation, Windows rapidly shifts back and forth from protected mode to real mode in order to write to and read from devices like disk drives. If your disk drive and controller are working normally with your DOS applications, they should work normally with Windows.

When Windows enters 386 enhanced mode, however, a different set of conditions ensue. Whereas in 386 mode, as in standard mode, Windows switches into real mode to access disk drives, it also has the ability on a 386 processor to relocate segments of memory for more efficient allocation to applications. If a disk driver reads information from one segment of memory and then tries to write back to that same segment — but Windows has relocated the address of that segment — the driver will write information to the wrong location or hang the computer.

To prevent this, Windows uses its disk-caching program, SmartDrive (installed in your CONFIG.SYS file as SMARTDRV.SYS), for all disk drive reads and writes while in 386 enhanced mode. SmartDrive is not necessary for ST506 and ESDI drives or for interfaces like IDE that emulate the ST506 specification; Windows in 386 mode reads and writes to these drives correctly without SmartDrive. But SmartDrive (or some other sophisticated disk-caching program) is required to communicate with system-level or *bus-mastering* interfaces, such as SCSI and other devices. (See the section on SCSI drives later in this chapter.)

Whether or not a SCSI drive is present, SmartDrive in Windows enhanced mode always handles disk read and write requests through a method known as *double-buffering*. All data is written to a "neutral" area of conventional memory, and then written to disk, so that the memory mapping Windows performs does not confuse the disk driver. For this reason, SmartDrive's performance in 386 enhanced mode is usually slightly slower than in standard mode. More information on double-buffering (including an undocumented way to disable it) is contained in the SmartDrive discussion later.

The Virtual Hard Disk IRQ Statement in SYSTEM.INI

Even with SmartDrive loaded, Windows in 386 enhanced mode may have difficulty with some nonstandard drives. In this case, you may see error messages such as:

```
"Drive C: Not Ready Error"
"Cannot Read from Drive C:"
"Cannot Write to Drive C:"
```

To provide the maximum compatibility with drives of all types, a setting in the [386Enh] section of the SYSTEM.INI file is available, which forces Windows to perform all read and write requests through the ROM BIOS chip in the computer system instead of handling the hard disk controller itself. This is accomplished by adding the following line to SYSTEM.INI under the [386Enh] label:

```
[386Enh]
VirtualHDIRQ=off
```

This statement stops Windows from "virtualizing" (handling) the hard disk interrupt request line (IRQ). Without this statement in SYSTEM.INI, Windows defaults to *on*. This statement is not case sensitive.

Disabling Windows' direct reads and writes will probably slow down these disk accesses, in return for better compatibility with nonstandard drives.

If your hard drive does not work under Windows, even with Windows' virtualization turned off, there may be some problem with the BIOS and drive in your particular configuration that would prevent it from working reliably with DOS applications as well.

Installation Problems with Various Drive Configurations

The Windows Setup program can run into various roadblocks during installation, related to the way disk drives are configured under DOS. Situations that can cause these problems include:

Drives larger than 32MB. SmartDrive version 3.0 can cause the loss of information on disk drives larger than 32MB unless the drives were partitioned and formatted with generic MS-DOS 3.*x*, 4.*x*, or 5.*x*. See the topic "Disks Larger Than 32MB" under the SmartDrive section of this chapter for more information.

DOS commands APPEND, ASSIGN, JOIN, or SUBST. These commands make one drive letter appear to DOS as a different drive letter, make a subdirectory look like a drive, and make a drive look like a directory. Commands like these should be removed from your configuration or temporarily cancelled before running Windows Setup. See the explanation of the SUBST command in Chapter 5.

LASTDRIVE=E. If your computer system has more than one hard disk drive letter, these letters are probably assigned first to drive C:, then drive D:, and so on. Unless there is a statement like LASTDRIVE=*x* in your CONFIG.SYS file, where *x* is the last drive letter in your configuration, DOS assumes that the last possible drive letter is E:. If this is not the case, Setup displays the error message "Cannot Read Drive F:" (where F: is the drive Setup ran into problems with) while trying to scan all your drives for software to assign icons to in Windows' Program Manager window. To fix this situation, add a line like LASTDRIVE=F (use the letter that matches the last drive in your system) in your CONFIG.SYS file, reboot your PC, and rerun Setup. The LASTDRIVE statement should not have a colon (:) after the specified drive letter, and you should not specify a letter higher than necessary since each drive letter requires 81 bytes of conventional memory.

SHARE protection. Before using Windows, you should make sure that DOS's SHARE.EXE program is loaded, to protect files on your hard disk from corruption. This is implemented by placing the following line in your AUTOEXEC.BAT file:

```
SHARE /F:2048 /L:20
```

This command allocates 2048 bytes of conventional memory "filespace" (/F:2048) in order to provide up to 20 "locks" (/L:20) on files that may be opened by Windows and other applications. If two applications try to open the same file (as routinely happens when files are moved in various File Manager directory windows), they might corrupt the file in the absence of Share protection to prevent this. The numbers shown in this example are the default values for SHARE.EXE. If you receive a message like "Not enough memory," increase these values. If, while using Windows, you receive the error message, "Share Violation: File Already in Use," SHARE.EXE has just prevented you from inadvertently corrupting a file.

Files accessed on a network do not require Share protection, since network operating systems normally prevent two applications from corrupting the same file. And SHARE.EXE may not be compatible with the operation of some networks. See Chapter 12 for more information.

Optimizing the Interleave of Your Hard Disk

One of the biggest improvements you can make to the performance of your hard drive is to optimize its "interleave." The *interleave* of a hard disk refers to the way information is stored on the disk.

The disk platters inside a hard drive are constantly turning while your PC's power is on. The surface of each disk platter is divided into *sectors*. When you write a file to disk, the disk controller places pieces of the file into different sectors. When you read from a file, the controller reads from those sectors in the same order that they were originally written. The file looks like one continuous stream to you, but it may actually be broken into several sectors on different physical areas of the disk.

As the drive platters are turning, the disk controller must wait until one complete sector has been read or written and the CPU has processed the information before it can work on the next sector. On older IBM XTs and ATs, the CPU could not handle the information from one sector in time to process information from the very next sector. Typically, two sectors would spin by before the CPU was ready to take information again. So the drives in these PCs were designed to write information in the first sector, then the fourth, then the seventh, and so on. This is called an interleave of 3-to-1. All of the sectors on the disk are eventually used, but two sequential sectors in the same file will normally have sectors from other files in between them.

As faster 386 computers became available, CPUs could handle data from disks with an interleave of 2-to-1 or 1-to-1. Since the speed of the disks' rotation was constant, this smaller interleave improved the performance of reading and writing files.

Most PC manufacturers made sure that the interleave of their hard disks was matched to the fastest rate that the CPU could accommodate. But sometimes this match-making did not occur. Some PCs were shipped with disk interleaves that were not as fast as their CPUs were capable of handling.

If this is the case with your PC, the disk interleave can be changed to its best value with an interleave optimizer like SpinRite II. This program analyzes your disk and CPU and changes the interleave (if you confirm the change) without destroying hard disk data. (Create a verified backup first, just for safety's sake.) You do not need to use a program like this if you can verify with the manufacturer of your PC that the interleave for your drives is already set to the best possible value. (SpinRite II is less than $100 and is available from Gibson Research, 22991 La Cadena, Laguna Hills, CA 92653, 800-736-0637 or 714-830-2200.)

SmartDrive

Introduction

Windows versions 2.*x* and 3.*x* include SmartDrive on the Windows distribution diskettes. SmartDrive is intended to speed up operations that require reading from a hard disk. For example, loading a spreadsheet or word processing file can be faster with a disk cache program because the cache keeps some or all of the file in memory (once it has been read from the disk in the first place), rather than making the program read from the slower hard disk every time the file is needed.

SmartDrive loads when it is included in the CONFIG.SYS file. It is important to note that SmartDrive must be listed *after* HIMEM.SYS, or whatever other memory-manager program is in use, such as Quarterdeck's QEMM386.SYS or Qualitas's 386MAX.SYS. Your CONFIG.SYS file might look like this:

```
DEVICE=c:\windows\HIMEM.SYS
DEVICE=c:\windows\SMARTDRV.SYS 512 256
```

In the above example, SmartDrive starts out with 512K of extended memory for its use as a disk cache. This first number on the command line is the maximum or *normal cache size*. This cache memory can speed up all applications that read from the disk, whether Windows is running or not.

When Windows starts, it reduces SmartDrive's memory to the second value (256K in this example), which is called the *minimum cache size*. Windows immediately reduces SmartDrive to this value when starting in standard or enhanced modes, to reclaim extended memory for Windows applications. When starting in real mode, Windows only reclaims SmartDrive memory as needed for applications.

The maximum and minimum cache size values can be anywhere from 128K to 8192K (8 megabytes). But SmartDrive cannot use more than the amount of actual RAM installed in your computer. The correct size for SmartDrive memory is the largest amount of RAM that will still allow all of your other applications to load and run normally. (If SmartDrive claims too much memory, your other programs may not run, displaying a "not enough memory" error message.)

SmartDrive can accept a memory-configuration option after the maximum and minimum cache sizes. Including the "/A" switch as shown below forces SmartDrive to use expAnded memory instead of extended memory:

```
DEVICE=c:\windows\SMARTDRV.SYS 512 256 /A
```

You would only use this option if you were running Windows solely in real mode. Since Windows cannot use expanded memory in standard mode and works faster with extended memory than expanded memory in enhanced mode, using the /A option is unnecessary in these cases.

 SmartDrive has an additional, undocumented option that may improve its performance in 386 enhanced mode. This option turns off the double-buffering that SmartDrive performs if a SCSI drive or other bus-mastering device is present in your system. You should not disable double-buffering unless you are certain that no such devices will be used in your PC.

To disable SmartDrive's double-buffering, the SmartDrive line in CONFIG.SYS must include the "/B-" (slash B minus) switch, as shown:

```
DEVICE=c:\windows\SMARTDRV.SYS 512 256 /B-
```

Although SCSI and other bus-mastering devices *require* double-buffering when using SmartDrive, some types of devices won't work with SmartDrive unless double-buffering is disabled. Some Adaptec disk controller boards fall into this category.

Disks Larger Than 32MB

The SmartDrive disk cache that came with Windows 3.0 can cause problems with disk drives that are larger than 32 megabytes in size. These problems can scramble files on your hard disk or corrupt the File Allocation Table (FAT) that DOS uses to keep track of all the files on your disk. In the most serious cases, the FAT may eventually be corrupted so badly that none of the files are readable. In that case, the disk can only be made usable again by putting it through a complete, low-level formatting, which erases any old data.

I personally have tried to help two different people who had destroyed all the information stored on their over-100MB disks by mistakenly using SmartDrive 3.0 with these very large disks (and I have spoken with other people who were hit with this disaster as well). In both cases, neither "undelete" utilities nor professional help could salvage this data once the FAT had been corrupted so badly that the disk became totally unreadable. A low-level format, and the restoration of some of the lost data from partial backups, was the only option left. If you use large hard disks, read the following carefully.

These problems only occur when a hard disk has been set up using a special utility program like one of those listed further. These utilities exist because DOS versions 2.*x* and 3.*x* do not have the ability to create a usable disk drive area (called a *disk partition*) larger than 32MB. Under DOS 2.*x* and 3.*x*, a hard disk that is physically, say, 80 megabytes in size would be divided into a C: drive of 32MB, a D: drive of 32MB, and an E: drive of about 16MB. With one of the special disk-partitioning utilities, however, it is possible to create a single area called drive C: that is the full 80MB in size.

SmartDrive will not scramble data on hard disk partitions larger than 32MB that were created using Microsoft's generic MS-DOS version 4.01 or higher. SmartDrive was written to be compatible with that version's method of creating large disk partitions. Additionally, Microsoft began shipping a new version of SmartDrive with its November 1990 interim release of Windows 3.0a, which recognizes unusual disk partitions and refrains from operating on them. But for users of the original Windows 3.0 SmartDrive, Microsoft has published a memorandum listing hard-drive partitioning utilities that SmartDrive may *not* be compatible with. The following list includes the product brand names as well as a specific line to look for in your CONFIG.SYS file that loads each utility's hard-disk driver program:

Product Name	Line in CONFIG.SYS
Golden Bow Systems Vfeatures Deluxe	DEVICE=FIXT_DRV.SYS
Ontrack Computer Systems Disk Manager	DEVICE=DMDRVR.BIN
Priam Systems Innerspace	DEVICE=EDVR.SYS
Storage Dimensions SpeedStor	DEVICE=HARDRIVE.SYS or DEVICE=SSTOR.SYS

If you're using Windows 3.0, SmartDrive, and any disk-partitioning utilities like those listed above, there are four alternative ways to prevent SmartDrive from corrupting your disk files (this will not correct any files that have already been affected):

Upgrade to Windows 3.0a or higher. This ensures that SmartDrive will not operate on disks partitioned with these utilities. (Windows 3.0a includes other improvements as well. See "Windows Version 3.0a Upgrade" in Chapter 3. Use Windows Notepad to study carefully any "readme" text files that may be included with the new Windows diskettes you receive, in case any new information about problems may be located there.) However, this does not provide the functionality of a disk cache with these drives. Call Microsoft at 206-637-7098 for details on receiving the upgrade diskettes.

Stop using SmartDrive. You should use this alternative if you cannot upgrade, use an alternative disk cache, or do not wish to repartition your hard drive into new partitions that are each 32MB or less. To stop using SmartDrive, simply delete the line that reads DEVICE=*c:\windows*SMART-DRV.SYS from your CONFIG.SYS FILE, and reboot your PC to make the change take effect.

Use an alternative disk cache program. Several disk cache programs that are compatible with Windows 3.*x* and third-party disk-partitioning utilities (and are generally faster than SmartDrive, too) are available. See the topic "Alternative Disk Caches" later in this chapter.

Backup and repartition your disk. This alternative requires that you make a verified backup of your hard disk, run a standard disk-partitioning utility to create disk partitions of 32MB or less, and restore your files from the backup. The backup is necessary because partitioning a disk eliminates any data files the disk previously held. Every release of DOS since version 2.0 includes the standard disk-partitioning utility FDISK.COM. The use of the FDISK program is explained in the DOS manual. After running FDISK to create partitions of 32MB or less, you must run the FORMAT command to initialize each partition. If you created hard disk partitions C:, D:, and E:, for example, you would run FORMAT C:, then FORMAT D:, and finally FORMAT E:. At that point, you can restore your data from the backup.

Although the last choice sounds like a lot of work, it may in fact be the best method to insure against file-corruption problems from *any* source. Many programs — not just SmartDrive — have difficulty operating with disk partitions larger than 32MB. These programs include older versions of many file-recovery and disk-optimization utilities, as well as other applications that write to disk files. If you do not have any single data file larger than

32MB, you should use standard-sized disk partitions, just to avoid any problems with these applications.

A hard disk divided into multiple 32MB partitions will also offer measurably better performance than one that is composed of one large partition, say, 80MB, because when you issue a command such as C:WIN, DOS has to search only the 32MB C: partition for the WIN.COM program, not the entire 80MB disk. It has been commonly reported that a 40MB hard disk with a 40-millisecond access time (the average time required for a drive to locate a given point on the disk surface) will be speeded up to an effective access time of 28 milliseconds if it is partitioned into two 20MB partitions instead of one 40MB partition.

If you are using both Ontrack Computer Systems' Disk Manager and Windows' SmartDrive, and you have not experienced any disk problems, it is possible that your hard disk was set up in a specific way that would avoid any of the incompatibilities described above. Several hard disk manufacturers — including Seagate and others — bundled Disk Manager with many of the drives they shipped over the years. Some of these drives may have been partitioned in a way that would not cause any problems.

SmartDrive may only pose a risk to your disk files, according to Microsoft, if one of the following two conditions are met:

1. The hard disk has more than 1024 cylinders ("cylinders" refers to the number of "tracks" that are on each magnetic surface inside the drive, much like the grooves on an LP record album).

2. The hard disk has been installed in a PC whose ROM BIOS chip does not automatically recognize and support that specific disk type. All hard disks in this situation require a disk driver to be loaded in CONFIG.SYS before they can be recognized by the PC.

Users of Ontrack Disk Manager can determine whether their hard drive was partitioned with more than 1024 cylinders with the following procedure:

STEPS:

Determining Your Hard Drive's Partitions

Step 1. Start Disk Manager in manual mode by issuing the command DM /M.

Step 2. Press "C" to choose the disk configuration choice from the menu.

Step 3. If the Actual Cylinder Count shown by Disk Manager is 1024 or less for each drive in the system, then Disk Manager does not conflict with SmartDrive. If more than 1024 cylinders are shown, that drive may experience difficulties.

Disk Manager users can also learn whether or not their PC's ROM BIOS automatically supports their hard drives, by doing the following:

STEPS:

Determining Whether Your Partitions Will Conflict with SmartDrive

Step 1. Issue the command VER at the DOS prompt. If the version of DOS that is displayed is lower than 3.30, this problem with the ROM BIOS will not occur and you can quit now. Otherwise, do step 2.

Step 2. Start Disk Manager in manual mode (DM /M) and press "C" to see your configuration.

Step 3. If Disk Manager reports that "Parameters Are Standard," the problem will not occur and you can quit. If "Parameters Are Replaced," do step 4.

Step 4. Compare Disk Manager's display of Setup Parameters to the Actual Parameters for every drive shown. If the Setup Head Count is exactly the same as the Actual Head Count, and the Setup Sector Count is exactly the same as the Actual Sector Count, the problem will not occur and you can quit. Otherwise, do step 5.

Step 5. Press "S" to select any drive with a difference between Setup and Actual. Press "P" to display the drive's partition table. If the drive includes the partition type "DOS," as well as any partition types that are marked "Read-Only" or "Write-Read," then that drive may experience problems with SmartDrive. Be sure to check all drives.

Alternative Disk Caches

In the early days after Windows 3.0 was introduced, few hard disk cache programs were capable of running under Windows in all of its modes. Usually, the protected modes used by WIN /S or WIN /3 interfered with the operation of these disk caches.

But several disk cache programs *are* compatible with Windows in real and protected modes, and these programs are generally faster than Windows' own SmartDrive utility. This is because SmartDrive generally caches individual "tracks" (one entire revolution) of a hard drive, while other disk-caching programs use more sophisticated algorithms.

One of the most versatile disk cache programs is PC-Kwik from Multisoft Corp. Sold separately, or bundled with other disk utilities such as the PC-Kwik Power Pak, PC-Kwik replaces SmartDrive and requires 10 to 50 percent less time than SmartDrive to perform most disk reads and writes. PC-Kwik uses whatever types of memory are available in your system (conventional, expanded, extended, and adapter segment memory), but releases memory whenever an application requests memory that PC-Kwik has in use.

Multisoft states that PC-Kwik is compatible with all four disk-partitioning utilities described earlier in the SmartDrive section, as well as Everex's EVDISK partitioning utility. (If you use one of these third-party disk-partitioning systems, be sure to read the manual and any "readme" files that come with PC-Kwik or any disk cache, in order to configure the cache to take maximum advantage of your system.)

In addition to PC-Kwik, Power Pak includes a RAM drive that replaces Windows' RAMDRIVE.SYS, a print spooler that replaces (and is faster than) Windows' Print Manager, and DOS command-line-recall and keyboard-accelerator utilities (useful only to DOS applications). The RAM drive and print spooler claim memory only when files are copied to the RAM drive or are in the process of being printed. The "memory lending" features of the disk cache, RAM drive, and print spooler mean that you do not have to decide in advance how much memory to reserve for each of these functions — each utility uses only the amount of memory it requires at the moment!

Windows 3.*x* users should make sure that the version of the PC-Kwik cache they use is 3.55 or higher, or Power Pak version 1.5 or higher. (At this writing, these packages are up to PC-Kwik version 4.*x* and Power Pak version 2.*x*.) The PC-Kwik setup program automatically installs in your CONFIG.SYS (unless you specify otherwise) the line DEVICE=C:\PCKWIK\PCK-WIN.SYS, a small device driver that optimizes memory for Windows 3.*x*. In addition, Multisoft recommends that the [386Enh] section of SYSTEM.INI should include the line VIRTUALHDIRQ=OFF so PC-Kwik can use its own advanced disk support routines instead of Windows' (this line is not case sensitive).

PC-Kwik alone costs well under $100, while the Power Pak is slightly higher. (Multisoft Corp., 15100 S.W. Koll Parkway, Beaverton, OR 97006, 800-234-5945 or 503-644-5644.)

Another disk cache for Windows, which has turned in even faster times than PC-Kwik, is HyperDisk from HyperWare, Inc. HyperDisk is compatible with OnTrack's Disk Manager 3.1 and higher, and Storage Dimensions' SpeedStor 5.14 and higher, when used with DOS 3.3 (and compatible with all versions of these disk-partitioning utilities when used with DOS 2.0 through 3.2). It is also compatible with versions of Golden Bow's Vfeature Deluxe that were released since the May 1990 introduction of Windows 3.0. HyperDisk correctly detects versions of Vfeature prior to this and disables itself if it would conflict. HyperWare also recommends that disk cache users use the line VIRTUALHDIRQ=OFF in the [386Enh] section of SYSTEM.INI.

Although it does not include all the utilities of Multisoft's PowerPak, HyperDisk does include numerous configuration options to optimize itself for 286 and 386 systems. Two levels of HyperDisk are available, each for less than $100. (HyperWare, 14460 Sycamore Ave., San Martin, CA 95046, 408-683-4911.)

Disk Swapping and Swap Files

SWAPFILE.EXE

When you start a new application or process (or switch to a different application) under Windows, but Windows does not have enough RAM available for the request, it moves some or all of a program that isn't being used out of memory and onto a hard disk. This is called *disk swapping*.

In real and standard modes, every time you start a DOS application under Windows, Windows creates an *application swap file* that corresponds to that program. When you switch from the DOS app back to Windows, Windows moves part or all of that application out of RAM and into this swap file; this provides more memory for Windows applications, which are now in the foreground, while the DOS app is in the background. These application swap files are named ~WOA*xxxx*.TMP; the ~ is a tilde, WOA stands for a Windows Old App (DOS) file, and *xxxx* is a random set of characters. Windows usually erases these files when they are no longer needed.

In 386 enhanced mode, Windows doesn't create application swap files to copy DOS apps out of RAM, but uses a single, large file into which it can move part or all of any DOS or Windows applications that aren't presently in use. This single file may be either a *temporary swap file,* which is created and destroyed every time you start and exit Windows, or a *permanent swap file,*which remains in place on your hard disk even when Windows is not running.

Whether you use a permanent or a temporary swap file, Windows has the ability to use this disk file as though it were RAM, if Windows is out of real RAM when an application requests some. This use of memory is called *virtual* memory, because it is "imaginary" or "not-real" memory. The important thing to remember is that, since virtual memory is not real RAM, but is actually a file on a much slower hard disk, whenever you start accessing virtual memory Windows will slow down dramatically. (The informal term "real RAM" should not be confused with the "real" mode of Windows.)

The program you use to create a permanent swap file is provided with Windows and called SWAPFILE.EXE. The "readme" text file that comes with Windows describes the Swapfile program as "a utility that can dramatically improve Windows' performance on some computers when you are running in 386 enhanced mode." The basis for this is that a temporary swap file is an ordinary DOS file, which may be broken into several different parts on different areas of your hard disk (this is called *fragmentation*). A permanent swap file, on the other hand, is created by SWAPFILE.EXE using only sectors of your disk that are completely contiguous with each other. Furthermore, Windows writes directly to this file (actually two hidden files named 386SPART.PAR and SPART.PAR), which is faster than writing to a file that uses the MS-DOS file system. Due to these concepts, the Swapfile program has become a "hot tip" as a Windows "performance enhancement" in several PC magazines.

Unfortunately, a swap file (permanent or temporary) improves the performance of Windows only if Windows is totally out of RAM to allocate to applications. *If Windows is this starved for memory, your Windows performance is already in the toilet.*

To improve the time required to switch between applications, make sure your system has enough RAM for each of the applications you need to run simultaneously. Switching between applications, both of which are in RAM, will always be many times faster than "paging" those applications on and off a hard disk. If your hard disk's "in use" light goes on when you switch between applications (or when an application is doing anything other than saving or opening a file), adding 1 to 2MB of RAM will make a bigger difference in the speed of these applications than any swap file will.

To illustrate this, one test result shows that Excel 3.0 calculates a 1.7MB spreadsheet in 63 seconds on a 386/25 with 2MB of RAM. But Excel requires only 17 seconds to perform the same calculations when the system is equipped with 4 or 8MB of RAM. This almost four-fold improvement in performance, due solely to more RAM, dwarfs any benefits that could be gained from faster hard disk transfers.

If you are stuck using Windows on a PC without adequate RAM, and choose to install a permanent swap file instead of RAM, there are just a few points to remember.

First, the size of the permanent swap file you create can be no larger than the largest contiguous, unused area on your hard drive. For this reason, you may have to run a disk optimization program (which rearranges all your disk files into one occupied area and one vacant area) before running SWAPFILE.EXE, in order to gain the space needed for a large enough permanent swap file. The file should be 1MB or more for Windows to use it to full advantage.

Second, you must start Windows in real mode (WIN /R) and have no other applications running except your Windows "shell," such as Program Manager, when you start SWAPFILE.EXE. Even applications that run "silently," without displaying an icon (like Novell Netware's NWPOPUP.EXE, which runs in the background to pop up messages from other network users), will interfere with SWAPFILE.EXE. The best way to make sure these programs are not running is to comment-out all the programs on your LOAD= and RUN= lines in your WIN.INI file (place a semicolon in the first column of these lines) and then restart Windows before running SWAPFILE.EXE.

Third, SWAPFILE.EXE cannot create permanent swap files on some hard disk types, like those in Zenith 386 machines. Zenith distributes a Zenith-specific version of Windows that you should use on Zenith 386s. For more information, see the Zenith section in Chapter 7.

Fourth, you cannot create a permanent swap file on a disk that is part of a network file server. (But if you're on a network, it may be to your advantage to specify that your *temporary* swap file be located on a network drive. See the following section "Why Not Disable Temporary Swap Files?"

Finally, once you have used SWAPFILE.EXE to establish a permanent swap file, you must not delete, move, or rename the hidden files 386SPART.PAR and SPART.PAR, or Windows won't be able to find them. To remove or resize these files, you must start Windows in real mode and run SWAPFILE.EXE again.

Why Not Disable Temporary Swap Files?

If you have plenty of RAM for Windows (4MB or more), and you don't want to take up disk space with an unnecessary permanent swap file, you might decide to eliminate the temporary swap files Windows creates. Since Windows only establishes temporary swap files in 386 enhanced mode, you could do this in the [386Enh] section of your SYSTEM.INI file.

Performance-wise, however, this would probably be a bad idea. On a 386-based system, Windows has the ability to *page* segments of memory that are as small as 4K. As applications request and release memory, Windows can move these 4K memory chunks around to create the best fit. For Windows to do this, however, it requires somewhere to page these 4K segments *to,* in case it suddenly runs out of RAM when an application requests more memory. The temporary swap file fills this need. If there is no temporary (or permanent) swap file in 386 enhanced mode, Windows reverts to paging segments of memory in much larger 64K chunks. This is less efficient and can result in Windows applications running "out of memory" when theoretically there is quite a bit free.

You can speed up the creation of temporary swap files, however, without totally eliminating Windows' use of them. When Windows starts in 386 enhanced mode, and there is no permanent swap file, Windows searches your PC's disks for a likely place to create a temporary swap file. It examines the amount of free space on your disks, and then creates a file according to an algorithm that leaves you enough free disk space to work with. (By default, Windows will not leave you with less than 512K after creating its temporary swap file.)

This examination of your disks can take a while. If Windows has to examine the drives on a network that your PC is connected to, it can take more than *one minute* (because of the large size of most network disks). Therefore, you can hasten the process of starting Windows in 386 mode by specifying the size you want the temporary swap file to be every time.

The following entries in the [386Enh] section of your SYSTEM.INI file would specify that you want a temporary swap file to be created in the root directory of the C: drive (it is not possible to specify a directory), 1024K in size, but leaving a minimum of 512K free on drive C: in any case:

```
[386Enh]
PagingDrive=c
MaxPagingFileSize=1024
MinUserDiskSpace=512
```

The drive letter that you specify for the temporary swap file will usually be a hard drive that is installed physically in your PC, not a drive on a network server. But you might find it preferable to specify a drive that is actually a network drive if (1) the network drive is faster than your "local" hard drive (as is often the case with today's high-performance network disks or disks that have large cache memory allotments), or (2) all your files are stored on the network and you do not have or need a local hard drive.

If you're going to use a network drive, be sure that the letter you specify is not the root directory of the network drive, for if you and any other network user specify the same root directory for temporary swap files, you will hang whenever both of you try to create swap files with the same names on the server. The drive letter you specify must actually be a network subdirectory that is "mapped" to *look* like a root directory. (For more information on this, see Chapter 12.)

The smallest paging file size that enables Windows to use 4K memory chunks, instead of 64K chunks, is 512K. Microsoft technical support, however, recommends that this value never be set lower than 1024K, since Windows needs some free space in the temporary swap file when, say, an entire 640K DOS app needs to be moved there.

The minimum disk space you force Windows to reserve for your own use is completely up to you. If there isn't enough free disk space, however, to honor both values you specified, Windows reduces the size of its temporary swap file, which at some point disables much of its virtual-memory management abilities.

If a permanent swap file exists, Windows ignores these settings in the [386Enh] section. And, of course, Windows ignores this section entirely if it starts up in real or standard mode, since it doesn't have the ability to use these swap files in those modes anyway.

What to Do If You Run Out of Hard Disk Space

If you do not have both enough hard disk space for Windows to create its own temporary or permanent swap file, and space for you to save your work, you can delete some of the files that Windows installed on your hard disk. The Windows manual includes a list of such "optional" files in the chapter called "Optimizing Windows." The list describes each file so you won't delete any files that you *do* wish to use. If you delete a file that you later need, you can expand it off the original Windows distribution diskettes. The procedure to expand compressed Windows files is explained later in this chapter, in the section on CD-ROM drives.

Fixing Corrupted Swap Files

If you see the message, "Corrupt Swap File Warning: Your swap file is corrupt," one of several things may have occurred. (This message is displayed only in regard to permanent swap files created with SWAPFILE.EXE, not temporary swap files created automatically by Windows in 386 mode.)

If you use SWAPFILE.EXE to create a permanent swap file (consisting of the two hidden files 386SPART.PAR and SPART.PAR), and you later delete, move, or rename one or both of these files, Windows will display the above error message. In this case, move the file(s) back to their original location, start Windows in real mode (with no applications other than the shell running), and run SWAPFILE.EXE to delete, move, or rename the file.

The error message can also occur if you give the 386SPART.PAR file a DOS read-only attribute (as you might have done if you marked all the files in a particular directory read-only). If this is the case, use File Manager to locate the hidden file and remove its read-only attribute, or use the command ATTRIB -R 386SPART.PAR at the DOS prompt.

The TEMP Variable _____

Setting the DOS Environment for Temporary Files

The location where applications write their temporary files can have an effect on how fast they write to disk. Many programs create a separate disk file when they are editing or sorting an open document.

Windows documentation states that the directory used by these applications to write their temporary files is determined by the following line, which should be placed in your AUTOEXEC.BAT file:

```
SET TEMP=c:\{directory}
```

where *c:* is the name of a nonremovable disk drive, and *directory* is an optional directory that exists on that drive. It is important to note that these temporary files, which are written by Windows applications, have nothing to do with the temporary swap file that is created by Windows in 386 mode and is used solely by Windows for its swapping purposes.

The speed of writing temporary files (in applications that do so) can be improved by setting this TEMP variable to the fastest drive available, if you have more than one. Additionally, this drive should contain at least 1MB of free space *after* Windows has claimed space for its own swap file.

The fastest possible drive to set the TEMP variable to would be a RAM drive. (Setting up a RAM drive is discussed in the following section.) However, you must ensure that this RAM drive is large enough for the temporary files your applications want to write, and that the RAM drive will not be filled with other files when Windows apps try to write temporary files there. Microsoft does not recommend setting the TEMP variable to a RAM drive unless it is at least 2MB in size.

Two anomalies affect the TEMP variable. The first is that some Windows applications, especially those that originated in the days of Windows 1.*x* or 2.*x,* look for a variable named TMP instead of TEMP (the result of an early miscommunication in the evolution of Windows). For example, some but not all modules of Micrografx Designer as recently as version 3.01, look for a variable named TMP when trying to write temporary files. For this reason, your AUTOEXEC.BAT file should include both lines, as follows:

```
SET  TEMP=c:\{directory}
SET TMP=c:\{directory}
```

The other anomaly is that some applications don't care what you set the TEMP variable to. Word for Windows 1.0 and 1.1, for example, like to write temporary files named ~WRD*XXXX*.TMP into whatever it thinks is the current directory. These files (where *XXXX* is a random set of characters) are usually deleted when you exit Winword. But if Winword hangs your system and you reboot, you may find files like this in directories at random. You can get rid of files like these and reclaim some disk space, by searching for them with a DOS utility program and deleting them — but don't do this while Windows is running.

RAM Drives

Windows includes a utility that turns part of the RAM in your system into a device that looks like a hard disk to DOS; this is called a *RAM disk*. This "imitation" hard disk will be several times faster than any hard disk in your system, since it reads and writes files as fast as the memory in your PC.

There is usually little need for a RAM disk when using Windows in 386 enhanced mode. A RAM disk takes away memory that Windows itself could just as easily allocate to applications and data. As long as all programs and the data files they open are in the Windows memory area, they will be as fast as if those files were in a RAM disk.

The exception to this rule is that a RAM disk can speed up certain operations if you have plenty of memory and can leave more than 4MB of RAM available for Windows after giving memory to a RAM disk and any disk cache program you use.

In this case, you might use a RAM disk (1) to speed up switching in real or standard modes from Windows to DOS applications (because it copies files to disk when starting DOS applications); (2) to speed up the copying of files to several floppies (these copies will go faster if the files are copied from a RAM disk instead of directly from your hard disk); or (3) to speed up the sorting or indexing of files by an application that reads through these files several times. For example, Word for Windows includes a command (the *rd* or *reference document* field) that creates tables of contents and indexes for a group of related documents, none of which are presently in memory. These tables and indexes are generated much faster if the files are first copied to a RAM drive, and Word for Windows is told that the files reside on drive *x:*.

To make Windows use a RAM drive in real or standard modes when switching to and from DOS applications, place the following line in the [NonWindowsApp] section of your SYSTEM.INI file:

```
[NonWindowsApp]
SwapDisk=x:\
```

where *x:* is the drive and directory of a RAM disk you have established. If you do not include this line in SYSTEM.INI, Windows is supposed to default to the drive specified in the SET TEMP= statement in your AUTOEXEC.BAT file, or (if there is no SET TEMP= statement) to the Windows directory itself.

To set up a RAM drive, you must insert a line like the following into your CONFIG.SYS file:

```
DEVICE=c:\windows\RAMDRIVE.SYS 1024 512 64 /e
```

The first number after RAMDRIVE.SYS indicates the size of the RAM drive in kilobytes (in this case, 1024K or 1MB). The second number indicates the sector size in bytes that will be used to store files (in this case, 512 bytes, the same as most hard disks). The final number indicates the number of files that may be contained in the RAM drive's root directory (in this case, 64).

The parameter "/e" after the last number indicates that the RAM drive is to be created in extEnded memory. You would use the parameter "/a" to create a RAM disk in expAnded memory. You should not create a RAM disk in expanded memory if you have extended memory, since an extended-memory RAM drive is usually faster.

The line in CONFIG.SYS that creates a RAM drive must be *after* the line that loads HIMEM.SYS, if the RAM drive uses extended memory.

SCSI Drives

Configuring for Multitasking Operation

Disk drives that use the Small Computer System Interface (SCSI, pronounced *scuzzy* or *sexy*) specification may have difficulty running under multitasking environments including Windows, QEMM386, and DESQview unless these environments are configured properly. Nothing is wrong with the SCSI drives or specification, but the software driver for the SCSI device may not be capable of functioning as expected when an operating environment puts the 386 processor into virtual-86 mode to start additional tasks.

Microsoft technical papers state that Windows will not operate correctly in 386 mode with any bus-master device, including SCSI drives, unless the SmartDrive disk cache utility is used. This is because SmartDrive sets aside a reserved memory area specifically for transfers to and from disk drives, in case a bus-master device is being used. SmartDrive writes disk information to this memory area, then writes from that area to the drive itself (using the SCSI disk driver).

This method is called *double-buffering* because the information is written to and read from the buffer separately for each disk operation. Double-buffering causes a slight slowdown in disk operations (compared with disk cache programs that do not use this method). Microsoft has released a memorandum, however, stating that this small performance impairment is worthwhile since SCSI drivers might corrupt disk information or freeze the system if double-buffering was not used with these drivers. SmartDrive automatically enables double-buffering when Windows is operating in 386 enhanced mode.

Additionally, you must insert the following line into the [386Enh] section of your SYSTEM.INI file to turn off Windows' virtualization (handling) of the hard disk interrupt request line when using SCSI drives:

```
[386Enh]
VirtualHDIRQ=off
```

Furthermore, you must *not* disable SmartDrive's double-buffering by using its /B- switch described earlier in this chapter.

Symptoms of 386-mode conflicts with SCSI or bus-master devices include (1) the system freezing in 386 mode when starting a second DOS application; and (2) corruption of data in files that were just written by a DOS application under Windows. The second case, corruption of data, is far less likely than the first. When switching from one application to another, a bus-master device driver usually becomes so confused (if it can't handle virtual-86 mode) that it hangs the entire system before any information, good or bad, can be written to the disk.

If you are using Quarterdeck Office Systems' QEMM386 to provide expanded memory management inside and outside Windows, you have additional options for configuring bus-master devices. To understand these options, a little information about these bus masters is necessary.

A bus-master device may be a hard disk controller card or some other device designed to transfer large amounts of data very quickly. The bus master does not use a PC system's *direct memory access channel* (DMA channel) to transfer information. The bus master handles its own direct memory access to devices, thereby eliminating the time that would be needed for the system's CPU to manage the DMA transfer itself. These bus-master transfers proceed without intervention by the CPU.

Bus-master transfers take place by writing information to a specific area of memory that is used by the SCSI drive or other device. In virtual-86 mode, however, Windows and other environments move physical memory addresses around at will in order to make memory available when applications need it. The bus master may write information to a physical address that is no longer located where the driver last found it. This will likely freeze the entire system.

QEMM386 can be run with a parameter that solves problems caused by bus-master drivers that cannot handle virtual-86 mode. Including the DISKBUF parameter on the QEMM line in your CONFIG.SYS file sets aside a small amount of conventional memory for this purpose, as follows:

```
DEVICE=c:\qemm\QEMM386.SYS RAM DISKBUF=2
```

The number 2 in this example stands for 2K of conventional memory. Setting aside this amount of memory for disk buffering solves any problems with bus masters if QEMM changes memory addresses in response to a multitasking environment, such as DESQview. Since Windows disables QEMM's memory-management routines and uses its own in 386 enhanced mode, however, this method still requires SmartDrive (or a compatible, alternative disk cache) for Windows applications to write to SCSI drives.

Several things can improve the performance of SCSI drives under multitasking environments. Most require that the SCSI driver be written by the manufacturer to be compatible with all modes of the 386 processor (including real mode, protected mode, and virtual-86 mode). Some steps, however, can be taken by the user. The following steps are listed from the most desirable to the least:

1. **Use SCSI drivers that are fully compatible**. Microsoft, IBM, Quarterdeck and others support an industry-wide specification called *Virtual DMA Services* (VDS). Drivers that are written to be compatible with this standard have no problem under multitasking environments. The

driver can find the actual, physical address of its data even when the processor is in virtual-86 mode and the addresses have changed. This method provides the best reliability, performance, and efficient use of memory. Windows' SmartDrive will not be necessary to write to a VDS-compatible drive. And QEMM (version 5.0 or higher) will not require any special parameters to work with such a drive.

2. **Configure the drive to use standard DMA**. The manual for your SCSI drive may describe a way to set the device to use BIOS transfers or standard DMA channels (rather than bus-master transfers). Since the CPU manages these transfers, QEMM can correct any problems when the device tries to write to memory addresses.

3. **Configure the driver for its own buffering**. The drivers of many bus-mastering hard disks have options to enable their own double-buffering. The manual for your SCSI drive may specify parameters for the device driver that are specifically for 386 operations. Early versions of the Adaptec drivers SCSCIHA.SYS and AHA1540.SYS allow 386 operations and double-buffering by adding the parameters "/v386" and "/b:64." In this case, "/v386" means virtual 386, while "/b:64" assigns a 64K memory area for DMA buffering. (64K might be more than you need in your particular situation — check the manual.) QEMM, again, should not require special parameters to work with a driver configured this way.

4. **Use SmartDrive and/or QEMM's DISKBUF parameter**. If none of the methods 1 through 3 are available, then you must use SmartDrive (or a compatible disk cache) under Windows, and QEMM's DISKBUF=2 parameter with other environments, to write reliably to SCSI or other bus-mastering devices. In this case, you may be able to improve the performance of SCSI transfers by increasing QEMM's DISKBUF parameter from 2 to 10. Transfer a large directory of files to your SCSI drive with DISKBUF=2 and time the results. Then change the value to 10, reboot the system, and time the same transfer. If there is no significant difference, go back to the value of 2. There is no reason to give up the additional 8K of memory if this amount of buffer memory does not improve performance. (Quarterdeck states that values larger than 10 should not have any additional benefit to performance.)

Contact the maker of your SCSI drive, if necessary, to ensure that your drive ships with a VDS-compatible driver (or that a VDS-compatible driver is in development).

CD-ROM Drives

Adding Support to Windows for CD-ROM

CD-ROM (Compact Disk Read-Only Memory) players allow PCs to access up to 600MB of data on relatively inexpensive compact disks. Windows does not necessarily provide support for CD-ROM players without some effort, however.

If you are using Microsoft's memory-resident program MSCDEX.EXE, which provides extensions to DOS that enable access to CD-ROM drives, you must add the file LANMAN10.386 to Windows' SYSTEM subdirectory for compatibility with Windows' 386 enhanced mode. This file is not copied to your hard disk when you install Windows with the Setup program.

To install this program, which is stored on the Windows distribution diskettes in a compressed form, you must first copy the file EXPAND.EXE from Windows Disk 2 (in either 5.25" or 3.5" format) to your Windows directory. (This makes it available in case you need it to install additional Windows files from diskette.) Then insert Windows Disk 4 (in 5.25" format) or Disk 5 (in 3.5" format) in a floppy drive and expand the necessary file with the following command:

```
EXPAND a:\LANMAN10.386 c:\windows\SYSTEM
```

This file is ordinarily used to support Microsoft's LAN Manager 1.0 network, but also provides functionality for CD-ROM drives. Once this file has been expanded to the SYSTEM subdirectory, you must add the driver to the [386Enh] section of your SYSTEM.INI file, as shown:

```
[386Enh]
DEVICE=LANMAN10.386
```

You must restart Windows for this change to take effect. Additionally, some CD-ROM players may not work under Windows 3.*x* unless they have been accessed once before Windows starts. This may be accomplished easily by placing any command that accesses the CD-ROM files (such as a DIR command) in your AUTOEXEC.BAT, after MSCDEX.EXE has been loaded but before loading Windows. This would look like

```
DIR x:
```

where *x:* is the drive letter that represents the CD-ROM drive.

Programs Prevented from Executing on CD-ROM

If you are using version 2.10 of Microsoft's CD-ROM extensions, you cannot directly run programs stored on a CD-ROM disk while in Windows' 386 enhanced mode. These programs will execute if you first copy them from the CD-ROM drive to another drive and then run them. You may still read the data files on the CD-ROM drive without copying them to another drive.

Version 2.10 of MSCDEX.EXE is dated 4/07/89. This problem was fixed in versions of this program released after 1990.

Accessing CD-ROM Collections

The Microsoft Bookshelf, a CD-ROM collection of books and technical information from Microsoft, provides a good example of some of the configuration questions regarding access to CD-ROM files under Windows 3.*x*.

The Bookshelf CD-ROM configuration requires at least the following steps to operate under Windows:

STEPS:

Operating the Microsoft Bookshelf CD-ROM Under Windows

Step 1. CONFIG.SYS. The following lines are typical of the elements that enable CD-ROM access:

```
FILES=30
BUFFERS=20
DEVICE=c:\windows\HIMEM.SYS
DEVICE=c:\windows\SMARTDRV.SYS 1024 512
LASTDRIVE=F
DEVICE=c:\cdrom\CDROM.SYS /D:MSCD1 /N:1
```

Step 2. AUTOEXEC.BAT. Several lines are usually necessary to set the DOS search path and environmental variables needed for Bookshelf:

```
PATH=c:\windows;etc.
SET CDPATH=c:\bkshlf;d:\software;d:\book
SET CDRAM=
c:\cdrom\MSCDEX.EXE /D:MSCD1 /M:8 /L:F
```

Step 3. **SYSTEM.INI**. The file LANMAN10.386 must be expanded off your Windows distribution diskettes and named in your SYSTEM.INI file (as described earlier in the CD-ROM section of this chapter).

Step 4. **BOOKSHELF PIF**. The PIF file that starts the Bookshelf program must have the /S (Standalone) parameter in the Optional Parameters box.

Floppy Drives _____

Floppy disk drives exhibit most of the same behavior as hard disk drives, with some exceptions because they are removable.

Some Windows applications are not particularly elegant in the way they handle your attempts to write to or read from a floppy drive that no longer contains a diskette. For example, you might try to save a file to a diskette in drive A:, but that diskette has already been removed or, in some cases, merely has a write-protect tab on it. In this case, you might see the error message, "Unable to save file A:*filename;* close one or more files in another Windows application and try again." Actually, other Windows applications have nothing to do with this situation and won't cure the problem. Simply insert a formatted diskette in the drive and try again.

Printing a job through the BIOS, instead of directly to a printer port (as explained in Chapter 13) can also cause anomalies if the last disk drive you accessed was drive A: and there is no longer a diskette in drive A:. In this case, when you try to print to a port such as LPT1.PRN= (as specified in the [Ports] section of your WIN.INI), you may receive the message, "System Error, Cannot Read From Drive A:." Reading is not the problem; when you insert a formatted diskette in A:, you will be able to print to the file.

Finally, some applications become "funny" after you open a file from a floppy diskette. Word for Windows 1.*x* creates temporary files in the same directory from which it opens documents. When this directory is on a floppy drive, exiting Word for Windows cleans up any temporary files it wrote. But if the diskette has been removed from that drive *before* exiting the application, Winword may refuse to exit (making it impossible for you to even close Windows) until you have found that diskette and placed it back into the drive so Winword can examine it for the presence of any possible temporary files. If you are in this situation and can't find that diskette, the only solution is to reboot.

Disk Drive Anomalies

The remainder of this chapter explains anomalies you may encounter with specific brands of disk drives and controllers.

Adaptec Controller Boards

Disabling Double-buffering May Be Required

Some Adaptec controller boards require that the double-buffering feature of Windows' SmartDrive disk cache in 386 enhanced mode be disabled. If this is the case (contact your Adaptec distributor for exact models involved), you must add the undocumented /B- switch, as described in the SmartDrive section earlier in this chapter, to the SmartDrive line in CONFIG.SYS, as follows:

```
DEVICE=c:\windows\SMARTDRV.SYS 512 256 /B-
```

Colorado Memory Systems (CMS)

Tape Drives Require Upgrade

Software that controls Colorado Memory Systems (CMS) tape drives may need to be upgraded to work with Windows 3.0. Tape backup controller cards that this might affect include the CMS AB-10 and DJ-10. Tape drives affected include the CMS Jumbo 120, and the Tallgrass TG-1140, which is similar in function to the Jumbo 120. Call Colorado Memory Systems at 800-346-9881 or 800-432-5858.

Columbia Data Products SCSI

Drivers Require Upgrade

Columbia Data Products SCSI drives use Western Digital 7000 FASST controllers, which require a software upgrade from the version that was current when Windows 3.0 was shipped. Although versions 3.3 through 3.35 of these software drivers may work under Windows 3.*x*, Columbia recommends that this software be upgraded to version 3.36 or higher.

The FASST SCSI controller requires configuration in your CONFIG.SYS similar to the following:

```
DEVICE=c:\directory\SSTBIO.SYS  /W:1
DEVICE=c:\directory\SSTDRIVE.SYS
```

Contact Columbia Data Products at P.O. Box 2584, 1070-B Rainier Drive, Altamonte Springs, FL 32714, 407-869-6700, or through their bulletin board at 407-862-4724.

Core Technologies

Disk Controllers Hang 386 Mode

The CNT-MCK and CNT-MCA disk controllers from Core Technologies require a fix to operate with Windows in 386 mode. The symptoms of this incompatibility include Windows crashing and returning you to the DOS prompt unexpectedly. This problem occurs on PS/2 and Micro Channel Architecture-type machines only. Call the technical support department of Core Technologies at 407-997-6033.

IBM

PS/2's Require DASDDRVR.SYS Patch

Several models of the IBM PS/2 family require a fix to their BIOS code to allow Windows and other applications to function properly with the PS/2 hard disks in these machines. This is done by loading a file called DASDDRVR.SYS (pronounced DAZ-dee driver) in your CONFIG.SYS file. Only the following PS/2's are involved:

PS/2 Models 70 and 80-041/071 (16 MHz models)
PS/2 Model 60-041/071
PS/2 Model 50-021 (the non-Z Model 50 with 20MB hard disk)

Operating with the wrong DASDDRVR.SYS version produces any of the following messages:

"Not ready error reading drive A:" at random intervals.

"General failure" when accessing a hard disk (intermittent).

"Track 0 bad, or invalid media" after formatting several 3.5" floppy disks.

Errors "301" or "8602" displayed after turning the system off then on quickly.

Errors "162" and "163" displayed, and date and time are lost.

A prompt for a password although you have not implemented password security.

Stating password already exists when you try to implement password security.

All of these problems are corrected by including the latest version of DASDDRVR.SYS in your CONFIG.SYS file. This version is number 1.03 or higher. Version 1.03 is 734 bytes in length, and is provided on IBM Model 50/60 and 70/80 Reference Disks.

When DASDDRVR.SYS is loaded from CONFIG.SYS, it checks the date of the PS/2 BIOS chip, as well as the exact model of the PS/2 it is running on. If this information matches the types of systems the driver is looking for, it loads a small memory-resident program that corrects the above problems. If not, the driver does not apply any patches or occupy any memory. DASDDRVR.SYS should be used if there is any doubt about whether or not it is needed, since it cannot hurt if it isn't needed.

Note that the IBM PS/2 Model 30-286 is also shipped with a disk file named DASDDRVR.SYS, but this file is not the same file as described above and operates on a completely different set of problems. Additionally, the Reference Disk for the PS/2 Model 55 *does* contain the same DASDDRVR.SYS file (734 bytes), but this was included on the disk mistakenly and is not necessary for the Model 55.

Iomega Corp.

Bernoulli Box Must Be "Locked" to Install Winword

Word for Windows 1.*x*'s installation procedure may display the error message, "Information file not in current directory," and fail to install on Iomega Bernoulli Box drive cartridges. This occurs because Word for Windows will not install itself onto removable media, such as floppy diskettes and removable Bernoulli cartridges, and deletes the SETUP.INF file on the original Winword Setup disk if this is the case. The solution is to "lock" the Bernoulli cartridges before installing Word for Windows. Then Word for Windows will recognize the Bernoulli Box drives as hard disks. The routine for locking Bernoulli cartridges is different for various models; the procedure is explained in the manual for your particular model. If you did not make a backup copy of the Word for Windows disks before trying to install from them, you must call Microsoft sales office at 800-426-9400 or 206-936-8661 to get a replacement Setup disk.

Additionally, if you try to install Windows 3.*x* to a Bernoulli drive, and Windows runs in real mode but hangs in enhanced mode, you may have a conflict between the way your Bernoulli interface board is physically set up and the parameters in CONFIG.SYS to the device driver RCD.SYS.

Without any parameters, RCD.SYS uses the Direct Memory Access (DMA) method for input/output to the Bernoulli drives. When loaded with an /F parameter, as in DEVICE=RCD.SYS /F, the driver uses "programmed" I/O instead of DMA. The switches on the controller board must agree with whichever method RCD.SYS is using.

Call Iomega at 800-456-5522 or 801-778-3000 for more information.

Plus Development Corp.

Configuring Impulse Hard Drives

The Plus Development Corp., which markets the successful Hardcard and Hardcard II add-in drives, has also developed Impulse hard drives which use their own disk interface known as the *Cluster Disk Interface,* or CDI. These drives require the line VIRTUALHDIRQ=OFF in the [386Enh] section of SYSTEM.INI to run correctly with Windows in 386 enhanced mode. In addition, it may be necessary to exclude the adapter-segment memory area C000-DFFF, which is used by these drives. The following statements in the [386Enh] section of your SYSTEM.INI file would accomplish this (these lines are not case sensitive):

```
[386Enh]
VirtualHDIRQ=off
EMMExclude=C000-DFFF
```

More information on CDI technology is available from Plus Development Corp. by calling 408-944-0410 or 900-740-4433.

Hardcard Driver Upgrade

The Plus Hardcard II 40 and 80 drivers must be upgraded to at least version 1.31 of the file ATDOSHC2.SYS to work with Windows 3.0. Version 1.30 of this driver can cause inaccurate reading of the Hardcard II drives under Windows. Version 1.31 corrects this, and may be identified by the wording "Revision C" on the original diskette label. If you do not have this version of the file, you can download it from Plus's bulletin board system. Set your communication program to 8 data bits, 1 stop bit, and no parity bits. Dial 408-434-1664 and use the password PLUS. Obtain the Hardcard II driver file by downloading ATDOSHC2.EXE. Another file, named HCII.EXE, includes both this driver as well as other disk utilities.

At this writing, no updated drivers were available for the older Hardcard 20 and 40 models. To run Windows in enhanced mode with older Hardcard drives, you must include the line VIRTUALHDIRQ=OFF in the [386Enh] section of SYSTEM.INI. This line is not case sensitive. Hardcards may also require a disk cache that uses double-buffering, such as SmartDrive, in Windows' enhanced mode.

Call technical support at Plus Development at 408-944-0410 or 900-740-4433.

Vertisoft

Double Disk Requires Upgrade

The Double Disk software from Vertisoft Systems that was current when Windows 3.0 shipped requires an upgrade for compatibility with all Windows modes. Double Disk allows you to create logical drives through a utility program. Version 2.14b or higher is required for full Windows functionality. Contact Vertisoft's technical support department at 803-836-6686, or call 201-780-8641 to order the upgrade.

Western Digital

WD1007A ESDI Controller May Hang

Windows may hang in 386 enhanced mode when starting up with a WD1007A ESDI hard disk controller in the system. Fix this by running SMARTDRV.SYS in the CONFIG.SYS file, and adding the statement VIRTUALHDIRQ=OFF (not case sensitive) to the [386Enh] section of the

SYSTEM.INI file. SMARTDRV.SYS puts a buffer between applications and the hard disk controller, which helps many controllers that might otherwise not work with Windows. And turning off direct writes to the hard disk interrupt (HD IRQ) can improve compatibility, although it may hurt performance somewhat.

Summary

This chapter has presented as much information as possible on the use and optimization of disk drives of all types. This includes:

▶ How Windows works with hard drives in real, standard, and 386 enhanced modes.

▶ What the SmartDrive disk cache does to improve performance of hard drives, and how to use documented and undocumented features of it to take advantage of caching.

▶ How to prevent problems when using disk cache programs with hard drives larger than 32MB.

▶ Alternative disk cache programs that offer better performance and more features than SmartDrive.

▶ Maximizing the use of the four different kinds of temporary and swap files that Windows and Windows applications create.

▶ Installing RAM drives for use with Windows and Windows applications.

▶ Configuring SCSI drives and other bus-mastering devices to work under Windows and multitasking environments in general.

▶ The anomalies of various drive models that could present problems for their reliability under Windows.

Chapter 9
Keyboards

In this chapter...

I'll cover the following topics:

▶ Preventing permanent damage from using your keyboard under Windows and DOS.

▶ Finding all the Windows shortcut keys that can speed up your work.

▶ Determining all possible key combinations on your keyboard that can be redefined in Windows.

▶ Understanding the character sets available to your keyboard under Windows and how they differ from the ones available under DOS.

▶ Dealing with changes between U.S. and non-U.S. keyboard layouts.

▶ Identifying anomalies in keyboards from various manufacturers that can interfere with the proper operation of Windows.

Your keyboard is one of the most important peripherals in your computer system. You may *look* at your monitor and *reach* for your mouse, but you *use* your keyboard almost constantly. This constant use makes keyboards so mundane that they become invisible, almost unnoticed. But the routine existence of keyboards does nothing to minimize their importance to your work, your comfort level, and even your health.

Windows handles the keyboard in general, and several important keystrokes in particular, very differently than most character-based DOS applications. Some of these differences give you more functions than you had under DOS, but all the keyboard enhancements will eventually affect your work in one way or another. You might as well find out about these features before having to learn them through trial-and-error.

Keyboards

The Biggest Threat to Your Health

Windows and PC software in general has been growing in sales at an explosive rate. But the growth of personal computing, and the proliferation of the keyboards that must be used to run DOS and Windows programs, has taken place without most people noticing a shocking fact:

> **Hand and wrist injuries caused by constantly repeated motions have become more prevalent than all other categories of job-related illnesses combined. A majority of *all* occupational illnesses in the U.S. (52 percent in 1989) are now repetitive-motion disorders such as carpal tunnel syndrome, which causes debilitating pains in sensitive hand and wrist tissue.**

Repetitive-motion disorders have been known for years, and do not afflict only office workers who use computer keyboards. Workers in automobile assembly lines and meat-packing plants, who make the same bolting or cutting actions over and over, commonly develop repetitive stress disabilities such as *tendonitis* and *carpal tunnel syndrome,* both of which cause tendons in the wrist to swell up and are accompanied by chronic pain.

But it is the widespread growth of the PC keyboard, and the speed with which these keyboards can be used (compared with older electric typewriters), that has caused a change in the nature and frequency of repetitive-motion disorders in the workplace and the home. And Windows — with its procedures requiring close hand-eye coordination of keyboard, mouse, and monitor — can only exacerbate this trend.

Repetitive-motion disabilities were responsible for only 18 percent of all job-related illnesses in 1981, according to the U.S. Bureau of Labor Statistics. But during the 1980s, a decade that coincided with explosive growth of PCs, these syndromes rose steadily in frequency, reaching 52 percent of job-related illnesses in 1989.

The connection between repetitive-motion disorders and computer keyboards is beginning to hit companies financially. U.S. West, Inc., the regional telephone company that provides services in several western U.S. states, spent $1.6 million from 1986 to 1990 on medical expenses related to repetitive-motion disabilities afflicting 240 of the operators in its Denver region.

The company plans to spend $13.5 million over an eight-year period to replace older office equipment with adjustable workstations and chairs.

Many other companies are affected as well. A study of 2,000 members of the Communications Workers of America, who are largely clerical workers, found that 20 percent could be diagnosed with either carpal tunnel syndrome or tendonitis. Workplaces will be hit hard as the chronic nature of repetitive-motion disorders adds up to major medical bills in the not-so-distant future.

Carpal tunnel syndrome leads to disabling pain that can leave victims unable to open a jar lid or button a shirt. After months or years of stress, tendons passing through the narrow bony structure in the wrist — the carpal tunnel — become enlarged and press on the median nerve to the hand. Surgery to relieve this pressure may mitigate the pain but is not always effective. Surgical procedures aimed at helping carpal tunnel syndrome sufferers is the second most frequently performed operation in the U.S. (after Caesarian births), according to Barbara Goldoftas, a Harvard University professor who won a National Magazine Award in 1990 for her reporting on the subject.

You can avoid repetitive-stress injuries by taking the following steps:

STEPS:

Avoiding Repetitive-Stress Injuries

Step 1. Move your keyboard so it is level with your wrists. Make sure your keyboard is located at standard "typing return" height, usually about 26.5 inches from the floor, not desktop height (29 inches). The best position for your wrist and lower arms when typing is parallel to the ground, not bent over to reach a keyboard awkwardly placed on an ordinary desktop surface. Of course, the typing returns that are built into the desks where many people work may not be adequate for your PC. Corporate purchasing agents continue to buy office desks with returns only 18 inches deep — enough for the Selectric typewriters of a bygone era but not today's keyboard-and-monitor combinations. If you are stuck with a configuration like this, get rid of the return by unscrewing it from your desk. Then buy a rolling stand 26.5 inches high and large enough to place your keyboard and monitor in a straight line of sight. In my own home, I've moved my work desk away from the wall and placed a small table behind the return to extend it into a 30" × 30" surface. This is the minimum you need for a keyboard, monitor, copy holder, and mouse pad.

Step 2. Adjust your chair to the height of your keyboard. Most office chairs can be raised to bring you level with your typing surface. If your company won't buy you an adjustable chair, buy a good, expensive one yourself (it's cheaper than disability insurance), put your name on it and take it with you to your next job.

Step 3. Make yourself take constant breaks. Even more important than adjusting furniture and chairs is taking tiny, frequent breaks that prevent stress in the wrists from building up. Electric typewriters used to enforce their own little microbreaks on you throughout the day; you needed to insert paper into the roller, apply white-out, and so on. With today's computer systems that allow the constant motion of tens of thousands of keystrokes an hour, it is important to pause for a breather now and then, no matter how much work pressure there is.

Repetitive-motion syndrome can be beaten by designing your work so it is comfortable and healthful. And good office design can pay off in more than just lower health-benefit expenses. Office workers can increase their productivity by 25 percent with proper adjustments in their workstations, according to the Center for Ergonomic Research at Miami University (Oxford, Ohio). Take whatever steps are necessary to organize your work area to fit your needs.

Using Keyboard Shortcuts

This section deals with the many shortcuts that are assigned to key combinations such as Ctrl+Insert and Ctrl+A by Windows and Windows applications. Additionally, you may want to redefine key combinations that aren't used by *any* Windows applications in order to support your own macros.

Microsoft also makes available an optional keyboard driver that allows you to press and release shift keys such as Ctrl and Alt *before* pressing the letter key of the combination. I provide information on this keyboard-and-mouse access driver in Chapter 10.

The Most Important (and Poorly Documented) Shortcuts

Despite the ease-of-use publicity about Windows, a novice Windows user is confronted with a bewildering array of new objects to click and shortcut keys to learn. These shortcut keys are difficult to memorize because the Windows manual does not include a chart of these keys in any one place, and some shortcuts are not documented at all. Once learned, furthermore, these shortcuts are difficult to remember because many of the key combinations are confusingly similar and do not follow any logical pattern.

Pressing Alt+Esc, for example, switches you from your current application to other applications running under Windows, while Alt+F4 exits the application that is running. Quick — do you remember which is which? Why is the act of exiting assigned to an F4 key combination instead of one based on the "escape" key? Haven't millions of DOS users learned that the Esc key is used to back out of applications?

Windows and Windows applications are full of other inconsistencies in the way they use shortcut keys — even in applications that were all written at Microsoft. Despite what you've heard that "all Windows applications work the same way," even as common an action as File Save is assigned to Ctrl+S in Windows Paintbrush but Shift+F12 in Microsoft Excel and Word for Windows. And applets like Windows Notepad and Recorder have no shortcut key for File Save at all!

Similarly, both Windows File Manager and Word for Windows have "Show All" options, and both programs use Ctrl+Asterisk to turn the Show All feature on and off. (File Manager shows all directories on a drive, while Word for Windows shows all editing marks in a document.) But the File Manager allows you to toggle Show All by pressing the Ctrl key and the asterisk key on the numeric keypad. In Word for Windows, Ctrl and keypad-asterisk doesn't work. You actually must press Ctrl+Shift+8 to get Ctrl+Asterisk (because there is an asterisk on top of the 8 key).

Worse, all Windows applications, such as Program Manager, which support multiple, smaller windows (*child windows*) inside their main application window allow you to jump quickly from child window to child window by pressing Ctrl+Tab. But not Word for Windows — Ctrl+Tab actually inserts a Tab character inside document tables. To cycle through child windows in Winword requires Ctrl+F6.

Despite these inconsistencies, there are many shortcut keys that work the same way in all or most Windows applications. I have gathered many of these together in Figure 9-1.

Key Combination	Result
Alt or F10	Pressed and released without any other keys, activates an application's menu bar. Then you can pull down any menu with the keyboard by moving to the menu name with a cursor arrow and pressing Enter or Down-Arrow.
Alt+{letter}	Activates the choice on an application's menu that has an underlined letter corresponding to the letter you pressed. Works the same way if you press and release Alt, then press the letter.
Alt+Down-Arrow	Displays the contents of a drop-down list box (such as color schemes available in the Colors section of the Windows Control Panel).
End	Moves to the end of a line (in a word processor).
Ctrl+End	Moves to the end of a document (in a word processor).
Enter	Selects a choice that is highlighted on a menu or in a dialog box.
Alt+Enter	In Windows' 386 enhanced mode only, switches a DOS application that is running full-screen to running in a small window (and back). For some reason, this doesn't work to toggle Windows applications from full-screen to a small window and back.
Esc	Closes dialog box or drop-down menu without taking an action.
Alt+Esc	Switches to another application running under Windows in a round-robin fashion each time you press this combination.
Ctrl+Esc	Brings up the Task List dialog box, which displays all running applications and allows you to switch to one, close one, or move all the applications into a Cascade or Tile arrangement. With a mouse, double-clicking an unoccupied space on the Windows Desktop (the patterned background) also brings up the Task List.
Alt+F4	Closes the current application. If the current application is your Windows "shell" program (such as Program Manager, File Manager, or MS-DOS Executive), this also exits Windows after you give confirmation.
Ctrl+F4	Closes a child window in Windows applications that support the Multiple Document Interface (File Manager, Word for Windows, etc.).
Home	Moves to the beginning of a line (in a word processor).
Ctrl+Home	Moves to the beginning of a document (in a word processor). *(continued)*

Figure 9-1. Shortcut keys in Windows. Many of these shortcut keys are important because a mouse cannot perform the same action, or performs it less conveniently.

Key Combination	Result
Alt+Hyphen	Pulls down an application's Document Control menu — the small horizontal icon at the extreme left of the application's main menu — which controls the size and other aspects of the document's child window. Do not confuse this with the Control menu (see Alt+Spacebar), which controls the application itself.
PrintScreen	Copies the entire Windows display to the Clipboard. It can then be pasted into Paintbrush or another graphics app and printed.
Alt+PrintScreen	Copies only the currently active window to the Clipboard. This could be the current foreground application, or a dialog box that has the keyboard focus within that app. May not work on 84-key keyboards and computers with old BIOS chips. In that case, try Shift+PrintScreen instead.
Spacebar	Toggles a choice that the selection cursor is on in a dialog box (see Tab).
Alt+Spacebar	Pulls down the Control menu, the long horizontal icon in the extreme upper-left corner of an application's window, which controls that application's size and other aspects.
Tab	Moves the selection cursor (a dotted rectangular box) to the next choice in a dialog box.
Shift+Tab	Moves the selection cursor in reverse order.
Alt+Tab	Switches to the application that was the current application before the application you are presently in. Switches back when pressed again. May not work on 84-key keyboards and computers with old keyboard BIOS chips.
Alt+Tab+Tab	Switches in turn to every application running under Windows (same as Alt+Esc) but displays only the title bar without redrawing the entire window. Hold down the Alt key while you press Tab repeatedly. Release the Alt key when the title bar of the application you want to switch to is highlighted. Undocumented feature. May not work on 84-key keyboards and computers with old keyboard BIOS chips.
Ctrl+Tab or Ctrl+F6	Jumps to the next child window in an application that supports the Multiple Document Interface, such as Program Manager and File Manager. (Ctrl+F6 in Word for Windows.)

Figure 9-1. Shortcut keys in Windows *(continued)*.

Undocumented Features of Ctrl+Esc and Alt+Tab+Tab

Two of the most useful and interesting key combinations are Ctrl+Esc and the undocumented Alt+Tab+Tab shortcut.

Ctrl+Esc — The Task List

Ctrl+Esc brings up a small window called the Task List. This window lists every application that is currently running under Windows. This is very useful in Windows because it is easy to open several applications and lose track of which ones are running (and where they are on the screen, if the one you want is hidden behind another window). Double-clicking on the name of one of the other running applications switches you to that window. Buttons in the Task List window also allow you to close any of the applications, or arrange all running applications on the screen in the <u>C</u>ascade or <u>T</u>ile patterns. The Task List can also be brought up by double-clicking your mouse on any unoccupied portion of the Windows Desktop area (the colored or patterned background). But if you are presently running an application full-screen and none of the Desktop is visible, Ctrl+Esc is the only way to access the Task List without reducing the size of your foreground window.

An undocumented feature of the Task List is that you can make *any* Windows application start up automatically when you double-click the Desktop or press Ctrl+Esc. Simply rename the Task List executable file TASKMAN.EXE (located in your Windows directory) to something else, and copy the executable file of another Windows application to the name TASKMAN.EXE.

For example, to make the Windows Calculator pop up over any application when you press Ctrl+Esc, rename TASKMAN.EXE to TASKMAN2.EXE and make a copy of CALC.EXE called TASKMAN.EXE. When you press Ctrl+Esc, or double-click the Windows Desktop, the Calculator pops up instead of the Task List. Once you've tried this, copy TASKMAN2.EXE back over TASKMAN.EXE and delete TASKMAN2.EXE to put your system back the way it was.

It isn't a good idea to use this renaming trick without a compelling reason, because you are interfering with an important Windows built-in function. In a moment I'll describe the preferred method, using the Windows Recorder. But renaming the Task List does work if you have a desperate need to start up one application from within any other in this exact way.

If you use this trick to start an application that takes a filename on its command line (such as the text editors Windows Write and Notepad), they display an error message when they start up similar to "Cannot find file *0123.*" This message can be dismissed with a click on its OK button, and the application then works as expected. What's happening is that the Windows code that handles Ctrl+Esc is trying to load a temporary file with a list of running applications into whatever program you have executed, expecting the program to be the usual TASKMAN.EXE Task List. Applications that don't look for parameters on their command line, such as the Calculator, don't even try to read the file and so won't display the error message.

A better way to make one application available from within another is to use the Windows Recorder to record a macro that starts the desired application. Then save that macro, with its own hotkey combination (such as Ctrl+Shift+A) in a Recorder file that you load in WIN.INI every time you start Windows. (See the description of Recorder's undocumented features in Chapter 2.) And a better Task List than Windows' Task List is provided by Task Manager (a shareware program on the diskettes included with this book).

Alt+Tab+Tab — The Undocumented Task Switcher

In addition to Ctrl+Esc, other shortcut key combinations allow you to switch among running applications. These include Alt+Esc, which opens a different application every time you press it, and Alt+Tab, which switches from your current foreground application to the application you previously used, and back.

 But the best way to switch among your running applications isn't documented at all. Just hold down the Alt key while you press the Tab key several times, pausing slightly between each press. Unlike Alt+Esc, which switches applications and redraws the window for every application in turn, Alt+Tab+Tab switches applications but redraws *only each application's title bar.* Since redrawing the entire window is always slower than just redrawing a title bar, Alt+Tab+Tab is a much faster method than Alt+Esc to cycle through all your running applications until you find the one you want. Simply release the Alt key when the desired application's title bar is highlighted, and that application's window will be fully redrawn and becomes the foreground.

Alt+Esc and Alt+Tab+Tab work with both Windows apps and DOS apps running under Windows, whether these apps are running full-screen, in a smaller window, or minimized as an icon. If an application is running as an icon, Alt+Tab+Tab does not restore the application's window but merely highlights the title under the icon (unless you let go of the Alt key to select that app). If a DOS application is running full-screen in text mode, Alt+Tab+Tab displays a text-mode banner line on-screen that represents the title bar of each application you are cycling to. The screen does not switch from text mode to graphics mode unless you let up on the Alt key; the window of the application you selected is then redrawn.

The Alt+Tab+Tab feature may have been left undocumented because 84-key keyboards and computers with older keyboard BIOS chips may not recognize the key combination "Alt" and "Tab." The IBM BIOS for its enhanced AT 101-key keyboard was one of the first to accept the Alt key as a way to modify the meaning of the Tab key. Test your keyboard to see which combinations of keys you can take advantage of. If you have a 101-key keyboard, you shouldn't have a problem with Alt+Tab+Tab or any of the other possible combinations.

Placing Your Own Macros on Key Combinations

The shortcut key combinations that are defined by Windows are all well and good. But the time comes when you want to define your own hotkeys. These hotkeys might invoke one of a series of Recorder macros (which can be made available within all Windows applications, as described in Chapter 2). Or they might apply only to macros in a single application, such as Excel, Word for Windows, or Amí.

In either case, you probably want to avoid redefining a key combination that is already in use by Windows, any Windows applications you have now, and any Windows applications you may acquire in the future. Unfortunately, there does not seem to be an ironclad rule about which key combinations Windows applications will always leave alone, to be defined as desired by users and microcomputer managers.

One way to determine which key combinations are "safe" for your redefined hotkeys is to look at the way Word for Windows uses key combinations. Winword grabs practically every combination of Ctrl, Alt, and Shift+Alt with every key on the keyboard. This pattern of assignments is shown in Figure 9-2.

The notable key combinations that are left "untouched" for you to redefine are:

◆ **Ctrl+Shift** plus A through Z and 0 through 9;

◆ **Punctuation marks** plus Ctrl, Alt, Ctrl+Shift, and Ctrl+Alt; and

◆ **Ctrl+Alt** (and Ctrl+Shift+Alt, not shown) plus almost any other character.

These combinations, then, are the best choices to redefine for your own macros, with the least chance of inadvertently interfering with a built-in function of a Windows app. (Word for Windows uses a lot of shortcut key combinations, but this does not ensure, of course, that some other Windows application won't come along and claim a hotkey that you devoted a lot of time to redefining.)

There are, however, a few notable exceptions to this list. For example:

◆ **Ctrl+Shift:** Winword doesn't use combinations of Ctrl+Shift with A through Z and 0 through 9, with the exception of Ctrl+Shift+8 as "Show All Marks";

◆ **Punctuation keys:** Winword uses the shift keys Ctrl, Shift, and Alt in combination with the hyphen (-) and equals (=) keys to make optional hyphens, superscripts and subscripts, and the like; and

◆ **Ctrl+Alt:** Even though most Windows applications make no use of Ctrl+Alt combinations (because you could accidentally hit Ctrl+Alt+Del), you'll find that Ctrl+Alt+F1 and Ctrl+Alt+F2 are reserved. This is because Windows requires that all key combinations involving F11 and F12 also perform the same action as when users press Alt+F1 and Alt+F2. Ctrl+Alt+F1 and Ctrl+Alt+F2, therefore, are hard-coded by Windows to do the same thing as pressing Ctrl+F11 and Ctrl+F12 (for 84-key keyboards, which lack F11 and F12 keys).

Alphanumeric Keys

Key	Key Alone	Shift+	Ctrl+	Ctrl+Shift+	Alt+	Alt+Shift+	Ctrl+Alt+
A	a	A	Show all in Define Styles			Show all in outline view	
B	b	B	Boldface text				
C	c	C	Center paragraph			Close pane	
D	d	D	Double underline text			Insert date field	
E	e	E	Close space before para.		Open Edit menu	Step through macro	
F	f	F	Font...		Open File menu	Show first line	
G	g	G	Unindent hanging paragraph		Open Help menu		
H	h	H	Hidden text				
I	i	I	Italic text				
J	j	J	Justify paragraph				
K	k	K	Small capitals text			Edit Header/Footer Link	
L	l	L	Left align paragraph				
M	m	M	Unnest		Open Macro menu		
N	n	N	Nest				
O	o	O	Open space before para.			Continue macro	
P	p	P	Point size...			Insert page field	
Q	q	Q					
R	r	R	Right align paragraph			Trace macro	
S	s	S	Assign style to paragraph			Start macro	
T	t	T	Hanging indent paragraph		Open Format menu	Insert time field	
U	u	U	Continuous underline text		Open Utilities menu	Step SUBs in macro	
V	v	V	Assign visible color to text		Open View menu	Show variables in macro	
W	w	W	Word underline text		Open Window menu		
X	x	X	Reset paragraph				
Y	y	Y					
Z	z	Z	Strikethru (search & repl.)				
1	1	!	Single line spacing			Show outline headings to 1	
2	2	@	Double line spacing			Show outline headings to 2	
3	3	#				Show outline headings to 3	
4	4	$				Show outline headings to 4	
5	5	%	1.5 line spacing			Show outline headings to 5	
6	6	<				Show outline headings to 6	
7	7	&				Show outline headings to 7	
8	8	*		Show all character marks		Show outline headings to 8	
9	9	(				Show outline headings to 9	
0	0	)					
Spacebar	Space	Space	Reset characters	Nonbreaking space	Open Control menu		
Backspace	Delete character left	Delete character left	Delete word left		Undo		
Enter	New paragraph	New line, same paragraph	Page break	Column break	Repeat		
Tab	Tab or next table cell	Backtab or prev. table cell	Insert tab in a table				

Figure 9-2: Shortcut keys assigned in Winword. This chart is in the WordBasic directory on the diskettes included with this book. Set Winword to View Draft before opening the file. Print it on a printer with Helvetica Condensed (such as a PostScript printer).

Punctuation Keys

Key Alone	Shift+	Ctrl+	Ctrl+Shift+	Alt+	Alt+Shift+	Ctrl+Alt+
Hyphen	Underscore	Optional hyphen	Nonbreaking hyphen	Open Doc. Control menu	Collapse outline	
Equal sign	Plus sign	Subscript	Superscript	Expand outline		
Backquote	Tilde					
Open bracket	Open brace					
Closed bracket	Closed brace					
Semicolon	Colon					
Single quote mark	Double quote mark					
Comma	Less-than sign					
Period	Greater-than sign					
Slash	Question mark					
Backslash	Vertical bar					

Function Keys

	Key Alone	Shift+	Ctrl+	Ctrl+Shift+	Alt+	Alt+Shift+	Ctrl+Alt+
F1	Help	Help using mouse pointer			Next field	Previous field	Lock field
F2	Move	Copy	Grow font	Shrink font	File Save As...	File Save	File Open
F3	Expand glossary name	Toggle case	Spike	Unspike			
F4	Repeat last action	Repeat search or Go To	Close document window		Close Word window		
F5	Go To...	Go back to previous point	Restore document window	Insert bookmark	Restore Word window		
F6	Next pane	Previous pane	Next document window	Previous document window	Next document window		
F7	Spell-check selection	Thesaurus	Move document window	Update source of field	Move Word window	Previous document window	
F8	Extend selection	Shrink selection	Size document window	Column (block) selection	Size Word window		
F9	Update fields	Toggle field codes view	Insert field	Unlink field; repl. w/result	Minimize Word window	Do field click	
F10	Menu	Icon	Maximize doc. window	Ruler mode	Maximize Word window		
F11	Next field	Previous field	Lock field	Unlock field	Next field	Previous field	Lock field
F12	File Save As...	File Save	File Open	File Print	File Save As...	File Save	File Open

Direction Keys

	Key Alone	Shift+	Ctrl+	Ctrl+Shift+	Alt+	Alt+Shift+	Ctrl+Alt+
Left	Left 1 character	Select left 1 character	Left 1 word	Select left 1 word	Left 1 word	Promote heading	
Right	Right 1 character	Select right 1 character	Right 1 word	Select right 1 word	Right 1 word	Demote heading	
Up	Up 1 line	Select up 1 line	Up 1 paragraph	Select up 1 paragraph	Previous region in pg. view	Move paragraph up	
Down	Down 1 line	Select down 1 line	Down 1 paragraph	Select down 1 paragraph	Next region in page view	Move paragraph down	
Home	Beginning of line	Select to beginning of line	Beginning of document	Select to beginning of doc.	Beginning of row in a table	Select to beginning of row	
End	End of line	Select to end of line	End of document	Select to end of document	End of row in a table	Select to end of row	
PgUp	Up 1 windowful	Select up 1 windowful	Top of window	Select to window top	Top of column in a table	Select to top of column	
Down	Down 1 windowful	Select down 1 windowful	Bottom of window	Select to window bottom	Bottom of column in a table	Select to bottom of column	
Insert	Toggle Insert/Overtype	Insert from Clipboard	Copy to Clipboard				
Delete	Delete right	Delete to Clipboard	Delete to end of word				

Numeric-Keypad Keys

	Key Alone	Shift+	Ctrl+	Ctrl+Shift+	Alt+	Alt+Shift+	Ctrl+Alt+
Keypad 5			Select entire document		Select entire table		
Grey +	Expand outline					Apply Normal style	
Grey –	Collapse outline					Expand outline	
Grey *	Show all levels					Collapse outline	

Figure 9-2: Shortcut keys assigned in Winword (continued).

Keyboard Characters

Taking Advantage of the Windows ANSI Character Set

One of the most important enhancements Windows makes available to the PC keyboard is a larger set of characters than the one that can be accessed under DOS. This character set is referred to as the ANSI set. ANSI stands for the American National Standards Institute, which works with the International Standards Organization (ISO), a United Nations agency, to establish language standards and many other types of agreements.

While the number of total characters possible under the ANSI standard is the same as under DOS — 256, the number of possible combinations in an 8-bit byte — more international characters and symbols are available in Windows because the ANSI set eliminates the line-drawing and math characters that are part of the PC-8 set present in most IBM-compatibles. By moving the IBM math characters into a new Symbol font, and deleting the line-draw characters entirely, Windows adds support for several accented letters needed in various languages, as well as for copyright and trademark symbols and the like. (Most Windows word-processing applications can draw lines without having to use text characters. And even those holdouts that couldn't draw lines in their original release — like Word for Windows 1.*x,* which was limited to drawing paragraph borders — gained that feature in later releases.)

The IBM PC-8 character set is shown in Figure 9-3. In the U.S. keyboard layout, the main keyboard provides keys for each of the alphabetic characters and punctuation marks, numbered 32 through 127. The other characters, under DOS, are accessed by holding down the Alt key, typing the appropriate character number on the numeric keypad (with NumLock *on*), and then releasing the Alt key. Alt+157, for example, produces ¥, the Japanese Yen symbol.

Although the PC-8 character set seems, to many people, a chaotic jumble of letters and signs, there is a natural order of sorts (no pun intended). The first 32 characters are control codes (including tab and carriage return characters); the next 32 are punctuation and numerals; the 32 after that include capital letters; exactly 32 places above that are the lowercase equivalents; and so on.

This kind of natural order also exists in the Windows ANSI character set, which is shown in Figure 9-4. This chart is also contained in the WordBasic directory on the diskettes included with this book. If you decide to view

CTRL & PUNC:		ALPHABETIC:		ACCENTS & LINE DRAW:			MATH:
0 ■	32	64 @	96 `	128 Ç	160 á	192 └	224 α
1 ■	33 !	65 A	97 a	129 ü	161 í	193 ┴	225 β
2 ■	34 "	66 B	98 b	130 é	162 ó	194 ┬	226 Γ
3 ■	35 #	67 C	99 c	131 â	163 ú	195 ├	227 π
4 ■	36 $	68 D	100 d	132 ä	164 ñ	196 ─	228 Σ
5 ■	37 %	69 E	101 e	133 à	165 Ñ	197 ┼	229 σ
6 ■	38 &	70 F	102 f	134 å	166 ª	198 ╞	230 µ
7 ■	39 '	71 G	103 g	135 ç	167 º	199 ╟	231 τ
8 ■	40 (	72 H	104 h	136 ê	168 ¿	200 ╚	232 Φ
9 ■	41)	73 I	105 i	137 ë	169 ⌐	201 ╔	233 θ
10 ■	42 *	74 J	106 j	138 è	170 ¬	202 ╩	234 Ω
11 ■	43 +	75 K	107 k	139 ï	171 ½	203 ╦	235 δ
12 ■	44 ,	76 L	108 l	140 î	172 ¼	204 ╠	236 ∞
13 ■	45 -	77 M	109 m	141 ì	173 ¡	205 ═	237 φ
14 ■	46 .	78 N	110 n	142 Ä	174 «	206 ╬	238 ε
15 ■	47 /	79 O	111 o	143 Å	175 »	207 ╧	239 ∩
16 ■	48 0	80 P	112 p	144 É	176 ░	208 ╨	240 ≡
17 ■	49 1	81 Q	113 q	145 æ	177 ▒	209 ╤	241 ±
18 ■	50 2	82 R	114 r	146 Æ	178 ▓	210 ╥	242 ≥
19 ■	51 3	83 S	115 s	147 ô	179 │	211 ╙	243 ≤
20 ■	52 4	84 T	116 t	148 ö	180 ┤	212 ╘	244 ⌠
21 ■	53 5	85 U	117 u	149 ò	181 ╡	213 ╒	245 ⌡
22 ■	54 6	86 V	118 v	150 û	182 ╢	214 ╓	246 ÷
23 ■	55 7	87 W	119 w	151 ù	183 ╖	215 ╫	247 ≈
24 ■	56 8	88 X	120 x	152 ÿ	184 ╕	216 ╪	248 °
25 ■	57 9	89 Y	121 y	153 Ö	185 ╣	217 ┘	249 ·
26 ■	58 :	90 Z	122 z	154 Ü	186 ║	218 ┌	250 ·
27 ■	59 ;	91 [	123 {	155 ¢	187 ╗	219 █	251 √
28 ■	60 <	92 \	124 |	156 £	188 ╝	220 ▄	252 ⁿ
29 ■	61 =	93]	125 }	157 ¥	189 ╜	221 ▌	253 ²
30 ■	62 >	94 ^	126 ~	158 ₧	190 ╛	222 ▐	254 ■
31 ■	63 ?	95 _	127	159 ƒ	191 ┐	223 ▀	255

Figure 9-3: The IBM PC-8 character set. In addition to nonprintable control codes, punctuation, and alphabetic characters, the PC-8 character set includes accented and line-draw characters, and math symbols. The latter are accessed using the Alt key and the numeric keypad.

this file (SPECIAL.WRD) in Word for Windows, click View Draft before opening the file. This will save you a great deal of time when Winword draws the screen for all the higher-order characters. The file may then be printed to any PostScript printer, or any printer that supports 9-point. Century, Symbol, and ZapfDingbats fonts. (This is a test of whether your printer is correctly supporting these typefaces!)

The ANSI characters numbered 0 through 127 are identical to their counterparts in the PC-8 character set. (These characters are also called the "ASCII" or "lower ASCII" character set, after the American Standards Committee for

Normal font
　　↓ Symbol font
　　　↓ Zapf Dingbats font
Character Number → 112　p　π　□

Num	Normal	Symbol	Ding	Num	Normal	Symbol	Ding
32				64	@	≅	✐
33	!	!	✁	65	A	Α	✑
34	"	∀	✂	66	B	Β	✒
35	#	#	✃	67	C	Χ	✓
36	$	∃	✄	68	D	Δ	✔
37	%	%	☎	69	E	Ε	✕
38	&	&	✆	70	F	Φ	✖
39	'	∋	✇	71	G	Γ	✗
40	(	(	✈	72	H	Η	✘
41	)	)	✉	73	I	Ι	✙
42	*	∗	☛	74	J	ϑ	✚
43	+	+	☞	75	K	Κ	✛
44	,	,	✌	76	L	Λ	✜
45	-	−	✍	77	M	Μ	✝
46	.	.	✎	78	N	Ν	✞
47	/	/	✏	79	O	Ο	✟
48	0	0	✐	80	P	Π	✠
49	1	1	✑	81	Q	Θ	✡
50	2	2	✒	82	R	Ρ	✢
51	3	3	✓	83	S	Σ	✣
52	4	4	✔	84	T	Τ	✤
53	5	5	✕	85	U	Υ	✥
54	6	6	✖	86	V	ς	✦
55	7	7	✗	87	W	Ω	✧
56	8	8	✘	88	X	Ξ	✩
57	9	9	✚	89	Y	Ψ	✪
58	:	:	✛	90	Z	Ζ	✫
59	;	;	✜	91	[	[	✬
60	<	<	✭	92	\	∴	✮
61	=	=	†	93	]	]	✯
62	>	>	☞	94	^	⊥	✰
63	?	?	✞	95	_	_	✿

Num	Normal	Symbol	Ding	Num
96	`	‾	✾	0128
97	a	α	❀	0129
98	b	β	❁	0130
99	c	χ	✳	0131
100	d	δ	✴	0132
101	e	ε	✵	0133
102	f	φ	❂	0134
103	g	γ	✶	0135
104	h	η	✷	0136
105	i	ι	✸	0137
106	j	φ	✹	0138
107	k	κ	✺	0139
108	l	λ	●	0140
109	m	μ	○	0141
110	n	ν	■	0142
111	o	ο	□	0143
112	p	π	□	0144
113	q	θ	❏	0145
114	r	ρ	□	0146
115	s	σ	▲	0147
116	t	τ	▼	0148
117	u	υ	◆	0149
118	v	ϖ	◇	0150
119	w	ω	❖	0151
120	x	ξ	❘	0152
121	y	ψ	❙	0153
122	z	ζ	❚	0154
123	{	{	❛	0155
124	|	|	❜	0156
125	}	}	❝	0157
126	~	∼	❞	0158
127			❦	0159

Num	Normal	Symbol	Ding	Num	Normal	Symbol	Ding	Num	Normal	Symbol	Ding
0160				0192	À	ℵ	①	0224	à	◊	➡
0161	¡	ϒ	❡	0193	Á	ℑ	②	0225	á	〈	➤
0162	¢	′	❢	0194	Â	ℜ	③	0226	â	®	➢
0163	£	≤	❣	0195	Ã	℘	④	0227	ã	©	➣
0164	¤	⁄	♥	0196	Ä	⊗	⑤	0228	ä	™	➤
0165	¥	∞	♦	0197	Å	⊕	⑥	0229	å	∑	➥
0166	¦	ƒ	❦	0198	Æ	∅	⑦	0230	æ	⎛	➦
0167	§	♣	❧	0199	Ç	∩	⑧	0231	ç	⎜	➧
0168	¨	♦	♦	0200	È	∪	⑨	0232	è	⎝	➨
0169	©	♥	♦	0201	É	⊃	⑩	0233	é	⎡	➩
0170	ª	♠	❈	0202	Ê	⊇	❶	0234	ê	⎢	➪
0171	«	↔	❉	0203	Ë	⊄	❷	0235	ë	⎣	➫
0172	¬	←	①	0204	Ì	⊂	❸	0236	ì	⎡	➬
0173		↑	②	0205	Í	⊆	❹	0237	í	⎢	➭
0174	®	→	③	0206	Î	∈	❺	0238	î	⎣	➮
0175	¯	↓	④	0207	Ï	∉	❻	0239	ï	⎰	➯
0176	°	°	⑤	0208	Ð	∠	❼	0240	ð		
0177	±	±	⑥	0209	Ñ	∇	❽	0241	ñ	〉	➱
0178	²	″	⑦	0210	Ò	®	❾	0242	ò	∫	➲
0179	³	≥	⑧	0211	Ó	©	❿	0243	ó	⌠	➳
0180	´	×	⑨	0212	Ô	™	→	0244	ô	⎮	➴
0181	µ	∝	⑩	0213	Õ	∏	→	0245	õ	⌡	➵
0182	¶	∂	❶	0214	Ö	√	↔	0246	ö	⎞	➶
0183	·	•	❷	0215	×	·	↕	0247	÷	⎟	➷
0184	¸	÷	❸	0216	Ø	¬	↘	0248	ø	⎠	➸
0185	¹	≠	❹	0217	Ù	∧	→	0249	ù	⎤	➹
0186	º	≡	❺	0218	Ú	∨	↗	0250	ú	⎥	➺
0187	»	≈	❻	0219	Û	⇔	→	0251	û	⎦	➻
0188	¼	…	❼	0220	Ü	⇐	↞	0252	ü	⎤	➼
0189	½	⏐	❽	0221	Ý	⇑	↟	0253	ý	⎥	➽
0190	¾	—	❾	0222	Þ	⇒	→	0254	þ	⎦	➾
0191	¿	↵	❿	0223	ß	⇓	↠	0255	ÿ		

Searching and Replacing Special Characters

Winword allows searching and replacing of formats and any special character. To enter a character like the Tab key into a search request, for example, simply type ^t (caret t) where the Tab character would appear.

^d Section/page break	^^ Caret character	**Character Formats:**	Ctrl+U Underline	Ctrl+C Centered lines
^n Newline (↵)	^? Question mark	Ctrl+B Bold	Ctrl+V Color; next color	Ctrl+E Close space before
^p Paragraph (¶)	? Any single character	Ctrl+D Double underline	Ctrl+W Word underline	Ctrl+J Justified lines
^s Nonbreaking space	(in search only)	Ctrl+= Subscript, 3 pts.	Ctrl+Spacebar	Ctrl+L Left-aligned lines
^t Tab character	^w White space (spaces	Ctrl++ Superscript, 3 pts.	Remove formatting	Ctrl+O Open space before
^- Optional hyphen	or tabs–search only)	Ctrl+F Font; next font		Ctrl+R Right-aligned lines
^~ Nonbreaking hyphen		Ctrl+H Hidden text	**Paragraph Formats:**	Ctrl+X Remove formatting
^1 A picture	**Replace With:**	Ctrl+I Italic	Ctrl+1 Single-spaced lines	
^14 Column break	^c contents of Clipboard	Ctrl+K Small capitals	Ctrl+2 Double-spaced lines	**Styles:**
^nnn Special character	^m contents of Search	Ctrl+P Point size; next size	Ctrl+5 1.5-spaced lines	^ystylename Stylename only

Figure 9-4: Special characters in Word for Windows (requires a PostScript printer). Three kinds of typefaces are available in a PostScript printer: Text (Century, Helvetica, and so on), Symbol, and Dingbats. Characters numbered above 127 are typed by holding down the Alt key and typing the number on the numeric keypad (with NumLock on).

Information Interchange, which codified them decades ago.) The next 32 characters, 128 through 159, are mostly nonprintable control codes. This is followed by 32 characters of legal and currency symbols, then 32 characters of uppercase accented letters, and finally 32 characters of lowercase accented letters.

In order to access the characters numbered above 127, Windows requires that you hold down the Alt key, type a *zero* (0) on the numeric keypad, then type the three digits of the character's number, as shown in Figure 9-4. Although this requires an additional keystroke, it *does* allow you to type in special characters using either the number used in the PC-8 set or the number used in the ANSI set. For example, you can type the Yen symbol (¥) in Windows using either Alt+0165 or Alt+157, whichever you remember. (There's a way to type these characters without having to remember such numbers; see the discussion later in this chapter.) If you type in the number of a character that doesn't exist in the ANSI set, such as line-draw characters, Windows displays either a blob or nothing at all.

Windows suppresses most of the characters numbered between 0128 and 0159. In the official ANSI sequence, those positions are designated for ligatures (such as the "fi" and "fl" combinations used by publishers) and eastern European language characters. These values between 128 and 159 are used by DEC VT-100 terminals as control codes, and since several Windows communication programs use the VT-100 protocol, the values are not used for printable characters by Windows.

Many Windows applications, however, put additional characters into the positions between 0128 and 0159. This chart shows the special characters available specifically for Word for Windows — other Windows applications may not support these conventions. Winword places "smart" quotes (curly quote marks that show the beginning and ending of quotations) and two sizes of dashes into the sequence from 0145 through 0151. But Notepad and Paintbrush, and many other Windows applications, support only the first two of these "publishing" characters, the single open and closed quote marks. Typing the other publishing characters into these applets — inserting a dash, say — results only in a rectangular blob. If you need smart double quote marks in Notepad or Paintbrush, you'll have to type two single quote marks.

Another anomaly with the way Winword and other applications use these publishing characters regards character 0149. Several books on Windows, and the Word for Windows *User's Reference* manual, state that the character 0149 produces a bullet (•). These sources are in error, however, because this bullet character shows up only when printed on an Adobe PostScript printer. All the Windows screen fonts display this character as a lowercase letter "o," and when character 0149 is printed to a LaserJet, an Epson, or many other printers, it also prints as a plain "o" instead of a bullet. The only way to reliably insert a bullet character into your documents is to use the bullet at position 0183 in the Symbol font. The chapter on WordBasic includes a macro that works in Word for Windows (and other word processors that support WordBasic) to make this Symbol bullet character available with a single keystroke, if desired.

Exploiting the Symbol and Dingbats Typefaces

The approximately 190 additional characters available in each of the typefaces named Symbol and Dingbats provide a wealth of richness to the keyboard under Windows. Support for these two faces varies, however. Windows includes a screen font for Symbol (in addition to Times Roman, Helvetica, and Courier), but not for Dingbats.

For people with LaserJet printers (but no PostScript cartridge), Microsoft used to include Symbol printer fonts for the LaserJet with the distribution diskettes for Windows 2.x, but these were left out of Windows 3.0. These Symbol fonts are now included with Word for Windows. To install Symbol printer fonts, you open the Control Panel's Printers icon, select your LaserJet printer driver, and click Configure Setup Fonts Add Fonts. You then specify *a:\symbol.w3* as the directory on the appropriate Word for Windows diskette from which Control Panel will install the fonts. Once you click OK out of the Control Panel, you can print the Symbol font in a variety of sizes on your LaserJet.

Access to the Dingbats font is a little more difficult. If you have a PostScript-capable printer, the font can be printed but you can't see it on your screen in Windows.

Purchasers of the IQ Engineering Super Cartridge 3, which provides Laser-Jet III printers with all the typefaces in a PostScript LaserWriter Plus (and more), enjoy an elegant solution to this problem. IQ Engineering provides a small Dingbats screen-font file (less than 8K in size) that the Control Panel can install into your \WINDOWS\SYSTEM directory. After installation, all Windows applications can display Dingbats on your screen. The file takes up so little disk space because it includes only a single 10-point. bitmap, but Windows automatically scales this bitmap to larger sizes if you use a

Dingbat character larger than 10- or 12-point. When scaled, the character becomes more jagged in appearance on the screen, but this is an acceptable trade-off to save space in memory and on your hard disk. (The IQ Engineering Super Cartridge 3 is covered in Chapter 13.)

Owners of Adobe's Font Foundry and the Dingbats typeface on a diskette (both items are included in the Adobe Type Manager Plus Pack) can generate screen and printer fonts for Dingbats in any size desired.

The real solution would be for Microsoft to simply include a Dingbats screen font in a future version of Windows, since so many people use PostScript printers — especially those who use desktop publishing applications.

Once you have access to the Dingbats font, many characters that are impossible to represent in any other typeface become available to you. I've even managed to print Dingbats characters that don't appear in the Dingbats character set. For example, I worked on a project where it was necessary for the participants to keep track of their progress on a printed chart, similar to the following example:

Phase 1 ❑
Phase 2 ❑
Phase 3 ❑

The "open ballot box" in this example is character 111 in the Dingbats typeface. The idea was that, as the project progressed, each of the completed phases would be changed to a solid black box (Dingbats character 110), like this:

Phase 1 ■
Phase 2 ❑
Phase 3 ❑

This method of printing out the progress of the project was fine, until it was decided that we needed to print a character for phases that were *half* completed. Looking at the special character chart, you see that there is no "half-filled" ballot box available. What I *did* find was Dingbats character 122, a black rectangle about half the size of the ballot box, which looks like this:

▮

Using the Word for Windows equation feature to print this character on top of the left edge of the open ballot box resulted in a totally new character — the half-filled ballot box I needed:

Phase 1 ■
Phase 2 ◨
Phase 3 ❑

A Word for Windows equation field resembles something produced by a 4-year-old hitting keys at random, but it works; fields look something like this:

{eq \o\al(❑,◨)}

To produce this example in Winword, you press Ctrl+F9 to insert the bold, curly braces which enclose the field. (You cannot simply type the braces.) Inside the braces, the keyword "eq" means *equation,* the "\o" means *overstrike the specified characters,* and "\al" means *align the characters on their left edge.* The two affected characters appear within the parentheses, separated by a comma. If you wanted to align the characters on their *right* edge, you would replace "\al" with "\ar"; to align them centered, "\ac" or no switch at all (centered is the default alignment).

Other Windows word processors make this kind of customized character much easier to generate. In Amí Professional, for example, you simply click Text Special Effects on the main menu, and specify your desired overstrike character (which may be any ANSI character) in the Special Effects dialog box. When you format a character in your text as Overstrike, that character prints with your specified overstrike character superimposed on it. (The two characters must be in the same font, such as Times, Symbol, or Dingbats.)

Once you understand the overstrike features of your favorite Windows word processing application, you can create special characters of your own for almost any need. To display a zero with a slash through it, for example, you would simply overstrike a zero with the slash character on your keyboard in whichever font you prefer (the Dingbats font is not required). Since a slashed zero is a frequently needed character in computer documentation, I'm surprised that Windows word processors don't simply allow you to specify in a document's dialog box that you want all zeroes printed this way. But until they do, you'll need to use this overstrike method.

Words and Phrases:		Company Names:	Major Place Names:
à la carte	exposé	Condé Nast	Ascunción, Paraguay
à la mode	jalapeño	Crédit Suisse	Belém, Brazil
adiós	lamé	Crédit Lyonnais	Bogotá, Colombia
appliqué	maître d'hôtel	Dom Pérignon	Brasília, Brazil
après ski	mañana	Estée Lauder	Córdoba, Argentina
attaché	moiré	Hermès	Curaçao, Lesser
Au révoir	naïf	Lancôme	Antilles
bête noire	naïve	Lazard Frères & Co.	Düsseldorf, Germany
cause célèbre	naïveté	Les Misérables	Génève, Switzerland
coup d'état	passé	Moët & Chandon	Medellín, Colombia
coup de grâce	paté	Nestle	México
crème de menthe	pièce de resistance	Plaza Athénée	Montréal, Canada
crème fraîche	pied à terre		Perú
crêpe	piña colada		Québec, Canada
crêpes Suzette	protégé		San José, Costa Rica
débridement	raison d'être		São Paulo, Brazil
déclassé	rêspondez s'il vous		Tiranë, Albania
décolletage	plaît (RSVP)		Valparaíso, Chile
décolleté	résumé		Zürich, Switzerland
décor	risqué		
découpage	roman à clef		
déjà vu	sautéed		
déshabillé	soufflé		
discothèque	tête-à-tête		
émigré	très chic		

Figure 9-5: Some accented words in English usage.

Using the Accented Characters

The Windows ANSI character set includes many accented letters that were unavailable in the IBM PC-8 character set. Although there still aren't enough to cover all the European languages, the set that is available gives writers a better ability to correctly spell proper names and places than the PC originally did.

If you use an English-language keyboard, you may be asking, "Why are the accented characters important? The English language doesn't have any words that need accents."

Au contraire, mon frère, as Bart Simpson likes to say. Since the English language has blithely stolen words left and right from almost every other language in the world, several words in English usage are properly spelled with accented letters. Some of these are listed in Figure 9-5.

Since Windows makes it possible to include accented characters just like any character on the keyboard, it's nice to have the ability to use these characters to properly accent foreign words in common usage.

Spelling checkers, including the one in Winword, won't catch unaccented words. I removed the accents from the list in Figure 9-5 and ran it through the spelling utility in Winword, which stopped on a few of them — but not in a single case did it suggest the correct spelling of the word. It did, however, suggest that my unaccented spelling of "bête noire" (which loosely translates as a "pet peeve") really should be changed to the name of your friend and mine, Pete Moire!

The Five ANSI Accents

One reason that many English-speaking computer users aren't more familiar with the accented letters in the ANSI set is that these letters seem to be a jumble of random, unrelated symbols. Actually, all the accented letters in the ANSI character set fall into one of five types. These accent types, and how to place them on hotkey combinations on your keyboard, are fully explained in Chapter 6. So I'll just list the five types briefly here:

1. Characters with an acute accent:

Á É Í Ó Ú Ý á é í ó ú ý

2. Characters with a grave accent (*grave* rhymes with "Slav" or "slave"):

À È Ì Ò Ù à è ì ò ù

3. Characters with an umlaut (also called a *dieresis*):

Ä Ë Ï Ö Ü ä ë ï ö ü

4. Characters with a circumflex (informally called a "hat"):

Â   Ê   Î   Ô   Û   â   ê   î   ô   û

5. Characters with a tilde, or an Iberian or Nordic Form:

Ã   Æ   Ç   Ð   Ñ   Õ   Ø   ¡   ¿

ã   æ   ª   ç   ð   ñ   õ   ø   º   ß

These characters largely occupy the positions numbered 0192 through 0224 — the uppercase letters start at 0192, while the lowercase versions are exactly 32 positions higher. On non-U.S. keyboards, those accented characters common in the national language are assigned to keys, so that pressing, say, the "ñ" key on a Spanish keyboard automatically inserts ANSI character 0241 into the document. On U.S. and other English keyboards, most of these characters require that you hold down the Alt key and type a four-digit number on the numeric keypad.

You should note that, when accented characters are used in your documents, they still sort correctly in alphabetical order. Windows applications use the "sort value" of each letter, not the numerical ANSI value, so that characters are sorted *a, á, b, c,* not *a, b, c, á,* as their numerical value might suggest.

A Modest Proposal for Accessing Accented Characters

Since it's hard to remember the number that stands for each of the higher-order characters, it's too bad Microsoft didn't develop a standard system for accessing these characters without having to memorize numbers. If I buy a $200 Brother electronic typewriter, it includes two "dead keys," which, in combination with the shift keys, automatically add an accent to the next letter pressed. For example, if I press the umlaut dead key (¨), then I press the letter "o," the letter is typed with an umlaut over it (ö). This is an easy way for a U.S.-style keyboard to access accented characters, without performing major surgery on the U.S.-standard layout. Yet a $5,000, U.S.-brand PC makes it difficult to use these characters.

A full set of macros to implement the following five key combinations is presented in Chapter 6 (along with undocumented key codes to place

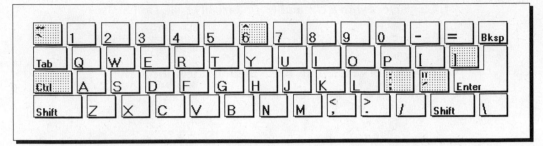

Figure 9-6: Ctrl keys used for accent macros.

macros on Ctrl+punctuation keys). The five keys that these macros are assigned to are shown in Figure 9-6. A short summary of the five rules is as follows:

RULES:

Implementing Key Combinations

Rule 1. Ctrl+´   adds an acute accent to the previous letter.

Rule 2. Ctrl+`   adds a grave accent to the previous letter.

Rule 3. Ctrl+^   adds a circumflex to the previous letter.

Rule 4. Ctrl+:   adds an umlaut to the previous letter.

Rule 5. Ctrl+]   changes the previous letter to another form.

In the case of a shifted key such as the colon [:] (Shift+semicolon), the Ctrl+key combination should work whether or not the Shift key is also pressed. Ctrl+semicolon, in the macros in Chapter 6, does the same thing as Ctrl+colon.

This solution won't be a great help to the touch-typist in French or German (or any other language that requires many accented letters), for these conventions require at least three keypresses for each accented letter. But for PC users with no choice but the U.S. keyboard, this method of accessing accented characters is a lot faster than looking up the numbers in the ANSI chart every time.

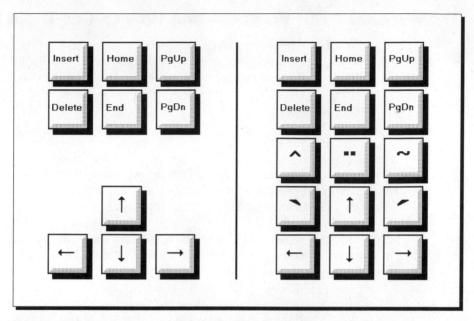

Figure 9-7: Space for extra accent keys on the 101-key keyboard.

A Better Way

A simpler method could become a standard for users of U.S. keyboards who sometimes need accented characters. Manufacturers could add a few keys to the standard U.S. keyboard, to the empty space between the dedicated cursor-arrow keys and the Insert/Delete keys. Five additional keys could fit in this space, for an acute, grave, circumflex, umlaut, or other accent — as shown in Figure 9-7.

If these accent keys were not needed, they could be redefined to act like any combination of the Ctrl, Shift, and Alt keys plus any ANSI character. Since these keys would be close to the frequently used arrow and insert keys, they could be programmed so that if one of the accent keys was hit accidentally, it would only affect letters of the alphabet, not the function of any other key in that dedicated area.

The Northgate OmniKey Ultra keyboard comes closest to this ideal, with 12 extra, definable SF (Special Function) keys in addition to the common F1 through F12 keys. When I have access to an Ultra keyboard, I set the SF keys to correspond to Alt+F1 through Alt+F12, then place the grave, circumflex, umlaut, acute, and other accents on SF5 through SF9, respectively. I describe this useful keyboard later in this chapter.

The Accents ANSI Forgot — and How to Get Them Back

The last topic in the accented-characters section of this chapter deals with several accents in worldwide use that somehow didn't make it into the ANSI specification, and how you can access these in Windows. Some of these are:

¯	macron
˘	breve
ˇ	inverted circumflex

These accents are used in several European languages, as well as in dictionaries and other documents to explain the pronunciation of words (for example, "lāt" to indicate the pronunciation of the word "late").

If you need these accents, you will have to build them through the equation or overstrike feature of your favorite word processor, as described earlier in the discussion of the Dingbats face.

All these accents exist as stand-alone symbols in either the Text or Symbol fonts. You'll find them in Figure 9-4 in this chapter, at the following positions:

94	^	Text font
126	~	Text font
168	¨	Text font
175	¯	Text font
180	´	Text font
184	¸	Text font
200	˘	Symbol font
218	ˇ	Symbol font

An interesting footnote, if you have Adobe Type Manager: ATM allows you to print three characters from Windows to a LaserJet printer that normally can't be printed from Windows to an Adobe PostScript printer. These characters appear at positions 0157, 0158, and 0159 in Text fonts, and consist of a dotless "ı" (useful for adding accents), a small circumflex, and a small tilde — perfectly sized to fit over a lowercase letter. Adobe apparently felt the need for more flexibility in accented characters than Windows provided, and added these three undocumented character codes.

The Ultimate Windows Keyboard

The Northgate Ultra

Windows applications make it possible to use a wide variety of keyboard shortcuts, and several apps such as Word for Windows make it relatively easy to redefine those shortcuts and place them on any key combination you like. This is a real treat when you can take advantage of a keyboard that has been specially designed to support as many Windows shortcuts as possible — the Northgate OmniKey Ultra keyboard.

The Ultra comes with two major advantages over normal 101-key keyboards. First, the 12 function keys F1 through F12 have been moved from the top of the keyboard back to the left side, where combinations such as Shift+F4 are an easy one-handed operation. Second, Northgate placed 12 *special* function keys, numbered SF1 through SF12, at the top of the keyboard where the "enhanced" F1 through F12 appear in other 101-key keyboards. Through software, the special function keys, such as SF1, can be set to send out key combinations such as Shift+F1, Ctrl+F1, and Alt+F1. (Alternatively, the special function keys can be set to act exactly like the 12 normal function keys for people who really like them along the top. This mode, however, defeats the purpose of having a keyboard with 24 function keys available instead of only 12.)

Northgate supplies a free utility named SFSET.COM that sets the modes of the special function keys. (Earlier versions of the Ultra keyboard named this program CLOUT.COM, for Command Line OmniKey Utility.) The following line, placed in your AUTOEXEC.BAT file, forces the keyboard to make the SF1 key equal to an Alt+F1 combination, SF2 equal to Alt+F2, and so on:

```
SFSET A
```

The most useful mode for the Ultra keyboard, I have found, is in fact its Alt-function key mode. Windows uses many combinations of Shift and Ctrl with function keys, so it would be dangerous to redefine these combinations with Recorder or in an application such as Word for Windows. But the Alt-function key combinations are so seldom used, they're ripe for redefining.

Word for Windows, in particular, is very suitable for redefinition of Alt and the function keys. Any macro created in Word for Windows can be placed on any key combination (see Chapter 6). Although Word for Windows already uses virtually every possible combination of Shift, Ctrl, and Alt with the 12 function keys, many combinations that involve the Alt key are unimportant and may be redefined without losing any serious functionality:

Alt+F1	Next field
Alt+F2	File Save As...
Alt+F3	unused
Alt+F4	Exit Winword
Alt+F5	Restore Winword window
Alt+F6	Next document window
Alt+F7	Move Winword window
Alt+F8	Size Winword window
Alt+F9	Minimize Winword window
Alt+F10	Maximize Winword window
Alt+F11	Next field (same as Alt+F1)
Alt+F12	File Save As... (same as Alt+F2)

Most of these Alt-function key combinations duplicate the commands in the Control Menu, including minimizing and restoring a Winword window, and moving and sizing the window with the keyboard (for those few Windows users without a mouse). Since all these commands are easily accessible from the keyboard by pressing Alt+Spacebar and the letter of the command (and these commands can all be performed more quickly with a mouse), it is no great loss to redefine Alt+F5 through Alt+F10 to another function or macro. (Alt+F3 isn't assigned by Word for Windows, anyway.) The only Alt assignments that must be preserved are Alt+F1 (Next Field), Alt+F2 (File Save As), and Alt+F4 (this fast Exit key works in all Windows applications). The Alt+F1 and Alt+F2 combinations are hardcoded by Windows to output the same codes as pressing F11 and F12. Because 84-key keyboards do not have F11 and F12 keys, Windows forces Alt+F1 and Alt+F2 to do whatever the F11 and F12 keys do in any application. So the functions assigned to these keys cannot be redefined in Word for Windows.

But this does not detract from the freedom that Northgate's extra 12 function keys brings to Windows users. With combinations of Ctrl and Shift, the 12 Alt-function keys can represent a total of 48 different commands (Alt, Alt+Ctrl, Alt+Shift, and Alt+Ctrl+Shift, times 12 keys) — minus the combinations such as Alt+F1 and Alt+F2 that are fixed.

With the Ultra keyboard's other benefits, such as the Ctrl and Caps Lock keys that can switch places to suit your preference and an unshifted asterisk key that is very handy for wildcard commands (*.*), Northgate has made the perfect Windows *and* DOS keyboard. They usually bundle them with orders for Northgate computers, but will sell the keyboard separately as well. It comes in a solid, "clicky" tactile-feedback model, and at this writing did not yet have a silent model. Northgate may be reached at 800-548-1993 or 612-591-0053.

Keyboard Anomalies _____

The remainder of this chapter describes unexpected behaviors of some brands of keyboards and workarounds for these situations, if possible.

NCR, Wang, Wyse Setup Errors

 When you run the Windows Setup program, certain keyboard BIOS chips prevent Setup from correctly detecting whether the keyboard is an 84-key XT-type or a 101-key AT-type. Some 101-key keyboards that incorrectly appear to Windows as 84-key keyboards are found on the NCR PC 925, the Wang PC 280, and the WYSEpc 286 and 386 machines. To fix this during Setup, you must manually change the selection "PC/XT-type keyboard (84 keys)" to whatever type the keyboard actually is (usually 101-key). Otherwise, certain keys (such as F11, F12, and so on) may not work as expected.

Shift May Disable Keypad Asterisk

Many people leave their PC's NumLock key *off* at all times and press the Shift key when they want to access the number keys on their numeric keypad. Pressing Shift has the effect of reversing the state of NumLock on these keyboards (usually older 84-key keyboards without a dedicated cursor-arrow keypad).

Windows 3.0 may interfere with the use of the keypad asterisk (*) and the Shift key, however, when running DOS applications under Windows. It has been reported with both Lotus 1-2-3 2.01 and Borland Quattro Pro that pressing Shift and the keypad asterisk (with NumLock *off*) does not insert an asterisk into the application. If your application exhibits this behavior, you must use NumLock to access the asterisk key, or use Shift-8 (*) on the top row of keys, which inserts an asterisk in all cases.

Changing to a Non-U.S. Layout

For people who commonly alternate between two national-language keyboard layouts, the easiest method of changing from one layout to another is by using the Control Panel's International icon. However, changing to a non-U.S. keyboard layout using the Control Panel in Windows 3.0 produces an unexpected message that asks you to insert a diskette with the appropriate country file. This happens even if you have previously installed this country file and it is present in your Windows subdirectory. Changing the path in the dialog box from "A:\" to your Windows SYSTEM directory will not help the Control Panel recognize this file. The only way to work around this behavior is to edit your SYSTEM.INI file with Notepad or another text editor, and change the line:

    keyboard.dll={filename}

in the [keyboard] section to include the filename of the desired layout. (Changing to a U.S. layout from a non-U.S. layout does not require this workaround.) This one-line editing workaround is faster than swapping diskettes, for people who need to work regularly with two different keyboard layouts.

Monterey International

Ctrl Key May Act Like Shift

When using the 104-key U.S. keyboard from Monterey International (Model K104) with Windows, the Ctrl key may act as though it were the Shift key when pressed. This keyboard may be set to three different configurations: A for AT, X for XT, and S for Standard. When the keyboard is set to A (as it might be when configured for an AT-compatible PC) and Windows is set up for a 101- or 102-key U.S. and non-U.S. keyboard, the Ctrl key sends the code for the Shift key. To get around this, change Windows Setup to "All AT-type keyboards (84-86 keys)" when the keyboard is configured for the A setting. This workaround, however, means that Windows will not recognize the F11 and F12 keys as well as other key combinations unavailable on 84-key keyboards.

Tandon

Caps Lock Can Trigger Keyboard Controller Failure

You may receive a message "Keyboard Controller Failure" when turning the Caps Lock key *off* when running Windows in standard or enhanced modes on Tandon PCs. This indicates that the Tandon ROM BIOS chip must be upgraded to version 3.61 or later. The current version in your PC can be determined by running the computer's setup program and looking for the version number in the upper-right corner of the display. Obtain the upgrade chip from Tandon at 805-378-7861.

Summary

This chapter has identified the following topics of importance regarding Windows and your keyboard:

▶ The danger to the health of your wrists and hands from keyboards that are awkwardly adjusted for rapid typing in DOS and Windows applications.

▶ Windows shortcut keys that can greatly speed up your work, including undocumented task-switching features.

▶ The Windows ANSI character set, and the Symbol and Dingbats character sets supported on many printers.

▶ Undocumented problems switching from U.S. to non-U.S. keyboard layouts, for those who work with two or more languages.

▶ Peculiarities of specific manufacturers and models of keyboards that can affect the proper operation of Windows.

Chapter 10
Mice and Pointing Devices

In this chapter. . .

I cover the following topics:

▶ Setting up mice and pointing devices on communication ports COM1 and COM2 or on a dedicated "mouse bus" port.

▶ Ways to use the compressed mouse drivers included with the distribution diskettes of Windows.

▶ Special mouse drivers for use by people who might have difficulty with the precision required by ordinary mouse drivers.

▶ A quick reference chart to some hard-to-find shortcuts that use the mouse.

▶ Considerations and anomalies regarding mice and pointing devices from several manufacturers.

While Windows has been designed from its beginning to allow almost all operations to be performed with the keyboard for those without mice, you will probably decide — if you ever try using Windows without a mouse — that the little rodents are indispensable for actually getting *work* done in Windows. Of course, Windows keyboard shortcuts are often faster than performing the same actions with a mouse, and the ability to work both ways is a great advantage for Windows users. (Even today, many actions on the Macintosh cannot be performed with the keyboard and *require* that you reach for the mouse and pull down a menu, such as selecting text point sizes in many Mac applications.)

This chapter includes items on pointing devices of all kinds: mice, trackballs, digitizing tablets, and so on. Included here is general information regarding all mice, followed by items on specific devices, arranged alphabetically by vendor name.

Mice

Choosing a Mouse Port

Mice can connect to a PC in one of two ways: through a serial communications port, usually a D-shaped connector labelled COM1 or COM2, or through a special "bus port" that is designed exclusively for use by mice. This connector is either built into the motherboard of a PC or is part of an add-in board that plugs into the computer's main bus slots. Whether you use a serial or a bus mouse is purely a matter of taste — there is little difference in performance or other considerations.

Although support for two additional serial ports, COM3 and COM4, began under DOS as far back as version 3.3, Windows 3.0 was released without the ability to recognize mice configured for these two new ports. Additionally, most PCs do not allow a device to use COM1 at the same time another device is using COM3, and the same is true of COM2 and COM4. (The exceptions, theoretically, are PCs with a Micro Channel Architecture or EISA bus, which are sensitive to the level of COM port in use.) Therefore, serial mice must be placed on only the first two serial ports or on a bus port, unless you have a later version of Windows that supports mice on COM3 or COM4.

One Button or Two?

While most Macintosh computers come with mice that have only one button, almost all PC mice are equipped with two, and both buttons are functional for various tasks in Windows. In addition, many companies sell mice with three buttons, and at least one company sells a kind of giant mouse with 40 buttons on it, programmable for various routines (see the section on the Prohance Powermouse later in this chapter).

Since the Microsoft Mouse sports only two buttons, Windows ignores the existence of the third button (the center button) if a mouse has one. This third button can become useful, though, with the addition of software. Whiskers, a shareware program on the diskettes included with this book, allows you to redefine mouse buttons to emulate the Enter key (handy for those dialog boxes that require an "OK" response) and other keys.

Using Mice Inside and Outside Windows

When you run Windows Setup, it automatically installs into your \WINDOWS\SYSTEM directory a small device file called MOUSE.DRV (2,896 bytes in size and dated 5/1/90 for the version shipped with Windows 3.0). If you indicate during Setup that you have a flavor of mouse other than a Microsoft-compatible mouse (as might be the case if you have a Hewlett-Packard, Logitech, or Mouse Systems brand mouse), another device file is installed (such as HPMOUSE.DRV).

These driver files are *not* supposed to be run in your CONFIG.SYS or AUTOEXEC.BAT files, unlike mouse drivers for some DOS applications. As long as these small files exist in your SYSTEM directory and are listed properly in your SYSTEM.INI file, Windows finds the proper file and loads it automatically to support the type of mouse you have.

Running a DOS application inside or outside Windows, however, does require that some mouse driver be loaded in your CONFIG.SYS (probably MOUSE.SYS) or AUTOEXEC.BAT (MOUSE.COM).

However, Windows 3.0 does not automatically install Microsoft Mouse drivers from the diskettes when installing itself. These files are in a compressed format on the diskettes and you must use the EXPAND.EXE utility provided with Windows to restore them before they can be used.

To do this, first insert Windows Disk #2 in a floppy drive and, at a DOS prompt, type:

```
COPY a:\EXPAND.EXE c:\windows
```

Copying the EXPAND.EXE utility to your Windows directory gives you permanent access to this utility whenever you may need it. (You should, of course, change A: and C:\WINDOWS to the appropriate drive and directory for your system.) The EXPAND.EXE file itself is not compressed, so it will work immediately.

Second, insert the Windows diskette with MOUSE.COM and MOUSE.SY$ into a floppy drive. (Notice the dollar sign [$] — compressed .SYS files are given the extension .SY$ to discourage people from using compressed drivers in CONFIG.SYS). Then, type:

```
EXPAND a:\MOUSE.COM c:\windows
EXPAND a:\MOUSE.SY$ c:\windows\MOUSE.SYS
```

Notice that MOUSE.SY$ is renamed to MOUSE.SYS by the second command.

You can now use the line DEVICE=C:\WINDOWS\MOUSE.SYS /Y in your CONFIG.SYS file, or the line C:\WINDOWS\MOUSE in your AUTOEXEC.BAT file, to load the mouse driver. (See the section on the undocumented /Y switch to MOUSE.SYS later in this chapter.)

Important: Many people copy mouse drivers directly into their C:\ root directory. I think it's better for the mouse drivers that come with Windows to be located in the WINDOWS directory. Since it's hard to tell one mouse driver from another (but it's essential that the latest Windows version be used), the line C:\WINDOWS\MOUSE.SYS in your CONFIG.SYS file immediately lets you know that you are using the current Windows mouse driver. The name of the directory itself is a little piece of self-documentation about the source of the driver.

Mouse Files May Hang Your System

The mouse drivers on the Windows distribution diskettes are in a compressed form, and if your system hangs as soon as it loads MOUSE.SYS or MOUSE.COM, it may be that you copied these files directly from the Windows distribution disks without decompressing them.

If a mouse driver is causing your system to hang on CONFIG.SYS, you must reboot from an original DOS floppy disk. Then, follow the procedure I just described, using EXPAND.EXE to decompress the drivers from the diskettes to your Windows directory.

To tell whether your drivers are compressed, check the size of the files. The compressed MOUSE.SY$ and MOUSE.COM drivers on the Windows 3.0 diskettes are about 19,000 bytes long. After decompression, these files are about 31,000 bytes. (In either case, the mouse drivers shipped with Windows 3.0 are dated 5/01/90, the same date as the other Windows files.) These files are larger than older mouse drivers from Microsoft, primarily because the full text of error messages for all the national languages that Windows supports has been added to the driver. When these mouse drivers are loaded, they detect the language for which your PC is configured. Only the messages in your language are loaded into RAM, requiring far less memory to run than the size of the disk files would indicate.

You Cannot Load MOUSE.COM Twice in 386 Mode

Loading the Windows Microsoft Mouse driver twice in different DOS sessions (virtual machines) in 386 enhanced mode may result in error messages or the mouse may "freeze."

If you run WIN /3 with no mouse driver loaded, for example, and then start a DOS session and type MOUSE, the expected message "Mouse driver installed" appears. But if you type EXIT to leave the DOS session (you will see a Windows message regarding "Pop-up Program Support"), start another DOS session, and type MOUSE, the driver reports "Driver not installed — interrupt jumper missing." Nothing is wrong with the "interrupt jumper" — a switch on a bus mouse board — but there is a conflict in the lowest 64K of memory. The first loading of MOUSE.COM initialized this area, but the second loading failed.

If you return to Windows at this point by pressing Alt+Tab, your mouse is immobilized until you Alt+Tab back to the DOS session and exit it. If you attempt to load the mouse driver in yet another DOS session, the mouse will become permanently stuck in Windows (until you restart Windows).

A potential workaround to this situation is to load MOUSE.SYS in your CONFIG.SYS (or MOUSE.COM in your AUTOEXEC.BAT) before starting Windows. The mouse driver should now be available to all DOS applications, whether started under Windows or not.

Undocumented /Y Switch in MOUSE.SYS

The Windows Setup program automatically adds a /Y switch to the end of the MOUSE.SYS command in CONFIG.SYS when installing for the Microsoft Mouse. This switch, which stands for "Yes," forces text-mode DOS applications that support a mouse to display the position of the mouse cursor as a rectangular block. If this switch is removed from MOUSE.SYS, the cursor becomes a graphical character called a "sprite" (with Video Seven-type graphics cards specifically).

Removing the /Y switch may cause a DOS application to have difficulty displaying the mouse cursor when you change applications and then change back. In a DOS application under Windows, you can press Alt+Tab to switch to other applications that are running at the same time. When you change back to the original DOS app (without the MOUSE.SYS /Y switch), it may display two mouse cursors — one normal cursor and one frozen in position on the screen.

Since it forces the cursor in text-based applications to display as a block (which is a legal text-mode character), the /Y switch may also prevent error messages when you start a DOS application that supports mice in a small window instead of full-screen. With a graphical mouse pointer, Windows may display the error message, "You cannot run this application while other high-resolution graphical applications are running full-screen." Windows does not allow a DOS application to display any EGA or VGA graphics unless the application is occupying the entire screen. If you receive this message, the DOS application is suspended until you maximize the DOS window (blow it up to the full screen) by pressing Alt+Enter. Starting a DOS application in a small on-screen window (and maximizing it with Alt+Enter) is only possible in Windows 386 enhanced mode.

MS-Mouse Driver Incompatible with Windows

Older Microsoft Mouse packages contain software that includes a driver file named MOUSE.DRV. The README file on the software disk says this file should be copied onto the original Microsoft Windows diskettes before installing Windows. This is incorrect. Using this driver with Windows 3.0 in standard or enhanced modes causes Windows to freeze the system.

The MOUSE.DRV file that shipped with the Microsoft Mouse (until some time after Windows 3.0 was introduced) is 3,699 bytes in size and is dated 3/15/90. The MOUSE.DRV file included on the Windows 3.0 distribution diskettes is 2,896 bytes in size and is dated 5/1/90. The file on diskette is in a compressed format. When installed by the Setup program, it expands to 4,896 bytes (but keeps its same 5/1/90 date).

Notice that the MOUSE.DRV driver file is *not* the same as MOUSE.COM or MOUSE.SYS, which are external commands loaded only when support for Microsoft mice is needed in applications outside Windows. MOUSE.DRV is loaded automatically by Windows for handling Microsoft-compatible mice, and is normally located in the Windows SYSTEM subdirectory. If you cannot find the correct MOUSE.DRV file in the SYSTEM subdirectory, or the wrong version has been copied to your Windows installation diskettes and you cannot recover the original, you will have to obtain a replacement copy from Microsoft sales and service (800-426-9400).

Expanding Mouse Accessibility _____

The Trace Access Pack

For people who have difficulty using a traditional mouse, Microsoft includes a driver on Disk 1 of its Supplemental Driver Library for Windows 3.0 that changes the behavior of the mouse. (This driver is included with some later versions.) The facilities of this driver are helpful to people with physical disabilities, and include using the keyboard or an alternate input device as a mouse. This driver is known as the Trace Access Pack, since it was developed by the Trace Research and Development Center at the University of Wisconsin at Madison.

Install this driver by changing the line in the [Boot] section of the SYSTEM.INI file from MOUSE.DRV=MOUSE.DRV to MOUSE.DRV=AP-MOU.DRV (case is not important). The original Trace Access Pack supported this change only if the original line read MOUSE.DRV, not HPMOUSE.DRV or others, but these additional mouse flavors might now be supported.

After changing the SYSTEM.INI file, you should copy the file AP-MOU.DRV from the Supplemental Driver Library diskette to the Windows \SYSTEM subdirectory. Then copy the files ACCESS.EXE and ACCESS.WRI to your WINDOWS directory. Finally, you create an icon in the Program Manager with the Title: Access and with the Command Line: ACCESS.EXE. (If you prefer not to clutter up your Windows directories with files that didn't come with Windows, you may copy all these files into a separate directory. In that case, the line in SYSTEM.INI must read MOUSE.DRV=c:*directory*\AP-MOU.DRV, and the icon in Program Manager must read c:*directory*\ACCESS.EXE.)

Other drivers that improve access to the keyboard are described in Chapter 9.

Using Mouse Shortcuts _____

For all the importance of the mouse in Windows, it is difficult to find a list, all in one place, of everything you can do with the mouse to save time. Various applications place a remarkable number of functions on left and right mouse clicks, combined with the Shift, Ctrl, and Alt keys. But these functions, which can be carried out much faster by a single mouse click than by the keystroke sequences that do the same things, don't save you any time if you don't know about them.

For this reason, I've gathered all the major mouse shortcuts in one widely used application, Word for Windows, into the chart in Figure 10-1. All the mouse actions in this chart may not be supported in all applications. But, for the sake of compatibility and ease of use, let's hope most applications come to agree on the same mouse actions for these functions. See also Chapter 3 for mouse shortcuts that work only in the File Manager.

Specific Mice

The remainder of this chapter is devoted to the installation, diagnosis, and troubleshooting of specific brands of mice, trackballs, and digitizing pads. You may want to look for the brand names of any products you own or use. Each vendor is listed in alphabetical order in the following sections.

Altra Felix Mouse

Requires Updated Driver Software

The driver software shipped with the Altra Felix mouse (formerly Lightgate Felix) prior to Windows 3.0 must be upgraded to work with Windows 3.0. Contact Altra at 1200 Skyline Dr., Laramie, WY 82070, 307-745-7538.

CalComp Wiz Mouse

May Be Configured with Mouse Systems Driver

The CalComp Wiz Mouse (a small digitizer pad and pointer) shipped prior to Windows for protected mode and may not work reliably with any of the mouse driver choices that you can install for Windows 3.0 in the Setup program. One symptom is that access times on hard disks may be extremely slow when using the Wiz. Microsoft Excel could require three to five minutes to load, for example, and applications running under Windows may spontaneously exit Windows, leaving you at a DOS prompt.

Obtain a new mouse driver by contacting CalComp Digitizer Co., 14555 N. 82nd St., Scottsdale, AZ 85260; 800-458-5888 or 602-948-6540.

If you have not yet upgraded to this mouse driver, you may still be able to use the Wiz with the following workaround: Run Setup (within Windows or at the DOS prompt in the Windows subdirectory) and change the Mouse

Mouse Action	What It Does
Mouse Click	Moves the insertion point to the position the mouse pointed to.
Mouse Drag	Highlights the area underneath the mouse pointer.
Click (in left margin)	Highlights the line that is pointed to.
Double-click	Highlights the word that is pointed to.
Double-click (in left margin)	Highlights the paragraph that is pointed to (or the row in a table).
Double-click (in Ribbon)	Opens Format Character dialog box.
Double-click (in Ruler)	Opens Format Paragraph dialog box.
Double-click (in Status Bar)	Opens Go To dialog box.
Double-click (in corner of document)	(Page View only) Opens Format Document dialog box.
Double-click (on Window Split Bar)	Splits display into two smaller windows. (The Window Split Bar is the solid black bar at the top of the vertical scroll bar.)
Shift+Double-click (on Split Bar)	Opens footnote window.
Shift+Click	Highlights the area between the place you pointed to and the previous location of the insertion point (same as dragging the mouse).
Ctrl+Click	Highlights the sentence that is pointed to.
Ctrl+Click (in left margin)	Highlights the entire document.
Ctrl+Shift+Click	Changes the formatting of highlighted text to the format of the text pointed to.
Right-click (at the top of a table)	Highlights the column pointed to.
Right-drag (at the top of a table)	Highlights all the columns pointed to.
Ctrl+Right-click	Moves highlighted text to the new position pointed to.
Ctrl+Shift+Right-click	Copies highlighted text into the new position pointed to.

Figure 10-1. Mouse shortcuts reference chart in Winword and other applications. "Click" means a left-button click, while "Right-click" means a right-button click.

selection to "Mouse System (or VisiOn) connected to COM1." (Change COM1 to COM2 if you are using the second serial port.) Save this configuration. Open your AUTOEXEC.BAT file with a text editor and add the following lines:

```
REM The following is required for Wiz with Mouse Systems driver.
MODE com1: 9600,N,8,1
ECHO 2 M>com1:
```

In the above lines, change COM1 to COM2 if necessary. Save AUTOEXEC.BAT and restart your computer to make the changes effective. According to CalComp technical support, setting the COM port in this way can make the Wiz work more reliably with the Mouse Systems driver under Windows.

DEC Mouse

Requires Upgraded Driver

If you use the mouse from Digital Equipment Corp. (DEC), but no mouse pointer appears on the screen in Windows, you need an upgraded mouse driver. Call DEC technical support at 800-332-8000.

DFI 200H Mouse

Requires Settings on Mouse and Driver

If you use the DFI Series 200H Mouse and the mouse pointer is unreliable or does not appear on the screen in Windows, check the mouse's settings to ensure it is operating in a mode compatible with Windows. First, the mouse must be set (with a switch on the side) to operate as a two-button mouse instead of as a three-button mouse. The switch positions are labeled "2" and "3."

Second, one of the following statements should be included in CONFIG.SYS or AUTOEXEC.BAT to load the mouse driver for the DFI 200H:

In CONFIG.SYS:
```
DEVICE=c:\dfimouse\DFIMOUSE.SYS
```

In AUTOEXEC.BAT:
```
c:\dfimouse\DFIMOUSE /Y
```

Use one method or the other to load this driver — do not load it in both places. If the driver is located in a directory other than C:\DFIMOUSE, change these statements to the correct directory.

GTCO Digitizer Pads

Require Upgraded Drivers

Drivers for the following digitizer tablets require an upgrade to work with Windows 3.0: GTCO Sketch Master, GTCO Micro Digi-Pad, and GTCO Type 5A Digi-Pad. The upgrades are free to registered customers; call GTCO at 301-381-6688.

Hewlett-Packard HP-HIL Mouse

Requires Special HP Drivers

The HP-HIL Mouse requires Hewlett-Packard drivers and does not work with the Microsoft Mouse drivers. Hewlett-Packard mouse drivers released prior to Windows 3.0 are not compatible with Windows protected modes. You must use the Windows 3.0 mouse drivers designed specifically for the HP-HIL Mouse.

To change these drivers, run Setup and change the Mouse setting from "Microsoft or IBM PS/2 Mouse" to "Hewlett-Packard Mouse." The Hewlett-Packard mouse driver files for DOS are located on Windows Disk #4 on 5.25" media, or Disk #5 on 3.5" media. These files are MOUSEHP.COM and MOUSEHP.SY$.

These two files are compressed on the Windows distribution diskette and will not work if they are simply copied from the diskettes to a hard disk. They must be expanded by running either the Setup program or the Expand program on Windows Disk #2. The following command at a DOS prompt decompresses these files:

```
EXPAND a:\MOUSEHP.COM c:\windows\MOUSEHP.COM
EXPAND a:\MOUSEHP.SY$ c:\windows\MOUSEHP.SYS
```

Notice that the second command renames MOUSEHP.SY$ to MOUSEHP.SYS. Compressed system files on the Windows distribution diskettes are given a .SY$ extension to prevent them from being used in a compressed format in a CONFIG.SYS command line.

A serious anomaly with HP-HIL mice, which connect to the keyboard of systems such as the HP Vectra PC, is that they cannot move on-screen while you are reading from or writing to your hard disk. This feature is built into this model, and it is impossible to configure Windows to avoid it. In character-based DOS applications that are not multitasking, this limitation is less noticeable than it is in Windows, which usually has several things going on at once.

IBM PS/2 Mouse

Old Driver Causes Black Buttons and Greenish Display

If dialog-box buttons such as OK and Cancel or the Minimize and Maximize buttons appear blacked out (although the colors are set correctly otherwise), you may need to upgrade the mouse software used with the IBM PS/2 Mouse. Another symptom is Windows starting in 386 enhanced mode with a greenish or yellowish tint to the normal colors. Version 1.0 of the IBM PS/2 MOUSE.COM file can be responsible for both of these problems.

If this is the case, use the Microsoft Mouse files included with Windows 3.0, or obtain version 1.1 of MOUSE.COM from IBM. The files on the Windows distribution diskettes are compressed and must be expanded with the EXPAND.EXE utility provided on Disk #2, by using the following commands:

```
EXPAND a:\MOUSE.COM c:\windows\MOUSE.COM
EXPAND a:\MOUSE.SY$ c:\windows\MOUSE.SYS
```

Notice that the second command renames MOUSE.SY$ to MOUSE.SYS. Either of these two mouse drivers will work with the IBM PS/2 Mouse. Load them in either CONFIG.SYS or AUTOEXEC.BAT (not both) by using the following commands:

In CONFIG.SYS:
```
device=c:\windows\mouse.sys /y
```

In AUTOEXEC.BAT:
```
c:\windows\mouse
```

If you don't know the version number of your IBM PS/2 Mouse driver, look at the file size and date of the driver file. MOUSE.COM version 1.0 is 12,539 bytes in size, dated 3/2/87. MOUSE.COM version 1.1 is 13,026 bytes in size, dated 12/5/89.

Kurta IS/ONE Digitizer Pad

Requires New Driver and Setup Procedure

The Kurta IS/ONE digitizer pad, a tablet with an electronic pen that acts like a mouse, requires a new version of the IS/Pensmith software driver for compatibility with Windows 3.0. Obtain this upgrade from Kurta by calling 415-899-1210. Change to this driver by running Setup from within Windows. Pull down the Options menu and choose Change System Settings. Change the Mouse selection to "No mouse or other pointing device." If this is the first time you have chosen this option, Setup asks you to insert Windows Disk #1 in drive A:. Instead, insert the diskette with the updated Kurta driver and click OK. The new driver supports the pen and digitizer.

Logitech Mice

Troubleshooting Serial Mouse Anomalies

Logitech is one of the largest, if not *the* largest, manufacturer of mice and trackballs for PCs. Many more Logitech mice have been sold than Microsoft Mice. Logitech mice, however, are often bundled with PCs or other equipment and may not be branded with the Logitech logo. Sometimes a small sticker on the bottom is the only identification of a mouse as having been manufactured by Logitech.

If you have a Logitech Bus Mouse, the Windows Setup program will detect it as a "Microsoft or IBM PS/2 Mouse." Since the Logitech Bus Mouse is compatible with the Windows driver for the Microsoft Mouse, this setting is correct, and you can continue the Setup program as you normally would.

The Logitech *Serial* Mouse, however, uses its own driver for Windows. The Logitech Serial Mouse exhibits its own sets of behaviors, separate from those of the Logitech Bus Mouse. You can take several troubleshooting steps if you have problems with Windows 3.0. (These steps also may apply to many other brands of serial mice running under Windows.)

The Logitech memory-resident programs LOGIMENU and CLICK are not compatible with Windows operation and may have to be removed from your AUTOEXEC.BAT file. (These programs interfere with the reliability of the Windows Setup program.) Look for a GOMOUSE.BAT file, since this batch file may load LOGIMENU and/or CLICK. If so, you can replace GOMOUSE.BAT with Logitech's MOUSE.COM program dated 10/2/89 to provide mouse support.

If your mouse pointer is visible but either won't move or doesn't show up at all, take the following steps:

STEPS:

Fixing Problems with the Logitech Serial Mouse

Step 1. Run the Setup program from within Windows and make sure the selection for Mouse is the Logitech Serial Mouse driver. If not, change it to "Logitech Serial Mouse," restart Windows, and test the mouse.

Step 2. If Setup, however, reports that the Mouse selection is *already* the Logitech Serial Mouse, and the mouse is one of the older, two-button Logitech Serial mice, change the selection to "Microsoft or IBM PS/2 Mouse" and restart Windows to test whether the mouse works as expected with *this* setting.

Step 3. If Setup reports that the selection for the Display is a Super VGA driver (800×600 resolution), change this to the regular Windows VGA driver to see if the mouse problem disappears. If so, there is a conflict between the Logitech Serial Mouse and the third-party Super VGA driver.

Step 4. If you have a Logitech Serial Mouse (including a Logitech Trackman) either on a PS/2 Mouse Port *or* connected to a Bus Mouse add-in card (using a converter on the connector in either of these two cases), then open your WIN.INI file with a text editor and add the following lines to the end of the file:

```
[MOUSE]
; This setting is for Logitech Serial Mouse on PS/2 Port or Bus
Port.
TYPE=2
```

Logitech reports that another setting used previously, type=3, is no longer valid with the Logitech Serial Mouse driver provided with Windows 3.0.

Step 5. If the above steps do not resolve the mouse problem, restart your system with plain vanilla CONFIG.SYS and AUTOEXEC.BAT files. While the system is performing its power-on routine, write down any BIOS and DOS messages that appear. Make sure that the BIOS date shown is 1988 or later, and that the DOS version is the correct one for the machine it's running on (don't use IBM's PC-DOS on a Hewlett-Packard PC that should use an HP version of MS-DOS, for example). Your plain vanilla CONFIG.SYS and AUTOEXEC.BAT files should look like the following, with the addition of any hard disk drivers or other drivers that are essential for your system to operate:

In CONFIG.SYS:
```
files=30
buffers=30
device=c:\windows\himem.sys
etc.
```

In AUTOEXEC.BAT:
```
prompt $p$g
path  c:\;c:\windows;c:\dos
etc.
```

Step 6. If booting with a plain vanilla configuration does not resolve the mouse problem, check that no other device is using interrupt request line 4 (IRQ4) if the serial mouse is connected to COM1, or interrupt 3 (IRQ3) if COM2. Two devices cannot use these interrupts simultaneously.

Step 7. Finally, turn off the PC, open the case, and look at the add-in card (if any) the COM port for the serial mouse is attached to. If there is a square chip on the board labeled WINBOND and a number such as W86C452P, replace the board with a later model.

Step 8. If replacing such a serial board is not possible, and all the other steps have failed, run Setup and change the Mouse selection to "Mouse Systems (or VisiOn) connected to COM1." (Use COM2 instead if appropriate.)

If you experience a problem with an erratic mouse pointer in Windows after starting a DOS application (including problems running COMMAND.COM) and then exiting or switching back to Windows, you may have a DOS mouse driver conflict. Make sure you are using version 4.10 of the Logitech Mouse DOS driver, which is supplied with version 4.01 of the Logitech MouseWare Utilities on the second diskette. (Note the similarity of the version numbers, 4.10 and 4.01, of the two applications.) If this is not the source of the problem, *and* you followed step 8 above by changing to the "Mouse Systems (or VisiOn)" mouse driver, then the erratic mouse pointer may be cured by starting DOS applications under Windows with a batch file like the following, where *program-name* is the command to run each program:

```
REM batch file to start program and reset mouse driver on exit
program-name
c:\logitech\MOUSE PC
```

Rerunning the Logitech mouse driver with the PC switch may clear the mouse hardware and allow the mouse pointer to work as expected when returning to Windows.

Model C7 Serial Mouse Unsupported by Generic CAD

Under the standard and enhanced modes of Windows, the version of Generic CAD that was current when Windows 3.0 shipped does not recognize the Logitech Model C7 Serial Mouse. This occurs even if the latest version of the Logitech mouse driver for DOS (4.10 or higher) is used. This is not a problem with the mouse, but is a feature of Generic CAD when Windows is using protected mode. The mouse operates normally in Generic CAD outside of Windows. For information on an upgrade, contact Generic Software at 206-487-2233.

Logitech Trackman

Uses Logitech Serial and Bus Mouse Drivers

The Logitech Trackman, a stationary trackball that performs the same functions as a mouse, is compatible with the Logitech mouse drivers. Windows does not show a selection in Setup for trackballs. If you have a Logitech Trackman on a serial port, use the Logitech Serial Mouse driver under Windows. If the Trackman is a Bus version, use the Logitech Bus Mouse driver.

Logitech Dexxa Mouse

Compatible with Microsoft Driver, Not Logitech

The Logitech Dexxa Mouse is *not* compatible with the Logitech Serial Mouse driver under Windows, and should not be set up for this driver. Instead, use the Setup program to select the "Microsoft or IBM PS/2 Mouse" driver for the Dexxa Mouse. This device is a two-button mouse with a resolution of 200 dots-per-inch of movement. If incorrectly installed as a Logitech Serial Mouse, the mouse pointer may be erratic or invisible.

Microspeed PC-Trackball

Requires Updated Driver to Work on Bus Port

The Microspeed PC-Trackball requires an updated driver to work with Windows 3.0 in standard and enhanced modes while plugged into the trackball's dedicated bus port. A symptom of this incompatibility is that Windows displays its logo screen when starting, but then quickly exits back to the DOS prompt. (Many other problems besides mice can also cause this type of "logo-then-exit" behavior.)

 If you cannot upgrade to the new driver immediately, a possible work-around is to attach the trackball to a serial port (COM1 or COM2) and run Setup to make sure that the Mouse selection is "Microsoft or IBM PS/2 Mouse."

Mouse Systems Bus Mouse

Should Be Set to Interrupt 2 Through 7

The Mouse Systems Bus Mouse may be set to use any interrupt request line (IRQ) from 2 to 15. Microsoft technical support, however, recommends that this mouse not be set to use any interrupt higher than 7 in order to avoid erratic operation. In addition, be sure (as with any mouse) that the Mouse Systems Bus Mouse is not set to use an IRQ that some other device in the system also uses.

A new driver, compatible with Windows 3.0, is available for the Mouse Systems Bus Mouse. You can get this driver by calling Mouse Systems technical support at 415-656-1117. The driver files are also available through the Mouse Systems bulletin board by dialing 415-683-0616 with your modem. The file is called WIN3DRV.EXE and is a self-extracting file that, when run, decompresses the necessary files onto your drive A:, after which they can be used with Windows.

After obtaining the necessary files, run the Windows Setup program from the DOS prompt while in the Windows directory. Change the Mouse selection to "Other," and insert the diskette containing the Mouse Systems driver when requested.

PC Tools and Mice

Microsoft Mouse Driver 7.04 Required

PC Tools technical support reports that PC Tools may not operate well with versions 7.0 or 7.03 of Microsoft Mouse driver software in CONFIG.SYS or AUTOEXEC.BAT. They recommend that Windows users upgrade to MOUSE.COM and MOUSE.SYS version 7.04, which is the version included with the Windows 3.0 distribution diskettes. Expand these files off the Windows diskettes using the Expand utility as described earlier in this chapter under "Using Mice Inside and Outside Windows." MOUSE.SYS should be used with the /Y switch as described earlier under "Undocumented /Y Switch in MOUSE.SYS."

Central Point Software, the maker of PC Tools, reports no problems under version 6.24b of the Microsoft Mouse driver, a much older version. If you have a copy of this vintage, it may be possible to load this version of MOUSE.SYS or MOUSE.COM in your CONFIG.SYS or AUTOEXEC.BAT (respectively), so DOS applications will find this mouse driver resident and still run Windows 3.0 with its built-in support for the Microsoft Mouse (when configured for the "Microsoft or IBM PS/2 Mouse" with the Setup program). Microsoft technical support suggests that the larger file sizes of the 7.0 and 7.03 mouse drivers may interfere with some aspects of PC Tools. The 6.24b version may occupy about 10-15K less memory in RAM — an area that may be conflicting with PC Tools.

If your mouse becomes inactive when you run the PCShell included with PC Tools 6.0 (dated prior to 4/5/90), there may be a conflict with HIMEM.SYS or MOUSE.SYS. If this is the case, take the following steps:

STEPS:

PCShell Troubleshooting

Step 1. Add the "/M:PS2" switch to HIMEM.SYS in your CONFIG.SYS file, as shown:

        DEVICE=c:\windows\HIMEM.SYS /M:PS2

This may eliminate the conflict on some machines (after you restart your PC to make the change effective). If this does not change the behavior, edit CONFIG.SYS back and go to step 2.

Step 2. Remove the /Y switch from the MOUSE.SYS line in CONFIG.SYS, if your system is *not* using a Video Seven graphics card. Restart your PC to make the change effective. If this does not change the behavior, edit the /Y switch back in.

Prohance Powermouse

Updated Driver and Custom Programs Required

The Powermouse is a large, 40-button mouse that can be configured to emulate certain keystrokes in applications when you press the various buttons. Version 5.26 of the Powermouse driver, POWER.COM, is required for compatibility with Windows 3.0. The previous version, 5.20, is 3,747 bytes in size, is dated 7/10/90, and is compatible with Windows only in real mode.

Two programs are bundled with the Powermouse to specify what keystrokes each of the buttons produce. The POWERPLS.EXE program is a terminate-and-stay-resident (TSR) program that may conflict with Windows. Use POWER.EXE, which is not a TSR, instead of POWERPLS.EXE.

Information about the loaded mouse driver can be viewed by typing a command like the following at a DOS prompt:

```
c:\prohance\TEST
```

For more information, call Prohance Technology at 408-746-0950.

Summasketch Digitizing Tablet

Drivers Require Upgrade

An upgraded driver program for the Summasketch Digitizing Tablet is required in order to use the pad with Windows 3.0. The drivers for this device included with Windows 2.0, 2.03, 2.1, and 2.11 are reported to interfere with the Setup program and cause Windows to exit back to a DOS prompt. Call Summagraphics Corp. at 203-881-5400.

Western Digital Motherboards

PS/2 Mouse Port Requires Upgraded BIOS

The PS/2 Mouse Port on Western Digital WDM2 or WDM20 motherboards causes Microsoft mice to act erratically in Windows standard and enhanced modes. This is due to an older keyboard ROM BIOS chip in these motherboards.

If you have this problem, take one of the following steps to work around it:

STEPS:

Getting Microsoft Mice to Work with Western Digital Motherboards

Step 1. Change your CONFIG.SYS line that loads HIMEM.SYS to include the /M:PS2 switch, as follows:

    DEVICE=c:\windows\HIMEM.SYS /M:PS2

The /M:PS2 switch is automatically written by Windows when installed for a PS/2-compatible machine, but Western Digital motherboards with a PS/2-style mouse port may not always be in a PS/2- type of computer. (In this example, if your HIMEM.SYS file is in a directory other than C:\WINDOWS, change the line to the correct directory.)

Step 2. Attach your mouse to a serial port (COM1 or COM2) instead of the mouse port. Run Setup, if necessary, to inform Windows of the new location of the mouse.

Step 3. Obtain a bus mouse, install the add-in board that comes with it, and attach the mouse to the mouse port in the bus mouse board.

Step 4. Replace the keyboard ROM BIOS by sending the motherboard to one of Western Digital's service centers.

Contact technical support at Western Digital at 714-932-7000.

Summary

In this chapter, I described little-known aspects of working with mice and other pointing devices from a variety of vendors, including:

▶ Differences between mice on dedicated bus ports vs. the COM1 and COM2 serial ports.

▶ How to decompress the mouse drivers that are included on the Windows distribution diskettes, so you can use them with DOS applications.

▶ The Access kit that modifies mouse and keyboard actions, in order to tailor them to individual preferences.

▶ How to save time with a mouse by using some little-known shortcuts, listed on a quick reference chart.

▶ Anomalies and troubleshooting secrets regarding specific brands and types of mice and pointing devices.

Chapter 11
Modems and Communications

In this chapter...

I explain communications under Windows.

▶ How you can correct communications devices that your PC (and therefore Windows) may not be identifying correctly.

▶ How communications ports fit within the limited number of devices that may be present within any personal computer system.

▶ How the newer communications ports — COM3 and COM4 — work and don't work under Windows, and how to take full advantage of them.

▶ Undocumented settings in SYSTEM.INI for com ports.

▶ Guidelines for trouble-shooting communications problems that can occur under Windows.

▶ Special factors to take into consideration when running modems at transfer rates higher than 2400 bits per second.

▶ Settings that can be useful with the Windows Terminal applet and other communications programs.

Communications

The subject of communications is one of the most frustrating aspects of personal computing. Once a PC begins communicating with another computer, any number of variables can go wrong and garble the connection. These include the communications settings in the PC, the settings in the distant computer, and the wiring (public telephone lines or dedicated lines) between the two.

The worst thing about troubleshooting communications connections is that the variables can be almost invisible. If the telephone connection between a PC and a distant computer is severed, the communications software at the

PC end is likely to halt with a terse "No Carrier" message. So what actually happened? Did the host computer "hang up," or did someone simply trip across the PC's modem cable, temporarily severing the link? Despite the attempts of many vendors to simplify PC communications and provide diagnostic tools to make the interaction between two computers more understandable, fixing "com" problems all too often still comes down to testing different variables, almost by trial-and-error, until something works.

This gauntlet of communications experimentation can be minimized by making sure that Windows itself is properly set up for comm programs. This chapter begins with the details required to run Windows and DOS communications programs reliably, followed by a section of settings for Windows' Terminal program (which also applies to many other communications programs) and some other communications software.

Com Ports 1, 2, 3, and 4 Under Windows

The earliest IBM PCs supported only two connections, or *ports,* through which outside devices could communicate *serially* with the computer (sending one bit of data at a time). These two ports were called *COM1* and *COM2*.

On the original IBM PC-1, and later on the IBM PC/XT, a serial port typically was part of an add-in board. A D-shaped bracket on the end of the board protruded out the back of the PC, and external modems could be plugged into this bracket via a *serial cable* with a 25-pin connector. Although a serial cable carries only one bit of data at a time, more than one pin is necessary for sending and receiving data, for electrical ground, and so on. Later, a D-connector with 9 pins was developed for the IBM PC/AT; the smaller bracket fits better in small-footprint PC cases.

Internal modems have become available, eliminating the need for a port and cable. They plug into a slot inside a PC and act as a port of their own. Most of these internal devices include switches or other methods that enable them to be set as either COM1 *or* COM2 boards, in order to avoid conflict with other boards in the PC. Two different devices cannot usually use the same port simultaneously.

Devices other than modems have emerged over the years that are designed to communicate with the PC through one of its two com ports. Different versions of the Microsoft Mouse, and other mice, were designed to plug into serial ports as well as special mouse ports. Other devices that require serial communications include scanners, printers, and plotters.

Interrupt Number:	Assigned To:
Nonmaskable Interrupt	Memory parity errors
0	Internal timer
1	Keyboard
2	EGA graphics adapter
3	COM2
4	COM1
5	Hard disk controller
6	Diskette
7	LPT1

Figure 11-1: Interrupts available on IBM XTs.

To accommodate the demands of these additional devices, DOS 3.3 (in 1987) added support for two more ports, named COM3 and COM4. These additional ports should theoretically double the number of serial devices that can be attached to or installed inside a PC. But a number of restrictions affect these ports. The most severe is that ports COM1 and COM3 cannot be used simultaneously by two different devices, nor can COM2 and COM4 be used simultaneously, on PCs with AT-type bus slots (called Industry Standard Architecture, or ISA).

The problem is that each com port uses up one of the PC's *hardware interrupts,* which are signals used by devices to get the CPU's attention. The original PC and XT have only eight possible hardware interrupts, numbered 0 through 7, and most of these are already in use by something other than com ports. The PC's internal clock, for example, interrupts the CPU about 18 times per second and uses the timer interrupt — number 0 — for this purpose. The first parallel port in a PC, named LPT1, uses interrupt 7, and so on. In addition, a special signal was provided for error-handling and is called the *nonmaskable interrupt* since it takes priority over all other interrupts.

The interrupts assigned to various devices in the IBM PC and XT are shown in Figure 11-1.

Interrupt Number:	Assigned To:
Nonmaskable Interrupt	Memory parity errors
0	Internal timer
1	Keyboard
2	Cascade to interrupts 8 through 15
3	COM2
4	COM1
5	LPT2
6	Diskette and hard drive
7	LPT1

Figure 11-2: Interrupts available on IBM ATs and higher.

With the AT, IBM added eight more interrupts, numbered 8 through 15. All these interrupts are reached by communicating through interrupt 2, which is said to be *cascaded* to the other interrupts. Some devices can be configured to use interrupts 8 through 15, but many cannot.

Interrupt numbering for the IBM AT was significantly modified. The interrupt assignments in the IBM AT (and almost all 286-and-higher ISA-compatible PCs), are shown in Figure 11-2.

COM1, by convention, uses interrupt 4 to communicate and COM2 uses interrupt 3. If devices that use these ports are not physically present in a PC, these interrupts are free for other devices to use. But since PCs frequently *do* include com ports, the makers of other devices that use interrupts (largely network adapter boards and mice) usually provide a way to switch their devices to interrupts other than 3 and 4, so as not to interfere with modems and other serial communications.

When COM3 and COM4 were added to the PC world with DOS 3.3, no interrupts could be taken in the first eight without eliminating numbers that were already widely used. So COM3 was given the use of the same interrupt as COM1 — interrupt 4 — and COM2 the same interrupt as COM4 — interrupt 3.

Two devices cannot control the same interrupt line on an ISA system without confusing everything in the process. As a result, two devices cannot use two different com ports assigned to the same interrupt simultaneously.

In an effort to allow more serial devices in a PC system, both the new Micro Channel Architecture (MCA) and Extended Industry Standard Architecture (EISA) provide a way for more than one device to use the same interrupt. As more and more add-ins are developed that are compatible with MCA or EISA, this form of *interrupt sharing* will eventually do away with the conflict.

Windows recognizes the existence of all four com ports — COM1, COM2, COM3, and COM4 — and provides settings in the Control Panel and the SYSTEM.INI file to configure the behavior of these ports. However, you must take several steps to make sure that all com ports in your system are configured properly. These steps are explained in the following sections.

Com Ports à la Mode

Since version 1.0, DOS has offered a program called MODE.COM to set parameters for your com ports. This program (which has many other functions besides configuring com ports) is typically used in a batch file to configure a port every time you start your PC. For example, to set COM1 to send characters at a rate of 2400 bits-per-second (bps), with no parity bit, eight data bits, and one stop bit, you would issue the following command at a DOS prompt:

```
MODE COM1 2400,N,8,1
```

If you are configuring COM1 to send data to a 9600 bps serial *printer,* you would add a comma and the letter P to the end of the command, as in MODE COM1 9600,N,8,1,P. This indicates that DOS should keep trying to send data even if the printer is temporarily busy printing.

Windows has its own method of configuring com ports that replaces the MODE command. The Control Panel includes a dialog box for Ports. This dialog box allows you to set the serial rate, data bits, and other parameters that Windows uses for each one. You must restart Windows for any changes you make to take effect. This dialog box is shown in Figure 11-3.

The DOS MODE command is also used to redirect data from one port to another. This is useful with programs that can only print to LPT1 through

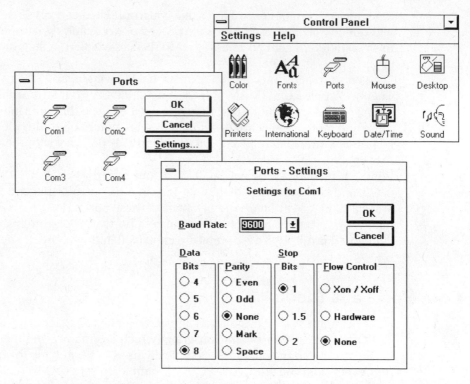

Figure 11-3: The Control Panel's Ports dialog box.

LPT3, when you actually need to print to a printer through a com port. The following commands at a DOS prompt would redirect data sent to LPT1 to COM1 instead:

```
MODE COM1 9600,N,8,1,P
MODE LPT1=COM1
```

Windows, however, ignores any such redirection commands that you specify. It always prints directly to ports, not through the ROM BIOS chip, which permits this kind of redirection. You must specify your communications and printer ports using the Control Panel. The Printers dialog box supports all ports from COM1 through COM4, and LPT1 through LPT3. This eliminates any reason to redirect a port so Windows can print to it.

(If you *need* to make Windows print through the BIOS, not directly to a port, you can change this behavior by redefining one of the ports in your WIN.INI file. To print through the BIOS using LPT1, change the line in the [ports] section of WIN.INI from LPT1:= to LPT1.PRN=, as shown:

```
[ports]
LPT1.PRN=
```

This makes Windows act as though it were printing to a file named LPT1.PRN. You can assign any printer to this port in the Control Panel. Windows then uses the BIOS to write to this "file." But DOS won't write to a file that has the same filename as one of its reserved device names, such as LPT1. Instead, DOS sends the information to the LPT1 port, ignoring the extension .PRN. This may be useful with third-party print spoolers or other programs that need to "see" what you are sending out a port. This is explained in more detail in Chapter 13. Don't add too many lines to WIN.INI — it can only handle 10 items in the [ports] section. If you're over the limit, comment-out unneeded lines by inserting a semicolon [;] in front of them.)

Identifying Addresses for Com Ports

Once a device attached to a com port has gained the CPU's attention by issuing a hardware interrupt, how does the CPU talk to that device? The same way it talks to most items in a PC — by using a particular address. Just as the CPU might route data to a DOS program located within the first 640K of memory addresses, the CPU routes data to and from a com port using that com port's address. This address is often called the *base port address* or *input/output (I/O) address.*

COM1, in the IBM PC and XT, was assigned the address (in hexadecimal numbering) of 03F8, and COM2 was assigned 02F8. When COM3 and COM4 were introduced, they were generally assigned 03E8 and 02E8 — exactly one "paragraph" of memory lower than COM1 and COM2. Although these addresses can be set by serial devices to a variety of values, most vendors have settled on these as standards. Most PC communications programs, such as Procomm Plus, as well as Windows' communications driver, COMM.DRV, therefore, assume that the four com ports possible in an AT-compatible system will use the interrupts and I/O addresses shown in Figure 11-4.

Port	Interrupt	I/O Address
COM1	4	03F8 hex
COM2	3	02F8 hex
COM3	4	03E8 hex
COM4	3	02E8 hex

Figure 11-4: Standard I/O addresses for com ports in ISA-bus machines.

MCA machines, such as IBM PS/2s, use different interrupts and addresses than ISA-bus machines. Windows usually detects when it is running on an MCA system and configures itself accordingly. MCA machines use interrupt 3 for all com ports COM2 and above, since MCA systems can be configured for interrupt sharing. Additionally, the I/O addresses for MCA machines are different for the ports above COM2 than the addresses in ISA machines, as shown in Figure 11-5.

Making Your PC Recognize COM3 and COM4

DOS 3.3 added support for four com ports, instead of the two that were supported in previous versions of DOS. But when DOS 3.3 shipped in 1987, the ROM BIOS chip in many PCs didn't look for this many com ports. The BIOS power-on routine stores the address of any com ports it finds in the "BIOS data area": bytes of memory in the lower 640K, where application programs looking for this information can find it.

If an older BIOS does not find and store this information on COM3 and COM4, Windows won't be able to use these ports — even if you have physical com port devices correctly configured for these port numbers.

You can quickly tell which com ports are valid in your system by issuing a MODE command to each port that is physically installed. For example, to find out whether COM3 is recognized (if you have three serial ports), issue a command like the following at a DOS prompt:

```
MODE COM3 9600,N,8,1
```

If you get the response, "Invalid parameters," but the same command works on another port, such as COM1, then COM3 is not being recognized.

Port	Interrupt	I/O Address
COM1	4	03F8 hex
COM2	3	02F8 hex
COM3	3	3220 hex
COM4	3	3228 hex
COM5	3	4220 hex
COM6	3	4228 hex
COM7	3	5220 hex
COM8	3	5228 hex

Figure 11-5: I/O addresses for com ports in MCA-bus machines.

If you have a Hayes-compatible modem with an external speaker, you can determine which port it is on by sending it commands to emit dial tones. For example, if you think your modem is on COM1 or COM2, you can check COM1 with the following commands at a DOS prompt:

```
MODE COM1 1200,E,7,1
COPY CON COM1
ATDT 12345
[Ctrl+Z]
```

This sequence of commands first configures the port, then copies what you type at the console (the keyboard) to COM1. The ATDT line gets the modem's attention (AT) and causes it to beep with five dial tones (DT 12345 — like pressing 1-2-3-4-5 on a touch-tone phone) *if* it is responding to COM1. If it doesn't respond, change the command to refer to COM2 or whatever other port you wish to test.

To correct an unrecognized com port, place in your AUTOEXEC.BAT a command that runs COMRESET.EXE (a program located on the diskettes included with this book). This program sets in memory the standard information about com port addresses shown in Figure 11-4. To set COM3 and COM4 with this program, for example, you would place the following line in your AUTOEXEC.BAT file:

```
COMRESET 3 4
```

If you can't use COMRESET.EXE for some reason, or you are working at a computer that doesn't have this program, you can do the same thing with the DOS Debug utility.

You can determine which ports are supported under your BIOS by displaying one line with Debug. To do this, type DEBUG at a DOS prompt. You will see a hyphen (-) at the left of your screen, which indicates that Debug is running. At this hyphen prompt, type D40:0 and press Enter. This command displays the bytes in memory starting at hexadecimal address 0040:0000. Immediately press Q to quit Debug. This session will look on your screen as follows:

```
DEBUG
-D40:0
0040:0000 F8 03 F8 02 E8 02 00 00-BC 03 78 03 00 00 00 00  ..........x.....
{several lines will appear}
-Q
```

Only the first line of the several that appear is important. The first two bytes indicate the I/O address of your COM1 port. In this case, Debug shows "F8 03" for this value, using the reversed byte-order typical of Intel processors. Reverse the order and you can see that the address is "03F8," the standard address for COM1.

The Debug line in this example shows a system with three com ports — a fourth port is not physically present in the system. This is indicated by the bytes "00 00" in the fourth com position on the Debug line. This system also has two parallel ports, LPT1 and LPT2. The I/O addresses for these ports are indicated in the right half of the line. The LPT1 port is at address 03BC ("BC 03"), and the LPT2 port is at address 0378 ("78 03"). There is no LPT3 or LPT4 in this system. (DOS 3.3 doesn't support LPT4, but there's a space for it in the BIOS data area, anyway.)

If you need to change these values, perhaps to set addresses for a com port your BIOS doesn't recognize, you can do this with a Debug script every time your PC boots up. This requires that you edit the values in the BIOS data area, by using Debug's E command. I don't recommend you do this unless you absolutely can't use COMRESET.EXE or a similar utility. You could write to an incorrect address and have to reboot your PC to recover.

But if Debug is your only alternative, you can set all four com ports to the standard ISA addresses by typing DEBUG and entering the following two commands:

```
E40:0 F8 03 F8 02 E8 03 E8 02
Q
```

The character "0" in these lines is always a zero, not the letter "O." Use the correct addresses and number of ports for your particular system. Once you've done this, you can put these two lines into a text file called, say, FIXCOM.SCR. You can make Debug run these two commands every time you boot up by placing the following command in your AUTOEXEC.BAT file:

```
DEBUG < c:\scripts\FIXCOM.SCR
```

Of course, as I've said, it's much easier to put COMRESET into your AUTOEXEC.BAT than to run this routine every time you boot up. See Section D, "Excellence in Windows Shareware," for more information on COMRESET.EXE.

Undocumented Com Settings in SYSTEM.INI

Windows' COMM.DRV driver handles communications in both real and standard modes. COMM.DRV uses all the standard settings for com ports as shown in Figure 11-4 earlier in this chapter.

In 386 enhanced mode, however, Windows uses an internal Virtual Communications Driver (VCD) that is designed to handle communications in a multitasking environment. If you have installed Windows on a 386, you can see that Windows uses this internal code by looking in the [386Enh] section of the SYSTEM.INI file for the line *device= *vcd*. The asterisk indicates that this driver is internal to Windows, not a separate file on disk, such as VCD.DVR.

Unfortunately, the VCD specifies nonstandard I/O addresses for COM3 and COM4 devices. The VCD expects to find COM3 at 2E8 instead of 3E8, and COM4 at 2E0 instead of 2E8 — the values shown in Figure 11-4. This is elaborated on in Windows' SYSINI2.TXT file, if you're curious.

You must add lines to your SYSTEM.INI file to override these default assumptions. These additional lines tell the VCD to use the industry-standard values for the com ports, instead of its own, nonstandard defaults. Microsoft has written an internal support memorandum stating that these defaults should be overridden "for proper functioning of the ports under enhanced-mode Windows." The four lines to add to the [386Enh] section of SYSTEM.INI are as follows:

```
[386Enh]
COM1Base=3F8h
COM2Base=2F8h
COM3Base=3E8h
COM4Base=2E8h
```

Lines such as these are also required for you to take advantage of shared interrupts on an MCA or EISA system. They must be set to the correct base port addresses for your particular system. In addition, on an MCA or EISA machine, you may need to add the following line to the [386Enh] section to use com ports that share the same interrupt number:

```
[386Enh]
ComIRQSharing=true
```

After restarting Windows to make the above lines effective, make sure that devices using COM3 or COM4 are configured to these values, by using any switches or configuration software that comes with these devices.

Lower Com Ports Must Be Used Before Higher

In general, you should configure the com ports in your system in consecutive order. In other words, if you have three com ports, it is better for them to be configured as COM1, COM2, and COM3, not as COM1, COM2, and COM4.

In addition, under real and standard modes in Windows, the COM3 and COM4 ports are not reliable until the devices on COM1 and COM2 have been used first. If you have a plotter on COM1 and a mouse on COM2, for example, you may have problems using a modem on COM3 until you have first sent something to your plotter. (This could be as simple as sending a one-byte "reset" command.) Microsoft suggests not using com ports 2, 3, or 4 until ports with the lower numbers 1, 2, and 3 have been "activated" or used by a serial device.

Setting the Time Between Programs Using the Same Port

By default, Windows in 386 mode requires two seconds between the time that one program stops using a com port and the time before it will assign the same port to another program. The SYSTEM.INI file contains settings that control this delay between applications that may be *contending* for the same port. Windows' default *contention delay* is the same as if you set all these lines to 2:

```
[386Enh]
COM1AutoAssign=2
COM2AutoAssign=2
COM3AutoAssign=2
COM4AutoAssign=2
```

If this contention delay is not enough to keep two communications sessions from conflicting, you can increase the delay up to a value of 999 seconds (over 16 minutes). Alternatively, you can set these values to -1 to make Windows display a message and give you a choice between two applications when they try to use the same port. A port setting of 0 (zero) allows any application to use that port at any time.

Troubleshooting Communications

Don't Switch Away in Real or Standard Modes

One thing that *definitely* interferes with DOS communications programs is switching away from them while Windows is in real or standard modes. These modes, unlike 386 enhanced mode, do not support multitasking of DOS applications and therefore suspend any application that is not currently in the foreground window. (Windows-based applications, however, can run in the background in any mode.) If you switch away from a DOS application engaged in a communications session (by pressing Alt+Tab or Alt+Esc to switch to another program), when you switch back to it, it will likely report that the session was terminated or that data could not be sent or received.

Don't Select Text in Windowed Sessions

If you are running a DOS communications program under 386 enhanced mode, and you switch to a "windowed" display (instead of full-screen), you may be tempted to drag your mouse across the window to highlight a block of text to copy to the Clipboard.

Selecting text in this way, however, suspends the DOS session while Windows changes the color of the window to indicate the area you're selecting. This can cause your communications connection to drop or become garbled.

You might prefer using Alt+PrintScreen to copy the whole window of the DOS session to the Clipboard — if this itself doesn't take the focus away from your communication link for too long.

Windows Doesn't Support Advanced FIFO Buffer

The original IBM PC and XT computers used an integrated circuit on IBM's communications adapter card called an "8250 Universal Asynchronous Receiver/Transmitter" (UART). Later, when the IBM AT was released, IBM replaced the 8250 with an improved chip, the 16450, which remained downwardly compatible with the 8250. With the PS/2 series of computers, IBM upgraded their communications chip to the 16550, which is integrated into the system board.

Several vendors besides IBM also use this chip. The new Hayes ESP Dual Enhanced Serial Port uses the 16550, coupled with coprocessor technology, to support high communications rates reliably.

The 16550 chip, and the related 16550A, is capable of using an advanced FIFO (first-in-first-out) buffer for improved communications. Windows 3.0, however, does not support this feature and will not operate correctly with it. Windows supports the 16550 chips only when they emulate the older 8250 UART. You must disable the 16550 buffer if it is in use and follow the procedures in the component manufacturer's manual.

PS/2s Limited in Port Speeds

If you use third-party file transfer software, such as Traveling Software's Lap-Link Plus or White Crane's Brooklyn Bridge, you may have found that you can achieve transfer rates up to 115,200 bps when communicating between two side-by-side machines linked with a serial cable. These speeds (much higher than most modem transfer rates) are possible because such software packages program the UART chip directly, instead of using the BIOS for transfer services.

Communications programs using Windows' COMM.DRV communications driver are limited to a transfer rate of 19,200 bps, however. It would be possible to replace this particular driver file with a third-party driver, but at this writing a reliable replacement is not commercially available. High-speed file transfers between machines must be performed at a DOS prompt.

Even when you use a DOS prompt, however, you may encounter some other limitations. IBM PS/2s, such as the Model 70, can run their serial ports under these file-transfer packages no faster than 38,400 bps instead of 115,200 bps. No workaround is possible, since this is a hardware limitation of the PS/2s.

Transferring Data Above 2400 bps

Windows-based communications applications, such as CrossTalk for Windows, DynaComm, and Relay Gold for Windows, may communicate through a com port at speeds up to 19,200 bps. DOS communication applications running under Windows' 386 enhanced mode, however, cannot reliably operate com ports faster than 9600 bps, and certain adjustments may be needed to enable these programs to transfer data at that rate reliably.

Windows should have no effect on programs running at 2400 bps or less; if you experience garbled data at these rates, a conflict between two devices on the same interrupt is more likely to be the cause. But communications under Windows at 9600 bps may be dependent on the speeds that the PC system itself is capable of sustaining. A 386 processor should be able to manage transfers at 9600 bps, but some other aspect of the hardware or software may slow down the efficient flow of data and cause characters or whole blocks of the transfer to be lost.

If You Lose Characters in Text-Only Transfers

If your data transfers consist of *text only,* and you are not sending or receiving any binary files, such as .EXE, .COM, or .ZIP files, then you should first change the method by which Windows in 386 mode sends characters into DOS applications that are receiving communications. This method is known as the *protocol.* Windows sends characters into such applications as fast as possible, by default. But this may cause text characters to be lost if the DOS app cannot keep up. In this case, a form of *flow-control protocol* is called for. If the DOS application supports flow control, it can issue a particular character when it is busy, and Windows will wait until the application is ready before sending any more data. This character is known as the *XOFF* character (pronounced "x-off," meaning transfer off), and the character used to resume is the *XON* character ("x-on," meaning transfer on). To enable this flow-control protocol between Windows and DOS communications applications, add the following line to the [386Enh] section of your SYSTEM.INI file:

```
[386Enh]
COM1Protocol=XOFF
```

In this example, change COM1 to the number of the specific port you wish to affect.

Important: The protocol should be set to XOFF *only* if plain text files are the only transfers made through this port. Transferring *binary* data files with the protocol set for XON/XOFF characters can garble the communication, because these characters appear at random in binary data.

If changing this setting doesn't prevent the loss of characters when transferring text at rates higher than 2400 bps, then leave the XON protocol set and begin increasing the communications buffer, as described in the next topic.

Increasing Your Communications Buffer

If communications transfers in 386 mode often lose characters after the first 128 bytes, one step to take is to increase the amount of *buffer memory* that Windows sets aside for these transfers. The default value is 128 bytes of memory for this buffer area. Increase this value 128 bytes at a time (to 256 bytes, then 384, and so on) by inserting the following line into the [386Enh] section of your SYSTEM.INI file:

```
[386Enh]
COM1Buffer=256
```

In this example, change COM1 to the number of the specific port you wish to affect, and change "256" to the multiple of 128 that represents the size of the buffer you need. This may not eliminate communications dropouts if the DOS comm program is basically unreliable. If the same problems arise when Windows is not running, then the program itself may be unreliable at that speed in your particular system, and a Windows-based communications program might prove to be more stable for this task.

Increase COMBoostTime for DOS Apps

If the preceding steps fail to prevent the loss of characters in a DOS communications program under Windows in 386 mode, you may need to increase the amount of time that Windows allows a DOS app to process characters in this situation. Windows allows two milliseconds (0.002 seconds) by default. You can increase this by adding a line to the [386Enh] section of your SYSTEM.INI. Start with four milliseconds and keep increasing by two, if necessary, as shown in the line below:

```
[386Enh]
COMBoostTime=4
```

The above setting affects all com ports, 1 through 4.

Lock Application Memory for Communications Programs

Running high-speed communications in Windows' multitasking 386 mode may require "locking" DOS applications' memory so that Windows does not move the memory and disrupt the communications session. DOS programs should be run from a PIF file, and DOS communications programs in this situation should have the Lock Application Memory box checked Yes in their PIF file. To find and change this setting, start the PIF Editor in its enhanced mode and click the Advanced button. The Lock Application Memory option is in the Memory Options section of the dialog box. Editing PIF files is explained in Chapter 5.

Turning Off the Timer for Kermit Transfers

Users of the *Kermit* protocol for transferring data may need to shut off the Kermit "timer" in the software on the PC side of the transfer, if all the preceding steps fail to eliminate the loss of data. Only about one second is allowed by the Kermit protocol between any two characters after the first communications packet has been received. Since Windows is buffering communications, it may appear that some transfers are taking longer than this (although Windows is actually continuing to process data normally). Turning off the timer does not affect the data that is sent or received.

Windows Terminal

How to Set Terminal to Auto-Answer Your Modem

The Windows Terminal applet bundled with Windows is fine for dialing out to communications services, but lacks many features of more sophisticated packages — letting someone dial in to *you*, for example.

Terminal has no menu command that sets your modem into an auto-answer mode. If it is necessary for you to have someone dial your computer for information (including dialing in yourself when you are away from your PC), you can configure a Hayes-compatible modem to do this in any one of the following ways:

STEPS:

Setting Terminal for Auto-Answer

Step 1. Before Windows starts, run any utility programs supplied with your modem that configure it for auto-answer.

Step 2. On the Terminal main menu, click Settings, then click Modem Commands. In the dialog box that appears, change the Originate setting from ATQ0V1E1S0=0 to ATQ0V1E1S0=1 (you are simply changing the value after the equals sign from 0 to 1). Click OK to accept this change. Dial any number. This sets your modem to auto-answer, and it will pick up the phone line the next time someone calls. Change the value from 1 back to 0 (and make a call) to undo this.

Step 3. If you will be present when you expect a call, type ATA in the Recorder window when your phone rings. This manually reconfigures your modem for auto-answer.

Adjustments Needed for CompuServe, GEnie, and BIX

Terminal automatically uses communications settings that correspond to those in use by most bulletin-board systems today. Specifically, a communications data stream is presumed to be made of eight bits of data and a single stop bit, with no parity bits included.

Connecting to on-line services such as CompuServe and BIX (the Byte Information eXchange) without changing these settings, however, results in unreadable "garbage" displayed on your screen. For services like GEnie, you may be able to read the response from the service but not the commands you are typing. (When using GEnie, set your modem to half-duplex.)

Before calling these services with Terminal, pull down the Settings menu, set Terminal Emulation to "DEC VT-100 (ANSI)," and click OK. Then open the Communications dialog box from the Settings menu and make sure the following options are selected:

For CompuServe or BIX:
Data Bits = 7; Parity = Even; Stop Bits = 1

For GEnie:
Data Bits = 8; Parity = None; Stop Bits = 1

You can save these settings by clicking File, Save As. For example, you could save the GEnie settings in a file named C:\TERMINAL\GENIE.TRM. Place this directory on your DOS Path, and you can start Terminal and load the appropriate settings for Genie simply by clicking File Run in the Program Manager or File Manager and typing GENIE.TRM.

Undocumented VT-100 ScrollLock Setting

The VT-100 emulation mode of Windows Terminal requires that the ScrollLock key be *on* to enable standard VT-100 cursor keys and the remapping of F1 to PF1, F2 to PF2, etc. This information is missing from the Windows user's guide, but the keyboard mappings are explained in the first page of Terminal's on-line Help Index while in VT-100 mode. Of course, if Terminal is in VT-100 mode with ScrollLock on, then F1 does not bring up Help as expected, because the F1 key has been remapped to PF1. To work around this and view the Help information, press Alt+H, then I, to start the Help Index from the keyboard.

VT-100 Bold Characters Not Bold on EGA

With an EGA display, bold VT-100 characters do not display as bold in Windows Terminal. Nothing is wrong with your display; this is a limitation of Terminal. The bold characters appear as bold at other resolutions.

Everex 2400 Modem

Changes Required in Terminal Settings

You'll need to alter the settings in Terminal in order for the Everex 2400 Modem to dial correctly. In Terminal, pull down the Settings menu and click on Modem Commands. Set the Modem Defaults to None; the default values in the dialog box disappear. Fill in the following values:

Dial Prefix:	ATDT
Hangup Prefix:	+++
Hangup Suffix:	ATH
Answer:	ATQ1E0S0=1
Originate:	ATQ1

Click OK and save these settings for any communication sessions you establish.

IBM Personal Communications/3270 (PCS)

If you use DOS programs that initiate communications sessions by using the IBM 3270 protocol, print and read the file 3270.TXT (in your Windows directory). This file contains new information on Windows' anomalies regarding 3270 software and hardware products.

PCS Uses Windows Hotkeys

The Personal Communications/3270 program (PCS) uses default key combinations Alt+Esc, Alt+Tab, and Ctrl+Esc to switch between a DOS session and the host computer. These combinations are also used by Windows to switch among Windows applications. You can use a keyboard definition file to redefine how PCS uses these keys (refer to the PCS manual).

Restrict PCS' Use of Expanded Memory

If no page frame is available in your system for expanded memory, you must create a PIF file for PCS that specifies EMS Required: 0 and EMS Limit: 0 in enhanced mode. This restricts PCS from trying to access any expanded memory. PIF files are explained in Chapter 5.

PCS Driver Is Incompatible with SmartDrive, RAMDrive

The expanded memory driver and emulator programs included with IBM's Personal Communications/3270 program, version 1.01, are not compatible with the SmartDrive and RAMDrive drivers included with Windows 3.0. The IBM files are named PCSX2EMS.SYS and PCSXMAEM.SYS. If SmartDrive or RAMDrive drivers are loaded into extended memory in your CONFIG.SYS file after these files, your machine will reboot. If they are loaded into expanded memory, you receive the error message "Expanded memory status show error."

Summary

This chapter has detailed some of the settings required for reliable communications under Windows. The topics covered:

▶ Making DOS and Windows recognize physical communications devices that may be properly configured in your computer but not identified by its power-on self-test routine.

▶ How the limited number of interrupts and port addresses in a PC can cause conflict between different devices attached to or installed in your computer.

▶ How COM3 and COM4 differ from the two ports that DOS has always supported, and how to make these ports accessible to Windows.

▶ How settings in SYSTEM.INI, including undocumented settings for COM3 and COM4, can affect the stability of your communications connections.

▶ Identifying and avoiding problems that can interfere with your communications sessions.

▶ How communications transfer rates above 2400 bits-per-second differ from slower rates, and how to make these faster transfers more reliable.

▶ Settings for specific hardware and software products to smooth their use with Windows.

Chapter 12
Networks

In this chapter. . .

I describe several of the little-understood aspects of setting Windows up on a network, including hard-to-find information on specific vendors' network software and hardware products. This includes:

▶ The concepts involved in networking Windows, and some of the benefits of running Windows from a network instead of on stand-alone PCs.

▶ Ways to configure the Program Manager to save you time when managing a network with dozens or hundreds of users.

▶ Secrets of configuring various applications to run under Windows on a network — steps that are not required to run those same applications on stand-alone PCs.

▶ Steps to take to prepare your PC and network for the installation of Windows, and anomalies that affect the installation process itself.

▶ How Windows' swap files work differently on a network than they do on a stand-alone PC, and how you must set them up for them to work efficiently or at all.

▶ Understanding some of the quirks that you might encounter when using the Windows Setup program with its /N (network) parameter.

▶ The importance of the SHARE.EXE program on PCs, and its possible conflicts with network software.

▶ Specific information pertinent to Novell Netware, Banyan Vines, and other network operating systems.

Windows 3.0 is the first version of Windows that is truly suitable for use on a company-wide local area network (LAN). Whereas previous versions of Windows operated on a network only with some difficulty — primarily because Windows 2.*x* was limited in the amount of memory it could make available on a PC running network software — Windows 3.*x* makes a networked graphical environment practical and appealing.

Networking Windows

Application Support for Networks

Besides the additional memory (up to 16MB plus virtual memory) that Windows 3.0 can make available to applications, two major developments have taken place in the Windows world that support the use of networks:

1. Windows applications tend to be "network-aware." When asked to read a file on a network, most current Windows applications work the same way whether that file is located on a remote network drive or just inches away on a PC's own hard disk. Several network features have been added to Windows itself, notably the ability to assign a distant network disk a drive letter from within File Manager and view that disk's files graphically, plus the ability to locate and print to any printer on the network. When Windows applications print to net-worked printers, they release the printer as soon as the last page is complete, allowing the next user to print to it immediately. (Compare this with Lotus 1-2-3 Release 2.01, which does not break the connection with a network printer when a printout is finished, but holds onto the printer until 1-2-3 is exited.)

2. Windows applications are conducive to individual configuration settings. Most of today's programs include an initialization file (identi-fied by the three-letter .INI filename extension) that contains prefer-ences for the program's menus and selection of tools. The bulk of the program can be stored in one central disk drive on the network, where it is easy to access and maintain, while each user keeps a specific setup that meets his or her needs in this .INI file.

Even with these advantages, installing and running Windows on a network can be a frustrating experience, due to the many different types of PCs, video monitors, and printers that exist in a typical company. Windows works a little differently with each of these devices. Learning to "tweak" the hundreds of settings that Windows provides to accommodate all these different pieces of hardware and software can feel like a thankless job. (These settings are described later in this chapter.)

But installing Windows on a network server, and running Windows and all Windows and DOS applications from that server, provides opportunities for major time savings for computer professionals.

Using the Program Manager to set up a single, master menu for all Windows users — with additional, personal menus that may be customized by each user to fit his or her needs — is one example of ways that network installation can save you days or weeks that would otherwise be spent building individual solutions for particular workstations.

Networking Program Manager

Program Manager Menus on a Network

Running Windows on a network allows you to maintain not only a single copy of each program on a network drive, but also a single master menu for all users in the Program Manager window.

By creating a master Program Manager "Group" file that contains icons for all applications that are licensed to users (including Windows accessories such as Notepad and Paintbrush), network managers can save many hours when a new program is licensed by placing the icon for this program on the master menu, instead of adding the new icon to every network user's Program Manager window individually.

An example that shows Program Manager set up on a network with a master "Programs" menu, and an individually customizable "Directories" menu, is shown in Figure 12-1.

Program Manager stores information about the group windows and related icons it displays in an undocumented file called PROGMAN.INI. On a stand-alone PC, this file is usually located in the Windows subdirectory. On a network, this file (along with all .INI files) should be moved to each user's personal subdirectory on the network, where .INI files may be written to when user preferences are changed through the Program Manager, Control Panel, or other Windows front-ends.

The PROGMAN.INI file is a plain text file that usually appears as follows:

```
[Settings]
Window=100 90 640 435 1
SaveSettings=0
MinOnRun=0
AutoArrange=0

[Groups]
Group1=C:\WIN\PROGRAMS.GRP
Group2=C:\WIN\DIRECTOR.GRP
```

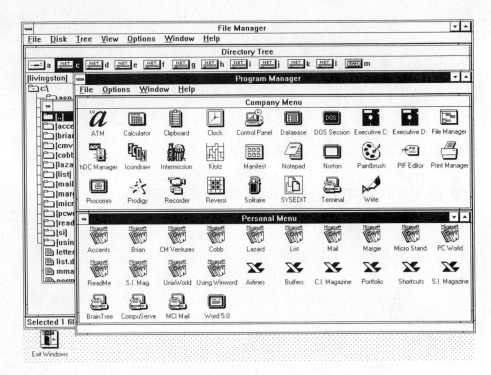

Figure 12-1: A Network master menu for applets (the Company Menu) and to start programs in particular directories (Personal Menu).

In the [Settings] section, the WINDOW= line indicates the location of the Program Manager window the last time Windows was exited and the "Save changes" box was checked *on*. The five numbers indicate the horizontal and vertical distance of the window in pixels from the upper-left corner of the screen, the horizontal and vertical width of the window in pixels, and whether or not the Program Manager window should load in its "unfolded" state (not as an icon). The other entries in the [Settings] section save values that were present in Program Manager's menus and dialog boxes when the configuration was last saved.

The [Groups] section offers the option of a single, master menu for network administrators. Each line in this section represents a different file containing the specifics for each group window displayed in the Program Manager. In this example, the user has two group windows: one for starting individual programs, and the other for starting programs in specific directories.

(Program Manager has truncated the name "Directories" when saving this file as DIRECTOR.GRP in order to conform to the DOS 8-character filename limit.)

The network administrator can use Windows on any workstation on the network to set up a group window containing all the icons (and the actions behind them) that will appear on the master menu. By changing the "Icon Spacing" value in Control Panel's Desktop and clicking "Arrange Icons" in Program Manager's Window menu, these icons can be made to fit in regular rows and columns within the space available for the group window. This file can then be copied to a read-only directory on the network. Let's say this file was moved to the N:\COMPANY directory and named MENU (with no extension — for reasons we shall see shortly).

Network users' PROGMAN.INI files would then be edited so that the GROUP= lines would read:

```
Group1=N:\COMPANY\MENU
Group2=C:\ZZ\DIRECTOR.GRP
```

The MENU group window now contains the programs all users have access to, while the DIRECTOR.GRP group window contains icons for those programs that are licensed to the particular user, with commands that start those programs in the specific directories used by that person. When a new program is added to the company-wide network, a change in the MENU file (by using Program Manager with supervisor privileges) makes that program immediately available to all Windows users on the network (the next time they start Windows).

Since the MENU group window is protected against unauthorized changes by its read-only status, use of this menu by anyone in the company cannot damage it. Users can still, however, drag icons from the company menu into their own personal group windows (by holding down Ctrl while dragging the icon with a mouse) and make their own customized routines with these icons. The properties of the Notepad icon, for example, could be changed from NOTEPAD.EXE to C:\MAILBOX\NOTEPAD.EXE to make Notepad automatically default to the C:\MAILBOX directory every time it is started. (The directory containing NOTEPAD.EXE — usually the Windows directory — must be on the DOS Path for this to work, of course as explained in Chapter 2.)

When a user exits Windows and checks the "Save changes" box to save the position and meaning of icons in his or her personal group windows,

Program Manager saves the personal .GRP files but finds that N:\COMPANY\MENU is read-only. Since it cannot write to that file, Program Manager displays the message "Program group file 'N:\COMPANY\MENU' is write-protected. Its contents will not be updated." This message is fairly straightforward (because we saved the MENU group without the usual .GRP extension, as mentioned previously). The message would be harder for the average user to understand if it used more cryptic computer filenames, such as "Program group file 'N:\PRGMS\GRP1.GRP' is write-protected..." Using the name of your company and the word MENU should make it understandable to everyone that the company menu cannot be changed by saving one person's Program Manager settings. Nevertheless, users should be informed in advance that this message will appear when saving their changes to the Program Manager, and that it is not an error.

Networking Application Software

For the most part, application software runs on a network under Windows just the same as it does on a stand-alone PC. A few exceptions, however, require a little advance planning on the part of network managers.

Word for Windows Won't Spell-Check

When you start Word for Windows from a network drive, the program seems to function as usual. When you start the spelling checker from the Utilities menu, however, Winword reports an error and won't spell-check because it needs to open and write to its spelling files; these files (if they are located in the Winword directory as they normally are) may be marked read-only on the network drive, along with all the other executables.

 The solution is to make a copy of the spelling files for each user of Word for Windows. A good place for these files is the user's personal network directory, since this directory must contain other Windows configuration-specific files and should be both readable and writeable.

If you locate the obscure reference to these spelling files in the Winword reference manual, however (it's under the WIN.INI section), you will be advised that six files need to be copied from the Winword directory to each user's personal directory — including spelling, hyphenation, thesaurus, and help files. These files total more than 1MB of disk space, and the thought of adding an additional megabyte of storage for every user may make you pause.

Fortunately, the reference manual is incorrect. All these files are not needed.
Simply copying three files, which total only about 200K, and adding a line to
each user's WIN.INI file is sufficient to restore the spelling checker to full
functionality. Locate the [Microsoft Word] section in WIN.INI (this section
refers to Word for Windows, not Microsoft Word for DOS), and add the
following two lines:

```
[Microsoft Word]
; The location of the LEX-AM.DAT and LEX-AM.DLL spelling files.
util-path=c:\zz
```

Then copy the LEX-AM.DAT, LEX-AM.DLL, and STDUSER.DIC files from the
Winword directory on the network to the user's personal directory. The first
two files are the dictionary and the executable spelling routine (DLL means
"dynamic link library") that checks against it. If you use a language other
than American English, the two letters after LEX- in the filenames will be
something other than AM — use the files that apply to you. The third file is
the standard user dictionary, which is customizable by the user in order to
add words that are unknown to the dictionary. Before the user defines any
new words, the STDUSER.DIC file is zero bytes in length (0K). The DOS COPY
command won't copy a zero-byte file — use XCOPY instead.

After you make these changes, restart Windows and Word for Windows. The
spelling checker will find the necessary files in a writeable format and will
work as expected.

Changing Winwords' Default Extension

Most word processors create documents by default that have filenames
ending with .DOC. This includes Word for Windows, Microsoft Word for DOS,
WordPerfect, MultiMate, and many others. On a stand-alone PC, this many
applications with files bearing the same extension might be manageable. On
a network, however, the confusion is enormous. Any time people work
together on projects and documents and use different software, the time
wasted in figuring out exactly which piece of software created which
document becomes frustrating for everyone.

This frustration is compounded since Word for Windows can read DOS
word processing files, but most DOS word processors (including Word for
DOS) cannot read Word for Windows files. To prevent attempts to load
Winword files into other word processors, you can add a single line to your
WIN.INI that changes Winword's default to something else. Companies seem

to be settling on the extension .WRD for Winword files. (The extension .WIN would be confused with other Windows files, and I've tried .WOR but everyone mispronounced it, so .WRD won out.) Place the following two lines in the [Microsoft Word] section of the WIN.INI file and restart Windows:

```
[Microsoft Word]
; Changes Winword's default document extension.
doc-extension=wrd
```

Distributing Winword Macros to All Users

One of Word for Windows' most powerful features is its capability to record and playback macros that can accomplish almost anything — open other applications, read and write multiple files under program control, and so on. Winword comes with its own version of Microsoft's Basic language (WordBasic), which provides commands to open and close files, loop numerous times, search and replace within documents, redefine any key combination, and many other functions.

One problem on a network is distributing new macros that have been written in the Basic language to all Winword users. Macros (even in Basic) can be very complicated (Microsoft distributes one macro in the EXAMPLES.DOC file supplied with Winword that is 11 pages long) and once a macro is written all users should be able to benefit from it without having to type it in themselves. These macros, however, are all stored in Winword's standard document template, which is a file called NORMAL.DOT. If this file is kept in the Winword directory and made read-only, individual users on the network cannot save changes to their preferred character and paragraph formats. If each user is given a separate copy, on the other hand, you cannot copy updated versions of NORMAL.DOT with newly written macros and key assignments to users' directories without eliminating the old file (containing users' own formatting preferences).

The best solution to this dilemma is to make a copy of the NORMAL.DOT document template (and other templates) for each user in his or her personal directory. Then make NORMAL.DOT *read-only* (with the DOS ATTRIB command), and create a template called LETTER.DOT. An AutoExec macro must be written for Winword to execute every time it starts. The AutoExec macro instructs Winword to use the character and paragraph formatting preferences contained in LETTER.DOT instead of NORMAL.DOT.

The Letter document template (and all other templates in the same directory) inherit all the macros and key assignments contained in NORMAL.DOT.

In this way, users may select any typeface, size, etc., which they need for their everyday documents. But whenever the computer staff develops new macro functions (or places additional functions on key combinations like Ctrl+Shift+A), simply copying a new version of NORMAL.DOT to all users' personal directories immediately distributes the changes to them (the next time they start Winword).

The following two lines must be inserted in WIN.INI under the [Microsoft Word] section for Winword to find document templates in a directory other than its own main directory:

```
[Microsoft Word]
; Sets the directory for NORMAL.DOT and other templates.
dot-path=c:\template
```

See Chapter 6 for details on several WordBasic macros that are necessary to handle the Normal template, Letter template, and other templates in this manner.

Word for Windows Requires NovellNet=Yes

In order for Word for Windows to open and save documents on a Novell network, the [Microsoft Word] section of WIN.INI must be edited to include two lines like the following:

```
[Microsoft Word]
; The following enables Winword to use Netware correctly.
NovellNet=Yes
```

If this is not included in WIN.INI, you may see the error message "Document name or path is not valid" when trying to open a document from a Netware drive, or "Not a valid filename" when trying to save a document. This occurs because, when Winword is reading from or writing to a subdirectory, it attempts to verify that the subdirectory and its parent directory are valid. If the user does not have enough privileges in the parent directory to write a file there, this test fails and Winword displays the above messages. Say, for example, that the user wishes to read from or write to a file in the DOCUMENT subdirectory under the ACCOUNTS directory on network drive N:, as follows:

N:	the root directory is read-only
\ACCOUNTS	this directory allows users no privileges
\DOCUMENT	the user has read/write privileges

The operation will fail because Winword cannot access the ACCOUNTS directory. Adding the NOVELLNET=YES statement causes Winword to simply change directories to the one containing the file the user wants (and change back after the operation is done), avoiding all such error conditions.

Excel Tutorial Won't Run from Network

Microsoft Excel should be upgraded to version 2.1d or higher for best results under Windows 3.0. Version 2.1c was required for Windows 3.0 compatibility, but 2.1d fixes some quirks that freeze PCs under certain conditions. (And Excel 3.*x* is even better.)

Excel won't run its Tutorial or Feature Guide on a network, because it wants to save a workspace file to disk in order to restore the environment after running the Tutorial files. Since the Excel directory will most likely be marked read-only, Excel can't write this file.

Apparently, the only solution is to copy the files necessary for the Tutorial and Feature Guide (or the entire Excel directory) to a directory on the network with both read and write access. Then, create an icon in the Program Manager marked "Excel Tutorial" and use this to start the Excel tutorial in the writeable directory. You can recopy the original Excel directory into this directory if these files become corrupted during multiple usage.

Before You Install Windows on a Network _____

The experiments of many people who have gone through painful trial-and-error with Windows on networked hardware and software have resulted in the following information. Learning from these experiences can save hours or days that would ordinarily be spent installing and trouble-shooting Windows.

1. **Consider your disk space needs.** Most people using Windows will need some kind of word processor and a spreadsheet, plus one or two other programs, such as a drawing package. Installing Windows, Microsoft Word for Windows, Microsoft Excel, and Micrografx Designer requires more than *24MB* of disk space on a 386-class system. That's *after* deleting large, unneeded bitmap files and *before* creating any document files or counting other programs, such as DOS. For this

reason alone, it makes perfect sense to store all Windows files — both program files and users' individual document files — on a network drive instead of locating them on individual disk drives in each PC.

At one typical company with hundreds of PCs, about 50 percent of the microcomputer staff's time was spent handling PC hard disk problems. This included requests for bigger hard disks to replace ones that were full; resurrecting files that had been accidentally deleted, copying files from place to place to accommodate people who moved around, and servicing hard disks that had suffered a total failure.

All of these problems are avoidable if all files — both programs and data — are stored in disk drives that are accessible through a network. People can move from desk to desk and still access their work. Damaged files can be restored quickly from a backup tape. It is easier to install larger disks, if needed, on a network than on multiple individual desks. And the access speed of network drives can be faster than local drives, because a much larger disk cache can be placed centrally on the network than most companies would spend on the same amount of memory for every desktop. It is not uncommon for a network hard drive to have a full 16MB of disk cache RAM, serving users' requests for files almost instantly. But few companies would buy 16MB or even 4MB of disk cache memory for every user of an individual hard disk.

Ask yourself the following questions before installing Windows programs on individual hard disks of your networked PCs:

Are all the PCs' hard disks backed up every night?

Can you upgrade each disk to a new software version in a single day?

Can you use virus-scanning programs to check each disk every night?

If you answered "No" to one or more of these questions, then you should seriously consider keeping all software and data files on network hard drives instead of on individual PC hard drives.

2. **Consider the power necessary for running Windows.** As a rule of thumb, you should estimate that each person who is now working with a character-based word processor or spreadsheet will need a PC that is twice as fast to accomplish the same amount of work on a graphically based program. This is because Windows applications are much larger than most character-based applications and must move around

more memory and pixels on the screen. You should plan hardware upgrades to fast 32-bit 386s at the same time that you move users to Windows 3.*x*.

If you are planning to switch from DOS to Windows applications without moving each person to a faster PC at the same time, you may meet serious user resistance. One company switched its word-processing pool practically overnight from a character-based DOS word processor to Word for Windows on 16-MHz 386s with a VGA display. Productivity dropped so much that the company had to hire an equal number of temporary secretaries as they had permanent secretaries, just to get out the same level of business documents they had always produced. The slowdown was because (1) the 16-MHz PCs took a long time to redraw the screen; and (2) the VGA display was too small — Word for Windows could show only 6 inches of a document's width, instead of 8 inches across as the secretaries were used to. Faster machines and Super VGA displays, which are capable of displaying the full 8-inch document width, were called for.

3. **Consider the investment in Windows applications.** Windows is at its best when running Windows-specific applications, not DOS programs. Despite its attractive icons, Windows does not make an ideal menuing system for starting older DOS apps. These programs almost always run more slowly under Windows than they did without Windows, unless specific tuning is performed on every Program Information File (PIF) that starts them. And many DOS apps have quirks that can both hamper Windows and diminish their own effectiveness, or prevent them from running under Windows at all. Moving to Windows almost always means investing in Windows-specific applications at the same time.

STEPS:

Installing Windows on a Network

Step 1. **Prepare a bootable floppy diskette.** Format a diskette in your A: drive and place the DOS System files on it by using the /S switch:

```
FORMAT A: /S
```

Copy your CONFIG.SYS and AUTOEXEC.BAT files from the hard disk to this floppy diskette. Also copy any essential drivers listed in

either of these two files, especially those that enable access to
your hard drive:

```
COPY CONFIG.SYS A:
COPY AUTOEXEC.BAT A:
COPY harddisk.drv A:
etc.
```

These steps are necessary to protect the configuration of the PC
used for the installation. Anything can happen (and usually
does), and making a bootable floppy diskette is a good precaution. Windows 3.0's SmartDrive program, for example, is incompatible with some larger-than-32MB hard disk partitioning
systems, and has irretrievably corrupted some of these drives.
This problem was corrected in the version of SmartDrive shipped
with Windows 3.0a (it detects this type of drive and disables
itself), but this example illustrates that accidents are always
possible.

Insert this bootable diskette in drive A: and make sure that if you
reboot your PC, this diskette will bring the system up normally.
You may need to change references in the CONFIG.SYS and
AUTOEXEC.BAT files from directories such as C:\DRIVERS to
A:\DRIVERS. Perform these changes with a text editor until the
bootable diskette works reliably. If something corrupts files on
your PC (making it impossible to access your hard drive, for
example), this diskette will get you running again so you can
diagnose the problem.

Step 2. Remove resident programs. The installation itself should
proceed from a PC that is as free as possible from memory-
resident programs. These programs are usually loaded automatically every time the PC is started, from the CONFIG.SYS file or the
AUTOEXEC.BAT file. Many memory-resident programs have no
effect on the Windows installation, but some are known to
corrupt Windows files during the Setup procedure. Ideally, *no*
programs should be resident in memory when installing Windows. To ensure this, you can rename CONFIG.SYS and
AUTOEXEC.BAT and save them for later with the following commands:

```
C:
CD \
REN CONFIG.SYS *.SAV
REN AUTOEXEC.BAT *.SAV
```

Create a simple, vanilla CONFIG.SYS with a text editor that says the following:

```
FILES=30
BUFFERS=20
BREAK=ON
```

Reboot the computer with Ctrl+Alt+Del. If possible, switch the PC to its slowest available speed. (Some PCs do not copy mass-duplicated diskettes perfectly when operating at a turbo speed.) With no AUTOEXEC.BAT in place, no memory-resident programs will be loaded, but the system will ask you to confirm the date and time. If the PC's battery is sound, the date and time should still be accurate, and two carriage returns will take you past these questions. When you see a bare "C>" prompt, you are ready to install Windows (see steps 3 and 4). After the installation is finished, copy CONFIG.SAV to CONFIG.SYS and AUTOEXEC.SAV to AUTOEXEC.BAT and reboot. If Windows won't start, or displays error messages, one of the programs in your CONFIG.SYS or AUTOEXEC.BAT is probably incompatible with Windows. You may have to remove all programs from these files and then add lines back to your CONFIG.SYS and AUTOEXEC.BAT one at a time to see which, if any, of your loaded programs are incompatible with Windows or prevent it from starting. Small programs that provide disk caching or accelerate the repeat speed of keys on the keyboard are likely to not work at all under Windows, and should be left out of your configuration after this installation.

Step 3.   Consider the location of programs on your disk. You should eliminate any DOS Path statement that references other programs on any hard disk. (This should have been accomplished by renaming AUTOEXEC.BAT to AUTOEXEC.SAV.) Eliminating the Path avoids the possibility that the Windows installation will accidentally run another application's programs or install itself over a previous version of Windows. If possible, install Windows 3.*x* into a new directory, and not into the directory that contained Windows 2.*x* or an earlier version. This ensures that all the new, updated Windows printer drivers and device drivers are copied during the installation. Older drivers will probably not work with Windows 3.*x*.

While your system is in this "vanilla" state, consider moving major applications to new directories with short names. All Windows applications should be located on your new DOS Path (to give you flexibility when starting Windows apps from the Program Manager), and the Path command is limited to 127 characters. (There may be ways around this, but the simplest way to avoid this limitation is not to approach it.) If you have Windows apps such as Word for Windows or Excel installed already in directories with long names such as C:\PROGRAMS\WIN-DOWS\EXCEL, move these to two- or three-letter directory names such as C:\XL. (Make sure the programs work in the new location before continuing — you may need to alter the directory name in batch file commands that use the old name, for example.) You will be adding many Windows applications soon, and the Path limit will hit you sooner than you may think.

Step 4. Install Windows to the network by one of two methods. Two methods have become popular for installing Windows on a network: the official method, which could be called *Expand,* and the method used by many large companies, which could be called *Masters.* The Expand method involves copying every possible Windows driver to a single directory on the network. The Masters method involves copying only those drivers that are needed and supported into specific subdirectories, from which they can be copied to the directories of users who need them.

The Expand method uses the EXPAND.EXE utility program included with Windows. All the files on the Windows distribution diskettes are compressed (except for EXPAND.EXE and SETUP.EXE) and do not work if simply copied to a hard disk. The Setup program that controls the Windows installation on individual PCs normally decompresses all the files it needs from the distribution diskettes and copies the expanded, working form of the files to the hard disk. Setup only copies those files needed for that individual PC, such as one printer driver, one display driver, and so on. The Expand method, by contrast, copies *all* the files in their decompressed form to a network drive. After this, individual PCs can be configured to use only those drivers they need from this pool.

To install Windows with the Expand program, insert Disk #2 of the Windows set (5.25" or 3.5" diskettes) into a floppy disk drive. Create a directory on the network for Windows (in keeping with the need for short directory names, we'll use N:\WIN in the following example, where "N" stands for the network drive), and copy EXPAND.EXE to that directory:

```
N:
CD \
MD win
CD win
COPY A:\EXPAND.EXE
```

Now that EXPAND.EXE is available, insert Disk #1 in the floppy drive and use Expand to decompress and copy all the files:

```
EXPAND A:\*.*
```

Insert Disk #2 and repeat this command. Continue through all the diskettes.

This does not quite complete the Expand procedure. Some files that have been expanded now need to be renamed. These files have the extension .SY$, such as MOUSE.SY$ and EMM386.SY$. When Setup copies these compressed files to a hard disk, it automatically renames them while expanding them, but the Expand program itself does not. These system files were given this unusual name so people would not accidentally copy them directly to their hard disks from the floppy diskettes and try to include them in their CONFIG.SYS files. MOUSE.SY$, for example, will freeze the PC every time it starts if the compressed driver of this name is listed in CONFIG.SYS. Once the PC hangs on CONFIG.SYS there is no way to regain control without a bootable floppy diskette.

Rename those files in your Windows subdirectory that have the .SY$ extension, by issuing the following command at the DOS prompt:

```
REN *.SY$ *.SYS
```

After these .SYS files have been expanded and renamed, they can be used normally in CONFIG.SYS if you ever need these drivers.

After this Expand procedure has been completed, any PC on the network can install a version of Windows customized to that PC's particular hardware configuration. Assume that an individual user with a 386-based PC, a graphics adapter and monitor, and a hard disk has logged onto your network. By simply setting the user's Path statement to include N:\WIN (the network directory containing all the Windows files) and creating a personal subdirectory with read-and-write access rights (call it C:\MYWIN), the user can create a working copy of Windows off the network by typing (in the personal subdirectory) the following command:

```
SETUP /N
```

The /N switch indicates to Windows' Setup program that only those files needed for network operation of Windows should be copied to the user's personal subdirectory. The bulk of the programs needed for Windows' operations will remain on the network drive. This means that only about 200K of files need to be copied to the user's personal directory, instead of the several megabytes that would be required for a full, stand-alone installation of Windows.

There are at least three problems with the Expand method of installing Windows to a network drive:

1. After expanding all the Windows files onto the drive, you still must run the SETUP /N command for each user who is to run Windows on the network, and this can be time-consuming.

2. Many new device drivers for Windows are available, particularly video drivers that can take advantage of the Super VGA resolution built into many video adapters, but SETUP /N won't let you install them from vendor-provided diskettes at setup time (you receive the message "Error building WIN.COM!").

3. With all of Windows' device drivers expanded into a directory on the network drive, it's possible for any user to run SETUP /N and install a new copy of Windows for any one of hundreds of possible combinations of desktop hardware — some of which may exhibit quirks running Windows that you will find difficult or impossible to trouble-shoot.

The last of these problems is the most serious. If your company has negotiated a site license for Windows, you may not have a legal problem with users installing copies of Windows for their own use. But the technical support problems involved when Windows is installed without planning and testing on many possibly incompatible PC configurations can be severe. If Windows doesn't print, runs poorly, or freezes on one of these configurations, what is the problem? An incompatible video board or PC motherboard? Or is it the way memory is set up? Trouble-shooting all these possibilities is very time-consuming and often never actually pinpoints the real problem.

For this reason, many companies find that converting to Windows is a perfect opportunity to upgrade their PCs at the same time. Over the years, most companies have collected a wide variety of different types of PCs, many with known shortcomings, because PCs have previously not been considered strategic assets — they were a convenience and nothing more, and if they worked at all they were worth the expense. Windows, however, makes it possible for companies to benefit from both the standardization of the user interface (making it easier to learn and use new programs) and the standardization of hardware to a minimum company-wide baseline (making information systems planning and maintenance much simpler).

Standardizing on one or two models for each type of component — monitors, printers, and so on — means that installation and maintenance are simplified many times over. Even with only two possibilities for each component — PC motherboard, video adapter, monitor, mouse, and printer — there are still 32 combinations to test for incompatibilities if some anomaly develops. (In most companies, there are literally thousands of possible combinations.) Additionally, Windows not only reveals some of the quirks of existing, older hardware and software, but also requires a higher level of performance from hardware in order to demonstrate the same level of user productivity previously achieved with character-based software. For all these reasons, many companies have decided that Windows installations deserve, at a minimum, a fast 386DX processor, a Super VGA display adapter and monitor, and access to a laser printer.

With this minimum as a company-wide baseline system for Windows, the *Master* method of installing Windows on a network may be greatly preferable to the *Expand* method. With the Master method, one copy of Windows is installed to a network drive, and is then reconfigured for each of the configurations the company can support. The configuration-specific files are copied to separate directories on the network drive. Setting up a new user, then, is as simple as copying the appropriate configuration files from the master directory into the user's personal subdirectory. It's not necessary to run SETUP /N for each user; using the Master method, new users may be set up in less than one minute.

Let's look at an example of how this works in practice. Say that a company plans to support VGA displays for executives who use PCs very little during the business day, but requires Super VGA displays for clerical workers who type important documents six to eight hours a day (Super VGA allows the full 8-inch width of a document to be seen in word processors and spreadsheet programs, while VGA allows only 6 inches.)

Install the master copy of Windows as usual with the SETUP command on Disk #1 (not SETUP /N), just as in a stand-alone installation to a hard disk. During this installation, specify VGA as the display type. When the installation is finished, copy VGA-specific files to a directory called N:\WIN-VGA on the network drive. These include the following:

> WIN.COM (which is specifically built for each configuration)
> All *.INI files (especially SYSTEM.INI and WIN.INI)

Also, depending on your configuration, it may be necessary to copy certain Windows files with other extensions to a user-specific directory:

> WINVER.EXE (Setup uses this to determine the version of Windows)
> _DEFAULT.PIF (controls DOS apps started without a PIF)
> *.GRP files (contain icons for particular applications)
> HIMEM.SYS (only if needed to boot a workstation)
> SMARTDRV.SYS (only if needed to boot a workstation)
> RAMDRIVE.SYS (only if needed to boot a workstation)
> EMM386.SYS (only if needed to boot a workstation)

These files should not be deleted from the Windows subdirectory, just copied. Next, run the Setup program again (from the DOS prompt, while the Windows directory is the current directory). This time, specify the Super VGA device driver for your particular configuration. After this installation is complete, copy the configuration-dependent files just listed to a directory called N:\WIN-SVGA.

Continue reconfiguring Windows in this way until each of the devices you support company-wide are included in the Windows directory. Then, store the original Windows distribution diskettes in a safe place (in case you need to support additional devices in the future) and delete WIN.COM and all *.INI files from the main Windows directory. These files will no longer be needed, because each user will have his or her own copy to start Windows. (See also Chapter 2 for renaming the file WIN.CNF to WI.COM and using the command WI instead of WIN to start Windows. This deletes the Windows logo that is displayed in graphics mode before Windows itself loads, and might eliminate the need to have different versions of WIN.COM for different users on your network.)

Each user must have a personal subdirectory on the network they can both read and write to. I usually create a directory on the user's C: drive (either a local drive or a network drive that is mapped to appear as the C: drive) called C:\ZZ. I chose the letters ZZ because when viewing the drive in the File Manager or other file utilities, ZZ sorts to the bottom of the list of directories and is less likely to be accidentally corrupted or erased by users. There is little need to access this directory after the appropriate Windows configuration files have been copied to it. But this personal directory must be located on the DOS Path and must precede the Windows directory in that path. A typical command for this in AUTOEXEC.BAT would look as follows:

```
PATH=c:\;c:\zz;n:\win;n:\bat;n:\util;n:\dos
```

where C:\ZZ contains the user's configuration-specific files, N:\WIN contains the master copy of Windows, N:\BAT contains batch files, N:\UTIL contains utility programs, and N:\DOS contains the version of DOS that is currently in use on the network.

Once the user's C:\ZZ directory is created (using the DOS command CD ZZ from the root directory), all that is required to make Windows run on that configuration is to copy files to that directory from the master configuration directory. If the user has a Super VGA display (and the rest of the desktop PC is standard), this command would look like:

```
XCOPY n:\win-svga\*.* c:\zz
```

After copying these files, typing WIN at the DOS prompt starts Windows. Since WIN.COM is in the user's C:\ZZ directory (and this directory appears in the Path prior to the Windows directory itself), DOS looks in the C:\ZZ directory for WIN.COM and runs it. Similarly, when Windows is loading and looks for its WIN.INI and SYSTEM.INI configuration files (and others), since they are not located in the Windows directory itself, Windows searches the directory that contains WIN.COM and finds these files there.

Once these master directories are installed on the network and verified as working, the process of adding new Windows users to the network is as simple as establishing that their hardware configuration meets one of the company-wide standards, and then copying one of the master sub-directories to their C: drive. If new device drivers become available in the future, this process can be repeated and the appropriate changes made to the SYSTEM.INI files in the directories of the affected users (SYSTEM.INI contains all the hardware specific information for Windows).

The one drawback of the master directory method of adding Windows users to a network is that you must ensure that hardware configurations that *look* compatible — two 386 PCs from two different manufacturers, for example —

actually *are* compatible. This requires testing each component for compatibility before simply assuming that to be the case (and copying particular configuration files to hundreds of such users). Performing this compatibility testing before making multiple Windows installations, however, is a good idea anyway and will help you catch any problems before they proliferate. This requirement alone makes it sensible to try to standardize as much as possible before the need arises to support Windows on a variety of incompatible configurations.

Swap Files on a Network

One well-advertised feature of Windows 3.*x* is its capability to use "virtual memory" in 386 enhanced mode. *Virtual memory*, in this case, means Windows' capability to move programs out of real RAM into hard disk storage in order to free up RAM to start other programs. Virtual memory means "imaginary" or "not real" memory — make-believe memory, in other words. Hard disk storage is imaginary RAM because a hard disk (unlike real memory) is not fast enough to run any programs. Windows only moves a program to hard disk storage to avoid an "out-of-memory" condition in which the user could not start any new programs at all.

When a Windows user starts a new application, but all the available RAM is in use by programs that were started earlier, Windows moves one of the earlier applications to hard disk storage in a process called *swapping*. Windows swaps the first application to disk and frees the RAM it was using, then loads the new application into that RAM. This process is slower than switching between two applications that are both in RAM. But the delay caused by swapping may be better than not being able to switch at all.

All this swapping has a different significance on a network than it does on a stand-alone PC. On a nonnetworked PC, Windows usually swaps programs into the directory on the user's hard drive that contains the WIN.COM program (which starts Windows) or to a special file called a *permanent swap file,* which is set up by using Windows' Swapfile application. On a network, this swapping could take place in a variety of areas.

In a network environment, Windows requires a swap area to which the user has network read *and* write access. This could very well be the personal subdirectory in which the user has his or her own WIN.COM, WIN.INI, and other configuration-specific files. This may be the C: drive in the user's PC or (especially if the networked PC does not have a local hard drive) a personal subdirectory on a network drive.

In the latter case, the process of setting up a swap file may take Windows a long time. This is because when Windows starts, it reads the drive in which it will create a temporary swap file and determines how big to make the swap file based on the amount of free space on that drive. A network hard drive may be 300MB, 600MB, or larger and may have hundreds of megabytes free. In this environment, Windows may take more than a minute to examine the drive and establish a large temporary swap file. Meanwhile, the user sees the Microsoft logo sitting motionless on the screen (or, even worse, a totally blank screen), making it appear as if the PC has frozen, when in fact, Windows is just searching network drives. Since it's impossible to create a permanent swap file on a network drive (because Windows wants to write to that file in a nonstandard format), a temporary swap file is a necessity. But the process of establishing one may seem a major impediment to using Windows on a network.

The solution is to establish in advance the maximum size of the temporary swap file. Windows' SYSTEM.INI file provides several settings that control the temporary swap file. These settings (shown with values in the [386Enh] section that might be set on a network), are as follows:

```
[386Enh]
Paging=Yes
PagingDrive=C
MaxPagingFileSize=1024
```

The PAGING= line controls whether or not paging, and therefore virtual memory, is enabled. This line may be set to Yes or No. (If the line is totally absent, Windows always defaults to Yes.)

If you have enough real RAM in your PC (say, 4MB), you might assume you could turn paging off entirely. After all, you would never need to swap an application to disk because you have enough RAM to run several applications at once.

This would be a mistake. Without a swap file to enable paging, Windows turns off not only the capability to swap applications to disk, but also some features that can be used to manage real RAM with a 386 processor. Specifically, on a 386, Windows can move chunks of RAM as small as 4K to accommodate the changing needs of applications for memory — *if* paging is enabled. If not, Windows reverts to chunks of memory that are 64K in size. With paging disabled, Windows gives applications 64K of memory at a time, whether they need that much or not. And Windows loses a great deal of its capability to reclaim memory when an application no longer needs it.

These are important reasons to leave paging enabled, even if you have a large amount of RAM available for applications. But how much disk space should be assigned to swapping? The minimum value that enables Windows' 4K memory management on a 386 chip is 512K, and the minimum size of a swap file that will do Windows much good is actually 1024K (1MB). Therefore, the MAXPAGINGFILESIZE= line should equal 1024 or higher. If the number is smaller than this (or Paging is set to No), Windows applications eventually display "out of memory" messages, even when their "Help About" dialog boxes show that 1MB or more is still available. Windows has plenty of memory available, but none that it can manage effectively.

Finally, what is the appropriate drive letter on which to establish the temporary swap file? On a PC with its own hard disk, the C: drive is a natural choice. A networked PC, on the other hand, does not need a local hard disk, and can use a personal subdirectory on a network drive (which can be labeled C:, D:, or almost any other letter).

On a network, however, specifying a network hard drive as the user's paging drive can cause problems. This is because the root directory of a network hard drive, such as N:\, may actually be the same as the root directory of the server machine itself. If multiple users have PAGINGDRIVE=N: in their SYSTEM.INI files and use Windows in 386 enhanced mode, their temporary files (all of which have the name WIN386.SWP) will be written over each other, causing Windows to halt with a thud. In this situation, do *not* use PAGINGDRIVE= statements in the users' SYSTEM.INI files. With no PAGINGDRIVE= statement, Windows will use the personal subdirectory where WIN.COM is located, which is a different writeable area for each user. There is no way to specify another subdirectory, other than the root, when using the PAGINGDRIVE= statement.

SETUP /N Anomalies

Loading Special Device Drivers

Windows' SETUP /N command is for individual network users to install Windows' configuration-specific files on their PCs. The SETUP /N command displays a menu of choices regarding the hardware configuration that the Setup program has detected: the user's type of PC (286, 386, 486), type of video adapter, type of mouse, and so on. This menu may be manually overridden in order to change one of the components that Windows detected. For example, the user's video adapter may be capable of displaying Super VGA resolution (800 × 600), but the Setup program detected this adapter as only a plain VGA (640 × 480). In cases like these, the Setup program allows the user to specify "Other" as the display type, and prompts the user to insert a diskette in a floppy drive that contains the driver for that device.

When Setup is begun with the /N switch for installation across a network, however, this "Other" procedure often does not work. Setup displays the message "Error building WIN.COM!" and refuses to continue.

There are two ways to work around this behavior. The first is to run Setup with one of the display drivers that comes with Windows — plain VGA, for example. Then, if the vendor of the customized display driver has provided instructions, copy the customized driver to the network directory that contains Windows and manually edit the line in SYSTEM.INI that refers to the VGA driver (changing it to refer instead to the customized driver).

If this method is not possible (because it is unclear what lines in SYSTEM.INI need to be edited), install Windows to a stand-alone, to a stand-alone PC by using the Setup program without any parameters. When the menu of choices is displayed, choose Other for the display type and insert the vendor's diskette in a drive when prompted. Setup accepts such a diskette when not running with the /N parameter. After the installation is completed, copy the SYSTEM.INI that resulted from the stand-alone installation to the user's personal directory on the network that contains his or her copy of WIN.COM. Make sure to also copy the device driver itself from the stand-alone hard disk to Windows' \SYSTEM subdirectory on the network. Examine SYSTEM.INI to make sure it does not contain any references to drive letters, such as C:\DEVICE.DRV. If the device driver is mentioned in SYSTEM.INI with no drive letter preceding it, then Windows (when starting up) will look for that driver in the \SYSTEM directory that is automatically placed below the directory containing Windows itself.

Disabling Auto-detection Using SETUP /I /N

If you see the error message "Error Building WIN.COM!" while running SETUP /N, the automatic hardware detection routine that Windows' Setup program performs may be conflicting with an adapter board installed in that PC. (This message may also mean that files named WIN.CNF or *filename*.LGO are corrupted or missing in the original Windows directory you are installing from.)

As an example, many ARCnet network adapter boards are set by default to use a base address of 2E0 (hexadecimal) to communicate with the CPU. When Setup examines the PC to determine whether or not the display is an IBM 8514 type, its detection routines conflict with the ARCnet board. (This situation may also produce the error message "Unknown File Copy Failure.") To get around this, you can either set jumpers to change the ARCnet adapter's base address from 2E0 to an address between 300 to 340, or use the following procedure:

Disable Setup's attempts to detect the PC's hardware components while running its network setup procedure by starting Setup with an /I switch (as in "Install"), followed by the /N switch. This looks as follows:

    SETUP /I /N

Strangely, these switches are order-sensitive. Whereas SETUP /I /N works, SETUP /N /I does not.

SHARE.EXE and Networks

On a stand-alone PC, it is necessary to run the following command once before starting Windows:

    SHARE /F:2048 /L:20

The DOS SHARE command (with its default values of 2048 bytes for file names and 20 file locks) prevents two applications — or two directory windows in the File Manager — from operating on the same data file simultaneously and corrupting it. The README file in the Windows directory specifically instructs readers to use this command, and I have seen several instances of damaged files without it.

Network disk-drive operation under Windows, however, does not require the use of SHARE, and some networks are incompatible with SHARE. The network automatically checks whether a file is in use by more than one application and refuses to allow multiple processes to open it unless the file is read-only or record-locked for multiuser access. Ask your network representative whether SHARE is required in your particular installation.

How Windows Sets
Itself Up for Networks

When the Windows Setup program detects that you are running a network when you install Windows (or you tell it to install for a particular network), Setup writes certain information into your SYSTEM.INI file. This is controlled by the file SYSTEM.SRC on the Windows distribution diskettes. Setup reads this file to determine which settings are appropriate for the network it detected (or you specified). If you are installing copies of Windows multiple times on a particular network, you can read this file and edit it to make Setup's behavior consistent with certain changes you want to make to every workstation on that network. (For example, you might specify a certain MAXPAGINGFILESIZE= line that you want every networked PC to use.)

In most cases, however, you'll want to use the defaults that Setup uses for the networks it recognizes. Some of these defaults are described in the following topics, which are broken into three different areas of your SYSTEM.INI file: (1) the [boot] section; (2) the [standard] section; and (3) the [386Enh] section.

For a complete description of what these sections and their individual settings do, you should print and read the SYSINI.TXT text files that Windows copies to your hard drive. (There are three different files, named SYSINI.TXT, SYSINI2.TXT, and SYSINI3.TXT, so they will fit into Windows Notepad.)

The [boot] Section of SYSTEM.INI

The [boot] section of SYSTEM.INI contains settings that configure Windows every time you start it. Most of these settings are for video, keyboard, mouse, and communications drivers. Setup writes a single line into this section, indicating the driver file that should be used when you start Windows. If you have a Netware network, for example, this line looks as follows:

```
[boot]
network.drv=netware.drv
```

At this writing, Windows supports the following networks and writes the following lines into SYSTEM.INI to specify the driver for each network:

Network:	Line in SYSTEM.INI
No network in use	network.drv=
3Com 3+Open LAN Manager 1.x	network.drv=msnet.drv
3Com 3+Open LAN Manager 2.0	network.drv=lanman.drv
3Com 3+Share	network.drv=msnet.drv
Artisoft LANtastic	network.drv=msnet.drv
Banyan Vines	network.drv=msnet.drv
DCA 10net	network.drv=msnet.drv
Digital Equipment Corp. DECnet DOS	network.drv=msnet.drv
IBM PC LAN	network.drv=msnet.drv
Microsoft Network	network.drv=msnet.drv
Microsoft LAN Manager 1.x	network.drv=msnet.drv
Microsoft LAN Manager 2.0 Basic	network.drv=msnet.drv
Microsoft LAN Manager 2.0 Enhanced	network.drv=lanman.drv
Novell Netware	network.drv=netware.drv
Ungermann-Bass Net/One	network.drv=msnet.drv

The [standard] Section of SYSTEM.INI

The [standard] section controls Windows' behavior in standard mode. Most networks require no special settings in this section. Only three settings in this section are of interest in network management:

The NETHEAPSIZE= setting sets aside a pool of memory in the lower 640K to buffer data moving to and from the network. A default of 8K is usually in effect, but this can be enlarged if necessary for your particular network.

The NETASYNCSWITCHING= setting prevents Windows from switching away from an application that has set up an asynchronous link across a network using NetBIOS. The default value is 0 (no), because switching away could cause this session to hang. But it can be set to 1 if switching is permissible.

The INT28FILTER= setting controls the percentage of interrupt 28 signals that are sent by Windows through to network software. This interrupt is used to determine whether the system is idle and it is safe to access a disk or perform other actions. The default is 10 (every tenth such interrupt will pass through), which is usually enough for network and communications software to coexist with Windows.

The [386Enh] Section of SYSTEM.INI

The [386Enh] section of SYSTEM.INI controls Windows' behavior in 386 enhanced mode. In this section, devices that begin with an asterisk (*) indicate support that is internal to the Windows kernel, not provided in a separate file on disk (such as *vnetbios, which is a "virtual" NetBIOS driver).

The Windows Setup program writes the following lines into the [386Enh] section for each of the following networks:

If no network is in use:

    network=*vnetbios,*dosnet

3Com 3+Share:

    network=*vnetbios,*dosnet

3Com 3+Open LAN Manager 1.*x:*

    network=*vnetbios,*dosnet,lanman10.386
    TimerCriticalSection=10000
    UniqueDOSPSP=true
    PSPIncrement=5

3Com 3+Open LAN Manager 2.0:

    network=*vnetbios,*dosnet
    TimerCriticalSection=10000
    UniqueDOSPSP=true
    PSPIncrement=5

Artisoft LANtastic:

    network=*vnetbios,*dosnet
    UniqueDOSPSP=true
    [*Important:* You must add the last line *manually* for Lantastic.]

Banyan Vines:

    network=*vnetbios,*dosnet,baninst.386
    TimerCriticalSection=5000
    [Other settings are required; see "Banyan Vines" later in this chapter.]

DCA 10net:

    network=*vnetbios,*dosnet
    TimerCriticalSection=10000
    [*Important:* You must add the last line *manually* for DCA 10net.]

Digital Equipment Corp. DECnet DOS:

    network=*vnetbios,*dosnet

IBM PC LAN:
```
network=*vnetbios,*dosnet
InDOSPolling=true
```

Microsoft Network:
```
network=*vnetbios,*dosnet
```

Microsoft LAN Manager 1.x:
```
network=*vnetbios,*dosnet,lanman10.386
```

Microsoft LAN Manager 2.0 Basic:
```
network=*vnetbios,*dosnet
```

Microsoft LAN Manager 2.0 Enhanced:
```
network=*vnetbios,*dosnet
```

Novell Netware:
```
network=vnetware.386,vipx.386,*vnetbios
```

Ungermann-Bass Net/One:
```
network=*vnetbios,*dosnet
```

If Windows is not operating properly on your network, one of these settings may have become corrupted or deleted. In addition, some feature of your particular network-and-workstation configuration may require changes to other settings in the [386Enh] section of SYSTEM.INI. The lines that might affect network operation are the following:

```
[386Enh]
AllVMsExclusive=
EMMExclude=
FileSysChange=
InDOSPolling=
Int28Critical=
NetAsyncFallback=
NetDMASize=
Network=
PSPIncrement=
ReflectDOSInt2A=
TimerCriticalSection=
TokenRingSearch=
UniqueDOSPSP=
```

There are too many possible interactions to describe all of them here, but if you need more information on these settings you should print and read the files NETWORKS.TXT and SYSINI*.TXT in your Windows directory (described earlier in this chapter). Additionally, you should read the technical material on networks provided by Microsoft, which is described at the end of this chapter in the "Other Networks" section.

Specific Networks

The remainder of this chapter describes configuration secrets for two network operating systems widely used by both smaller businesses and large corporations — Novell Netware and Banyan Vines.

Novell Netware

Version 3.01 of Shell Programs Is Required

Windows runs on versions of Netware from 2.10 on up, but several files must be upgraded to version 3.01 or later to run correctly under all Windows modes. You can tell what version of the Netware "shell" program a networked PC is running by typing the following command at the DOS prompt in the directory containing the Netware files:

    IPX I

If the response is version 2.15 or lower, the shell programs must be upgraded. The following version 3.01 components are required; the table shows the filename, size in bytes, and DOS file date:

Filename	Size	Date
IPX.OBJ	19,166	05/07/90
LOGIN.EXE	70,301	07/28/89
NET3.COM	48,544	05/08/90
NET4.COM	48,907	05/08/90
NETBIOS.EXE	23,088	04/20/90
SHGEN.EXE	26,321	05/04/89

In addition to these files, other Netware utilities (including MAKEUSER.EXE and BINDFIX.EXE) must be upgraded before use with version 3.01 of the shell programs.

Obtain these files by calling Novell at 800-346-7177. Press "2" when prompted by a recording and request part number 883-976-001. Novell was charging $30 for this upgrade at the time of this writing.

A driver program is included with the upgrade that allows some network adapter boards to work under Windows' enhanced mode when configured for interrupt request line 2 (IRQ2). This interrupt, available only on AT-class PCs or higher, actually "cascades" to IRQ9 and makes available interrupts that are not present on XT-class systems.

A network adapter board configured for IRQ2 may freeze the PC when Windows starts in 386 enhanced mode, even if it works fine in real or standard mode. Correct this problem by running the INSTALL program included with the upgrade disk. The INSTALL program copies the VPICDA.386 driver into the \SYSTEM subdirectory under Windows. It also changes one of the SYSTEM.INI lines to DEVICE=VPICDA.386 from DEVICE=*VPICD (the asterisk in the old line indicates that Windows uses a driver that is internal to the Windows program itself, instead of a separate file on disk).

ROOT Parameter Helps Map Drives to Users

Version 3.01 of Netware offers a new parameter called ROOT that is useful when mapping network drives to drive letters on users' networked PC systems. This parameter makes a directory located on a network disk drive appear as the root directory of a separate drive letter to the user. This can be useful in providing network users with their own separate, writeable areas of the network drive, each of which has a single drive letter instead of a directory name. It is common, for example, for networked PCs that do not need a local hard drive to be mapped to a directory on a network drive that looks and acts exactly like a local C: drive.

Under Netware 3.01, if a network server is named SERVER and a network drive is named SYS, the command to map a directory named PUBLIC/HOME to look like a user's C: drive would be:

```
MAP ROOT c:=server/sys:public/home
```

In addition to providing the user with a C: drive to store data files (and Windows' configuration-specific files such as SYSTEM.INI), this method has an important security benefit. Mapping a network subdirectory to appear as a root directory prevents an unauthorized user from moving from the subdirectory up to the real root directory of the network drive (where other users' files might become accessible).

Options for the NETWARE.INI File

Using the Network icon in the Control Panel under Netware for the first time automatically creates a NETWARE.INI initialization file. This file contains several default commands that are always available under Windows when running Netware, such as connecting to or detaching from remote file servers, and enabling or disabling messages from other users.

The NETWARE.INI file, however, is a plain text file that can be edited with Notepad (or any text editor) to add additional commands (such as short-cuts for attaching to remote printers or other devices). These commands are then displayed every time the Network icon is double-clicked in the Control Panel.

When NETWARE.INI is first built (in the Windows directory), it reads as follows:

```
[MSW30-Utils]
Attach A File Server=<Attach
Detach A File Server=<Detach
Disable Broadcast Messages=<No Messages
Enable Broadcast Messages=<Messages
```

The first line [in brackets like this] indicates that the following lines are Microsoft Windows 3.0 utilities. This must remain the first line in the file. The less-than sign (<) after the equals sign in the following lines indicates that these default utilities are always present. Other commands can be added, such as a command to attach to a laser printer in the Shipping department and set it for landscape mode. In that case, the file would look as follows:

```
[MSW30-Utils]
Attach A File Server=<Attach
Detach A File Server=<Detach
Disable Broadcast Messages=<No Messages
Enable Broadcast Messages=<Messages
Shipping Laser/Landscape=Capture L=1 J=0
```

All the titles preceding the equals signs in the file cannot add up to more than 512 characters (this is a Windows limitation). Additionally, none of the commands to the right of the equals signs can be longer than 128 characters.

The [Netware] Section in SYSTEM.INI

You may want to add a separate section headed [Netware] to your SYSTEM.INI file to control two aspects of DOS sessions under Windows on your network: (1) whether one DOS session can "see" network printers, drives, and so on, that were logged onto in a second DOS session, and (2) whether network drives you logged onto in a DOS session remain connected after you exit Windows.

Under most network operating systems (those listed earlier in this chapter that use the Microsoft Network driver MSNET.DRV or the LAN Manager driver LANMAN.DRV), network printers and drives that you log on to in one DOS session are immediately usable in any other DOS sessions you are running. In other words, if you attach in one session to Printer A so you can print to it from WordPerfect, another DOS application that was already running could then print to that printer, too. This is called *global visibility,* since printers, drives, and other network resources that you attach to in one DOS session become immediately visible (usable) to other DOS sessions. One DOS session, in fact, can *delete* the connection to a network device — which can cause problems if another DOS session wants to keep using that device.

The Netware driver, NETWARE.DRV, however, uses a method called *inherited visibility.* Under this method, DOS applications that you start under Windows get a list of network resources that were available to other DOS applications at that time, therefore *inheriting* the list.

Changing the connections to any network printers, drives, etc., in one DOS session does not change the list of devices available to the other DOS sessions. In addition, one DOS session cannot delete any connections previously made in another DOS session — therefore, one DOS session breaking another's connection is not possible.

This situation, of course, affects Windows only in 386 enhanced mode, because more than one DOS session is only possible under enhanced mode. Furthermore, any connection to network devices made from within Windows (as opposed to within a DOS session under Windows) is immediately available to all Windows applications.

To change Netware's behavior so network connections made or broken in one DOS session affect all other DOS sessions, add the following *separate* section to the SYSTEM.INI file:

```
[Netware]
NWShareHandles=true
```

In addition to *global* and *inherited* visibility, some third-party network drivers may use a method called *local visibility*. If a network driver has this capability, network connections made within a DOS session affect only that session. Making or breaking a connection would not affect any other DOS session under Windows.

The other setting in the [Netware] section of SYSTEM.INI controls whether connections to network drive letters that you made within Windows remain active when you exit Windows. For example, if you log onto network drive *x:* in Windows in order to read a file, can you still change to drive *x:* at a DOS prompt after you exit Windows?

By default, Netware restores all your drive mappings when you exit Windows to the same condition that was in effect when you *started* Windows. To change this behavior so your drive mappings remain in effect, add the following separate section to the SYSTEM.INI file:

```
[Netware]
RestoreDrives=false
```

NWPOPUP.EXE Requires Initialization

The file NWPOPUP.EXE is included with Windows as a background application that displays network messages on-screen that are sent to you by other Netware users. Windows automatically adds this application to your LOAD= statement in WIN.INI if you install for a Netware network. However, NWPOPUP may not initialize correctly when Windows starts, preventing users' messages from being displayed. This is corrected as soon as you run a DOS application — even if it is just a DOS icon running in the background. To work around the initialization problem, you can load a background DOS session as an icon by placing a statement such as the following at the beginning of your WIN.INI file:

```
LOAD=nwpopup.exe dos.pif
```

The start-up of a DOS task in this way seems to initialize NWPOPUP and allow it to display messages over foreground Windows applications. This behavior is fixed in future versions of this program.

NWPOPUP Interferes with Swapfile

The NWPOPUP.EXE utility that displays Netware messages is a "silent" application and does not show a minimized icon while running in the background. This may interfere with the operation of SWAPFILE.EXE, which is included with Windows to create a permanent swap file on a hard disk. NWPOPUP is operating normally, but Swapfile requires that no other Windows application be running in the background while it creates the hard disk file. If Swapfile complains that it cannot run, check the WIN.INI LOAD= line to see if NWPOPUP is running. If so, comment-out the LOAD= and RUN= lines by adding a semicolon to the beginning of each line, as follows:

```
; LOAD=nwpopup.exe winfile.exe
; RUN=excel.exe
```

This will prevent any application from being in memory while using the Swapfile utility. Another way to remove NWPOPUP from memory while running Windows is to open the Control Panel, double-click on the Network icon, and run the command Disable Broadcast Messages (this command is displayed in the dialog box). When you close the Control Panel, you can run Swapfile (if no other programs are in the background).

Solving Printing Problems

If Windows applications will not print to a Netware printer, or print garbled, the following items should be checked, in this order:

1. **SET TEMP.** Before entering Windows, the command SET TEMP=C:\ must be issued (where *C:* is a directory with valid Create, Write, and Delete rights). Without this environmental variable, Windows may not print correctly.

2. **Printer driver.** Check which driver and port are selected in the Printers section of the Control Panel.

3. **Netware shell.** Version 3.01 or higher is necessary to operate Windows under Netware.

4. **Netware driver.** From the Program Manager, click File Run and type SETUP to ensure that Netware is shown as the network driver installed.

5. **Workstation printers.** Windows requires that printers be attached to a server, and will not work with utilities that print from one workstation to a printer attached to another workstation.

If the above points are verified, then you may need to change the print configuration by using Netware's PRINTCON print console utility. Use the Edit Print Job Configuration option. The correct settings should be as follows:

PRINTCON Choice	Correct Setting
Suppress Form Feed	Yes
File Contents	Byte Stream
Print Banner	No
Auto Endcap	No
Enable Timeout	No

These settings in PRINTCON have the same effect as issuing the following CAPTURE command at the DOS prompt:

```
CAPTURE NB NA TI=0 NFF NT
```

The No Banner (NB) option avoids scrambled pages by eliminating an initial, text-mode banner page from printing while Windows is printing in graphics mode. The options No Automatic Endcap (NA) and Timeout=0 (TI=0) prevent Netware from terminating a print job before a Windows application has formatted all output pages. The No Form Feed (NFF) option should be selected, since Windows always adds a form feed of its own after print jobs. And, finally, the option No Tab Expansion (NT — the same as saying File Contents: Byte Stream, as shown in the example lines) prevents Netware from expanding Tab characters into spaces. Tab characters (ASCII character number 9) occur randomly in graphics output and should not be converted or expanded when sent to the printer by the network.

CAPTURE Version 2.12 vs. 3.01

Solving printing problems under Netware 2.12 may require that the CAPTURE.EXE utility shipped with version 3.01 of the Windows SHELL kit be replaced with the utility of the same name bundled with version 2.12 of Netware, according to a Microsoft technical note. The 2.12 version of CAPTURE.EXE is dated 3/1/89 and is distributed by Novell on its Public2 diskette.

The CAPTURE program is typically placed in Netware's Z:\PUBLIC directory. If it's necessary to replace the 3.01 version with the 2.12 version for acceptable printing, follow these steps:

STEPS:

Replacing CAPTURE Version 2.12 with Version 3.01

Step 1. Log in as a supervisor and change to the Z:\PUBLIC directory.

Step 2. Issue the command FLAG CAPTURE SRW.

Step 3. Insert the Public2 diskette and COPY A:\CAPTURE.EXE Z:\PUBLIC.

Step 4. Issue the command FLAG CAPTURE SRO and reboot.

When the network session is loaded again, version 2.12 of CAPTURE will be in effect instead of version 3.01. Contact Novell Technical Support at 800-LANSWER for more information.

EMSNET*x*.COM and XMSNET*x*.COM Anomalies

A PC attaching itself to a Netware network typically loads a network software program first, called NET3, NET4, or NET5 (for DOS versions 3.*x,* 4.*x,* or 5.*x*). Because this program takes up memory in the lower 640K of the PC, similar programs have been developed that load this application into expanded or extended memory instead. These programs are called EMSNET*x*.COM and XMSNET*x*.COM, respectively (where *x* is the version of DOS on the PC).

Several network users have reported different results or problems running EMS or XMS versions of Netware NET*x* programs, compared with NET*x* itself. These problems disappear when NET*x* is loaded instead of EMSNET*x* or XMSNET*x*. If you experience difficulty running Windows in standard or enhanced modes with these Netware programs in expanded or extended memory, it may be necessary to use NET*x* exclusively. Windows in standard and enhanced modes uses the protected mode of the 286 and 386 processors, instead of the "real" mode of XT-class computers, and this may cause incompatibilities with how Netware drivers use expanded or extended memory. Contact Novell in such cases at 800-LANSWER.

File Manager Problems Dragging Files

The Windows File Manager will not allow you to use a mouse to drag files from one directory to another under Netware if you do not have at least Search privileges in the parent directory *above* the directory to which you are trying to drag the files. This situation would look like the following diagram:

Moving *from* directory ABC...   ...*to* directory XYZ

C: N:

\ABC   \XYZ

File Manager does not allow the files to be dragged by a mouse from directory ABC to directory XYZ unless you have Search privileges in the root directory N:\. This behavior also occurs if you use the keyboard to run the File Move or File Copy commands from the File Manager menu (or press F7 or F8 to start those commands) and specify a destination for the files such as N:\XYZ instead of N:\XYZ*filename*.

To avoid this problem, users should be granted search rights to the parent directories above those directories into which they need to move files. Or the root directories of network drives should be created with the MAP ROOT command under Netware 3.01 or higher so that the root directories are actually network subdirectories. This problem can also be avoided when issuing Move and Copy commands from the keyboard by specifying a destination such as N:\XYZ*.* instead of N:\XYZ.

Accessing Parent Directories

DOS uses a peculiar convention to refer to the directory *above* the subdirectory you are in currently. This "higher" directory is called the *parent directory*. In any DOS command, you can type two periods (..) to represent this parent directory. Using DOS's change-directory command, for example, typing

CD ..

changes to the parent directory. If you were in, say, the C:\DOCS\MEMOS directory, CD .. results in C:\DOCS becoming the current directory. Another DOS convention is that a single dot refers to the *current* directory. The command

COPY . A:

copies all files in the current directory to the A: drive — without requiring you to type *.* to represent "all files."

In the File Open dialog box of a Windows application, clicking a directory name that looks like

   [..]

may be the only way for a user to move from the current directory to the one above it.

Netware does not automatically display these "double dot" and "single dot" conventions. In order to force Netware to display these when it provides Windows applications with a list of filenames in the current directory, you must add the line SHOW DOTS=ON to the SHELL.CFG file that configures Netware's behavior.

If you are using a workstation where this change has not yet been made by a system administrator, you can work around the missing "double dots" in File Open dialog boxes by typing ".." as the name of the file you wish to open. When you click OK, Windows applications switch to the parent directory and display the filenames in *that* directory (exactly what you want).

Increasing Your File Handles

Netware ordinarily allows processes to open as many as 40 files at a time. Under Windows, however, this number can quickly be exceeded as applications (including Windows itself) use files, dynamic link libraries, and so on.

Microsoft recommends that you increase the setting of the FILE HANDLES= setting in your SHELL.CFG file from 40 to 60 if you have this problem.

Conserving Your Dynamic Memory Pool

Administrators of Netware 286 (which is more prevalent at this writing than Netware 386) may find that network users of Windows are helping to deplete the memory area called "Dynamic Memory Pool 1." This area of memory is used by Netware 286 to keep track of which users are logged in, what drives they are mapped to, and so on.

Under some versions of Windows and Netware's shell program, an entry a few hundred bytes in length is created in the pool every time someone on the network starts a DOS application under Windows. This entry is not deleted until the person exits the DOS session. Under early releases of version 3.01 of the Netware shell programs, however, this entry was never deleted, and exiting the session added even more bytes to the pool.

Since the pool (under Netware 286, not 386) is fixed in size at only a few tens of kilobytes, it gradually fills throughout the day. Serious consequences ensue as soon as someone opens a session that fills the pool entirely — the server crashes, knocking out the entire network. Several businesses experienced these crashes every day, occurring seemingly at random around 2 or 3 p.m., until this problem was diagnosed.

You can monitor the utilization of Dynamic Memory Pool 1 by viewing the "Summary" option of Netware's SYSCON program. If the depletion of this pool is a problem on your network, you should use version 3.01D or higher of the Netware shells. (This solves other Netware problems as well.) Reducing the number of drives that users are mapped to when they start Windows can also reduce the memory consumed in the pool by a few bytes.

If these solutions are not sufficient, two statements in SYSTEM.INI under the [Netware] section (described in the topic "The [Netware] Section in SYSTEM.INI" earlier in this chapter) can help reduce memory pool usage: set NWSHAREHANDLES=TRUE and RESTOREDRIVES=FALSE.

Banyan Vines

Banyan Vines has a smaller installed base than Novell Netware, but is commonly used in some of the world's largest corporations because it can communicate with LAN servers located in different cities and countries. Vines' Global Naming Service (not available in Netware) means that a user can log onto a Vines network in any office, even in another country, and access resources of a company's worldwide network. The international features of Vines are enhanced by the fact that each user's account can specify a national language, so that messages from the network automatically appear in the language most familiar to the user.

Vines requires version 4.0 to run Windows 3.0, with the addition of what Banyan refers to as a "site-specific" patch numbered 0h (zero hex). Once this patch disk has been added to the network servers, Vines network users may use network drives, printers, and other resources while within Windows. With the 0h patch in place, the Vines server reports that the version it is running is 4.00 (0) — a rather odd numbering system but one that is familiar to Banyan administrators.

NetBIOS Support Needed to Print

To print to network printers from Windows, each Vines user must load some form of NetBIOS program, which provides communications across the network to the attached printers. The NetBIOS program, however, is needed only by Windows, not by most DOS programs, so there is a way to load the memory-resident NetBIOS so that it affects only Windows' extended memory and does not take conventional memory away from DOS programs.

This method takes advantage of the fact that when Windows loads, it looks for a file called WINSTART.BAT and (if found) runs any commands in that batch file before starting the rest of the Windows desktop. This batch file must be located in the Windows directory but otherwise is a normal batch file that may contain all the usual statements and programs. The significance of this particular batch file is that any memory-resident programs loaded by WINSTART.BAT remain resident only within Windows and do not affect (and are not present in) any DOS sessions that are subsequently started from Program Manager. By contrast, memory-resident programs started *before* Windows take up memory in every DOS session started within Windows, whether or not the functions of that resident program are needed by that session.

One way to provide the NetBIOS support needed for Windows to print to networked printers under Vines is to load the PCNETB program that is included in every Vines installation. To load this program in WINSTART.BAT, with appropriate error checking and warning messages, the batch file would look like this:

```
@echo off
echo Starting Windows programs...
if not exist z:\pcnetb.com goto :ERROR
    z:\pcnetb
    goto :END
:ERROR
    echo There is a problem with the network printer support.
    echo Call the Computer Center at ext. 1234 to report this.
    echo Press any key to continue.
    pause > nul
:END
```

In the above WINSTART.BAT, the batch file first informs the user, "Starting Windows programs..." This message is helpful since Windows can take several seconds to load programs at first, during which a blank screen causes the PC to appear frozen. The batch file then confirms that

PCNETB.COM is actually available from the network — if the server has gone down since the user first logged in, this file will not exist (as far as DOS is concerned) and an error message should be displayed. If available, PCNETB is loaded from the Z: drive (Vines uses the convention that Z: represents the network drive containing the network operating system and utilities).

Since PCNETB.COM occupies about 40K of memory inside Windows, you should obtain a much smaller utility called TSR2A.COM from your Banyan representative and substitute that file for PCNETB.COM in the above batch file. (Later revisions of TSR2A.COM may have similar but slightly different names.) To print to Vines networked printers, Windows needs only to have interrupt 2A redirected — not full NetBIOS support — and TSR2A.COM performs this function while occupying just a few hundred bytes of memory. Use PCNETB only for those programs that require full NetBIOS to function across the network.

DOS Polling Support Required in SYSTEM.INI

Vines appears to Windows as though it were Microsoft Network (MS-NET) compatible. Although it does not appear among the list of networks in the Windows Setup program, Vines is supported by Windows, which automatically detects a user's connection to Vines and installs the MS-NET driver that enables most Vines features.

Windows also edits the SYSTEM.INI file automatically when a Vines network is detected. The Setup program inserts the line TIMERCRITICALSECTION=5000 in the [386Enh] section of SYSTEM.INI. In case a user is running Windows on a networked 386 and starts multiple applications, one of which requires calls to the network, this line ensures that Windows halts all other applications for five seconds (5000 milliseconds) while the calling program finishes the critical task it started.

Vines, however, requires an additional line for correct operation that is not automatically written by Windows Setup. This line makes sure that network software running a DOS routine is not interrupted in the middle. You must manually edit the [386Enh] section of Vines users' SYSTEM.INI files to read as follows:

```
[386Enh]
; The following two lines are required for Banyan Vines.
TimerCriticalSection=5000
InDOSPolling=Yes
```

Since these two lines slow down network performance slightly, Banyan intends to eliminate the need for them in a future upgrade to Vines. Using these lines in the meantime, however, is very important in order to eliminate Unrecoverable Application Errors (UAEs) in Windows. Without the INDOSPOLLING=YES statement, users of Windows applications under Vines receive UAE messages seemingly at random during the workday. A simple action like clicking a mouse or opening a file may occur at the exact split-second that some other network operation needs to take place, freezing Windows and forcing a reboot. Including the INDOSPOLLING=YES statement eliminates these random errors.

Windows Files May Not Be Execute-Only

Vines provides a command to make executable files on a network drive read-only and also prevent these files from being copied to floppies or other disks. These files are said to be *execute-only* files, and are thus protected against unauthorized copying and distribution. Windows executables, however, do not run properly under Vines if made execute-only, and must not be marked in this way. All the Windows files should instead be marked with a read-only attribute by changing to the Windows directory and issuing a DOS ATTRIB command, as follows:

```
ATTRIB +R *.* /S
```

The /S switch in the above line indicates that the ATTRIB command should operate on all subdirectories of the current directory. This applies the read-only attribute to Windows' \SYSTEM subdirectory, which contains the Windows kernel and many other executable programs, in addition to the main \WINDOWS directory. The read-only attribute helps make Windows files on the network drive available to multiple users without the danger of accidentally erasing or corrupting these files.

File Manager Cannot Drag Files to Network Drives

Under Vines version 4.00 (0), it is impossible to drag files with the mouse in File Manager from one subdirectory to another subdirectory located on a network drive. It *is* possible under Vines to drag files to a directory that is *not* on a network drive, such as a floppy disk or a local PC hard disk. This behavior also affects the File Move and File Copy commands typed from the keyboard in the File Manager menu (or pressing F7 or F8 to start those commands).

Vines uses Windows' network support as though Vines were a Microsoft Network (MS-NET), but this does not include support for dragging files to network drives under Vines. In later versions of Vines, Banyan released its own network support program to provide full functionality under Windows File Manager.

To avoid this problem, first select files to be moved or copied with a mouse, then issue the File Move or File Copy command from the keyboard and specify a full destination path in the resulting dialog box, such as N:\XYZ*.* instead of N:\XYZ.

Print Manager Not Needed But Reports Errors

It is unnecessary to use Windows' Print Manager under Vines. The print spooler in Vines handles printing to networked printers, so Windows' spooler isn't needed. If you start the Print Manager while running Vines, however, it will load and display the message "General Network Error" as the status of any network printer to which the user is currently attached. There is nothing wrong with the printer or the print job. The MS-NET Windows driver that is loaded to support Vines simply does not detect or report any printer status information. A future driver from Banyan will provide additional functionality to the Print Manager under Vines.

Other Networks

If you are running Windows on a network, you should print the file NETWORKS.TXT that Windows copies to your hard drive. This file contains revisions to previously printed material on how Windows operates with various networks.

And for more information on other network operating systems not described here, you should obtain a Microsoft technical paper called "Windows 3.00 and Networks," by Kai Kaltenbach. This paper contains detailed specifications for installing Windows on particular vendors' networks and using network resources within Windows. Call Microsoft Product Support at 206-454-2030.

Summary

In this chapter, I've explained many of the differences between running Windows on a network and running it on a stand-alone PC. These include:

▶ Ways you can configure the Program Manager to save time, by developing one master menu for network users and individual menus that can be customized as needed.

▶ Configuration anomalies that affect applications when running on a network, but not on stand-alone PCs.

▶ Preparatory steps that can help you have a successful, trouble-free Windows installation on your network.

▶ Changes you must make to Windows' swap files to ensure that these files do not hang your server or cause unacceptable performance delays.

▶ Quirks in the Windows Setup program when you use it with the /N network parameter.

▶ How SHARE.EXE differs on stand-alone PCs and ones that are connected to a network.

▶ Specific configuration advice regarding Netware, Vines, and other network operating systems.

Chapter 13
Printers

In this chapter. . .

I provide information on printing devices and the way Windows uses them, including:

▶ The difference between the way DOS character-based applications print and the way Windows prints.

▶ Using the Control Panel to set up your printer to obtain the best performance and use of its features.

▶ Little-known settings in your WIN.INI and SYSTEM.INI files that control aspects of your Windows applications' communication with printers.

▶ How to get the best printing performance under Windows from different types of printers.

▶ Specific information on Hewlett-Packard LaserJet and Adobe PostScript printers, including undocumented ways to preserve and restore LaserJet soft font information that is ordinarily destroyed when installing new versions of Windows.

▶ Configuration secrets for dot-matrix printers, which lost support under Windows 3.x that was built into Windows 2.x.

▶ Settings and workarounds necessary for a variety of specific brands and models of printers under Windows.

Printers

Windows uses printers in a different way than most character-based DOS applications. Many DOS applications print only text and produce printouts by sending plain ASCII text to whatever printer is attached to your computer. By contrast, Windows often prints to printers in graphics mode, even when the output appears to contain nothing but text. Windows, in general, attempts to use the highest graphics resolution that a printer is capable of (with some exceptions, which are described in this chapter). As a result, printers often behave differently under Windows than they do when used by DOS character-based applications.

This chapter includes information on printing from Windows to any printer, followed by sections on Hewlett-Packard LaserJet printers, PostScript laser printers, dot-matrix printers, and several specific brands of printers (and their quirks). A brief discussion of printers on local area networks is included in the "Performance" section of this chapter, but most information on network printing problems is contained in Chapter 12.

The Drivers Windows Left Out

Windows supports a large number of printers — hundreds of different models. But in the upgrade from Windows 2.11 to 3.0, support was dropped for a few. These include the following printer models:

NEC Pinwriter P2/P3
Olivetti Cicero PG 301
Olivetti PG 208 M1
Toshiba P321, P321 SL, P321 SLC
Toshiba P341, P341 E, P341 SL
Toshiba P351 C, P351 SX
Toshiba P1340, P1350
Ricoh PC Laser 6000
Xerox 4020 Color Inkjet

If you use one of these printers, you will need to configure them to use another printer emulation supported by Windows 3.x.

Additionally, the first million or so copies of Windows 3.0 were shipped with support information on the following printers in the SETUP.INF file on 5.25" diskettes, but not on the 3.5" diskettes:

NEC Pinwriter P6, P7, P2200, P5200
NEC Silentwriter LC 860, LC 860 Plus

If you are installing Windows 3.0 on 3.5" diskettes and you have an NEC Pinwriter model, you can work around the lack of this information by installing for the NEC Pinwriter P5300. After installation, use the Printers Configuration box of the Control Panel to reconfigure the printer for the correct model. An NEC Silentwriter can be installed as an HP LaserJet printer.

Supplemental Printer Drivers

In addition to the printer drivers included with Windows 3.0, Windows 3.0a shipped with even more printer drivers, including upgraded drivers for PostScript printers and HP LaserJet IIs and IIIs. The PostScript driver includes support for a few Adobe document-structuring conventions, and corrects a problem selecting printer bins from Word for Windows 1.1. The LaserJet drivers support the use of additional memory to enhance performance, and the LaserJet III driver adds support for scalable soft fonts and cartridges. Users of Windows 3.0 can obtain these and other new drivers by calling Microsoft Sales and Service (800-426-9400 or 206-936-8661).

Creating Custom Drivers

The development of drivers for printers not supported by Windows requires a detailed knowledge of the specific printer, as well as the Windows Software Development Kit (SDK) and Device Development Kit (DDK). There are, however, companies that specialize in developing these drivers for customers who need to use particular devices as yet unsupported by Windows. Two of these companies are: GDT Softworks (800-663-6222) and Paradise Software (800-367-5600).

Using Control Panel to Configure Printers _____

Obtaining Information on Your Printer

The use of the Control Panel's Printers dialog box to configure printers is well-documented in the Windows manual and doesn't need repeating here. But a few less-known features about the Control Panel's support for printers bear mentioning.

First, it may be possible for you to obtain information about a printer that is unavailable in the manual by opening the Control Panel's Printers dialog box, highlighting your printer's name, then clicking Configure Setup Help. This choice does not bring up help on using the Control Panel, as many people think, but on aspects of using your specific printer with Windows. Most of the information is on PostScript printers, but LaserJets and other printers are also mentioned. Try it and find out what's available about your printer.

Second, it may not be obvious that changing your selected printer in the Control Panel does not necessarily change the Control Panel's "default printer." Many Windows applications automatically print to the default printer, unless you switch to a different printer in the application's own Printer Setup dialog box. To change the default printer in the Control Panel, you must highlight the name of your printer and press Alt+D.

If you have *no* default printer selected (the Default Printer box says "No Default Printer"), or the port that your default printer is connected to is "None," the File Print option on the menu of Windows applications will probably be greyed out (unavailable). Options appear as soon as you specify the default printer and click OK in the Control Panel.

Finally, although the Control Panel clearly shows all your available printers, which one is selected and which one is the default, this is not true of all Windows applications. Windows applets such as Notepad and Cardfile do show all your available printers when you click their Printer Setup menu choices. This includes whether these printers are "active," "inactive" (assigned to the same port that an "active" printer is already assigned to), or assigned to port "None." However, the printer that is highlighted in these applets' Printer Setup dialog boxes is not your current default printer — it is the *first* printer in the list, whatever that happens to be. If you click Printer Setup to see what printers are available, and then click OK instead of Cancel, the applet will now print to whatever printer was first on the list — which may not be what you want.

Other Windows applications display printers differently in their Printer Setup dialog boxes. Applications such as Excel and Word for Windows may list in their Printer Setup dialog boxes only printers that are "active," not those that are "inactive." This makes it impossible to switch between two printers on the same port (if you have two printers on an A-B switch box, for example). You must use these applications' Run choice from their Control menus, open the Control Panel, switch the two printers, and then return to your application.

In other cases, Excel may display a printer that is "inactive" as being connected to Port: None, even if it is presently assigned a port in the Control Panel. (Excel versions 2.0 and 2.1 also ignore any printers installed in your WIN.INI file after encountering any printer driver with a full pathname longer than 25 characters.)

If you need to assign two printers to the same port and have them both accessible ("active") from within Windows applications, see the section "Using WIN.INI Settings," later in this chapter.

Print Manager

Windows includes a print-buffer application called Print Manager (PRINTMAN.EXE). This application is otherwise known as a print spooler. When the Print Manager is turned *on* in the Control Panel's Printers dialog box, applications that print documents are actually printing to an area of memory controlled by the Print Manager. This is usually faster than printing to an actual printer, and you are able to use the application again sooner than if you had to wait for each page to be printed directly to the printer.

When the Print Manager receives a print job from an application, it copies the print file to a temporary file on a disk drive determined by the TEMP environmental variable. This variable is specified by the SET TEMP=*c:* in your AUTOEXEC.BAT file, where *c:* should be the fastest drive in your system. This may be a RAM drive, if you have enough memory to establish a RAM drive of 2MB or more. A RAM drive smaller than this can cause problems because temporary files may run out of room, causing unexpected errors.

Print Manager is one of the few print spoolers ever written that does not restart itself automatically when you refill a printer's paper tray. You usually receive a "Cannot Print" message, and you must find the Print Manager icon on the icon line, open the Print Manager's window, and click its <u>R</u>esume button to restart your print job.

Print Manager also has a limit of 20 print jobs at any one time. If you have a directory full of several small files, and you use a feature such as Word for Windows' File Find to select and print them all unattended, you might exceed this limit and receive an error message.

But if you can keep your paper tray full, and don't try to print too many files at once, Print Manager usually does return you to your main application faster than if you printed directly to the printer without using a spooler.

You may be able to get faster overall printing performance, however, by using a third-party print spooler that is compatible with Windows and turning Print Manager off. One of these compatible print spoolers is included in the PC-Kwik Power Pak, a set of utilities that also includes a Windows-compatible disk cache (described in Chapter 8). Power Pak is available from Multisoft Corp., 15100 S.W. Koll Parkway, Beaverton, OR 97006; 503-644-5644.

With any third-party print spooler (which will also speed up printing from DOS applications, unlike the Windows print spooler), you should be sure to follow any instructions regarding installing their product to work with

Windows, such as redirecting printer ports, as described in the following section.

Using WIN.INI Settings

Setting Up Multiple Printers on the Same Port

If you use a PostScript laser printer for some jobs and a dot-matrix or color printer for other jobs, you can connect them to the same port with an A-B switch box that determines which one gets each print job.

But Windows does not allow you to configure two different printers on this port and switch between them within applications. When two printers are assigned to the same port in the Control Panel, one of them must be "active" while the other is "inactive."

Most Windows applications cannot use their own Printer Setup dialog box to switch active printers to inactive and vice versa. Instead, when you want to print to Printer A rather than Printer B, you must leave your application, start the Control Panel, make the active printer inactive and the inactive printer active. You can then return to your application and switch it to the printer that formerly was unavailable.

There is a way, however, to assign two printers to the same port and make them both "active," so you can switch between them within your applications.

The secret is in the [ports] section of your WIN.INI file, which contains a list of the ports available in your system. When you install Windows, this section probably looks like this:

```
[ports]
LPT1:=
LPT2:=
LPT3:=
COM1:=9600,n,8,1
COM2:=9600,n,8,1
COM3:=9600,n,8,1
COM4:=9600,n,8,1
EPT:=
FILE:=
```

In this section, the lines starting with LPT represent the number of printer ports in your system. The lines starting with COM establish settings for communicating to serial printers at 9600 bps, with no parity, eight data bits, and one stop bit. The EPT:= line is used for IBM's "enhanced" printer port, and the FILE:= line is used to print documents to a file on disk instead of to a printer. (If you assign a printer to the FILE:= port in the Control Panel, instead of a real port, Windows asks you for a filename every time you send a job to that printer.)

To assign two printers to the same LPT port, change the definition for the port you want to share in WIN.INI. If you want to assign two printers to LPT1, for example, delete the LPT1:= line and add lines to the ports section as follows:

```
[ports]
LPT1.PS=
LPT1.DOT=
```

You may use any extension, up to three letters, after the term LPT1. Replacing the colon (:) with a period and an extension makes it look to Windows like you are printing to a filename instead of to a printer port. Since you can assign a printer to print to any filename you want, Windows prints to these filenames just as though it were printing to ordinary DOS files on disk.

DOS, however, does not allow files to be saved with names that are the same as its reserved device names (LPT1, COM1, CON, NUL, etc.). Instead, if you try to copy a file to a name like LPT1.PS, DOS sends that information out the LPT1 port, ignoring the extension completely.

This difference between the way Windows and DOS treat reserved filenames allows two printers to be active in the Control Panel, even though they are assigned to the same port. After you make the above change to your WIN.INI (and restart Windows), open the Control Panel's Printers dialog box. Assign one printer to the LPT1.PS port, and the other printer to the LPT1.DOT port. (Pick extensions that are meaningful for the types of printers in your system.) Make one printer the default printer by highlighting it and pressing Alt+D. Then click OK to exit the Control Panel. Both of these printers will now be available to switch between in any Windows application.

When you make this change in your WIN.INI file, you should also comment-out the EPT:= line (if you don't have such an IBM port), and the lines for any com ports you don't have in your system. This is because Windows can only read up to ten lines in the [ports] section of the WIN.INI file. To comment-out lines, place a semicolon (;) and a space in front of them. While you're doing this, add a comment at the top of the section as a reminder that only ten lines are allowed.

After doing this, your WIN.INI [ports] section might look like this:

```
[ports]
; Windows allows no more than 10 lines in this section.
LPT1.PS=
LPT1.DOT=
LPT2:=
LPT3:=
COM1:=9600,n,8,1
COM2:=9600,n,8,1
; COM3:=9600,n,8,1
; COM4:=9600,n,8,1
; EPT:=
FILE:=
```

When writing to a filename such as LPT1.PS, Windows writes the file through routines in your ROM BIOS. This might be slower than writing print information directly to your LPT1 and other printer ports. Test a long print job before and after making this change. If there is a significant difference when Windows prints through the BIOS instead of printing directly, then you may need to add a separate printer port to your PC so that each printer can have a separate port assigned to it in the Control Panel, eliminating the need for this redirection.

(Despite the fact that DOS doesn't allow files to be created with reserved device names, Banyan Vines 4.0 [and possibly other versions] *does* create actual disk files called LPT1.PS if you use this trick in WIN.INI. This can cause a problem, because if you have a file such as LPT1.PS on your hard disk, DOS will not recognize a command like DEL LPT1.PS to delete it! If you find yourself in this situation and the file in question is the only file with that extension in that particular directory, first issue the command REN *.PS JUNK.PS to rename the file. Then the command DEL JUNK.PS will work.)

In any case, what *doesn't* work is the redirection method DOS provides to send information destined for one port out to another port instead (the MODE command). You might try to send information out the LPT2 port, but have DOS redirect it to LPT1 instead, with the following DOS command:

```
MODE LPT2=LPT1
```

Windows simply ignores any such DOS redirections, when Windows writes directly to the port hardware.

The [PrinterPorts] and [Devices] Sections

Windows provides two sections in WIN.INI to specify which printers you have assigned to which ports. These sections are the [PrinterPorts] section and the [Devices] section.

If you inspect these sections in your WIN.INI file, you should find that the same printers are listed in both sections, assigned to the same ports in each case. The [PrinterPorts] section also includes values that indicate the number of seconds allowed for a printer to respond before Windows displays an error message (the *timeout* values).

The [PrinterPorts] section is new to Windows 3.0, but the [Devices] section is included for older applications that look for installed printers in this area of WIN.INI. This is why Excel and Winword's Printer Setup dialog boxes cannot "see" printers that are inactive, but the Control Panel can.

Control Panel looks in the [PrinterPorts] section for timeout information, but writes settings to both sections when you make a change to your printers' configuration. Both of these sections need to reflect the same information.

Printing to a File

Windows provides a convenient way to print to a disk file, instead of printing directly to a printer. One of the ports listed in the [ports] section of WIN.INI is called FILE:= (the colon before the equals sign is important). When you use the Control Panel to assign a printer to this "port," Windows requests a filename to print to every time you print to that printer. This can be used to save a series of print jobs and print them at a later time, or to trouble-shoot printer problems, since you can save a copy of the print job to a disk file and examine it for errors (if you know how to decode a printer language).

You can also specify in advance the name of the file to which you want to save the print job. You would do this by adding a line to the [ports] section of WIN.INI, as follows:

```
[ports]
MYFILE.PRN=
```

If you do this, any print jobs sent to a printer attached to this "port" will overwrite previously existing files with this name. It may be easier just to use the generic filename FILE:=.

One of the problems with printing a job to a disk file is that you may run out of disk space in the middle of the job. If so, the job is canceled, and in protected mode Windows displays the message "Insufficient Disk Space." In real mode, the message is a noninformative "Cannot Print," although the problem, again, is lack of disk space.

Even worse, when this happens you may find that the Help About box in the Program Manager reports that your System Resources have been reduced by 20 to 60 percentage points. The area of memory consumed by the buffer for the print job has not been reclaimed by Windows, and nothing you do can get it back. At this point, you should exit and restart Windows, which clears this memory.

Using SYSTEM.INI Settings

Setting the Time Between Two Apps Using the Printer

If you change the configuration of two printers in WIN.INI as just described, you may need to change a printer port setting for 386 enhanced mode.

In 386 mode, Windows controls the use that applications make of the printer, so that two applications cannot try to access a printer port at the same time. By default, Windows requires that 60 seconds elapse between a DOS application's use of a printer port and any other application printing to that port.

If you often switch printers while in 386 mode, or use the PrintScreen key to dump the screen to the printer in a DOS session and then switch to a Windows application, this amount of time may be too restrictive. You may get unnecessary error messages.

For this reason, you may want to change the LPTxAUTOASSIGN= statements in the [386Enh] section of your SYSTEM.INI file, where x stands for the printer port you use. To set these ports for an elapsed time of 2 seconds instead of 60, change these lines to look as follows:

```
[386Enh]
LPT1AutoAssign=2
LPT2AutoAssign=2
LPT3AutoAssign=2
```

IBM's EPT Printer Port

Using EPT with Windows

The line EPT:= in the [ports] section of your WIN.INI file refers to an "enhanced" printer port developed by IBM for some of its PS/2 computers. The IBM Personal Pageprinter, a PostScript clone, must be attached to an EPT port to work with Windows and other programs. The EPT port is usually located on a proprietary IBM board inside a PS/2. The purpose of this board is to encourage buyers of an IBM Personal Pageprinter to purchase parallel port boards from IBM, instead of standard parallel boards from third parties.

You may receive the message "The Print Manager cannot write to EPT" when using the Pageprinter. You must take the steps described in the following sections to print to an IBM Personal Pageprinter from Windows.

Fix the EPT Settings in Your SYSTEM.INI File

You must add a line to the [386Enh] section of SYSTEM.INI to ensure that commands sent to the EPT port by one application will not affect commands sent by other applications. You must also set the LPT1 port so it does not issue any "contention" warnings. The following two lines added to the [386Enh] section of your SYSTEM.INI accomplish this:

```
[386Enh]
local=EPT
LPT1AutoAssign=0
```

The line LOCAL=EPT is case sensitive and the term EPT must be in all caps. No colon is required after the name of the port. The line LPT1AUTOASSIGN=0 can also be set by opening the 386 icon in the Control Panel, selecting the LPT1 port, clicking "Never Warn," then clicking OK. This prevents the LPT1 and EPT ports from causing error messages when EPT is used to print to the Pageprinter. Restart Windows after making these changes to your SYSTEM.INI file.

Updating the Pageprinter Software

You must use version 1.3.1 of the IBM Personal Pageprinter Adapter Program. The files must be updated using a corrective service disk (CSD) available through IBM dealers. Earlier versions of this program have files dated January 1, 1989. The updated files, which you must use instead of the earlier files, have dates at least as recent as the following:

PPEPT1.SYS	7-31-89
PPCTL.EXE	6-19-89
PPCTLGPR.FPS	6-19-89
PPTSR.COM	7-10-89
README.TXT	8-11-89
DEFAULT.CHL	7-17-89
DEFAULT.CHE	7-17-89

If you have the IBM Personal Pageprinter II Model 031, the installation program has been updated from version 1.0 to 2.0. You should use Installation Disk #1, version 2.0, and install the Pageprinter software so it supports Windows 3.*x*. When this installation diskette asks for Disk #2, insert Disk #1 from version 1.0 of the software.

Initializing the Printer Before Starting Print Manager

You cannot use the Windows Print Manager with the Personal Pageprinter, unless you take the following steps:

STEPS:

Using Print Manager with Personal Pageprinter

Step 1. Open the Control Panel's Printers dialog box and turn *off* the Print Manager check box.

Step 2. With the PostScript printer driver selected, click the Control Panel's Configure Setup Options Header buttons to send a PostScript header file to the printer. Alternately, you can send any small print job to the printer, with the Options in the Control Panel set to Download Header Each Job.

Step 3. Turn the Print Manager back on.

To use the Print Manager, you must perform these steps every time Windows is started. You could record these actions in a macro with the Windows Recorder, then play the macro every time you start Windows, using the undocumented features of the Recorder described in Chapter 2.

Using Font Downloaders

You cannot use soft font downloading programs like the downloader provided with the Adobe Type Library to the Pageprinter on an EPT port. You must use the downloader provided with the Pageprinter.

Drivers You Should Always Install

No matter what kind of printer is actually connected to your PC, there are two printer drivers you should always considering installing, along with the ones you need for your everyday printing.

The Generic/Text Driver

Most people naturally think the Generic/Text printer driver is only for those lowly dot-matrix printers, so out of the mainstream that they don't have their own printer driver for Windows. And that *is* one of the uses for this driver.

But more importantly, the Generic/Text driver is one of the fastest ways to get plain text output from a Windows application to your LaserJet or any other printer that supports both ASCII text and graphics.

For example, If you print to a LaserJet an Excel spreadsheet that consists of only a single size and style of type, Excel forms a full-page graphic image, complete with bitmapped fonts, gridlines, and borders. You could remove the gridlines, and so on, but it may be easier to simply switch to the Generic/Text driver before printing. When you print to this text-only driver, Excel simply prints ASCII text corresponding to the contents of each cell — and the printout is as fast as a DOS PrintScreen.

For other applications, the Generic/Text driver may be the only way to print just text. The Windows Cardfile applet normally prints a "stack" of cards to a LaserJet as three or four graphic images of index cards per page, which wastes paper. Printing a stack from Cardfile to the Generic/Text driver, however, prints only the text. And if you assign the driver to the FILE:= port (using the Control Panel's Printers dialog box), you end up with an ASCII text file of the stack, which you can edit, sort, and so on.

If you use the Generic/Text driver to dump ASCII text to an otherwise Windows-supported printer, you'll probably want to assign the driver to a port such as LPT1.PRN, as described earlier in the "Using WIN.INI Settings" section.

And if you use any Windows ANSI characters other than those on the main keyboard (the characters numbered above number 127), you should configure the Generic/Text driver so it prints any such characters your printer is capable of. The Generic/Text driver can convert any higher-order character into a plain ASCII character (such as converting the Japanese Yen symbol ¥ into the letter Y), or pass these through if your printer can handle them as is. You specify which ones your printer supports in the Control Panel's Printers dialog box. Select the Generic/Text driver, then click Configure Setup Characters. (The Help option in this driver's dialog box is fairly helpful, if you're interested.)

The PostScript Driver

Even if you don't have a PostScript printer, you may still have a use for the Windows PostScript driver. With the PostScript driver installed and made the default printer, all the PostScript typefaces appear in the type selection boxes of word-processing and spreadsheet applications. These typefaces space themselves on-screen as they would if you printed to a PostScript printer. You can use the Print Preview function of many applications to see how a page would look if typed in, say, Helvetica Compressed, even if your own printer does not have that face.

Most importantly, you can print a file using the PostScript driver and take a copy of that file to a facility that *does* have a PostScript printer. Using a command like COPY MYFILE.PS LPT1, you should be able to print your file directly to any true PostScript printer.

If you use tricks like this to redefine the capabilities of your printer, remember these points: When you change printers in the Control Panel, applications like Windows Write immediately support the new typefaces and fonts that are available in the new printer driver. But Word for Windows (and some other applications) build a font list and don't recognize the new driver fonts until you rebuild the list by clicking File Printer Setup, then clicking OK. You should do this in Word for Windows every time you change the default printer.

Printing from the Help Application

The Windows Help engine (WINHELP.EXE) is one of the most useful undocumented programs within Windows 3.x (along with others like SysEdit and the Executive, discussed in Chapter 3). WinHelp allows developers to release hypertext-like, on-line documentation, complete with keywords in different colors that jump to different parts of the text when double-clicked. These hypertext files (.HLP files) are completely self-contained and cannot be edited by users, although tools are emerging to let companies edit and distribute their own, original files.

The Help engine does have a few quirks, however. As distributed in Windows 3.0 and 3.0a, the Help engine duplicates the last line of every page on the top line of the *next* page as well. This only affects those few Help topics that are longer than one printed page, of course, so you may never encounter this problem.

A more difficult design problem is that, although you can print a copy of the Help topic you are currently viewing, there is no way to print *all* the Help topics in a particular file. This makes the .HLP format (until this problem is fixed) a poor way to distribute an entire manual, which users could both print and refer to on-line.

Another problem sometimes occurs when the Help engine prints to printers that support scalable type (type fonts of any size). Since the Help engine prints to the smallest available size of a printer's default font, this sometimes shows up on scalable printers, such as PostScript and LaserJet III printers, as 4-point text — almost too small to read. (In truth, this affects the Word for Windows and Excel Help engines, which are separate applications, more often than the WinHelp engine itself.)

 If you get 4-point text when you print a Help topic, you can work around the problem by installing the Generic/Text printer driver (as described earlier in the section "Drivers You Should Always Install") and using WinHelp's Printer Setup menu to switch to that driver. This should force the printout to use the printer's medium, fixed-pitch default font, such as Courier.

Fixing 'SoftRIP' Errors

When you are printing a complex document, you may see the message "Cannot print. SoftRIP Error" before your print job aborts. This message indicates that you need to close some windows, especially window objects that display icons, to free System Resource memory.

SoftRIP stands for a "software raster imaging processor." This program converts printing instructions into a bitmap that is sent to the printer. This full-page bitmap is called a raster image (as opposed to a vector-based image, which contains line-drawing instructions but not the actual bitmap). High-end PostScript typesetters contain separate boards that convert PostScript instructions into bitmaps; these boards are called hardware rasterizers. Windows, however, does not have such a board and must use a software program and available memory to perform this instruction-to-bitmap conversion.

Situations that can cause Windows' rasterizer program to run out of memory include printing an image to a printer that does not have its own internal memory buffer, such as an HP PaintJet. Images that are particularly sensitive to available memory include pictures that use graduated shading patterns, shaded ovals, or other geometric forms.

When the conversion process runs out of memory, it displays the "SoftRIP Error" message. Although this does not necessarily indicate an out-of-memory situation, the "SoftRIP" message probably means that GDI.EXE, the executable that displays objects in Windows' graphical display interface, has exhausted the 64K area it uses to track these objects. (This area is one of the factors in the "free percentage" of System Resources reported by the Help About box in Program Manager.)

Some of this memory can be freed, and you can start the print job again, by closing applications that are running in the background. You can also free System Resources by turning off program features that display icons. This includes the Ruler and Ribbon in Word for Windows, and the Tool Bar in Excel, each of which display buttons that qualify as icons.

You can permanently increase the free percentage of System Resources by reducing the number of program groups in the Program Manager. Moving icons out of a program group, then minimizing that group, highlighting it, and clicking File Delete, saves about 2 percent of System Resources the next time you start Windows.

You can also use the Control Panel to remove screen fonts that you don't use — namely, the Roman, Modern, and Script fonts for dot-matrix printers — and to delete soft fonts from the printer section of your WIN.INI. Restart Windows to make these changes take effect.

Improving Printing Performance

How Windows Prints

Since Windows often sends data to printers in graphic form, and printing graphics is much slower than printing plain text, speeding up print jobs under Windows requires some understanding of how Windows uses printers.

In theory, programmers of Windows applications do not have to worry about what printer a person is using while running their programs. A Windows program should be able to send general printing instructions to Windows itself, which figures out which printer driver is in use and correctly converts the general instructions into specific instructions for that device. This principle is called *device-independence*. No matter the printer, a Windows program can just send out information and Windows sends commands the best way for the currently selected device.

In reality, Windows programs that assume device-independence print very slowly. To print efficiently, Windows applications need to know which printer driver is in use so they can feed information in the best way for that particular driver.

Most printer drivers receive information from Windows applications in *bands*. These bands start at the top of the page and proceed to the bottom of the page. Each band is one-inch high or so. The Windows application copies to each band any text and graphical information that is to be printed in that band. This continues until the end of the page is reached.

The LaserJet and PostScript drivers, which most Windows users select, however, do not follow this procedure.

The LaserJet driver first provides Windows applications with a single text band that covers the entire page, followed by a series of graphics bands. If an application does not compensate for this method, it prints every page to the LaserJet driver twice, because it receives two requests per page. Graphics copied into the text band (and text copied into the graphics bands) are ignored, but slow down the whole process.

The PostScript driver does not distinguish between text and graphics. Only one band is presented to applications — one whole page.

When printers are set to landscape mode instead of portrait mode, a different set of rules apply. Drivers like the one for the IBM Proprinter present Windows applications with a series of bands to fill up from left to right across the page. The LaserJet driver requests these bands from right to left, but not by using the same text-vs.-graphics method described earlier. And the PostScript printer, again, uses a single band to cover the entire page.

Printing performance under Windows, then, is not a matter of speeding up Windows *per se*. Each individual Windows application must know and use these printer driver anomalies in the most efficient way to gain good printing performance.

Speeding Up Application-Dependent Printing Performance

Since the speed of printing is more dependent on individual applications than on Windows as a whole, the steps you might take to improve performance will vary. Check the following items to see which ones apply to the applications you use.

1. **Print at 150 dpi.** If your application prints primarily text (and a few horizontal and vertical gridlines), you may get better performance when printing to LaserJet printers by setting the printer driver to 150 dpi (dots-per-inch) resolution in the Control Panel, instead of 300 dpi. This is because applications such as Word for Windows and Excel actually send perpendicular lines to a LaserJet as a series of filled rectangles, and these can occupy a lot of memory (and therefore take a long time to send to the printer).

   Changing the LaserJet driver from 300 dpi to 150 dpi affects only graphics, not text. And the filled rectangles that applications send out are usually at least two pixels wide, anyway (they would be too thin if they were only one pixel wide). So you don't lose any actual resolution.

Even when printing graphics embedded in the text of applications like Word for Windows, you will find that Winword automatically sends images to a LaserJet at a 150 dpi resolution. Any graphic that you assign a scaling factor of 100 percent in Winword actually prints twice the size of the same graphic printed from Windows Paintbrush (with its Use Printer Resolution switch turned on). This is because Winword correctly assumes that you want a graphic (when printed on a LaserJet printer) to appear about the same size as when printed to a lower-resolution device, such as a dot-matrix printer. Therefore, since the LaserJet's 300 dpi resolution would make every graphic very tiny if each dot maintained a one-to-one correspondence, Winword compensates by duplicating every pixel.

2. **Don't print through a serial cable.** Many people print to devices such as the Apple LaserWriter (a PostScript printer) using a com port and a serial cable. This is because, to discourage PC users, Apple has never included a parallel port in its LaserWriters — only an AppleTalk port, with a serial port thrown in as an afterthought.

Using a serial port set to 9600 bits per second, however, slows Post-Script printers down *at least four times,* compared to their throughput when using a parallel port or an AppleTalk port. This is especially noticeable when printing any graphics (including horizontal and vertical gridlines).

To eliminate this bottleneck, do one of the following: (a) purchase only PostScript printers with parallel ports, such as models from QMS and other manufacturers; (b) purchase an inexpensive AppleTalk board, insert it into any PC that is attached to an Apple LaserWriter, and run a cable from that to the printer; or (c) purchase a program that reprograms the LaserWriter to accept data through its serial port at 57,600 bits per second, instead of 9600.

A program that reprograms the LaserWriter's serial port to this speed is available from Legend Communications, Inc., 54 Rosedale Avenue West, Brampton, ON, Canada L6X 1K1; 800-668-7077 or 416-450-1010. If you use this program (PSPlot), you must also, of course, change the speed of your PC's serial port, as explained in the product's documentation. Legend also provides programs that allow you to print ASCII text files, Novell banner pages, and HPGL and Epson graphics on a PostScript-only printer.

3. **Use Print Manager optimally.** If you use Print Manager as a spooler for print jobs, you should make sure it is configured the way you want. Print Manager's Options menu can set the buffer to high, medium, or low priority. (You set the options by running PRINTMAN.EXE.) If you want faster printouts, set the priority to high. On the other hand, if you want to quickly regain control over your applications after sending a print job, set the priority to low.

4. **Don't use Print Manager with a network printer.** If your printer is a networked printer, the network probably has its own spooler program. If you use Windows' Print Manager, it writes your print jobs to a disk file and then writes them out to the network print spooler, which writes them to *another* disk file before finally printing them. Use the Control Panel's Printers dialog box to turn the Print Manager off. See Chapter 12 for more suggestions.

Printing to a Network

Use a Spooler That Prints from RAM

Most of the information in this book about printing over a network is contained in Chapter 12. But it's appropriate to mention here one of the factors that can affect printing from Windows.

If your network print spooler is like most, it receives print jobs from network users, then writes them to disk and waits a certain period of time to make sure that the print job is over before sending it on to the printer. Both the disk-writing stage and the waiting period are wasting your time.

You should make sure that your network uses a print spooler that prints directly from RAM to your selected printer as soon as your print job is received. Such print spoolers start printing the first page as soon as it is formed in memory, instead of waiting until the entire file has been written to disk. Since printers are even slower than disk drives, these print spoolers still must write to a disk file every time they receive a print job. But they can send parts of a print job from the disk to the printer as soon as the printer is ready to print another page. This means that you can start looking at the first few pages of a long print job even before your application has finished sending the entire job to the printer.

Since Windows always indicates the end of a print job, intelligent network spoolers also do not have to wait to see whether a print job contains anything else before ending one print job and starting another. This improves printing performance for everyone on the network.

The vast majority of network print spoolers are what I would call "dumb" spoolers, writing and waiting needlessly for every printout, no matter how short. One company that makes an "intelligent" print spooler is Software Directions, Inc., 1572 Sussex Turnpike, Randolph, NJ 07869; 800-346-7638 or 201-584-8466. Its PrintQ LAN product writes directly to printers from RAM and supports Novell and other local area networks.

Printing to Print-Sharing Devices

One other type of print spooling can affect Windows users who share a printer. Windows works well with print-sharing devices that use parallel cables or have enough memory to handle print jobs while waiting for the printer to become available. But Windows seems to have difficulty working with cheaper print-sharing devices that use serial cables and do not have any substantial amount of internal buffer memory.

In cases where a device does not have enough memory to hold an entire print job, the device may become confused by delays from Windows applications that are sending data. A Windows program, of course, can take several seconds to format a large graphic or a complex page before it has another page to send to the printer. This delay can cause the serial device to stop one print job in the middle and start another. This usually results in two jobs that don't look like what the authors intended.

You might be able to eliminate such problems if the print-sharing device has a way to "lock" onto a port once it receives a print job from that port. Since Windows applications always correctly indicate the end of their print jobs, this is a more reliable method than a timeout period to determine when one job is over and another can safely begin.

Specific Printer Types

The remainder of this chapter describes the configuration of LaserJet, PostScript, and dot-matrix printers. This is followed by sections on other specific printer models.

If you need more information on how Windows addresses printers and soft fonts, contact Microsoft to obtain a copy of Microsoft Technical Notes: "Windows 3.0 Printing and Fonts," by Kai Kaltenbach.

LaserJet Printers

Using the Correct Character Set

Most PCs in the U.S. use an IBM-standard character set called the PC-8 set. This term refers to the eight data bits used to specify each of the 256 possible characters that a PC can display and print (numbered from 0 to 255). This character set is also called the lower-ASCII set (for the first 128 characters) and the upper-ASCII set (for the other 128).

Windows uses a different character set than the IBM PC-8. Windows' character set is called the ANSI set and consists of 256 characters determined by the International Standards Organization (ISO), of which the American National Standards Institute is a member. This character set is shown in Chapter 9.

All Windows printer drivers recognize the ANSI character set. When a Windows application prints a document that contains ANSI characters numbered higher than 127, the printer driver tries to print the same characters to the printer. If the printer doesn't support a certain ANSI character, as on some HP DeskJets and other printers, the driver prints a blank or a random character. If you use Windows' Generic/Text driver, you can specify which characters your printer can print by using the Control Panel command Configure Setup Characters.

When you open a DOS session under Windows, and press the PrintScreen key to send the display to your printer, you may be surprised to find that HP LaserJets do not always print exactly what you see on your screen. This is not a problem with Windows. DOS sessions under Windows use the IBM PC-8 character set (if you are in the U.S.), but most HP LaserJets sold in the U.S. do not leave the factory configured to print this character set.

In other countries, LaserJets are usually configured for the character set used in that area. In the U.S., HP sets these printers to use a character set known as Roman-8. This character set, unfortunately for you, is used by almost no PC manufacturers. When you send a DOS PrintScreen to a Laser-Jet set to Roman-8, many of the characters on the screen print as garbage — especially borders and boxes used in menus and other applications.

This problem is easy to correct. All LaserJets allow you to fix their internal character set to the standard IBM PC-8 set, by using the control panel on the front of the printer. Different LaserJet models do this in slightly different ways, so you'll have to check the manual that comes with your printer or call Hewlett-Packard. But all models have a Menu button that you press to display a list of character sets. From this list, you choose PC-8 (sometimes called US-8 or IBM-8) and press a Reset key.

Whenever I visit a U.S. company, I notice that about 90 percent of their LaserJets have never been changed from the factory settings to support the standard PC character set. Users seem unsure why their PrintScreens have so much garbage on them. In cases like this, I like to change the LaserJet settings to Norwegian, just to see how long it will take someone to figure out why all their printouts have slashes and accents through the letters. (I don't do this! Really! Just kidding! I would *never* change someone else's print settings, but you get the idea that you need to know how to set and fix these defaults.)

LaserJet IIIs can be configured to default to a character set called Windows — but don't choose this character set. Windows printer drivers automatically print all the ANSI characters correctly to LaserJet IIIs when they are configured for the PC-8 character set. All you do by configuring a LaserJet III to default to the Windows character set is garble DOS PrintScreen jobs.

Memory Overflow Problems under Windows

Since Windows can use the full 300-dpi resolution of the HP LaserJet, it often "pushes" the printer harder than character-based applications do. This can lead to garbled printing or the failure of the printer to print anything at all, if one of the following problems occurs: a shortage of memory in the printer to store the entire page that is being sent from a Windows application, or a mismatch between the capabilities of the printer and the Windows driver that is selected to communicate with it.

A Windows-printed page is often full of graphics information, even if the printed output appears to contain only ordinary text. Gridlines (such as those in an Excel spreadsheet or a Word for Windows tabular chart), for example, are not text but are actually small, filled rectangles printed in graphics mode. It doesn't take very many gridlines for a formatted page to become as large as a full-page graphic, which can cause a memory-overflow error, and halt a LaserJet printer with insufficient memory.

The LaserJet Plus and LaserJet II include 512K of memory as a standard feature. The LaserJet III includes 1MB, twice as much. But even this amount does not guarantee that a page cannot exceed this amount and freeze the printer. Memory boards can be purchased from HP or third-party vendors and added to LaserJets to increase their capacity to store incoming pages (as well as downloaded fonts), and this may be the only way to permanently end memory-overflow problems.

An alternative to memory add-ons, however, is available through the Windows Control Panel. Open the Control Panel (or start Printer Setup from the File menu of many Windows applications). After selecting the installed LaserJet printer, click Configure Setup. Set the print resolution to a lower setting than 300 dpi, such as 150 dpi. This may be a low-enough resolution to allow a print job that previously choked the printer to get through. Graphics printing will be much coarser at 150 dpi than at 300 dpi, but if the output consists of nothing but text and rectangular gridlines, there may be no difference between printed pieces at the two resolutions.

Printing Performance on LaserJets

The question often arises, "What is the fastest way to print to a LaserJet printer under Windows?" This question is complicated by the fact that when a LaserJet is printing in its ordinary, fixed-pitch Courier typeface, it can usually output seven or eight pages a minute, but this rate drops substantially when a proportional typeface is used. With the revolution in desktop publishing, more and more correspondence uses proportional typefaces, and a business letter printed in Courier looks increasingly old-fashioned.

Hewlett-Packard recognized this change when it discontinued the Laser-Jet II, its best-selling laser printer, in 1990, replacing it with the LaserJet III for about the same price. The LaserJet III directly supports typeface *outlines* that can be scaled to almost any size, from 4-point type on up, and includes the CompuGraphic Corp.'s proportional typefaces CG Times (a version of Times Roman) and CG Univers (a sans serif typeface with slightly more-weighted strokes than Helvetica). Additionally, the new Resolution Enhancement technology in the LaserJet IIIs makes the somewhat-jagged 300-dpi resolution of the printer look like noticeably-smoother 600-dpi output. (And all LaserJet IIs can be upgraded to LaserJet IIIs with an HP circuit board swap.)

This new generation of LaserJets solved the problem of scalable type for HP users, but left unanswered the question of the best way to add typefaces to the basic two and get the best performance out of the printer regardless of the exact font used. A choice of only two typefaces quickly becomes tiresome. Times Roman is now the most over-used typeface in desktop publishing — its too-thin hairline strokes tend to make poor Xerox copies and faxes — while Helvetica has become the world's most boring sans-serif type family.

Two solutions overcome the limitations of the LaserJet III. One is to add a PostScript cartridge to the LaserJet, and the other is to add an HP-compatible "supercartridge" that provides the same fonts as a PostScript printer, but in HP's native Printer Control Language format. The first solution is represented by HP's Adobe-authorized PostScript cartridge, which requires an additional 1MB of printer RAM on top of the 1MB included with the LaserJet III. The other is typified by the Super Cartridge 3 from IQ Engineering (685 N. Pastoria Ave., Sunnyvale, CA 94086; 408-733-1161), a company that includes former HP engineers.

HP's Adobe cartridge and memory upgrade are the top-of-the-line approach to printer capabilities. With this combination, the LaserJet III becomes a printer as capable of the most elaborate PostScript typographical and shading effects as any Apple LaserWriter, and usually at a lower total cost. And because Apple LaserWriters have never included a parallel printer port, the LaserJet III/PostScript cartridge combination generally prints much faster on PC networks than LaserWriters do, since PC managers tend to connect LaserWriters to networks through their much-slower serial ports. (For the record, if you use an Apple LaserWriter on a PC network, you should purchase an inexpensive AppleTalk network card and place it in the PC that is acting as the print server. Print jobs can be sent to a LaserWriter at over 38,000 bps through an AppleTalk port, while serial ports are usually limited to 9600 bps.)

IQ Engineering's Super Cartridge 3, however, exploits many of the features of the LaserJet III and offers an attractive alternative to the PostScript cartridge. The Super Cartridge uses HP's own fast-scaling engine to provide text printing that, in the tests described further, was virtually as fast as the LaserJet III's own text output speed. While the IQ cartridge will never enable a LaserJet to print "encapsulated" PostScript graphics (.EPS files), it does print bitmap graphics and graphic files in HPGL format (HP Graphics Language, a vector format originally developed for plotters but equally adept at drawing lines in a LaserJet III). And it provides several typefaces that PostScript printers almost never include — notably, a handy Prestige Elite fixed-pitch font that is more compact and attractive than HP's Courier, and a beautiful Garamond Old Style typeface that is much more pleasant to look at than Times Roman.

What effect, if any, do these two printer enhancements have on LaserJet printing performance? To find out, I conducted some controlled print runs under a variety of configurations for the LaserJet III. First, the LaserJet III was tested in its original state, using Windows' LaserJet III printer driver but no font cartridges or other font-support programs. Then, the LaserJet was upgraded in turn with IQ Engineering's Super Cartridge 3 (with support for the installed cartridge through a printer configuration file in the Control Panel) and with HP's Adobe PostScript cartridge (complete with a switch-over to Windows' PostScript printer driver). Finally, the same tests were conducted on a cartridgeless LaserJet III with font support provided by Adobe Type Manager's installable screen and printer font software. I used a Northgate Slimline 386/20 with 4MB of RAM, and a LaserJet III with 3MB of RAM. Windows 3.0 printer drivers were used, and all jobs were printed by Word for Windows 1.1. The LaserJet was turned off and on again between every test to clear the printer's *font cache,* which can have a dramatic effect on the performance of print jobs the second or third time they run. Type-faces were named in the terminology of the device being tested, except for the original LaserJet III itself — the PostScript cartridge was told to print "NewCenturySchlbk," for example, while the IQ cartridge was told to print "IQ Schoolbook."

The results turned in under these conditions indicate that the IQ cartridge succeeded in printing complex text jobs and graphics files with virtually no speed degradation compared with the HP's built-in font-scaling capabilities. And, in most cases, the IQ cartridge was significantly faster than either the HP PostScript cartridge or the Adobe Type Manager add-in type-scaling program for Windows.

In the first test, a one-page chart of special characters available under Windows was sent to the printer and to its various alternative font-genera-tors. The chart includes all characters in Windows' ANSI character set, numbered 32 through 255, in the typefaces Century, Symbol, and Zapf Dingbats. It is similar to the figure of special Windows characters that appears in Chapter 9.

The LaserJet III, in its native mode, cannot print this special-character chart properly, because the printer lacks the necessary Dingbats font (it success-fully converts the Century font to CG Times, however, and is capable of printing the Symbol font if you installed the HP Symbol files when you ran Word for Windows Setup). All the font-support alternatives, however, had no problems with the chart, although they required noticeably differing times to produce this one page:

Character Chart	1st Run (in minutes)	2nd Run (in minutes)
IQ Super Cartridge 3	1.67	1.60
HP Adobe PostScript Cartridge	4.00	1.48
Adobe Type Manager software	9.60	5.30

In the second test, a three-page text-only document was sent to the LaserJet. This document consisted largely of 12-point New Century Schoolbook type, with a few lines in 14-point and 24-point for emphasis. The plain LaserJet III converted this type specification to the printer's internal CG Times typeface. The other font-support alternatives printed the correct fonts, but the IQ cartridge ran at normal LaserJet speeds while the PostScript options slowed significantly until font-caching had stored the fonts in the printer's memory:

3-Page Text Job	1st Run (in minutes)	2nd Run (in minutes)
LaserJet III without font support	0.92	0.92
IQ Super Cartridge 3	1.00	0.95
HP Adobe PostScript Cartridge	1.60	0.95
Adobe Type Manager software	1.57	1.50

Finally, to test the effect of font-generators on graphics printing (a slow process under Windows in many situations), I printed an almost-full-page bitmap to the LaserJet. This file consisted of the CHESS.BMP bitmap (included with Windows) converted to a .PCX file in Paintbrush, enlarged to 300 percent of its original size, and printed by Word for Windows. The PostScript cartridge took twice as long to print this graphic as any other alternative. Presumably, this is due to the performance-inhibiting effect of the Windows PostScript driver, since the other alternatives all generated their output using the Windows 3.0 LaserJet III printer driver:

Graphic File	1st Run (in minutes)	2nd Run (in minutes)
LaserJet III without font support	0.90	0.87
IQ Super Cartridge 3	0.95	0.88
HP Adobe PostScript Cartridge	2.32	2.32
Adobe Type Manager software	0.92	0.88

If you already have a PostScript printer, there is certainly no need to replace it with a LaserJet III. The PostScript language gives a laser printer a broad array of text-manipulation special-effects that cannot be matched in HP's Printer Control Language, and the best PostScript printers are faster on some jobs than the latest LaserJets. But for straight text-and-graphics printing performance, the HP format, with IQ's Super Cartridge for additional font choices, is a strong competitor.

I would like to thank Christine Rivera of Micro Dynamics Plus, an excellent PC training facility in New York City, for her support with these performance trials.

New Driver May Not Replace Old When Installed

Certain problems when printing to a LaserJet printer under Windows 3.0 can be the result of installing Windows into a directory containing an old copy of Windows 2.x. In some cases, the new LaserJet III print driver file does not replace the old LaserJet print driver that was a part of the earlier Windows version.

The old print driver actually works under Windows 3.0 in real mode, but problems occur in standard and enhanced modes. You may see an "incompatible printer" message when attempting to print, or the system may freeze entirely when printing. In the LaserJet printer setup dialog box, no paper sizes will be shown as available, and other choices, such as fonts, may be unavailable as well.

If you installed Windows 3.0 into a Windows 2.x directory and are experiencing these problems, you must delete the old driver and replace it with the updated file. To do this, open the Control Panel, select the LaserJet printer, and click <u>R</u>emove. Then, minimize the Control Panel, open the WIN.INI file with Notepad, and search for and delete the section headed [HPCL5A,LPT*n*] (where *n* is the number of the printer port you had configured the LaserJet printer for) and all the lines in that section. Finally, delete the actual HPPCL5A.DRV file from your hard disk.

To install the new LaserJet III driver, run the Control Panel and click Install. Insert the Windows distribution diskette with the LaserJet III driver — Disk #6 on 3.5" media, Disk #5 on 5.25" media. After installation of the new driver, the printer should immediately work as expected.

Additional Troubleshooting Steps

If you continue to have problems with a LaserJet printer, further trouble-shooting may be necessary. On most LaserJet printers, you can print a test page without requiring an application program (and without even being attached to a computer). If the printer won't even print this page, the problem is probably within the printer, not Windows. On a LaserJet III, you print this page by turning *off* the On Line button, then holding down the Test button until the display panel reads "Self Test." The resulting page should show the amount of memory installed in the printer as well as other information, such as the number of pages the printer has printed in its lifetime.

If the printer prints, but is having some intermittent difficulty, you can disable the LaserJet III's "Autocontinue" option. Autocontinue is a feature that allows the printer to attempt to continue printing after encountering an error. Turning this feature *off* permits you to read the error message displayed in the printer's display panel if there is an intermittent problem, then continue printing by pressing the Continue button.

To turn off Autocontinue, press the On Line button to turn off the light, then press and hold the Menu button for five seconds, or until "AUTO CONT" appears in the display panel. If the display says, "AUTO CONT=OFF," you don't need to change it — press the Menu button repeatedly until READY appears in the display, then turn the On Line light back on. If the display says, "AUTO CONT=ON," press the plus (+) key to change the display to OFF. Press the Enter key (on the printer) to make this setting the default (an asterisk [*] appears to indicate that this has become the default). Press Menu repeatedly to return to READY, then press On Line. Printer errors will now cause a message to be displayed in the window, which may help identify the cause of printing problems.

Overlapping Lines May Require a Margin Change

If Notepad or another Windows application overlaps the first two lines of the page when printing to a LaserJet, the problem may not be the printer. LaserJet printers usually cannot print closer than 0.25 inches from the top or bottom of the page. If the Top Margin or Bottom Margin in the Page Setup dialog box are set to zero, lines sent to the printer may be outside the printable area of the page, and the overlapping effect occurs. This affects LaserJet models II, IIP, IID, and III. PostScript printers are also affected if you try to print outside the printable area, but unlike LaserJets, PostScript printers in this situation usually omit the lines instead of overlapping them. To correct this, use a Top Margin of 0.25 inches or more.

Using the Symbol Font with LaserJets

Windows includes four screen fonts — Courier, a fixed-pitch typeface; Tms Rmn and Helv, proportional typefaces; and Symbol. The LaserJet I and II printers include the Courier printer font, and LaserJet IIIs include proportional typefaces similar to Times Roman and Helvetica. But in order to use Windows' Symbol face, supported in virtually all Windows applications, you must install Symbol soft fonts.

The Symbol typeface is present in all PostScript printers, even the earliest ones, and contains a wealth of useful characters. These include a true bullet (•); copyright and trademark bugs (©, ®, and ™); true vertical and horizontal lines, which were left out of the ANSI character set (| and —); real arrows and an "Enter key" symbol for documentation (←, ↑, →, ↓, ↔, and ↵); and many others.

Windows 2.*x* included Symbol fonts for LaserJet printers, but these were left out of Windows 3.0. These fonts are now included with applications such as Microsoft Word for Windows. To install these fonts, find the Word for Windows diskette (or other applications' diskette) that contains a sub-directory called \SYMBOL.W3. This directory contains Symbol fonts compatible with Windows 3.*x*. (Windows 2.*x* fonts won't work.)

Start the Control Panel's Printers dialog box and highlight your LaserJet printer driver. Click Configure Setup Fonts. In the dialog box that appears, click Add Fonts and specify the correct directory containing the Symbol font files in your floppy drive. Click OK. The dialog box should list the Symbol fonts in sizes from 8-point to 24-point. Select these fonts by clicking on them, then click Copy. This copies files to your hard disk and adds them to your WIN.INI file. Click Exit, then click OK until you have closed the Control Panel completely. Any documents you send to your LaserJet containing Symbol characters will now download these characters to your printer and print them in the nearest available size.

Undocumented Support for Soft Fonts

One of the downsides to installing soft fonts in your WIN.INI file is that if you install a new version of Windows over an old one, the printer section of WIN.INI is rewritten and all your soft font information is lost. (This is another good reason, as explained further in Chapter 15, why you should *not* install a new version of Windows into the same directory as an old version.)

The LaserJet printer driver, however, has undocumented features that allow it to save and regenerate your installed soft font information, even across Windows installs. These features assist both Microsoft and anyone who must frequently reinstall new versions of Windows.

The LaserJet font installer program (part of the Control Panel printer driver) copies soft fonts to a directory typically named PCLFONTS on your hard drive. It also copies to your disk a Printer Font Metrics (.PFM) file, which Windows applications use to determine the size and weight of the fonts you can print. It is the lines in WIN.INI that refer to your files in the PCLFONTS directory, and the .PFM file, that are lost when you reinstall Windows.

You can generate a fonts-installed directory in a file called FINSTALL.DIR by using one of the LaserJet driver's undocumented features. After installing Windows, you use another undocumented feature to recreate the soft font lines in your WIN.INI file.

To generate FINSTALL.DIR, open the Control Panel's Printers dialog box. Highlight the LaserJet driver, then click Configure Setup Fonts. *Hold down the Ctrl and Shift keys* while clicking Exit. This displays a dialog box, in which you define the directory to create FINSTALL.DIR. This file should be in the same directory with the soft fonts, probably C:\PCLFONTS. Click OK after you have specified the directory. This writes the FINSTALL.DIR file.

When you need to restore the soft font information into your WIN.INI file, click Configure Setup Fonts as before. This time, hold down the Ctrl and Shift keys while clicking the Add Fonts button. This displays a dialog box that asks you for the location of the FINSTALL.DIR file. Specify the directory that contains this file and your soft font files and click OK.

You will see your soft font files in a list box on the right of the dialog box that appears. Select the fonts by clicking each one with your mouse, then click Add. When asked for a directory to install these fonts, type in the directory where they already exist and click OK. In a few moments, these fonts are displayed on the left side of the dialog box, as well as the right. No files have actually been copied. Only your WIN.INI file has been updated with the correct information.

Landscape ProCollection Fonts Cause UAE

The HP ProCollection cartridge can cause the error message "Unrecoverable Application Error" when applications print using these fonts in landscape orientation while Windows 3.0 is in 386 enhanced mode. This occurs on the HP LaserJet II printer and on printers that emulate the LaserJet II and use the LaserJet II printer driver. The only solution is not to set up the printer dialog box for landscape orientation while in Windows' enhanced mode, or to deselect the ProCollection cartridge in the Control Panel. A later version of the printer driver corrects this behavior.

The ProCollection also tends to print everything from Windows Notepad, Calendar, and Cardfile in **bold**, rather than normal, when using the HPPCL.DRV LaserJet driver. Remove the selection of the ProCollection cartridge in the Control Panel to make text from these applications print nonbold on the LaserJet.

LaserJet IID Can Incorrectly Duplex

When printing more than one copy of a document on an HP LaserJet IID while using the feature of the IID that allows printing on both sides of the paper, the first page of the second copy is printed on the *back* of the last page of the first copy. This occurs because there are an odd number of pages in the document and the Windows printer driver is not detecting that a new page is needed for the second (and subsequent) copy. The only workaround is to make sure that such print jobs contain an *even* number of pages, by inserting a page break or blank page at the end of the document.

Rounded Boxes Print Unevenly

Applications that are capable of printing rounded boxes, such as Windows Paintbrush and Aldus PageMaker, print the rounded corners thicker than the straight lines when printing to LaserJets using the LaserJet driver shipped with Windows 3.0. These diagrams printed correctly with the Windows 2.*x* driver. This behavior is corrected in newer versions of Windows 3.*x*. But if you don't have the newer driver, the older one could possibly be used to print these boxes, but only under the real mode of Windows 3.0.

PostScript Printers

Aside from plain vanilla LaserJet printers, Adobe PostScript printers are the most popular type of laser printers used in business today. PostScript printers often use the same printer drum and other components as ordinary LaserJets. But all PostScript printers are capable of printing type in any size requested and of printing "Encapsulated PostScript" graphics that remain sharp even when output at many times their original size (unlike bit-mapped graphics files enlarged on a LaserJet).

With the introduction of plug-in cartridges from Adobe and HP, it has become quite easy to convert LaserJets to PostScript printers. Once the cartridge is in place (and one or two megabytes of additional RAM is added to the printer to form PostScript images), the newly enhanced LaserJet has all the brainpower of any other genuine Adobe PostScript printer — at a lower cost than almost any other PostScript device. The Adobe name guarantees compatibility; under close inspection, third-party PostScript "clones" reveal bugs that can make complex graphics print differently than expected.

The only drawback of the Adobe cartridge in a LaserJet is that it won't work if installed incorrectly. The printer must be turned off before the cartridge is inserted or removed — just pushing it into the slot won't enable the PostScript features (and the cartridge can be damaged by excess voltage if the printer is powered-on when inserted). And, of course, while the cartridge is installed, the printer no longer thinks it's a LaserJet. Adobe's cartridge for the LaserJet II family allows the user to switch the printer back into LaserJet mode by issuing a software command, but HP's licensed cartridge for the LaserJet III doesn't.

While PostScript provides a great deal of convenience, troubleshooting problems on PostScript printers is often quite different from troubleshooting plain HPs. Fortunately, some undocumented features can make this task easier.

Obtaining the Latest on Your PostScript Driver

If you use a PostScript printer, you should definitely open the Windows Control Panel, highlight the printer driver, then click Configure Setup Help. This opens a window onto a wealth of information about PostScript printers in general and PostScript printer models in specific. If you see something on a printer you use, you can print the text of the item directly to your printer from the Help window.

Error Handler Option Hidden in Control Panel

All PostScript printers support an error-handler mode, which forces the printer to print a sheet when an error occurs instead of simply halting. This sheet contains a message that may indicate the type of problem that stopped the printout. (If Windows is set to print to a file instead of to the printer directly, this message is saved to the file — where it can be examined with a text editor — instead of printed.)

Windows' PostScript printer driver has an option that instructs the attached PostScript printer to begin working in error-handler mode, but this option is hidden and does not appear in Control Panel's Printer dialog box.

To enable error handling, open the Control Panel and run the Printers icon. Make sure that the PostScript printer is selected (highlighted) in the resulting dialog box. Click Configure, then Setup, then Options. In the dialog box that appears, press Alt+E, just as though an option were visible in which the first letter of Error-Handler was underlined as a choice. Click OK several times to close the Control Panel's dialog boxes. The Error Handler information has been invoked and will remain in effect until the printer is reset or turned off.

Verifying a Correct Connection

Sometimes, a PostScript printer may seem not to react to any Windows applications. Since a PostScript printer does not respond to a PrintScreen command (a common way to test whether a LaserJet or dot-matrix printer is working), it may be difficult to tell whether a PostScript printer that does not print Windows jobs is improperly configured or is not receiving commands at all. To prove that a PostScript printer is properly connected and receiving commands, type the following at a DOS prompt:

```
copy con com1
showpage
[Ctrl+Z][Enter]
```

In the first line of this sequence, the COPY CON command copies whatever you type at the console (the keyboard) to the device on port COM1. (Substitute another port if your printer is on COM2, LPT1, etc.) On the next line, the PostScript "showpage" command is similar to a LaserJet's "eject page" or form-feed command. When you press Ctrl+Z, Enter (which sends the keystrokes and returns the keyboard to normal), the PostScript printer will emit a blank page if it received the command. If nothing happens, then something is wrong with the port, the cable, or the printer itself, but not with Windows.

Driver Doesn't Save Scaling Factors

When selecting a file and choosing File Print in the Windows File Manager, the file always prints to a PostScript printer at 100 percent scaling, even though the PostScript driver may be set in the Control Panel for 50 percent, 200 percent, or any other scaling factor. This does not indicate a problem with the printer, but is inherent in File Manager and the Windows 3.0 PostScript printer driver.

This driver also fails to save any scaling factors other than 100 percent when exiting Windows and starting it again. You must set this value every time you start Windows if you regularly need an enlargement or reduction in your PostScript printing. This is a design decision that prevents people from setting an unusual scaling factor, then forgetting why their printouts are too large or too small the next time they use Windows.

Driver Cannot Change Printer Resolution

Although PostScript printers can suffer insufficient memory problems when processing complex pages sent to them by Windows (just like LaserJets, as described previously), Windows' PostScript printer driver does not have an option to lower the printer's resolution temporarily to reduce the memory required to print a page, as the LaserJet driver does. PostScript printers can fall back from 300-dpi resolution to 150 or even 75 dpi if they lack the memory to store a complex image at the higher density. (The image that is printed will certainly be coarser, but it might have a better chance of printing at all.) But the Windows 3.0 PostScript driver does not allow this to be specified. The PostScript driver included with Windows 2.x offers the choice of printer resolutions in this situation, however. It can be used to print under Windows 3.0 (by reinstalling the driver file, using the Control Panel's Printer Install option), but only in real mode.

Missing Lines May Require a Margin Change

If your PostScript printer drops out lines at the top or bottom of pages when printing from Notepad or other Windows applications, you may have the Page Setup dialog box set to a Top Margin or a Bottom Margin of zero. Most PostScript printers cannot print closer than 0.25 inches from the top and bottom margin. For more information, see "Overlapping Lines May Require a Margin Change" in the HP LaserJet section of this chapter.

Sending PrintScreens to PostScript Printers

One of the most frustrating things about PostScript printers is that, for all their power and flashy graphics, if you send most of them a plain ASCII text file (like a DOS PrintScreen), they sit there dumbly and do nothing. All text sent to a PostScript printer must be "processed" into a PostScript "envelope" first. (Newer printers from QMS and other companies can automatically switch into LaserJet mode when they detect a print stream that contains plain ASCII text, but this is not yet true of most PostScript printers.)

To overcome this, add a program to your system that captures ASCII text and converts it on-the-fly into a form that Adobe PostScript can handle. One such program is sold by Legend Communications, and was described earlier in the section "Improving Printer Performance." Another program, called Trading Post, is produced by the LaserTools Corp., 1250 45th St. #100, Emeryville, CA 94806, 415-420-8777. Trading Post is usually installed to look for plain-text output on your LPT1 port. It reformats this text and sends it to your PostScript printer on LPT2, COM1, or whichever port you use. You print from Windows applications (all of which support Windows' PostScript driver) to the PostScript printer using the actual port. But PrintScreen output, along with any DOS application that doesn't support PostScript, is directed to a port that Trading Post is monitoring.

This system even works well across a network. Trading Post redirects plain text to ports that may be spooled to a network printer as easily as it redirects output to printers directly connected to your PC.

Beyond Windows' PostScript Driver

If Windows' PostScript printer driver limits your printing capabilities, you may want to replace it with a third-party PostScript driver from such companies as Micrografx and QMS.

The PostScript driver that comes with Windows 3.*x*, a product of Microsoft and Aldus Corp., leaves out many features that users of the Macintosh PostScript print driver take for granted. The Windows driver, for example, cannot reduce the printer's resolution from 300 dpi to 150 or 75 dpi to make draft copies print faster (although this was a feature of the PostScript driver in Windows 2.*x*). It also cannot reset the printer, show the font list, or print out how much RAM is available.

The Micrografx PostScript driver, by contrast, offers many options. You can install and download PostScript fonts to the printer, or specify that they should automatically download when you print. If you ever print to high-resolution PostScript typesetters, you can specify the minimum width to use for hairline rules, which look fine on a coarse laser printer but often become nearly invisible on a 2500-dpi imagesetter. And, of course, the Micrografx driver is reported to be faster than the Windows driver, but I haven't tested this.

Micrografx's PostScript driver is included with its Designer 3.*x* package, or is available separately for under $200. Contact Micrografx at 1303 Arapaho, Richardson, TX 75081-2444; 800-272-3729 or 214-234-1769.

The complete features of QMS' PostScript driver were not announced at this writing. Contact QMS at 1 Magnum Pass, Mobile, AL 36618; 205-633-4300.

Dot-Matrix Printers

Windows Doesn't Automatically Install the Correct Fonts

When Windows version 2.*x* was installed with a dot-matrix printer selected as the output device, it also installed a range of fonts appropriate for that printer's resolution. Windows 3.0 does not automatically install these fonts. Microsoft has issued a technical paper stating that it was necessary to leave out the installation of the appropriate fonts in order to "complete the development of the Windows 3.00 Control Panel in time to ship the product." As a result, you may need to install these fonts manually to get acceptable printing on a dot-matrix printer.

Since dot-matrix printers are much lower-resolution devices than laser printers (which are more appropriate for the graphics output of Windows), special bit-mapped printer fonts are usually not produced for dot-matrix printers. Instead, Windows uses the same *screen fonts* that it uses to display text on-screen as a model for the pattern of dots that it will use for each letter printed on a dot-matrix printer.

The appropriate font for a dot-matrix printer, then, depends on that printer's resolution — how close together it can print two dots. Dot-matrix printers fall into two groups: 9-pin printers (lower resolution) and 24-pin printers (higher resolution).

24-pin dot-matrix printers (so-called because the print head has 24 tiny cylinders that can strike the ribbon and create an image) usually print with a resolution of 180 dpi, both vertically and horizontally. Because the resolution is the same in both directions, 24-pin printers are said to have a 1-to-1 *aspect ratio* — just like laser printers. Some 24-pin printers claim a resolution of 360 dpi, which is higher than most laser printers' 300 dpi resolution. But these dot-matrix printers are not sharper than a laser printer, because one dot printed by a 24-pin printer is many times larger than a single dot from a laser printer, creating a fuzzier image.

24-pin printers should ordinarily be used with the screen fonts that Windows installs for VGA or 8514/A monitors. These screen fonts have a 1-to-1 aspect ratio, like 24-pin printers, but unlike the EGA and CGA screen fonts (these are not as tall as the VGA fonts, in order to compensate for the different resolutions of EGA and CGA displays).

The VGA screen fonts were drawn with the assumption that 96 dots in a line of characters will represent one inch in a document (when displayed on a VGA display). Since a 24-pin printer prints at 180×180 dpi, VGA screen fonts print at about one-half the size that is shown for the font in the Control Panel and in applications. The 8514/A screen font assumes that 120 dots represents one inch, so these fonts print at about two-thirds the stated size. Setting a 24-pin printer to print at 360×360 dpi means that VGA and 8514/A fonts will print about one-fourth and one-third the stated size, respectively. For this reason, it is better to leave these printers set for a resolution of 180×180 dpi when printing from Windows (unless you like the reduced effect). Similarly, it is better not to set the printer for a resolution with an aspect ratio that is not 1-to-1, such as 180×360 dpi, which results in elongated letterforms.

Windows identifies the screen fonts on its distribution diskettes by the last letter in the filename of the font file. The VGA screen font is known as "E" and the 8514/A font as "F." The Times Roman, Helvetica, Courier, and Symbol fonts that are included with Windows have filenames like the following:

VGA Screen Fonts	**8514/A Screen Fonts**
TMSRE.FON	TMSRF.FON
HELVE.FON	HELVF.FON
COURE.FON	COURF.FON
SYMBOLE.FON	SYMBOLF.FON

If you installed Windows for a VGA display, the VGA screen fonts are already installed but you may wish to install the 8514/A screen fonts to obtain additional type sizes. If you installed Windows for other than a VGA display, these screen fonts were probably not installed, and you may want to install both the VGA and the 8514/A fonts.

9-pin printers usually offer a resolution of 120 dots horizontally and 72 dots vertically. This resolution, which does not have a 1-to-1 aspect ratio, is best served with the screen font identified by the letter "D," which also does not conform to the 1-to-1 ratio. If your 9-pin printer can be set all the way down to a very coarse 60×72 dpi resolution and you wish to use this setting (for faster performance, perhaps, or less ribbon wear), you may want to also install the "C" font.

To install any of the above fonts manually, use File Manager or the MS-DOS Executive to find the diskette in your Windows distribution disks that contains the font files you wish to install. Open the Control Panel and click Fonts. When the Font dialog box appears, showing those screen fonts that are already available, click Add. Select the drive that contains the diskette, select the filename(s) you wish to install, and click OK. The Control Panel copies the files to your hard disk and displays a sample of each font.

Each installed screen font takes up a small amount of Windows memory. If you are extremely low on memory, you can use the Fonts dialog box to remove screen fonts. If you do this, Control Panel does not delete them from your hard disk, and they can be added back later. Do not remove the Helv font for your screen resolution, since this font is used in almost all Windows dialog boxes.

Screen fonts often removed by Windows users include the *vector fonts,* Modern, Roman, and Script. These fonts do not have a bit-mapped image, but only consist of straight lines (or *vectors*) describing each letter's strokes. (For this reason, they are sometimes called *stroke fonts*). Dot-matrix printer users, however, may not want to remove these fonts (though they seem to occupy about 5K of memory every time Windows loads). This is because the vector fonts are the only fonts that can be used to print both characters of any size and symbols from Windows' entire 255-character ANSI character set on printers without proportional fonts of their own. Most dot-matrix printers fall into this category, so the vector fonts may be useful when other fonts are limited. Printers such as the Epson LQ-500 and the Hewlett-Packard DeskJet and DeskJet Plus (ink-jet printers that are similar to a dot-matrix) do not include the second 128 characters in the ANSI character set.

Windows Write and other Windows applications such as Word for Windows and Excel, however, can remap these characters to print on these printers if the characters are formatted in the Modern, Roman, or Script fonts. See the Epson and HP sections later in this chapter for more information.

Printer Anomalies

The rest of this chapter describes configuration information for specific models of printers when used with Windows.

Epson Dot-Matrix Printers

Older Epson 24-pin dot-matrix printers may not be able to print the 128 characters in Windows' upper-ANSI character set. The Epson models that *do* support all the characters in Windows are the LQ-500, LQ-850, LQ-1050, and LQ-2500.

 You may be able to work around this limitation with other Epson printers (and all dot-matrix printers) by using the vector fonts built into Windows (Roman, Modern, and Script) instead of the bitmapped screen fonts (Tms Rmn, Helv, and Courier). The vector fonts draw characters on printers as a series of lines, rather than storing an exact bitmap of the characters themselves. This can allow printers to print characters that they do not ordinarily support.

Support by Windows applications is uneven for the upper-ANSI characters using the vector fonts, however. You may find that Windows Write and major applications such as Word for Windows and Excel print these characters to older dot-matrix printers, while such Windows applets as Notepad and Cardfile do not.

Additionally, Epson printer models named the Series 80, FX, RX, and older models of the MX line may require that you upgrade their ROM chip to use them with Windows 3.*x.* You can find the version of your ROM in these printers by holding down the Line Feed button when you turn the machine's power switch on. If the machine prints three or four lines during its self-test and then stops, the newer ROM is already installed. If the machine keeps printing lines after the first three or four, the ROM is an older model and should be replaced.

The replacement is a chip called Dots Perfect that can be ordered from Epson. Versions of the chip are specific to different models of the Epson line. The upgrade enables graphics printing on these models. Contact Epson at 800-873-7766 for information.

Hewlett-Packard DeskJet Printers

Neither the HP DeskJet nor the DeskJet Plus printer can print characters above 127 in Windows' ANSI character set. (They do not support the upper-ASCII characters from DOS, either.) It may be possible to access these characters by using Windows' vector fonts, Roman, Modern, and Script, as with the Epson printers described in the previous topic.

Additionally, the DeskJet printer drivers in Windows 2.*x* and 3.*x* do not support any landscape internal or cartridge fonts. If you try to print to a DeskJet from an application such as Excel while in landscape mode, Windows tries to substitute a vector font for the screen font visible on your monitor. These vector fonts are the only ones that will print on DeskJets in landscape mode.

Hewlett-Packard PaintJet Printers

The PaintJet series supports Windows soft fonts that may be installed in your WIN.INI file and downloaded to the printer as needed. You may be able to install more than 25 such fonts, but the driver will recognize and list as available only the first 25. (Each size and weight counts as a different font.) To use other fonts, it is necessary to remove a few.

If colored lines print at random on a PaintJet XL (a faster model of the PaintJet), you may have to turn *off* the Compression and High-Speed Direct LPT check boxes in the Control Panel for the PaintJet driver. These options enhance the performance of the PaintJet XL but may be responsible for the appearance of random lines.

Additionally, the PaintJet driver supports a Presentation Mode option on the PaintJet XL. This mode deposits more ink, in order to make deeper colors on transparency sheets. If you configure the PaintJet's hardware switches to force it into Presentation Mode, but you do not obtain deeper colors, Windows is probably overriding the printer's hardware switches. If you do not have the Presentation Mode option checked *on* in the Control Panel, the PaintJet driver switches the printer out of Presentation Mode before printing.

Hewlett-Packard Plotters

If you have trouble printing to an HP plotter with the printer driver in Windows 3.0, try assigning the printer to FILE:= in the Control Panel, then print a job to this file. Examine the size of the resulting file by using File Manager or a DOS DIR command. If the file is less than 10K in size, the driver is malfunctioning. If it is larger than 10K, try copying it directly to the printer from DOS, using the command COPY /B MYFILE.HP COM1 (replacing the filename and port with the actual names for your system). The /B switch ensures that the entire binary file is copied. If this file does not print, make sure your com port is correctly configured for the plotter, and try again. If it still does not print, try one of the following workarounds.

First, reconfigure the printer in the Control Panel so it looks like a Colorpro with GEC, 7470A, and 7475A plotters. This driver may produce better results.

If this does not correct the problem, you can use the Windows 2.*x* driver for HP plotters, if you start Windows 3.*x* in real mode.

IBM 4019 Laser Printer

The IBM 4019 laser printer supports four different emulations. These are ASCII mode (IBM calls this the PPDS mode), LaserJet II, Plotter emulation (HPGL), and PostScript. The PostScript emulation requires the installation of a PostScript option.

The Windows driver for the IBM 4019 supports the printer in ASCII mode. In the other emulations, use a LaserJet or PostScript driver.

The IBM LaserPrinter E is the same as the 4019, except it has governor ROMs that slow it down from a text speed of 10 ppm (pages per minute) to 5 ppm. This allows the printer to be priced lower than the 4019 and compete with Hewlett-Packard's LaserJet IID. The LaserPrinter E is not listed in Windows printer drivers, but works with the IBM 4019 driver.

The 4019 also supports a Print Sharing Device that is designed to allow workstations on a Token-Ring network to use the printer. When turned on, this interface constantly polls the network, looking for print streams. If short documents print from Windows to this printer, but longer ones print only partial jobs or disappear entirely, the Print Sharing Device may be flushing its buffer while waiting for Windows' Print Manager to send information.

Set the device's switches to a maximum delay of 60 seconds to allow Print Manager to print to the device without being timed out.

NEC SilentWriter LC890

If the characters in the first column of your Windows printouts are clipped on an NEC SilentWriter LC890, you must upgrade the printer ROM chips. This upgrade can be obtained from NEC dealers.

Additionally, the LC890 will not recognize the Letter/Legal switch on its optional paper bin. You must set the paper length using the printer's front panel instead of these switches.

QMS Jetscript

You must send a text file to the QMS Jetscript (a licensed Adobe PostScript printer) before starting Windows in order to print from Windows applications. The following text file can be created with Notepad or any text editor; the characters must be in all lowercase:

```
serverdict begin 0 exitserver
statusdict begin
0 setdefaultparallel
0 setparallel
start
```

Give this file a name like REVERSE.ON to indicate that it turns *on* the Reverse channel. Copy this file to the printer using a command such as COPY REVERSE.ON LPT1. For more information, contact QMS Technical Support at 205-633-4300.

PacificPage PostScript Cartridges

If print jobs sent to a PacificPage PostScript cartridge disappear before producing any output, but the same jobs sent to a genuine PostScript printer print normally, you may need to upgrade to a new revision of the PacificPage interpreter (an unlicensed PostScript clone).

Pacific Data Products suggests increasing to 99 the values for Device Not Selected and Transmission Retry in the printer driver's Configure Setup dialog box under the Control Panel. If this does not fix the problem, contact PacificData at 619-552-0880.

Texas Instruments OmniLaser

The TI OmniLaser requires a ROM version of 1.4 or higher to work reliably with Windows 3.*x*. On older versions, it may be necessary to use only the printer's parallel port if you experience problems or messages such as "Can't Write to Printer."

The OmniLaser 2115 printer requires Firmware version 2.613 or 2.635 to print reliably. If you upgrade to this level, the ROM version in the printer is no longer important. You can find the printer's Firmware version by printing a status page.

For more information, contact Texas Instruments at 800-336-5236 or 512-250-7407.

Summary

In this chapter, I have explained details of Windows' printing architecture, and the way it treats different types of printers. This includes:

▶ How Windows writes to most printers in high-resolution graphics mode, and how to override this in some cases.

▶ Ways to use the Control Panel to get maximum features and performance out of your printer.

▶ Settings in your WIN.INI and SYSTEM.INI files that you can adjust to configure your printers to your liking.

▶ The use of the Generic/Text driver and PostScript driver, even if you don't have one of these printers attached to your system.

▶ Considerations that can affect the printing performance you achieve with various devices under Windows.

▶ Printer-specific information on the major classes of printers used with Windows: LaserJet, PostScript, and dot-matrix printers.

▶ Configuration information on individual models of printers from different printer manufacturers.

Chapter 14
Video Boards and Monitors

In this chapter. . .

I cover the following topics:

▶ How different video standards and resolutions affect Windows.

▶ How Windows makes your screen fonts look similar to your printout, and how it differs from the way the Macintosh does this.

▶ How to avoid memory conflicts between video boards and other devices in your computer, and what steps you can take when devices *do* conflict.

▶ Specific configuration information for VGA, Super VGA, 8514/A, EGA, and CGA displays.

▶ The three different types of screen fonts that Windows uses, how these are controlled by settings in your WIN.INI and SYSTEM.INI files, and how you can change them to get just the size and look you want.

▶ Configuration anomalies affecting specific video boards from a variety of manufacturers.

This chapter contains information on the subsystem that displays Windows' graphical user interface — your video board and monitor. If your video board matches your monitor's capabilities, the Windows performance you experience has much more to do with your video board than with your monitor. Therefore, I have concentrated on video board configuration and troubleshooting issues in this chapter.

For information on screen savers, which blank your Windows screen to provide security and prevent images from burning into your screen, see Chapter 3.

Video Standards

Good display graphics lie at the heart of Windows' appeal. While most PC programs prior to Windows 3.0 ran only in text mode, Windows and all Windows applications require a PC equipped with a graphics display.

Many graphics standards prevail in the PC world, however, and not all video graphics boards are compatible with all PC display monitors. When pushing graphics boards and monitors to their highest resolutions, furthermore, vendors may introduce incompatibilities that show up in Windows (exquisitely sensitive as it is to graphics hardware) as garbled screens or hopelessly frozen PC systems.

Figure 14-1 — PC Video Graphics Board Standards — lists several available standards, from the lowest resolution to the highest. Each standard may be capable of several modes (a VGA-standard board, for example, can be switched to any of 17 different modes, including the earlier CGA and EGA modes), but only the most commonly used modes are shown in the table.

In the table, the Windows Support column indicates "No" for those resolutions that are not supported by drivers in the Windows 3.0 diskettes, and "with driver" for those resolutions that require driver software on a separate diskette provided by the graphics board vendor.

Some video boards can provide higher resolutions or display more colors when more memory is installed on the graphic adapter itself. These resolutions are shown in the table. A board offering 1024×768 resolution, for example, may be able to display only 16 colors with 512K of RAM installed, but can display 256 colors with 1024K (1MB) installed.

Boards that offer a resolution of 1024×768 differ from each other in another important respect. Some of these boards, such as the IBM 8514/A adapter, are not truly capable of displaying 1024×768 resolution in one pass each time the screen is redrawn (refreshed). Instead, the screen is refreshed in two passes: first the odd-numbered scan lines (horizontal lines that make up the picture) are drawn, then the board draws the even-numbered lines. This allows the board and compatible monitors to be made less expensively, since they really only need to be capable of displaying 512×768 resolution at a time. Drawing the screen in two passes fills in the complete image. But this method of refreshing the screen causes a flickering effect that most

PC Video Graphics Board Standards			
Video Standard	**Resolution(s)**	**Colors**	**Windows Support?**
CGA	320 × 200	4	No
	640 × 200	mono	Yes
Hercules Monochrome	720 × 348	mono	Yes
EGA	640 × 350	16	Yes
VGA	640 × 480	16	Yes
	320 × 200	256	No
Super VGA (256K)	800 × 600	16	with driver
Super VGA (512K)	800 × 600	256	with driver
IBM 8514/A (512K)	1024 × 768 interlaced	16	Yes
IBM 8514/A (1024K)	1024 × 768 interlaced	256	Yes
Other 8514/A (512K)	1024 × 768 noninterlaced	16	Yes
Other 8514/A (1024K)	1024 × 768 noninterlaced	256	Yes
XGA	1024 × 768 interlaced	256	with driver
TIGA (512K)	1024 × 768 noninterlaced	16	with driver
TIGA (1024K)	1024 × 768 noninterlaced	256	with driver

Figure 14-1: A sampling of video standards. This is a list of the most common video boards and modes available for PCs.

people notice after a minute or two (except on specially prepared monitors). Vendors other than IBM (such as Paradise and ATI) manufacture 8514/A-compatible boards that can be switched to display a noninterlaced image. Monitors capable of displaying noninterlaced 1024 × 768 resolution include the Mitsubishi Diamond Scan and the NEC 4D. Interlaced displays should only be used in environments where people look at the screen intermittently — as in airline terminals, where a quick glance finds the time of a departing flight. In a workplace, where people look at the display for several minutes at a time, use only noninterlaced video.

Differences Between Windows and Mac Video

Although the Macintosh has a reputation for desktop publishing uses, Windows actually has an advantage over the Mac in displaying text on the screen. Windows screen fonts are easier to read on-screen, and this is particularly apparent at smaller point sizes.

Most businesses require that certain legal text, footnotes, headers and footers, indexes, and other matter be typed in sizes as small as 8 points. In some spreadsheets, entire business models must be formatted using 8-point type in order to fit the necessary information into a single page.

A comparison of type of the same point size in Windows and on the Mac is shown in Figure 14-2. The Windows screen font allows a height of six pixels to define each letter in words such as "screen," where each letter is the same height. The Macintosh allows only three pixels to define each letter. Small type in Windows on a 640×480 VGA display is tiny but clearly readable. Macintosh type of the same size on a 640×480 display is nearly illegible. This makes it difficult to type or proofread legal matter and spreadsheets in small type on a Mac.

One company in the financial services industry, which performed an extensive side-by-side comparison of Windows and Macintoshes, found that this difference alone was one of the most significant reasons to choose Windows for all their new PC installations. (Another was that a Super VGA system with an Intel 386/33 processor was priced $2,000 less than a Macintosh with comparable performance.)

The reason that type looks different on Windows is because Windows (on a VGA or Super VGA display) uses 96 dots on the screen to represent text that will be one-inch wide on your printout. The Macintosh uses 72 dots on the screen to represent this same printed inch. This correspondence between screen pixels and the width of objects on your printouts is sometimes called a *logical inch.*

All WYSIWYG systems (what-you-see-is-what-you-get) try to match the appearance of your screen to the eventual look of the material you get from your printer. Windows has enough dots within its logical inch on-screen to make fairly fully formed fonts, even in small point sizes. The Macintosh, with fewer screen pixels to represent the same printed area, must reduce the detail in its screen fonts. This cannot be overcome without investing in far more expensive video boards and displays than are usually purchased with Macintosh systems.

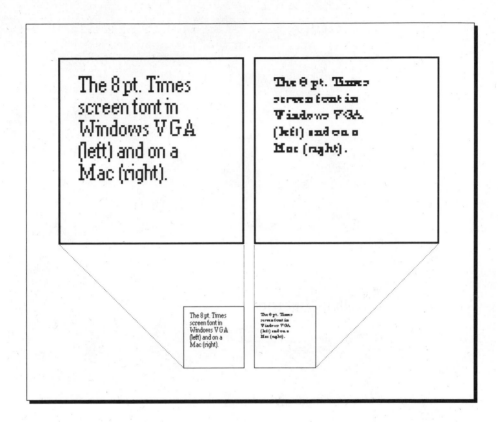

Figure 14-2: Type comparison of a Windows VGA screen (left) and a Macintosh screen (right).
Small type on a Windows VGA screen is more readable than the same size on a Macintosh, because Windows uses a larger screen area; both boxes are 100 pixels square.

The screen shots comparing Windows and Macintosh type were taken directly from the screen of comparably equipped computers with 640×480 displays. The boxed areas enclose squares that are 100 pixels on each side. The enlarged boxes are blown up to three times the original size. In these screen shots, one pixel is the size of the dot over the letter "i" or the period at the end of the sentence.

Using Super VGA vs. Plain VGA

One disadvantage of this use of more pixels per inch is that Windows displays a smaller portion of your documents than a Macintosh can. On an ordinary VGA display, a word processor such as Word for Windows can

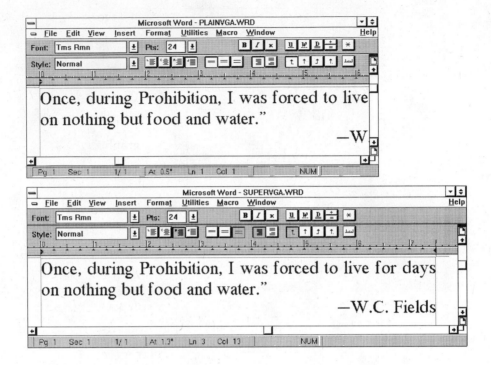

Figure 14-3: VGA vs. Super VGA displays.

only show 6 inches of text on each horizontal line — even though most people's letters are 8.5 inches wide. This is shown in Figure 14-3. When working on documents more than 6 inches wide, typists using Windows on a VGA display must scroll left and right as they type, in order to see the entire width of each paragraph. Super VGA displays, by comparison, allow Word for Windows to show a full 8 inches width on each line. This eliminates the need for back-and-forth scrolling.

One of the most popular graphics resolutions today, therefore, is the Super VGA standard (800×600), recently codified by the Video Electronics Standards Association, an industry-wide group of adapter board and monitor manufacturers. This standard is widely supported because most of the "multiscanning" monitors that computer users purchased over the past several years, starting with the NEC Multisync, are inherently capable of 800×600 displays.

IBM's VGA boards (640×480) do not take advantage of the 800×600 capabilities of multiscanning monitors — which now include the NEC 3D, Mitsubishi Diamond Scan, Sony Multiscan, and many others. But it costs very little to make a VGA-compatible board that is also capable of driving a monitor at 800×600 resolution. For this reason, most VGA adapter boards sold today by companies other than IBM and Compaq have circuitry for displaying Super VGA as well as ordinary VGA resolution.

Many boards provide additional, proprietary graphics resolutions besides those shown in the table. Many "enhanced" EGA and VGA boards, for example, provide resolutions of 640×480 with 256 colors or 1024×768 with 16 colors. When these boards venture above a resolution of 800×600, though, they almost always use interlacing to achieve the appearance of high resolution, complete with flickering. And there is no standard for these proprietary resolutions. If the vendor provides a driver for Windows 3.0, then all Windows applications can use that vendor's specific graphics resolutions. But most software-driver development for Windows will continue to be within those graphics standards indicated in the table. (Note: High resolution adapters combined with poorly optimized drivers will have a significant impact on speed.)

The following sections of this chapter include information on the most common video standards used with Windows — VGA, EGA, CGA, and 8514/A — and information about specific brands of video graphics adapters and monitors.

VGA

Troubleshooting Video Problems

A wide variety of VGA graphic adapter boards exists. Enhancements to the boards of various manufacturers may result in desirable features or performance, but can also lead to erratic or frozen displays under Windows. You may have encountered one of these problems if you experience the following symptoms:

1. While installing Windows, the Setup program freezes during Disk #2, at the point when Setup would normally switch to a graphics display to complete the remainder of the installation.

2. After installing Windows, you cannot start Windows in standard or 386 enhanced modes.

3. After starting Windows, the display is full of snow or the colors are wrong, even though they are set correctly in the Control Panel.

4. DOS applications started under Windows abort, or Windows terminates them with the message "This application has violated system integrity" (which means that the DOS application attempted to write to an area of memory that belongs to some other application or function).

If this is the case, and nothing else, such as a memory-resident program, is at fault, the video adapter may be the culprit.

One of the most common sources of conflict between Windows and video adapters is the memory space that these adapters claim. As we have seen previously, video adapters may have 512K, 1MB, or more of video memory. This video memory is in addition to, and separate from, the 640K of conventional memory that all PCs are capable of supporting. It is also separate from a PC's expanded memory and extended memory. Video memory must be provided with its own address space. This address space begins exactly where the 640K of conventional RAM ends. Examine Figure 14-4, "A 386 PC with 1MB of RAM."

The table shows that, of the 1MB of RAM, the first 640K is located at the memory addresses between 0 and 640K and becomes what is known as *conventional memory*. The remaining 384K of RAM does not continue upward at the 640K line. Instead, it "jumps" to the address at 1024K. This 384K is located at the memory addresses between 1024 and 1408K and becomes what is known as *extended memory*.

The addresses between 640 and 1024K are reserved for use by hardware add-ins — video adapter boards, network adapter boards, ROM BIOS chips, and so on. This area of memory is called the *Adapter Segment Memory* because of this use of these addresses by adapter boards and other devices. The Adapter Segment is also known as high memory, upper memory, and upper-memory blocks. These terms are confusing, because Microsoft also calls the first 64K of extended memory the *High Memory Area* (HMA), which is used by Microsoft's HIMEM.SYS driver. So we'll refer to the 384K area between 640 and 1024K only as the "Adapter Segment" to keep the distinction clear.

	Decimal Address	Hex Address
	1408K	16000
384K of Extended Memory		
	1024K	10000
ROM BIOS Chip	960K	F000
PS/2 Additional ROM BIOS Chip	P896K	E000
64K EMS Page Frame	832K	D000
VGA ROM BIOS Chip	768K	C000
Hercules, CGA, & Text-Mode RAM	704K	B000
VGA & EGA Graphics RAM	640K	A000
	320K	5000
640K of Conventional Memory		
	0K	0000

Figure 14-4: A 386 PC with 1MB of RAM. Different video boards occupy different areas of memory in the A000, B000, and C000 ranges.

There are six 64K blocks of memory within the Adapter Segment. Although there are many exceptions, each of the six blocks is typically used by a certain type of adapter or device. It is in the Adapter Segment that VGA boards most often conflict with Windows' use of memory, so it's important to know how this memory is being used.

The six blocks of memory are usually refered to by their first memory address, in hexadecimal numbering. The 64K at the 640K line is known as "A000" (pronouced *A thousand*), the second 64K is known as "B000," and so on.

These blocks often are allocated in the following way to different devices:

A000: VGA and EGA graphics adapter RAM chips. VGA and EGA adapters "swap" parts of their video memory in and out of this 64K area continuously.

B000: Hercules monochrome graphics RAM takes the first 32K of this area; the second 32K is occupied by CGA graphics RAM, or EGA or VGA text-mode RAM (this is why two color adapters cannot coexist in the same PC — they both would claim this same area).

C000: VGA adapters place their ROM BIOS chips here; some BIOSs take as little as 24K of this area, while others occupy 32K of it.

D000: A 64K "Page Frame" is often placed in this block of memory, in order to provide EMS (Expanded Memory Specification) access to DOS applications. The total available expanded memory is "paged" in and out of this area continuously. (Within certain restrictions, the Page Frame may be located in any 64K block of the Adapter Segment that is not in use.)

E000: IBM PS/2s place an extra ROM BIOS chip here, in addition to the normal ROM BIOS found in almost all other PCs at F000.

F000: The ROM BIOS chip located here is depended upon by most DOS applications to provide basic routines to support disk I/O and other functions.

Problems with VGA boards usually arise because they occupy a block of memory that Windows cannot detect. When Windows starts, it examines all the memory locations in the Adapter Segment, looking for holes that it can fill with memory for running Windows applications. Windows avoids memory locations that appear to be occupied by a device. But if Windows claims a memory location that looks free, and that location is later required by a device that previously was dormant (such as a video card exercising a new function), the conflict will eventually cause the screen to fill with garbage or freeze entirely.

If you experience a video-related problem, take the following steps:

STEPS:

Fixing Video-Related Problems

Step 1. Before starting Windows, make a backup copy of the SYSTEM.INI file, then open SYSTEM.INI with a plain text editor and look for the section headed [386Enh]. Add a line that says the following:

```
[386Enh]
EMMExclude=A000-CFFF
```

The line excludes Windows' use of any memory areas in the first three 64K blocks of the adapter segment (blocks A, B, and C). In hexadecimal numbering, memory location "CFFF" is one less than "D000."

This line eliminates memory-use conflicts between Windows and almost all VGA cards. Save SYSTEM.INI and start Windows. If the video problem disappears in 386 enhanced mode, then a memory-address conflict probably was causing the problem.

If Windows is now operating normally, pull down the Program Manager's Help menu, and click About Program Manager. This displays a dialog box showing the amount of RAM available to Windows. This amount may change when the specific area of the memory conflict has been identified and a smaller amount of memory has been excluded from Windows' use in the SYSTEM.INI file.

Open SYSTEM.INI with Notepad and change the EMMExclude line to read:

```
[386Enh]
EMMExclude=C000-CFFF
```

Save SYSTEM.INI, then exit and restart Windows. If it continues to operate normally, edit SYSTEM.INI again to the following:

```
[386Enh]
EMMExclude=C000-C7FF
```

If Windows works well with this setting, you can continue to reduce the amount of memory that is excluded from Windows. If not, you must increase the amount that is excluded. To *reduce* the amount, change the "7" in the last EMMExclude line above to

6, then to 5, 4, or 3. To *increase* it, change to 8, then 9, A, B, C, D, or E. Few VGA adapter boards require that this line be set lower than C7FF or higher than CBFF.

Step 2. If Step 1 did not fix the problem (or you are not running Windows in 386 enhanced mode), check the VGA board's manual to see if it automatically switches modes (this is usually called an "auto-switch" or "auto-emulation"). Windows does not work well when video boards change modes without being instructed to do so. Disable the auto-switch feature, if possible, and start Windows again.

Step 3. If you still have a problem, run Setup from a DOS prompt in the Windows subdirectory and change the selection for the Display. If it is already set for "VGA," change it to "QuadVGA, ATI VIP VGA, and 82C441 VGAs." Boards based on an 82C441 or similar chip work better with this driver than with the plain VGA driver. If you are already using the "Quad VGA" driver, change it to "VGA." Alternatively, if the VGA board maker provides a driver that is Windows 3.0-compatible, change to this driver. Or, if you are already using a special driver, change back to "VGA" or "Quad VGA." Save the setup and restart Windows.

Step 4. If this fails, copy CONFIG.SYS and AUTOEXEC.BAT to backup names, then remove all programs from these files and restart your PC with this "vanilla" configuration. Preserve any hard-disk drivers or other programs that are essential, but remove everything else. Your plain vanilla CONFIG.SYS and AUTOEXEC.BAT files should look like the following:

In CONFIG.SYS:
```
files=30
buffers=20
device=c:\windows\himem.sys
etc.
```

In AUTOEXEC.BAT:
```
prompt $p$g
path c:\;c:\windows;c:\dos
etc.
```

Step 5. If all these steps fail to correct the video problem, it may be necessary to replace the ROM BIOS chip on the video board itself. Contact the manufacturer to see if an upgrade chip is required.

If the Bottom of Your VGA Display Is Missing

If you installed Windows for a VGA display, but the bottom one-sixth of your display is missing or seems to be "off the bottom" of your monitor, you may be using a VGA driver with an AT&T display adapter. Many of these video adapters display only 640×400, not 640×480 (like true VGA displays), and must use Windows' AT&T video driver. Several laptops, such as the NEC ProSpeed 386, also run at 640×400 resolution.

Monochrome VGA

May Require "VGA" Instead of "Mono" Setup

All VGA-compatible boards are capable of displaying both color and monochrome images. If a VGA board sending a VGA signal is connected to a color analog monitor, it will display color. If connected to a monochrome analog monitor, it will display only two colors (the image and a background color, usually black).

If you are using a VGA adapter with a monitor that can display only monochrome images (most VGA-capable laptop computers fall into this category) and you are having problems with the display, run Setup from the DOS prompt in the Windows subdirectory. If the selection for the Display is "VGA with Monochrome Display," change it to the ordinary "VGA" driver. If the selection is already "VGA," change it to "VGA with Monochrome Display."

Some VGA boards have difficulty switching into specific monochrome modes of VGA, but display color VGA on monochrome screens just fine. If this is the case, changing the display driver may fix your problem. After this change, it may be necessary to remedy some of the Control Panel's colors to make the monochrome screen as readable as possible.

Super VGA

Supporting 386 Mode and More Than 16 Colors

Super VGA boards that have difficulty running Windows in 386 enhanced mode should respond to the same troubleshooting techniques described above for VGA adapters. Specifically, these lines in the [386Enh] section of

SYSTEM.INI should prevent any conflict between most Super VGA boards and Windows for the same memory addresses:

```
[386Enh]
EMMExclude=C400-C7FF
```

If this does not fix the problem, change "C7FF" to "CBFF." Once the problem goes away, reduce the area that is excluded, as described in the VGA discussion.

Video graphics boards that should be detected properly by Windows upon start-up include those from IBM, Paradise, Video Seven, and many others. If problems occur with one of these boards, the cause may be a memory-resident program that does not work under Windows' 386 enhanced mode, rather than the graphics board itself.

Many Super VGA boards include the capability to display 256 colors under Windows (at various resolutions). These boards always come with a special driver that is Windows 3.0-compatible. If you have a 256-color driver installed, but are having trouble displaying images with that many colors, the Windows application you are trying to use may be the cause. Windows programs are designed to support only a certain number of colors. Microsoft PowerPoint can recognize over 16 million colors (24-bit color), but Windows Paintbrush can only recognize 256 colors (8-bit color). Other programs have their own limitations. In addition, remember that if a 256-color image is loaded into Paintbrush while a 16-color driver is in control, and that image is saved by Paintbrush, the image will be reduced to only those 16 colors that the driver knows about.

8514/A and VGA

Requires Excluding Memory for Pass-Through VGA

The 8514/A adapter was introduced by IBM in 1987 and has been duplicated by several manaufacturers since that time. Register-compatible clones of the 8514/A are commonly available from such companies as Western Digital (Paradise) and ATI.

Most 8514/A video boards connect to a separate VGA board in your computer through a connection called a *pass-through cable*. This cable allows a monitor to be attached to an 8514/A board, but display signals from either the 8514/A or the VGA. The 8514/A displays graphics at 1024×768, while the VGA displays graphics at 640×480 as well as text modes. Some 8514/A compatibles include a VGA adapter as a "daughter board" that attaches directly to the 8514/A board.

In either case, if you have installed Windows for an 8514/A display you may need to specifically exclude areas of Adapter Segment memory used by the VGA board, because when installed for an 8514/A adapter, Windows does not automatically detect the memory used by all VGA boards. This requires a statement like EMMEXCLUDE=C400-C7FF in the [386Enh] section of your SYSTEM.INI file, as discussed earlier in the section "Troubleshooting VGA."

Additionally, if you have an 8514/A adapter connected to an older VGA, and you have problems switching between two different full-screen DOS sessions under Windows, you might need to upgrade the digital-to-analog converter (DAC) on the VGA board. This problem might manifest itself by displaying only a blank screen when you switch from one DOS session to another.

 If you are at a DOS prompt when this occurs, you might be able to refresh the screen and continue working by issuing the command MODE CO80. This switches DOS into an 80-column color mode (even if it was already in that mode) and may repaint the screen.

Dual VGA Monitors

Running Windows at 1600 × 600, Side by Side

In case Super VGA or 8514/A resolution don't provide enough screen real estate for you, the Colorgraphics Communications Corp. makes a Dual VGA Plus card that displays up to 800×600 on each of two or more side-by-side monitors. The company provides a driver for Windows that allows a full 1600×600 screen area, doubling the workspace that Windows can use. Open applications can be moved from one monitor to the other for more convenient viewing.

I haven't tested this adapter, but if you need such a capability (perhaps for stock trading, where several monitors are commonly assigned to each broker), the company provides models for both the AT and the MCA bus. Contact Colorgraphic at 404-455-3921.

EGA

Difficulties in Changing to an EGA Configuration

If you installed Windows for a screen resolution other than EGA, and then reconfigured it in the Setup program for an EGA adapter, the Windows Setup may not copy the EGA.SYS driver and add it to your CONFIG.SYS. In this case, exit Windows, change to your Windows directory, and run the Setup program from the DOS prompt. Change the video mode to some mode other than EGA (perhaps a mode that you previously installed) and exit. Then run Setup and change the video mode to EGA. This should result in the EGA.SYS driver being copied to your hard disk and installed properly in your CONFIG.SYS. This driver is necessary for some EGA mode-switches.

Driver Must Be Loaded After MOUSE.SYS

Loading the MOUSE.SYS 7.04 driver that is provided with Windows 3.0 in your CONFIG.SYS *prior to* loading the EGA.SYS driver (version 2.10.18) results in the message, "Warning! Overwriting an old copy of the EGA Device Driver." Change the order of these two drivers in your CONFIG.SYS so the mouse driver loads *after* the EGA.SYS driver.

CGA

Forcing a VGA Adapter to Display CGA

Windows will run on a CGA display, although Microsoft often discourages it. Since the CGA color graphics mode (320×200 resolution) is too coarse to display menus and dialog boxes, when Windows is installed for CGA it forces the CGA adapter into a monochrome mode in which the resolution is doubled to 640×200. This is still very coarse.

One of the few good reasons to install Windows with a CGA display is if you have a VGA adapter that does not support Windows 3.0. If the VGA board is downwardly compatible with EGA and CGA, but Windows does not work with the board in VGA or EGA modes, the CGA driver may work as a last resort to use Windows on that system. Another reason to run the CGA driver on a VGA system is to test software that may be used later by people with CGA only.

Forcing an unsupported VGA adapter to display Windows by installing the CGA driver, however, results in problems starting DOS applications under Windows. On a 386 system running Windows in enhanced mode, the error message "386 Display Type Mismatch" may be displayed. In real mode and standard mode, the DOS application may run fine until you switch away from the DOS program and then back to it.

This is caused by installing Windows for CGA before installing several VGA support files that Windows needs in order to display text on a VGA system. Although Windows is set up to display CGA graphics, a text-based DOS application is displaying a text mode that is being processed on VGA hardware.

The solution is to install Windows for VGA first, then run Setup again and change the Display selection from "VGA" to "CGA." When you install Windows for VGA graphics, the Setup program copies several virtual device drivers to your hard disk, where they are available to the other Windows programs.

When you run the first installation and Windows attempts to start up in graphics mode on an unsupported VGA, of course, it will scramble the display or freeze the system. This is to be expected. Reboot the system, change to the directory containing Windows, run Setup from the DOS prompt, and change the Display selection to "CGA."

Once this is completed, start Windows (it should display in CGA mode). The following changes should improve compatibility with DOS text display, especially in enhanced mode. Open the SYSTEM.INI file with Notepad. Change one line in the [boot] section, as follows:

Before:

[boot]
386grabber=cga.gr3

After:

[boot]
386grabber=vga.gr3

Change a line in the [386Enh] section as follows, and save SYSTEM.INI.

Before:

[386Enh]
display=vddcga.386

After:

[386Enh]
display=*vddvga

These changes allow Windows to handle text mode on a VGA adapter, even though Windows is in CGA mode. A "grabber" is a program that displays DOS text under Windows. Restart Windows to make these changes take effect.

Using Self-Configuring Adapters

If your display adapter has the capability to switch modes automatically, you may need to turn off this capability in order to install or run Windows in 386 mode. This feature is often called "auto-switch" or "auto-configure," and may be triggered when the board detects a change from EGA to VGA software, and so on.

These boards use a hardware interrupt called a *nonmaskable interrupt*. Windows cannot handle the changes the board makes to its video mode in this way.

Improving Your Video Performance

The performance of your video adapter is one of the biggest factors in the overall perceived performance of Windows. Unfortunately, if your video adapter is installed correctly, there is little you can do to speed it up, other than replacing it with a faster adapter.

Since new video adapters are released every month, I haven't attempted to rate the performance of different brand-name video boards here. The latest and fastest boards are constantly superceded by newer, zippier boards, and any ranking immediately becomes obsolete.

Instead, there are a few general rules that you can follow to try to optimize your video board's performance in your particular system:

RULES:

Optimizing Your Video Board's Performance

Rule 1. Try your video board's 16-color mode if you are using a 256-color mode, or even a monochrome mode if you are using color. The extra information present in a display with more colors may not be worth it if you do not use these colors and need the fastest possible performance from Windows.

Surprisingly, the same often does not hold true for lowering the *resolution* (as opposed to lowering the number of colors) of most video boards. Using Windows' plain VGA driver, instead of your board's own Super VGA (800 × 600) driver, may not result in a noticeable improvement in performance. This is because most video board manufacturers concentrate on improving the performance of their products at their highest resolution, since that is what computer magazines usually test.

And I've found that the 1024×768 boards that I've tested performed faster than boards operating at 640×480 resolution — even though the higher-resolution boards have to update 250 percent as many pixels as the VGA boards. This is because 8514/A manufacturers invest more in performance improvements to justify the higher cost of their products.

Rule 2. Use the latest version of your board's software driver for Windows. Upgrading the software may make a bigger difference in your board's video performance than replacing the hardware. Video board manufacturers are constantly revising their software drivers for better performance. But these revisions often are not widely publicized to buyers of the company's boards (due to the hassle and expense of taking orders from customers, although I think this is a poor way for companies to try to save money). In many cases, the only way to find out about the latest revision is through a computer bulletin board system, onto which companies copy the new version and allow owners to download it themselves. (There is no question of copy protection, since the software won't work at all without the proper video board.)

Rule 3. Make sure your video board is operating in 16-bit mode, if it can be switched from 8-bit to 16-bit operation. You should first check to see whether configuration settings are implemented properly, to allow the board to operate in 16-bit mode. You should then check whether any devices in your system might be forcing your video board to slow down to 8-bit transfers. PCs do not allow devices using 8-bit and 16-bit transfers to coexist within 128K regions of the Adapter Segment memory. If one 8-bit device exists within a 128K region, the PC forces the other devices in that region to use 8-bit transfers as well. This affects the regions addressed as A000-BFFF, C000-DFFF, and E000-FFFF.

The most critical area is C000 to DFFF, because this is where most VGA boards place their ROM BIOS chip. This 128K region is a common address for network adapter boards, which often are limited to 8-bit transfers. Monochrome boards, located between A000 and BFFF, can also slow down VGA boards.

If you find a board that may be forcing your video board into 8-bit mode, try to move the 8-bit device into a memory address at E000 or above. Make sure this does not interfere with other devices or with an expanded memory page frame, which may be situated at E000 to EFFF.

Rule 4. Test your video adapter's performance with your own suite of applications, not a set of synthetic video benchmarks. Windows' performance is only meaningful to you in terms of the speed with which you can use your applications. Unfortunately, specialized video benchmark tests may not be good indicators of the performance you will experience in applications.

Video benchmarks are often designed to measure low-level hardware commands, such as transfering bits from one memory location to another or drawing 1,000 lines. CAD applications such as AutoCAD may make use of these functions, but Windows applications do not. In testing several video boards, I found that their scores on bit-block transfer tests and the like had no relationship to their performance in Word for Windows, Excel, Paintbrush, and other Windows applications.

Instead, run a consistent suite of your own applications on different video boards, or on a single video board after trying some of the configuration changes described in the previous points in this section. Load your largest word-processing document, your largest spreadsheet, and your largest graphic. Time each trial carefully, and reboot your PC between tests. You'll gain more practical data than you will by using artificial, circuit-level benchmarks.

Screen Fonts

Changing Your Screen Fonts

Windows supports two different kinds of fonts: printer fonts and screen fonts. Printer fonts are described in Chapter 13. Screen fonts are divided further into three types: typographic fonts, system fonts, and windowed DOS fonts.

The differences between these types of screen fonts, and how to change their size to suit your needs, is described in the following topics. Before proceeding with these topics, you will need to copy the EXPAND.EXE program from Disk #2 of your Windows distribution diskettes into your Windows directory. Once there, it can be used to expand any Microsoft files you may need.

Changing the Size of Typographic Fonts

Typographic fonts are controlled by the [fonts] section of your WIN.INI file. These fonts, including Tms Rmn and Helv, are used by applications that support proportional type. If you have a VGA display, your [fonts] section probably looks like this:

```
[fonts]
Helv 8,10,12,14,18,24 (VGA res)=HELVE.FON
Tms Rmn 8,10,12,14,18,24 (VGA res)=TMSRE.FON
Courier 10,12,15 (VGA res)=COURE.FON
Symbol 8,10,12,14,18,24 (VGA res)=SYMBOLE.FON
```

You probably don't need to change these fonts, since your applications expect them to be a certain size for your display. If you installed a VGA board with an "extended" resolution of 1024×768, however, Windows may not have installed the 1024×768 typographical fonts if your board is not compatible with IBM's 8514/A adapter. In that case, you would benefit from switching these fonts to the 8514/A resolution fonts, which have the same name as the VGA font files but end with the letter F instead of E.

Find the Windows diskette that contains these files. Then, change to your C:\WINDOWS\SYSTEM directory and issue the following commands from a DOS prompt:

```
EXPAND  a:\HELVF.FON
EXPAND  a:\TMSRF.FON
EXPAND  a:\COURF.FON
EXPAND  a:\SYMBOLF.FON
```

This decompresses and copies these files to your System directory. Now open your WIN.INI file in Notepad or your favorite text editor. Immediately click File Save As and name the file WIN.VGA to make it easy to switch back if you don't like the new fonts. Then change your [fonts] section to refer to HELVF.FON instead of HELVE.FON, and so on. Restart Windows to make the change take effect.

Changing the Size of System Fonts

System fonts come in three flavors: fixed fonts for displaying fixed-pitch characters in applications such as Notepad that cannot handle proportional fonts; OEM fonts, for displaying fixed-pitch characters in the IBM PC-8 character set (explained in Chapter 9); and the System font, for displaying Windows menus. The System font should not be confused with the font Windows uses to display text in dialog boxes — Windows uses the first sans-serif font it finds in the typographic [fonts] list in WIN.INI to display dialog boxes (this is usually Helv).

System fonts are controlled by the [boot] section in your SYSTEM.INI file. It is useful to change the size of these fonts if you would like to display more lines in windows of text editors. If you have good eyes, and you would like the type to be smaller so you can get more lines on the screen, you can change from VGA system fonts to EGA. If you would like the text to be larger, you can change from VGA to 8514/A fonts.

If you installed Windows for a VGA system, your [boot] section of SYSTEM.INI probably looks like this:

```
[boot]
fixedfon.fon=vgafix.fon
oemfonts.fon=vgaoem.fon
fonts.fon=vgasys.fon
```

These lines represent your fixed-pitch font, your IBM PC-8 font, and your System menu font. The fonts for EGA resolution are named EGAFIX.FON, EGAOEM.FON, and EGASYS.FON. The same fonts for 8514/A resolution are named 8514FIX.FON, 8514OEM.FON, and 8514SYS.FON. You will also find similarly named fonts for CGA resolution, but these are "squashed-looking" when used on a VGA display.

Change to your C:\WINDOWS\SYSTEM directory and expand these font files from your Windows distribution diskettes. Then, open your SYSTEM.INI file with Notepad or a text editor, save a copy as SYSTEM.VGA to make it easy to go back, and change filenames such as VGAFIX.FON to EGAFIX.FON (if that's the new size you want). Restart Windows to make your changes take effect.

Changing the Size of Windowed DOS Fonts

Windowed DOS fonts are for displaying character-mode DOS applications when you run them in a small window in 386 enhanced mode.

When you install Windows for an 8514/A display, Windows copies a font file for windowed DOS applications that is appropriate for EGA or VGA displays. This may make DOS windows look too small to read comfortably on a large 8514/A display. You can read your windowed DOS apps more easily if you change this font to one more suitable for the 8514/A resolution.

The fonts used by Windows to display DOS applications in windows are controlled by the following lines in the [386Enh] section of your SYSTEM.INI file:

```
[386Enh]
EGA80WOA.FON=EGA80WOA.FON
EGA40WOA.FON=EGA40WOA.FON
CGA80WOA.FON=CGA80WOA.FON
CGA40WOA.FON=CGA40WOA.FON
```

These four files are used when an application is in an EGA/VGA text mode displaying 80 or 40 columns, or a CGA text mode with 80 or 40 columns. The acronym "WOA" stands for Windows Old Application, Microsoft's term for DOS applications.

To enlarge the display of characters in a windowed DOS app, you must change to your C:\WINDOWS\SYSTEM directory and expand the file 8514FIX.FON from one of the Windows distribution diskettes (as discussed in the previous topic on System fonts). This decompresses this file and copies it to your System directory.

After doing this, open SYSTEM.INI with Notepad or a text editor and immediately save it to a new name like SYSTEM.VGA to make it easy to go back. Then change the line in SYSTEM.INI that says EGA80WOA.FON=EGA80WOA.FON to say EGA80WOA.FON=8514FIX.FON. Save the file and restart Windows to make your change take effect.

Correcting Erroneous Font Displays

If a Windows application displays a different typeface than the one you just selected, there may be a problem in the [Fonts] section of your WIN.INI file. This could occur when screen fonts are added with installer programs such as Bitstream's or Hewlett-Packard's.

Windows applications look through the WIN.INI file to load fonts from filenames listed there. The first file that matches the requested typeface is used to display the font on the screen. If two typeface files have similar characteristics, the application may display the incorrect font since the next font on the list was never encountered.

The Symbol and Zapf Dingbats typefaces, for example, are both considered members of the "symbol" family of typefaces since they are neither "serif" nor "sans-serif" typefaces. (If you request to display or print a typeface that is unavailable, Windows tries to display or print another face in the same "family" of typefaces.) If the [Fonts] section of your WIN.INI contains both Symbol and Zapf Dingbats, try changing the order of these faces, as shown here:

Before:

```
[Fonts]
Symbol 8, 10, 12, 14, 18, 24 (VGA res)=symbole.fon
ITCZapfDingbats 8, 10, 12, 14, 18, 24 (VGA res)=zd24e.fon
```

After:

```
[Fonts]
ITCZapfDingbats 8, 10, 12, 14, 18, 24 (VGA res)=zd24e.fon
Symbol 8, 10, 12, 14, 18, 24 (VGA res)=symbole.fon
```

For similar reasons, if you attempt to print a document with Times Roman text to a laser printer that does not have a Times Roman font, but you installed Symbol fonts for laser printers when you ran Windows Setup, the Times Roman text might print in the Symbol font because it matches the size you requested or has other features that are similar to the formatted text.

Plasma Displays

Changing the Color Scheme to Display Help Text

Plasma displays are usually used on laptops and portables. They display a monochrome image, using a bright red-orange color against a black background.

Windows' Help displays may be difficult to read on a plasma display because some of the Help text is in the color green. If this is the case, run the Control Panel and select Colors. Choose "Flourescent" in the Color Scheme dialog box. Click the Color Palette button. Choose "Window Background" in the Screen Elements dialog box. Click once on the color that is 4th from the left and 6th from the top in the Basic Colors area. Choose "Title Bar Text" and select the same color.

If this color arrangement is easier to read, save it by clicking the Save Scheme button. (This button was greyed-out until you chose Color Palette in the steps above.) Enter a name for the scheme in the resulting dialog box, such as "Plasma." Click OK and exit the Control Panel. Test the Windows Help function to see if the new colors are an improvement.

Video Anomalies

The remainder of this chapter describes particular configuration settings for a variety of specific video adapters.

AST

Windows cannot detect some memory that is used by the AST VGA Plus board. You must insert the line EMMEXCLUDE=C000-C500 into the [386Enh] section of your SYSTEM.INI file to work with this board.

Additionally, if you use the AST 3G Plus II EGA board, you must turn off its auto-switching feature (the AST manual refers to it as "auto-emulation") by turning switches 5 and 6 *off.* You must make sure the board has a BIOS version of 3.0 or later, and on earlier versions of the board with an emulation switch on the back, you must turn the emulation switch to its *off* position.

ATI

The ATI VIP and EGA Wonder boards require that you turn *off* switch 8 to disable these boards' auto-switching features to work with Windows. This also disables some 132-column text modes and other features of these boards, as described in their manuals.

Everex

Everex's EV-673 EGA/VGA video board requires a separate file named VDD673.386 to work under Windows' 386 enhanced mode. You can obtain this file by contacting Everex at 415-498-1115 or dialing their bulletin board with your modem at 415-438-4650. The correct version is dated 8/8/90; do not use older versions.

Copy this file to your C:\WINDOWS\SYSTEM directory. Then change the line in the [386Enh] section of your SYSTEM.INI file that says DISPLAY=*VDDVGA to say DISPLAY=VDD673.386. When you restart Windows, Everex's virtual display driver loads instead of the internal one that Windows previously used.

Quadram

The EGA Prosync video board from Quadram will not work under Windows when the device driver EGA.SYS is loaded in your CONFIG.SYS file. It is necessary to remove this line to use the EGA Prosync. Otherwise, you may experience garbage when you move your mouse or switch between Windows and a DOS application.

Sigma

The Windows Setup program hangs your computer when it switches to video mode during the installation of Disk #2 if a Sigma VGA/H card is present. Other symptoms include your system hanging when HIMEM.SYS is loaded. Sigma recommends that you upgrade to their Legend board, which supports Windows even when its auto-emulation and RAM shadowing features are enabled.

Additionally, you may need to replace the SETUP.INF file on the Windows distribution diskettes with a file by the same name provided by Sigma if you are installing Windows on a system with a Sigma monitor and video subsystem. Contact Sigma at 415-770-0111 for more information.

Video Seven

Requires /Y Switch in MOUSE.SYS

The Windows Setup program automatically adds a /Y switch to the end of the MOUSE.SYS command in CONFIG.SYS when installing for the Microsoft Mouse. This enables Windows to properly handle Video Seven-type graphics cards. If this switch is removed from MOUSE.SYS, these cards display a graphically based cursor in DOS text-based applications, called a "sprite." The /Y switch forces these applications to display the position of the mouse cursor as a rectangular block (a legal text-mode character). This avoids problems when Windows is starting text-mode DOS programs.

For more information, see "Undocumented /Y Switch in MOUSE.SYS" in Chapter 10.

BIOS Revisions Required for Video Seven Boards

The following is a list of BIOS versions that Headland Technology, the manufacturer of Video Seven boards, supports for the use of Windows:

FastWrite	1.1 or 1.18
Vega	1.47, 1.48, or 1.78
VRAM	1.1 or 1.18

Contact Headland Technology at 800-248-1850 in the U.S. and Canada, 800-553-1850 in California, or 415-656-7800 for more information.

Summary

This chapter describes many of the troubleshooting steps required to configure video boards for Windows in all modes. The topics covered include:

▶ The difference between the way Windows and the Macintosh form a correspondence from screen fonts to actual printouts.

▶ Configuration secrets of VGA, Super VGA, 8514/A, EGA, and CGA displays.

▶ Ways to improve the performance of your video board.

▶ How Windows determines which screen fonts to use, and how you can change the size of these fonts to suit your own display preferences.

▶ Anomalies that require configuration steps for a variety of video boards from different manufacturers.

SECTION

C

CONFIGURING YOUR SYSTEM

Chapter 15
Installing and
Configuring Windows

In this chapter. . .

I cover the following topics:

▶ How you can get better results from Windows by setting up your PC in certain ways *before* installing Windows.

▶ The ideal configuration to install Windows and avoid potential installation problems.

▶ Issues you should be aware of when running Windows' Setup installation program.

▶ Completing the installation after Setup has finished copying files to your hard disk.

▶ Permanently establishing the best configuration for your PC under Windows, or switching between a Windows configuration and an alternate configuration.

This chapter is devoted to information on setting up your computer and installing Windows. This chapter is not for beginners only — experts, too, should read this chapter for several secrets regarding the Windows setup procedure. But this chapter is where beginners and those who haven't yet installed Windows should definitely begin this book. I include step-by-step information on how to prepare your PC for Windows, and how to set up Windows in the best way for your system.

Additionally, if Windows represents your first exposure to a PC, I have included a sidebar in this chapter on "The Least You Need to Know About DOS."

Avoiding Installation Problems

Your computer system may be configured in a way that can halt Windows' installation process or interfere with its files being copied accurately to your hard disk. Windows' SETUP.EXE program is even more sensitive to variations

The Least You Need to Know About DOS

If you are a DOS beginner, or are starting to use Windows after working on another graphical environment, like a Macintosh or Sun, this section is for you.

Windows does not "protect" you from the way that DOS stores information on your disk drives — you can see exactly where everything is stored on your drives and organize it as you like. It's sometimes said that DOS is hard to learn, but if you know a few terms, you can use the Windows File Manager (or a similar program) to do everything you need.

1. **Disk drives.** Most PCs have two or more disk drives for storing information. These drives are identified by the letters A through Z, followed by a colon (:). The first **floppy diskette** drive in your PC is drive A:, the second diskette drive (if you have one) is B:, the first **hard drive** is C:, and so on.

2. **Subdividing a disk.** Drives are subdivided into **directories,** also called **folders.** These directories make it easier to find your documents than if everything was stored in one huge list. For example, if you occasionally write letters to politicians, you might keep track of letters written to your Governor in a directory called GOVERNOR under your LETTERS directory. You create a directory in the File Manager by using the File Create>Directory command.

The **backslash** is a special character in DOS that indicates your level in a drive's directory structure. The directory C:\LETTERS\GOVERNOR has two backslashes in it — this indicates that you are two levels down from the C:

drive's main directory, called the **root directory.** The root directory of drive C: is indicated by a backslash with no directory name after it, such as C:\. All other directories **branch** off this main directory, which is why all the directories on a drive are called a **tree.** In Windows, the File Manager starts up by showing you the directory tree of the current drive, from which you can choose to display any folder.

3. **Storing documents in files.** All documents must be given names. Each document is called a **file,** and DOS allows each **filename** to have from 1 to 8 characters, followed by a period, followed by 0 to 3 more characters called the filename's **extension.** Names like MYFILE.DOC and README.TXT are legitimate DOS filenames. A filename can contain any letter or number, plus any of the punctuation marks found above the number keys on your keyboard (except the asterisk). Extensions indicate what type of information is in each file. The extension .DOC probably means a document created by a specific word processor, while .TXT probably means a plain text file that any text-editing program like Windows Notepad can read. Most programs require that you type only the first eight letters when naming a file, and will automatically add the proper extension for you.

The File Manager allows you to use a mouse to select a file, or any group of files in the current directory window, then copy, move, or delete them all. This is explained if you click File Manager's Help Procedures menu choice, then click the topic Selecting More Than One File.

in hardware and software than Windows itself. The following checklist describes what to avoid when installing Windows. This discussion is followed by an almost-foolproof means to eliminate *all* such installation concerns.

TSRs That Interfere with Windows' Installation

The following programs and components can either interfere with the file-copying process essential for Windows' installation or hang your computer entirely:

> The DOS APPEND, FASTOPEN, and SHARE commands.
> Iomega Corp.'s Bernoulli Box removable drives that aren't "locked."
> Logitech's LOGIMENU and CLICK mouse programs.
> The Micronics Memory Manager (MICEMM4G.EXE or similar name).
> Absence of a FILES=30 statement in CONFIG.SYS — or no CONFIG.SYS at all.
> The Sigma VGA/H video adapter card (version 2.02).
> The Sun Tech memory card driver, RMS.SYS.

A way to easily neutralize the effect of these items on the Windows Setup program is described later in the section, "The Best Configuration for Installation."

Hard Disks Larger Than 32MB

If you have a hard disk larger than 32MB, and this disk uses any method other than DOS to manage this many megabytes, you will probably find a line in your CONFIG.SYS file that loads a device driver from one of the following companies:

Product Name	Line in CONFIG.SYS
Golden Bow Systems'	DEVICE=FIXT_DRV.SYS
	Vfeatures Deluxe
Ontrack Computer Systems'	DEVICE=DMDRVR.BIN
	Disk Manager
Priam Systems'	DEVICE=EDVR.SYS
	Innerspace
Storage Dimensions'	DEVICE=HARDRIVE.SYS *or*
SpeedStor	DEVICE=SSTOR.SYS

If one of these is in your CONFIG.SYS file, installing the SmartDrive disk cache program that comes with Windows 3.0 can irretrievably scramble information on your hard disk. The version of SmartDrive that comes with Windows 3.0a will probably not install at all.

If you are in this situation, read the section on disks larger than 32MB in Chapter 8 before installing Windows.

Check Your Computer Type for Anomalies

If you have one of the following models of PCs, before installing Windows you should read the advice about configuring Windows for these models in Chapter 7:

Advanced Logic Research (ALR)
    Powerflex or 486 VEISA

All Charge Card

Amstrad

Apricot

AST Research Premium/286,
    PS/2 Rampage Boards,
    or Fastboard

AT&T 386, 6300, or 6300 Plus

Austin

Club American

Compaq 286, SLT/286, 386, 486,
    or SystemPro

CompuAdd 316SL

Dell 286 and 386SX

Epson

Everex 386/25

Gateway 2000 386

Head Start LX-CD

Hewlett-Packard

IBM PS/1 and PS/2 286

Intel Inboard 386/PC

Microsoft Mach 20 Accelerator

NCR 486 and 925

Northgate 286 and 386

Olivetti

Packard-Bell Legend or Victory

Tandy 1000, 2500 XL, or 3000

Toshiba Laptops

Zenith 286, 386SX, or 386

Use the Right DOS

If your PC is currently using a version of DOS that is meant for some other brand of PC, you will have problems running Windows. For example, if you have a Hewlett-Packard Vectra PC, you should use only HP-DOS, not IBM's

PC-DOS or Microsoft's generic MS-DOS. You can find out what version of DOS you have by typing VER at a DOS prompt. If you don't see a copyright notice that names the manufacturer of your PC, make sure the version of DOS you are using is approved by your PC manufacturer before installing Windows. Install the correct version before proceeding.

Have Enough Hard Disk Space

Windows requires more than 6,300,000 bytes of free disk space to install, if you have a 386-class PC. On a 286-class machine, Windows still requires over 4,400,000 bytes to install.

Additionally, when loading itself in 386 enhanced mode, Windows requires at least 1.5MB of free disk space on the drive where Windows is installed. If this much space is not available when Windows loads, it disables most of its memory-management features, losing both performance and the capability to open an optimal number of windows. Free disk space is used by Windows to create a temporary swap file (which must be at least 1MB in size to be effective), after leaving at least 500K free for your needs.

(You can make Windows use a drive *other* than the one containing Windows, if necessary, by using the command PAGINGDRIVE=*x,* as described later in this chapter.)

To find out how much free space is available on a disk, change to that drive and type DIR at a DOS prompt. If you don't have enough free space, now is the time to remove some unnecessary files to make room for Windows.

Take Your Mouse Off COM3 or COM4

Windows can't use mice that are attached to COM3 or COM4. So if this is your situation, you'll have to relocate your mouse to COM1, COM2, or a bus-mouse port before installing Windows.

Have the Right Kind of Memory

Windows requires a certain amount of memory to run efficiently — and that memory must be of a certain kind, depending on the mode you want to run Windows in.

In general, you should provide Windows with a total of 4MB of memory. Windows will run in all its modes — real, standard, and 386 enhanced — with as little as 2MB. But bulky applications such as Word for Windows and Excel run as much as four times slower with only 2MB rather than 4MB.

Additionally, if you run Windows in 386 enhanced mode, and your 386 has only 2MB of memory, Microsoft recommends that you have 5 to 6MB of free disk space on the drive that Windows will use for temporary files. Otherwise, Windows either may crash when printing files or not be able to open DOS applications.

This is a good time (before installing Windows) to add memory to your PC, or to reconfigure your memory for Windows' use.

The following are rules of thumb to follow when configuring your memory for Windows and DOS applications:

Mode:	Memory configuration:
Windows in real mode	Configure all memory (above the conventional 640K) as expanded memory, by using the expanded memory manager that came with your memory board.
Windows in standard mode	Configure as much memory as possible as *extended,* and (if your DOS applications need expanded memory) configure the rest as *expanded.*
Windows in 386 mode	Configure all memory as extended memory. Use a 386 memory-manager such as Windows' EMM386.SYS or Quarterdeck's QEMM386.SYS to convert extended to expanded for DOS applications that need it.

The Best Configuration for Installation

The best way to avoid problems when installing Windows is to (1) have a way to return to your old configuration (as it was *before* you installed Windows); and (2) install Windows without any memory-resident programs loaded in your machine.

This requires that you take two steps before installing Windows: make a bootable diskette for your machine, and change to a "vanilla" configuration — one that loads no unnecessary programs or device drivers.

You may think these steps are unnecessary. However, I can assure you that I have seen several people spend many hours to recover from errors caused by Windows or other programs — all of which could have been avoided if they had taken a few minutes to make a bootable diskette and simplify their configuration.

Everyone needs a bootable diskette, not just because of Windows, but because of the many things that can cause a hard disk to fail to boot up. Your hard disk doesn't need to fail completely — a single error in your CONFIG.SYS file or a bad byte in the boot track (track 0) is all it takes. A bootable diskette — containing any commands and device drivers that are essential for your system — can make the difference between a quick recovery from an error, or a long, tedious process. Your bootable diskette allows you to access your hard drive and correct any problems, even if your hard drive is incapable of starting your system.

(For the greatest security, you should also make a complete backup of your computer before installing Windows. I know more than one person who lost valuable hard disk data as a result of errors made while installing Windows. I can't describe for you a complete backup procedure in this chapter — if you need to back up your hard disk, you must use the procedure prescribed by whatever backup software you prefer.)

Make a Bootable Diskette

Take the following steps to create a bootable diskette for use when your hard drive is incapable of starting your system:

STEPS:

Creating Your Own Bootable Diskette

Step 1. **Prepare the diskette.** Format a diskette in your A: drive and place DOS' "system" files on it by using the FORMAT /S switch:

```
FORMAT A: /S
```

Step 2. Copy the configuration files. Copy your COMMAND.COM, CONFIG.SYS, and AUTOEXEC.BAT files from the hard disk to this floppy diskette. Also copy any essential drivers listed in either of these two files. Especially important to copy are drivers that enable access to your hard drive:

```
C:
CD \
COPY COMMAND.COM A:
COPY CONFIG.SYS A:
COPY AUTOEXEC.BAT A:
COPY harddisk.drv A:
etc.
```

Step 3. Test the diskette. Insert this bootable diskette in drive A: and reboot, to make sure that this diskette will bring your system up normally. You may need to change lines that name directories on your hard drive, like C:\DRIVERS, to directories on the floppy, like A:\DRIVERS. Perform these changes with a text editor until the bootable diskette works reliably.

Creating a Vanilla Configuration

I always change to plain "vanilla" CONFIG.SYS and AUTOEXEC.BAT files when installing *any* application, not just Windows. Using this vanilla configuration has saved me many problems during the application installation and testing stage — but *especially* with Windows and other applications that write directly to hardware. To install itself, Windows doesn't need to know that you have expanded memory, keyboard accelerators, or any of the other stuff that exists in most DOS environments — it's better to do without these when running Setup.

All Windows needs to know (hardware-wise) when you run Setup is what kind of video board and mouse you have — and you usually don't require special software drivers for Windows to detect these devices.

If you're installing Windows on a networked PC, you should activate any software that controls Token-Ring or Ethernet boards, or other boards that claim a space in memory above 640K. Check Chapter 12 before installing Windows, if this is your situation.

STEPS:

Creating a Vanilla Configuration

Step 1. **Rename your configuration files.** Rename CONFIG.SYS and
AUTOEXEC.BAT to names like CONFIG.SAV and AUTOEXEC.SAV (.SAV as
in "save"). Don't use the names CONFIG.OLD and AUTOEXEC.OLD,
because Windows uses these names.

This requires the following commands:

```
C:
CD \
REN CONFIG.SYS *.SAV
REN AUTOEXEC.BAT *.SAV
```

Step 2. **Recreate CONFIG.SYS.** With a text editor, create a vanilla
CONFIG.SYS that says the following:

```
SHELL=C:\COMMAND.COM /P /E:512
STACKS=0,0
FILES=30
BUFFERS=20
BREAK=ON
```

The SHELL= command establishes the location of your
COMMAND.COM file. The /P parameter specifies that this is a
permanent copy of COMMAND.COM and that it should run
AUTOEXEC.BAT. The /E:512 parameter specifies an environment
size of 512 bytes, in DOS 3.2 or higher. If you use DOS 3.1, specify
/E:32 instead. (In DOS 3.1, the number 32 is multiplied by 16,
providing you with an environment of 512 bytes.) You can't
specify an environment size in versions of DOS prior to 3.1.

The STACKS= command allows multiple interrupts to stack up
without hanging your PC. Stack space isn't needed in DOS 3.3 or
higher, so you save some memory by specifying zero stacks,
each of them zero bytes in length. If you use DOS 3.2, change this
line to STACKS=9,192. You can't specify the number or size of
stacks in versions of DOS prior to 3.2.

(Later in this chapter, we'll copy lines such as these into your
normal CONFIG.SYS after installing Windows.)

Step 3. Add any necessary drivers. If any other lines are required in your normal CONFIG.SYS, add them to your vanilla CONFIG.SYS now. *Don't* add lines for temporary storage devices such as the Iomega Bernoulli Box. Windows' Setup program gets confused by these "extra" devices when it searches all your disks for software during installation.

(If you require a device driver to access your hard drive, be sure to read the section "Hard Drives Larger Than 32MB," near the beginning of this chapter.)

Step 4. Recreate your AUTOEXEC.BAT. Create the following vanilla AUTOEXEC.BAT file with a text editor:

```
ECHO OFF
PATH=C:\;c:\bat;c:\util;c:\dos
PROMPT=$p$g
SET TEMP=c:\temp
SET TMP=c:\temp
```

Change the directories shown in this PATH= statement to match the necessary directories in your own system. Make sure *not* to include in this PATH= statement, however, directories that contain software that isn't necessary for this installation or directories that contain previous versions of Windows.

The statement PROMPT=PG displays a DOS prompt that includes the current directory path ($P) and a greater-than sign ($G).

The statements SET TEMP= and SET TMP= establish the directories that applications use to write temporary scratch files. You need both lines because applications such as Micrografx Designer and Microsoft Word for DOS look for the variable TMP, not TEMP. If you have several drives, use an empty directory on the fastest one. (If a TEMP directory doesn't exist on that drive, create it now.) Don't use a RAM drive for your temporary directory, unless you have a RAM drive larger than 2MB (and don't use a RAM drive during the installation).

We'll also copy lines like these into your normal AUTOEXEC.BAT after installing Windows, later in this chapter.

Step 5. Add any necessary software. If any memory-resident programs are essential to start your computer, add them to your vanilla AUTOEXEC.BAT at this point. But leave out programs that aren't needed for the installation, such as keyboard accelerators and other utilities.

Step 6. Reboot your PC. At this point you should reboot your PC with Ctrl+Alt+Delete, in order to make sure that the new configuration works. If it *doesn't* work, and your PC hangs at the point that it loads the new CONFIG.SYS, insert your bootable diskette in drive A:, reboot, and then examine your configuration files for errors. Test this until it succeeds, before installing Windows.

What You Need to Know About Setup

You are now almost ready to begin running Windows' Setup program. Before you do, you should check the following items:

1. **Use short directory names for applications.** Setup asks you for a directory name in which to install Windows. It then scans your hard drives and installs icons for your applications into the Windows Program Manager. After installation, the Program Manager allows you to change to any directory before starting a program — but only if that program is on the Path. (This is explained in Chapter 2.) Because the PATH= statement can be no longer than 127 characters long, you will soon run out of space unless you use short directory names for Windows and other applications.

For example, you should install Windows in a directory called C:\WIN instead of C:\WINDOWS. To do this, simply change the C:\WINDOWS default to C:\WIN when asked what directory to install Windows into. Be careful to completely erase the extra letters you don't want in the directory name — if you move the cursor to the left and press the Spacebar to erase "DOWS" from C:\WINDOWS, Setup can't handle the extra spaces and will hang. Use the Backspace or Delete key instead of the Spacebar.

To avoid running out of space in the Path, you may want to rename existing directories that use long names, before installing Windows.

This way, when Setup catalogs your software during the Windows installation process, the directory names it finds won't have to be changed later.

While you're doing this, it's a good idea to leave version numbers out of directory names that contain applications. You might think it is a good idea to install Windows 3.0 into a directory such as C:\WIN30. But when you upgrade to Windows 3.1, if you install it to a directory called C:\WIN31, your batch files that refer to C:\WIN30 won't work any more and you'll have to edit them all by hand. (For many reasons, discussed in other chapters, it isn't a good idea to install a new version of Windows into the old version's directory.)

A better way to handle version numbers is to use them only in directory names for *old* versions of software that you keep on your hard drive (in case you need to go back to them). For example, install Windows 3.0 in a C:\WIN directory; when upgrading to Windows 3.1, first rename C:\WIN to C:\WIN30, then install Windows 3.1 into C:\WIN. By keeping the same directory name when you install new versions of software, you won't have to change your batch files.

2. **Know the options for your particular PC.** On the Hardware Compatibility List included in the Windows distribution box, PCs with asterisks (*) require an extra step when running Setup.

If your PC is one of these, you must not accept Setup's default, which describes your system as an "MS-DOS or PC-DOS System." You must change this computer type to one that specifically configures Windows for your type of PC.

At this writing, the computer systems that require this step are:

AST Bravo/386SX

AST Premium 286, 386/SX, 386/25, 386/33, 386C, 486/25, and 486/33

Everex Step 386/25

NCR PC386SX

NCR PC925

NEC PowerMate SX Plus

NEC ProSpeed 386

Toshiba 5200 and T1600

Zenith Z-386/16, Z-386/20, Z-386/25, and Z-386/33

These particular machines aren't "incompatible" — Windows simply cannot detect the memory addresses used by some options on these machines. You must specifically identify these PCs in order for Setup to write Windows' SYSTEM.INI to avoid conflict with a particular feature of these computers. See Chapter 7 for more information.

3. **Set up for some drivers you don't think you'll need.** I recommend that you let Setup install Windows drivers for the printers you have, of course. But you should also tell it to install the Generic/Text printer driver and the PostScript printer driver — even if you don't have these types of printers.

Why? Because these printer drivers give you capabilities that no other drivers provide. Complete details are explained in Chapter 13. Briefly, the Generic/Text driver enables you to convert material from any application into plain-text format, and the PostScript driver enables you to produce files that can be used by people who *do* have PostScript printers or imagesetters (and produce Print Preview displays that let you know what these pages will look like). It's a *lot* easier to install these drivers now, even if you don't use them, than it is to install them later.

4. **When you install printers, configure them, too.** Setup copies the printer drivers you specify, but it doesn't configure the drivers for the model of printer you have. When installing printers during Setup, click the Configure and Setup buttons, and make sure the options you find in these dialog boxes match your particular printer model. You should also click the Help button and print any text files you find that are *hidden within the driver itself.* These "help" files often contain crucial information that isn't printed in a manual.

5. **Let Setup rewrite your configuration.** When Setup asks if you would like it to write changes into your CONFIG.SYS and AUTOEXEC.BAT file (or whether you would like to do this yourself), let Setup write these changes. You've already preserved your original files (and Windows will do it again, to files like CONFIG.OLD and AUTOEXEC.OLD). Setup usually does a good job of writing the lines that Windows needs. Make sure to transfer these lines into your normal CONFIG.SYS and AUTOEXEC.BAT when you switch back to your normal configuration (as described later in this chapter).

The exception to this rule is when you are installing Windows inside the "DOS compatibility box" of the OS/2 operating system. OS/2 configuration files are different from their DOS cousins. Setup may refuse to write into these files if it detects them. But, in any case, don't let Setup write to your CONFIG.SYS and AUTOEXEC.BAT if you use OS/2.

6. Write-protect your original Windows diskettes. Some OEM versions of DOS can write garbled information to the Windows diskettes. Placing write-protect tabs on these diskettes avoids this potential problem.

Write-protect tabs are also absolute protection against a destructive computer virus attaching itself to one of the files in your Windows distribution diskettes. (A computer virus is a program that copies itself into other programs, then erases your files or causes other problems. You can scan your disks for viruses using the SCAN.EXE program described in "Use This First!" in the "Excellence in Windows Shareware" section.)

You should always write-protect the original software diskettes you receive for any application — especially DOS — for both of these reasons.

(On 5.25" floppy disks, a diskette is write-protected when the tab is *closed*. On 3.5" disks, a diskette is write-protected when the tab is *open*.)

Running Windows' Setup Program

After taking the steps described so far, you are ready to run Setup. This part of the installation is adequately described in the Windows manual. If the diskette drive you are using for the installation is drive A:, you type the following commands at a DOS prompt:

```
A:
SETUP
```

If you implemented the steps in the checklist earlier in this chapter, Setup should copy most of the Windows files to your hard drive without incident, after which it starts Windows. You are now ready to complete the installation.

Completing the Windows Installation

After Setup has completed its file copying, exit Windows and return to the DOS prompt. Setup does not copy from the diskettes several Windows files you may need. It's best to go ahead and complete the installation at this time.

You should copy three types of files from the Windows diskettes: the Windows Expand utility, Windows mouse drivers, and any printer fonts you need.

Copying the Expand Utility

Place Windows distribution Disk #2 (either 5.25" or 3.5" format) in a floppy drive. Type the following command at a DOS prompt to copy EXPAND.EXE from the diskette to your Windows directory:

```
COPY a:\EXPAND.EXE c:\win
```

This utility enables you to install compressed files from the Windows diskettes. Since the Windows directory is on the Path, you can now use Microsoft's Expand utility any time — as we will in the following topics.

Copying the Windows Mouse Drivers

If you ever want to use a mouse in a non-Windows program, you should use the updated Microsoft mouse drivers included on the Windows diskettes (if your mouse is Microsoft-compatible). But the Windows Setup program does not automatically copy these drivers to your hard disk for you.

You should expand these drivers off the Windows distribution diskettes, whether or not you think you'll ever need them. The two drivers — MOUSE.COM and MOUSE.SY$ — are small and take up little room on your hard disk.

Find the diskette that contains files named MOUSE.*, and issue the following command at a DOS prompt to expand them into your Windows directory:

```
EXPAND a:\MOUSE.COM c:\win
EXPAND a:\MOUSE.SY$ c:\win\MOUSE.SYS
```

Notice that the second command line in this example renames MOUSE.SY$ to MOUSE.SYS. The diskette file MOUSE.SY$ has a dollar sign in its name to discourage people from copying this file to their hard drive and using the compressed file in their CONFIG.SYS. In its compressed form, loading this file in CONFIG.SYS hangs your machine — and, since most people have never made a bootable diskette, this leaves them *no way* to start their machine.

After expanding these mouse drivers, you can load them in CONFIG.SYS or AUTOEXEC.BAT as needed for your DOS applications.

Copying Printer Fonts

If you have a dot-matrix printer of any kind, the Setup program may not have copied to your hard drive the fonts needed by Windows to print to this printer. Formerly, if you installed a printer driver for a dot-matrix printer, Windows 2.*x* copied whichever fonts were appropriate. This capability was "lost" in Windows 3.0, however.

If you use a dot-matrix printer, see the "Dot-Matrix Printers" section of Chapter 13 for information on how to install these fonts manually.

Switching to Your Permanent Configuration

Determining the Best Settings for Your CONFIG.SYS

Once you have completed the installation steps to this point, you are ready to create your permanent CONFIG.SYS for Windows.

Windows Setup has added lines to your "vanilla" CONFIG.SYS and it probably looks like this:

```
DEVICE=HIMEM.SYS
DEVICE=c:\win\SMARTDRV.SYS 2048 1024
SHELL=C:\COMMAND.COM /P /E:512
STACKS=0,0
FILES=30
BUFFERS=20
BREAK=ON
```

The first two lines, which load HIMEM.SYS (Windows' extended memory manager) and SmartDrive (Windows' disk cache program), are typical of the edits that Setup makes when installing Windows. You probably want to modify both of these lines. Additionally, if you have enough RAM, you may want to add a RAM drive to improve Windows' performance when writing temporary files. These steps are described below.

Moving HIMEM.SYS

It is a bad idea to have device drivers in the root directory of your C: drive, and this is particularly true of HIMEM.SYS. You will certainly want to upgrade to a new version of Windows at some point in the future, and if the new version of Windows installs *its* version of HIMEM.SYS into the root directory of your C: drive, your original HIMEM.SYS will be lost, and it will be difficult for you to go back to the old version of Windows in case you have a problem.

Most computer managers recommend that files other than COMMAND.COM, CONFIG.SYS, and AUTOEXEC.BAT be located in directories other than the root directory. This not only helps keep versions separate, but also acts as a form of self-documentation. If you have a device driver in your root directory named, for example, C:\DEVICE.DRV, how do you know what this driver does? On the other hand, If you placed it in its own directory, it might have a name such as C:\INTEL\DEVICE.DRV. You could then try to identify this driver by looking for an Intel component in the system.

This is a good time to copy HIMEM.SYS directly into your Windows directory, delete it from the root directory, and change its line in CONFIG.SYS to the following:

```
DEVICE=c:\win\HIMEM.SYS
```

Finding the Best Size for SmartDrive and RAMDrive

The Windows Setup program tends to establish a fairly large memory allocation for SmartDrive — possibly more than you need.

Setup writes two numbers at the end of the line that loads SmartDrive. These numbers represent the amount of memory (in kilobytes) that SmartDrive claims when Windows is *not* running, and the amount it shifts to when Windows *starts* running. This looks something like the following:

```
DEVICE=c:\win\SMARTDRV.SYS 2048 1024
```

Microsoft has created a technical-support memo that its staff uses to recommend the best size for SmartDrive and RAMDrive memory allocations under Windows. These recommendations are based on the amount of memory you have, and whether you primarily use Windows in standard or enhanced mode. The guidelines also help you decide whether or not to make Windows use the RAM drive when writing temporary files. Their recommendations are as shown on next page (my recommendations follow):

Standard mode usage:

Memory (MB)	SmartDrive	RAMDrive	TEMP=RAMDrive?
1	0	0	No
2	0	0	No
3	512	512	No
4	1024	1024	No
5	1024	2048	Yes
6	1024	2048	Yes
7	1536	2560	Yes
8	2048	3072	Yes
9	2048	4096	Yes
10	3072	4096	Yes
11	4096	4096	Yes
12	4096	4096	Yes

Enhanced mode usage:

Memory (MB)	SmartDrive	RAMDrive	TEMP=RAMDrive?
1	0	0	No
2	0	0	No
3	512	0	No
4	1024	0	No
5	1024	1024	Yes
6	1024	1024	Yes
7	1536	1536	Yes
8	2048	2048	Yes
9	2048	3072	Yes
10	3072	4096	Yes
11	4096	4096	Yes
12	4096	4096	Yes

The above recommendations reflect Microsoft's estimation that you should reserve at least 2MB of RAM for Windows itself in standard mode and 2.5MB in enhanced mode. Additionally, Microsoft estimates that you should not use a RAM drive for temporary Windows files, unless you have a 2MB RAM drive in standard mode or a 1MB RAM drive in enhanced mode. (Enhanced mode has the ability to manage chunks of memory in smaller segments.)

These recommendations are fine if you only run Windows' applets, such as Notepad and Solitaire. But if you use large applications and documents, such as Word for Windows, Amí, Micrografx Designer, and Excel, I would amend these recommendations. You may get better performance by reserving as much as 4MB for Windows and using a smaller SmartDrive than Microsoft recommends, if memory is tight.

Independent tests generally show that SmartDrive's beneficial effects level off after 512K of memory has been allocated to SmartDrive. You can test this by changing the line that loads SmartDrive to the following and rebooting your machine:

```
DEVICE=c:\win\SMARTDRV.SYS 512 512
```

Start Windows, then immediately open your largest document, timing every step. Then, open your second-largest document, close it, reopen the first document, close that one, and finally reopen the second document. This establishes the time it takes your application to read these files, both before and after they are in the disk cache.

After these tests, change SmartDrive to the following and reboot:

```
DEVICE=c:\win\SMARTDRV.SYS 1024 1024
```

Perform exactly the same series of actions as before. If your application is not noticeably faster with 1024K (1MB) devoted to SmartDrive, set it back to 512K and let other applications have the extra memory.

Determining the proper size for RAMDrive requires a different test. If you place the following line in your CONFIG.SYS, DOS creates a RAM drive 2MB in size in extended memory (if you have that much memory):

```
DEVICE=c:\win\RAMDRIVE.SYS 2048 /E
```

This RAM drive is assigned to the next letter after the last *real* hard drive in your system. Let's say that your only hard drive is C:, and your RAM drive is assigned the letter D:. If you place the following commands in your AUTOEXEC.BAT file, Windows applications will write temporary files into the root directory of your RAM drive:

```
SET  TEMP=D:\
SET  TMP=D:\
```

The best reason for setting a DOS environmental variable TEMP to a RAM drive is that it benefits Windows' print spooler, Print Manager. When you print from an application, Print Manager first writes your application's print file to this RAM drive (which is much faster than writing to a hard drive). Then, Print Manager lets you use your application for other work, while it feeds the print file (a segment at a time) to your printer.

You can see how large a RAM drive you need by starting the Windows File Manager and opening a directory window showing the root directory of the RAM drive. (You'll have to copy a small file to the root directory of your RAM drive before File Manager will let you open a directory window for it.) Then, start an application, position it side by side with the File Manager window, and print your largest document (especially one with full-page graphics). You can watch the temporary file(s) grow and shrink in the RAM drive's root directory as Print Manager buffers your job. It makes sense to have a RAM drive larger than the largest document you'll ever print, but not much larger if you're tight on memory.

If you need to switch between two different configurations — one of which assigns memory for a RAM drive, the other of which does not — you can use a single AUTOEXEC.BAT routine to set the correct TEMP= variable in either case. Let's say that sometimes you have a RAM drive named D:, while other times you have only your C: hard drive, with a directory named JUNK for temporary files. Insert the following lines in your AUTOEXEC.BAT:

```
SET TEMP=C:\JUNK
IF EXIST D:\NUL SET TEMP=D:\
```

The DOS IF EXIST statement cannot test for a directory or a drive — only for filenames. To test for a drive or directory, you must test for a file named NUL. This is a reserved DOS device name for a do-nothing device. It always exists in every directory, so you can test for it to determine whether a drive or directory exists.

In this example, your AUTOEXEC.BAT first sets TEMP to C:\JUNK. But if your RAM drive D: exists, the TEMP variable is quickly changed to the root directory of that drive instead.

Establishing the Right Size for Your Swap File

If you use 386 enhanced mode, it automatically creates a temporary swap file every time you load Windows. Windows determines the size of this swap file by examining the drive that Windows is installed on, then creating a temporary file that leaves you 500K of free space or more. The swap file is used to move programs out of memory and onto your disk, if Windows runs out of real RAM.

You may be able to get slightly better performance when starting and operating Windows by taking one of the following actions: (1) specifying a different drive for the temporary swap file than the one that Windows is installed on; (2) specifying a specific size for that swap file; or (3) establishing a permanent swap file.

STEPS:

Improving Performance in Windows

Step 1. Specify a drive for your swap file. If you have several hard drive letters, and one of them has more space than the one you installed Windows on, you can make Windows use that drive for temporary swap files. To do this, make a copy of your SYSTEM.INI file with File Manager or your favorite utility — call the copy SYSTEM.BAK or similar. Then, open your SYSTEM.INI file with Notepad or another plain-text editor and insert the following line in the section headed [386Enh]:

```
[386Enh]
PagingDrive=x
```

where x is the letter of the drive for Windows' swap file. It doesn't make any sense, by the way, to specify a RAM drive. If Windows frequently runs out of memory, reduce your RAM drive's size and leave the additional memory for Windows to claim.

Step 2. Limit the size of the swap file. You can specify the size of temporary swap files once, instead of each time you start Windows. (This really only saves time on a network drive, where it can take up to one minute to establish the swap file. If you use a network, be sure to read the section on swap files in Chapter 12 before doing this). Though Windows uses this file to swap applications if it runs out of real RAM, the file also enables some of Windows' memory-management functions, so it's important to keep it at a healthy size (as explained a little later).

You specify the temporary swap file's size by inserting the following line into your [386Enh] section:

```
[386Enh]
MaxPagingFileSize=1024
```

where you replace *1024* with the actual size (in kilobytes) that you want for the swap file.

Alternatively, you can specify the minimum amount of free disk space you want Windows to leave on your drive after creating its temporary swap file. You specify this by inserting the following line:

```
[386Enh]
MinUserDiskSpace=500
```

where you replace *500* with the actual amount (in kilobytes) you want Windows to leave free.

Make sure, if you use either of these methods, that Windows always has the ability to create at least a 1MB temporary swap file. If space on this drive gets tight, Windows will establish a smaller swap file, but won't warn you that it's running out of space. After this swap file falls below 512K, Windows' ability to manage 4K memory segments on a 386 is impaired. When this occurs, Windows reverts to 64K segments, its performance slows, and you may not be able to open as many windows as usual until you free enough disk space to restore Windows' normal disk-paging functions.

Step 3. Establish a permanent swap file. If you usually run more programs under Windows than you have real RAM for, Windows will constantly copy applications out of memory, onto your hard drive, and back. If you are in such a situation, this swapping process may go faster if you create a permanent swap file for use in 386 mode, instead of letting Windows establish temporary swap files when it starts. This will still be many times slower than adding RAM, but if you are starved for memory, you can take the following steps to configure a permanent swap file.

A permanent swap file is faster than a temporary swap file because Windows only establishes permanent swap files that are *contiguous*. This means that the entire file resides on one, unbroken area of your hard disk. You should, therefore, use a disk "optimizer" program, such as those provided with Norton Utilities, Mace Utilities, and PC Tools Deluxe, before establishing a permanent swap file. These "optimizers" move all your files closer together (physically), so you have one large, unbroken area on your drive.

After doing this, you must remove all programs from the LOAD= and RUN= lines in your WIN.INI file. Windows will not create a permanent swap file if programs other than the Windows "shell" (such as Program Manager) are running. This includes programs that run "silently" (without displaying a window on the screen), screen-saver programs that run in the background, and so on.

You must start Windows in real mode, using the command WIN /R. Then, pull down Program Manager's File menu, click Run, and type SWAPFILE in the dialog box that appears.

When you click OK, the Swapfile program displays the amount of space available on your hard drive for a permanent swap file. You must choose a size that will leave you enough disk space for other programs, because the permanent swap file claims space that cannot be used by programs other than Windows. (Temporary swap files, on the other hand, are always deleted when you exit Windows, so the space can be used by any DOS app.) A 1MB swap file may be enough if you always switch only between the same two programs under Windows. Otherwise, you should create a permanent swap file of 2MB or more. If Windows tells you that it is out of memory after you create this permanent swap file, of course, you may need to delete it (using SWAPFILE again) and create a larger one.

More information on swap files is contained in Chapter 8.

Establishing Expanded Memory for DOS

In 386 enhanced mode, DOS applications you start under Windows are provided with expanded memory. But if you need these same applications to have access to expanded memory on your 386 system when Windows *isn't* running, you need to insert a line into your CONFIG.SYS file that converts extended memory into expanded memory. Windows includes a device driver called EMM386.SYS that provides this function. (Other memory managers, such as Quarterdeck Office Systems' QEMM386, have advanced features beyond those in EMM386.SYS, and are discussed in Chapter 16.)

To establish 512K of expanded memory outside of Windows, for example, you would enter a line like the following into your CONFIG.SYS file — *after* the line that loads HIMEM.SYS:

```
DEVICE=c:\win\EMM386.SYS 512
```

The README.TXT file included with Windows states that, in order to start Windows in 386 enhanced mode after installing EMM386.SYS, you must include the parameter D=48 at the end of this DEVICE= line. This is not entirely accurate. The D=48 parameter, an undocumented feature of EMM386.SYS, is required only if you receive this error message when loading EMM386.SYS:

```
EMM386 DMA buffer is too small.
Add D=nn parameter and reboot.
```

In that case, add the switch D=48 to the end of the line that loads EMM386.SYS. This should establish enough buffer space for both the memory manager and Windows.

Another undocumented "feature" of EMM386.SYS is that you can't start Windows in standard mode if any of EMM386.SYS's expanded memory is in use. This would be the case, for example, if you loaded Windows' SmartDrive in your CONFIG.SYS after loading EMM386.SYS, and you configured SmartDrive to use expanded memory. (You can configure SmartDrive to use expanded instead of extended memory, as explained in the Windows manual, but I don't recommend it because of problems like this — and because extended memory is faster.) The problem can also be caused by *any* DOS program that uses expanded memory, such as a network driver like Novell's EMSNET3 or other memory-resident programs, before you start Windows in standard mode.

If you encounter this problem, when you try to start Windows you will receive the error message:

```
Cannot run Windows in standard mode; check to ensure that you are not
running other protected-mode software, or run in real mode.
```

The problem is not "other protected-mode" software, but DOS software that is using EMM386.SYS's expanded memory. Until this is corrected in a later version of Windows, you must refrain from letting programs claim any EMM386.SYS memory before you start Windows in standard mode.

EMM 386.SYS also cannot provide expanded memory to any DOS application you run under Windows in standard mode; you must use another memory manager, such as QEMM386.SYS, for this.

Making Your Changes to CONFIG.SYS Permanent

After completing the above steps, you can transfer the changes that both you and Windows made to your CONFIG.SYS file into your original CONFIG.SYS, which you earlier renamed CONFIG.SAV or similar.

To do this, use a text editor to copy the lines from CONFIG.SYS into CONFIG.SAV. Remove any duplicate lines from CONFIG.SAV. Rename CONFIG.SYS to CONFIG.VAN. Then remove any lines from CONFIG.VAN, other than the ones needed for your "vanilla" configuration. You can use CONFIG.VAN in the future when installing new versions of Windows or other software. Finally, rename CONFIG.SAV to CONFIG.SYS. After making the changes described below to your AUTOEXEC.BAT, you'll be ready to reboot with these new files.

Making Changes to Your AUTOEXEC.BAT

Your AUTOEXEC.BAT file should not require as many changes as you and Windows probably made to your CONFIG.SYS. The lines you wrote into your "vanilla" AUTOEXEC.BAT already include most of the statements that Windows needs, such as SET TEMP=C:\TEMP.

You must, however, be sure to add the DOS SHARE.EXE command to your AUTOEXEC.BAT before making your changes permanent. This small DOS program ensures that two applications won't try to open the same file, thereby garbling it (Windows sometimes makes it possible for this to happen without you knowing about it). Two different directory windows in File Manager, for example, can operate on the same file momentarily, causing a loss of data.

Or try this — insert a text file into a document in Word for Windows, then close the document you were working on. You've closed all the files, right?

Wrong. Without closing Word for Windows, switch to File Manager and try to delete the text file. If SHARE is loaded, it will warn you that two applications are trying to operate on the same file. Word for Windows still has the text file's "file handle," until you close Word for Windows itself.

To prevent accidents like this that can corrupt your data files, add the following lines to your AUTOEXEC.BAT file:

```
REM The following provides 2048 bytes of Filespace for 20 Locks.
SHARE /F:2048 /L:20
```

This sets aside enough memory to "lock" any open files so they can't be corrupted, and the remark documents the syntax of the DOS command that does this. If you later receive a message like, "Not enough locks," you can increase either of the two numbers in this command. But without some remark to remind you and others what these switches do, this kind of message might be hard to decipher.

It's important to note that SHARE.EXE should *not* be loaded when you actually install Windows because, ironically, the Setup program is not compatible with it and may hang.

At this point, your vanilla AUTOEXEC.BAT probably looks something like the following:

```
ECHO OFF
PATH=c:\win;c:\;c:\bat;c:\util;c:\dos
PROMPT=$p$g
SET TEMP=c:\temp
SET TMP=c:\temp
REM The following provides 2048 bytes of Filespace for 20 Locks.
SHARE /F:2048 /L:20
```

Use a text editor to insert these lines at the beginning of your original AUTOEXEC.BAT, which you previously renamed AUTOEXEC.SAV or similar. Eliminate any duplicate lines that have been created in AUTOEXEC.SAV, such as two separate PATH= statements. Rename AUTOEXEC.BAT to AUTOEXEC.VAN. Then remove the SHARE statement from AUTOEXEC.VAN. You can use AUTOEXEC.VAN with your CONFIG.VAN the next time you need to install new software. Finally, rename AUTOEXEC.SAV to AUTOEXEC.BAT.

Congratulations! You're Ready to See If It Works

After all these steps, you're ready to reboot your machine. This is the acid test, because any device drivers or memory-resident programs in your original CONFIG.SYS and AUTOEXEC.BAT files will now take effect. If any of them are not compatible with Windows, your computer could either crash immediately or after an indeterminate period of time. If this happens, comment-out any lines that load device drivers and programs you don't absolutely need. Then add them back, one at a time, to find out which ones might be causing the problem. (See Chapter 16 for trouble-shooting procedures regarding conflicts between devices.)

If your PC hangs as soon as it loads a device driver in CONFIG.SYS, you will need the bootable floppy you created earlier in this chapter. Boot from this floppy and change any conflicting lines before trying to reboot from your hard disk.

How to Forget About Backup

I would like to conclude this chapter with a topic that is particularly important to Windows users — a way to totally forget about ever having to back up your computer, but still have complete peace of mind.

Windows uses your computer in many ways most other DOS software does not. It opens a lot of files, uses protected mode, and writes directly to your hardware. In short, it does a lot of things that make it *more* likely, not less, that something will happen to accidentally delete or corrupt your valuable data files.

As you probably know, most PC hard disk drives have an average life expectancy of only two to four years. A disk drive can die suddenly and for no apparent reason, like a tire going flat. When it dies, your disk can take with it all the data it contains. Obeying Murphy's Law ("if anything can go wrong, it will"), your hard disk will die when it is least convenient to you — perhaps just before that big report is due or when the government wants to see all your tax records (which you carefully recorded on what used to be your hard drive).

Although most PCs don't come with little tape drives for automatic backup, the majority of PCs sold today *do* include a feature that allows them to automatically back up your system every day — with little effort on your part.

This feature is *the B: drive* of your computer. If you have two floppy drives — and most PCs today ship with one 5.25" drive and one 3.5" drive — and you have DOS 3.2 or later, you can add five lines to your AUTOEXEC.BAT that can eliminate the need for you to worry about backup for a long, long time.

This simple method isn't the most elegant — you can easily improve it, as I'll explain later — but it's absolutely free. And it's far better than the backup method that 95 percent of PC users rely on, which is *no backup at all.*

This method requires that you perform one complete backup of your system, perhaps just after you've installed Windows, by using whatever backup software you prefer. This backup should turn off all the "flags" that DOS uses to tell which files have been written but have not yet been backed up.

Then, add the following five lines to your AUTOEXEC.BAT:

```
XCOPY C:\*.* B:\ /S /M
IF NOT ERRORLEVEL 1 GOTO :OKAY
ECHO Your backup diskette is full — place an empty one in drive B:
PAUSE > NUL
:OKAY
{place the remainder of your batch file here}
```

The first line of this batch file uses the DOS XCOPY command to copy every file that needs backing up from drive C: to B:. The /S switch performs the copy on all subdirectories on that drive, and the /M switch copies only modified files (and turns off their backup flag, or "archive bit," so they won't be copied the next time AUTOEXEC.BAT runs). This requires, of course, that you leave a formatted diskette in drive B: whenever you're not actually using that drive in your work. (Most computers don't complain if there's a diskette in drive B: when they boot up — they only boot off drive A: or drive C:.)

The second line detects whether you have more files to back up than would fit on one diskette. If the XCOPY command runs out of space on the target diskette (or encounters some other error), it sets the DOS errorlevel variable to a number higher than zero. In this case, your batch file displays a message reminding you to insert another blank, formatted diskette. It isn't important to copy all the remaining files right now. Your AUTOEXEC.BAT will get them the next time you start your PC. What's important is to have *some* method like this working for you over time.

You could add a "loop" to this batch file to make it fill up multiple diskettes, for example. Or you could substitute a better backup program than XCOPY. (Don't use the DOS BACKUP command, because it doesn't reliably produce copies that can be restored.) There are many good ones, including Fastback, Norton Backup, PC Tools Deluxe, and so on.

But right now, if you have a B: drive and DOS 3.2 or higher, you can have a functioning backup system working for you by adding just five lines — and without buying anything.

I use this method myself. I happen to like XCOPY, because it writes files that I can read right off the diskettes without going through a "reconstitution" process, as with compressed files (and XCOPY is free). I buy preformatted diskettes, which used to be expensive, but are now less than 10 cents above the cost of nonformatted diskettes, from national sources such as Global Computer Supplies (11 Harbor Park Drive, Port Washington, NY 11050, 800-845-6225 or 516-625-6200).

When a diskette fills up, I remove it from my PC and store it at another location, along with all the other diskettes I've made this way. Although this means I have to make a trip if I need to retrieve a lost file, it's much better than not having the backups at all. If a fire totally destroys my computer, my insurance will pay for another one, but more likely my hard disk will crash some day. In either case, I'll be able to restore every file back to the state it was in the last time I turned on the PC.

Of course, you'll need a special backup program that compresses data and works across multiple floppy diskettes if you write files every day that are larger than the size of a single floppy. But few people create more than a megabyte of documents in a single day (except those who scan large images).

Summary

This chapter describes in detail the preparation required for a trouble-free installation of Windows, and how to configure various settings for best performance. This includes:

▶ How to avoid installation problems that might be caused by certain hardware and software.

▶ Configuring your system temporarily into a "vanilla" state that minimizes problems when installing Windows or any new piece of software.

▶ Decisions required when you run Windows' Setup installation program.

▶ Determining the best settings for Windows features, such as disk cache, RAM drives, and swap files.

▶ Making this configuration a permanent part of your PC's start-up routine.

Chapter 16
Using Memory Managers

In this chapter...

I describe the use of the two most popular memory managers used by Windows sites, QEMM386 from Quarterdeck Office Systems and 386Max from Qualitas Inc., and I cover the following topics:

▶ The capabilities products like QEMM give you that are not available through HIMEM.SYS.

▶ How you can identify and take advantage of "holes" in your system's memory between the 640K line and 1MB — a mysterious Sargasso Sea of your PC that can entangle you in memory conflicts, seemingly out of nowhere.

▶ Using QEMM386 to trouble-shoot and correct problems encountered with extended memory and Windows' use of protected mode.

▶ How Qualitas exploits proprietary features of IBM PS/2s to provide more memory above 640K.

Windows' memory-management program, HIMEM.SYS, is usually installed automatically when you run the Windows Setup program. Setup copies HIMEM.SYS to your hard disk (usually in the root directory of your C: hard drive) and adds the following line to your CONFIG.SYS file:

```
DEVICE=HIMEM.SYS
```

HIMEM.SYS, or a compatible memory manager like the ones described in this chapter, is required to run Windows in standard or enhanced modes (but not real mode). It allows Windows applications to use any extended memory you have in your system (on AT-class systems or higher). Additionally, HIMEM.SYS can convert *extended* memory (under Windows in 386 mode) into *expanded* memory for DOS applications that require such expanded memory. (See specific configuration options of HIMEM.SYS for different types of computers in Chapter 7.)

But HIMEM.SYS can convert 386 extended memory into expanded memory for DOS programs *only* when they are running in a Windows DOS session, not when they are running outside Windows.

For this reason, Windows also includes an expanded memory management program for 386-class PCs called EMM386.SYS. You can give DOS applications (while outside Windows) 512K of expanded memory by including a line like DEVICE=C:\WINDOWS\EMM386.SYS 512 in your CONFIG.SYS file.

Using both HIMEM.SYS and EMM386.SYS, however, consumes more of the 640K of conventional memory available in your PC than using a single memory manager that provides all these functions. This has created a demand for integrated, third-party memory managers, which replace both HIMEM.SYS and EMM386.SYS and provide other features as well.

Quarterdeck's QEMM386.SYS

Replacing Windows' HIMEM.SYS

Quarterdeck Office Systems' expanded memory manager for 386s, QEMM386.SYS (also referred to simply as QEMM), is the most widely used third-party memory manager for Windows. Industry surveys consistently rate QEMM as one of the top ten best-selling PC business software programs of all types — selling almost as many copies as Windows itself. This is because QEMM makes more memory available for all DOS applications, whether or not they are running in a DOS session under Windows. QEMM is therefore practical for all 386 users, not just Windows users.

QEMM386.SYS provides all the services that HIMEM.SYS does. First, QEMM provides applications with extended memory access according to Microsoft's Extended Memory Specification (XMS). This includes providing Windows with all the XMS memory it needs to start in standard and enhanced modes. Second, QEMM manages the High Memory Area (HMA), the first 64K of extended memory, which both QEMM and Windows use to gain additional memory for real-mode applications (including Windows itself in real mode).

QEMM's advantages over HIMEM.SYS are that it provides these important additional features for Windows users:

1. QEMM can convert 386 extended memory into expanded memory for all DOS applications when Windows is not running.

2. QEMM can place memory-resident programs (such as disk caches, mouse drivers, and network software) into extended memory, where these programs work just as they did before but take up little or no conventional memory between 0K and 640K.

3. QEMM can *limit* the amount of extended memory that Windows claims when starting in standard and enhanced modes; HIMEM.SYS assumes that Windows should receive *all* extended memory, therefore leaving none for non-Windows programs that might require extended memory.

The ability to "load high" certain programs (which would otherwise take up memory in the lower 640K) has become very important to many computer users. As an illustration, some programs, called *network shells* — which are required to be in memory before you can use a network — take 50 to 100K away from other DOS programs. Loading the shell programs for Novell's Netware, for example, can prevent some large programs, such as Lotus's Freelance Plus, from having enough memory to start up.

How QEMM Manages the First Megabyte

A diagram of the conventional 640K of RAM that all PCs can address, and the area between 640K and 1MB, is shown in Figure 16-1. This figure shows a "memory map" produced by Manifest, an excellent diagnostic program that Quarterdeck includes with every QEMM386 package.

In this figure, the first 640K of memory (called *conventional* memory) is shown as the first ten rows in the large chart. This 640K of memory occupies the address rows labeled 0000, 1000, 2000, and so on up to 9000.

The 384K memory area between 640K and 1MB is shown as the next six rows in the chart. These rows are labeled A000, B000, C000, and so on up to F000. These labels are hexadecimal numbers. In hex numbering, the next number after 9 is A, the next number after A is B, and so on.

In order to understand the use of hexadecimal numbering, I visualize these numbers as the odometer on a car. When a car using a *decimal* odometer reaches 999 miles, of course, the next mile turns the odometer over to 1000. In hexadecimal numbering, the mile after 999 is 99A, then 99B, 99C, 99D, 99E, 99F, *then* the last digit turns over and our hex odometer reads 9A0.

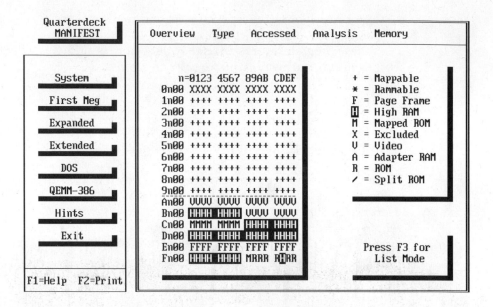

Figure 16-1: One of Manifest's diagnostic screens. The large chart in the center of the screen shows the first 1MB of memory addresses. The top ten rows (0000 through 9000) represent 640K of conventional memory. The next six rows (A000 through F000) represent the 384K of memory addresses between 640K and 1MB. By filling the space with different letters, Manifest shows how these addresses are being used. Some of the memory above 640K is being used by a video adapter board (V) and a ROM BIOS chip (R). In addition, QEMM has added a Page Frame (F) and moved some extended memory to create High RAM (the reversed H's). By counting the H's (each of which represents 4K), we can see that QEMM has made an additional 164K of High RAM available. Some DOS programs can be loaded into this area, conserving the lower 640K.

Visualizing these hexadecimal numbers on an odometer, you can turn the odometer forwards and backwards to add and subtract these numbers in your head. It is often necessary to subtract 1 from a hexadecimal number in order to configure memory managers to use certain memory boundaries. You might have to specify, for example, the entire area from the E000 line to the F000 line, *not including* F000 itself. You must specify the address that is *one before* F000.

Using our hex odometer, we can see the numbers around the F000 line rolling up or down, as in this example:

```
F003
F002
F001                                    ↑
F000              Higher Memory Addresses
EFFF
EFFE
EFFD
EFFC              Lower Memory Addresses
EFFB                                    ↓
EFFA
EFF9
```

The memory address before F000 is EFFF. The last address within the first megabyte is FFFF. The first address after FFFF is 10000 — the beginning of *extended* memory.

The area above 640K (from A000 to FFFF) is not occupied by RAM chips, as with the lower 640K. It is reserved for the memory that resides on adapter boards and devices in a PC — video adapters, network adapters, read-only memory (ROM) chips, and so on. But, as we shall see in this chapter, a variety of other uses have been made of this memory in addition to simply providing addresses for memory on adapter boards.

This 384K memory area has been called a variety of names — high memory, upper memory, shadow memory, the Twilight Zone, etc. The most accurate name for this area, I believe, is *adapter segment* memory, because of the adapter boards that use addresses in this area.

Both Windows and QEMM make use of addresses in the adapter segment. On a 386, Windows and QEMM can move pieces of a machine's extended memory from addresses *above* 1MB to addresses *between* 640K and 1MB. This can provide more memory for some operations. Both programs can relocate extended memory into the adapter segment, for example, to create a 64K "Page Frame" that is used by applications that access expanded memory. QEMM does this by itself; Windows requires the services of the HIMEM.SYS driver.

Only one memory manager can be in control of the 386 processor at a time. Therefore, when HIMEM.SYS is loaded, it can prevent other 386 memory managers from being used. Since HIMEM.SYS does not have the ability to load resident programs in memory locations higher than 640K, in some configurations there is not enough conventional memory for users to start Windows or load their other large programs — inside *or* outside Windows.

At the request of many companies that rely on 386 memory managers, Microsoft made a solution available. A separate software program was released that allowed 386 memory management programs such as Quarterdeck's QEMM and Qualitas Inc.'s, 386Max to take over the functions usually provided by HIMEM.SYS. This separate program, called WINHIRAM.VXD, is included with the distribution diskettes for QEMM and other memory managers. (The VXD stands for Virtual eXtended memory Driver.) WINHIRAM.VXD contains all the program code necessary for 386 memory managers to perform EMM services for Windows. In future versions of Windows, WINHIRAM.VXD will be included on the Windows distribution diskettes directly. As Microsoft adds features to Windows, updated versions of this memory driver will continue to work with third-party memory managers. This will make programs such as QEMM automatically compatible with newer releases of Windows, and make upgrades to QEMM and 386Max necessary less frequently.

The first release of QEMM that supports Windows 3.0 is QEMM 5.1, which was shipped in the fall of 1990. This release was quickly followed by QEMM 5.11, which fixes two bugs related to memory paging and the IBM PS/2 series of computers. Anyone who purchased QEMM 5.10 during the short time it was available should upgrade to version 5.11. Quarterdeck provides free upgrade diskettes to registered users of version 5.10. The QEMM version number you have is displayed on the screen when QEMM is first loading during the PC start-up process.

The QEMM Installation Process

In most cases, QEMM 5.1 requires no special parameters to support Windows correctly. Installing QEMM with its default settings enables it to provide applications with expanded memory (the type Windows uses in real mode) or extended memory (the type Windows uses in standard or 386 enhanced modes). When you install QEMM, answer "yes" to the question, "Fill All High Memory with RAM?" This will utilize any extended memory in your system in such a way that you can load programs above 640K and provide an expanded memory area for Windows and other applications. It is not necessary to configure QEMM to "leave alone" some extended memory for Windows to use. Give QEMM all extended memory, and it will provide it to all applications that need it, including Windows.

Before using QEMM386.SYS, your CONFIG.SYS file might look like this:

```
FILES=30
BUFFERS=20
DEVICE=c:\win\HIMEM.SYS
device=c:\win\mouse.sys
etc.
```

When you run QEMM's installation program, it adds itself to your CONFIG.SYS file automatically, just before the line that loads HIMEM.SYS. The designers of QEMM chose not to delete your HIMEM.SYS line, preferring to let you edit your CONFIG.SYS file yourself. Having the two programs both loaded in CONFIG.SYS causes no operational problems, because HIMEM.SYS finds that another memory manager (QEMM) is already in place and does not load itself. However, in this situation, the HIMEM.SYS driver does beep when trying to load and displays the message "Error: An Extended Memory Manager is already installed." It is better to start up without this needless delay. If your CONFIG.SYS looks as follows, remove the HIMEM.SYS line with a text editor:

```
FILES=30
BUFFERS=20
DEVICE=c:\qemm\QEMM386.SYS ram rom
DEVICE=c:\win\HIMEM.SYS
device=c:\win\mouse.sys
etc.
```

If you install Windows *after* having installed QEMM, then the line containing HIMEM.SYS will be inserted into CONFIG.SYS by Windows just *above* the line containing QEMM. Again, having both programs loaded causes no fatal problems. In this case, neither HIMEM.SYS nor QEMM386.SYS beeps or displays an error message. When QEMM loads, it detects the HIMEM memory manager and requests that HIMEM transfer control of the memory to QEMM (which HIMEM does). Thereafter, QEMM provides extended and expanded memory to any Windows or non-Windows application that requests it. However, in this situation, HIMEM.SYS still occupies 2.8K of memory below 640K, which now serves no purpose. So it is better to delete the HIMEM.SYS line from your CONFIG.SYS in this situation, just as described above.

After installing QEMM, and removing HIMEM.SYS, run the Optimize program provided on the QEMM distribution diskettes. This program automatically loads all the other device drivers in your CONFIG.SYS and AUTOEXEC.BAT for testing purposes. It keeps track of how much memory each driver (such as a mouse driver) required, and adds lines to CONFIG.SYS and AUTOEXEC.BAT that load these drivers into appropriately sized "holes" in memory between 640K and 1MB. This saves memory below 640K. Backup copies of both CONFIG.SYS and AUTOEXEC.BAT are automatically made so you can go back to the old configuration if necessary. Many computer systems report 100MB or more of additional DOS memory after Optimize has found the best arrangement of TSR's in adapter-segment memory.

Tuning Your SYSTEM.INI File for QEMM

If you often use Windows in 386 enhanced mode, you may want to add the following lines to the [386Enh] section of your SYSTEM.INI file to facilitate QEMM's memory management:

```
[386Enh]
VCPIWarning=false
SystemROMBreakPoint=false
```

VCPI stands for the Virtual Control Program Interface, an extended memory management specification used by programs such as Lotus 1-2-3 Release 3.0, Oracle, Mathematica, and many other large programs. (A complete list may be found in Chapter 5.) Since Windows ordinarily cannot run such programs, it displays a warning message when you start them. QEMM, however, is compatible with these programs. Additionally, some programs make a call for VCPI memory, but run without using VCPI as soon as they detect that they are running in a DOS session under Windows. Therefore, setting VCPIWARNING=FALSE gets rid of the unnecessary message.

Setting SYSTEMROMBREAKPOINT=FALSE allows QEMM, instead of Windows, to handle certain ROM BIOS instructions known as the "break point."

Making Room for Translation Buffers

When QEMM is installed, it normally examines the area between 640K and 1MB every time you start your 386. It then moves some extended memory into "holes" in the adapter segment — addresses that are not already being used by an adapter or other device.

Windows, however, also wants to use memory in this area. This area is primarily used for two purposes: (1) to create a 64K expanded memory "page frame" for use by DOS applications running under Windows, and (2) to create "translation buffers." These translation buffers are a memory area used when Windows is in protected mode (either standard or enhanced mode). When Windows must send a message to a device that can operate only in the lower 1MB of memory — such as writing to a hard disk — Windows uses the translation buffers to send the information. Since this area of memory is lower than 1MB, any DOS device can write to and read from it.

When Windows starts in 386 enhanced mode with QEMM running, it normally requests (and receives) control of the 64K expanded memory page frame that QEMM previously established. No special arrangements by the user are necessary to give Windows control of this page frame. On the other hand, Windows may not be able to find enough memory between 640K and 1MB to establish its translation-buffer area. In that case, Windows places the buffers in conventional memory, using up some memory below 640K that DOS applications running under Windows could use. The size of the translation buffers varies from PC to PC, but on one system I checked, this buffer ate up 13,600 bytes if it was located in conventional memory instead of somewhere between 640K and 1MB.

You can find out the size of these translation buffers on your system by the following procedure.

STEPS:

Finding the Size of Translation Buffers on Your System

Step 1. Use DEVICE=HIMEM.SYS in your CONFIG.SYS during this test, not DEVICE=QEMM386.SYS.

Step 2. Place the line EMMEXCLUDE=A000-EFFF in the [386Enh] section of your SYSTEM.INI file. Reboot your computer and start Windows in 386 enhanced mode (WIN /3). The EMMEXCLUDE statement excludes all memory addresses between 640K and 1MB that Windows could use. Therefore, Windows' translation buffers will *have* to be located in conventional memory, below 640K.

Step 3. Once Windows is running, start a DOS session. At the DOS prompt, give the command CHKDSK. (*Do not use* CHKDSK /F in a DOS session — but CHKDSK alone is all right. See Chapter 5 for details.) Write down the amount of memory that CHKDSK reports is free.

Step 4. Take the EMMEXCLUDE= line out of your SYSTEM.INI file. Exit and restart Windows. Start a DOS session and repeat the CHKDSK command. If the free-memory figure is higher than before, this is the size of the translation buffers on your system. If the figure is no different, then there is not enough room between 640K and 1MB for Windows to place the translation buffers there under your current configuration.

To allow Windows to place its translation buffers above 640K (with QEMM installed), you must exclude some memory between 640K and 1MB from QEMM's use. If QEMM doesn't claim some area within this range (at least 16K), Windows finds the area "unused" and places the translation buffer there.

An excellent prospect for this area, if you are using an EGA or VGA display adapter, is the memory area that would ordinarily be used by a Hercules or other monochrome video board. If you have no monochrome adapter, QEMM manages the memory area otherwise used for monochrome displays. This is a 32K area of memory, located in the addresses B000-B7FF. You can exclude QEMM's use of this area by changing the line in CONFIG.SYS that starts QEMM386.SYS to look like this:

```
DEVICE=c:\qemm\QEMM386.SYS RAM EXCLUDE=B000-B7FF
```

This should also result in Windows reporting some additional memory in the Help About dialog box under the Program Manager. Any memory in this area not needed for translation buffers can also be managed by Windows as part of its "virtual memory" scheme in 386 mode.

If you *are* using a monochrome adapter, or using a monochrome *and* an EGA or VGA adapter, you must find another area between 640K and 1MB to exclude from QEMM's use, so Windows can have that area for translation buffers.

Troubleshooting Windows 3.*x* Problems

Certain problems running Windows 3.*x* can be corrected by adding parameters to the QEMM line in CONFIG.SYS to "tune" Windows' and QEMM's behavior. Often, these problems are not *caused* by the installation of QEMM, but were present in the first place and merely *detected* by QEMM. Other problems with Windows or DOS applications may be caused simply by using any memory manager to change your memory configuration. Then, a previously invisible conflict becomes all too apparent.

Conflicts between two programs can often be discovered by stripping CONFIG.SYS and AUTOEXEC.BAT down to the bare minimum of those commands which are needed to run. Each line containing a memory-resident program can then be added back in until the problem occurs, thereby identifying one of the two conflicting programs. But this method is tedious and time-consuming. Before resorting to mere experimentation, you can take certain definite steps based on the symptoms described next.

If Windows 386 Mode Won't Start or Hangs When Exiting

1. **Use QEMM's RAM parameter.** Windows 386 mode requires QEMM386.SYS to be loaded with a RAM parameter in CONFIG.SYS. A typical line would look like this:

   ```
   DEVICE=c:\qemm\QEMM386.SYS RAM
   ```

   This parameter causes QEMM to fill free memory areas between 640K and 1MB with extended memory, and convert it into memory that Windows and other applications can use.

   If for some reason you do not want QEMM to fill this area with RAM (and so you don't use the RAM parameter), you *must* exclude a certain area between B000 and B7FF from QEMM's use, in order for Windows to use this area. If you don't have a monochrome adapter in your system, both QEMM and Windows try to manage this area. (Using the RAM parameter gives this area to QEMM, and Windows stays away from it.)

   If you don't use the RAM parameter, the line that loads QEMM386.SYS in your CONFIG.SYS file might look like this:

   ```
   DEVICE=c:\qemm\QEMM386.SYS EXCLUDE=B000-B7FF
   ```

2. **Use QEMM's NOSORT parameter.** If your PC has memory chips of a different speed on its motherboard than on an add-in memory board, QEMM "sorts" this memory for efficiency. This would be the situation if you have a memory board such as an AST RAMpage board or an Intel AboveBoard, in addition to memory on your motherboard. QEMM provides the fastest memory to the first several applications that request memory, reserving any slower memory until all the faster memory is in use. This "sorting" feature, however, is turned off by

Windows when starting in 386 mode, and QEMM can no longer manage the sorted memory. It's better to avoid conflict in this situation by using the parameter NOSORT to tell QEMM not to sort the memory, as shown in the following example line. It doesn't hurt to use the NOSORT parameter, even if it is not needed (although it may make a slight difference in the performance of a few applications).

```
DEVICE=c:\qemm\QEMM386.SYS RAM NOSORT
```

3. **Use QEMM's NOFILL parameter.** If your PC would ordinarily have less than 640K of memory on the system board, you can use QEMM to "backfill" memory from an add-in memory board so the system shows a full 640K of conventional RAM, with the remainder as expanded or extended memory. Like the memory-sorting feature, however, this QEMM feature is also disabled by Windows when it enters 386 mode, and Windows cannot handle this backfilling. It should be shut off as shown in the following example:

```
DEVICE=c:\qemm\QEMM386.SYS RAM NOFILL
```

4. **Upgrade from QEMM 5.10 to 5.11 on PS/2s.** This is especially important on IBM PS/2 machines, which use more memory because of a larger ROM BIOS than most other PCs require. Quarterdeck offers a free upgrade to version 5.11 for registered users of QEMM 5.10. If it's necessary to use QEMM 5.10 on a PS/2, you must tell QEMM not to use the PS/2's "extended BIOS data area," by using the parameter NOXBDA as follows:

```
DEVICE=c:\qemm\QEMM386.SYS RAM NOXBDA
```

If Windows Still Won't Run in 386 Mode

1. **Make sure there is no adapter memory conflict.** Both QEMM and Windows in 386 mode make use of areas of memory between 640K and 1MB. If either QEMM or Windows tries to use any part of this memory that is also being claimed by an adapter board, the system will eventually hang or display garbage on the screen.

   To make sure there is no conflict, first eliminate both QEMM's and Windows' use of *any* adapter segment memory, except 64K for an expanded memory page frame (Windows requires this page frame in 386 enhanced mode). If this solves the problem, then some device is probably using adapter-segment memory in the area you excluded.

This test requires a change in both the QEMM386.SYS line in CONFIG.SYS and in Windows' SYSTEM.INI file.

If you are certain, for example, that no device is using the 64K area that starts at D000 (and this area can therefore be used for the page frame), the QEMM386.SYS line would look like this:

```
DEVICE=c:\qemm\QEMM386.SYS RAM X=A000-CFFF FRAME=D000 X=E000-FFFF
```

In the above line, the X= statements mean EXCLUDE= (as shown in previous examples). In case you need to keep this line in CONFIG.SYS short, QEMM interprets X= exactly the same as EXCLUDE=.

The parameter X=A000-CFFF tells QEMM to exclude all of the A, B, and C memory areas from its use. (At least some of these memory addresses are always used by video cards.) Similarly, X=E000-FFFF excludes the E and F areas (which are used for ROM BIOS chips). The FRAME=D000 parameter forces QEMM's 64K expanded memory page frame into the only remaining area, from D000 to DFFF. If you know that a hardware adapter is using any memory in the D area, you should change these values so the page frame does not overlap that adapter's memory usage. The page frame, for example, could be placed at D400 or D800, instead of D000. The beginning of the page frame must start on a 16K memory boundary, so it could not start at D200 (which is only 8K higher than D000).

After saving your changes to the CONFIG.SYS file, open Windows' SYSTEM.INI file with a text editor. Search for several lines that begin with the bracketed statement: [386Enh]. Add lines to exclude Windows' use of expanded memory in the same areas that we excluded QEMM from, as follows:

```
[386Enh]
EMMExclude=a000-cfff
EMMExclude=e000-ffff
```

Save these changes and restart your computer by pressing Ctrl+Alt+Del. If Windows still won't start, or hangs in 386 mode, use one of Quarterdeck's diagnostic programs as described next.

2. **Run QEMM.COM to look for conflicts.** Included on the distribution diskettes with QEMM386.SYS is a separate program called QEMM.COM. After starting your computer with QEMM386.SYS in CONFIG.SYS (even if Windows won't start), you can run QEMM.COM to see a picture of how

your computer uses adapter-segment memory. At the DOS prompt, type QEMM and press Enter. You will see a display like the following:

Area	Size	Status
0000-9FFF	640K	Conventional
A000-BFFF	128K	Video
C000-C7FF	32K	Mapped ROM
C800-D7FF	64K	High RAM
D800-DBFF	16K	Adapter RAM
DC00-EFFF	80K	High RAM
F000-FFFF	64K	ROM

The "Status" column shows how each area of memory is presently used. The first 640K, of course, is "conventional" memory. The next 128K is used by the video adapter (in this hypothetical example). The next 32K is a ROM chip (probably the VGA video ROM) to which QEMM has assigned (mapped) some faster memory. The next 64K is a "high RAM" area that QEMM can use to store programs and data, and the final 64K is where this system's ROM BIOS chips are plugged in.

The area of memory that is probably causing the conflict is shown above as D800-DBFF, which is labeled "adapter RAM." Notice that this 16K of memory is located in the same block of memory that we had previously forced QEMM to use for the expanded memory page frame (in the discussion under point number 1). If QEMM was using this area for the page frame or any other function, either QEMM or Windows would have problems as soon as the adapter board tried to use any of its RAM.

An adapter like this could be an add-in board for a scanner, a printer accelerator board, a specialized video board, or anything that connects to some other peripheral in the system. You must either change the memory addresses that this adapter uses, or set QEMM to avoid using the same memory as this board. It is usually easier to change QEMM's command line.

Other messages from QEMM.COM might reveal other components that might conflict. For example, the D800-DBFF area shown above could have been identified as "ROM," "mapped ROM," or simply "RAM." If an area like this is identified by QEMM.COM as anything other than "Mappable," "High RAM," or "Unused," then that area is probably in use by some piece of add-in hardware and must be left alone by QEMM386.SYS and every other memory manager.

To fix this conflict, the QEMM line in CONFIG.SYS must be edited to specifically exclude the adapter's memory addresses. You can remove the exclusions shown above in the previous QEMM example, and type in the following exclusion instead:

```
DEVICE=c:\qemm\QEMM386.SYS RAM EXCLUDE=D800-DBFF
```

Windows' SYSTEM.INI file probably also needs to be reedited to reflect the information about this adapter board. (If the device does not become "active" until after the QEMM386.SYS line in your CONFIG.SYS, then QEMM may not detect the device, but Windows will. In this case, you do not need to exclude the contested memory area from Windows' use, since Windows will avoid the area on its own.)

Take out the EMMEXCLUDE= lines from the previous SYSTEM.INI example, and replace them with the following line:

```
[386Enh]
EMMExclude=D800-DBFF
```

Now both QEMM and Windows will leave this particular memory area alone. Restart your system by pressing Ctrl+Alt+Del. From the DOS prompt, start Windows. If everything operates normally, the previous problems were almost certainly because Windows and the adapter board were both trying to use the same area of memory.

(*Important:* Note that Windows "rounds up" memory addresses that you tell it to exclude or include with EMMEXCLUDE= and EMMINCLUDE= statements. If you make a mistake and specify EMMEXCLUDE=D800-DC00 instead of EMMEXCLUDE=D800-DBFF, for example, Windows rounds the address DC00 up to the next multiple of 16K, therefore excluding D800 to DFFF.)

3. **More troubleshooting with QEMM.COM.** If the previous diagnostic routine does not help Windows work properly, QEMM.COM provides additional tools to locate memory conflicts. To use these tools, configure QEMM386.SYS as follows and restart the system, but do not try to start Windows:

```
DEVICE=c:\qemm\QEMM386.SYS RAM ON
```

The ON parameter ensures that QEMM will remain enabled during the following procedure. (Usually, QEMM is not fully enabled unless another application program has requested the use of expanded or extended memory.)

It is now necessary to "exercise" your system — each piece of software and hardware in the system must be used briefly. This has the effect of using every area of memory at least once, by one or more programs. Afterwards, QEMM.COM can show you all the areas of memory that were accessed. There may be one or more memory areas that are never touched except in certain circumstances. If these areas are unidentified, either QEMM or Windows may hang if they also try to use these areas. Exercising the system tends to reveal these areas.

To exercise the system, do the following. Start each software program you have, one at a time. In each program, open a document, spreadsheet, or graphic (whatever formats the program supports). Print a document on each printer attached to your system. If the application has a "Shell" or "DOS Command" option, shell out to DOS then return to the application. Exit to DOS, if necessary, to format a diskette in each floppy drive you have.

After this, issue the following command:

```
QEMM ACCESSED
```

QEMM.COM displays a chart showing every area of memory in the first megabyte of memory addresses. Each 4K region of memory will show up as either Accessed (read from), Written, or Unused. Make a note of the Accessed and Written areas of memory, especially those areas between 640K and 1MB. You should probably not allow QEMM and Windows to use these areas. Change accordingly the X= lines for QEMM386.SYS, and the EMMEXCLUDE= lines in SYSTEM.INI, as described earlier.

4. **Avoid page frames outside C000 to F000.** Windows cannot work in 386 mode if any part of the expanded memory page frame is below 640K or above F000. QEMM386.SYS can place the page frame in either of these areas. If QEMM starts up and does not find a free 64K area between 640K and 1MB, it can place the page frame below 640K at memory address 9000 (this number is 64K below A000). Alternately, QEMM can establish a page frame in, say, E800 to F7FF, if there is no ROM BIOS code there and you included this area (with the QEMM parameter INCLUDE=nnnn-F7FF). QEMM tries to place the page frame as high in memory as possible (to leave the biggest possible hole for other uses). If QEMM can claim an area from E800 to F7FF for the page frame, it will do so; but Windows will not function properly with the page frame there. Similarly, the page frame cannot usually go into the A or B areas of adapter segment memory, because video boards

almost always use up these areas. If QEMM.COM shows the page frame to be anywhere except entirely between C000 and EFFF, move it into the "safe" area by changing the FRAME= parameter to QEMM386.SYS as discussed previously.

5. **Disable shadow RAM.** Many PCs move some of their extended memory into the memory areas used by their ROM chips. This makes the ROM instructions execute in RAM, which is faster than the ROMs in which the instructions would otherwise have to be found. This might interfere with Windows' operation if Windows cannot properly detect the use of this memory. Disable the "shadow RAM" feature by following the instructions for your PC. Or disable it through QEMM's NOSHADOWRAM parameter, as follows:

```
DEVICE=c:\qemm\QEMM386.SYS RAM NOSHADOWRAM
```

6. **Exclude QEMM's or Windows' use of monochrome video memory.** Both QEMM and Windows in 386 mode can use an area of memory from B000 to B7FF that is normally used only by monochrome video graphics adapters (such as the Hercules adapter). If you have no such adapter, but Windows won't start in 386 mode, exclude this area of memory from QEMM, as in the following example. Doing this usually results in an increase in the amount of available memory that Windows reports when you click <u>H</u>elp in the Program Manager and then click <u>A</u>bout Program Manager. (This is discussed earlier in this chapter in the topic "Making Room for Translation Buffers.") Check this number before and after making the following change in CONFIG.SYS:

```
DEVICE=c:\qemm\QEMM386.SYS RAM EXCLUDE=B000-B7FF
```

Whether or not you use QEMM, you can eliminate Windows' use of this area, if necessary. (If QEMM is *not* excluded from the monochrome area, and claims it, Windows automatically avoids it.) The SYSTEM.INI file supports a command that prevents Windows from accessing the B000-B7FF area. This command is called DUALDISPLAY=TRUE.

If your system has a dual display (both a color and a monochrome graphics adapter and two monitors), then the monochrome adapter is almost certainly using B000 to B7FF. If you have only a color EGA adapter and monitor, Windows tries to claim the B000 to B7FF area for itself. If you have a VGA adapter and monitor, Windows avoids B000 to B7FF in case you switch into a VGA-monochrome mode, which uses this memory area.

Setting the following line in the [386Enh] section forces Windows to *act* as though a monochrome adapter is present and avoid that memory area:

```
[386Enh]
; The following disables Windows' use of B000-B7FF.
DualDisplay=true
```

You can also use the line EMMEXCLUDE=B000-B7FF in the [386Enh] section to accomplish this exclusion. But these two different commands may have a different effect, depending on whether you have an EGA or VGA system.

7. **Make sure Windows has enough file handles.** Windows' documentation states that there should be a FILES= line in your CONFIG.SYS that allocates at least 30 *file handles,* which are tiny areas of memory where DOS keeps a list of which files are open. Additionally, you should establish up to 20 *buffers,* each of which is a 512-byte chunk of memory where DOS keeps information to speed its access to files on your hard disk. (If you are using SmartDrive, you can reduce the number of buffers to 10. Other disk cache programs recommend setting your BUFFERS= statement as low as 3, since these caches provide better performance than DOS' own buffer memory.) Your CONFIG.SYS file should look like this:

```
FILES=30
BUFFERS=20
```

QEMM includes two small utility programs that allow the memory used by these two CONFIG.SYS lines to be located *above* 640K, instead of below. This frees more memory for DOS applications. Moving ten buffers out of your 640K area, for example, would save 5K in conventional memory.

To do this, you might think you could set your CONFIG.SYS file to look like this:

```
FILES=1
BUFFERS=1
```

Then your AUTOEXEC.BAT file would use QEMM's utility programs FILES.COM and BUFFERS.COM to add additional file and buffer space above 640K, as follows:

```
C:\QEMM\LOADHI FILES +29
C:\QEMM\LOADHI BUFFERS +19
```

However, Windows may not load if there are fewer than 15 file handles in conventional memory below 640K. Nor will Windows load if there is no FILES= statement in CONFIG.SYS or no CONFIG.SYS at all. Make sure to begin with at least 15 file handles in CONFIG.SYS. Then, if you want to add more in your AUTOEXEC.BAT you can use QEMM's FILES.COM to load them above 640K, Windows will find at least the 15 file handles it needs below 640K.

But if you continue to have problems with Windows after making sure at least 15 file handles are below 640K, it's probably not because of the additional file handles and buffers in the adapter-segment memory. But try eliminating file handles and buffers above 640K and placing them all in CONFIG.SYS if you experience any problem.

8. **Remove TSR's that require expanded memory.** You may have in your CONFIG.SYS or AUTOEXEC.BAT file a line that loads a terminate-and-stay-resident (TSR) program which allocates some expanded memory for itself. (Such programs often require a parameter such as "/E" or "/A" to specify expanded memory.) This allocation may conflict with how Windows manages expanded memory. This conflict may have been present before the installation of QEMM, but altering your memory configuration made it noticeable. Microsoft has published a technical paper for software developers that lists several expanded-memory functions that may *not* be used before Windows is loaded. Some of these functions are fairly widely used by older TSR programs, therefore making these programs unusable with Windows, especially in 386 enhanced mode. If you find that Windows works properly after one of these TSR's has been removed from your CONFIG.SYS or AUTOEXEC.BAT files, contact the author of the program to see whether a newer version is available that meets the guidelines published by Microsoft.

9. **Look for bus-master boards.** A *bus-mastering device* is usually a board in your system that controls external peripherals, such as scanners, printers, and SCSI hard disk drives. Most adapter boards are not bus masters. Bus masters are so called because they momentarily take over the system's internal bus that controls each of the slots, and transfer large quantities of data during that instant. This transfer can be much faster than would normally be possible between devices, because the board speaks directly to a particular device. This is called *direct memory addressing* (DMA). This addressing method does not require the board to go through the CPU (286, 386, or whatever), which would delay the transfer.

Bus-master devices may assume they can write directly to an address in memory that will always remain exactly where it was originally. Under Windows, this is not a safe assumption. Windows (in 386 mode) can change locations of memory at any time, to accommodate the memory demands of different programs.

The best bus-master boards ship with device-driver software that meets a specification supported by IBM, Microsoft, and Quarterdeck (among others). This arrangement is called *Virtual DMA Services* (VDS). A bus master using VDS-compatible software will not cause problems under QEMM or Windows in 386 mode. The VDS spec allows the device to find and use the correct memory addresses, no matter where they may physically be located in memory.

Additionally, bus masters will not cause any problems with Windows if they communicate with devices using a ROM BIOS chip or a standard DMA channel, instead of their own DMA. Many bus-master devices can be configured to use the former method instead of the latter.

If you have a bus master device, and it cannot be configured in one of the above ways, you must configure QEMM and Windows to "buffer" that device. Both QEMM and Windows have settings that take a small part of memory and make it available exclusively for the bus master to use. This eliminates problems in 386 mode.

Under Windows, this buffering is turned on automatically in 386 mode by using either the SmartDrive disk cache program or a disk cache program compatible with this feature.

Outside of Windows, QEMM has the capability to buffer bus-master devices. This capability is enabled by adding a DISKBUF parameter to the QEMM line in CONFIG.SYS, as follows:

```
DEVICE=c:\qemm\QEMM386.SYS RAM DISKBUF=2
```

In the above example, "2" stands for 2K of conventional memory that is dedicated to the bus master. This amount should ensure enough memory to correct any problems in 386 mode. It might be possible to improve the transfer speed of the bus-master device by increasing this number up to 10. Try performing a large transfer, such as copying a large directory to a disk drive attached to the bus-master board, with the setting at 2. Then change it to 10, reboot, and try it again. If this is no faster than the same transfer at a setting of 2, leave it at 2. Quarter-deck states that numbers higher than 10 should have no additional benefit.

If you have a bus-master hard disk drive (such as a SCSI drive), see the Disk Drive section for more information.

10. **Swap between QEMM and HIMEM, if necessary.** If all of the above procedures fail to help Windows run in 386 enhanced mode, as a last resort you can switch from using QEMM to using HIMEM.SYS. This does not require reinstalling either QEMM or Windows. Simply place the word REM before the DEVICE=QEMM386.SYS line in CONFIG.SYS. (Since REM is not allowed in CONFIG.SYS files prior to DOS 4.0, this will cause your system to beep and display the message "Unrecognized Command in CONFIG.SYS" when you restart your PC. But this message is harmless and can be ignored.) Then add the line DEVICE=*c:\windows*\HIMEM.SYS right above the old QEMM line. Be sure to remove any other state-ments in CONFIG.SYS or AUTOEXEC.BAT that require the presence of QEMM (such as any LOADHI lines). Then press Ctrl+Alt+Del to reboot your system. If Windows works normally, something about your QEMM line in CONFIG.SYS may have been causing the problem, and another one of the QEMM parameters listed in the QEMM manual may be necessary.

If any of the above reveals a true conflict between QEMM and Windows, it may be necessary to contact Quarterdeck's technical support line at 213-392-9851.

Difficulties Running Windows Applications in 386 Mode

If your Windows applications run slowly, hang, or display the message "Unrecoverable Application Error — Terminating Application" while run-ning Windows in 386 mode under QEMM386.SYS, the problem is almost certainly *not* with QEMM. When Windows loads, it's own internal expanded memory manager requests total control over memory from QEMM. QEMM grants the request, disabling its own functions. Any problems with memory when Windows is in control is Windows' responsibility, until you exit Windows and QEMM is reactivated.

You might create a problem with the hand-off from QEMM to Windows' internal EMM driver, however, if you mistakenly changed some of Windows' settings in the SYSTEM.INI file. In the [386Enh] section of SYSTEM.INI, there are two settings that affect the EMM driver. If these settings are not present, Windows uses default values. But if you typed the default values into the SYSTEM.INI text file, they would look like this:

```
[386Enh]
EMMSize=64
NoEMMDriver=False
```

The SYSINI.TXT text file that comes with Windows explains that the default setting for EMMSIZE= allocates the largest amount of your system memory as expanded memory that it can. You would only want to change this setting if one of your applications has the habit of grabbing *all* expanded memory for itself, leaving no memory for other applications. If one application exhibits this behavior, you will notice it because you cannot return to Windows and start any other DOS application or session while the first DOS program is running.

You might make the mistake of thinking that, since QEMM386.SYS is both an expanded *and* extended memory manager, there is no need for Windows to load its own driver. In this case, you might read SYSINI.TXT and conclude that you could type in EMMSIZE=0, or NOEMMDRIVER=TRUE, or both. The SYSINI.TXT file encourages this, in a way, by stating that the statement NOEMM-DRIVER=TRUE prevents Windows in 386 mode from loading its expanded memory manager.

If you make these changes, you will find out the hard way that Windows *requires* its own EMM driver to be loaded in order to run in 386 enhanced mode. Because of a bug in Windows 3.0, the NOEMMDRIVER= statement is "broken" and does not have the desired effect, no matter how you set it. The statement is not, in fact, implemented. Setting EMMSIZE=0, however, defi-nitely *does* have an effect. Even though Windows' EMM driver may be loaded, if it has no access to expanded memory, Windows cannot run and load applications.

Leave these settings out of SYSTEM.INI (so it can use the defaults) and let Windows load its EMM driver and request control of memory from QEMM. Then the system should run normally.

Other things that can allow Windows to start in 386 mode, but cause problems later, include the use of "shadow RAM" and loading certain incompatible programs above 640K (using LOADHI or another such pro-gram). You may have to disable your system's use of shadow RAM or use QEMM's NOSHADOWRAM parameter, as described above. Alternatively, some of the programs you load before Windows may not work the same way or at all if they are loaded high, instead of in conventional, 640K memory. You may have to use some conventional memory to load these programs, or not use them in conjunction with Windows if they prove incompatible.

If Windows Displays Garbage in 386 Mode

If you see random characters on the screen, perhaps accompanied by some beeping noises, when starting Windows in 386 mode, and you are dumped out to the DOS prompt, there may be a problem with the file WINHIRAM.VXD that Microsoft provides to vendors of Windows 3.0-compatible 386 memory managers. Check to see that this file exists in the same directory that QEMM386.SYS is loaded from. If it's there, make sure it is identical to the one that came on your original QEMM distribution disks. Older versions of this file may not work with newer versions of QEMM, and vice versa. If you have any doubt, you can compare the two files by issuing DOS' COMP command, as follows:

```
COMP c:\qemm\WINHIRAM.VXD  a:\WINHIRAM.VXD
```

If COMP reports that "Files Compare OK," then the two files are exactly identical. Additionally, the message "EOF Marker Not Found," despite its negative sound, is a *good* message, since two files may be identical, even if they have no end-of-file marker. However, if you get the message "File Compare Error" or "Files Are Different Sizes," you should copy the original file from the diskette on top of the hard-disk file as shown below, then compare them again:

```
COPY a:\WINHIRAM.VXD  c:\qemm\WINHIRAM.VXD
```

Some computer makers' versions of DOS include a utility called FC (File Compare) instead of COMP. If so, use that command instead of COMP.

If Windows Runs Slowly in 386 Mode

Windows uses hard disk space in 386 mode for swapping among applications and for creating a print file before sending jobs to the printer. Windows should have a minimum of 2MB of free space (and may be able to use more) on the drive that it uses for .TMP and temporary swap files. This drive is the one specified in your AUTOEXEC.BAT file with the following lines:

```
SET TEMP=c:\directory
SET TMP=c:\directory
```

These statements must be present for Windows and some Windows applications to write temporary scratch files, which are deleted as soon as they are no longer needed. (Some modules of Micrografx Designer as recently as 3.01 look for the TMP rather than the TEMP setting, which is why both are included.) The directory that you specify should be on the fastest drive in your system — a RAM drive, if you have enough memory for one that is 2MB or larger.

Installing QEMM and/or other programs on your hard disk may have reduced the free space on the drive with your TEMP directory just below the point where Windows can use it efficiently. In this case, look for another disk that has more free space or create more free space on your disk (or add more memory). The performance of Windows might be improved when swapping by optimizing your disk with a disk-utility program and then creating a permanent swap file on your disk by using the Swapfile program described in your Windows manual. However, swapping to a hard disk will always be slower than using real RAM. If your hard disk access light comes on frequently while you are using Windows (indicating that Windows is out of memory and is swapping a program to disk to free some up), better performance may only be possible by adding more extended memory.

Networks and QEMM

Network software that uses expanded or extended memory before starting Windows can cause problems. For example, Novell's XMSNET program (which utilizes the XMS standard to request extended memory into which to load itself) has a known problem that is fixed by upgrading from QEMM 5.10 to 5.11. If you are using a network and loading network software in expanded or extended memory, and Windows is having problems that are not rectified by any of the other procedures discussed in this section, load the network software in low memory and try Windows again.

Additionally, if your network uses diskless workstations (with no hard disk or floppy drives installed), you might need a utility that enables QEMM to load Windows' required WINHIRAM.VXD file from anywhere on a network. This utility, called QEMMFIX, allows a diskless workstation to boot up off a network disk drive, then load Windows at any time, even if the drive letter that originally contained WINHIRAM.VXD has changed (which is often the case after logging onto a network). QEMMFIX is available free through Quarterdeck's bulletin board system. Call the BBS with your modem at 213-396-3904. (See Chapter 12 for more information about running Windows on a network.)

For more information on QEMM, contact Quarterdeck Office Systems, 150 Pico Blvd., Santa Monica, CA 90405; 213-392-9851.

Qualitas's 386Max

Qualitas Inc.'s 386Max (formerly called 386-to-the-Max) has become a notable alternative to Quarterdeck's best-selling QEMM memory manager. 386Max, however, is used less often by Windows users than by users of DOS applications on 386s, because 386Max does not work with Windows 3.0 in standard mode — only in real and enhanced modes.

This is because Windows uses some unorthodox methods to access memory in standard mode. Qualitas determined that making 386Max compatible with Windows in this mode would require significant changes to their product every time a new, minor upgrade to Windows was released. Since standard mode is the fastest of Windows' three modes (as explained in Chapter 7), this is a handicap for 386Max users.

Qualitas's products are worth considering for some of their specialized features, particularly support for a larger conventional memory space on IBM PS/2 computers, and support for a concept called *instancing* under Windows. These are explained in the topics that follow.

Cleaning Out the PS/2's Attic

IBM PS/2s require a much larger memory area between 640K and 1MB than other brands of PCs for their ROM BIOS chips. The PS/2 ROMs incorporate lines and lines of code for little-used functions such as Cassette Basic (for the tape-recorder storage used by people in 1981 who didn't have a hard disk or any floppy drives) and OS/2. For this reason, PS/2s claim 128K of memory between 640K and 1MB for these ROM chips, while other PC manufacturers' ROMs require only 64K or less.

Qualitas's special version of 386Max for PS/2s, called Blue Max, "cleans out" the areas of these extra-large ROMs that you aren't using. These adapter segment memory addresses are then available for Blue Max to relocate TSR's and other programs, saving more conventional memory. Blue Max might give you an additional 30K of conventional memory on a PS/2, above the amount you could reclaim with QEMM.

Support for 386 Instancing

The other noteworthy capability of 386Max and Blue Max are their support for *multiple instances* of devices (such as mice) and device drivers (such as ANSI.SYS) in multiple DOS sessions under Windows' enhanced mode. This is called *instancing,* and 386Max automatically provides it for those devices and drivers that require it.

To understand this, visualize two DOS sessions that you have started under Windows in 386 enhanced mode. Both DOS sessions display a bare C> prompt. If you loaded DOS's display-and-keyboard driver ANSI.SYS in your CONFIG.SYS file, you can change the color of the prompt and other text that appears when you type commands. If you give an ANSI command to change the colors in DOS Session number 1, you notice that the colors also change in DOS session 2.

386Max allows you to give an ANSI command that affects only DOS session 1. What's happening is that ANSI.SYS maintains a small area of memory to store its screen colors and other details. Ordinarily, all DOS sessions share this one memory area — therefore, their colors and prompts must be the same. 386Max maintains a different memory area for each DOS session. A change in one does not necessarily control the settings in any other.

This can be important for tricky situations, such as running mice in two different DOS applications simultaneously.

Qualitas can be contacted at 7101 Wisconsin Avenue, Bethesda, MD 20814; 301-907-6700, fax 301-907-0905.

Summary

In this chapter I've explained the use of memory-management alternatives that provide you with more capabilities than HIMEM.SYS. Some of the topics covered include:

▶ The concept of filling unused spaces in the memory areas between 640K and 1MB with useful RAM, freeing up memory below 640K.

▶ How the configuration options in Quarterdeck's QEMM can be used to determine the use of this memory and avoid memory conflicts among various devices and software programs.

▶ What to look for when various error conditions occur under Windows in standard and enhanced modes.

▶ How special features of IBM PS/2s and certain device drivers can be exploited by Qualitas's 386Max and BlueMax products.

Chapter 17
Configuring DOS 5 for Windows

In this chapter. . .

I describe some of DOS's new features, including:

▶ New and updated commands and programs for DOS.

▶ Smoother operation for Windows, and the ability to provide additional conventional memory for DOS sessions running under Windows.

▶ Reasons why you might *not* want to take advantage of some memory-management features of DOS 5, and use third-party memory managers instead.

▶ Details on configuring your CONFIG.SYS and AUTOEXEC.BAT files to gain the most conventional memory.

▶ Which programs are safe to load into memory areas higher than 640K and which programs aren't.

▶ Anomalies affecting several hardware and software products running with DOS 5.

Microsoft released its first version of DOS 5 in mid-1991. This version of DOS, tailored with Windows in mind, offers several features that were unavailable in previous versions.

What DOS 5 Gives You

New and Improved Features

A partial list of the new features of DOS 5 includes:

Clearer Windows. Several tweaks were made to DOS 5 that provide slightly smoother operation for Windows 3.*x,* including the elimination of some obscure causes of Unrecoverable Application Error messages. This alone justifies the upgrade to DOS 5.

Loading DOS in high memory. If you have a 286 or higher, you can load DOS into HIMEM.SYS's High Memory Area (the first 64K of extended memory). This saves about 40K of conventional memory, which DOS applications (and DOS sessions under Windows) can use.

Loading drivers and TSRs above 640K. Some device drivers and terminate-and-stay-resident (memory-resident) programs can be loaded by DOS between the 640K and 1MB area. This saves most of the conventional memory that these programs would use if loaded normally in CONFIG.SYS or AUTOEXEC.BAT, which, again, can be used by DOS applications or DOS sessions.

New utilities. Some of the new programs included with DOS 5 are:

UNDELETE and UNFORMAT programs to recover from mistaken DEL and FORMAT commands.

EDIT, a full-screen editor that replaces the Edlin line editor.

HELP, a utility that explains DOS commands (all DOS commands also support a new "/?" switch to display help text).

SETVER, which reports an earlier DOS version number to applications that run fine under DOS 5 but have to "see" the version they expect.

DOSKEY, which allows you to recall previous commands you issued at a DOS prompt, and give new, shorter names ("aliases") to long DOS commands.

QBASIC, an interpreter for Microsoft's QuickBasic programming language.

Improved utilities. A few of the many improved programs that appear in DOS 5:

FORMAT can now delete all files from a previously formatted diskette in seconds, rather than requiring a complete reformat.

DIR can display directories sorted by name, extension, size, or date, and search through entire disks to find any filename.

DOSSHELL, a graphical program introduced with DOS 4.0, can now display a Windows-like Program Manager and File Manager side by side, and switch between two or more running DOS programs (but not run them simultaneously, like Windows, or run Windows apps).

For Windows users, the most interesting DOS 5 feature is DOS's ability to provide more conventional memory to DOS sessions under Windows. This is described in the remainder of this chapter.

Why You May Not Want to Load Programs High

If you load DOS and DOS programs into memory above the 640K line, you are using up extended memory that is moved into this area for that purpose. Windows and all Windows applications use extended memory (in standard and enhanced modes), so loading programs high can slightly reduce the amount of memory available to your graphical applications.

The only real reason to load DOS and other programs high is if you have a very large DOS application that will not run (or won't run in a DOS session under Windows) unless you increase the amount of conventional memory available to it. Additionally, a few DOS programs run faster for each additional 64K of memory they can claim. But if you don't have such a demanding program (Lotus Freelance Plus would be an example), there is no benefit to moving your DOS TSRs out of conventional memory.

Additionally, some DOS TSRs won't work, or will cause problems when other applications try to run, if they are loaded higher than 640K. It's difficult to predict which combinations of programs will have this type of conflict. Loading a TSR high never improves its performance or its compatibility. You can avoid some trial and error by leaving as many programs as possible in conventional memory.

Why You May Want to Use a Third-Party Memory Manager

Although DOS 5 provides the ability to load itself and TSRs above 640K, you may still want to use third-party memory managers, such as Quarterdeck's QEMM386 (discussed in the previous chapter), which provide additional capabilities that DOS 5 doesn't.

QEMM386 includes an Optimize program that tests all your memory-resident programs and recommends the best order to load them to gain the most memory. Also included is Manifest, a great diagnostic utility that shows you exactly what's in different areas of your system's memory. Additionally, QEMM386 ships with the Vidram utility, which moves the 640K line to provide DOS character-based applications with up to 736K of conventional memory. DOS 5 does not include any of these features.

DOS 5 also does not allow you to specify the exact area of memory above 640K that a TSR should be loaded into. The first TSR you load high is placed by DOS into the largest free area available; the second TSR goes into the largest area left after that, and so on. If your memory-resident programs (such as network drivers) must be loaded in a certain order, but one that is loaded later in the sequence requires the use of a larger memory area, you may not be able to load all your programs by using DOS alone. Programs like QEMM386 allow you to specify the area of memory to use when loading each program high. This can provide a much better "fit" and result in freeing more useful memory for other applications.

Additionally, some of DOS 5's load-high features are not compatible with Windows 3.x in standard mode.

Finally, disk operating systems from vendors other than Microsoft usually have features not included in the current version of MS-DOS. Digital Research, makers of DR-DOS, usually releases new memory-management features before the same features become available in MS-DOS. Contact Digital Research at 70 Garden Court, Monterey, CA 93940, 800-443-4200 or 408-649-3896, for more information.

If DOS 5 meets your needs, however, the following discussion covers ways that you can configure it for the maximum conventional memory usage under Windows. Some of this material assumes that you have read or are familiar with the concepts described in the previous chapter (on using memory managers). Additionally, before you make any of the changes to your CONFIG.SYS file discussed in the following topics, you should make a bootable diskette as described in Chapter 15. Make absolutely sure that you can boot your PC from this diskette before making any of these changes — any errors in your CONFIG.SYS can cause you to lose the ability to use your PC at all without a bootable diskette.

Configuring DOS for Upper Memory

Setting Up Your CONFIG.SYS

To load DOS into memory above 640K, you must have a 286-based system or higher, with enough extended memory for the HIMEM.SYS extended memory manager to claim 64K at the 1MB line. You must ensure that two lines appear at the beginning of your CONFIG.SYS file, in the following order:

```
DEVICE=c:\dos\HIMEM.SYS
DOS=HIGH
```

If you have enough extended memory, DOS probably configured these lines for you when you upgraded to DOS 5. The command line DOS=HIGH in CONFIG.SYS gives DOS the ability to load some of itself into the 64K area that HIMEM.SYS makes available in extended memory. This frees about 40K of conventional memory for use by other applications.

To load other programs above 640K requires a 386-based system or higher, with enough extended memory that DOS can relocate extended memory into the "empty" segments between 640K and 1MB. In addition to the lines used to load DOS itself above 640K, you must add the parameter UMB onto the DOS= line, and add a line that loads the DOS expanded memory manager EMM386.EXE. This looks as follows:

```
DEVICE=c:\dos\HIMEM.SYS
DOS=HIGH,UMB
DEVICE=c:\dos\EMM386.EXE  NOEMS/Y=c:\dos\EMM386.EXE
```

The UMB parameter stands for upper memory blocks. This term is used in the DOS 5 manual to refer to the memory addresses between 640K and 1MB. This is the same area referred to in Windows documentation as adapter segment memory and reserved memory. All these terms mean the same thing. These terms are distinct, however, from the upper memory area, which is the 64K of extended memory just *above* the upper memory blocks area.

Adding the UMB parameter makes it possible for DOS to support the use of upper memory blocks by EMM386.EXE. If you want to force DOS to load itself into conventional memory, and *not* allow EMM386.EXE to load programs above 640K, you might specify the following in your CONFIG.SYS, which is the default:

```
DOS=LOW,NOUMB
```

The NOEMS parameter to EMM386.SYS allows the expanded memory manager to fill the empty area in the upper memory blocks with extended memory (for use in loading programs high). But it does not provide any expanded memory for DOS applications. Instead, more memory is available to load programs high.

The /Y parameter is an undocumented feature of EMM386.EXE that helps Windows find this file when loading in enhanced mode. 386s will not load Windows in standard mode with EMM386.EXE invoked. If you want EMM386.SYS to have the ability to load programs above 640K, *and* you want DOS applications to have the use of expanded memory, use the parameter RAM instead of NOEMS, as follows:

```
DEVICE=c:\dos\EMM386.EXE RAM/Y=c:\dos\EMM386.EXE
```

If you want to provide expanded memory to DOS applications, but not convert *all* extended memory into expanded memory, you can limit the amount of memory that EMM386.EXE converts by placing a number representing your kilobyte limit on the command line, as follows:

```
DEVICE=c:\dos\EMM386.EXE 512 RAM/Y=c:\dos\EMM386.EXE
```

The NOEMS parameter *does* allow Windows in 386 enhanced mode to provide expanded memory to DOS applications that are running in DOS sessions under Windows. So you might want to use NOEMS instead of RAM if you only use your DOS expanded-memory programs under Windows.

If you don't need to provide applications with expanded memory (because your DOS programs don't need it, and no Windows programs use it), you can gain more memory in your upper memory blocks by telling EMM386.EXE to include the 64K area beginning at E000. EMM386.EXE ignores this 64K area in case you're using an IBM PS/2 system, or some other component that uses up this much memory. If you're sure that this memory segment is free, add it to the area made available to EMM386.EXE by using the following line:

```
DEVICE=c:\dos\EMM386.EXE NOEMS I=E000-EFFF/Y=c:\dos\EMM386.EXE
```

If certain areas of memory need to be *excluded* from use, perhaps because a board activates this memory area after CONFIG.SYS has been loaded, you can use an X= switch to do the opposite:

```
DEVICE=c:\dos\EMM386.EXE NOEMS X=C400-C7FF/Y=c:\dos\EMM386.EXE
```

Loading Programs into Upper Memory Blocks

Once you have made the preceding changes to your CONFIG.SYS, reboot your PC to make the changes take effect. If everything works normally, and your system starts up and displays the DOS C> prompt (or whatever prompt you like to display), you are ready to determine which programs to load into upper memory blocks. If your system hangs, reboot with your bootable diskette and edit the lines in your CONFIG.SYS until your PC boots normally.

At this point, you can run the program EMM386.EXE as a command from the DOS prompt, and it will report the starting address of the upper memory blocks where programs can be loaded above 640K. This report may not be very useful, since it will probably say that the largest upper memory block available is 0K. The reason is that these blocks are already allocated to DOS and EMM386.EXE is not counting them. But you *can* use them to load programs high.

To find the amount of memory that your TSRs are presently occupying and the size of "holes" in your upper memory blocks into which you can move these programs, give the following command at a DOS prompt:

```
MEM /P | MORE
```

The MEM command, with its Program switch, displays a long list showing the addresses at which all programs in memory are presently loaded. The vertical bar (|) sends this list to the MORE utility, which displays only one screen at a time if the list is longer than a single screen.

MEM also displays the size of each program in memory. Memory addresses and memory sizes are displayed in hexadecimal code. The first byte of memory is at location 000000. The first byte above 640K is at location 0A0000, and the last byte of the upper memory blocks is at location 0FFFFF. Memory blocks marked "Free" above 0A0000 are empty spaces in memory, into which you can load TSRs.

DOS loads programs into upper memory blocks, as mentioned earlier, by placing each program into the largest available empty memory area. Look through the MEM list to find a TSR that has a small enough size to fit into an available Free space. If this TSR is a device driver that you load from CONFIG.SYS, you can load it high by using the new DEVICEHIGH= statement, as shown:

```
DEVICEHIGH=c:\dos\ansi.sys
```

After making this change, reboot and run the command MEM /P | MORE again. You should see that your driver now occupies a space in memory above 0A0000.

Some drivers take up more memory after they start running than they do when they are first loaded. This can cause your system to hang, because these drivers do not "see" enough memory above themselves. If this is the case, you can specify an amount of memory for the exclusive use of such a driver. This amount is specified, again, in hexadecimal code. The following command line, for example, would allocate 4K to a driver (since 1000, in hexadecimal code, is equal to 16^3, or 4096 bytes):

```
DEVICEHIGH SIZE=1000 c:\device\driver.sys
```

To load a program into upper memory blocks in your AUTOEXEC.BAT file (or at a DOS prompt), you use the new LOADHIGH command. The following command loads into an upper memory block a TSR in your C:\UTILITY directory:

```
LOADHIGH c:\utility\tsr.com
```

The LOADHIGH command doesn't work to load batch files, only .COM and .EXE executable files. (You can use LOADHIGH *within* a batch file to load an executable, however.) And, of course, many TSRs and utilities won't work when loaded above 640K. Some of these are described later in this chapter.

Programs Safe to Load Above 640K

Microsoft documents that the following DOS 5 drivers are safe to load above 640K using the DEVICEHIGH= line in your CONFIG.SYS file:

> ANSI.SYS
> DISPLAY.SYS
> DRIVER.SYS
> EGA.SYS
> PRINTER.SYS
> RAMDRIVE.SYS

Additionally, the following DOS memory-resident utilities are safe to load using the LOADHIGH command in your AUTOEXEC.BAT file:

> APPEND.EXE (but you shouldn't use this with Windows)
> DOSKEY.COM
> DOSSHELL.COM
> GRAPHICS.COM

KEYB.COM
NLSFUNC.EXE
MODE.COM
SHARE.EXE
PRINT.EXE

Programs You Shouldn't Load Above 640K

It's not possible to list all the programs that may have difficulty or hang your system when loaded above 640K. But the following are a few known cases.

Don't try to use the DEVICEHIGH= statement on HIMEM.SYS or EMM386.SYS. These drivers must be loaded before you use any DEVICEHIGH= statement, and they must be in conventional memory, anyway.

Don't load SmartDrive high. I've received conflicting information on this, but it's better not to experiment with all the files on your hard drive. Load SmartDrive normally for safety's sake.

Don't use the DEVICEHIGH= statement on the FILES= or BUFFERS= lines in your CONFIG.SYS. Leave buffers and file handles in conventional memory, until you receive notice that these tricks work with DOS 5.

DOS 5 Anomalies

The following topics describe other considerations you should take into account when using DOS and Windows programs with DOS 5.

Running EMM386 Under Windows

If you start a DOS session and try to run the EMM386 program to see a report of your memory, you receive the error message, "EMM386 Driver Not Installed." This message, of course, means that the EMM386 driver *is* installed. But Windows' own expanded memory manager has disabled it and does not have the ability to report to you on your memory status. You must run EMM386 outside Windows to get a report.

Additionally, DOS 5 installs a read-only file named WINA20.386 in the root directory of your boot disk (probably your C: drive), if you have a system that can run Windows in enhanced mode. You can move this support file out of your root directory if you place the undocumented command SWITCHES=/W in your CONFIG.SYS, and the line DEVICE=C:\DOS\WINA20.386 in the [386Enh] section of your SYSTEM.INI.

DOS 4.x Drives Larger Than 32MB

If you used various versions of DOS 4.x to create a hard disk drive letter larger than 32MB, once you upgrade to DOS 5, you *must not boot that system with a DOS 4.x diskette*. Doing so risks rendering unreadable all the information on that drive. DOS 5 changes the partition information on these larger-than-32MB drives, if they were created with a version of DOS 4.x that used *logical sectoring*. This includes the OEM versions of DOS 4.x from Zenith, Toshiba, NEC, Wyse, and many other computer manufacturers.

Once you upgrade to DOS 5, collect any bootable diskettes that were formatted using DOS 4.x and store them in a safe place where they will never be used to boot your PC.

Third-Party Disk Partitions Larger Than 32MB

DOS 5 may refuse to run its automatic upgrade utility, SETUP.EXE, if you used a third-party disk partitioning utility to create hard disk drive letters larger than 32MB.

These third-party products include the following manufacturers, with the name of their product and a device driver that you may find in your CONFIG.SYS file:

Manufacturer:	Product:	Device Driver:
Golden Bow Systems	Vfeature Deluxe	FIXT_DRV.SYS
Hewlett-Packard	MultiVol	MULTIVOL.SYS
Hewlett-Packard	Volume Expansion	HARDRIVE.SYS
Ontrack Systems	Disk Manager	DMDRVR.BIN
Storage Dimensions	SpeedStor	HARDRIVE.SYS *or* SSTOR.SYS

You may be using one of these drivers without being aware of it. Many of these drives were partitioned at the factory and never required that you run any utility to partition these larger-than-32MB drives yourself. Seagate, for example, shipped drives for years bundled with Ontrack Disk Manager. Hewlett-Packard distributed MultiVol or Volume Expansion with its HP-DOS in both versions 3.2 and 3.3.

If you use *any* drive letters that are larger than 32MB, you should assume that you may have a problem. More information about these drivers is also described in Chapter 8. And it's worth repeating here that you should avoid creating drive letters larger than 32MB unless you are absolutely forced to by the existence of a single data file that is larger than 32MB. Drives partitioned into separate letters of 32MB or less have a faster average access time than huge drives, boosting your performance.

If you use one of the disk-partitioning utilities listed above, you must read the README.TXT file on the DOS 5 diskettes for instructions on how to make these disk drivers compatible.

Networks

In general, network driver software will work with DOS 5 installed, if you use the version of the network driver that is specific to DOS 4. However, network drivers that try to use extended or expanded memory, instead of loading themselves into conventional memory, may not work after DOS 5 is installed — specifically such drivers as Novell's XMSNET4. Other network drivers that support DOS 4 may not work with DOS 5 until you establish a SETVER command in your AUTOEXEC.BAT that "fools" these drivers into thinking they are still running under DOS 4.

For a variety of rules that apply to different network configurations, you must consult the DOS documentation — particularly the README.TXT text file that is included with the DOS distribution diskettes you receive.

Applications That Directly Use Extended Memory

Applications that use interrupt 15 to access extended memory, and do not request extended memory from HIMEM.SYS, may require that you force HIMEM.SYS to leave some extended memory alone so these programs can use it.

This includes such programs as Paradox, Oracle, and some versions of expanded memory managers, including QEMM and Turbo EMS.

You can set aside extended memory for these programs by using the switch /INT15=*nnnn* on the HIMEM.SYS line. For example, to set aside one megabyte of extended memory for DOS applications, you would edit the HIMEM.SYS line in your CONFIG.SYS as follows:

```
DEVICE=c:\dos\HIMEM.SYS /INT15=1024
```

It may also be necessary to use switches when loading an application that uses extended memory, to tell it how much memory it should limit itself to.

Microsoft CD-ROM Extensions

Versions of Microsoft's MSCDEX.EXE CD-ROM extensions that were compatible with DOS 4 also work under DOS 5.

101-Key ROM BIOS Support

Some programs, including IBM DisplayWrite III, Lotus Express, and Lotus Metro, do not provide support for 101-key keyboard extended BIOS commands. You can make these programs work by adding the line SWITCHES=/K to your CONFIG.SYS file, which forces DOS not to use 101-key commands. This means that you cannot access (through DOS 5) key combinations that exist only on 101-key keyboards, such as F11 and F12.

Quarterdeck Manifest

You must use at least version 1.01 of Quarterdeck's Manifest memory diagnostic utility with DOS 5.

Summary

This chapter presents an overview of the new memory-management features introduced with DOS 5, and how these features can be used with Windows. This includes:

▶ Commands and utilities that are new or improved in DOS 5.

▶ How you can gain additional conventional memory for all your DOS sessions under Windows by moving device drivers and memory-resident programs into upper memory blocks.

▶ Some programs that definitely *do* and *do not* work when moved into memory areas higher than 640K.

▶ Specific problems affecting various hardware and software products under DOS 5.

Chapter 18
WIN.INI and SYSTEM.INI Reference

In this chapter...

I provide documentation for almost 200 settings in your WIN.INI and SYSTEM.INI files — the two most important files that initially configure Windows every time it starts — including two types of information:

▶ Recommendations on a few WIN.INI and SYSTEM.INI settings that may not be obvious, or may not be adjustable with Windows' Control Panel.

▶ Reference charts that describe, in one line if possible, what every setting does — providing you a way to scan the list for options that you might want to investigate further.

Understanding WIN.INI and SYSTEM.INI

How These Files Are Documented

Since WIN.INI doesn't appear in your Windows manual's index — and the SYSTEM.INI listing leads only to a discussion of settings for temporary swap files — you might think that most of the options in these files are undocumented features.

In fact, Microsoft included an adequate description of each option in a series of text files that were copied to your hard disk when you installed Windows. You should print these text files — they have names like WININI.TXT, WININI2.TXT, SYSINI.TXT, SYSINI2.TXT, and SYSINI3.TXT — read them, and file them in a convenient place for a permanent reference to these options. These files were broken into smaller pieces by Microsoft since Notepad couldn't open them if they were all saved in one big file.

Given the existence of these reference files, it isn't necessary for me to go into detail on all these options here in these pages. You could write a book (and I'm sure Microsoft will) just explaining in detail what each of these options does and their possible uses.

Instead, I thought it more valuable to create a quick reference to these options — a reminder of what each option does, condensed into a single line, if possible. This allows you to learn a little about each option — you can study Microsoft's text files if you need further information. The reference charts for both WIN.INI and SYSTEM.INI appear at the end of this chapter.

 The Windows initialization files that *are* undocumented are those that control Program Manager, File Manager, and the Control Panel — PROGMAN.INI, WINFILE.INI, and CONTROL.INI. If you're interested in the inner workings of these files, you can examine them and print them out with Notepad. They're almost self-explanatory.

Additionally, undocumented settings in WIN.INI for major Windows applications such as Word for Windows and Excel are described in Chapter 4.

The Structure of an .INI File

Both WIN.INI and SYSTEM.INI share a similar structure. This structure also applies to most .INI files in Windows applications. (It is often preferable for an application to maintain its own, separate .INI file, rather than writing everything into Windows' own WIN.INI.)

An .INI file consists of sections, each of which starts with a section heading in square brackets. The left bracket must be in column 1. This heading is followed by a series of lines, with a keyword or words on the left, followed by an equals sign (=) and a number or text value for that keyword. Remarks, which have no effect on any values, are indicated by a semicolon (;) in column 1 of a line. This looks like the following:

```
[SectionHeading]
; This line is a remark, which Windows ignores.
Keyword=value
```

You should proceed with caution before adding or changing anything in WIN.INI or SYSTEM.INI. Always copy these files to another file, such as WIN.BAK, before making a change to the original. Windows performs little error-checking on these files, and it may be difficult to find a mistake if Windows won't start or has other problems after you make a change. For example, Windows 2.*x* would inform you (when loading) if a filename you specified for a screen font did not exist on your hard disk. Windows 3.*x* "lost" this ability, so if you type a filename wrong, you won't receive any warning when you start Windows — but your font file won't be loaded.

Additionally, lines in WIN.INI and SYSTEM.INI cannot be longer than 127 characters — the same as the DOS limit on command lines. This mostly affects the LOAD= and RUN= lines in the [Windows] section of WIN.INI. People often cram numerous programs into these lines, bringing them dangerously close to the limit. And applications such as the IdleWild screen blanker in Microsoft's Windows Entertainment Pack write their own names into the LOAD= line of WIN.INI over and over again, if you configure them to load themselves automatically. This can eventually cause unexpected results in Windows, since the extra characters are written over other parts of Windows' memory.

You also must keep WIN.INI smaller than 32K in size. You will probably never approach this limit, unless you install scores of fonts into this file.

Indicating Your Preferences

Most keyword settings in .INI files are specified with either a numerical value or a simple choice of two options, such as Yes or No. Windows and Windows applications use a few conventions to turn options on or off:

To Turn an Option On:	To Turn an Option Off:
true	false
yes	no
on	off
1	0

In SYSTEM.INI, all the values that turn options on or off are interchangeable. For example, the SYSTEM.INI setting FILESYSCHANGE=ON forces DOS applications to report to Windows' File Manager any disk writes they make, which slows these applications down. You probably want to make sure this is disabled, by editing the line to FILESYSCHANGE=OFF. It's also disabled if you type FILESYSCHANGE=FALSE, FILESYSCHANGE=NO, or FILESYSCHANGE=0.

But don't count on this in WIN.INI. For example, the WIN.INI setting SPOOLER=YES turns on Windows' Print Manager, and SPOOLER=NO turns it off. But settings like SPOOLER=TRUE, SPOOLER=ON, and SPOOLER=1 *also* turn it off. Windows only looks for the value "yes."

The Windows documentation for SYSTEM.INI calls its yes-no options "Boolean values." But they're actually just on-off switches.

In all cases, Windows reads changes you make to WIN.INI and SYSTEM.INI only when you exit and restart Windows. But if you want to make a Windows *application* read a change you just made, you can trick Windows into reinitializing its copy of WIN.INI. After making your change to WIN.INI, open the Control Panel's Printers dialog box. Don't change any printer settings — just click OK. The Control Panel writes all your printer defaults into WIN.INI. But if you've changed WIN.INI's date or time since Windows first started, the Control Panel first reads your new WIN.INI into memory, and *then* writes its printer information. Now you can start any Windows application that configures itself through WIN.INI, and it will use your new settings.

Of course, you must make sure that you edit .INI files *only* with applications that can read plain text files. Notepad is ideal, and the DOS 5 Edit program or Edlin is fine if Windows won't start and you need to correct an error in an .INI file before trying again.

Secrets of WIN.INI

Programs=

The PROGRAMS= line, in the [Windows] section of WIN.INI, specifies which extensions represent programs that Windows should try to run when you double-click filenames with these extensions. (You can also pull down the File Run menu in Program Manager and File Manager and run them by typing the filename.)

This line should look like the following:

```
Programs=com exe bat pif
```

If you install Windows 3.*x* into a directory that contains a previous version of Windows/386, however, this line in your WIN.INI may not be updated. Windows/386 didn't require you to have the extension "pif" on this line, but

Windows 3.*x* does. You won't be able to run PIF files in Windows 3.*x* unless
that extension is listed.

Many people, myself included, like to use PIF files to run all batch files from
Windows, instead of running the batch file directly. If this makes sense to
you, you should remove the extension "bat" from the PROGRAMS= line and
add it to the [Extensions] section of WIN.INI in association with Notepad.
This way, when you double-click on a .BAT file, you can edit it in Notepad,
then double-click that batch file's PIF to see how it runs.

This would look like the following in your WIN.INI:

```
[Windows]
Programs=com exe pif

[Extensions]
bat=notepad ^.bat
```

Wallpaper=

The WALLPAPER= setting, in the [Desktop] section, specifies the filename of a
bitmap that Windows displays as the background. Instead of using a regular
.BMP bitmap file, however, you can compress your bitmap files and run them
as "run length encoded" files, or .RLE files. This compression saves disk
space, since .BMP files can be very large.

You can compress these files by using either PaintShop or WinGif,
shareware programs located on the diskettes included with this book. The
procedure is described in Chapter 3.

ButtonFace= and Other Undocumented Colors

The [Colors] section of WIN.INI supports a variety of color settings that
cannot be specified by using the Colors icon in the Control Panel. These
settings include:

```
ButtonFace=
ButtonShadow=
ButtonText=
GrayText=
Hilight=
HilightText=
```

BUTTONFACE= is probably the most interesting of these settings. All of the Button settings determine the colors used to display dialog-box buttons, such as OK and Cancel. However, BUTTONFACE= also controls the color of icons used in the File Manager to indicate files and directories. When you start Windows, all these File Manager icons are a bland grey color — quite a staid look. If you specify BUTTONFACE=255 255 255, however, all these icons become white, making the File Manager more pleasant to look at, in my opinion. (And you can speed up the File Manager as explained in Chapter 2, which makes File Manager more pleasant to work with, too.) This also fills your OK buttons and such with white, lightening their look.

All these settings are described in the WIN.INI Reference Chart, later in this chapter.

Secrets of SYSTEM.INI

Undocumented Com Port Settings

If you use serial ports COM3 or COM4 on your PC, you need to set these ports a certain way in the [386Enh] section of SYSTEM.INI to use them in enhanced mode with most communication software. This is explained, in more detail than is possible in the SYSTEM.INI Reference Chart, later in this chapter.

NoEMMDriver=

When Windows starts in 386 enhanced mode, it loads its own expanded memory manager (EMM), which takes over from any other EMM you might have in your CONFIG.SYS file.

The NOEMMDRIVER=TRUE setting in the [386Enh] section of SYSTEM.INI is supposed to prevent this memory manager from loading. This would save a little extended memory, which could be used by other Windows applications.

However, in Windows 3.0, specifying NOEMMDRIVER=TRUE merely disables Windows' *use* of expanded memory functions, but doesn't actually disable the expanded memory manager or save any memory. Microsoft refers to this setting as being "broken." This condition also affects the settings

IGNOREINSTALLEDEMM=YES and EMMSIZE=0. The problem may be fixed in a later release of Windows, but it isn't critical — there is little need for you to try to disable Windows' own EMM anyway.

WindowUpdateTime=

The WINDOWUPDATETIME= setting in the [386Enh] section controls the priority given for updating the display of DOS applications that you run in a window instead of full-screen. (This is only possible on a 386.) Windows' SYSINI3.TXT file is in error in its description of this setting. The text file states that the default of WINDOWUPDATETIME=50 represents the number of milliseconds of time that *Windows* receives *in between* updates of the windowed DOS screen. This suggests that *lowering* the value of the setting would give your windowed DOS app more time, therefore making it run faster.

In fact, the numerical value in this setting represents the relative *timeslice* that your windowed DOS app receives, in proportion to the timeslices of all other applications that are running. You will get better performance out of your DOS applications if you specify WINDOWUPDATETIME=200, or whatever value is appropriate for your particular system. More information on how to find out the optimum value is in Chapter 5.

The [386Enh] Section

The [386Enh] section of SYSTEM.INI is only relevant if you start Windows in 386 enhanced mode. But since this section has more options than any other — and these options are crucial to users of enhanced mode — I have broken the reference chart for this section into logical subsections. This should make it easier for you to find and examine the options that might be pertinent to your system.

This section specifies the filenames of several device drivers that Windows loads in 386 enhanced mode for keyboard and mouse handling, and so on. In many cases, the driver is built into one of Windows' own executable files. If Windows is using an "internal" driver such as this, it is indicated in SYSTEM.INI by an asterisk (*) preceding the filename. This makes Windows look for a driver such as *VDDVGA internally, instead of looking for a file named VDDVGA.DRV in the C:\WINDOWS\SYSTEM subdirectory.

If you need to replace an internal driver with a separate, third-party driver — perhaps one provided for a new piece of hardware or software — you should know that you can almost always specify a full directory name in front of the filename in SYSTEM.INI or WIN.INI. This allows you to dedicate the \SYSTEM subdirectory to Microsoft files, and makes it much easier to avoid filename problems the next time you upgrade to a new version of Windows.

The [386Enh] section in SYSTEM.INI itself, of course, is still one long section — not broken up the way I have organized it.

How the Reference Charts Are Organized

I have illustrated each setting in WIN.INI and SYSTEM.INI by using typical default values that might be initialized when you first install Windows. This assumes that you use a VGA display, a U.S.-type keyboard, and so on. Change these assumptions to suit your particular system.

Where these default values are true for your computer system, you can use these charts to help you restore your WIN.INI and SYSTEM.INI files to their original state, if you make a mistake that renders them useless. (Prevent this by copying these files to backup names, as described earlier, before making any changes.)

Where a setting has no default values, the words *(no default)* appear after the keyword of the option. In some cases, this means that the keyword will work even if *nothing* appears after the equals sign (=). In other cases, Windows won't work at all unless there is *some* valid value after the equals sign.

In cases where the word None appears after an equals sign, Windows is actually using the letters N-O-N-E as a string — displaying this when you run Setup, for example. If a keyword works with *nothing* after the equals sign, I leave this space blank.

WIN.INI Reference Chart

[Windows] section *(Controls keyboard, mouse, printer defaults, and so on.)*	
Beep=yes	Sounds a beep with each error message.
BorderWidth=3	Width in pixels of window borders, from 1 to 49.
CursorBlinkRate=530	Number of milliseconds between cursor blinks.
Device=*{no default}*	Specifies which printer in the [devices] section is default.
DeviceNotSelectedTimeout=15	Seconds Windows waits for a device to respond.
Documents=*{ext1} {ext2} ...*	Extensions shown as "document" icons in File Manager.
DoubleClickSpeed=452	Milliseconds allowed between clicks for mouse double-clicks.
KeyboardSpeed=31	Milliseconds before a held-down key is repeated.
Load=*{filename1} {filename2} ...*	Programs Windows should load as minimized icons.
MouseSpeed=1	Determines whether Windows will "accelerate" the mouse. 0=No acceleration. 1=Doubles movement after MouseThreshold1 (see below). 2=Also quadruples movement after Mouse-Threshold2.
MouseThreshold1=5	Pixels per mouse-interrupt that trigger MouseSpeed=1.
MouseThreshold2=10	Pixels per mouse-interrupt that trigger MouseSpeed=2.
NetWarn=1	Displays a warning message if your network isn't available.
NullPort=None	Text used in Control Panel for a printer assigned to no port.
Programs=com exe bat pif	Extensions Windows runs when you double-click them.
Run=*{filename1} {filename2} ...*	Programs that Windows should run windowed, not as icons.
Spooler=yes	Turns Print Manager on or off.
Swapdisk=	*Obsolete.* Use SWAPDISK= in SYSTEM.INI instead.
TransmissionRetryTimeout=45	Seconds Windows waits for a busy device to become unbusy.

[Desktop] section *(Controls appearance of desktop and spacing of icons.)*	
GridGranularity=0	Pixels used for a spacing grid that windows "lock on" to.
IconSpacing=77	Pixels between icons on icon line and in Program Manager.
Pattern=None	A bit pattern specified by Control Panel Desktop.
TileWallpaper=0	Tiles the wallpaper bitmap if set to 1; otherwise, centers it.
Wallpaper=None	Specifies a bitmap filename; can be an .RLE file.
WallpaperOriginX=0	Pixels from left edge of screen to shift a tiled wallpaper.
WallpaperOriginY=0	Pixels from top of screen to shift a tiled wallpaper.

[Extensions] section *(Specifies associations and the command to run for each.)*		
ext=filename {switches} {^.ext}	*ext*	is an extension associated with a program.
	filename	defines the program Windows runs.
	switches	are any command-line parameters needed.
	^.ext	indicates document name is passed to program.

[Intl] section *(Settings for date, time, currency, and other defaults.)*

iCountry=1	Specifies countries by their international area code, except 1=U.S., 2=Canada.
iCurrDigits=2	Number of digits after the currency separator (sDecimal).
iCurrency=0	Specifies currency formats: 0=$1; 1=1$; 2=$ 1; 3=1 $.
iDate=0	Date formats: 0=12/31/90; 1=31/12/90; 2=90/12/31. *Obsolete — Win 3 apps use format specified by sShortDate.*
iDigits=2	Number of digits after the decimal separator in numbers.
iLZero=0	Specifies leading zeros in numbers: 0=.5; 1=0.5.
iMeasure=1	Specifies measurement system: 0=Metric; 1=English.
iNegCurr=0	Specifies display of negative numbers: 0=($1); 1=−$1; 2=$−1; 3=$1−; 4=(1$); 5=−1$; 6=1−$; 7=1$−.
iTime=0	Specifies 12- or 24-hour clock: 0=1:00; 1=13:00.
iTLZero=0	Specifies leading zeros in times: 0=6:30; 1=06:30.
s1159=AM	String that follows times before noon in 12-hour format.
s2359=PM	String that follows times after noon in 12-hour format, or after all times in 24-hour format (such as "h" in 1830h).
sCountry=United States	Descriptive string for the country selected in Control Panel.
sCurrency=$	Specifies the symbol used to indicate currency.
sDecimal=.	Separator between whole and decimal currency amounts.
sLanguage=USA	Language, for apps that use different spell checkers, etc. dan=Danish; dut=Dutch; eng=Intl. English; fcf=French Canadian; fin=Finnish; frn=French; ger=German; ice=Icelandic; itn=Italian; nor=Norwegian; por=Portuguese; spa=Spanish; swe=Swedish; USA=U.S. English.
sList=,	Punctuation used to separate items in a list (e.g., a comma).
sLongDate=dddd, MMMM d, yyyy	Specifies long date format, including punctuation. dddd, MMMM d, yyyy appears as Tuesday, January 1, 1991. Month: M=1; MM=01; MMM=Jan; MMMM=January. Day: d=1; dd=01; ddd=Tue; dddd=Tuesday. Year: yy=91; yyyy=1991.
sShortDate=M/d/yy	Specifies short date format, using codes as in sLongDate.
sThousand=,	Punctuation used in numbers over 999 (e.g., a comma).
sTime=:	Punctuation used in time strings, such as 6:30:59.

[Ports] section *(No more than 10 ports may be specified in this section.)*

LPT*n*:=	Parallel port number *n*.
LPT*n*.OS2=	Must be used if running Windows under OS/2. No colon.
LPT*n*.ext=	Any extension makes Windows use BIOS, not direct to port.
COM*n*:=9600,n,8,1{,p}	Com port *n*, baud rate, parity, word length, and stop bits. P is optional and indicates hardware handshaking.

EPT:=	"Enhanced" parallel port used on some IBM PCs.
FILE:=	Devices ask for a filename before printing to this "port."
filename=	Devices write to this filename when assigned to this "port."

[Fonts] section *(Specifies the typographic fonts loaded by Windows.)*

Name=filename	Specifies a font file, which may include a directory name.

[PrinterPorts] section *(Must specify the same printers as in the* [devices] *section.)*

Name=filename,port,15,45	Specifies the driver file in the \SYSTEM or other directory. After the port, numbers specify DeviceNotSelectedTimeout and TransmissionRetryTimeout. These override the default settings described in the [Windows] section.

[Devices] section *(Active devices — used only by Windows 2.x apps.)*

Name=filename,port	Specifies the driver file and port (or "None").

[Colors] section *(Controls the color of window elements, such as title bars.)*

Name=red green blue	0=no color; 128=$1/2$ intensity; 255=full intensity.

Set the following in Control Panel:

ActiveBorder=128 128 128	Inside the foreground window frame.
ActiveTitle=0 64 128	The title bar of the foreground window.
AppWorkspace=255 255 232	Area child windows are drawn on, as in Program Manager.
Background=192 192 192	The Windows Desktop.
InactiveBorder=255 255 255	Inside the frame of background windows.
InactiveTitle=255 255 255	The title bar of background windows.
Menu=255 255 255	Area underneath menu choices.
MenuText=0 0 0	The menu choices themselves.
TitleText=255 255 255	Text inside the title bar.
Scrollbar=224 224 224	Color on either side of the "thumb" in scroll bars.
Window=255 255 255	Background area of an application's main "client" window.
WindowFrame=0 0 0	Lines that make up the edges of a window.
WindowText=0 0 0	Text inside "client" windows.

Change the following manually:

ButtonFace=192 192 192	*Tip:* 255 255 255 makes File Manager folders white.
ButtonShadow=64 64 64	Makes lower-right shadows of buttons dark grey.
ButtonText=0 0 0	Makes text of buttons, such as "OK," black.
GrayText=192 192 192	Makes unavailable menu items light grey (note spelling).
Hilight=64 64 64	Makes highlighted background dark grey (note spelling).
HilightText=255 255 255	Makes highlighted text white (note spelling).

SYSTEM.INI Reference Chart

[Boot] section *(Specifies driver files in \SYSTEM or other directory.)*

286grabber=vgacolor.gr2	Real & standard driver that displays (grabs) DOS sessions.
386grabber=vga.gr3	386 enhanced driver that displays DOS sessions.
comm.drv=comm.drv	Serial communications driver.
display.drv=vga.drv	Driver for a specific video resolution.
fixedfon.fon=vgafix.fon	Fixed-pitch font used in menus by Windows 2.*x* apps.
fonts.fon=vgasys.fon	Proportional font used in menus by Windows 3.*x* apps.
keyboard.drv=keyboard.drv	Driver for a specific flavor of keyboard.
language.dll={no default}	Dynamic Link Library for language support (U.S., if blank).
mouse.drv=mouse.drv	Driver for a specific flavor of mouse.
network.drv={no default}	Driver for network support (no support, if blank).
oemfonts.fon=vgaoem.fon	Font file that displays the IBM PC-8 character set.
shell=progman.exe	Program that starts applications on LOAD= and RUN= lines.
sound.drv=sound.drv	Driver that makes the "beep" (or other sounds).
system.drv=system.drv	Hardware driver; replaced by Adobe Type Manager, etc.

[Boot.description] section *(Text used in Windows Setup to display current choices.)*

display.drv={no default}	Display resolution, *e.g.,* VGA.
network.drv={no default}	Network, *e.g.,* No Network Installed; Novell Netware; etc.
language.dll={no default}	Language selected, *e.g.,* English (American).
keyboard.typ={no default}	Keyboard, *e.g.,* Enhanced 101 or 102 key U.S. and Non U.S.
mouse.drv={no default}	Mouse, *e.g.,* Microsoft or IBM PS/2.

[Keyboard] section *(Settings for differences between keyboards.)*

keyboard.dll={no default}	Filename that handles keyboard (internal, if blank).
oemansi.bin={no default}	Filename for non-U.S. characters (internal U.S., if blank).
type=4	Specifies major keyboard types. 1=IBM PC or XT 83-key keyboard. 2=Olivetti ICO 102-key keyboard. 3=IBM AT 84- or 86-key keyboard. 4=IBM enhanced 101- or 102-key keyboard.
subtype=0	Distinguishes between flavors of major keyboard types. Type 1, Subtype 2=83-key Olivetti M24 or AT&T 6300 301. Type 1, Subtype 4=AT&T 6300 Plus 302-type keyboard. Type 2, Subtype 1=102-key Olivetti M24 ICO-type.

[NonWindowsApp] section *(Controls DOS sessions.)*

NetAsyncSwitching=0	Prevents switching away from applications that use async network BIOS calls. Set to 1 to enable switching away.

ScreenLines=25	Lines displayed in DOS sessions; apps can override this.
SwapDisk=*c:\directory*	Drive and directory Windows copies DOS sessions to when switching away in real and standard mode. If blank, uses the SET TEMP= directory or, if none, the Windows directory.

[Standard] section *(Controls Windows in standard mode.)*

Int28Filter=10	Every tenth interrupt 28 (DOS idle) is sent to TSRs loaded before Windows. Larger values improve Windows' speed but hang network drivers. Setting to 0 halts all TSRs.
NetHeapSize=8	Size in kilobytes of buffer for network transfers (if any network).
PadCodeSegments=0	Set to 1 to work around bugs in Intel's C2 version of 80286.
ReservedLowMemory=0	Sets aside *n*K for certain, rare non-Windows applications.

[386Enh] section — Disk *(Controls temporary swap file and disk space.)*

MaxPagingFileSize=*nnnn*	Limit in kilobytes of temporary swap file. Use 1024 or higher.
MinUserDiskSpace=500	Size in kilobytes Windows leaves free when creating a swap file.
Paging=yes	If no, prevents swap file and disables 386 memory features.
PagingDrive=*C*	Drive letter for swap file. If blank, uses Windows drive.
VirtualHDIrq=on	Set to off to make Windows write to drives through BIOS.

[386Enh] section — Drivers *(Internal Windows drivers and installable filenames.)*

CGANoSnow=no	If yes, Windows writes to CGA displays so as to avoid snow.
Device=*filename or *internal*	Driver Windows loads, from the \SYSTEM or other directory.
Display=*vddvga	Display handler. Same as DEVICE=.
Ebios=*ebios	Extended BIOS handler. Same as DEVICE=.
EISADMA=no	Set to no to turn off direct memory access on EISA PCs.
Global=*AAA*	Device name, in all caps, forced to be global to the system.
IRQ9Global=no	Set to yes if floppy drive reads hang your system.
Keyboard=*vkd	Keyboard handler. Same as DEVICE=.
Local=CON	Device name, in all caps, handled separately in each session.
Mouse=*vmd	Mouse handler. Same as DEVICE=.
MouseSoftInit=true	Disable if a mouse in a windowed DOS app is a problem.
NMIReboot=false	If true, causes a reboot on a nonmaskable interrupt.
TranslateScans=no	Set to yes to correct some nonstandard keyboards.
UseInstFile=false	*Obsolete.* If true, Windows looks for INSTANCE.386 file.

[386Enh] section — DOS Apps *(Statements that affect DOS sessions [virtual machines].)*

AllVMsExclusive=false	If true, DOS apps run exclusive full-screen, ignoring PIFs.
AltKeyDelay=.005	Increase if app requires more time to process the Alt key.
AltPasteDelay=.025	Increase if app can't paste after receiving an Alt key.

CGA40WOA.FON=*filename*	Fixed-pitch font for apps in CGA 40-column mode.
CGA80WOA.FON=*filename*	Fixed-pitch font for apps in CGA 80-column mode.
EGA40WOA.FON=*filename*	Fixed-pitch font for apps in EGA 40-column mode.
EGA80WOA.FON=*filename*	Fixed-pitch font for apps in EGA 80-column mode.
FileSysChange=on	Forces DOS apps to inform File Manager of all disk writes.
KeyBoostTime=.001	Time an app gets increased priority with each keystroke.
KeyBufferDelay=.2	Seconds Windows waits when app's keyboard buffer is full.
KeyIdleDelay=.5	Seconds Windows ignores idle calls after you press a key.
KeyPasteDelay=.003	Seconds Windows waits between pasting keystrokes.
KeyPasteTimeout=1	Seconds Windows waits before using slow-paste method.
MinTimeSlice=20	Smallest number of milliseconds a DOS session gets.
PerVMFiles=10	Increase to 20 if DOS app needs more file handles.
VCPIWarning=true	Displays a message when starting a DOS-extender app.
WindowUpdateTime=50	Priority that a windowed DOS app receives. *Tip:* try 200.

[386Enh] section — Memory *(Statements that affect Windows' memory allocation.)*

DMABufferIn1MB=no	If yes, places buffer below 1MB for 8-bit bus master cards.
DMABufferSize=16	Memory in kilobytes for direct memory access transfers.
DualDisplay=no	If yes, Windows always leaves B000-B7FF alone.
EMMExclude=*xxxx-yyyy*	Excludes adapter segment memory from Windows' use.
EMMInclude=*xxxx-yyyy*	Forces Windows to include memory it otherwise ignores.
EMMPageFrame=*xxxx*	Specifies the starting address for the 64K page frame.
EMMSize=65536	Amount of memory for mapping as expanded memory.
HighFloppyReads=yes	Turns DMA verify to E000-EFFF into a read.
IgnoreInstalledEMM=no	If yes, forces Windows to use unknown memory manager.
MapPhysAddress=*n*	Specifies range in megabytes to allocate linear address space.
NoEMMDriver=false	If true, Windows omits loading its memory manager.
ReservePageFrame=true	Puts buffers below 640K, instead of stealing from EMS.
SystemROMBreakPoint=true	Uses break point above F000.

[386Enh] section — Networks *(Statements that affect Windows and networks.)*

InDOSPolling=no	Set to yes if software requires critical section for INT21.
Int28Critical=true	Disable if software needs critical section for INT28.
NetAsyncFallback=false	If true, forces Windows to allocate memory for NetBIOS.
NetAsyncTimeout=5.0	If NETASYNCFALLBACK=TRUE, seconds for critical section.
NetDMASize=0	DMA buffer in kilobytes for NetBIOS (default=32 on MCA).

NetHeapSize=12	Size in kilobytes for network data transfer buffers.
Network=*vnetbios, *dosnet	Internal device to handle networks, or device filename.
PSPIncrement=2	Number of 16-byte increments to add to new DOS sessions.
ReflectDOSInt2A=false	If true, Windows sends INT 2A to network software.
TimerCriticalSection=0	Milliseconds Windows halts during some network activities.
TokenRingSearch=true	Set to false if this search conflicts with a device's memory.
UniqueDOSPSP=false	Set to true to start apps as specified by PSPIncrement.

[386Enh] section — Ports *(Statements that configure com and parallel ports.)*

COMnAutoAssign=2	Seconds Windows holds com port after one app uses it. 0=Any app can use that com port at any time. −1=Windows asks before it assigns the port to any app.
COMnBase=*address*	Set COM3Base=3E8h and COM4Base=2E8h for com apps.
COMBoostTime=2	Milliseconds to allow app to process com port interrupts.
COMnBuffer=128	Number of characters buffered for each com port.
COMnIRQ=x	COM1 & 3 are usually 4, COM2 & 4 are usually 3. Set to −1 to disable a com port if it conflicts with another device.
COMIrqSharing=false	Set to true on MCA and EISA machines that share IRQs.
COMnProtocol=	Set to XOFF only if your transfers consist of plain text.
LPTnAutoAssign=60	Seconds Windows holds parallel port after one app uses it. 0=Any app can use that parallel port at any time. −1=Windows asks before it assigns the port to any app.
SGrabLPT=n	Forces printer interrupts on LPTn to go through Windows.

[386Enh] section — System *(Statements that control Windows' own virtual machine.)*

SysVMEMSLimit=2048	Limit in kilobytes on expanded memory Windows can claim. 0=No expanded memory. −1=Unlimited expanded memory.
SysVMEMSLocked=no	Allows Windows to swap its expanded memory to disk.
SysVMEMSRequired=0	Expanded memory in kilobytes required to start Windows.
SysVMV86Locked=false	Allows Windows to swap its virtual memory to disk.
SysVMXMSLimit=2048	Limit in kilobytes on extended memory for drivers. −1=No limit.
SysVMXMSLocked=no	Allows Windows to swap extended memory to disk.
SysVMXMSRequired=0	Extended memory in kilobytes required to start Windows.
WindowKBRequired=256	Conventional memory in kilobytes required to start Windows.
WindowMemSize=-1	Allows Windows to claim all conventional memory. Set this to a positive value in kilobytes if Windows can't load in 386 mode.
WinExclusive=no	If yes, Windows halts all DOS sessions when in foreground.
WinTimeSlice=100,50	Foreground, background time (1–10000) for Windows apps.

Summary

In this chapter I presented a few pieces of information on settings in your WIN.INI and SYSTEM.INI files, including:

▶ Descriptions of some little-understood settings in WIN.INI and SYSTEM.INI.

▶ Quick reference charts that summarize all the settings in WIN.INI and SYSTEM.INI, in one line if possible, to give you a way to glance down the list looking for items that might require attention in your specific system.

For detailed information on each of these settings, print the WININI*.TXT and SYSINI*.TXT files that were copied to your hard drive when you installed Windows.

SECTION
D

EXCELLENCE
IN WINDOWS
SHAREWARE

The Best in Windows Shareware

How to Use This Windows Shareware

One of the biggest Windows secrets is the existence of scores of Win 3 programs that cost one-half to one-tenth the cost of widely advertised programs. These programs are called *shareware,* and I have gathered the best of these programs together in the disks that accompany this book.

Windows Shareware

Shareware is a revolutionary form of software distribution, in which you receive a fully functional, free trial version of a program *without sending any money!* You can try the program to see if you like it, before incurring any expense. If you *do* like the program, you can register it with the author, after which you receive technical support, upgrades to new and improved versions, and many other goodies, as described later in this chapter.

Compare this with the Windows software you see advertised in most PC magazines. This software costs $100 to $500 or more. You cannot usually try these programs before you buy them. If you find, after installing a program you've bought, that the program doesn't meet your needs, most companies do not allow you to return the software and get your money back. These packages are definitely "try at your own risk."

Shareware programs, by contrast, usually cost only $20 to $50 to register. The cost of shareware is a fraction of the cost of other commercial software, because the developers of these programs don't spend money on advertising and marketing, and so don't add such expenses to their product. The shareware authors take the entire risk of distributing their program. If people don't like it, no one registers. Fortunately, so many people *do* register that it makes the existence of shareware possible.

Shareware is usually distributed by electronic bulletin boards, such as CompuServe, GEnie, and many others. Once a shareware author sends a copy of his or her program to the operators of these bulletin boards, PC users with modems can call in and receive a copy of the program through their phone line (which is called "downloading"). This method of distribution costs the shareware author nothing per copy, unlike the expensive packaging of software with high overhead.

There are two difficulties with this method of distribution from the PC user's point of view, however. The first is that you must pay for the time you spend using the phone lines, the bulletin board, or both, when you download programs. The second is that amateur programmers worldwide have sent literally thousands of programs to these bulletin boards. Most of these programs don't run under Windows at all. If designed for Windows, they may run only under Windows 2.*x* — or they run under Windows 3.*x*, but are error-prone or so simplistic that you wouldn't use them for more than a few minutes before giving up. Finding the "gems" among this remarkable variety of programs would require you to spend weeks copying programs and trying them.

I have combed through descriptions of over 1,000 programs, and personally tested more than 100, to bring you the *Windows 3 Secrets* disks. On these disks are a "Baker's three dozen" of the best Windows shareware programs available at this time. Their scope is impressive. Some of these programs are simple utilities which do only one thing, but do it well. But others are powerful, major applications, with as many configuration options as the most expensive software programs you can find.

None of these programs is the last word in software — each of them continues to evolve and build upon previous versions. None of them may be perfect for your needs — and no software can ever anticipate all the variations in different people's sometimes-incompatible PC hardware and software. But each program has some unique trait that qualifies it to bear our "Excellence in Windows Shareware" title. I think you will enjoy using many of them.

I would like to thank George Lynch for his assistance in organizing these programs. He runs a New York-based, professional training service specializing in Windows applications, such as Word for Windows. Contact: George Lynch, 92 Prospect Park West, Brooklyn, NY 11215; 718-768-5358.

Published Documentation

I've published here portions of the documentation for most of the programs included on the disks. The documentation ranges from a mere page to tomes of nearly 100 pages. At the insistence of the program authors, I have not edited or rewritten the documentation, but reprint it here in their own words (fortunately, most of the program authors are quite literate).

As this book developed I found a number of last-minute programs so outstanding that I just had to include them for you — but I ran out of room for documentation, no matter how hard the typesetters crammed. Rather than leave these programs out, I've included them with their full documentation on the disks. For your convenience, in the book I've put at least the introductory material and in some cases the installation and tutorial — so that you can get a flavor of the program, which should be enough to motivate you to print the rest of the documentation (or register and get it from the vendor). You'll also find the registration form for each package, to make it easy to register.

Free Programs and Shareware Programs

The *Windows 3 Secrets* disks contain both free programs and shareware programs.

Free programs have no technical support, no upgrade policy, and no printed manuals for distribution. They may be copyrighted, which gives their authors the right to control their distribution; or "public-domain," which permits any type of use.

Shareware programs are not free or public-domain programs. They are copyrighted, commercial programs, which include (depending on the policies stated for each program) technical support, bound manuals, free or inexpensive upgrades to advanced versions with additional features, or other benefits for those who register.

The free programs on the *Windows 3 Secrets* disks are:

ComReset	Mark30
GNUchess	WinExit
Klotz	WordBasic Macros
Lander	W.BAT

The shareware programs on the disks are:

Almanac	Paint Shop	Viruscan
ApplicationTimer	PKZIP	Whiskers
Desktop Navigator	Puzzle	WinBatch
Hunter	RecRun	WinClock
Icon Fixer	RunProg	WinEdit
Icon Manager	SnagIt	WinGIF
Launch	Task Manager	WinPost
Magic	Unicom	WinSafe
MetaPlay	Utility Pak	Zip Manager

Some of the above programs are DOS programs, which have been included because they support an important Windows function — setting your com ports for Windows, converting files into a Windows format, compressing files, scanning for viruses, or protecting Windows files from corruption.

The DOS-based programs on the disks are:

ComReset
PKZIP
Viruscan
WinSafe

What You Receive If You Register

Most of the shareware programs display the author's name and address when they first start, to let you know where to register the program for technical support, etc. This display goes away in a few seconds, or when you click OK. But in all cases, the name-and-address display goes away permanently when you register.

Other than this one data display, all of these programs are fully functional Windows utilities. Some programs have "big cousins" which provide advanced features that are not present in the shareware version. But this in no way prevents you from using those functions that each program offers in its "junior" version.

I have not accepted any programs that are merely self-running advertisements for another product ("rolling demos"). Nor have I allowed any programs that utilize a copy protection scheme, a timed expiration date, a limited number of executions, or any other self-destructing mechanism. (The *Windows 3 Secrets* disks themselves are write-protected to defend them against viruses — but this is not copy protection.) Furthermore, all these programs are 100 percent Windows 3.*x*-compatible (not counting the DOS programs, of course); none are Windows 2.*x* programs.

The primary incentive these programs use to encourage you to register them is the quality of their support and upgrade policies. If you register, depending on the conditions stated in the chapters that describe each program, you receive:

♦ At the very least, a permanent license to use the program on your PC.

♦ In most cases, the ability to upgrade to a future version of the program, with features that may significantly enhance the version you have.

♦ Technical support, if you have questions or configuration problems regarding your particular type of PC — usually provided by an electronic mail system (in which you receive a response directly from the authors in a few hours), by regular mail, or, in some cases, by telephone.

♦ Sometimes, a printed manual with more detail or with better illustrations than can be provided in the shareware version — and, if you register multiple copies for a company installation, enough printed manuals for each of your staff.

♦ In a few cases, a disk that contains a registered version of the program, along with other "bonus" shareware programs not listed in this book.

♦ In all cases, the registration of shareware encourages the development of new Windows shareware programs, which could be the next Windows "killer app" — and which you can, again, try out in advance, like all shareware.

I myself am a paid, registered user of each and every one of the shareware programs in this book. I can say that the "treats" I find in my mailbox as a result of registering are truly a joy. This includes everything from upgraded versions of programs to announcements of entirely new programs (based on ideas so great that I wish I'd thought of them first!).

The Association of Shareware Professionals

As shareware grew into an accepted distribution method for software over the last several years, authors of shareware felt a need for a cooperative organization. The Association of Shareware Professionals (ASP) was formed in 1987 to "strengthen the future of 'shareware' (user-supported software) as an alternative to software distributed under normal retail marketing methods."

The ASP certifies programs as meeting their criteria for shareware and sponsors events at computer industry events. If you are a software author, the ASP may help you find distribution channels for your program. At this writing, membership was very reasonable — $50 for the first year, $75 thereafter. For more information, write the Executive Director, Association of Shareware Professionals, 545 Grover Road, Muskegon, MI 49442-9427, or send a message to CompuServe 72050,1433.

The ASP Ombudsman Program

To resolve any questions about the role of shareware, registrations, licenses, and so on, the ASP established an Ombudsman to hear all parties. Not all of the shareware authors who have programs on the disks in this book are members of the ASP. But if you have a support problem with an author who is, and you cannot settle it directly with that publisher, the Ombudsman may find a remedy. Remember that you cannot expect technical support for any program unless you are a registered user of that program.

As the Association's literature describes it, "ASP wants to make sure that the shareware concept works for you. If you are unable to resolve a shareware-related problem with an ASP member by contacting the member directly, ASP may be able to help. The ASP Ombudsman can help you resolve a dispute or problem with an ASP member, but does not provide technical support for members' products. Please write to the ASP Ombudsman at P.O. Box 5786, Bellevue, WA 98006, or send a CompuServe message via easyplex to ASP Ombudsman, 70007,3536."

General License Agreement

Each of the shareware programs on the accompanying disks has its own license agreement and terms. These are printed in the chapter describing each program, or in a text file enclosed with the program on the disk. In general, you should assume that any shareware program adheres to at least the following license terms suggested by the ASP, where *Program* is the specific shareware program, and *Company* is the program's author or publisher:

The Program is supplied as is. The author disclaims all warranties, expressed or implied, including, without limitation, the warranties of merchantability and of fitness for any purpose. The author assumes no liability for damages, direct or consequential, which may result from the use of the Program.

The Program is a "shareware program," and is provided at no charge to the user for evaluation. Feel free to share it with your friends, but please do not give it away altered or as part of another system. The essence of "user-supported" software is to provide personal computer users with quality software without high prices, and yet to provide incentives for programmers to continue to develop new products. If you find this program useful, and find that you continue to use the Program after a reasonable trial period, you must make a registration payment to the Company. The registration fee will license one copy for one use on any one computer at any one time. You must treat this software just like a copyrighted book. An example is that this software may be used by any number of people and may be freely moved from one computer location to another, as long as there is no possibility of it being used at one location while it's being used at another — just as a book cannot be read by two different persons at the same time.

Commercial users of the Program must register and pay for their copies of the Program within 30 days of first use or their license is withdrawn. Site-license arrangements may be made by contacting the Company.

Anyone distributing the Program for any kind of remuneration must first contact the Company at the address provided for authorization. This authorization will be automatically granted to distributors recognized by the ASP as adhering to its guidelines for shareware distributors, and such distributors may begin offering the Program immediately. (However, the Company must still be advised so that the distributor can be kept up-to-date with the latest version of the Program.)

You are encouraged to pass a copy of the Program along to your friends for evaluation. Please encourage them to register their copy, if they find that they can use it. All registered users will receive a copy of the latest version of the Program.

Each of the programs and documentation thereto are published and distributed with this book with the written permission of the authors of each. The programs herein are supplied as is. Brian Livingston and IDG Books Worldwide Inc. individually and together disclaim all warranties, expressed or implied, including, without limitation, the warranties of merchantability and of fitness for any particular purpose; and assume no liability for damages, direct or consequential, which may result from the use of the programs or reliance on the documentation.

Installation of Shareware Programs

Complete installation instructions for the Windows 3 Secrets disks are on the last page of this book.

Use This First!

Preface to Viruscan, Clean-Up, and Vshield _____

by Brian Livingston

Computer viruses are programs that secretly copy themselves into other programs on your disks. After a random period of time, destructive viruses erase all the files on your hard drive, or take other harmful or irritating actions.

Before using your PC again, you should insert the *Windows 3 Secrets* Disk #1 in a floppy drive and use it to search your hard drive(s) for viruses. To do this, type the following command at a DOS prompt:

```
A:\SCAN C: D: E:
```

Include only as many drive letters as you have hard drives: C:, D:, E:, and so on. The SCAN.EXE program does not write anything to your hard drive (unless you use special parameters, as explained later in this chapter). If your system is free from computer viruses, you will see the message, "No viruses found." If you see a message that indicates that SCAN.EXE *did* find a virus, you should immediately read the information in this chapter on how to remove the virus before you proceed.

I feel so strongly that everyone should be able to scan their PC for viruses that the SCAN.EXE program is stored in a uncompressed, immediately usable form in the root directory of Disk 1. You can use this disk to test any PC — the disk is write-protected, so it cannot itself be infected. The SCAN.EXE program is *also* located, with Clean-Up, Vshield, and other programs from McAfee Associates, in the \VIRUSCAN directory on the disk. You should install these programs from this directory and use them on a regular basis.

Since McAfee Associates updates its virus-detection programs approximately once a month for registered users, you should definitely register to benefit from these updates. Dozens of new strains of computer viruses appear each month — most of which are mere variations on the 10 or 12 viruses that are responsible for 95 percent of all virus incidents.

In the future, virus protection will be built into DOS — which caused the problem in the first place by providing no mechanisms to detect "rogue" programs — but until then, you must check for viruses yourself.

For more information, contact the Computer Virus Industry Association, 4423 Cheeney St., Santa Clara, CA 95054, 408-727-4559. Their bulletin board system contains updated anti-virus programs and other text files, which are available by dialing 408-988-4004. In other countries, you should view the AGENTS.TXT file after installing the Viruscan programs from the *Windows 3 Secrets* disks. This text file lists representatives of these anti-virus programs in most parts of the world.

For a complete explanation of viruses, obtain a copy of *Computer Viruses* by John McAfee and Colin Hayes (St. Martin's Press, 175 Fifth Ave., New York, NY 10010, $16.95).

VIRUSCAN and CLEAN-UP

by McAfee Associates

These instructions tell how to identify a virus with the VIRUSCAN program and remove the virus with the CLEAN-UP program. They are intended to provide the person with a virus infection an emergency means to identify and remove an infection. They are not meant to replace the program documentation. Please read through the documentation for detailed instructions. Files on the diskette ending in a .DOC extension have been formatted for printing on a printer with a minimum of 60 lines per page. Files ending in a .TXT extension have not been formatted.

VIRUSCAN (SCAN.EXE)

1. Copy all the VIRUSCAN files to a floppy disk.
2. WRITE PROTECT THE DISK!!!
3. Insert the disk into the infected PC and type:
   SCAN C: D: E:
   This will allow VIRUSCAN to run on the C:, D:, and E: drives. If you do not have D: and E: drives, leave them out.
4. If infected files are found, they may be ERASED by running VIRUSCAN with the /D (overwrite and delete) option:
   SCAN C: D: E: /D
   Running VIRUSCAN with the /D option will delete files in a way that is non-recoverable. Use this option only if you do NOT want to recover any of the infected files. Otherwise use the CLEAN-UP universal virus disinfectant.
5. Turn computer off to remove the virus from memory.

CLEAN-UP (CLEAN.EXE)

1. Copy all the CLEAN-UP files to a floppy disk.
2. WRITE PROTECT THE DISK!!!
3. Power down the infected system and then boot from a clean, write protected system master diskette. Note: If you are unable to reference all of the logical drives on your hard disk after you have booted from a floppy, then check to make sure that you have included on the floppy — and in your CONFIG.SYS — any special-purpose device drivers necessary to access your hard disk.

4. Insert the CLEAN-UP disk into the infected PC and type:
   CLEAN C: D: E: [virus ID code]
   This will allow CLEAN-UP to disinfect viruses on the C:, D:, and E: drives. If you do not have D: and E: drives, leave them out. For the Jerusalem virus, the ID code is [JERU]. For the Stoned virus, the ID code is [STONED]. For other viruses, use the ID code generated by SCAN, or check the VIRLIST.TXT file. Remember to include the square brackets, "[" and "]". If you are disinfecting a file-infector virus, such as the Jerusalem virus, it is recommended that you add the /A switch to the command line to check all files. This will ensure that the virus is removed from any overlay files that may not use the default overlay extensions recognized by CLEAN-UP. If you know that none of your programs use overlays, then the /A switch is not necessary.
5. Turn the computer off and then re-boot from the hard disk.

An Important Note: You have now completed a virus disinfection of your computer system, however, you may have other computers and floppy disks that are infected. You now have a clean PC from which to scan and clean them. Please take the time now to read through the VIRUSCAN and CLEAN-UP documentation to show you the fastest and safest way of removing your computer virus infection.

VIRUSCAN

Version 6.8 74-B
Copyright © 1991 by McAfee Associates

Synopsis

VIRUSCAN (SCAN.EXE) is a virus detection and identification program for the IBM PC and compatible computers. VIRUSCAN will search a PC for known computer viruses in memory, the boot sector, the partition table, and the files of a PC and its disks. VIRUSCAN will also detect the presence of unknown viruses.

SCAN works by searching the system for instructions, sequences or patterns that are unique to each computer virus, and then reporting their presence if found. This method works for viruses that VIRUSCAN recognizes. To detect unknown viruses, VIRUSCAN can create a validation code or "CRC check" for .COM and .EXE files and append it to them. If the file has been modified in any way, SCAN will report that infection may have occurred. VIRUSCAN can also look for new viruses from a user-supplied list of virus search strings. VIRUSCAN runs on any PC with 256Kb and DOS version 2.00 or greater.

Authenticity

VIRUSCAN runs a self-test when executed. If SCAN has been modified in any way, a warning will be displayed. The program will still continue to check for viruses, though. If SCAN reports that it has been damaged, it is recommended that a clean copy be obtained. VIRUSCAN versions 46 and above are packaged with the VALIDATE program to ensure the integrity of the SCAN.EXE file. The VALIDATE.DOC instructions tell how to use the VALIDATE program. The VALIDATE program distributed with VIRUSCAN may be used to check all further versions of SCAN. The validation results for Version 74-B should be:

FILE NAME: SCAN.EXE
SIZE: 80,951
DATE: 02-15-1991
FILE AUTHENTICATION
Check Method 1: BD20
Check Method 2: 0D35

If your copy of SCAN.EXE differs, it may have been modified. Always obtain your copy of VIRUSCAN from a known source. The latest version of VIRUSCAN and validation data for SCAN.EXE can be obtained off of McAfee Associates' bulletin board system at (408) 988-4004.

Overview

VIRUSCAN (SCAN.EXE) scans diskettes or entire systems for pre-existing computer virus infections. It will identify the virus infecting the system, and tell what area of the system (memory, boot sector, file) the virus occupies. An infected file can be removed with the overwrite-and-delete option, /D which will erase the file. The CLEAN-UP program is also available to automatically disinfect the system, and repair damaged areas whenever possible.

VIRUSCAN Version 74 identifies all 217 known computer viruses along with their variants. Some viruses have been modified so that more than one "strain" exists. Counting

such modifications, there are 475 virus variants. The ten most common viruses which account for over 95% of all reported PC infections are also identified by SCAN. The accompanying VIRLIST.TXT file lists describes all new, public domain, and extinct computer viruses identified by SCAN. The number of variants of each virus is listed in parentheses after the virus name.

All known computer viruses infect one or more of the following areas: the hard or fixed disk partition table [also known as the master boot record]; the DOS boot sector of hard disks and floppy disks; or one or more executable files within the system. Executable files include operating system files, .COM files, .EXE files, overlay files, or any other files loaded into memory and executed. A virus that infects more than one area, such as a boot sector and an executable file is called a multipartite virus.

VIRUSCAN identifies every area or file that is infected, and indicates both the name of the virus and CLEAN-UP I.D. code used to remove it. SCAN will check the entire system, an individual diskette, sub-directory, or individual files for existing viruses. VIRUSCAN will also check for new, unknown viruses with the Add Validation and Check Validation options. This is done by computing a code for a file, appending it to the file, and then validating the file against that code. If the file has been modified, the check will no longer match, indicating that viral infection may have occurred. SCAN uses two independently generated CRC (Cyclic Redundancy Check) checks that are added to the end of program files to do this. Files which are self-checking should not be validated since this will "set off" the program's self-check. Files which are self-modifying may have different values for the same program depending upon the modifications. VIRUSCAN adds validation codes to .COM and .EXE files only. The validation codes for the partition table, boot sector, and system files, are kept in a hidden file called SCANVAL.VAL in the root directory.

VIRUSCAN can also be updated to search for new viruses via an External Virus Data File option, which allows the user to provide the VIRUSCAN program with new search strings for viruses. VIRUSCAN can display messages in either English or French. VIRUSCAN works on stand-alone and networked PC's, but not on a file server. For networks, the NETSCAN file server-scanning program is required.

Operation

IMPORTANT NOTE: WRITE-PROTECT YOUR FLOPPY DISK BEFORE SCANNING YOUR SYSTEM TO PREVENT INFECTION OF THE VIRUSCAN PROGRAM.

VIRUSCAN will check each area or file on the designated drive(s) that could be host to a virus. If a virus is found, a message is displayed telling the name of the infected file or system area, and the name of the identified virus. SCAN will examine files for viruses based on their extensions. The default executable extensions supported by SCAN are .BIN, .COM, .EXE, .OV?, .PGM, .PIF, .PRG, .SYS and .XTP. Additional extensions can be added to SCAN, or all files on disk can be selected for scanning. To run VIRUSCAN type:

> SCAN d1: ... d10: /A /AV /CV /D /E .xxx .yyy
> .zzz /EXT d:filename

> /FR /MANY /NLZ /NOMEM /REPORT d:filename
> /RV /X

Options are:

/A Scan all files for viruses
/AV Add validation codes to specified files
/CV Check validation codes for files
/D Overwrite and delete infected file
/E .xxx .yyy .zzz Scan overlay extensions .xxx .yyy .zzz
/EXT d:filename Scan using external virus data file
/FR Display messages in French
/M Scan memory for all viruses (see below for specifics)
/MANY Put SCAN into loop checking drive(s)
/NLZ Skip scanning of LZEXE compressed files
/NOMEM Skip memory checking
/REPORT d:filename Create report of infected files
/RV Remove validation codes from specified files
/X Scan for extinct and research viruses (removed for this version of SCAN)
(d1: ... d10: indicate drives to be scanned)

- The /A option will cause SCAN to go through all files on the referenced drive. This should be used if a file-infecting virus has already been detected. Otherwise the /A option should only be used when checking a new program. The /A option will add a substantial time to scanning. This option takes priority over the /E option. The /AV option allows the user to add validation codes to the files being scanned. If a full drive is specified, SCAN will create validation data for the partition table, boot sector, and system files of the disk as well. Validation adds ten (10) bytes to files; the validation data for the partition table, boot sector, and system files is stored separately in a hidden file in the root directory of the scanned drive.

- The /CV option checks the validation codes inserted by the /AV option. If the file has been changed, SCAN will report that the file has been modified, and that viral infection may have occurred. Using the /CV option adds about 25% more time to scanning. **Note:** Some older Hewlett-Packard and Zenith PCs modify the boot sector or partition table each time the system is booted. This will cause SCAN to continually notify the user of boot sector or partition table modifications if the /CV switch is selected. Check your system's manual to determine if your system contains self-modifying boot code.

- The /D option tells VIRUSCAN to prompt the user to overwrite and delete an infected file when one is found. If the user selects "Y" the infected file will be overwritten with hex code C3 [the Return-to-DOS instruction] and then deleted. A file erased by the /D option cannot be recovered. If the McAfee Associates' CLEAN-UP program is available, it is recommended that CLEAN be used to remove the virus instead of SCAN, since in most cases it will recover the infected file. Boot sector and partition table infectors cannot be removed by the /D option and require the CLEAN-UP virus disinfection program.

- The /E option allows the user to specify an extension or set of extensions to scan. Extensions should include the period character "." and be separated by a space after the /E and between each other. Up to three extensions may be added with the /E. For more extensions, use the /A option.

- The /EXT option allows VIRUSCAN to search for viruses from a text file containing user-created search strings. The syntax for using the external virus data file is /EXT d:filename, where d: is the drive name and filename is the name of the external virus data file. For instructions on how to create an external virus data file, refer to Appendix A.
  Note: The /EXT option is intended for advanced users and computer anti-virus researchers to add their own strings for detection of computer viruses on an interim or emergency basis. When used with the /D option, it will delete infected files. This option is not recommended for general use and should be used with caution. The /FR option tells VIRUSCAN to output all messages in French instead of English. The /M option tells VIRUSCAN to check system memory for all known computer viruses that can inhabit memory. SCAN by default only checks memory for critical and "stealth" viruses, which are viruses which can cause catastrophic damage or spread the infection during the scanning process. SCAN will check memory for the following viruses in any case:

1554	1971	1253	2100
3445-Stealth	4096	512	Anthrax
Brain	Dark Avenger	Disk Killer	Doom-2
EDV	Fish6	Form	Invader
Joshi	Microbes	Mirror	Murphy
Nomenclature	Plastique	Polish-2	P1R (Phoenix)
Taiwan-3	Whale	Zero-Hunt	

If one of these viruses is found in memory, SCAN will stop and advise the user to power down, and reboot the system from a virus-free system disk. Using the /M option with another anti-viral software package may result in false alarms if the other package does not remove its virus search strings from memory. The /M option will add 10 to 40 seconds to the scanning time.

- The /MANY option is used to scan multiple diskettes placed in a given drive. If the user has more than one floppy disk to check for viruses, the /MANY option will allows the user to check them without having to run SCAN multiple times. If a system has been disinfected, the /MANY and /NOMEM options can be used to speed up scanning of disks.

- The /NLZ option tells VIRUSCAN not to look inside files compressed with the LZEXE file compression program. SCAN will still check the programs for external infections.

- The /NOMEM option is used to turn off all memory checking for viruses. It should only be used when a system is known to be free of viruses.

- The /REPORT option is used to generate a listing of infected files. The resulting list is saved to disk as an ASCII text file. To use the report option, specify / REPORT on the command line, followed by the device and filename [See EXAMPLES below for samples].

- The /RV option is used to remove validation codes from a file or files. It can be used to remove the validation code from a diskette, subdirectory, or file(s). Using /RV on a disk will remove the partition table, boot sector, and system file validation. This option can not be used with the /AV option.

- The /X option is used to check for extinct viruses. An extinct virus is defined as a virus from which there have been no infection reports in the preceding twelve (12) months, or a virus that was created as a research tool and does not exist outside of a few tightly-controlled copies. Viruses that are extinct are listed in the accompanying VIRLIST.TXT file preceded with an asterisk "*" next to the virus name. It is recommended that VIRUSCAN initially be run with the /X option but subsequent runs need not use the /X option. **Note:** Viruses are currently not separated into an "extinct" category. This option has been removed from VIRUSCAN until further notice.

Examples

The following examples are shown as they would be typed in.

SCAN C: To scan drive C:
SCAN A:R-HOOPER.EXE To scan file "R-HOOPER.EXE" on drive A:
SCAN A: /A To scan all files on drive A:
SCAN B: /D /A To scan all files on drive B:, and prompt for erasure of infected files.
SCAN C: D: E: /AV /NOMEM To add validation codes to files on drives C:, D:, and E:, and skip memory checking.
SCAN C: D: /M /A /FR To scan memory for all known and extinct viruses, as well as all files on drives C: and D:, and output all messages in French.

SCAN C: D: /E .WPM .COD To scan drives C: and D:, and include files with the extensions .WPM and .COD
SCAN A: /CV To check for known and unknown viruses (via the validation codes) on drive A:
SCAN C: /EXT A:SAMPLE.ASC To scan drive C: for known computer viruses and also for viruses added by the user via the external virus data file option.
SCAN C: /M /REPORT A:INFECTN.RPT To scan for all viruses in memory and drive C:, and create a text file called INFECTN.RPT on drive A:

Exit Codes

VIRUSCAN will set the DOS ERRORLEVEL upon program termination to:

Error Level	Description
0	No viruses found
1	One or more viruses found
2	Abnormal termination (program error)

If a user stops the scanning process, SCAN will set the ERRORLEVEL to 0 or 1 depending on whether or not a virus was discovered prior to termination of the SCAN.

Virus Removal

What do you do if a virus is found? You can contact McAfee Associates for assistance with manually removing the virus, for disinfection utilities, and for more information about the virus. The CLEAN-UP universal virus disinfection program is available and will disinfect the majority of reported computer viruses. It is updated frequently to remove new viruses. The CLEAN-UP program can be downloaded from McAfee Associates BBS. (It is also included on your InfoWorld *Windows 3 Secrets* diskette.)

It is strongly recommended that you get experienced help in dealing with viruses, especially critical viruses that can damage or destroy data [for a listing of critical viruses, see the /M option under OPTIONS, above] and partition table or boot sector infecting viruses, as improper removal of these viruses could result in the loss of all data and use of the disk(s).

If CLEAN-UP is not available, then:

For Boot Sector and Infectors: Power down the infected system and boot from an uninfected, write-protected diskette. Use the DOS SYS command to attempt to overwrite the boot sector. This works in many cases. Run VIRUSCAN to see if the virus has been eradicated. If this does not work, do a file-by-file backup of the system (in other words, do not backup the boot sector) and do a low-level format of the disk. For a floppy diskette, copy the files off the infected diskette using the DOS COPY command, not XCOPY or DISKCOPY which will transfer the virus. Reformat or discard the infected floppy disk.

File Infectors: Power down the infected system and boot from an uninfected, write-protected diskette. Run VIRUSCAN with the /D and /A options. Scan all original disks for viruses and replace programs from them if clean.

Partition Table Infectors: Power down the infected system and boot off of an uninfected, write-protected diskette. Proceed to do a file-by-file backup of the system (in other words, do not backup the partition table). Then do a low-level format of the disk.

Disinfection utilities are available for the majority of reported computer viruses; these programs can be downloaded from McAfee Associates' BBS at (408) 988-4004.

Tech Support

In order to facilitate speedy and accurate support, please have the following information ready when you contact McAfee Associates:

- Program name and version number.
- Type and brand of computer, hard disk, plus any peripherals.
- Version of DOS you are running, plus any TSRs or device drivers in use.
- Printouts of your AUTOEXEC.BAT and CONFIG.SYS files.
- The exact problem you are having. Please be as specific as possible. Having a printout of the screen and/or being at your computer will help also.

McAfee Associates can be contacted by BBS or fax twenty-four hours a day, or call our business office at (408) 988-3832, Monday through Friday, 8:30AM to 6:00PM Pacific Standard Time.

McAfee Associates: (408) 988-3832 office
4423 Cheeney Street: (408) 970-9727 fax
Santa Clara, CA 95054-0253: (408) 988-4004
BBS 2400 bps
U.S.A.: (408) 988-5138 BBS HST 9600
(408) 988-5190 BBS v32 9600

If you are overseas, please refer to the AGENTS.TXT file for a listing of Agents for McAfee Associates product support or sales.

Appendix A: Creating a Virus String File with the /EXT Option

The External Virus Data file should be created with an editor or a word processor and saved as an ASCII text file. Be sure each line ends with a CR/LF pair. Note: The /EXT

option is intended for emergency and research use only. It is an temporary method for identifying new viruses prior to the subsequent release of SCAN. A sound understanding of viruses and string-search techniques is advised as a prerequisite for using this option. The virus string file uses the following format:

```
#Comment about Virus_1
"aabbccddeeff..." Virus_1_Name
#Comment about Virus_2
"gghhiijjkkll..." Virus_2_Name
. .
"uuvvwwxxyyzz..." Virus_n_Name
```

Where aa, bb, cc, etc. are the hexadecimal bytes that you wish to scan for. Each line in the file represents one virus. The Virus Name for each virus is mandatory, and may be up to 25 characters in length. The double quotes (") are required at the beginning and end of each hexadecimal string. SCAN will use the string file to search memory, the Partition Table, Boot Sector, System files, all .COM and .EXE files, and Overlay files with the extension .BIN, .OV?, .PGM, .PIF, .PRG, .SYS and .XTP. Virus strings may contain wild cards. The two wildcard options are:

Fixed Position Wildcard: The question mark "?" may be used to represent a wildcard in a fixed position within the string. For example, the string:

```
E9 7C 00 10 ? 37 CB
```

would match "E9 7C 00 10 27 37 CB", "E9 7C 00 10 9C 37 CB", or any other similar string, no matter what byte was in the fifth place.

Range Wildcard: The asterisk "*", followed by range number in parentheses "(" and ")" is used to represent a variable number of adjoining random bytes. For example, the string:

```
E9 7C *(4) 37 CB
```

would match "E9 7C 00 37 CB", "E9 7C 00 11 37 CB", and "E9 7C 00 11 22 37 CB". The string "E9 7C 00 11 22 33 44 37 CB" would not match since the distance between 7C and 37 is greater than four bytes. You may specify a range of up to 99 bytes.

Up to 10 different wildcards of either kind may be used in one virus string.

Comments

A pound sign "#" at the beginning of a line will denote that it is a comment. Use this for adding notes to the external virus data file. For example:

```
#New .COM virus found in file FRITZ.EXE from
#Schneiderland on 01-22-91
"53 48 45 45 50" Fritz-1 [F-1]
```

Could be used to store a description of the virus, name of the original infected file, where and when it was received, and so forth.

Special thanks to Robert Brown, Christopher Morgan, and Robert Wright for their assistance with the VIRUSCAN documentation.

Registration

A registration fee of $25.00 US is required for the use of VIRUSCAN by individual home users. Registration is for one year and entitles the holder to unlimited free upgrades off of McAfee Associates BBS. Diskettes are not mailed unless requested. Add $9.00 US for diskette mailings. Registration is for home users only and does not apply to businesses, corporations, organizations, government agencies, or schools, who must obtain a license for use. Contact McAfee Associates for more information. Outside of North America, registration and support may be obtained through the agents listed in the accompanying AGENTS.TXT text file.

CLEAN-UP

Version 6.8 74-B
Copyright © 1991 by McAfee Associates

Synopsis

CLEAN-UP (CLEAN.EXE) is a virus disinfection program for IBM PC and compatible computers. CLEAN-UP will search though the partition table, boot sector, or files of a PC and remove a virus specified by the user. In most instances CLEAN-UP is able to repair the infected area of the system and restore it to normal usage. CLEAN-UP works on all viruses identified by the current version of the VIRUSCAN (SCAN.EXE) program. CLEAN-UP runs on any PC with 256Kb and DOS version 2.00 or greater.

Authenticity

CLEAN-UP runs a self-test when executed. If CLEAN has been modified in any way, a warning will be displayed. The program will still continue to remove viruses, though. If CLEAN reports that it has been damaged, it is recommended that a new, clean copy be obtained. CLEAN-UP is packaged with the VALIDATE program to ensure the integrity of the CLEAN.EXE file. The VALIDATE.DOC instructions tell how to use the VALIDATE program. The VALIDATE program distributed with CLEAN-UP may be used to check all further versions of CLEAN. The validation results for Version 74-B should be:

FILE NAME: CLEAN.EXE
SIZE: 105,937

DATE: 02-15-1991
FILE AUTHENTICATION
Check Method 1: 207E
Check Method 2: 04B4

If your copy of CLEAN.EXE differs, it may have been modified. Always obtain your copy of CLEAN-UP from a known source. The latest version of CLEAN-UP and validation data for SCAN.EXE can be obtained off of McAfee Associates' bulletin board system at (408) 988-4004.

Overview

CLEAN-UP searches the system looking for the virus you wish to remove. When an infected file is found, CLEAN-UP isolates and removes the virus, and, in most cases, repairs the infected file and restores it to normal operation. If the file is infected with a less common virus, CLEAN-UP will then display a warning message and prompt the user, asking whether to overwrite and delete the infected file. Files erased in such a manner are non-recoverable.

Verify the suspect virus infection with the VIRUSCAN program before running CLEAN-UP. VIRUSCAN will locate and identify the virus and provide the I.D. code needed to remove it. The I.D. is displayed inside the square brackets, "[" and "]". For example, the I.D. code for the Jerusalem virus is displayed as "[Jeru]". This I.D. must be used with CLEAN-UP to remove the virus. The square brackets "[" and "]" MUST be included. The common viruses that CLEAN-UP is able to remove successfully, and repair and restore the damaged programs are:

1260	1591	1701	1704
4096	Alabama	Alamed	Ashar
Dark Avenger	DataLock	Disk Killer	EDV
Fish	Flip	Invader	Jerusalem A
Jerusalem B	Jerusalem E	Joshi	KeyPress
Liberty	Music Bug	Pakistan Brain	PayDay
Ping Pong B	Plastique	Slow	Stoned
SunDay	Suriv03	Taiwan 3	Taiwan 4
V800	VacSina	Vienna	Violator
Whale	Yankee Doodle	ZeroBug	Bloody
New Jerusalem			

An important note about .EXE files: Some viruses which infect .EXE files cannot be removed successfully in all cases. This usually occurs when the .EXE file loads internal overlays. Instead of attaching to the end of the .EXE file, the virus may attach to the beginning of the overlay area, and program instructions are overwritten. CLEAN-UP will truncate files infected in this manner. If a file no longer runs after being cleaned, replace it from the manufacturer's original disk.

An important note about the Stoned Virus: Removing the Stoned virus can cause loss of the partition table on systems with non-standard formatted hard disks. As a precaution, backup all critical data before running CLEAN-UP. Loss of the partition table can result in the LOSS OF ALL DATA ON THE DISK.

Operation

IMPORTANT NOTE: POWER DOWN YOUR SYSTEM AND BOOT FROM A CLEAN SYSTEM DISK BEFORE BEGINNING. RUN THE CLEAN-UP PROGRAM FROM A WRITE-PRO-TECTED DISK TO PREVENT INFECTION OF THE PRO-GRAM.

Power down the infected system and boot from a clean, write-protected system diskette. This step will insure that the virus is not in control of the computer and will prevent reinfection. After cleaning, power down the system again, reboot from the system disk, and run the VIRUSCAN program to make sure the system has been successfully disinfected. After cleaning the hard disk, run the VIRUSCAN program on any floppies that may have been inserted into the infected system to determine if they have been infected.

CLEAN-UP will display the name of the infected file, the virus found in it, and report a "successful" disinfection when the virus is removed. If a file has been infected multiple times by a virus (possible if the virus does not check to see if it has already attached to a file) than CLEAN-UP will report that the virus has been removed successfully for each infection. To run CLEAN-UP type:

```
CLEAN d1: ... d10: [virus ID] /A /E .xxx /FR /
MANY /M
/REPORT d:filename
```

Options are:

/A Examine all files for viruses
/E .xxx .yyy .zzz Clean overlay extensions .xxx .yyy .zzz.
/FR Display messages in French
/MANY Check and disinfect multiple floppies
/REPORT d:filename Create report of cleaned files
d1: ... d10: indicate drives to be cleaned
[virus ID] Virus identification code - provided by the VIRUSCAN program when it detects a virus. For a complete list of codes, see the accompanying VIRLIST.TXT file

- The /A option will cause CLEAN to go through all files on diskette. This should be used if a file-infecting virus is detected.

- The /E option allows the user to specify an extension or set of extensions to clean. Extensions must be sepa-rated by a space after the /E and between each other. Up to three extensions may be added with the /E. For more extensions, use the /A option.

- The /FR option tells CLEAN-UP to display all messages in French instead of English.

- The /MANY option is used to clean multiple floppy diskettes. If the user has more than one floppy disk to check for viruses, the /MANY option will allows the user to check them without having to run CLEAN multiple times.

- The /REPORT option is used to generate a listing of disinfected files. The resulting list can be saved to disk as an ASCII text file. To use the report option, specify /REPORT on the command line, followed by the device and filename.

Examples

The following examples are shown as they would be typed in on the command line.

CLEAN C: D: E: [JERU] /A To disinfect drives C:, D:, and E: of the Jerusalem virus, searching all files for the virus in the process
CLEAN A: [STONED] To disinfect floppy in drive A: of the Stoned virus
CLEAN C:\MORGAN [DAV] /A To disinfect subdirectory MORGAN on drive C: of the Dark Avenger, searching all files for the virus in the process
CLEAN B: [DOODLE] /REPORT C:YNKINFCT.TXT To disinfect floppy in drive B: of the Yankee Doodle virus, searching all files in the process, and creating a report of disinfected files named YNKINFCT.TXT on drive C:

Registration

A registration fee of $35.00 US is required for the use of CLEAN-UP by individual home users. Registration is for one year and entitles the holder to unlimited free upgrades for the duration of the year. Upgrades must be obtained from the McAfee Associates bulletin board. Diskettes are not mailed with registrations unless specifically requested. Add $9.00 US for diskette mailings. Registration is for home users only and does not apply to businesses, departments, organizations, government agencies, or schools, who must obtain a site license for use. Contact McAfee Associates for more information. Outside of North America, registration and support may be obtained through the agents listed in the accompanying AGENTS.TXT text file.

VSHIELD Version 3.0 74-B
VSHIELD1 Version 0.2

Copyright © 1991 by McAfee Associates.

Synopsis

VSHIELD is a virus prevention program for IBM PC and compatible computers. It will prevent viruses from infecting your system. When VSHIELD first loads it will search the PC for known computer viruses in memory, the partition table, boot sector, system files, and itself and then install itself as a Terminate-and-Stay-Resident (TSR) program. It will then scan all programs before allowing the system to execute them. If any program contains a virus, VSHIELD will refuse to allow it to execute. It will also not allow the system to be warm-booted from any diskette which contains a boot-sector virus. VSHIELD can optionally check files that have been validation coded by the VIRUSCAN (SCAN) program for new, unknown viruses. Complete documentation to VSHIELD appears on the accompanying disk.

VALIDATE

Version 0.3
Copyright © 1991 by McAfee Associates

VALIDATE is a file-authentication program that may be used to check other programs for signs of tampering. VALIDATE uses two discrete methods to generate Cyclic Redundancy Checks (CRC's), which are then displayed for the user to compare against the known value for the program(s) validated. The known validation data can be published by the author of the program or be obtained from a trusted information database. The dual CRC checking provides a high degree of security. Complete documentation for VALIDATE may be found on the accompanying disk.

Registration for McAfee Associates Programs

Registration is required for the use of the VIRUSCAN, SHIELD and CLEAN-UP program series in a home environment. This form should be used to register a program.

Registered users of the VIRUSCAN programs receive free technical support and assistance with virus infections in the form of walk-throughs of virus removal. The McAfee Associates bulletin Board is available (9 lines) for access to the latest versions of the VIRUSCAN series and for downloads of virus related information. A registered user may obtain free upgrades of the registered programs for a period of one year after registration, provided they are downloaded from the BBS. Diskettes are not mailed to registered users unless specifically requested. Diskettes are mailed first class in the U.S. and by airmail for foreign countries. For such mailings, please add $9.

Corporate, business and organizational users require a site license for the use of the VIRUSCAN programs. For site license information please contact McAfee Associates at the address or phone number below.

REGISTRATION FORM For Individual Home Users

PROGRAM: # COPIES: AMOUNT:

CLEAN-UP ($35 per copy) _____ $ _____

VIRUSCAN ($25 per copy) _____ $ _____

VSHIELD ($25 per copy) _____ $ _____

SENTRY ($25 per copy) _____ $ _____

FSHIELD ($25 per copy) _____ $ _____

VCOPY($15 per copy) _____ $ _____

- ADD - $9 for Diskette (5.25" 360K only) $_____

(All programs and documentation fit on one diskette)

TOTAL $_____

PAYMENT BY:

Check/Money Order No._____ enclosed for $_____

OR CHARGE:MasterCard _____ Visa _____

Card Number _____

Name on Card _____ Exp. Date _____

Signature _____

MAILING ADDRESS:

NAME _____

ADDRESS _____

_____

CITY/STATE/PROVINCE _____

COUNTRY/POSTAL CODE _____

HOME PHONE _____

OFFICE PHONE _____

SEND TO:

McAfee Associates
4423 Cheeney Street
Santa Clara, CA 95054-0253
U.S.A.
(408) 988-3832 Voice —
    Use this number for questions/bug reports
(408) 988-4004 BBS —
    Use this number for obtaining program upgrades
(408) 970-9727 FAX

File and Program Management

Desktop Navigator and Task Manager

Desktop Navigator

Copyright © 1991 by METZ Software

Overview

Desktop Navigator is a comprehensive, yet easily understood file and directory manager for Microsoft Windows. Desktop Navigator is a Windows application program that combines several important and time-saving features into one cohesive, menu operated program. With Desktop Navigator you can quickly change drives, directories, or process files. Powerful features such as the ability to move an entire directory tree to another directory and/or drive are also included. Display options include a 12 or 24 hour clock on screen, a memory display that details both DOS and Expanded EMS RAM, an edit field which lets you specify the type of file to be displayed, a graphical directory tree, and a comprehensive file display. Desktop Navigator uses about 30K of memory.

If you like Desktop Navigator, please register it. Registering this application will provide you with the following benefits: Product support, free upgrades, prioritized consideration of your requests, and the means for METZ Software to continue development of this and other MS Windows products. Plus, the diskette you receive will contain all of the latest versions of our products. We also give you a license number which turns off the built-in registration reminders. We apologize for the lack of formal documentation or online help, fortunately, the ThreadZ File F/X applications do have both. [See a description of ThreadZ File F/X at the end of this chapter.] Also, you can call METZ Software if you have any questions, problems, or suggestions (please use our support number: 206/641-4525). We will be glad to help you any way we can.

Layout

Desktop Navigator has the following components within its display area:

Digital clock: Displays current date and time. Configurable from the Configuration/DeskNav menu selection.

Free memory: Displays the size of the largest block of available conventional memory that is free. If EMS 4.0 memory is installed, the amount that is free is displayed also, separated by a plus sign. This gives you a good idea of how much memory remains available on your system.

File specification: Is an edit box which allows you to specify the type of files to be displayed. Wild cards and actual filenames are allowed.

Directory Tree: Contains a graphical display of directories on the current drive. Single click with mouse, or use the keypad to change directory selection. Press a character to select the next directory beginning with that character.

Files: Listbox containing a list of files based on the file specification and selected directory. This listbox allows multiple selection - use the shift key and mouse or keyboard to select more than one entry.

Status: Displays statistics regarding the listed files.

Keyboard users: Use the tab key to switch between the last three items.

Menu Items

File

Run: Allows you to run an application and specify parameters.

Run with: Allows you to run an application and pass it the selected files.

Status: Displays information about the currently selected files.

Select all: Causes all listed files to be selected.

Deselect all: Causes all selected files to be deselected.

Print: Sends the selected files to the printer.

Copy: Will copy the selected files to another drive/directory.

Move: Will move the selected files to another drive/directory.

Rename: Allows you to individually rename the selected files.

Delete: Will delete the selected files.

Attributes: Allows you to modify the file attributes for the selected files.

Sort by: Allows you to choose the preferred file sorting method.

Exit: Closes Desktop Navigator.

Exit Windows: Quick exit from windows.

Directory

Status: Displays information about the currently selected directory.

Create: Use to create a sub-directory under the currently selected directory.

Rename: Allows you to rename the selected sub-directory.

Copy: Copies the selected directory and all the files and sub-directories under that directory to a selected destination. The destination can be on another drive.

Move: Moves the selected directory and all the files and sub-directories under that directory to a selected destination. The destination can be on another drive.

Delete: Allows you to delete a directory and its contents, which includes sub-directories and their contents. If the root directory is selected, all files and subdirectories on the disk can be deleted.

Refresh: Since it is possible for another application to modify the directory structure, the Refresh option will reload the directory tree, ensuring that it is current.

Drive

Displays all available disk drives, select the drive you wish to change to.

Status: Displays drive and memory information.

Configuration

DeskNav: Information regarding your DeskNav preferences. The default application to run will be used when you double click on a file that has no registered extension in the WIN.INI file. NOTEPAD.EXE is the default.

Screen Saver: Configure and customize your own screen saver/blanker.

Print: Allows you to set the DeskNav print options.

Printer Setup: Allows you to select and/or set up system printers.

Windows

Arrange: 'Tiles' windows on the screen based on grid for arranging windows in the DeskNav configuration dialog.

Tile: Positions windows on the screen using the entire screen.

Cascade: Positions active windows from top left to bottom right of screen.

Clear: Closes down all applications other than Desktop Navigator and MS-Dos Executive.

Close Icons: Closes all iconized applications other than Desktop Navigator and MS-Dos.

Icon: Iconizes all the iconizable applications.

Maximize: Zooms all applications that are active and can be zoomed.

Optimize: Sizes all applications to use the optimal desktop area.

Restore: Sends the Restore system menu command to all applications.

Utilities

File Finder: Allows you to specify a file (wild cards are allowed) to search for and the drives to search. Files found are listed in the files listbox, and can be operated upon by the File menu options.

Lock System: Password protect your system while you are not using it.

Tools

Customize: Allows you to customize the Tools menu. Update lets you add applications to the Tools pulldown menu and choose from several execution options.

Using Desktop Navigator

With the directory tree containing a list of directories, you can easily move about within your system. Use a mouse to scroll and select directories. Use your cursor keys, or press the first character of the desired directory Once you have selected a directory you can then select one or more files from the right hand listbox (to do so, hold down the shift key while selecting the files). Press enter (or double click with mouse) to have all the selected files executed. Or, you can use the Files menu to process your selections. The File Copy/Move functions will deselect or remove each file as it is processed from the right hand listbox. If the destination disk becomes full, the remaining files will still be selected so that you may continue with the operation. File attributes are automatically processed.

Running Non-Windows applications from Desktop Navigator may require an appropriate .PIF file (see the Microsoft Windows Users Guide). Select the .PIF file to run instead of the .EXE or .COM file.

File Descriptions

This release is a demonstration version and as such is not to be sold. Desktop may only be distributed for free (or at cost) as the following group of files:

DN.EXE or DESKNAV.ZIP Archive file containing the following files:
DESKNAV.EXE The Desktop Navigator program (required)
METZDLL.EXE METZ Software dynamic link library. (required)
DESKNAV.DOC This file
DESKNAV.TLS Sample tools file
DESKNAV.BMP Sample bitmap for screen saver
METZ.ORD METZ Software order form
APPS.WRI METZ Software application descriptions
CLP2FILE.EXE Clipboard to File utility for screen saver bitmap
CLP2FILE.DOC Clipboard to File documentation
METZTSR.COM METZ TSR DOS program for screen saver support
METZTSR.DOC METZ TSR DOS program description and instructions
THREADZ.TXT Special announcement concerning ThreadZ File F/X

Release Notes

METZDLL.EXE is a link library for Desktop Navigator. It must be located somewhere in your environment path. We recommend placing it in your Windows directory. (METZDLL.EXE is also used by other METZ Software applications.) Your comments and suggestions are always welcome, and help make this application a better product. Information in this document is subject to change without notice and does not represent any commitment on the part of METZ Software. No warranties of any kind are associated with this product. Thank you for your support.

Task Manager

Copyright © 1991 by METZ Software

Introduction

After realizing how convenient the Microsoft Windows 3.0 Task List application was, and yet how limited it is in usefulness, we decided to improve on the concept, and

thus created Task Manager. Task Manager has the basic tools found in the Microsoft Task List application, as well as several additional features.

For your convenience, the license number "MASCOT" will allow you to evaluate this application for a limited time without the usual reminder screens popping up.... We apologize for the lack of formal documentation or on-line help; fortunately, the ThreadZ File F/X applications do

have both. (For more information on File F/X, see the section near the end of this chapter.) Also, you can call METZ Software if you have any questions, problems, or suggestions (please use our support number: 206/641-4525). We will be glad to help you any way we can.

Overview

Task Manager is a comprehensive, yet easily understood replacement for the Microsoft Task List application. To install Task Manager, rename your old Microsoft TASKMAN.EXE to TASKMAN.OLD, then place the new TASKMAN.EXE and METZ.DLL in your Windows 3.0 directory. You can then access TaskMan by double-clicking on your Windows background (Desktop) or by pressing Ctrl+Esc.

Task Manager provides the same basic functionality as the Microsoft Task List app, as well as the ability to quickly run programs and files, and a customizable Tools menu. Additional Task Manager features include a fully customizable screen display blanker (screen saver), Windows arrangement functions, directory tree display, file finder, point-and-shoot file manager, and system memory and disk space display. Task Manager uses under 25K of memory.

Installation

TaskMan should be installed b*efore* you run Windows, since the system can lock up if TaskMan is already running when you replace it. Please rename or backup your original Microsoft TASKMAN.EXE for safe keeping. Copy the new TASKMAN.EXE and METZ.DLL to your Windows 3.0 directory. Be sure to backup your Microsoft taskman.exe.

TaskMan can also be used as a replacement for the Microsoft Program Manager. Change the SHELL=PROGMAN.EXE setting in the file SYSTEM.INI to SHELL=TASKMAN.EXE. When you run TaskMan as the shell, you can still run an application when starting Windows, e.g., WIN NOTEPAD. TaskMan will run the application and add it to the TaskMan Run box. Another nice feature is that TaskMan will leave you in the directory you were in before you ran windows, so the TaskMan File Manager will default to your current DOS directory. TaskMan will also launch the applications listed on the LOAD= and RUN= lines of your WIN.INI FILE. If you decide not to use TaskMan as your shell, add TaskMan to the LOAD= line of your WIN.INI file so that you can use the screen saver feature and to speed up TaskMan's own initialization process. When TaskMan is installed you can access it by double-clicking on the Windows background (Desktop) or by pressing Ctrl+Esc.

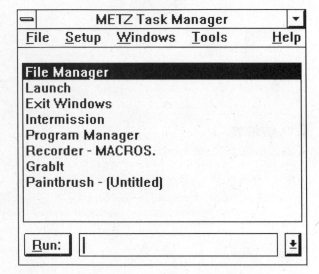

Using TaskMan

Some menu items are greyed while TaskMan is loading directory information in the background (while other applications are running). You can add TaskMan to the LOAD= line of your WIN.INI to speed up this process. You can create a custom bitmap for the screen saver using the included application CLP2DISK.EXE. Please see the section on the Clip to Disk application later in this section for more information. **Important:** Running Non-Windows applications from Task Manager may require an appropriate .PIF file (see the Microsoft Windows User's Guide).

File Descriptions

This release is a demonstration version and as such is not to be sold. Task Manager may only be distributed for free (or at cost) as the following group of files:

MTM.EXE or TASKMAN.ZIP Archive file containing the following files:
TASKMAN.EXE The Task Manager program (required)
METZ.DLL METZ Software dynamic link library (required)
TASKMAN.DOC This file
TASKMAN.TLS Sample tools file
METZ.ORD METZ Software order form
APPS.WRI METZ Software application descriptions
CLP2DISK.EXE Clipboard to Disk utility for screen saver bitmap
CLP2DISK.DOC Clipboard to Disk documentation
METZTSR.COM METZ TSR DOS program for screen saver support
METZTSR.DOC METZ TSR DOS program description and instructions
THREADZ.TXT Special announcement concerning ThreadZ File F/X

Release Notes

METZ.DLL is a dynamic link library for Task Manager. It must be located somewhere in your DOS environment Path. We recommend placing it in your Windows directory. We have tried to be as consistent with Microsoft Windows interface specifications as possible. Please see the Microsoft Windows User's Guide for more information regarding the Windows interface. Your comments and suggestions are always welcome, and help make this application a better product. METZ Software relies heavily on user input, so be sure to give us your suggestions and comments. Information in this document is subject to change without notice and does not represent any commitment on the part of METZ Software. No warranties of any kind are associated with this product. Thank you for your support.

• This application has an implementation that will prevent screen saver timeouts while you are working in a DOS application under Windows. Other screen savers will timeout even if you are actively typing away within a DOS Window or the timeout will occur only after you are inactive in any DOS Window as well. Please read the METZ TSR section of this section or METZTSR.DOC, and install the METZTSR.COM application if you wish to prevent timeouts while you are working in a DOS Window.

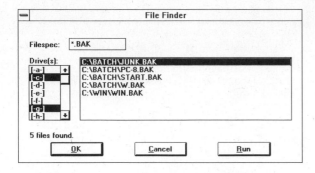

- You can override the optimize default area by placing the following line in the file TASKMAN.INI:

  OPTIMIZE=25,55,200,350

  The values are the pixel positions of the optimization area and can be set to your preferences. In the example, 25 is the left position, 55 is the top position, 200 is the width, and 350 is the height. When you select Optimize from the Windows menu, these coordinates will be used to position the open windows.

- Optimize can be set to Cascade the windows as well. Add the word cascade to the end of the OPTIMIZE= line.

  OPTIMIZE=25,55,200,350,CASCADE

  TaskMan will then Cascade the windows after optimizing them to your specifications.

- TaskMan saves up to 20 items for the run line in a combo box. You can select items in the list by pressing Alt+Down-arrow or clicking on the down-arrow with the mouse. The list is saved from session to session.

- You can double click on files listed by the File Finder and File Manager to execute or load that file.

- TaskMan uses the PROGRAM= setting in the WIN.INI when searching for applications entered on the run line that have no extension. For example, if you type COMMAND on the TaskMan run line and press enter, TaskMan will append each of the extensions listed in the program= section of the WIN.INI, in the order they are listed, in an attempt to find the executable filename. You can change the PROGRAMS= setting in the Setup TaskMan dialog. For best results be sure that the PROGRAM= settings are listed in order of your priority. We are recommending PROGRAMS=EXE PIF COM. Add BAT. if you wish to run batch files as well.

METZ Clipboard to Disk Application

Overview

METZ Clp2Disk is a utility that will copy a bitmap from the clipboard to a file. The bitmap saved by Clp2Disk can be used with a METZ Software application screen saver.

Using Clp2Disk

If you wish to create your own custom bitmap for use with the Screen Blanking option available in a METZ Software product please follow these steps:

1. Using a graphics application such as Microsoft PaintBrush, create an image.
2. Cut or Copy the image to the clipboard.
3. Run CLP2DISK.EXE. If the clipboard contains a bitmap, Clp2Disk will display it on the screen.
4. Select Save As to place the bitmap in a file.
5. The file you saved can now be used with the METZ Software product.

Non-Registered Users

This product is provided at no charge to METZ Software users to support the METZ Software products. Use for any other purpose requires payment of a registration fee. Please contact METZ Software for more information.

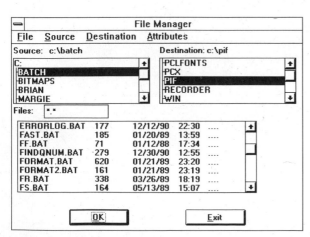

METZ TSR

Overview

METZ TSR is a DOS application that is to be used in conjunction with the various METZ Software Microsoft Windows applications. This TSR (Terminate and Stay Resident) program is an application that prevents a METZ Software application inactivity-timeout while you are running a DOS application under Windows. In the past, the inactivity timeout could occur while you were still working in the DOS application. Now, with METZ TSR installed, it will only occur after the specified interval of keyboard and mouse inactivity has elapsed, regardless of whether you are running a DOS application.

If you use any of the METZ Screen Savers or the METZ Lock product and run DOS applications under Microsoft Windows, we suggest that you install METZ TSR. To install this product, either add a line containing METZTSR to your AUTOEXEC.BAT file or type METZTSR at the DOS prompt.before you run Microsoft Windows.

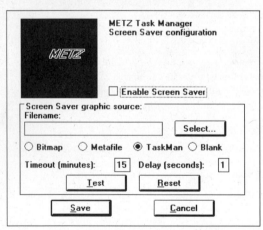

Many METZ Lock users have asked for an option to prevent Ctrl+Alt+Del from resetting their system. This can now be accomplished by adding a command line option of /! to the TSR when it is first run. For example, METZTSR /! will disable the Ctrl+Alt+Del keystroke combination from DOS and under real and standard mode Windows. METZ TSR will work with the following METZ product versions or greater:

- METZ Lock 1.4
- Task Manager 1.0
- Desktop Navigator 2.5
- METZ Desktop Manager 3.2

Previous versions are not affected by this TSR. METZ TSR is also compatible with the ThreadZ File F/X product. METZTSR.COM uses only 464 bytes of memory. METZTSR uses the function number 169 when it is installed. If, by chance, you have another TSR installed which uses the same function number, you can override the default function with an /f option:

METZTSR /f###   where ### is the new number between 128 and 255. You will also need to add the same function number to the WIN.INI file under the section pertaining to the particular METZ Software application:

- [METZ Lock]
- Function=###

The METZ Software application will not attempt to interface with the TSR if FUNCTION=0 in the WIN.INI file. This product is a METZ Software application; use for purposes other than the support of our products requires a license agreement from METZ Software.

ThreadZ Forms Alliance with METZ Software

ThreadZ Software Design Group, Inc., developers of utilities for Microsoft Windows, and METZ Software, developers of shareware utilities for Windows, have announced the formation of a special alliance, the goal of which is to facilitate timely software development and provide easy access to solution-oriented products. The first result of this alliance is the incorporation of two of METZ Software's shareware programs into a retail product called ThreadZ File F/X. ThreadZ File F/X is a group of four utilities and a bonus of ThreadZ Task Manager, presented in an "a la carte" manner so as to facilitate ease of use:

F/X File Manager, simplifies the create, delete, copy, rename and move functions in Windows 3.0 using an intuitive tree directory display.
F/X File Find, a search program enabling users to locate files on.any attached hard drive, provides for the use of DOS wildcards, specific file extensions, or even file creation dates as search.criteria.
F/X File Undelete provides a list of deleted files, states the likelihood of a successful recovery, and, when prompted, will attempt.to undelete the chosen file.
F/X Text Search allows users to search a file, path name, directory or an entire disk for a text string. A list of matching files is displayed and may be printed as a report.
The ThreadZ Task Manager, a distinctive replacement for Windows' Task List, utilizes a menu which may be used to launch applications and lets you arrange your windows the way that works best for you!
ThreadZ File F/X retails for $129.95. ThreadZ can be reached at 4018-1488th Ave. N.E., Redmond, WA 98052-5516, or by calling 800-767-6292 in the U.S. and Canada, 206-869-6292 elsewhere.

Microsoft Windows Applications Currently Available from METZ

METZ Desktop Manager: METZ Desktop Manager is designed to provide you with a friendly menuing system plus several utilities. With Desktop you can easily create menus and sub-menus which directly access your applications and data (across directories and drives). Additional features such as a customizable screen blanker, windows arrangement functions, directory tree display, file finder, point and shoot file management, and an automatic menu generator are also included.

METZ Phones: METZ Phones is a Microsoft Windows application designed for maintaining lists of names, phone numbers, and addresses. If you have a Hayes compatible modem, Phones has the capability of dialing the phone for you.

METZ Dialer: METZ Dialer is a popup, speed dialer which, when coupled with a Hayes compatible modem, provides a quick and convenient method of dialing phone numbers. A customizable pulldown menu allows you add names and numbers you frequently call.

METZ Lock: METZ Lock is a security application for Microsoft Windows. Lock can be used to prevent unauthorized use of your system while unattended.

METZ Runner: METZ Runner is a utility which provides a quick method to run applications and files.

METZ Time: METZ Time is a digital, popup, date and time display which can be placed anywhere on the screen.

METZ Freemem: METZ Freemem is a moveable, digital, display of free conventional and free expanded memory.

Non-Registered Users

Use of Desktop Navigator or Task Manager for purposes other than evaluation requires payment of the registration fee. Once you register and receive a license number you are automatically allowed to upgrade to future releases. It is important that you register this application to help ensure continued support and development. Our intention is to provide useful, user-friendly applications at a low cost, and your support helps make that possible. All available functionality is enabled in this version to provide you the ability to effectively evaluate this application. Ordering information is included in the file METZ.ORD and in the registration form at the end of this chapter. All orders will receive a disk containing the latest versions of our products.

METZ Software Order Form

METZ Software Support (206) 641-4525 • Sales 1-800-447-1712 • Fax (206) 644-6026

P.O. Box 6042 International (206) 641-4525 Bellevue, Wa., 98008-0042, U.S.A.

Product Quantity Price Task Manager, license #, _____ x $30 = _____

and diskette METZ Desktop Manager, documentation, _____ x $30 = _____

license #, and diskette Desktop Navigator, license #, _____ x $30 = _____

and diskette METZ Phones, license #, _____ x $20 = _____

and diskette METZ Runner, license #, _____ x $10 = _____

and diskette METZ Dialer, license #, _____ x $10 = _____

and diskette METZ Lock, license #, _____ x $10 = _____

and diskette METZ Time and diskette _____ x $10 = _____

METZ Software update/demo disk only _____ x $ 5 = _____ (included with all orders)

Purchase orders under $100 add $10 = _____ (do not add P.O. charge to credit card orders)

Wash. state residents add 8.2% sales tax _____

Diskette format: ___ 5.25" ___ 3.5"   Total: _____

Payment by: ___ MasterCard ___ Visa ___ Check ___ P.O.   Card #:_____ Exp. Date:_____

Purchase Order #:_____

Signature: _____

Name: _____

Address: _____

Phone #: _____

Comments: _____

Where did you find our product(s): _____

What other Microsoft Windows products are you looking for?_____

For credit card or purchase orders, you may send this information electronically to: GENIE: A.METZ COMPUSERVE: [73567,1637]

Launch 1.7

Copyright © 1991 by David Stafford

Launch is the popular utility that lets you start programs directly from the Windows Desktop, without having to go through Program Manager or File Manager. Your favorite programs are only one mouse click away!

Installation is a snap: just copy Launch to your hard disk. Launch will create a default menu the first time it runs (or anytime it cannot find LAUNCH.INI). You can install Launch in your WIN.INI or SYSTEM.INI so it will load automatically. The on-line help contains more detailed instructions. Once Launch is installed, just hold down the left mouse button once on an unoccupied part of the Desktop. Your Launch menu will pop up automatically.

You will notice that the behavior of Launch's menu is a little different when you select the middle or right mouse button. The menu appears to be "sticky" and you don't need to constantly depress the mouse button. The menu section begins with [Menu]. Each subsequent line contains a menu item, followed by an equals sign and the name of the program to run, with (optionally) any command-line arguments. Remember that you can Launch any program that you can run from the File Manager or the DOS Executive. This includes PIFs, batch files and non-Windows programs. You can also specify a path to a program (as in C:\QEDIT\Q.PIF).

Launch supports the [Extensions] section of WIN.INI. You can list a document name in the Launch menu (or enter a document name in the Run box) and the associated program will be launched when the document is selected. The easiest way to edit LAUNCH.INI is to simply to enter LAUNCH.INI in the Run box. The editor will be started automatically. Loading Launch a second time will read the updated LAUNCH.INI file.

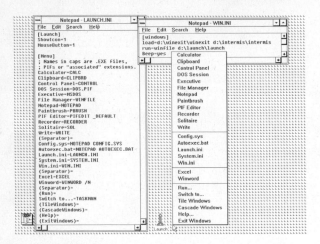

Setting Up Your LAUNCH.INI File

Launch needs an INI file that contains the options and the menu description. If LAUNCH.INI is not present in the same directory as LAUNCH.EXE, Launch will create it. You can customize LAUNCH.INI to suit your specific needs. An example INI file is included at the end of this subject. The configuration section begins with [Launch]. There are two items that you can configure: ShowIcon and MouseButton.

- ShowIcon determines whether or not the icon is displayed. A value of 1 (the default) displays the icon and a value of 0 directs Launch to hide the icon.

- MouseButton selects which mouse button to use for popping up the Launch menu. The acceptable values are:
    1. Left button (the default).
    2. Middle button (if your mouse driver supports it).
    3. Right button.

Special Menu Options

Separator A menu bar separator into the menu.
ExitWindows Pops up an "Exit Windows" dialog box.
ExitLaunch Exits Launch.
Help The Launch help system.
About The Launch "About" box.
Run Pops up the "Run" dialog box.
TileWindows Tiles the windows on your desktop.
CascadeWindows Cascades the windows on your desktop.
ArrangeIcons Rearranges the icons on the desktop.

Note that these require an equals sign even though no program is associated with the menu item. Each option is enclosed in parentheses (rather than square brackets).

Example LAUNCH.INI file:

```
[Launch]
ShowIcon=1
MouseButton=1

[Menu]
Edit LAUNCH.INI=LAUNCH.INI
Notepad=NOTEPAD
Calculator=CALC
File Manager=WINFILE
Solitaire=SOL
(Separator)=
(Run)=
Tasks...=TASKMAN
```

```
(Help)=
(TileWindows)=
(Separator)=
(ExitWindows)=
```

You can include special options just before the command in the menu. Options are enclosed in a [] (square brackets) pair. This is a new feature with Launch 1.7, and the only option presently available is to specify the subdirectory to change to before executing the command. This is an important and much-requested feature, because some programs insist on being run from their own directory. Look at the LAUNCH.INI below for examples.

Example LAUNCH.INI file:

```
[Launch]
ShowIcon=1
MouseButton=1

[Menu]
Edit Menu=[C:\LAUNCH] LAUNCH.INI
Notepad=NOTEPAD
Calculator=CALC
File Manager=WINFILE
Solitaire=SOL
(Separator)=
(Run)=[C:\APPS]
Tasks...=TASKMAN
(Help)=
(TileWindows)=
(Separator)=
(ExitWindows)=
```

You can include Launch in the RUN= line of WIN.INI or run it as the Windows shell by putting it in the SHELL= line of SYSTEM.INI (in place of Program Manager). Launch uses less memory and requires fewer system resources than Program Manager. Using Launch is easy. Simply hold down the mouse button over the empty desktop and the Launch menu will pop up. (The mouse button is configurable. See the LAUNCH.INI subject.)

The Run box can not only launch programs, but data files as well! Launch will even search your PATH (and the Windows directories) for the program or data file. Launch supports the [Extensions] section of WIN.INI. For example: if you enter "WIN.INI" in the Run box, NotePad will be launched with your WIN.INI file loaded. You can enter a command in the Run box, similar to the way you would enter it on the DOS command line. The Run box will keep track of the last 25 selections. You can use the arrow keys to scroll through past selections, or you can click on the down-arrow button with the mouse. Double-clicking on the Launch icon will bring up the help information. You can hide the Launch icon if you do not want it to appear on your desktop.

Upgrade Information

A major upgrade of Launch is in progress. Some of the features of Launch 2.0 will be:

- Support for multi-level menus.
- Keyboard support.
- Better configurability.
- Change to a specific directory before launching a program.

Launch follows the small-is-beautiful principle. It does just one thing and it does it well. Launch stays out of your way when you are not using it, and requires very little computing resources. Please feel free to distribute this program. All I ask is that you be careful and remember to include all three files (LAUNCH.EXE, LAUNCH.TXT, and LAUNCH.INV) together.

Disclaimer: This program comes with the same fine warranty that the big guys give you: none. I have done my best to make this a solid program, but I cannot assume any responsibility for its use. If you get a rash, or your computer turns into a bubbling pool of metal (or anything else bad happens), I am not liable. If you have any trouble, please let me know, and if it turns out to be a problem with Launch I will do my best to fix it.

Registration

This is the eighth release and as you can see, I have put a lot of time into Launch. This program is distributed as shareware. The cost is only $29.95 (4,000 yen in Japan). Site licenses are also available (see the chart below). Checks can be drawn on an American or Japanese bank. Due to customer request, I have upgraded the upgrade policy. Originally, you were entitled to one minor upgrade free. The new policy is that all minor upgrades are now free. This policy is not limited to new customers; if you registered an earlier version of Launch, you are entitled to free minor upgrades. I have sent new registration numbers to all Launch customers, but if I somehow missed you, or you have lost it, just let me know and I will send you another.

When you mail your registration you will receive a registration number that will disable the dialog box that appears when Launch is started. Your registration number will be valid for all minor upgrades. Support is available for registered users via CompuServe, MCI Mail or regular mail.

Don't forget to include your name, address and version number (this is 1.6). If you include your CompuServe or MCI Mail address, you will receive your registration number faster. Other registrations are sent via airmail. Comments and suggestions are welcome. Ideas from people using Launch have made it a better program.

I would like to thank the people who have registered. Your support for my efforts has enabled me to continue to maintain and improve Launch.

David Stafford
Kamakura NS Bldg 4-F
Onaricho 4-16
Kamakura, Kanagawa 248 Japan
CompuServe: 72411,2670 or 76666,2542
MCI: DSTAFFORD 361-6512
Site license information.

Qty	Cost	Qty	Cost
1-9	$25	50-99	$15
10-49	$20	100+	$10

Recorder Run 2.01

Copyright © 1991 by e-Image

Using Recorder Run

Recorder Run (RECRUN.EXE) is a Windows 3.0 application designed to allow users to assign icons in the Program Manager to a macro sequence that has been recorded with the Windows Recorder (RECORDER.EXE). It appears that this feature is sought-after by many Windows users. Using Recorder Run is quite simple:

1. Create a macro with Recorder.
2. Identify a unique keyword in the Macro Name field of the macro you would like to run with Recorder Run.
3. Set up a new Group Item in the Windows Program Manager to call RECRUN.EXE with 2 parameters on the command line, just like this:
   RECRUN.EXE <.REC-File-Path> <Macro-Keyword>
4. Assign this Program Item a name.
5. From the Program Manager, double click on the new icon to start your macro.

Macro Keywords

The macro keyword is the most important part of the Recorder Run system. Before recording a macro with RECORDER.EXE, the user fills in a profile of the macro, i.e., its name and some other information about the macro. Recorder Run uses the Macro Keyword in its search through the Recorder's Listbox, and looks for the first macro with the given keyword in its name. Therefore, the user should attempt to keep the macro keywords unique.

Hint: A good choice of Macro Keyword is the accelerator description string which appears in the left column of the Recorder's Listbox, e.g., Ctrl+F1. These are always unique.

—	Program Item Properties
Description:	This Runs a Recorder Macro
Command Line:	RECRUN MACROS.REC Ctrl+Shift+F1
OK	Cancel	**B**rowse...	Change I**c**on...

Recorder File Pathnames

The recorder file pathname is simply an MS-DOS pathname which directs RECORDER.EXE to the file containing your macro definitions. Usually this pathname would end with a .REC extension, since this is the convention for RECORDER.EXE data files.

Speed Hint: Keep all your RECRUN macros in one file, and don't use the full pathname for <.REC-Pathname>. Instead,

save the file in your Windows directory. The result is that RECRUN will only have to bring up RECORDER.EXE once. Every time after that, it's just a quick SendMessage, and your macro will execute quicker.

Recorder Run Programmer's Description

This topic explains how Recorder Run works from a Windows programmer's perspective. Recorder Run uses the following algorithm to perform its function:

1. Check the Windows desktop for a Window registered with the Class "Recorder".
2. If the document loaded in RECORDER.EXE is <.REC-Pathname>, then skip to 5.
3. Close that Window by sending a WM_SYSCOMMAND (SC_CLOSE) message to its hWnd.
4. Execute a new instance of Recorder with the <.REC-Pathname> specified on RECRUN.EXE's command line.
5. Search the strings in Recorder's Listbox for an occurrence of the macro keyword.
6. If the keyword is found, then select that macro and send a ListBox notifier message to the Recorder.EXE Window, pretending (sneaky) it came from the Listbox itself.

That's it. Pretty simple.

Registration

Simply install RECRUN.EXE and RECRUN.HLP into your Windows directory, and then execute RECRUN.EXE with File Manager. The About... box for RECRUN will be displayed, and you can check the RECRUN.HLP file for instructions as to how it works. If you find RECRUN.EXE helpful, please register. $10.00 U.S. buys a license for one machine.

e-Image
Attn: RECRUN Registration
#106-9803-82 Ave.
Edmonton, Alberta
Canada T6E 1Y8
CompuServe: 76376,43

We will issue a confirmation letter for the # of licenses.

WATCH for upcoming Windows applications from e-Image!

Name _____

Address _____
_____
_____

RunProg

Version 1.06
Copyright © 1991 by David A. Feinleib

Introduction

RunProg allows you to run a program maximized, minimized, normal size, hidden, or at specified coordinates. In addition, RunProg can run up to 25 programs from your WIN.INI file at sizes you specify.

```
┌─────────────────────────────────────────────┐
│ ⊟          Program Item Properties           │
├─────────────────────────────────────────────┤
│ Description:  │ Notepad                      │
│                                              │
│ Command Line: │ RUNPROG [0 0 640 420] NOTEPAD.EXE│
│                                              │
│  ┌────────┐ ┌────────┐ ┌─────────┐ ┌───────────┐ │
│  │   OK   │ │ Cancel │ │ Browse..│ │Change Icon..│ │
│  └────────┘ └────────┘ └─────────┘ └───────────┘ │
└─────────────────────────────────────────────┘
```

Using RunProg

If you want to put a new icon in the Program Manager, click File New, select "Program Item", and type:

{directory}RUNPROG.EXE [xxx] Program-Name {directory}

Where:
directory directory in which RUNPROG is located
xxx size at which to run program
Program-Name name of program to run
directory directory in which to start; the directory which will appear if you select File Open from the program you run

For example, if RunProg is located in C:\WINDOWS and you want to add WORD.EXE which is located in D:\WORD, run it maximized and have it start in the directory C:\DOCS, you would type:

C:\WINDOWS\RUNPROG.EXE [Max] D:\WORD\WORD.EXE C:\DOCS

It is not necessary to specify a document directory. Click OK when you are done. To select the correct icon for the program you have entered, click File Properties, select "Change Icon" and in the edit box, type Program-Name, where, continuing the example above, you would type:

D:\WORD\WORD.EXE

Click "view next" until you see the appropriate icon and then click OK.

If you want to modify an old program in the Program Manager, click File Properties, and follow the steps outlined above. If the program you want to run is in your Path, you need not specify the entire path of the program to be run.

Using RunProg from the WIN.INI File

RunProg can run up to 25 files from your WIN.INI file at sizes you specify. Note that you can still use RunProg from the Program Manager if you run programs from the WIN.INI file. To use RunProg from your WIN.INI file, you must place RUNPROG.EXE on either the LOAD= or the RUN= line in your WIN.INI file. If you have other programs on the line, separate them with a space.

If you have run RunProg before, find the section in your WIN.INI file shown as [RunProg]. If you have not run RunProg before, you can either run RunProg once from the Program Manager so that RunProg will create its section, or you can create a section. To create a section for RunProg, go to the bottom of the WIN.INI file and type:

[RunProg]

In this section, you must list the files that you want RunProg to run. You may list up to 25 files in the form:

ProgramX=[Size] PROGRAM

For example, if you wanted to run three programs, you might type:

Program1=[Max] C:\WINDOWS\NOTEPAD.EXE
Program2=[Min] C:\WINDOWS\TERMINAL.EXE
Program3=[Norm] C:\WINDOWS\PBRUSH.EXE

Save the changes that you make to the WIN.INI file and restart Windows; the programs you have entered will be run at the sizes specified.

Options

To use RUNPROG.EXE, you must specify the way the program you want to be run should be displayed. The following options are available:

[Max] Shows the program maximized
[Min] Shows the program minimized
[Norm] Shows the program in its normal size
[Hide] Runs the program hidden
[X Y Width Height] Shows the program at specified size

The option must have brackets around it. It may be in uppercase, lowercase, or any combination of case. If you run RunProg with no parameters, a screen will come up which describes RunProg's options and shareware registration. Please note that if you run a program hidden, there is no way to make it visible. This option is useful for running programs that take no user input but perform a certain function and then close themselves. If you are using this option with a DOS application, make sure that in the applications PIF file, you specify that the application's window should be closed when the program terminates. If you run a DOS application hidden that does not close itself, you may have trouble exiting Windows.

For the "specified size option," you must specify four numbers: the X coordinate, the Y coordinate, the Width, and the Height. If the coordinates are specified incorrectly, the program will be run at the default coordinates. The program to run should be specified after the option.

Liability

RunProg is supplied as is. The author disclaims all warranties expressed or implied, including, without limitation, the warranties of merchantability and of fitness for any purpose. The author assumes no liability for damages, direct or consequential, which may result from the use of RunProg.

How to Contact Me

Comments and suggestions (with or without the registration fee) would be greatly appreciated. Please send them to:

David Feinleib
1430 Mass. Ave. Suite 306-42
Cambridge, MA 02138
BIX: "pgm"
CompuServe: 76516,20
FidoNet:1:101/310 David Feinleib

Registration for RunProg

RunProg is shareware. You may make copies of this program and give them to others as long as the documentation is provided with the program, both unaltered. Registered versions of RunProg which do not have a shareware reminder message are available for $10.00 + $2.75 for 5 1/4 inch, $4.75 for 3 1/2 inch. You will be able to receive support by BIX, CompuServe, FidoNet, or mail. Please include your name, address, and current version number. See above for the address.

Site licenses, LAN licenses, and substantial quantity discounts are available. Customization of RunProg is available but is not included in the shareware registration fee. The fee charged for customization will depend on the amount and significance of the customization. Please contact me for more information regarding the above two items. Thanks!

Thanks very much to Scott McIntosh, who was a great help in creating and testing this program.

Graphics

Icon-Fixer

Version 1.01
Copyright © 1991 by Robert F. Nee

Introduction

Icon-Fixer is a utility for Microsoft Windows 3.0 which lets you specify icons to use in place of the boring, default DOS Icon. When a DOS window is minimized, Icon-Fixer steps in and displays a user specified icon instead. The user may also specify which DOS windows should have their icons "fixed."

Installation

Icon-Fixer was designed for users running in Standard or Enhanced modes; it will not work in real mode. Icon-Fixer consists of two files, ICON.EXE and ILIB.DLL. These two files may be placed anywhere the user wishes. In addition Icon-Fixer relies on a initialization file named ICON.INI that it expects to find in the same directory as the executables. If this file does not exist it will be created.

If you wish to have Icon-Fixer run every time Windows is started, edit the WIN.INI file in your Windows directory. Assuming you placed ICON.EXE and ILIB.DLL in a directory named C:\WINDOWS\UTILS, the top of the file should look similar to the following:

```
[windows]
load=c:\windows\utils\icon ...
```

After making this change, save and re-start Windows.

Using Icon-Fixer

Once Icon-Fixer is installed and running, you may select the icon to use for each minimized DOS window. The user may assign up to 20 icons to DOS window titles. This is similar to assigning an icon to a program in the Program Manager. The icons you assign in the Program Manager are separate from associations made with Icon-Fixer however.

Associations are made in Icon-Fixer by clicking on the Icon-Fixer icon and choosing "Associate" from the system menu. This brings up a dialog box which shows a list of the current associations. A box also shows a picture of the currently selected association. To make a new association click the Add button. Enter the window title and the filename of the icon to use for the new association. The "Window Title" is the line that appears in the title bar of the DOS window or under it when it is minimized. This is usually specified in the .PIF file. It is not case sensitive. You may browse through your icon files by clicking on the Browse button. Click OK to set this association or Cancel to abort.

You may delete any associations you have made by clicking on the title in the list box and pressing the Delete button. Double click on a title to edit an association. In order to save the associations you have made and update the ICON.INI file for the next time you run Icon-Fixer, click on the Save button. Association are not saved automatically.

It is important to note how Icon-Fixer matches the titles of DOS windows with the titles specified by the user. Icon-Fixer will match titles up to the length of the title in the association. In other words "DOS" will match DOS windows with titles of "DOS Window" and "DOS Box" but not "MSDOS".

Options

The Options dialog-box on the Icon-Fixer menu allows the user to alter the way Icon-Fixer behaves. The settings of all options are saved so they will be the defaults next time you run Icon-Fixer.

The Hide Window option (available only to registered users) hides the Icon-Fixer Icon to get it out of the way. Icon-Fixer may be unhidden by running a second copy of the program. It is recommended that you only hide the

Icon-Fixer window after you have tailored it to your liking. If the hidden option is set when starting Icon-Fixer, the icon will be displayed for 8 seconds and then hidden. Clicking on the icon during this time will prevent it from being hidden.

A Note About Icon Files

The icon file format contains two bitmap images: one that contains the image and one that specifies what parts of the image are transparent. One of the things that makes Icon-Fixer possible is the large number of icon files in the public domain, and several good icon editing packages. Unfortunately, some of these editors and many of these icons have a serious flaw. They ignore the transparency bitmap and substitute a white background. While these icons are fine for the Program Manager, which has a white background, they are less appealing as application icons or for use with Icon-Fixer. Icon-Fixer can still use these icons but they will display with a white background.

Limitations of This Version

This release of Icon-Fixer has some minor limitations that will be addressed in future releases. I invite users to provide feedback as to which of these is most important. Only single-icon icon files are supported. Future versions will support icons in DLLs and files with multiple icons in them. A maximum of only 20 associations can be made.

Licensing Agreement

Terms

The license to use this program is effective until terminated and is non-transferable. You may terminate the license by destroying all copies of this program. Failure to comply with any of the terms of this license will also result in termination.

Warranty

This program is provided as is without any warranty express or implied. In addition, Robert F. Nee specifically disclaims all warranties, expressed or implied, including but not limited to implied warranties of merchantability and fitness for a particular purpose with respect to defects in the program license granted herein. In no event shall Robert F. Nee be liable for any claims for lost profits or any other commercial damage, including but not limited to special, incidental, consequential or other damage. In no case shall Robert Nee's liability exceed the license fees paid for the right to use the licensed software. Some states do not allow the exclusion or limitation of incidental or consequential damages, so the above limitation or exclusion may not apply to you.

User Registration

Icon-Fixer is not provided free. You are permitted to use Icon-Fixer for 30 days free of charge. If you continue to use it after this trial period you are asked to please register it. Registered users will receive a registration number that will enable the Hide Window feature as described above. This is not crippleware, I am simply trying to provide an incentive for users to register. Besides, who wants to pay for something they already have? The last page of this chapter provides an order form that may be used for registration.

Once you receive your registration number, click on the Register button in the About box and enter your name and registration number. This information will be saved and the Hide Window option will be enabled.

If you have any suggestions for future improvements, or if you are experiencing problems with Icon-Fixer, please feel free to contact me. Thank you.

Internet mail address: <nee@cf_su20.sbi.com>

CompuServe address: 70461,2034

GEnie mail address: RNEE

Snail mail address: Robert F. Nee

　　　　　　　　　222 Willow Avenue #6

　　　　　　　　　Hoboken, NJ 07030

Icon Manager

Version 1.1
Copyright © 1991 by Impact Software

Contents at a Glance

Acknowledgements: I would like to express my sincere appreciation to the following individuals. Each person contributed uniquely to this project in one important way or another. The results you see in this program would not be the same without any one of them.   *- Len Gray*

Special Thanks:
　　Burton L. Alperson
　　Scott Baker
　　Laura Cox
　　James Curran
　　Russ Mueller
　　Barry Simon

Introduction

Welcome to Icon Manager!

Icon Manager provides you with a complete set of tools which allow you to create, modify, extract, and organize full-color icons for use with Microsoft Windows 3.0. Special attention has been given to attempt to make every feature as straight-forward and easy to use as possible. To fully enjoy the power and features of Icon Manager, please take a few minutes to read the installation procedure, and especially the information provided on the different file formats that Icon Manager supports and the section on Putting it All Together. Icon Manager features include:

- Support for four different file formats:

  .ICO   Icon resource files (.ICO), usable by Program Manager, which contain only one type of icon.

  *.ICL   Icon library files, also usable by Windows Program Manager, which can contain multiple icon images.

  *.ICA   Icon archive files which allow you to store multiple icons like libraries but save over 20% of your disk space (save over 30% compared to icon resource files). Additionally, archive files remember the exact placement of each of your icons as well as the size of the document window.

  *.EXE   Icon Manager will extract all icons it can find in Windows executable programs from any version of Windows. These images can then be edited or copied directly into any of the three file types described above.

- A Multiple Document Interface (MDI) design which allows up to 50 files to be open simultaneously and provides auto-arrange functions for open and iconized windows.

- A straight-forward drag 'n' drop interface allows icons to be effortlessly moved or copied from file to file or in and out of the bitmap tool.

- The bitmap tool provides import and export support for engineering icons in conjunction with paint applications like Windows Paintbrush. The clipboard is used to transport bitmap images between applications. Special support is provided for creating the transparent and inverse screen attributes of icons.

- A screen capture feature allows you to easily duplicate any area of your video display into the bitmap tool.

- A convenient button bar provides quick access to frequently used editing switches.

INSTALLATION

Setup Procedure

Hardware and Software That You Will Need

Icon Manager requires an IBM Personal Computer or compatible, equipped with the Microsoft Windows operating environment, level 3.0 or higher. A color monitor of at least EGA resolution is recommended. Although Windows will make adjustments internally to display Icon Manager images on CGA or monochrome monitors, an extra level of effort is required by users to conform to the restrictions imposed by these types of monitors. Icon Manager creates icons of the highest color range and resolution currently supported by Windows for the best possible end results on high-performance color monitors.

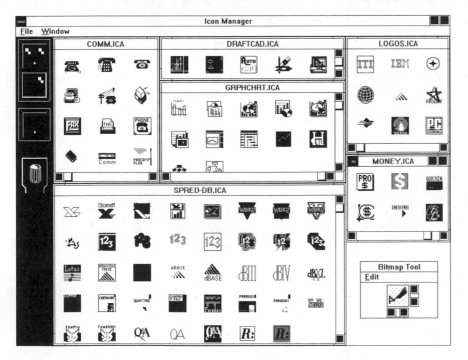

The installation will require approximately 75K bytes of file space for program installation. Maintaining icon images will require more disk space depending on the quantity and format of the icons. More information on icon disk requirements can be found in Chapter 4, Icon File Format Considerations.

Installing Icon Manager

Icon Manager does not require any sophisticated installation procedure. Simply copy the executable file ICONMAN.EXE into the sub-directory of your choice. This can be your Windows sub-directory (frequently C:\WINDOWS) or another directory which suits your own organizational preferences.

Placing ICONMAN.EXE in your Windows sub-directory means that you won't have to specify a pathname for Icon Manager when you create a program item in Program Manager. If you also store your icon files in your Windows directory, you won't have to specify a pathname when performing the Change Icon... procedure of the Proper-ties... dialog (see Chapter 2, Using Icons in Program Manager). This strategy is the most straight-forward to use, however using it for all of your Windows applications can become impractical from a disk organization and management perspective. Placing Icon Manager into a separate sub-directory used only for saving icons makes file management much easier. The best strategy that we suggest is to create a sub-directory with a short pathname such as C:\ICONS. This can be easily typed into Program Manager with your filename and provides the advantages of a discreet file location for your icons.

You'll probably want to create a program item for Icon Manager under Program Manager. This part of the installation is good practice for preparing to customize your Program Manager desktop with new icons. If you haven't explored this portion of your Windows environ-ment, now is a great time! To begin, first highlight the group that you would like to place Icon Manager in by clicking on it with the mouse. Select 'New...' from Program Manager's File menu, make sure the Program Item radio button is selected, and click on OK. In the Command Line edit box enter d:\ICONS\ICONMAN.EXE where d: is the disk drive that you chose to install Icon Manager to. Click on OK and you should see Icon Manager appear in your program group. If you cannot see the Icon Manager icon, try using the Arrange Icons command from File Manager's Window menu as well as the group's scroll bar controls if all of the icons cannot be displayed at once.

OPERATION

Introduction to Icon Manager

The Main Display and Menu

Icon Manager displays an empty main window with a menu at the top and a button bar down the left side when started. The main menu bar contains two primary selections, File and Window. Both contain standard sub-menus for their class within Windows.

The File Menu

The File menu contains selections allowing files to be created, opened, closed, saved, and renamed (Save As...). Additional selections are provided for exiting the program and displaying the About... dialog. When opening or saving a file, a dialog is provided which allows the selection of the file format and the disk directory to be used for the open or save procedure. The four radio buttons which appear in the lower right area of the dialog allow choosing the file format to be opened or to be used when saving the file. The Program format is not available during a Save or Save As... operation. The listboxes provide easy access to select an existing file for action or to change the file drive or directory.

In addition to opening individual files, a pushbutton control labeled Open All will be activated when opening an icon resource file and multiple icon resource files exist in the currently selected directory. Use Open All to open an untitled document which contains all of the icon resource files in the current directory. This command is provided to assist users establish icon archive and library files using from their collection of icon resource files.

Opening any file that contains multiple icon images will cause a new document window to be opened in Icon Manager, in which the icons will be displayed. If an icon resource file is opened which contains only one icon image, the icon will be placed into the screen cursor, much like dragging an icon for a copy or move operation. Click the left mouse button over the area you would like to drop the icon. If you do not have an open file to place the icon, you can drop it into the Bitmap Tool tempo-rarily.

When you open a multiple icon file for editing by Icon Manager, the file is read into a temporary workspace area where all editing changes are made without affecting the original file. The file must be saved to make any modifica-tions made during the session permanent. You can make changes to your files and then save them only when you are satisfied with the results. Icon Manager will remind you to consider saving a file if you forget and try to close the file or exit the program without saving changes that you have made.

When saving an icon file, the icon resource file radio button will only be active and available if you are saving a file containing a single icon image. This file format will not accept multiple icon images.

The Window Menu

The Window menu contains standard selections for arranging and selecting the windows within a Multiple Document Interface program. An additional menu selection, Arrange Window , is provided to arrange the icons within the currently active document window.

The Tile and Cascade options are both used to automatically arrange the open document Windows within Icon Manager. Tile will size all of the open windows to approximately equal size and place them flush against each other across the entire main window. Cascade will arrange the Windows in a waterfall pattern beginning from the upper left hand corner of the main window, each window on top of each other but slightly lower and offset to the right so that you can easily select any window by clicking on its title bar.

The Arrange Icons selection will arrange any minimized document windows appearing as icons in a neatly organized pattern across the bottom of the main window. This selection is a standard option provided by the Multiple Document Interface and should not be confused with the next selection, Arrange Window. The latter selection is an extra feature which has been added to Icon manager's menu to allow the arrangement of the icons that you have placed within a document. Choosing Arrange Window will make sure that all icons in your document are positioned in an even pattern with consistent spacing between each image. Note the icons are not associated with a document position in their native file types, only icons stored in an icon archive file are guaranteed to appear in the same position between saving the file and reopening it. You can force the sequence of an icon library file by choosing the Arrange Window command before saving. Icon Manager performs an internal sort when arranging a window so the icons will appear in the same order when using the View Next command within Program Manager.

Select the Close All option to clear your main workspace and begin a fresh editing session. Icon Manager will prompt you to save any files that have been modified before closing them.

The Button Bar

A button bar is displayed to the left of the main window containing three buttons and a trash can. The top two buttons are used to toggle the action invoked when you drag an icon within Icon Manager. The top button selects a copy operation, while the button directly underneath selects a move operation. Each button displays the current selection state by visual depression as well as a green indicator for a selected button or a red indicator if deselected. Please note that some operations are restricted by the type of file being used. You cannot move an icon from an executable (because it never really is removed from the program) nor can you drag an icon into an executable file.

Directly under the copy/move buttons is a third button which conveniently toggles the Bitmap Tool on when required or out of your way for maximum viewing/

workspace area. Under the Bitmap Tool button is a trash can area. Use the trash can with the move action selected to remove unwanted icons from your files (or select the copy operation if you just want to have fun throwing things into the trash can!). Simply drag the icon over the trash can and then drop it and Icon Manager will dispose of the image.

Working with Icon Manager Files

Organizing icons using Icon Manager is a breeze! First, select either a copy or move operation by clicking the appropriate button at the top of the button bar. Now, simply point at the icon you wish to copy or move, click the left mouse button down, drag the icon to where you would like it to be, and release the left mouse button to drop the icon into its new location. This drag and drop procedure can be used to move or copy an icon within its original document, between documents, or in and out of the Bitmap Tool (described in the next chapter). The cursor will change to a monochrome representation of the icon during the drag operation to provide visual feedback that it is being moved. This cursor shape will revert to a DO NOT image of a circle with a diagonal line through it whenever the cursor is positioned over an area of the screen which cannot accept the icon. When dragging an icon from an executable file, the icon will temporarily display in monochrome to confirm the operation, and then switch to the do not cursor style because the icon cannot be copied into the executable file. Move the cursor to the Bitmap Tool or another document window type to continue your copy operation.

As you fill an icon window on your display you will probably want to size and shape the window as it becomes full, making room for more icons. Experiment using the window sizing frames and the Arrange Window command to become comfortable with growing your own icon libraries. You will find that you can drop icons in any area of the icon document, even on top of each other, and later use the Arrange Window command to expand the internal size of the icon document and neatly separate each image.

The Bitmap Tool

The Bitmap Tool is used to engineer bitmap operations and to allow icons to be created and modified. It can be used to import and export bitmaps to and from paint applications such as Windows Paintbrush where you can create or modify the design of an icon. The Bitmap Tool also provides features for capturing a bitmap directly from your video display, and a tool which allows the transparent/inverse portion of the icon to be created or removed when importing or exporting icon bitmap images.

The Viewport

The focal point of the Bitmap Tool is a square viewing window called the Viewport. The Viewport is used to display a bitmap image which is precisely 32 by 32 pixels square (the size of a high resolution icon). Any bitmap used by the BT must be at least 32 by 32 pixels in size. Larger images can be worked with, activating scroll bars outside of the Viewport which are used to position the desired 32x32 portion of the bitmap within the Viewport window. Oversized images can be placed into the Viewport using the Paste command from the BT Edit menu or by using the Capture feature of the BT.

The Bitmap Tool Edit Menu

The Bitmap Tool contains a few standard selections and a couple of special features unique to Icon Manager. The first three choices, Paste , Copy All , and Copy Viewport , refer to the cut and paste operations which are associated with the Windows clipboard. The Paste command will paste any currently available bitmap contained in the Windows clipboard into the icon viewport (the image must be at least 32 by 32 pixels in size). The Copy All is the reverse of this procedure, placing a copy of the bitmap currently in the Bitmap Tool into the Windows clipboard. Copy Viewport is a special instance of the Copy command which only transfers the 32 by 32 pixel portion of the bitmap which is visible in the Viewport into the clipboard. Use these three commands to import and export bitmap images between Icon Manager and your favorite paint application.

Following the copy/paste selections is the Capture selection. This feature is used to capture bitmap images from your video display into the Bitmap Tool. When you select Capture , Icon Manager will make its own windows transparent, exposing the entire Windows desktop which remains. It will also turn the cursor into a crosshair + shape. Icon Manager will retain control of the cursor to allow you to execute the screen capture. Point the crosshair cursor to one corner of the area you would like to capture. Press the left mouse button down just like you would do when dragging an icon, and drag the cursor to the opposite corner of your capture area. As you drag the cursor you will see the screen flash an inverse rectangle the size of your clip. Release the left mouse button to complete the capture operation. Icon Manager will reappear with the captured image displayed inside the Bitmap Tool's Viewport. Use the scroll bar controls to position the 32x32 area you wish to work with inside the viewport, or choose the Copy All command to copy the entire bitmap that you captured into the clipboard for pasting into another application.

Note: The inverse display action provided during screen capture is not meant to be used to precisely line up your clip. It is only provided to give you positive feedback that the capture operation is being performed. It would be not be kosher to change the color of another window's client area as this may cause extremely undesirable results if the application was updating the area when the change was made. Icon Manager can only briefly invert these areas during the instant that it has control of the system, and must revert the screen to its original colors before relinquishing control to Windows. Don't get caught up trying to clip a precise area. Clip an oversized area that insures you have the portion of the screen you need and then address the excess later in Paintbrush or with the Viewport's scroll bar adjustment.

The last two selections appearing on the Bitmap Tool's Edit menu are Add Screen Inverse... and Remove Screen Inverse.... These options are used to create the transparent and inverse screen areas of an icon, or to substitute a color from the 16 color palette for these areas when editing them in a paint application. Using both a transparent and an inverse screen portion in your icon will limit your icon design to fourteen colors. This should not be too restrictive for most icon designing. The only icon we are aware of today that uses all sixteen colors is for the program Mypal, a color palette application, and it does not use any screen or inverse screen area.

The dialogs for color/screen substitution are straightforward, allowing you to easily point and click on the color(s) you want to exchange. A Reset button can be used to start over, and a check box labelled Available Colors Only can be activated to display only the colors which have not been used within your icon image. This is a handy feature to use when you are substituting colors for the transparent/inverse areas before exporting an icon to Paintbrush. By selecting Available Colors Only, you can quickly see what colors can be used to uniquely identify these areas.

The background color that is used to preview your image against is initially set to gray. You can change this color to examine how the icon will appear against different backgrounds by clicking any of the color buttons with the right mouse button.

Icon File Formats

Icon Manager can read four different file formats and will create or write three of these. The following section describes each of the file formats in detail and explains a few strategies behind using each type.

Icon Resource File (.ICO File)

An icon resource file can contain no more than one icon, but may contain several different representations of that icon suitable for display on different types of video monitors. Icon resource files commonly have the file extension of ICO . These files were originally editable only by the SDKPAINT program which accompanies the Microsoft Software Development Kit. Several utilities are now available from both shareware and commercial vendors that allow manipulation of icons and their data. Many of the icons that are currently available through shareware channels were produced by PBIcon (Icon Manager's predecessor) or other shareware programs. These icons contain only one representation of the icon (the high resolution 32 by 32 pixel, 16 color format) used by most color monitors of EGA or higher resolution. Other commercial packages provide capabilities to software designers which allow the creation of up to three additional representations of icons to be stored into these resource files. These are 32x32 monochrome (2 color), 32x32 three plane color (8 color), 32x32 four plane color (16 color) and 32x16 CGA (2 color). Windows examines the different representations contained in the file and chooses the best one for the current display at program execution time. This allows the designer the ability to take advantage of color capability and to avoid using colors that will not appear as intended, without worrying which video display it will be used with.

The size of an icon resource file depends directly on what type and how many representations of the icon it contains. For the readily available icons described above which contain a 32x32 16 color image only, that size is 766 bytes. One portion of the data which makes up 128 of these bytes is the AND mask. This data is a 32x32 monochrome bitmap used to provide screen transparency and inverse screen color to the color portion of the icon. The capability to create or alter this portion of the icon has been overlooked by the early shareware programs. Most users do not notice the lack of an icon's transparent area because they use the default Application Workspace color of white that Windows installs with. You can easily spot the difference between Icons that do or do not have a transparency mask by changing your application workspace color to light gray or cyan from the Control Panel's colors module. Icon Manager allows you to create a transparency mask by using any one or two colors of the 16 color palette available to you to specify transparent or inverse screen icon areas.

Icon Library (.ICL File)

An icon library is a collection of icon resource files which have been specially formatted with header and directory information to appear to Windows as a runtime link library of resources, or DLL. The header information and two types of directories (one for the icon resource files and another for the individual icons' representations) require an additional amount of disk space above and beyond the size of the resource files alone. The advantage of an icon library is the ability to collect or group multiple icons (by category perhaps) to allow the user to select an icon from the file using the 'View Next' button within Program Manager's dialog box. Of course, storing too many icons in an icon library or including icons for a wide-variety of applications can make this process tedious and time consuming for the user. This is one of the tasks that Icon Manager is meant to ease. By organizing your icons into icon resource files and icon libraries in advance using Icon Manager, it should be much easier to find and select the icon or icons that best meet your needs, no matter how extensive your icon libraries become.

Icon libraries are stored using the file extension of ICL by Icon Manager. Programs offered by other vendors may also create icon library files, such as Icon Designer by hDC, which uses the extension of IL . The use of different extensions is not meant to add confusion to their usage, but to maintain a distinction between processors. Icon Manager will read icon library files which are created by the current 1.1 release of Icon Designer. We do NOT recommend a casual interchange of data between the two programs, nor do we commit to supporting the use of icon libraries maintained by Icon Manager within any other application.

Icon Archive (.ICA File)

An icon archive file is a special file format maintained and used by Icon Manager to help you get the most out of your disk space and program operation. These files are stored using the file extension of ICA. Because Icon Manager deals exclusively with high-resolution color icons and does not need to assemble the resources into sophisticated link directories, icon archive files can save you over 20% of the disk space that an icon library would require. This savings is even greater when compared to storing individual icon resource files (something that might surprise you), due to the overhead required by individual file space allocation on your hard drive. A typical hard drive allocates file space in 512-byte sectors. Two sectors are required for a 766 byte file, of which 258 bytes, or over 33% of the total disk space, is wasted.

The most efficient way to manage icons, if you are primarily concerned with disk space, is to store only those icons that you are currently using in icon resource files and keep all of your remaining icons in icon archive files. Icon libraries can be used discriminably where convenient, and can require less space than multiple icon resource files if you are changing your icons frequently.

You should use icon archive files to store icons that you do not require on a regular basis, but want to keep available for possible future use. In addition to saving disk space, archive files use a small portion of their data area to maintain information about where each icon has been placed within your library window, as well as the size of the window when you last saved the file. This adds one more convenience to the operation of these files.

Executable

Icon Manager will read and extract icons from both pre-3.0 Windows executables as well as current programs. Icon Manager processes each icon representation that it finds within the executable, and converts it, if necessary, to either a monochrome or color 32x32 pixel icon resource in the current 3.0 format. Yes, although Icon Manager likes to work with 16 color icon formats, it will preserve the attributes of a monochrome icon which it reads from either an existing icon library file or executable file, until such time that you edit that icon using the bitmap tool to export it to your paint application. No need to waste any more space until it's needed! Icon Manager will not write icons back into executable files.

Putting It All Together

The following sections provide information to help you get the most out of using Icon Manager within your Windows environment. We begin by explaining some strategies of organizing your Program Manager desktop. Next is an explanation of how to use other Windows programs and files created by Icon Manager to customize your Program Manager desktop. Don't look for this information in your Windows User's guide, it isn't there. The last section of the chapter is devoted to special tips to help you use Windows Paintbrush to create and modify icon designs.

Customizing Program Manager

The whole concept behind Icon Manager is to provide the tools required to allow you to customize your desktop within Program Manager. Adding custom icons to your desktop is not the only important topic here. Customizing your desktop using the Properties dialog of Program Manager can significantly improve your user interface through organization of your program groups and specialization of the icons they contain.

Let's begin by taking a look at the program groups that comprise a standard Windows installation. These are the Main, Accessories, Games, Windows Applications, and Non-Windows Application groups. They provide an organizational scheme that meets the requirements of your initial Windows installation. If you have not made any significant changes to this configuration, you are missing out on much of the power Program Manager is meant to provide.

Few users actually run all of the programs that are installed as icons into program groups. The best way to start creating the most potent desktop for your computer is to eliminate the program icons that you do not currently have a use for, and to collect the infrequently used icons into a group of their own. Program items and their icons require Windows system resources that could be used by your applications when they execute. This isn't meant to suggest that you should remove all of your program groups and items to give your applications more memory. It is only mentioned to make you more aware of considerations which you might find interesting and

prudent. Deleting the program icons from Program Manager will not delete the programs from your system, it only removes the 'quick access' startup features of Program Manager. You can restore any program items that you delete whenever you desire.

You will most likely want to organize your desktop by eliminating, renaming, and adding program groups. But before we do that, let's consider new program items that you will want to add. Any DOS applications that you run from within Windows can be entered into a program group and depicted with a custom icon. You may want to follow the standard installation format of placing these items into a DOS program group, however you may find that placing these programs into groups related to your own tasks provides a friendlier and more efficient interface.

In addition to adding DOS program items, consider adding specialized program items that provide initialization information to your applications. Most Windows applications accept command line parameters which are processed by the programs when they are started. The most straight-forward command line parameter is a filename to begin processing. For example, Windows Notepad and Windows Write will accept the name of a text document to load at startup rather then entering File, Open..., and so forth after starting the program. If you run programs like these and frequently start with a beginning template document of some kind, adding a program item which specifies the command line information can be a very powerful tool. This becomes even more evident with more sophisticated applications such as Microsoft Excel or Word for Windows. The macro facilities that are supported by these programs can allow an entire customized process to be initiated by specifying command line document and/or workspace parameters. You may choose to create several instances of the same program in different program items to specify different types of tasks which the program initializes for. Refer to the manuals for your Windows applications to see what command line parameters are accepted, and consider delving further into any macro capabilities supported by programs that you use frequently.

The most suitable desktop layout will be different for everyone. There is no rule of thumb as to how many groups you should have or how many items in each group. You will find the best layout for yourself by refining your desktop over time. It is best to avoid a large number of groups containing few items in each; this not only wastes system resources in a manner of speaking, in most instances it is also more difficult to work in a more cluttered environment.

There are several short-cut methods to placing program items within groups. One of these is simply dragging the icon of the program from File Manager and dropping it into a program group of Program Manager. The most straight-forward way to create a program group or item is by selecting the New... dialog selection from Program Manager's File menu and typing in the information directly. (For information on managing program groups and items refer to Chapter 3 of your Windows User's Guide.)

Using Icon Files with Program Manager

The focal point of customizing program items is the Properties... dialog selection under Program Manager's File menu. This is one area that the Windows User's Guide does not cover in much detail. Before you add custom changes to program items, first create your program groups and enter raw program items into the groups using any of the procedures described in the Windows User's Guide. The following information describes how you can add command line parameters and customize the icons for your program items after this foundation has been laid.

First, highlight the program item that you wish to customize. Now select Properties... from the File menu. A dialog box will appear, which contains two text edit boxes. The first box can be used to enter the title that you would like to be displayed underneath the icon in the program group. You can use a custom title instead of the default program name by choosing a short, descriptive title of the action or task that the icon represents. Choosing too long a title will cause the text of adjacent icons to overlap each other. The second text edit box is used to enter the command line for the program. This always includes the name of the program (the fully qualified pathname is required if the program is not in your Windows directory or in your DOS program search path). It can optionally contain added command line parameters for the application to use at startup (e.g., WRITE.EXE BUSLETR.WRI). If you are satisfied with the information that you enter into the edit controls and you do not wish to change the icon at this time, select OK to update the program item with the new information.

To select a different icon for the program item, select the Change Icon... button from the properties dialog. A dialog will be displayed which includes an edit box that initially contains the name of your Windows application, or PROGMAN.EXE if you have added a DOS application. This filename is the location where Program Manager obtains an icon for its display. Windows programs can contain more than one icon. Selecting the View Next button will step through the available icons in the file, one at a time. When you see the icon that you would like to choose, select OK to confirm your choice. You will have to select OK once again to close the properties dialog and complete the update.

The icon information is transferred into one of Program Manager's data files when the program item is created or updated. It is read from the file specified in the Change

Icon dialog, not from the command line of the Properties dialog. This means that you can replace this name with the name of any other file containing icons that is in a format which Program Manager can process. This includes other Windows programs, icon resource files (*.ICO), and specially-constructed icon library files.

To change the icon of a program item to one found in another file, follow the instructions above for selecting the Properties... dialog and the Change Icon dialog. Enter the name of another Windows program, or an icon resource or library file (*.ICO or *.ICL) created with Icon Manager. (*.ICA icon archive files cannot be read by Program Manager). Select the View Next button and you should see a new icon appear in the preview area. Select View Icon again for Windows programs or icon libraries to select other icons in the file. If a message box appears saying No icons found in file , double-check the name you entered into the file name edit box to be sure that it is correct. You may have to specify the complete drive and pathname of the file if it is not in your Windows directory or your DOS program path. When you see the icon that you would like to use in the preview area of the Change Icon dialog, select OK to confirm your selection and then OK once again on the Properties dialog to complete the update.

Working in Paintbrush

Windows Paintbrush (or any other Windows paint application which can use the bitmap data format) can be used to create or modify icons. Here at Impact Software we felt that more could be done to support icon users by working on icon management tools rather than by designing a complete paint application just to add a few extra features (i.e., defining the transparent/inverse screen portion of the icon). Windows Paintbrush provides an extremely rich set of drawing tools in addition to the pixel-by-pixel editing which is found in most icon paint programs. In the future, OLE (Object Linking & Embedding) additions to Microsoft Windows will allow programs like Icon Manager and Windows Paintbrush to seamlessly operate together as one program.

This section provides a few tips and tricks to make creating and modifying icons using Windows Paintbrush a little easier. You should consult your Windows User Guide (Part II, Windows Accessories, Chapter 8, Paintbrush) for a complete description of how to use Paintbrush and its features.

Pasting Into Paintbrush: When you initially Paste an image into Paintbrush it will be placed flush in the upper left corner of the drawing area. This is NOT the ideal position to conduct editing. When you select the Zoom In option Paintbrush wants to use this upper left area to provide a true-life sized display of the zoomed area for your examination. Attempting to zoom in to this location in the drawing area produces undesirable operation of the editing process. The very first action you should perform when pasting an icon into Paintbrush is to position the cursor over the icon image, depress the left mouse button, and drag the image to the center of your screen (or maybe the bottom right corner if you intend to use the Shrink + Grow feature to produce an oversized image).

Sizing Considerations: Icon images used by Icon Manager must be 32 by 32 pixels in size. There is no magic algorithm that can be used to shrink a large picture into a small icon while retaining all of the information contained in the larger picture. Keep your images 32 by 32 pixels whenever possible to avoid messy resizing operations. This is not meant to imply that you shouldn't use oversized images to work with. Using the Zoom In option is a must for editing these small images; however, this feature limits the drawing tools to only the paintbrush and the fill tool. You should find your own comfort level between the convenience of using oversized images and the difficulty that you associate with resizing to and from the 32-pixel-square icon image. If you choose to work on oversized images and later shrink to icon size, the following tips will help you along the way.

Using 32X32.BMP: A bitmap image is provided with Icon Manager in the file 32X32.BMP which can help you create and size your icons. This image can be placed onto your drawing area by selecting Paste From... on the Edit menu and selecting the file 32X32.BMP from your d:\ICONS sub-directory. As when pasting an icon into the drawing area, immediately drag the pasted image from the upper left corner into a more suitable position in your drawing area. This bitmap consists of a black square surrounded by a dotted red square. The area INCLUDING the black line is exactly 32 by 32 pixels square. This represents the actual area of your icon image. The dotted red line represents the beginning of the area OUTSIDE of the icon.

The reason for providing two separate outlines becomes clear when you want to use Paintbrush's Pick tool if you are going to Shrink + Grow. The clipping rectangle of the Pick tool does not work consistently across all four boundaries of the rectangle. You will find that the tool includes pixels that are contained underneath its top and left boundaries, but does not include pixels that are directly underneath the right and bottom boundaries. The 32x32.BMP bitmap can help you position the crosshair cursor more accurately during a Pick operation.

Picking to Shrink + Grow: To Grow an image, select the Pick tool and position the crosshair cursor directly over the top left corner of the dotted line, and then gently easing the mouse one pixel down and one pixel left. When the crosshair is in place, gently depress the left mouse button to begin the Pick operation without disturbing the crosshair. Now drag the crosshair down to the bottom right corner, this time placing the left

and upper extensions of the crosshair directly on top of the dotted red line (remember, these pixels will not be included in the pick operation). Now you can select Shrink + Grow from the Pick menu. Create a new, larger square by defining a new image area with the cursor while holding down the SHIFT key to maintain a perfectly square area. When you release the left mouse button you should acquire a perfectly resized image.

Use a similar approach to reversing this operation. Carefully choose the upper left corner of your from pick and use the SHIFT key to cut out a perfect square. Line up the destination area within 32X32.BMP just as you would to pick an image from it (see instructions above). Shrinking an image almost always results in minor variances to the position of pixel colors when multiple colors appear close together or intermixed. You will always want to examine the icon image with the Zoom In feature to examine the image for areas which can be improved with a small touch up.

Copying an Icon Out of Paintbrush: Before you copy your icon to the clipboard, remember to consider preparing a transparent area for the icon. Most icons benefit from having their outer areas transparent, avoiding the white square often seen by users who select a color other than the default white for their application workspace background. You may also opt to create an inverse screen portion for your icon, although this is rarely used. Simply paint the transparent and inverse screen areas with colors that are not used in the rest of your icon. You can specify these colors later in Icon manager's Bitmap Tool as the screen and/or inverse areas to complete the construction of the icon.

Copying an icon out of Paintbrush is a simple operation. Choose the Pick tool and clip an area which includes your icon. There is no need to make a precise clip as long as the clip contains all of the image area for your icon. Choose Copy from the Paintbrush Edit menu. Now activate Icon Manager and select Paste from the Bitmap Tool menu. The image will appear in the Viewport. If the image is larger than 32 by 32 pixels, the scroll bar controls will activate to allow you to smoothly scroll the desired 32-pixel square into view.

Registration

Licensing Icon Manager

If you use this software and find it of value, you may obtain a license for its use and support the continuing development of quality Windows shareware. Our licensing agreement appears on the following registration form, along with pricing information for the software license and related materials.

Registration Form

License request for Icon Manager

Copyright © 1991 by Leonard A. Gray

Icon Manager is licensed on a per user basis. The license grants the user the right to install and use the software on one or more computers so long as the total number of users does not exceed the license quantity.

Please type or *print clearly* the following information:

Name/Company _____

Street _____

City _____ State/Prov _____ ZIP/Postal Code _____

Country _____ Phone _____

____ VISA ____ MasterCard ____ JBM

Credit Card Number _____

__ Diner's Club __ Carte Blanche

Expiration _____ Name As Appears on Card _____ Signature _____

Type	Qty _____	Price	Total
Basic Registration	_____ x	$19.95=	_____
Update Diskette	_____ x	$6.50=	_____ Disk Size: __ 5.25 __ 3.5

(Included free! Over 300 original and enhanced icons from various contributors)

Operations Manual	_____ x	$3.50	_____
(HP LaserJet III quality - 8.5 x 11)		Sub-total	_____
California residents add 6.5% sales tax.			_____
Outside U.S. and Canada			_____
add $5.00 shipping per set of diskette/manual			_____
Grand total:			_____

We accept checks and money orders in addition to payment by credit card (must be paid through a U.S. bank).

License requests from outside the United States: Registrations will be processed upon receipt of the current equivalent of U.S. funds in check or money order (must be drawn or paid through a U.S. bank) or credit card request subject to the currency exchange rates used by your credit card company. Mail your completed registration request to:

Impact Software
12140 Central Avenue
Suite 133
Chino, CA 91710
U.S.A.

Thank you for supporting the shareware software concept and encouraging the future development of Windows shareware!

Windows is a trademark of Microsoft Corporation.

Impact Software
Chino, California
U.S.A.
Voice: (714)590-8522
Data: (714)590-0500 (Public BBS: eight bits, no parity, one stop)

Magic Screen Saver

Version 1.13
by Will S. Stewart & Ian C. MacDonald
Copyright © 1990,1991 by Software Dynamics

What Is Magic?

Magic is a configurable screen saver/security utility designed specifically for Microsoft Windows 3.0. If your computer is left unattended, Magic fills your screen with colorful animation, as well as providing password protection for your computer. Much thanks to the many users of Magic worldwide who have supported, criticized, and paid shareware fees since our initial release!!

A static screen image left unattended for a long time can damage the computer screen as the image gets burned into the display. A screen saver saves the computer monitor from this damage by blanking or changing the display if the computer is not used for a set amount of time (timeout period). After the timeout period, Magic puts your computer into Sleep mode. In Sleep mode, the screen is blanked and a changing moire colour pattern moves around the screen. Since the moire pattern is constantly changing, no spot on your monitor gets burned in, and the computer doesn't look like it is turned off (as simply blanking the screen would do). Any user action (like moving the mouse or pressing a key) brings back (wakes up) the user's normal Windows display. Magic also provides computer security by requiring a password before waking up from Sleep mode. This can prevent unauthorized snooping to your computer while it is running.

Overview of Features

- Saves monitor from damage due to image burn-in.
- Password protection in Windows (works across reboots).
- Stimulating colour screen saver graphics.
- Configurable active icons.
- Can be set to not interfere with communication programs.
- Includes an Installer program.

How Do I Install It?

Once installed, Magic can run in background without any maintenance from the user at all. Magic is best used as an 'init' program for Windows. That means that it is automatically loaded as Windows boots up and will work as long as Windows is in operation. To install Magic in the Windows boot-up process, do the following:

With the Installer

(Note: You *must* use the installer if your version of Magic is personalized.)

1. Start up the installer program. **Note:** The files MAGIC.EXE and MAGICLIB.DLL for the new version have to be in the same directory as the installer.
2. Check the "Modify Win.ini" box [default] if you want to have Magic run automatically every time Windows is started. **Note:** If the WIN.INI file has already been modified, it will not be changed again. The installer will make a backup of your WIN.INI file (WININI.OLD) if it has to be modified.
3. Click on the "Start" button to start the installation process.

Manually

1. Open the WIN.INI file in your Windows directory with Notepad, or any text-editing program.
2. Several lines down from the top of the file, you will find a line like the following:
   ```
   load =
   ```
   These lines tells Windows what programs to load as it boots up. Change this line to read as follows:
   ```
   load = magic.exe [+any other startup programs]
   ```
3. Save WIN.INI and Windows will now know to automatically run Magic. All that's left is to copy the files MAGIC.EXE and MAGICLIB.DLL into the same directory (the Windows directory) as your WIN.INI file.
4. Restart Windows and Magic will start up automatically if you did steps 1-3 correctly.

Note: The manual method does not allow the registration information from a personalized copy of Magic to be transferred to the new version. If you copy the newer files over your existing personalized files, the personalized information will be destroyed. The installer *will* preserve the registration information in a personalized version.

How Do I Use Magic?

Magic's colorful animation both saves your monitor from damage and shows off Windows' graphics capabilities. While no user configuration (beyond installation) is necessary, you can easily configure Magic to suit your work environment and preferences. After the timeout period (in minutes), Magic will go to sleep, blanking your monitor and filling it with the animated magic pattern. As

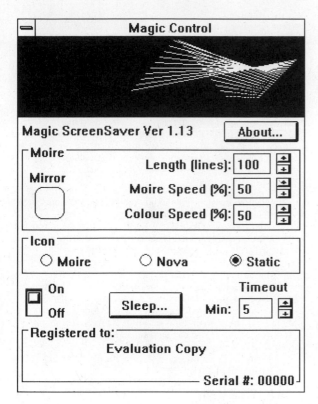

Magic Control

Magic ScreenSaver Ver 1.13   About...

Moire
Mirror

Length (lines): 100
Moire Speed [%]: 50
Colour Speed [%]: 50

Icon
○ Moire   ○ Nova   ● Static

On
Off   Sleep...   Timeout Min: 5

Registered to:
Evaluation Copy

Serial #: 00000

opposed to waiting for the timeout, you can make Magic go to sleep immediately by putting the mouse in the Sleep Corner of your monitor. (see Sleep/Wake Settings). If you move the mouse or hit a key, Magic "wakes up" and returns your normal Windows display.

Note: If you put Magic to sleep manually (putting the mouse in the Sleep Corner), only a mouse movement will wake Magic up. If you have an evaluation copy of Magic, hitting the spacebar will bring up a credit screen, as opposed to waking up Magic.

In normal operation, Magic appears on the Windows desktop as an icon, but selecting the Control Panel menu option (or double clicking on the Magic desktop icon) opens up Magic's Control Panel options.

The Control Panel

Magic's Control Panel allows you to change every feature of its operation to suit your preferences.

Sleep Preview Window

At the top of the Control Panel is the Sleep Preview Window. This area shows a preview of the graphics that

will fill the screen in Sleep Mode. If you change the moire graphics settings, the Sleep Preview Window will reflect those changes.

About Magic

Below the Sleep Preview Window is the Magic version number and an About button. Clicking on the About button presents more information about Magic, how to contact its creators, and the benefits of registering.

Moire Graphics Control

The moire graphics can be configured to your liking with three scrollbar controls and the Mirror button. The number of lines in the moire pattern can be varied from 1 to 150. The MAX setting (beyond 150) sets the moire to infinite length. The speed of the moire animation and the speed of the colour changes can be varied from 1 to 100%. You can use the mouse to click on the controls' up and down arrows, or you can use the up and down arrow keys. The Mirror button allows you to vary the symmetry of the Moire pattern on the screen. Clicking the Mirror button steps you through the mirroring options. You can choose no mirroring, vertical sym metry, horizontal symmetry, or both horizontal and vertical symmetry.

Magic Icon

Magic appears as an icon on the Windows desktop. You can select from 3 different behaviors for the Magic icon. These modes for the icon only affect the icon, not the Sleep animation.

Moire: In this mode, the Magic icon show a miniature moire pattern in the icon (except when the control panel is shown). This animation only occurs when your computer is idle, so it does not slow down processing. If the computer is busy, the icon animation stops until the computer is idle again.
Nova: In this mode, the Magic icon shows a star. As Magic approaches Sleep mode, the star collapses to show how close you are to Sleep mode. As the computer goes to Sleep, the star visually goes Nova and explodes to indicate that Sleep mode is starting.
Magic: In this mode, the icon is always the Magic application icon (a rabbit coming out of a Magician's hat) and does not animate on the Windows desktop.

On/Off Switch

Magic resides in background, takes very little memory, and should not interfere with well-behaved software running under Windows. However, programmers developing Windows software may wish to have a completely clear system for debugging their own programs. Therefore, Magic has an on/off switch to completely enable or disable Magic without actually closing it. When the switch is in the OFF position, Magic is totally disabled and will not enter sleep mode or look for a Sleep timeout. When disabled, the Magic icon changes to an overworked software developer catching some much needed rest (Z's).

Sleep Time Setting

You can set how long the computer must be inactive before entering sleep mode. Similar to changing the Moire graphics settings, you can click on the arrows or use the arrow keys to change the number of minutes of inactivity before entering Sleep mode.

Sleep Button & Sleep Window

You may wish Magic to enter Sleep mode on command. By putting the cursor in the Sleep Corner (of your screen), Magic enters Sleep mode immediately. You can also invoke Password mode by holding the Ctrl key down when putting Magic to sleep manually.

You may also want Magic to not go to sleep, regardless of the timeout. By putting the mouse in the Wake Corner, Magic will be inhibited from going to sleep. If you put the mouse in the Wake Corner, the cursor will change to a small 'W' to show that Magic will stay awake. The 'Sleep' button leads to the Sleep window, where the Sleep/Wake Corners can be set, and you can enter the password window.

Sleep/Wake Corners

The Sleep window shows the current Sleep Corner and Wake Corner settings on 2 rectangles which each represent your monitor. The smaller squares in the corner of each 'monitor' represent the Sleep & Wake corners respectively. By clicking the mouse in a different corner of the rectangle (representing your monitor), you can move the Sleep & Wake corners. Magic will not allow you to set the Sleep & Wake corners to be the same. For example, if the Sleep Corner is set for the lower left corner of the Sleep rectangle (in the Sleep Window), this means that placing the mouse in the lower left corner of your monitor will put Magic to Sleep immediately.

The Wake Corner works similarly with the Wake rectangle in the Sleep Window. By default, the Wake Corner is the lower right corner of your monitor. Placing the mouse in the Wake corner of your monitor keeps Magic from going to Sleep. If you put the mouse in the Wake Corner, the cursor changes to a 'W' for a couple of seconds to show that you are in the Wake Corner.

Password Protection

Magic can be used for computer security, as well as saving your screen. If Password mode is enabled, the correct password must be entered before Magic will come out of Sleep mode back to your Windows display. Clicking on the Password... button (in the Sleep window) opens the Password Configuration dialog where you can type in a new password or toggle Magic's Password mode. When entering a new password, all keypresses show up as asterisks (*) for security. You must type the password in both the Password and Confirm fields to ensure that it is correct. When what you type in the Confirm field matches what you typed in the Password field, the OK button will be enabled. Clicking on the OK button stores the changes you have made to the Password settings. The Cancel button disregards any changes and reverts to the previous password (if any).

The Always Use Password checkbox allows you to toggle Magic's password mode. If checked, Magic will always require your password to wake up. Leave the box unchecked if you only occasionally want Magic to require a password. To invoke password checking with this mode, hold down the Ctrl key and put the mouse in the Sleep area. You must hold the Ctrl key down *until* Magic falls asleep to enable password checking. To let you know that you do have password mode enabled when Magic goes to sleep, Magic will display "Password Mode will be Enabled.." on your screen for 3 seconds before starting the moire animation. You can also select a blank screen mode for the screen saver by holding down the Shift key while you manually put Magic to sleep. This mode is only temporary in that you have to hold down the Shift key each time Magic is put to sleep. By selecting a Moire Length of 0 in the control panel, Magic will always use the plain blank screen while asleep.

Wrap-Around Password Protection

In Magic v1.13 (or later), password security works across restarts. If Magic is asleep with the password mode enabled and someone restarts your computer, Magic will enter password-protected Sleep mode as soon as Windows restarts. Of course, Magic must be set to load automatically with Windows for Magic to protect across restarts (see How Do I Install It?). Until the proper password is entered, Windows cannot be accessed.

Compatibility

Magic takes very little memory and processing time. It should not interfere with well-behaved Windows applications or DOS programs. In fact, Magic only gets processing time when all other applications are idle, such as when a word processing program is waiting for keyboard or mouse input. If you see Magic's animation slow down, it is usually because some other program is busy on your computer (for example, printing a letter). Only when your system is idle will Magic's animation operate at full speed, since it will not be slowing down any other program.

Communications

Previous to v1.11, Magic did not detect communications programs and could slow down serial communications activity. With v1.11 or later, the user can select up to four (4) serial ports for Magic to monitor. If a communication program uses a monitored serial port, Magic stops animating until the serial port is freed again. In this way, Magic does not slow down communications programs (uploads/downloads) on your computer.

Telling Magic to Monitor a Serial Port

All the settings for Magic are in the [Magic] section of the WIN.INI file (in your Windows directory). You need line(s) like the following in your WIN.INI file to tell Magic to monitor a serial port.

```
[Magic]
..
(other Magic settings)
..
WatchComPorts=n, n, n, n
(where n = 1 for COM1, 2 for COM2,...)
```

Note: If you use a serial mouse, *do not set Magic to monitor the mouse's serial port.*

If you do not have a serial port selected for Magic to monitor in your WIN.INI file, Magic won't detect communication activity and may slow down communication programs. By default, Magic does not monitor any serial ports. The Moire icon mode can slow down communication programs. Therefore, when you are going to be using communications, we recommend that you use the Nova or Magic modes for the icon. Since printer servers, networks, terminal programs, etc. all use communications, you should use the Nova or Magic icon modes for minimum interference.

DOS Apps

Since DOS applications do not report messages to Windows, Magic currently disables its screensaving whenever a DOS program is active.

Other Screen Savers

You should not try to use Magic and other screen saver utilities at the same time. The nature of screen savers causes them to interfere, with each other.

Windows Configurations

Magic works well in various configurations of Windows including CGA, EGA, VGA, and SVGA, using Pubtech File Organizer, HP NewWave, or off-the-shelf Windows 3.0. If you have a problem, please let us know. Magic v1.13 is a fully-compatible Windows 3.0 application. It will run only under Win 3, not under Windows /386 or 2.x (old versions of Windows).

Who Made Magic?

The Magic Screen Saver is a shareware program by Bill Stewart and Ian MacDonald of Software Dynamics. Much thanks to the many users and programmers who have supported our efforts & provided constructive criticism from around the world. As shareware, you are entitled to try an evaluation version of Magic out for 15 days free, upload it to online services, and give copies to associates, subject to the following conditions:

1. A lot of time and effort went into writing and testing Magic. If you don't use Magic, you'll throw it out. If you do use it, pay the modest shareware fee of $25 U.S. (or equivalent) to the authors. By paying the shareware fee, you will become a registered user of Magic, receive notice of all upgrades, and receive a personalized version of Magic (without the periodic "payup" screen) in the mail.

   Paying the small shareware fee for something you find useful encourages the free exchange of information currently enjoyed by the software community. It also encourages us, the authors, to support and upgrade the program. Not paying is both unlawful and uncool.

2. You may give an evaluation copy (non-personalized) of Magic to others, but may not distribute Magic for direct or indirect profit by any means, except through agreement with the authors.

3. You may not alter MAGIC.EXE, MAGICLIB.DLL, or this documentation in any way. When distributing Magic, you must include this documentation with the package.

4. While every effort has been made to test Magic in various environments, neither the authors nor Software Dynamics are liable for any damages caused directly or indirectly through the use or misuse of Magic. We provide Magic AS IS, & provide no guarantee that any specific features will be added in the future, nor any guarantee of its fitness for any specific purpose. We do not guarantee compatibility with future versions of system software, Windows, or any other products, although future versions of Magic will be upgraded to stay current with changes in DOS and Windows if we continue to receive user support through shareware.

The Shareware Fee

To register as an authorized user of Magic, send us the modest shareware fee. If you send us $25 U.S., you will be registered, we will notify you of all upgrades (in advance of their release), and we will mail you a personalized copy of the most recent version of Magic (without the periodic "payup" screen). Users who have already sent us $20 U.S. are still registered, but if you send an additional $5 U.S. (to cover the cost of the disk and shipping) we will send you a personalized copy of the latest version of Magic (with a serial number and without the periodic "payup" screen). We also offer licenses for sites or LANs that have many Magic users. The sliding fee scale makes Magic less expensive per user as the size of your group increases. The fee scale is as follows:

# of Units	Cost per Unit (U.S.)
1-9	$25
10-19	$15
20-49	$13

# of Units	Cost per Unit (U.S.)
50-99	$11
100-199	$9
200-499	$7
500 or more	$5

Please add $5 U.S. to any order for each additional master disk you require. Also, please specify the size and format (DSDD 3.5 inch, for example) of the disks you need. If you do not provide your disk preference, we will use DSDD 3.5 inch disks. Feel free to fax us purchase orders for Magic group licenses. We accept government and corporate purchase orders only for orders with 10 or more users. Orders for less than 10 users must be prepaid by check.

Once you receive your personalized copy of Magic, you will be able to update to later versions by downloading the new version from online services. If you have a personalized copy of Magic, the version you download will be personalized (no "payup" screen), as well. Minor upgrades will be posted on all major online services. Registered users can use these online services to get new versions. Therefore, users do not need to keep sending us $5 every time there is a new release. If you do not have access to online services, you can request that we mail out the new version (send $5 for shipping and handling).

Please send payment by check in U.S. or Canadian dollars, or pounds sterling, since these currencies are the easiest to negotiate. If using a currency other than U.S. dollars, calculate the registration fee in U.S. dollars and send us the equivalent in your currency.

Registration Form

To help our efforts to map out who is using Magic & on what hardware/software, please include the following information with your shareware payment to help us make Magic even better. It will also make it easier for us to inform you of upgrades, etc.

Name: _____

Address: _____

_____

Company: _____

Online Accounts: _____

Phone No: (voice) _____

Phone No: (fax) _____

Computer: _____

Amt of Memory: _____

Graphics Card: _____

How you obtained Magic: _____

Concerns, Questions, Feedback: _____

_____

We appreciate and encourage all user feedback that will help us improve the product. For any questions, comments or complaints, you can contact us by mail, voice, or online services as detailed below:

Software Dynamics
3530 15th Street SW, Suite 4
Calgary, Alberta
CANADA T2T 4A3
Voice: (403) 243-0296
Fax: (403) 287-9333
CompuServe: 71621, 1163
Connect: STEWART1
AOL: ZenMaster3

Many thanks for your support,

Will S. Stewart
Ian C. MacDonald
Software Dynamics

MetaPlay

Version 1.5
by Steve Goulet
Copyright © 1991 by GDG Systems Inc.

What Is MetaPlay

MetaPlay is a program that is used to view metafiles. Windows metafiles (.WMF) are files containing graphical pictures in a vector-based format. Using some of the more advanced features of MetaPlay, one can use it to create a slide show, add hypertext-like capabilities to Microsoft Word or Microsoft Excel, or one can use it to convert a metafile to a bitmap for use in a desktop publishing program. Under Windows 3.0, these bitmaps could then be used to create some very impressive wallpaper. Included with this version of MetaPlay is a powerful script language facility that enables you to make slide show presentations with your metafiles, and enhance them with text and graphics.

General Features

Supports metafiles larger than 64K, up to what memory allows. While this option is fine for viewing metafiles, please note that the clipboard does not support metafiles of this size in Windows 2.x. MetaPlay, when running under Windows 3.0, supports both bitmaps and metafiles larger

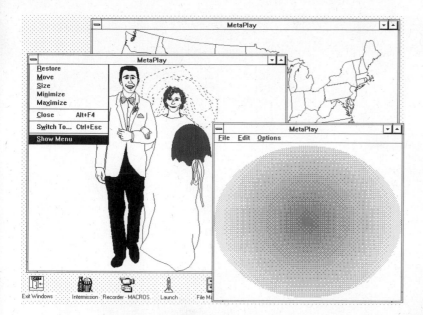

Size Window to Metafile When this option is selected a scaling factor is requested. The height and width of the metafile are multiplied by this factor and the window is sized accordingly. There are maximums and minimums for window sizes on various adapters, and the program will not let you select a scaling factor outside of these bounds. This option can be very useful if someone wishes to create several similar bitmaps of the same size. He or she can create several metafiles, and then use the same scale factor on all of them to produce bitmaps of the same size. Of course, the metafile size in the metafile headers must be the same.

Background Color Many exported metafiles contain no background colour. This does not create a problem when viewing a metafile, but may create one when converting it to a bitmap. Selecting a background colour with this option will set the background colour of the bitmap.

Metafile Stats Selecting this option will display a dialog box containing technical information regarding the selected metafile. The statistics on the left side of the box are values from the header. These values are defined by Aldus and are too lengthy to list the meanings here. Anyone familiar with the header format will recognize what they are. The values on the right are calculated by the program. These values should be self explanatory.

Bitmap Stats This option displays a dialog box containing information about a bitmap that would be created if the metafile was copied to the clipboard or saved to disk. Note: All units in the above dialog boxes are in pixels, except for those that are marked as being in inches, and the width to height ratios (W/H).

than 64K, both from the clipboard and disk. MetaPlay can load metafiles and save them to disk as bitmaps, or copy them to the clipboard as metafiles or bitmaps. It can also copy metafiles from the clipboard and save these files to a disk metafile.

Menu Options

Open Select this option to load in a new metafile.

Save As Bitmap Select this option to convert the metafile to a bitmap and save the bitmap to disk. Windows 3.0 users should note that under version 1.0 of MetaPlay, the disk based bitmap format is only compatible with Windows version 2.xx. We will correct this problem when the Software Development Kit becomes available.

Save As Metafile Select this option to save a metafile to disk.

Copy As Metafile This option will send a copy of the metafile to the clipboard.

Copy As Bitmap Select this option to convert the metafile to a bitmap and copy it to the clipboard.

Paste Select this option to copy a metafile from the clipboard into MetaPlay. The metafile can now be saved to disk for later playback.

Autoscale This feature will cause the metafile to keep its given aspect ratio when displayed in the window. This default for this is on. When this feature is disabled the metafile will occupy the whole window regardless of size.

Command Line Options

MetaPlay has a wide variety of command line options to customize playback. A command line in Windows takes the following format:

    PROGNAME.EXE option1 option2 option3 etc...

In this case, the program name (PROGNAME) is METAPLAY.EXE. The options that follow can include a filename. For example to load the file GDG.WMF the command line would be:

    METAPLAY.EXE GDG.WMF

This assumes that both METAPLAY.EXE and GDG.WMF are in the current directory or you have specified a path that has included these files in it.

To distinguish between the filename and other options, all other options take the format /L=NN where L is the letter of the option and NN is an number or string, depending on the option. Here is a list of available options and what they do:

/PX=NN This will initially Position the window at the X coordinate given by NN. NN is not actually a pixel position but a percentage of the width of the screen. For example, if one wanted the window to start in the middle of the screen one would put /PX=50.

/PY=NN This will initially Position the window at the Y coordinate given by NN. NN is not actually a pixel position but a percentage of the height of the screen. For example, if one wanted the window to start half way down the screen, one would put /PY=50.

/SX=NN This is the initial width of the window given in a percentage of the screen width. For example, if one wanted the window to be half as wide as the screen, one would put /SX=50.

/SY=NN This is the initial height of the window given in a percentage of the screen width. For example, if one wanted the window to be half as high as the screen, one would put /SY=50.

/X If this parameter is specified then the initial display of the window will be full screen (maximized under Windows terminology).

/T=NN This represents the amount of time to delay before automatically closing the window. If not specified, the window will stay open indefinitely. NN is the time given in seconds.

/K If this option is specified, the window will automatically be closed when the next keystroke is passed to the window.

/M If this option is specified, the menu will show initially. The default is to not show the menu.

/NA If this option is specified, initially the AUTOSCALE feature will be disabled. It is, by default, enabled.

/NB If this option is specified, the initial window will be drawn without a border. Use this option with care since, if a window is opened in this mode, it cannot be sized or closed from the system menu but must be closed with the above /T=NN or /K options or by typing ALT+F4 when the window is active.

/C="Text" This option allows specification of the text that will appear in the window caption. If omitted, it defaults to MetaPlay. This option will be very important if MetaPlay is used with our scripting facility, since it is by this name that the scripting facility identifies the window.

Any combination of these options are allowed on a command line. For example, to center the image on the screen, give it a caption of "Demo," and display it for only three seconds, the command would be:

```
METAPLAY.EXE GDG.WMF /PX=25 /PY=25
           /SX=50 /SY=50 /C="Demo" /T=3
```

MetaPlay Script Files

MetaPlay script files are ASCII text files containing a series of instructions which direct MetaPlay to perform certain actions, such as displaying a metafile or drawing a line. MetaPlay script files can be loaded from the command line by prefacing the file name with the @ character. For example to run the DEMO.SCR the command line would be:

```
METAPLAY.EXE @DEMO.SCR
```

Note that the full file specification must be given — but the extension does not necessarily have to be .SCR, although we do recommend using the .SCR specification.

The MetaPlay script language is a very simple language that currently supports over 35 functions to help you present your slide show. Here is a list of its functions and the parameters that go into them.

Boxtext — "String",xStart, yStart, Width, Height. This command puts the text in "String" on the screen, using the current font, in a box specified by the parameters that follow. This function is very useful when used in conjunction with the Settextvalign and Settexthalign functions.

Close — None. This command causes METAPLAY to terminate its execution.

Ellipse — xStart, yStart, Width, Height. This command draws an empty ellipse on the screen. See rectangle for a description of the parameters.

Fill — xStart, yStart. This command fills an area of the screen starting at xStart and yStart with the current brush color, stopping at the current pen color.

Fillrect — xStart, yStart, Width, Height. This command draws a filled rectangle on the screen. The rectangle border is drawn with the color of the pen, and it is filled with the brush color.

Fillellipse — xStart, yStart, Width, Height. This command draws a filled ellipse on the screen.

Line — xStart, yStart, Width, Height.This command draws a line on the screen. Width and Height are the width and height of a box that would bound the line.

Lineto — xPos, yPos. This command draws a line from the current pen position to the specified coordinates. See Moveto.

Moveto — xPos, yPos. This command moves the current pen position to the specified coordinates. It doesn't draw anything on the screen. See Lineto.

Playmetafile — filename, xStart, yStart, Width, Height. This command is used to display a metafile on the screen. The first parameter is the filename of the metafile to be played and a full file specification must be given. The *xStart* and *yStart* parameters tell MetaPlay where to position the metafile in the MetaPlay window. These parameters must be integers, with a value that corresponds to a percentage of the window height or width. For example, if you want your metafile to be displayed with the upper left corner of the metafile in the center of the MetaPlay window, *xStart* and *yStart* would be 50 and 50 (half way down, half way across). All coordinates are measured from the top left corner of the window. The width and height parameters specify the width and height of the area in which the metafile will be played in terms of a percentage of the total MetaPlay window width and height. For example, if you wish your metafile to take up three quarters of the width and height of a screen, *Width* and *Height* would be 75 and 75.

Playtextfile — filename, xStart, yStart, Width, Height. This command is used to display a text file on the screen. The parameters are the same as those used in Playmetafile, where *xStart, yStart, Width* and *Height* define a box in which the text file will be displayed.

Rectangle — xStart, yStart, Width, Height. This function is the same as fillrect, except that the rectangle is not filled.

Setautocenter — ON or OFF. The autocenter feature will cause Metafiles to be centered within their bounding box. Use this function to turn it on of off.

Setautoscale — ON or OFF. The autoscale feature will cause metafiles to be scaled to preserve their proper aspect ratio. Use this function to turn it on of off.

Setbackgroundcolor — Redvalue, Greenvalue, Bluevalue. This command sets the color that is used to fill in the background of text. This function only has meaning if the text mode is set to opaque. See Setbrushcolor and Settextmode.

Setbrushcolor — Redvalue, Greenvalue, Bluevalue. This command sets the current brush color. The brush color is the color that all fills, and the interior of circles and rectangles are drawn with. *Redvalue, Greenvalue* and *Bluevalue* must be integers between 0 and 255. These values represent the amount of that color that will be used in the brush. For example to create a white brush all values would be 255. A black brush would have all values 0.

Setmapmode — ANISOTROPIC or ISOTROPIC or TEXT. This command changes the mapping mode that MetaPlay uses to display its metafiles and text. The default mode is ANISOTROPIC, meaning things are scaled relative to the size of the window. In ISOTROPIC mode, things are scaled relative to the size of the window, but an x versus y perspective is maintained. In TEXT mode, the coordinates are no longer relative to the window; rather, they are screen pixels in this mode. Use this mode with caution, as it does introduce device dependencies.

Setpencolor — Width. This command moves the current pen thickness or width. A value of 0 is the default, which will produce a single pixel line. This value is a percentage of the screen width.

Setextcharset — OEM or ANSI. This function sets the character set that the font will use.

Settextcolor — Redvalue, Greenvalue, Bluevalue. This command sets the text color. See Setbrushcolor and Settextmode.

Setextfacename — String. This function tells MetaPlay to try to use the font that has a facename defined by String. This value can be in quotes.

Setextfamily — DONTCARE ROMAN SWISS MODERN SCRIPT or DECORATIVE. This command tells MetaPlay to use a font from the specified family. If it is set to DONTCARE, MetaPlay will use the system font or try to find a good match based on other text characteristics.

Setexthalign — LEFT CENTER or RIGHT. This function sets the horizontal alignment of the text display (from any of the text displaying functions) about its given coordinates.

Setextheight — Height. This function sets the desired height of the font that is to be used in subsequent text operations. If set to 0 (the default), MetaPlay will use the system default.

Setextpitch — FIXED or VARIABLE. This function tells MetaPlay to use FIXED or VARIABLE pitch fonts.

Setextstrikeout — ON or OFF. This function turns text strikeout on or off.

Setextitalic — ON or OFF. This function turns text italics on or off.

Setextmode — OPAQUE or TRANSPARENT. If the mode is set to TRANSPARENT, text is drawn by overwriting what is on the screen. If mode is set to OPAQUE the space between the letters is filled with the background color.

Setextunderline — ON or OFF. This function turns text underlines on or off.

Setextvalign — TOP CENTER or BOTTOM. This function sets the vertical alignment of the text display (from any of the text displaying functions) about its given coordinates.

Setextweight — Weight. This function sets the desired boldness of the font that is to be used in subsequent text operations. 0 is very very light, 400 is normal text and 700 or above is bold.

Setextwidth — Width. This function sets the desired width of the font that is to be used in subsequent text operations. If set to 0 (the default), MetaPlay will use the system default.

Text — "String", xStart, yStart. This command puts the text in "String" on the screen using the current font at the specified location.

Wait — Delay. This command is used to pause for the specified duration. *Delay* is the amount of time to wait, specified in tenths of a second. For example, to pause for 2 seconds the command would be Wait 20.

Waitkey — None. This command causes the program to wait at that point until a key is pressed.

Limitations

Due to the unavailability of the Windows Version 3.0 Software Development Kit in Canada at this writing, we are unable to save a bitmap in a form compatible with the new .BMP format used by Windows 3.0 programs and by Windows PAINT. However bitmaps can still be moved into PAINT thru the clipboard, enabling one to touch them up and use them as wallpaper. This gives people a very powerful way to create bitmaps with any drawing package, so long as it supports metafile export or metafile copying to the clipboard. We will issue a new release when the bitmap save feature is compatible with Windows 3.0.

Registration

GDG Systems
4451 P.H. Mathieu
Lachinaie QC
Canada
J6W 3T8
(514) 597-9755

Enclose $25.00 in U.S. dollars, or the Canadian equivalent, for MetaPlay (including shipping and handling). In Canada, add 7% GST and/or 8% VAT. Thank you.

Name _____

Address _____

_____

Telephone (   ) _____ ( ) Day ( ) Eve

Paint Shop

Version 1.50
by Robert Voit
Copyright © 1991 by JASC, Inc.

Overview

Over the last decade numerous painting programs and computer scanners have provided you, the user, the opportunity to acquire thousands of pictures to be used as you desire. The format of the files that these pictures are saved in vary widely. There is no standard to these picture files. This results in your ability to acquire pictures for which you have no program that supports that particular file format. Paint Shop was designed to help you make use of those files.

Paint Shop is a Windows Program. Its purpose is to allow you to display, print, alter and save pictures that use various picture file formats. With the advent of the graphical user interface, you now have the ability to create high quality documents without the high priced desktop publishing programs. For example, you can use Paint Shop to open a PCX file, dither the picture to black and white, mark off the part of the picture you desire, copy that part to the clipboard, and paste it into Microsoft's Write. Use Write to put the text into your document, then print the document. You have just done desktop publishing with what was provided in Windows and Paint Shop.

Paint Shop is distributed as a shareware program. This gives you the opportunity to try Paint Shop for the 30 day free trial period. This method of distribution was selected to provide you with the opportunity to obtain a quality application at a price substantially less than comparable commercial applications. See the section entitled Licensing for information on obtaining a license number.

Operational Considerations

Due to memory requirements for holding large pictures, Paint Shop will run the best in Windows 386 enhanced mode. Paint Shop can also be run in Windows' standard mode. Remember that large pictures take quite a bit of memory. If you do not have enough memory to complete an operation of Paint Shop, a message telling you this will appear. If Paint Shop can not recover your original picture when an out of memory error occurs then Paint Shop will reset. Paint Shop resets by clearing the present picture from memory and the client area. Just re-open the picture file to get the original picture back into Paint Shop.

Loading and Saving of GIF pictures and dithering of any picture is done in the background. This allows you to

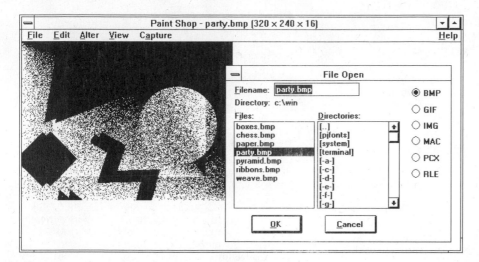

another application but do not want to shut down Paint Shop.

Open

Open lets you open a picture file. Select the file format of the picture that you would like to view. See the section File Formats for more information on the various file formats supported. The different file formats that are supported are aligned along the right side of the file open dialog box. Switch to the proper drive and directory by double clicking the drive or directory in the Directories list box. Now select the file to open from the Files list box by double clicking on the file name. Paint Shop will now read the file and display the picture.

Save As

Save As lets you save a file using a specified picture file format.

Select the format that you would like to save the file as. See the section File Formats for more information on the various file formats supported. The name of the file will automatically be changed to provide for the proper file name extension. You may alter the file name if you desire. You may save the file to a different drive or directory by double clicking the desired drive or directory in the Directory list box. When you are ready, click on the OK button. Paint Shop will now save the file using the file name and file format that you have specified. If the file name already exists in the current directory, Paint Shop will prompt you, asking if you would like to overwrite the existing file. Select OK to overwrite the original file. Select Cancel to abort the file save operation.

Delete

Delete will delete the file of the currently displayed picture. Before deleting the file you will be asked if you are sure that you want to delete the file.

Print

Print allows you to print the current picture. Paint Shop uses the printer resolution that you have selected. If your picture is too big for the size of your paper, the picture will be shrunk to the size required to fit the paper. The speed of the print operation depends on the type of printer used, picture size, and the selected printer resolution. The larger the picture and the higher the resolution the longer it will take. Just one step down in

continue to work in Windows as Paint Shop is taking care of the processing of your picture. Paint Shop does allow for multiple instances (more than one copy of Paint Shop may run at the same time). Paint Shop has a built in Help system. All menu commands along with additional information may be obtained by selecting HELP - INDEX.

Installation

Paint Shop is made up of 3 files:

PS.WRI The User's Manual
PS.HLP The On-Line Help file
PS.EXE Paint Shop program

The only files that are required to run Paint Shop are PS.EXE and PS.HLP. Copy these two files to any directory that you desire. They must be in the same directory. Use your DOS reference manual for instructions on creating directories and copying files. Once the files are where you want them, add Paint Shop to your Program Manager. Use your Windows manual for information on how to add an application to Program Manager. You are now ready to run Paint Shop. Start Paint Shop the same way you would start any other Windows program.

Menu Items

File

New

New will clear the current picture from memory and the screen. This is useful if you need more memory for printer resolution will change your print time dramatically.

Printer Setup

Printer Setup will activate the printer's setup dialog box. You can use this option to change the printer's configuration. Most printer setup dialog boxes have their own help system. Use this help system to get additional information on the various options available in the setup dialog box.

Exit

Exit will shut down Paint Shop.

Edit

Copy

Copy will copy the currently marked area to the clipboard. See Operations-Marking for information on how to mark an area of the picture. If there is no marked area, Paint Shop will copy the entire picture to the clipboard.

Paste

Paste will paste the picture on the clipboard into Paint Shop. Once the picture is in Paint Shop, you can treat it as any other picture.

Alter

Flip

Flip will turn the picture upside down.

Mirror

Mirror will create a mirror image of the picture.

Rotate Right

Rotate Right will rotate the picture 90 degrees to the right.

Rotate Left

Rotate Left will rotate the picture 90 degrees to the left.

Stretch/Shrink

Stretch/Shrink can be used to change the size of the picture. When this option is selected a dialog box will allow you to change the dimensions of the picture. You may select one of the standard VGA sizes, or Custom Size. If you select Custom Size, enter the new width and height in the edit boxes. After making your selection for the new width and height click the OK button. If you do not want to change the size of the picture, select Cancel.

Trim

Trim will reduce the picture to include only the area that is marked. See Operations-Marking for information on how to mark an area of the picture.

Dither Color

Dither Color will dither the picture from 256 colors down to 16 colors. The 16 colors that result will be the 16 default colors that Windows uses.

Dither Mono

Dither Mono will dither the picture from 256 or 16 colors down to 2 colors. When you select Dither Mono a dialog box will appear allowing you to determine the way that the picture should be dithered. No single method for dithering will do a good job on all pictures. Thus Paint Shop gives you the options to have the picture dithered the way you would like it dithered. This allows for 24 different outcomes. The different possibilities are set up by the selections you make using the Dither-Mono dialog box. Your choices fall into 3 categories. You must select one choice from each of the 3 categories. These categories are: Palette weight, Palette color and Dither type.

Palette weight: You may select weighted or non-weighted. A weighted palette will set more of the original colors to black and white, instead of dithering out the color to appear as different levels of grey. You will find that edges are usually sharper using a weighted palette.

Palette color: You may select Grey, Red, Green or Blue. When a picture is dithered, it is done relative to the grey values of the original palette. You may obtain better dithered pictures if the picture is dithered relative to one of the components of the original palette. In other words, only using one of the components from Red, Blue or Green. For example, a picture with a lot of flesh tones comes out better if you only use the Red palette component. A picture that is mainly green will look better if you use only the Green palette component.

Dither type: Paint Shop uses a technique called error diffusion to do the dithering. Within error diffusion there are 3 algorithms that are most popular. They are Floyd-Steinberg, Burkes and Stucki. They each give different results.

The best choice of each of the 3 categories is completely subjective. The best choice can usually be narrowed down by selecting a Weighted palette and using the Floyd-Steinberg Dither type. Then dither against Grey, Red, Blue and Green. This will tell you the best Palette Color with which to dither. After finding the best palette color then try a non-weighted palette. Since all the dither types will have about the same outcome for weighted and non-weighted palettes, you will now know the answer to Palette Weight and Palette Color. Next, use your Palette Weight and Palette Color that you've found to be best, and dither using the other 2 Dither Types. The more you use the dithering option the better you get at knowing what will be the best selections without having to go through the above routine.

Greyscale

Greyscale will change the picture's colors to the greyscale values of the original colors. The picture is still a colored picture. It will just be various shades of grey.

Invert

Invert will invert the colors of a black and white picture. Black will become white and white will become black. Many pictures come with a black background. When printing these pictures the background will be printed. By using Invert the background would become white and the resulting picture would not have the background printed.

Prep for MAC

Prep for MAC takes care of all the work necessary to prepare a picture for saving as a MAC file. MAC files should have a white background, Prep for MAC gives you the option to invert the picture colors during the prep operation. The preparation process does four steps:

1. Reduces the picture so that neither the width nor the height exceed the maximum allowed by MAC pictures. If Paint Shop reduces the size of your picture, the aspect ratio will be maintained.
2. Dithers the picture, if necessary, to black and white. This step will use a weighted palette, grey color and Floyd-Steinberg dithering. If you wish different options for the dithering, then dither the picture with Alter-Dither-Mono before using Prep for MAC.
3. Inverts the picture colors, if you selected this option.
4. Pads any area outside of the picture with a white background, to bring the picture to the proper size of a MAC picture.

View: Full Screen

Full screen viewing will display your picture outside of a window. Press any key or mouse button to return to windowed operations.

Capture

After selecting Capture-Area or Capture-Full Screen a dialog box will provide you with different options of what to do with Paint Shop. These options are: Hide Paint Shop, Make Paint Shop an Icon, and Leave Paint Shop Alone. Hide Paint Shop will make Paint Shop disappear from the screen during capturing. Make Paint Shop an icon will reduce Paint Shop to an icon during capturing. Leave Paint Shop alone will result in Paint Shop staying right where it is during capturing.

Area

Area will allow you to capture a designated part of the screen. After making your selection on what to do with Paint Shop the cursor will turn into a "t". To select the area to be captured, move the cursor to the beginning point. Hold down the left mouse button. Move the cursor to the ending point. Release the left mouse button. During the selection of the area the area will be outlined and the size of the area will be displayed in the center of the area.

Full Screen

Full Screen will capture the entire screen. After making your selection on what to do with Paint Shop, Paint Shop will capture the screen.

Capture Notes

An individual window may be captured without having to use the Capture-Area option. Follow these steps to capture just one window.

1. Select the window you want to capture by making it the active application.
2. While holding down the "Alt" key press the "Print Screen" key.
3. Start Paint Shop, if it is not already running.
4. Select "Edit-Paste" from the Paint Shop menu.

Once you have captured all or part of the screen you can do anything with the picture that you would like, including saving or altering the picture.

Help

Index

Index will call up Paint Shop's built in help system. If you are unfamiliar with using built in help systems, select the Help-Using Help option.

Using Help

Using Help will explain how to use built in help systems.

About

Displays general information about Paint Shop. Press the OK button to close the About box.

Operations

File Association

Picture files may be opened using file association. File association is the association of the file name extension within File Manager. See your Windows manual for information on how to setup associations to file name extension in File Manager.

Marking

Marking is the operation of defining a specific area of the picture for a future copy or trim operation. To mark an area of a picture, move the cursor to the upper left point of the area to be marked. While holding down the left mouse button, move the cursor to the lower right corner of the area to be marked. Release the left mouse button. The area that is marked will be outlined with the size of the area displayed in the center of the marked area. You may now use Edit-Copy to copy the marked area to the clipboard, or you may use Alter-Trim to make the marked area the current picture.

File Formats Supported

Pictures that may be used by PC computers are saved in many different formats. Paint Shop supports a limited number of these formats. It is the intention of Paint Shop to make the handling of these various formats as simple for the user as possible. Paint Shop will make all decisions possible about a file format. This section explains the various file formats and the way Paint Shop will handle those formats.

BMP

The BMP files come in 2 different formats. These formats will be referred to as Windows and OS/2. OS/2 BMPs were the first of the two different formats designed. The pictures that are saved using this format may be used with OS2's Presentation Manager. An enhanced BMP file format was released with Microsoft Windows. This is the reason for the reference to Windows and OS/2 BMP formats. BMP files can be used as "wallpaper" for the background when running in Windows. See your Windows documentation on how to use a BMP file as wallpaper. Within the Windows BMP format, two different types of encoding can be used. These are RGB and RLE. The OS/2 format only supports one type of encoding, RGB.

Files that use the RGB encoding scheme have no encoding done. The data that makes up the picture is simply saved to a file. This makes for some very large BMP files. The RLE (run length encoding) scheme does some compression of the data that makes up the picture. The RLE encoding is further broken down into two different formats: RLE4 and RLE8. RLE4 is the RLE compression routine used for picture data of 16 or fewer colors. RLE8 is the compression routine that is used for pictures of 17 to 256 colors.

Paint Shop supports all formats and encoding schemes of BMP files.

No work is required by the user to properly open a BMP file. When saving a file as a BMP, the user will have to select either OS/2 or Windows. Since the OS/2 format only supports the RGB encoding, all files saved as OS/2 will use RGB encoding. When saving as a Windows BMP, Paint Shop provides the option of saving the file as either an RGB or an RLE encoded file. If you select RLE encoding, Paint Shop will determine the proper RLE (RLE4 or RLE8) encoding to be used.

GIF

There are 2 GIF file versions; 87a and 89a. Version 87a was the first of the two versions to appear. Version 89a added new features to the 87a format. None of these new 89a features are used by Paint Shop. Both of these versions may use an encoding method referred to as interlacing.

Interlacing is when a picture is saved by using four passes instead of just one. On each pass certain lines of the picture are saved to the file. If the program decoding a GIF file displays the picture as it is decoded, the user will be able to see the four passes of the decoding cycle. This will allow the user to get a good idea of what the picture will look like before even half of the picture is decoded. Some communication programs allow the user to download GIF files and view them as they are downloaded. If the picture is interlaced, the user will be able to decide if the picture is one they like before half the download is complete. If the user does not like the picture, the download can be aborted. This results in the saving of time and money for the person downloading the picture. Paint Shop supports both 87a and 89a GIF file formats. Paint Shop also supports interlacing. No work is required of the user to open a GIF file.

When saving a picture as a GIF file, the user has the option of saving the file as an 87a or 89a version. Since Paint Shop does not use any of the new features of the 89a version, all GIF files should be saved as 87a. This will allow older GIF viewers to display the pictures that are created by Paint Shop. The user will also have the opportunity to save the picture as an interlaced GIF. If you intend to upload the picture to a bulletin board, it would be advantageous to save it as an interlaced picture. Some GIF files contain more than one picture. Paint Shop will only process the first picture in the file.

IMG

Paint Shop supports black and white IMG pictures of any size. If your picture is colored, you will have to dither it to black and white before saving the picture as an IMG file.

MAC

MAC files come from the Macintosh program MacPaint. Mac pictures are very specific. They must have a width of 576 and a height of 720. MAC pictures are black and white. Mac pictures should have a white background. You will be given the option of inverting the picture during the

Prep for MAC operation. If your picture is using a black background, then you should select the invert option. If the picture is already on a white background then do not invert. If you would like to see what the picture will look like when it is inverted, select the Alter-Invert menu option.

In order to save a picture as a MAC picture, the above requirements must be met. This can be accomplished by using the Alter-Prep for MAC menu command. Paint Shop provides the option to saving the MAC picture with or with out (W/O) a header. The MAC header is the information that is necessary for the picture to move back and forth (via BBS(s)) between the Macintosh and PC. Therefore, all pictures should be saved with the header. The option to save with out the header exists only because some PC applications want the MAC picture without the header.

PCX

There are 4 PCX file versions:

Version 0 Black and white pictures
Version 2 16 or fewer colors with palette information
Version 3 16 or fewer colors without palette information
Version 5 256 or fewer colors

Paint Shop will read all PCX file versions. If the file is a version 3, Paint Shop will use the default VGA colors used by Windows as the palette. This may result in a different looking picture than you would see when using some other picture viewer.

When saving a picture as a PCX file, Paint Shop will decide which version to use. The reasoning is to create the oldest version possible for that picture. This will allow older applications (which do not support the newer versions) to use the PCX files created by Paint Shop. Paint Shop will use the following method to determine how to save a file as PCX file:

- If the picture is black and white then the version will be 0

- If the picture is from 3 to 16 colors then the version will be 2

- If the picture has more than 16 colors, version 5 will be used

RLE

RLE files are BMP files that use one of the RLE compression routines. Since an RLE compression routine is used, the file format is that of a Windows BMP file. The only difference between a RLE file and a Windows BMP file that uses RLE coding is the file name extension. For more information on the RLE encoding and Windows BMP file formats, please refer to the BMP file format.

Licensing

You may use Paint Shop for a free 30 day trial period. If you continue to use Paint Shop after the 30 day trial period, you are required to obtain a license number. Use the registration form at the end of this document to register Paint Shop.

Licensing Agreement
You may not transfer your license without written permission from JASC, Inc. You may physically transfer Paint Shop from one computer to another provided the program is used on only one computer at a time.

Term
The license to use this program is effective until terminated. You may terminate the license by destroying all copies of this program. It will also be terminated upon failure to comply with any of the terms or conditions of this agreement.

Warranty
This program is provided as is without warranty of any kind. In addition, JASC, Inc. specifically disclaims all warranties, expressed or implied, including but not limited to implied warranties of merchantability and fitness. In no event shall JASC, Inc. be liable for any claims for lost profits or any other commercial damage, including but not limited to special, incidental, consequential or other damage. Some states do not allow the exclusion or limitation of incidental or consequential damages, so the above limitation or exclusion may not apply to you. In no case shall JASC, Inc.'s liability exceed the license fees paid for the right to use the licensed software.

Governing Law
This statement shall be construed, interpreted, and governed by the laws of the state of Minnesota.

Agreement
By licensing Paint Shop you agree to the above licensing agreement.

Support

Registered users may obtain support by contacting JASC, Inc. via Email on CompuServe (72557,256) or calling JASC, Inc. at 1-612-934-7117. Phone support is from 9am-5pm central time, Monday through Friday.

Distribution

Copies of Paint Shop may be freely distributed, provided that PS.EXE, PS.HLP, and PS.WRI are distributed together. No fee, charge or other compensation may be accepted for the distribution of Paint Shop. Except, Public Domain Disk Vendors and BBS(s) may charge a nominal fee for distribution of the program. The recipient of Paint Shop must be informed, in advance, that the fee paid to acquire Paint Shop does not relieve the recipient from paying the Registration Fee for Paint Shop if the recipient uses Paint Shop.

Bundling with Other Products

Paint Shop may only be bundled with other products with the written permission from JASC, Inc.

WinGIF

Copyright © 1991 by SuperSet Software Corp.

Procedures

How to View an Image

WinGIF can be used to view files in GIF, PCX, BMP, and RLE formats. To view an image file in any of these formats, choose the File Open command, highlight the image file name and select Open. WinGIF will then display the image.

If the image contains more colors than your Windows driver is able to display, the image will not look correct when you first open the file. To get the best possible view of such images from your Windows driver, use WinGIF's ability to dither the image by using either the Edit VGA 16 Dither or the Edit Monochrome Dither commands.

GIF or PCX to BMP Conversion

To create a BMP file suitable for use as Windows wallpaper from an existing image in GIF or PCX format, first load the GIF or PCX file using the File Open command. After WinGIF finishes opening your file, you might notice that the colors don't look right, we'll fix that later; for now, resize the image to the desired size using one of the Resizing commands in the Edit menu. Several of the most common screen sizes have their own menu items, but if you want to specify an exact size, you may do so

using the Edit Resize command at the bottom of the edit menu.

Now that your image is the correct size, it is time to correct the colors. The most common reason colors are not correct is because the source image had more colors than your Windows display can show. WinGIF solves this problem by dithering your image. You may choose one of two dithering commands in the edit menu: the Edit VGA 16 Dither command or the Edit Monochrome Dither command. If you have a color EGA/VGA display, choose the former; otherwise, choose the latter. The next step is to use the commands in the Edit Palette submenu to fine-tune the image and then choose the Edit Palette Accept Palette command to accept the colors.

Finally, you are ready to save your image as a BMP file. Use the File Save command and choose BMP as the file type. Save the file in your windows directory if you want control panel to show your BMP file as one of the choices for wallpaper.

Exiting WinGIF

Choosing the File Exit command or double-clicking on the System Menu will exit WinGIF. You will not be prompted for a confirmation unless WinGIF is currently processing a command.

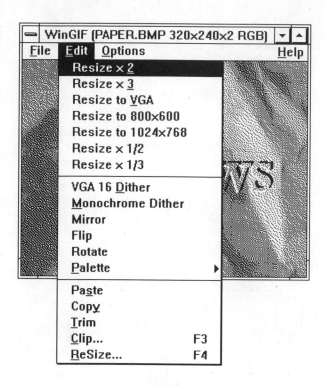

How to Interrupt Processing in WinGIF

To interrupt WinGIF while it is processing during a File Open or a dithering command, you can either press the ESC key or double-click on the system menu and answer no to the message that asks you if you want to quit WinGIF.

Selecting a Region

You may select a portion of an image by positioning the mouse cursor on the top-left or bottom-right corner of the region desired and then pressing the left mouse button and dragging the mouse to the opposite corner. You can also directly select a region by entering its position directly into the Edit Clip dialog box. Selecting a region is necessary before using the Edit Trim command and is optional before the Edit Clip and the Edit Copy commands.

Commands

File Menu

The File menu includes commands that enable you to open and save files, and to print

- Open...
- Save...
- Printer Setup...
- Print Exit

Opening Files

Choosing the File Open menu command brings up the open dialog box. Choose an image file encoded in BMP, RLE, GIF, or PCX format, then click the OK button to open the file. This command is affected by the following option menu options: Clean Background, Decode to Screen, Auto Minimize. Also see How to Interrupt Processing.

Saving Files

Choosing the File Save menu command brings up the save dialog box. Choose an image file name and then click on the Format button to choose between the RLE 4, RLE 8, BMP, PCX or GIF format, then click the OK button to save the file. When you have chosen a format, the other options in the save dialog box are enabled or disabled as appropriate for your format. The options labeled 1, 4, 8 and 24 bpp determine the number of colors available for you picture. The option Interlace GIF, available only if the GIF format, saves the image in interlace mode.

The File Printer Setup Command

This command brings up the printer setup dialog box. This dialog box differs with each printer driver you may be running. Changes made with this command will affect only WinGIF and not other applications.

Printing Files

Choosing the File Print command will begin printing the currently loaded image according to the options set with the File Printer Setup Command and the Options Full Page Print Command.

Exiting WinGIF

Choosing the File Exit command or double-clicking on the System Menu will exit WinGIF. You will not be prompted for a confirmation unless WinGIF is currently processing a command.

Edit Menu

The edit menu in WinGIF provides commands for manipulating and editing the currently loaded graphic image. It also provides tools for copying and pasting to the clipboard

- Resize × 2
- Resize × 3
- Resize to VGA
- Resize to 800×600
- Resize to 1024×768

- Resize × 1/2
- Resize × 1/3
- VGA 16 Dither
- Monochrome Dither
- Mirror
- Flip
- Rotate
- Palette
- Paste
- Copy
- Trim
- Clip...
- Resize...

Resizing the Image

The following commands may be used to resize an image after it has been loaded:

Edit Resize × 2 Doubles the size of the image
Edit Resize × 3 Triples the size of the image
Edit Resize to VGA Resizes to the standard VGA resolution 640×400
Edit Resize to 800×600 Resizes to the standard SVGA resolution 800×600
Edit Resize to 1024×768 Resizes to the standard SVGA resolution 1024×768
Edit Resize × 1/2 Resizes to 1/2 original size
Edit Resize × 1/3 Resizes to 1/3 original size
    Edit Resize... Resizes to any specified resolution and contains options for performing dithering at the same time and for preserving the original image's scale.

Dithering the Image

Two commands are available to dither an image after it has been loaded. These two commands are as follows:

    Edit VGA 16 Dither Change the image to use a standard EGA/VGA 16 color palette.
    Edit Monochrome Dither Change the image to use only black and white.

These commands are affected by the Clean Background, Decode to Screen, Alt Dither Palette, Shadow Dither, and Auto Minimize options. These two dithering options are also available from the Edit Resize... dialog.

Mirroring the Image

The Edit Mirror command produces a mirror image (left-right swapped) of the currently loaded image. Choosing Edit Mirror a second time reverses the action.

Flipping the Image

The Edit Flip command flips the currently loaded image so that the top and bottom portions are swapped. Choosing Edit Flip a second time reverses the action.

Rotating the Image

The Edit Rotate command rotates the current image clockwise 90 degrees. Choosing Edit Rotate three more times reverses the action.

Palette Manipulation

The Edit Palette menu item brings up the submenu below. These commands allow you to alter the current image's palette . The cumulative results of any of these commands except Accept Palette are reversible using the command Restore Palette.

- 256 Grays
- 64 Grays
- 16 Grays
- 8 Grays
- 4 Grays
- Contrast +
- Contrast -
- Brightness +
- Brightness -
- Accept Palette
- Restore Palette

Changing the Palette to Greyscale

Five commands under the Edit Palette submenu allow you to change your palette from color to greyscale. These commands are the 4, 8, 16, 64, and 256 Grays commands. Note that a greyscale display is not the same as a monochrome display. If you have a monochrome display (one that can display only black or white) you should use the Monochrome Dither command.

Changing the Image Contrast

You may use the Contrast - and Contrast + commands from the Edit Palette submenu to increase or decrease the contrast in your image.

Changing the Image Brightness

You may use the Brightness - and Brightness + commands from the Edit Palette submenu to increase or decrease the brightness of your image.

The Edit Palette Accept-Palette Command

When you select this command, WinGIF first sorts the colors in the palette in order of descending use in the image, then frees any palette entries that are not used in the image. This can make the palette smaller and it can also eliminate problems with pictures that use all the colors that Windows can display. (Windows normally reserves 20 colors from a 256 color display. Sorting gives accurate color for the most used colors.) If you load an image with WinGIF on a 256 color display and notice some areas of the picture do not look correct then using this command may solve the problem. It is a good idea to always choose this command right before saving an image since the palette associated with the image might be made smaller. This command is not reversible with the Restore Palette command.

The Edit Palette Restore-Palette Command

This command changes the image palette to either the original palette or the last one accepted with the Accept Palette command. This allows you to make changes with the commands in the Edit Palette submenu and later be able to restore the original palette.

Pasting from the Clipboard

The Edit Paste Command loads any image in the Windows clipboard into WinGIF. The clipboard image must be encoded in Windows bitmap or DIB format.

Copying to the Clipboard

The Edit Copy command copies the current image into the Windows clipboard. WinGIF exports the Windows bitmap and DIB formats to the Windows clipboard. If you Select a Region before choosing Edit Copy, only the selected region will be copied to the clipboard.

Trimming the Image

To trim an image, first Select the Region that you would like to keep and then choose the Edit Trim command. Trimming may also be done without a mouse from within the Edit Clip command.

Clipping the Image

You may provide precise coordinates for trimming or clipboard copies by using the Edit Clip command. This command prompts you for an X and Y Origin. This origin is the top-left corner of the region to be kept. It also asks for the X and Y Dimensions which are the width and height, respectively, of the region. Pressing OK returns you to the image and shows you where your region is. You may then choose Edit Clip again to modify your region or to press Trim which will trim your image using the region. If you Select a Region with the mouse before choosing Edit Clip, the selected region will automatically be entered in the X and Y Origin and Dimension fields.

The Resize Dialog

The Resize dialog is invoked using the Edit Resize... command. This dialog lets you resize your image to any resolution, maintain the original scale, apply an new scaling factor, or perform dithering and resizing at the same time.

The Width and Height fields let you specify the size of the image exactly. If you have the Resize to Scale option checked then whenever you change the Width or Height and press TAB, the other dimension (Height or Width) is updated automatically to preserve the original image's

scale. Entering a number in the Scale Factor field and pressing TAB automatically changes the values in the Width and Height fields by the scale you enter (i.e. entering 2 in the Scale Factor field will double the width and height values).

The No Dither, VGA Dither, and B/W Dither options determine which, if any, dithering should be performed at the same time as the resizing. VGA Dither corresponds to the Edit VGA 16 Dither command and the B/W Dither corresponds to the Edit Monochrome Dither command. Stretching and dithering in one step will significantly reduce the memory requirements from those for stretching and dithering separately. Pressing OK performs the resizing (and dithering, if selected).

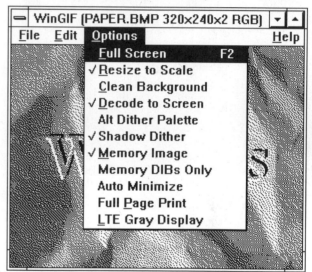

Options Menu

The options menu in WinGIF provides access to WinGIF options which affect may affect how other commands operate. All of the commands in the options menu except for Full Screen toggle on and off as you select them. When options are changed their new setting is saved in the WINGIF.INI initialization file.

- Full Screen
- Resize to Scale
- Clean Background
- Decode to Screen
- Alt Dither Palette
- Shadow Dither
- Memory Image
- Memory DIBs Only
- Auto Minimize
- Full Page Print
- LTE Gray Display

Full Screen Option

The Options Full Screen command shows your image on a full screen, using all available colors in the color palette. Normally windows reserves 20 colors from SVGA displays for system use. In this mode this feature of windows is disabled to give a full 256 colors. To return to the normal Windows display, press any key.

Resize to Scale Option

The Options Resize to Scale command toggles the Resize to Scale option. This option affects the commands Resize to VGA, Resize to 800×600, and Resize to 1024×768. When this option is turned on, the scale of the original image is preserved when the commands above are chosen. The resulting image is the largest scaled image which can fit inside the specified dimensions. By their nature, the Resize × 2, Resize × 3, Resize × 1/2 and Resize × 1/3 always preserve scale whether this option is on or not.

Clean Background Option

The Options Clean Background command toggles the Clean Background option. When this option is on, the screen will be erased before showing a new or modified image with the File Open, VGA 16 Dither, or Monochrome Dither command.

Decode to Screen Option

The Options Decode to Screen command toggles the Decode to Screen option. When this option is on, the WinGIF window will show its progress during the File Open, Edit VGA 16 Dither, and Edit Monochrome Dither commands. When this option is off, you will not see the results of the commands above until WinGIF is finished processing the entire image.

Alt Dither Option

The Options Alt Dither command toggles the Alternate Dither option. When this option is on, WinGIF will use an alternate dithering palette during the Edit VGA 16 Dither. It is best to experiment to see whether the default dithering algorithm or the alternate dithering algorithm yield the best results for an image.

Shadow Dither Option

The Options Shadow Dither command toggles the Shadow Dither option. When this option is on, WinGIF will attempt to darken the dark areas of an image during the Edit VGA 16 Dither and Edit Monochrome Dither commands. It is best to experiment to see whether the Shadow Dither option yields the best results for an image but generally this option is recommended. Similar and also more dramatic results can be achieved by enhancing contrast and adjusting brightness before dithering.

Memory Image Option

The Options Memory Image command toggles the Memory Image option. Most users will want to keep this option on. This option should be turned off only when available memory in your system is very low, or when you are running in Windows real mode.

Memory DIBs Only Option

The Options Memory DIBs Only command toggles the Memory DIBs Only option. This option should be turned on when available memory is getting low. Screen update times will be slower with this option on.

Auto Minimize Option

The Options Auto Minimize command toggles the Auto Minimize option. When this option is on, WinGIF will automatically make itself into an icon at the bottom of the screen whenever opening a GIF file or dithering an image.

Full Page Print Option

The Options Full Page Print command toggles the Full Page Print option. When this option is on, WinGIF will tell windows to size images while printing to fill the page as well as possible while still maintaining the original image's scale.

LTE Gray Display Option

The Options LTE Gray Display command toggles the LTE Gray Display option. When this option is on, WinGIF will choose colors that result in a greyscale display on a Compaq LTE 386/20. This command can also be used with some success on other systems; the result being an abstract and sometimes pleasing posterization of your image.

Help Menu

The help menu in WinGIF provides access to the Windows Help program and to an About box which gives information about the program and how to register your copy of WinGIF.

Keyboard Shortcuts

The following keys may be used within WinGIF:

F1 Help
Shift F1 Help Mode
F2 Full Screen
Shift F2 Show Image in Full Window (hide menu and title bar)

Alt F2 Show Image in Full Window and use the full palette
F3 Clip
F4 Resize
F5 Accept Palette
F7 Brightness -
F8 Brightness +
F9 Contrast -
F10 Contrast +
ALT F7 thru ALT F10 Same as F7 thru F10 but in larger increments
Cursor Keys Scroll the Image.

Registration

WinGIF is a shareware product. Please support the shareware concept and register by sending $15 to the address below. Use beyond a 15-day evaluation period is prohibited without registration. When you register, you will receive an I.D. number that eliminates the name-and-address screen that appears when WinGIF loads.

SuperSet Software P.O. Box 1036 Orem, UT 84059

Name _____

Address _____

_____

_____

Text Editing and Searching

Hunter

Copyright © 1991 by Peter Eddy

How to Use Hunter
Finding Files

To find a file using Hunter, select Filespec from the Criteria menu option and enter the file name or names you wish to find. Multiple file names should be separated by a space. File names can contain wildcards. Wildcard characters are * (matches any number of characters) and ? (matches any single character).

Finding Text in Files

To find text within files you must tell Hunter what kind of files to search under the Filespec command and what text to look for with the Grep command. (A "grep" is a string of characters.) Both of these options are available under the Criteria menu option. Having done this, select Go! from the menu.

Make Options Default

Selecting Make Options Default instructs Hunter to remember all the option settings under the Options menu, and to automatically load them the next time it's run. To save filespec options, select Make Default on the filespec dialog box.

Commands
Criteria Menu

The Criteria Menu includes commands that let you specify exactly what kind of information you're looking for.

Filespec: The Filespec dialog is where you tell Hunter what type of files it should look for. Under file name, you can select multiple file names which may (and probably will) consist of wildcard characters such as *.DOC *.TXT, for all document and text files.

File Age and Size: Hunter will optionally search for files that are of a certain age and/or size. To do this, select a logical operator and enter a number in the appropriate edit box. For example "< 5" Days Old reads "Less than five days old." The combination ">= 1000000" Bytes in Size reads "Greater than or equal to 1 million bytes (1MB) in size." If you do not wish to use an age or size limit, simply clear any values in the appropriate edit boxes; the logical specification will then have no effect.

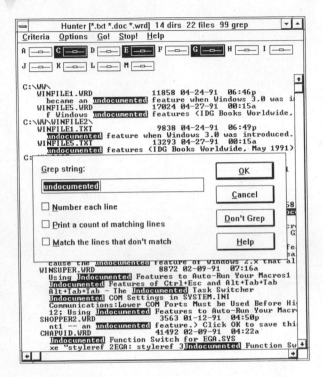

similar to, but more powerful than, wildcard characters for DOS file names.

Regular Expressions: Hunter uses regular expressions to locate patterns in files. In these expressions, upper and lower case differences are always ignored and blank lines never match. An ordinary character (not mentioned below) matches itself. The following characters have special meaning:

^ A circumflex at the beginning of an expression matches the beginning of a line. Use ^dear to find all lines in files that begin with the word dear.

$ A dollar sign at the end of an expression matches the end of a line.

. A period matches any character except a new line.

: A colon matches a class of characters described by the following:

:a Matches any alphabetic, i.e., A to Z, regardless of case.

:d Matches digits (0 to 9).

:n Matches alphanumerics (alphabetic or digit).

: A colon followed by a space matches spaces, tabs and other control characters including newline.

* An expression followed by an asterisk matches zero or more occurrences of that expression. For example, fo* matches f, fo, foo, etc.

+ An expression followed by a plus sign matches one or more occurrences of that expression. For example fo+ matches fo, foo, etc.

[ ] A string enclosed in square brackets matches any character in that string, but no others. If the first character in the string is a circumflex, the expression matches any character except a new line and the characters in the string. For example [xyz] matches any string containing an x, y, or z, while [^xyz] matches abc but not axb. A range of characters may be specified by two characters separated by -. For example [a-z] matches alphabetics, while [z-a] never matches anything.

- An expression followed by a minus sign optionally matches the expression. A minus sign appearing within square brackets is treated as an ordinary character if it is the first or last character in the expression.

\ The backslash quotes any character. It's usually used to match one of these special characters. Example: \$ matches a dollar sign, \\ matches a backslash. Optionally the backslash can be followed by ascii digits representing the character value: \65 matches A and a.

Hidden and System Files: Hunter will also search for hidden and/or system files. Very rarely do most users create hidden files so this option is not normally selected. System files are those files marked for use by DOS itself. Normally system files are also hidden, so select both hidden and system to find these files.

Make Default: Push this button to cause the currently selected filespec options to become the default.

Finding Text Within Files

To locate text in a file, select Grep from the Criteria menu, enter the text you wish to find in the edit box and press the OK button, then select Go! from the main menu bar. All files specified under the filespec option will be searched for the text you have entered. Hunter does not distinguish between upper and lower case.

Turning off Text Search: After you've entered text in the Grep dialog box, Hunter will continue to look for that text every time you select Go! until you change the text, push the Don't Grep button, or close the application.

Advanced Searching: Hunter is not limited to simple search strings. The search string can contain very handy items called regular expressions which are

Examples:

colou-r Matches color or colour: The u is optional with the - sign.

:d:d:d[-]:d:d:d:d

Matches telephone numbers: Three digits followed by a space or a dash ([-]), then four more digits. Note that the special character -, need not be quoted within brackets.

(-:d:d:d[ )\-]- -:d:d:d[-]:d:d:d:d

Matches long distance telephone numbers: An optional open parenthesis ((-) followed by three digits (:d:d:d), optionally separated by a space, a closed parenthesis, or a dash ([ )\-]), optionally followed by a space (-), followed by three more digits, a space or a dash (-), followed by four more digits. Note that this complex regular expression is unnecessary: The expression for local telephone numbers above will also match long distance numbers.

(-800[ )\-]- -:d:d:d[-]:d:d:d:d

Matches 800 telephone numbers only.

:d:d-/:d:d-/:d:d:d-:d-

Matches dates like 3/1/61 and 10/4/1991

Options Menu

The options menu lets you control things like where and how Hunter looks for files and the colors it will use.

First File Only: When this option is selected, Hunter will stop searching as soon as it has found the first file that meets the search criteria.

Use Environment Path Only: Selecting this option instructs Hunter to search only the directories listed in the PATH environment variable. This option is useful for finding duplicate executable file names.

Show File Statistics: Selecting this option instructs Hunter to display found files size (in bytes), last modification date, and last modification time. When disabled, only the file names will be displayed.

Monitor Progress: When this option is selected Hunter will display in the title bar the current number of files found, directories searched, and strings matched (if you're using Grep).

Color Settings: You can change the colors Hunter uses for the background, for directory and file names, and for found text. For best results, run a short text search before you change colors. If you select Make Options

Default after changing colors, Hunter will use the new color selections the next time it's run. Otherwise, the color selections will be in effect for the current session only.

Make Options Default: Selecting Make Options Default instructs Hunter to remember all the option settings under the Options menu, and to automatically load them the next time it's run. To save filespec options, select Make Default on the filespec dialog box.

Load Default Options: If you change settings and later decide you wish you hadn't, you can restore all settings to the last time you ran Make Options Default by selecting this option.

Go! and Stop!

The Go! command tells Hunter to begin the search. Once you select Go! you can select another application and let Hunter look for the information you specified in the background. You may stop the search at any time by selecting the Stop! command.

The Stop! command stops the search immediately and displays whatever information Hunter has found. You may begin the search again by selecting Go!

Registration

Registration for Hunter is $30.00 and includes a free upgrade to version 3.0. Planned version 3.0 features include:

- Saving of results to text file
- Search by Directory Tree
- Command Line Options
- Clipboard Interface

Published, distributed, and supported by: The National Windows User Group (WUGNET) P.O. Box 1967 Media, Pennsylvania 19603 CompuServe I.D. Number: 76357,2064.

Name _____

Address _____

City, State, Zip _____

Please indicate: 5.25" disk ( ) 3.5" disk ( )

Hunter technology is also available for licensing; contact WUGNET.

WinEdit 1.0G

Copyright © 1990,1991 by Steve Schauer

Acknowledgements

WinEdit was designed & written by Steve Schauer. Additional programming by Morrie Wilson and Bob Foster. The Control Bar was written by Dave Edson. Local memory routines were written by Dan Quigley. The regular expression routines are based on code written by Allen I. Holub, as published in the C Gazette. Our thanks to the many beta-testers for their invaluable comments & suggestions.

Introduction

WinEdit is an ASCII text editor designed to take full advantage of the Windows 3.0 graphical environment. WinEdit is first and foremost a programmer's editor, with features designed for creating and maintaining program source code. With its ASCII file format, ability to edit files of almost unlimited size, and word-processing features such as headers and footers, WinEdit also serves as an effective "front end" for desktop publishers and word processors, including PageMaker, Word For Windows, and Ventura Publisher.

Features

- Uses all available Windows memory to load up to 16MB of text files.
- Multiple Document Interface allows an unlimited number of document windows.
- Run your favorite compiler or other programming tool from within WinEdit. WinEdit will monitor the compiler's output and allow you to review any warning or error messages.

- Regular expressions can be used in search and replace operations for powerful text manipulation capabilities.
- Full access to the Windows SDK help and C 6.0 language help by clicking on any SDK or C language key word. (Requires the Windows help file SDKWIN.HLP provided with the Microsoft SDK and Microsoft QuickHelp provided with Microsoft C 6.0.)
- Print half sized "two-up" pages side by side in land-scape mode - ideal for source listings or early drafts of desktop publishing documents.
- Headers and footers - WinEdit can optionally place the document name, date, and time in the header or footer of any printout.
- Easy to use - on-line help is always available. All major program features are available through the pulldown menus and dialog boxes. Most-used features have accelerator keys as well for lightning fast operation.
- Fast - one of WinEdit's design goals is speed in all critical operations. WinEdit loads large files quickly, updates and scrolls the screen instantly, and keeps up with the fastest typist.

Getting Started

Installing WinEdit

WinEdit requires only one file to run: WINEDIT.EXE. Copy this file to a directory on your path, and you can start. You should also copy the WinHelp file, WINEDIT.HLP, to the same directory. If you are running Windows in 386 enhanced mode, you can copy the file EDTEMP.PIF to your Windows directory to allow WinEdit to compile from within a window. That's it!

Entering License Information

Choose this menu selection from the System Menu to enter your license number and ID when you register your copy of WinEdit. Registering brings you wonderful benefits:

- Gets rid of that pesky reminder window that comes up when you start the program
- Entitles you to one hour free telephone support for 90 days
- Gets you the latest version of WinEdit

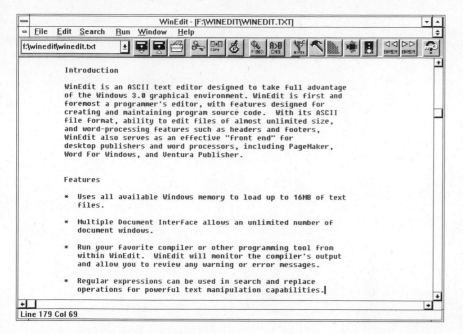

WinEdit - [F:\WINEDIT\WINEDIT.TXT]

File   Edit   Search   Run   Window   Help

f:\winedit\winedit.txt

```
Introduction

WinEdit is an ASCII text editor designed to take full advantage
of the Windows 3.0 graphical environment. WinEdit is first and
foremost a programmer's editor, with features designed for
creating and maintaining program source code.  With its ASCII
file format, ability to edit files of almost unlimited size,
and word-processing features such as headers and footers,
WinEdit also serves as an effective "front end" for
desktop publishers and word processors, including PageMaker,
Word For Windows, and Ventura Publisher.


Features

*   Uses all available Windows memory to load up to 16MB of text
    files.

*   Multiple Document Interface allows an unlimited number of
    document windows.

*   Run your favorite compiler or other programming tool from
    within WinEdit.  WinEdit will monitor the compiler's output
    and allow you to review any warning or error messages.

*   Regular expressions can be used in search and replace
    operations for powerful text manipulation capabilities.
```

Line 179 Col 69

PgDn: Moves down one window
Ctrl+Home: Moves to the beginning of the document
Ctrl+End: Moves to the end of the document

Selecting Text

Shift+Left or Right Arrow: Selects text one character at a time to the left or right. Or, if the character is already selected, cancels the selection.
Shift+Down or Up Arrow: Selects one line of text up or down. Or, if the line is already selected, cancels the selection.
Shift+Home: Selects text to the beginning of the line.
Shift+End: Selects text to the end of the line.
Ctrl+Shift+Left Arrow: Selects the previous word.
Ctrl+Shift+Right Arrow: Selects the next word.
Shift+PgUp: Selects the previous screenful.
Shift+PgDn: Selects the next screenful.
Ctrl+Shift+Home: Selects to the beginning of the document.
Ctrl+Shift+End: Selects to the end of the document.
Keypad +: Copies current line to clipboard if no selection, or copies current selection.
Keypad -: Cuts current line to clipboard if no selection, or cuts current selection.

Help Keys

F1: WinEdit Help Index
Shift+F1: Extended Help

Commands

File Menu Commands

New: Opens a new window with a new, untitled document
Open: Opens a new window with an existing document. WinEdit can read an ASCII text file as large as available Windows memory.
Save: Saves the current document. The window remains open. If the document is UNTITLED, WinEdit prompts you for a document name.
Save As: Saves a document after prompting you for a new name.
Print: Prints the current document using the print settings entered in the Page Setup dialog box.

• Gets you a printed User's Manual
• Encourages the authors of this program to continue bringing you new and better products instead of breaking down and getting a real job

Basic Operations

WinEdit follows the standard conventions for Windows programs. Refer to Chapter 2 of your Microsoft Windows User's Guide for instructions on using menus, selecting text, working with dialog boxes, working with documents, and using Windows Help.

WinEdit Keys

Use the following keys in WinEdit:

Moving the Insertion Point

Up Arrow: Moves up one line
Down Arrow: Moves down one line
Right Arrow: Moves right one character
Left Arrow: Moves left one character
Ctrl+Right Arrow: Moves right one word
Ctrl+Left Arrow: Moves left one word
Home: Moves to the beginning of the line
End: Moves to the end of the line
PgUp: Moves up one window

Page Setup: Allows you to set the margins, headers, footers, printer font, and page layout.
Printer Setup: Sets printer options for WinEdit before printing.
Preferences: Allows you to choose the screen font WinEdit uses, the tab size, whether the Control Bar is shown, and startup file loading options.
Exit: Closes all open windows and exits WinEdit. If there are any unsaved files, WinEdit prompts you before exiting.

Edit Menu Commands

Undo: Restores the line the insertion point is on to the same state it was in when the insertion point first moved into it.
Cut: Removes the current selection from the document and places it on the clipboard.
Copy: Places a copy of the current selection on the clipboard without removing it from the document.
Paste: Pastes the text in the clipboard into the document at the insertion point.
Delete: Removes the current selection from the document without changing the contents of the clipboard. If there is no selection, removes the character to the right of the insertion point.
Select All: Selects all the text in the document.

Search Menu Commands

Find: Searches for text in a document.
- Find: Type the text you want to find.
- Match case: Select this box to match the upper and lower case exactly.
- Next: Search forward starting at the insertion point.
- Previous: Search backward starting at the insertion point.

Repeat Last Find: Repeats the last search using the same options, without opening the Find dialog box.
Change: Searches for text in a document and replaces the found text with text you specify.
- Find: Type the text you want to find.
- Replace with: Type the text you want to insert in place of the found text.
- Match case: Select this box to match the upper and lower case exactly.
- Search backwards: Search backward starting at the insertion point.
- Confirm before: When text is found, you will be prompted changing before the change takes place.
- Change All: Start at the beginning of the document, and search the entire document. You will be prompted before each change takes place if the Confirm before changing box is selected.

Next Error and Prev Error: If any warning or error messages have been captured from the output of one of the Run Menu items, these menu choices allow you to review the messages and the corresponding source code.
View Compiler Output: Loads the captured compiler output into a document window.

Run Menu Commands

The commands on this menu allow you to run other programs from within WinEdit. Use the Configure... command to enter the necessary command to run the program. Select the Capture Output box and WinEdit will run the program you configure and save its output. When the program finishes, WinEdit will allow you to review any warning or error messages that have occurred, along with the corresponding source code. WinEdit constructs a DOS batch file to execute when you choose to capture output. For this reason, to run a Windows application from the Run Menu, do not choose to capture output.

WinEdit Project Files

WinEdit saves the information from the Configure... dialog box in a private INI file with an extension of .WPJ (WinEdit Project File). Choose the Save... pushbutton to save the contents of the dialog box in a .WPJ file. Choose the Open... pushbutton to load an existing .WPJ file.

Window Menu Commands

Tile: Arranges all open document windows side by side so that all windows are visible.
Cascade: Arranges all open document windows in an overlapping pattern so that the title bar of each window is visible.
Arrange Icons: Arranges all document icons into rows.
Close All: Closes all open document windows. If a document has changes that need saving, you will be prompted to save the document before closing.
Document Name- Each open window is listed on the menu by name. Choose the name and that window will become the active document window.

Procedures

Changing Printers and Printer Options

Select Printer Setup from the File menu to change printer settings. WinEdit will make the requested changes to your printer settings for this editing session only. The default Windows settings will not be changed. To permanently change a printer setting, use Control Panel. Select Page Setup from the File menu to change the printer settings for margins, header, footer, printer font, and page layout.

WinEdit will remember these settings from session to session.

Compiling (Running Other Programs)

The first five commands on the Run menu are user-configurable commands to execute another program. You may configure these commands to execute any .EXE or .BAT program by typing the command text in the appropriate Configure... edit box.

If the program supports DOS redirection (as most compilers and linkers do) you can select the Capture Output box to have WinEdit capture the program's output in a file. When the program finishes, WinEdit will allow you to review any warning or error messages that have occurred, along with the corresponding source code. WinEdit constructs a DOS batch file to execute when you choose to capture output. For this reason, to run a Windows application from the Run Menu, do not choose to capture output.

Copying, Cutting, and Pasting Text

To copy and paste, or cut and paste text:

1. Select the text.
2. Choose Copy from the Edit menu to copy the selected text to the clipboard. Or choose Cut from the Edit menu to cut the text to the clipboard.
3. Move the insertion point where you want the text to appear. Or select text you want the pasted text to replace.
4. Choose Paste from the Edit menu.

Creating New Documents

Choose New from the File menu to open a new, untitled document window.

Deleting Text

To delete text without sending it to the clipboard:

1. Select the text.
2. Choose Delete from the Edit menu or press the Delete key.

If there is no selection, Delete deletes the character to the right of the insertion point.

Extended Help

Press Shift+F1 or click the Right Mouse Button on any Windows SDK function, message, or data structure name and WinEdit will access the SDKWIN.HLP topic for that item. If the word is not a valid Windows SDK topic, WinEdit will pass the word to QH.EXE (Microsoft's QuickHelp program, supplied with most Microsoft language products). This will allow you online access to any language or library keyword covered in the QuickHelp database.

For SDK Help, the WinHelp file SDKWIN.HLP must be in either the current directory, the Windows directory, or a directory listed in your PATH statement. For QuickHelp, QH.EXE must be in either the current directory, the Windows directory, or a directory listed in your PATH statement. In addition, you must have an environment variable "HELPFILES=" defined which tells QH.EXE where to look to find the appropriate QuickHelp database files.

Printing Documents

Choose Print from the File menu to send the current document to the printer.

Printing Headers and Footers

Choose Page Setup from the File menu to configure header and footer text. Type the text you wish to appear at the top and bottom of each page. You can use the following special characters in headers and footers:

%f The document name will appear.
%d The file date and time will appear, unless the file has been changed, in which case the current date and time will appear.
%p The page number will appear.

Saving Documents

Choose Save from the File menu to save a document. Choose Save As to save the document with a new name, or to save an untitled document.

Setting Preferences

Choose Preferences from the File menu to choose a screen font, default tab size, whether or not to show the Control Bar, and startup file loading options.

Setting Margins

Choose Page Setup from the File menu to change the margins used for printouts. You can enter the measurements for top, bottom, left, and right margins. The margin settings are in inches or centimeters, corresponding to the English or Metric Measurement setting in Control Panel.

Undo

Choose Undo from the Edit menu to restore the current line to the state it was when the insertion point was first moved in to it.

Using Regular Expressions

A regular expression is a search or replace string that uses special characters to match text patterns. WinEdit supports UNIX-style regular expressions.

When WinEdit conducts a search using regular expressions, it must check character by character in your text. For this reason, searches using regular expressions are slower than regular searches.

The following table describes the regular expression characters recognized by WinEdit.

\   Escape. WinEdit will ignore any special meaning of the character that follows the Escape expression. Use the Escape if you need to search for a literal character that matches a regular expression.

.   Wild Card. Matches any character. For example, the expression 'X.X' will match 'XaX', 'XbX, and 'XcX', but not 'XaaX'.

^   Beginning Of Line. The expression matches only if it occurs at the beginning of a line. For example, '^for' matches the text 'for' only when it occurs at the beginning of a line.

$ End Of Line. The expression matches only if it occurs at the end of a line. For example, '(void)$' matches the text '(void)' only when it occurs at the end of a line.

[]   Character Class. The expression matches any character in the class specified within the brackets. Use a dash (-) to specify a range of character values. For example, '[a-zA-Z0-9]' matches any letter or number, and '[xyz]' matches 'x', 'y', or 'z'.

[^]   Inverse Class. The expression matches any character not specified in the class. For example, '[^a-zA-Z]' matches any character that is not a letter.

*   Repeat Operator. Matches zero or more occurrences of the character that precedes the '*'. For example, 'XY*X' matches 'XX', 'XYX', and 'XYYX.

+   Repeat Operator. Matches one or more occurrences of the character that precedes the '+'. For example, 'XY+X' matches 'XYX' and 'XYYX, but not 'XX'.

Software License

WinEdit is not and has never been public domain software, nor is it free software. Non-licensed users are granted a limited license to use WinEdit on a 21-day trial basis for the purpose of determining whether WinEdit is suitable for their needs. The use of WinEdit, except for the initial 21-day trial, requires registration. The use of unlicensed copies of WinEdit by any person, business, corporation, government agency or any other entity is strictly prohibited.

A single user license permits a user to use WinEdit only on a single computer. Licensed users may use the program on different computers, but may not use the program on more than one computer at the same time.

No one may modify or patch the WinEdit executable files in any way, including but not limited to decompiling, disassembling, or otherwise reverse engineering the program. A limited license is granted to copy and distribute WinEdit only for the trial use of others, subject to the above limitations, and also the following:

1.   WinEdit must be copied in unmodified form, complete with the file containing this license information.
2.   The full machine-readable WinEdit documentation must be included with each copy.
3.   WinEdit may not be distributed in conjunction with any other product without a specific license to do so from Wilson WindowWare.
4.   No fee, charge, or other compensation may be requested or accepted, except as authorized below:
    a.   Operators of electronic bulletin board systems (sysops) may make WinEdit available for downloading only as long as the above conditions are met. An overall or time-dependent charge for the use of the bulletin board system is permitted as long as there is not a specific charge for the download of WinEdit.
    b.   Vendors of user-supported or shareware software approved by the ASP may distribute WinEdit, subject to the above conditions, without specific permission. Non-approved vendors may distribute WinEdit only after obtaining written permission from Wilson WindowWare. Such permission is usually granted. Please write for details (enclose your catalog). Vendors may charge a disk duplication and handling fee, which, when prorated to the WinEdit product, may not exceed eight dollars.

Limited Warranty

Wilson WindowWare guarantees your satisfaction with this product for a period of 90 days from the date of original purchase. If you are unsatisfied with WinEdit within that time period, return the package in saleable condition to the place of purchase for a full refund. Wilson WindowWare warrants that all disks provided are free from defects in material and workmanship, assuming normal use, for a period of 90 days from the date of purchase. Wilson WindowWare warrants that the program will perform in substantial compliance with the documentation supplied with the software product. If a significant defect in the product is found, the Purchaser may return the product for a refund. In no event will such a refund exceed the purchase price of the product.

EXCEPT AS PROVIDED ABOVE, WILSON WINDOWWARE DISCLAIMS ALL WARRANTIES, EITHER EXPRESS OR IMPLIED, INCLUDING, BUT NOT LIMITED TO IMPLIED WARRANTIES OF MERCHANTABILITY AND FITNESS FOR A PARTICULAR PURPOSE, WITH RESPECT TO THE PRODUCT. SHOULD THE PROGRAM PROVE DEFECTIVE, THE PURCHASER ASSUMES THE RISK OF PAYING THE ENTIRE COST OF ALL NECESSARY SERVICING, REPAIR, OR CORRECTION AND ANY INCIDENTAL OR CONSEQUENTIAL DAMAGES. IN NO EVENT WILL WILSON WINDOWWARE BE LIABLE FOR ANY DAMAGES WHATSOEVER (INCLUDING WITHOUT LIMITATION DAMAGES FOR LOSS OF BUSINESS PROFITS, BUSINESS INTERRUPTION, LOSS OF BUSINESS INFORMATION AND THE LIKE) ARISING OUT OF THE USE OR THE INABILITY TO USE THIS PRODUCT EVEN IF WILSON WINDOWWARE HAS BEEN ADVISED OF THE POSSIBILITY OF SUCH DAMAGES.

Use of this product for any period of time constitutes your acceptance of this agreement and subjects you to its contents.

Association of Shareware Professionals Ombudsman Statement

Wilson WindowWare, the producer of WinEdit, is a member of the Association of Shareware Professionals (ASP). ASP wants to make sure that the shareware principle works for you. If you are unable to resolve a shareware-related problem with an ASP member by contacting the member directly, ASP may be able to help. The ASP Ombudsman can help you resolve a dispute or problem with an ASP member, but does not provide technical support for members' products. Please write to the ASP Ombudsman at P.O. Box 5786, Bellevue, WA 98006 or send a CompuServe message via Easyplex to ASP Ombudsman 70007,3536

WINEDIT Order Form 1.0G

Name: _____
Company: _____
Address: _____
_____
City: _____ St:_____ Zip: _____
Phone: (_____)_____ Country: _____
____ WinEdit (s) @ $59.95 : _____.____
    Foreign air shipping (except Canada) @ $9.50 : _____.____
                        Total: _____.____
Disk Size(circle one)   5.25" acceptable   3.5" required
Please enclose a check payable to Wilson WindowWare; or you may use Visa, MasterCharge, or EuroCard. For credit cards, please enter the information below:
Card #:__ __ __ - __ __ __ - __ __ __ - __ __ __
Expiration date: ____/____
Signature: _____

Where did you get your copy of WinEdit? _____
_____
What version of WinEdit have you been evaluating? _____
_____

Send to: Wilson WindowWare
           2701 California Ave SW #212
           Seattle, WA 98116
           USA

or call: (800) 762-8383 (orders only)
           (206) 937-9335
           (206) 935-7129 (fax)

(Please allow 1 to 2 weeks for delivery)

WinPost Version 2.0

Copyright © 1991 Nobuya Higashiyama

Introduction

WinPost provides a mechanism for manipulating on-screen reminder notes for Microsoft Windows 3.0. Up to 32 "notes" can be in use at any given time. WinPost will save the state of all notes upon program termination, so the next time you bring up the program, the notes will look exactly the same as when you exited the program. It also has a "Layout" feature, which allows the user to assign individual notes to one or more "layouts" so that the user can choose to display only notes belonging to a particular "layout".

Controller Icon

When you start WinPost, it will appear as an icon. This is called the Controller Icon, and it cannot be maximized into a window.

When you click on the icon, it will display a system menu with the following menu items:

Move Allows the user to move the icon.
Close Terminates the program.
Switch To... Allows the user to switch to another window.
Create a note Selecting this menu item brings up a pop-up menu which is used to select a note size. The user selects one of three sizes (1.5" by 2", 3" by 3" or 3" by 5"), or the default size (see Configuration section below). If a maximum number of notes (32) is already in use, a dialog box with an error message will appear.
Show all notes Selecting this menu item will display all active notes. All hidden notes are redisplayed, and notes covered by other windows are brought to the front. Notes Icon will also disappear (see below).
Hide all notes Selecting this menu item will hide all active notes. It will also create a Notes Icon to indicate the fact that at least one note is hidden.
Layout... Selecting this menu brings up the Layout Dialog (explained below), which allows the user to select, add or delete note layouts.
Configure... Selecting this menu brings up the Configuration dialog (explained below),which allows the user to customize various parameters.
Save To Disk Allows the user to save information about notes to disk.
About WinPost... Displays information about the author.

Layout Dialog

This dialog box is used to select the active layout. Each note is assigned to none, one or more layouts by the user. When the user selects a particular layout, all notes which do not belong to the selected layout behave as though they do not exist. This feature can be used to create notes specific to a particular task or an application, so that numerous notes can be assigned to various layouts to reduce the amount of notes showing at one time.

The user selects the active layout by selecting the appropriate layout description in the listbox and pressing the "Use" button, or double-clicking on the desired description. Pressing the "Cancel" button terminates the dialog box without changing the current layout. Selecting a layout and pressing the "Delete" button deletes the selected layout. Pressing the "Add..." button brings up another dialog box which prompts for the description of a new layout (31 character limit).

A reserved layout named "All" is used to select all notes. When a new layout is selected, all notes which do not belong to the selected layout will disappear as though they no longer exist. However, information pertaining to

these notes are still kept so that they will be displayed once again if a layout to which these notes belong is selected.

Configuration Dialog

This dialog box is used to customize various parameters.

Font Selection: The user may change the font used by the note windows. Two combo boxes are used to configure the font. The "Face Name" box is used to select the font face, and the "Point Size" box is used to select the font size. When a new font face is selected, the "Point Size" list box is opened, showing the available point sizes for that font.
Note Color: The user selects the desired color of the note windows.
Default Note Size: The user selects the default note size by pressing one of the radio buttons.
Auto Save Timer: The user may opt to have WinPost save the contents of all notes periodically so that not all work is lost if the system crashes before the user has had a chance to write to disk or terminate the program. The user specifies how often WinPost should save to disk (in minutes); setting this parameter to zero disables the Auto Save feature.

Once all the parameters have been configured, the user may save the configuration by pressing the "Accept" button. Pressing the "Cancel" button will abort the dialog without making any changes.

Note Window

Each note is an editable window. Standard editing operations are available. Contents and the position of each window is saved whenever you end the program; when you run the program again, all the notes will be restored. A note window can be moved just like a normal window; its size, however, cannot be changed. Each note window also has the standard system menu gadget. System menu will show the following menu items:

Move Allows the user to move the window.
Switch To... Allows the user to switch to another window.
Delete this note Selecting this menu item deletes this note.
Hide this note Selecting this menu item hides this note.
Change caption... Allows the user to change the note window title bar caption. A dialog box will appear, prompting the user for the new caption.
Assign to Layout... Selecting this menu item brings up a dialog box which is used to select the layout(s) to assign this note to. More than one layout may be selected. The user assigns the layouts by selecting the appropriate entries in the list box. Pressing the "Select

all" button selects all layouts. Once the appropriate layouts are selected, pressing the "Accept" button saves the layout assignment. The user may cancel the operation by pressing the "Cancel" button.

Undo Undoes the last editing operation.

Cut Deletes the selected text and copies it into the system clipboard.

Copy Copies the selected text into the system clipboard.

Paste Copies the content of the system clipboard at the cursor position.

Notes Icon

If there is at least one note that's hidden, a Notes Icon will be displayed. This icon operates just like a standard application icon. Just like the controller icon, it cannot be maximized into a window. **Cl**arification: a note window that is covered by another window is not considered to be "hidden" — a note is "hidden" when you select "Hide all notes" menu item on the Controller Icon, or "Hide this note" menu item on the Note window menu. When you click on the Notes Icon, it will display a system menu with the following menu items:

Move Allows the user to move the icon.

Switch To... Allows the user to switch to another window.

Show all notes Selecting this menu item will show all active notes (just like selecting the menu item by the same name on the Controller Icon).

Mouse Shortcuts

Several common operations can be selected by using various mouse shortcuts. The following shortcuts are available:

Controller Icon

- Double-clicking the left mouse button creates a new note of default size.

- Single-clicking the right mouse button hides all notes.

- Double-clicking the right mouse button hides all notes except one; series of double-clicks can be used to cycle through all notes one at a time.

Notes Icon

- Double-clicking the left mouse button shows all hidden notes.

Note Window Menu Gadget

- Double-clicking the left mouse button hides that note.

[Note: If you are using Whiskers 2.x to re-define your right mouse button, you cannot use Whiskers' "Exclude" dialog box to restore the right mouse button's original meaning

when clicking WinPost's Controller Icon (right mouse button hides all notes, etc.). This will be corrected in the registered version of Whiskers. —Brian Livingston]

License

This version of WinPost is NOT public domain or free software, but is being distributed as "shareware". Non-registered users of this software are granted a limited license to make an evaluation copy for trial use for the express purpose of determining whether WinPost is suitable for their needs. At the end of this trial period, you should either register your copy or discontinue using WinPost.

By registering this software, you will ensure continued support and updates of this product. Plus, registered users will receive a copy of this software without the registration notice window. A WinPost registration entitles you to use the program on one CPU. You may make as many copies as you wish, but only one CPU may actively be running this program at one time. If other people need to use it, then you should purchase a site license. See the following section for information about site licensing or quantity discounts.

Corporate Site Licenses and Quantity Purchases

All corporate, business, government or other commercial users of WinPost must be registered. We offer quantity discounts as well as site licensing. Corporate site licensing agreements allow duplication and distribution of specific number of copies within the licensed institution. Duplication of multiple copies is not allowed except through execution of a licensing agreement. Site license fees are based upon estimated number of users. Note that with a site license, only one copy of the program will be sent. You will be responsible for distributing additional copies. Please call or write for more information.

ALL PRICES AND DISCOUNTS ARE SUBJECT TO CHANGE WITHOUT NOTICE. WARNING: YOU MAY NOT USE WinPost WITHIN YOUR ORGANIZATION WITHOUT A PRIOR PURCHASE OR LICENSE AGREEMENT.

Disclaimer

User of this program acknowledges this disclaimer of warranty:

"This program is supplied as is. The author disclaims all warranties, expressed or implied, including, without limitation, the warranties of merchantability and of fitness of this program for any purpose. The author assumes no liability for damages, direct or consequential, which may result from the use of this program."

Support

For all questions, bug reports, comments and suggestions, please contact: Nobuya Higashiyama 7337 Chaparral Road Columbus, OH 43235 (614) 798-0910. If you leave a message regarding technical support, calls will be returned for registered users only.

WinPost 2.0 ORDER FORM

Name: _____

Title: _____

Company: _____

Address: _____

_____

_____

City: _____ State: _____ Zip: _____

Phone: _____

Please check one of these two order categories:

[ ] New Registration

Number of licenses _____ @ $20.00 each Total _____

Please call or write for site license and quantity discounts

[ ] Upgrade from Version 1.0 or 1.1. No Charge

This applies only to those who have registered WinPost previously via a donation of $10 or more

Add shipping/handling (for both new and upgrade registrations)

$5.00 domestic, $10.00 international _____

Select diskette type: [ ] 5.25"   [ ] 3.5"

Total (payable by check/money order) _____

Remit to:

Nobuya Higashiyama 7337 Chaparral Road Columbus, OH 43235 (614) 798-0910

Communications

COMRESET Version 1.0

Copyright © 1991 by FBN Productions

This simple program is used to initialize serial ports on an IBM PC-compatible computer. It was designed specifically because Microsoft Windows 3.0 running in 386 enhanced mode does not fully reset the com ports if you use serial communications applications under Windows. Run COMRESET to reinitialize the ports installed in your machine after you exit Windows, if you are having trouble with communications applications that normally work correctly but fail after you run Windows on your system.

List the numbers of the com ports you want to reset on the COMRESET command line. (Generally, you should reset all the ports that are installed in your system.) Include only the number, and separate each with a space. COMRESET recognizes only ports COM1 through COM4 and will exit with an error message (and without doing anything) if you specify a port that is out of range. If a com port is specified but does not actually exist in your system, COMRESET will note it with an error message, but other existing ports you may have specified will still be reset. Example: To reset ports 1, 2 and 4, enter the command:

```
COMRESET 1 2 4
```

at the MS-DOS prompt.

COMRESET assumes that the serial ports are at the "standard" addresses and interrupts for COM1 through COM4:

Device	Port	IRQ
COM1	03f8h	4
COM2	02f8h	3
COM3	03e8h	4
COM4	02e8h	3

Custom versions of the program to address other ports can be produced on request.

This program is a product of:

FBN Productions
917 W. Columbia Ave.
Champaign, IL 61821

This is a free program, and you may distribute it as you desire. For further information or source code, contact FBN Productions at the address above or through the FBN BBS at (217) 359-2874.

UNICOM

Release 2.0
Copyright © 1990 by Data Graphics

Contents at a Glance

Section 10 - Command Summary
Appendix A - Communication Error Codes
Appendix B - Product Support

Introduction

UNICOM is a data communications application specifically designed for users of the Microsoft Windows operating environment, versions 2 and 3. UNICOM will perform all data communication tasks in the *background* while other applications are running. You may switch to another Windows application at any time. UNICOM Release 2.0 includes the following features:

- Built-in file transfer protocols that include XMODEM Checksum, XMODEM CRC, XMODEM 1K (old YMODEM), YMODEM G, YMODEM Batch, ZMODEM, ZMODEM Resume, Kermit, CompuServe B, Quick B and ASCII.
- Color ANSI-BBS, VT52 and TTY Terminal Emulation, supporting user-selectable terminal fonts that span ANSI and OEM character sets.
- A 250-line Scrollback Buffer is easily operated with the use of a vertical scroll bar.
- A user-configurable Utility Menu allows instant access to your favorite Windows or DOS applications.
- A new Script Language supports more than 35 commands with a Trace Mode for debugging.
- A Script Scheduler allows pre-programmed execution of up to eight script files, each at specific days and times.
- Directory assisted batch dialing and redialing is supported for users with Hayes-compatible modems.
- An Online Help System allows instant access to general help and script command topics. The user manual is also available for direct reference from the online help.
- A unique journaling feature lets you record mouse and keyboard operations for later playback.
- Chat Mode makes keyboard communication simple. Two separate windows appear. Type your message in one window and view received characters in another.
- User definable Hot Keys can allow any UNICOM menu selection to be assigned to a function key for one-button access to UNICOM program options.
- Keyboard macros, File logging, Printer Logging, File Paste and Print Screen.

UNICOM provides some unique features that support the Windows environment. You can:

- Transfer the contents of a Clipboard from one computer directly into the Clipboard of another. This provides you with the ability to transfer many types of Windows-unique data formats between computers.

Some of these formats include: Excel Spreadsheets (SYLK, DIF), Bitmap Images (from Paint), Metafile Pictures (from Designer), Text (from Notepad) and any format that can be placed on the Clipboard.

- Operate your computer in a multi-user mode with UNICOM's host mode. A built-in command processor allows a validated remote user to examine or transfer files on a designated disk drive. This operation is transparent to any user who may be at the keyboard directly operating other Window applications.
- Operate multiple program instances. Advanced users with the appropriate hardware configuration may initiate simultaneous background file transfers with multiple remote systems.
- Send a Screen Snapshot directly to the Clipboard.

About This Manual

This manual is your reference to installing and operating UNICOM on a computer equipped with Microsoft Windows. The manual is divided into 10 sections:

1. "Getting Started" describes how to install and start UNICOM on your computer.
2. "Setting Up UNICOM" details all user configurable program options.
3. "Operating UNICOM" describes the purpose and use of all operating features.
4. "Using the Dialing Directory" explains how to automatically dial (and re-dial) remote host systems. This section also includes information on how to maintain the dialing directory.
5. "Transferring Files" will illustrate how to send and receive text or binary files using XMODEM, YMODEM, ZMODEM, Kermit CompuServe B, Quick B and ASCII file transfer protocols.
6. "Transferring the Clipboard" describes the steps necessary to transmit and receive Clipboard formats between two computers equipped with UNICOM software.

   The remaining sections may be found on the accompanying disk:

7. "Using Script Files" describes how to automate manual communication tasks with UNICOM's script command language.
8. "Host Mode Operation" will detail built-in features that support remote password protected access to your files.
9. "Advanced Operation" describes how UNICOM may be operated to perform simultaneous multiple file transfers between multiple remote computers.
10. "Command Summary" lists and describes all menu commands.

Hardware and Software Requirements

UNICOM requires Microsoft Windows version two or three to be installed and properly configured on your computer. Before installing UNICOM on your computer check the following:

1. If a BUS mouse is installed in your computer, make sure the mouse interrupt level does not conflict with interrupts reserved for serial port operation. The BUS mouse interrupt is set via a jumper on the interface board. Consult your mouse installation manual.
2. Your serial port(s) (COM1 and COM2) or (COM3 and COM4) should be set for interrupt operation using IRQ4 and IRQ3 respectively. The interrupt levels are typically selected via jumpers located on your serial interface board or on the motherboard. Consult your computer reference manual.
3. Microsoft Windows version 2 may contain a BUG in the communication port driver. If your version of Windows is dated before April 1989, you should update to Windows 3 or obtain a replacement communication port driver (named COMM.DRV) from Microsoft and reinstall Windows 2 using this replacement file.
4. A Hayes-compatible modem must be present to support UNICOM's directory-assisted dialing and call hang-up features.

The modem dip switch settings should be set to the manufacturer's DEFAULT positions. The modem must be configured to return VERBOSE responses. Also, please note that certain operations such as Clipboard to Clipboard transfers require enough temporary memory and disk storage to hold the data being transferred. This storage is released after the transfer operation is completed.

Section One — Getting Started

Installing UNICOM Software

The UNICOM 2.0 distribution disk should contain the following files:

UNICOM.EXE The UNICOM executable program
UCLIB.DLL UNICOM Runtime Support library
UNICOM.DIR A sample dialing directory
UNICOM.KEY A sample keyboard macro file
UNICOM.CFG A default program configuration file
UNICOM.WRI UNICOM online manual
UNICOM.HLP Online Help Text File
UCSCRIPT.HLP Script Online Help Text File
UC-READ.ME UNICOM release notes
CMPUSRV.SCR An example UNICOM login script file

To Install UNICOM

1. UNICOM requires that Microsoft Windows 2.x or 3.x be installed and working on your computer.
   If you are upgrading from a previous version of UNICOM, do not mix your old UNICOM.CFG with that of a new UNICOM release. UNICOM configuration files are not compatible across releases.
2. Insert the distribution disk in your floppy disk drive.
3. Copy the files to any directory on the destination drive where you wish to store UNICOM. You will need to remember this directory path and enter it into the UNICOM file path window from within the program setup menu.
   The support file: UCLIB.DLL must be placed in a directory listed in your search path as defined by your MS-DOS PATH environment variable. This PATH environment variable is set in the MS-DOS AUTOEXEC.BAT file. Consult your DOS operating manual for more information about the DOS PATH environment variable.
4. Before running UNICOM, it is a good idea to check the items listed in the previous Hardware and Software Requirements section.
5. Activate UNICOM and enter your license number by pressing the ENTER LICENSE NO. button that appears on an opening start-up screen. The license number is printed on your receipt and *should be saved for future reference* should the program need to be re-installed. Licensing disables the opening startup screens and prevents their return during program operation.

Should UNICOM be moved to another computer, or if Windows was reinstalled, it may be necessary to enter the license number again to disable the built-in nagware screens should they reappear.

Running UNICOM

UNICOM may be activated from DOS using the following syntax:

    UNICOM [configfile]

By omitting the optional [configfile] parameter, UNICOM will look for a default configuration file named UNICOM.CFG. From DOS, type the command (depending upon your windows version):

    WIN UNICOM

    -or- WIN386 UNICOM

To activate UNICOM from the Microsoft Executive or File System, doubleclick (using a mouse) on the file: UNICOM.EXE. When invoked without a configuration file parameter, additional UNICOM instances will attempt to access a configuration file named UNICOM2.CFG. If this file cannot be located, the port settings will default to COM2, 1200, N, 8, 1. When UNICOM is activated for the first time, a file path setup window will appear prompting you to enter a UNICOM files, upload and download directory.

The files directory should be set to the drive and directory where UNICOM has been installed. The download directory should be set to the drive and directory where files received from data transfers are to be stored. The upload directory should be set to the drive and directory where UNICOM will first look to locate files for upload selection.

Enter the pathnames into the edit fields within the dialog box. Paths defined here are valid only for the current UNICOM session. To make the paths permanent, activate the SAVE SETUP option from within the SETUP menu. Paths are stored in your Windows WIN.INI file. An error message will be displayed if any of the path fields contain an invalid directory or if UNICOM could not locate its executable files in the directory specified in the FILES DIRECTORY field.

At the start of each program run, the configuration file 'UNICOM.CFG' is accessed (from the file path set previously) to determine what communication port will be used and other operating parameters. If UNICOM cannot locate this file, the port will default to COM2, 1200 baud, No Parity, 8 data bits and 1 stop bit. Should a communication port fail to open, UNICOM will display a message box to indicate the failure. The port configuration dialog window will be displayed automatically. A valid communication port should be selected.

When a communication port is successfully opened, UNICOM will try to initialize the Hayes compatible modem if the port was configured for a modem connection. Should the message "Modem Not Responding" appear, this means UNICOM could not get the modem's attention. Make sure the communications port and modem are configured properly. Ensure that the modem is set to return VERBOSE responses.

Section Two - Setting Up UNICOM

Communication Port Settings

To select and configure a communications port, select the COMM PORT option from the Setup menu. A setup window will appear displaying the current port configuration as shown in Figure 1.

Select the communication characteristics desired from this window using a mouse or keyboard. COM1 through COM4 are shown as available options. If your computer or

Figure 1

version of Windows does not support a particular port, an error message will be displayed if an attempt is made to configure it.

Configuration Option Descriptions

Port: Physical Communication Device: Com1 - Com4
Baud Rate: Port Operating Speed (Bits Per Second) (300 bps to 19,200 bps)
Parity: Specifies the character parity for the currently selected port. NONE means no parity bit is provided. EVEN, ODD, MARK, SPACE specify that parity operation as follows:

- EVEN - Parity bit set to provide an even number of set bits.
- ODD - Parity bit set to provide an odd number of set bits.
- MARK - Parity bit always set.
- SPACE- Parity bit always clear.

Stop: 1 or 2 Stop Synchronization Bits
Word: Defines the number of data bits that make up the character size.
Handshake: Is a means by which your computer (and the remote host) will control incoming and outgoing data. Most computers require a handshake to avoid losing

data. Handshakes may be performed using hardware (RS-232 pins) or special ASCII control characters. UNICOM provides selection of the following hand-shake types as supported by the Windows comm port driver:

EIA: specifies that RS-232 pin 4: Request to Send (RTS) performs receive flow control and pin 5: clear to send (CTS) for transmit flow control. RTS will be dropped when the receive queue is full and raised otherwise. Character transmission will be suspended when CTS is dropped by the external device and resumed when it is raised.

None: specifies no handshake. A software-specific handshake is up to the application program (such as an XMODEM protocol transfer) driving each end of the communication link.

Xon/Xoff: interprets DC1 (CTL Q) and DC3 (CTL S) characters as special flow control characters. When UNICOM receives a DC3, it will suspend any transmission until a DC1 (Xon) is encountered. Likewise, when UNICOM's receive buffer is full, a DC3 (Xoff) is transmitted to the remote computer to cause it to suspend (provided the remote recognizes XON/XOFF) transmission. UNICOM resumes the suspended remote transmission (when ready) by transmitting a DC1.

Connection: Instructs UNICOM to treat the remote connection as a modem or a direct computer-to-computer link. If set to MODEM, UNICOM will assume that a modem is connected and try to initialize it during program startup, host and modem configuration operations.

Disable Error Report: Controls the reporting of hardware detected communication errors from the communication port driver built-in to Windows.

- Parity - When selected, disables reporting of parity errors detected in received characters.

- Framing- When selected, disables reporting of improperly synchronized transmissions due to poor line quality or mismatched communication settings.

- Overrun- When selected, disables reporting of a UNICOM transmit or receive buffer overflow.

Select the port and the desired characteristics from the above options and press the CONFIGURE button to activate the port. To restore the port settings to the original configuration (as stored in the program configuration file), press the DEFAULT button then press CONFIGURE. **Note:** COM3 and COM4 are not supported by the Microsoft port driver provided in release 2.x of Windows.

Terminal Settings

Terminal characteristics may be modified by selecting the TERMINAL option. A terminal setup window will appear displaying current options 3.

Terminal: ANSI-BBS, VT52 or TTY emulation.
Color: When this feature is enabled, color ANSI-BBS emulation will be used. Color terminal escape sequences received from a remote host control foreground and background colors displayed on your screen.
Newline: This option will automatically generate a linefeed upon receipt of a carriage return. If characters seem to wrap around on a single line with your particular host, enable this option.
Local Echo: Some hosts do not echo characters back when typed from the keyboard. Half duplex systems typically operate this way (such as GEnie). Enable this option to instruct UNICOM to echo characters that are typed from the keyboard. Should characters appear double on your screen, disable this option.
Autowrap: Some remote hosts do not generate a linefeed after reaching the end of line. Should characters fail to wrap around to the next line, enable this option.
Erase on Backspace: Once enabled, backspace characters received will be translated into BS-SPACE-BS to erase the character on your screen. This translation is normally performed by the remote host. If characters are not erased using backspace with your particular host, enable this option.
Font Selection: One listbox contains the name of all available fixed and variable length fonts found in your installed version of Windows. The size listbox contains the available size(s) for the font highlighted in the font name listbox.

Hayes Compatible Modem Settings

UNICOM provides a modem setup window containing user selectable options for Hayes compatible modems. Select the MODEM option from the Setup menu. A Modem Setup window will appear (shown in Figure 2) containing the current modem settings.

The purpose of this window is to construct a modem init string that will be sent to the modem upon activating UNICOM or by pressing Accept. The modem setup window supports two types of init strings: User Entered and Selected. The init string type is selected using the two radio buttons located at the top of the window. When selected, the User Entered radio button will instruct UNICOM to transmit the modem init string defined in the edit box for modem initialization. If the Selected radio button is chosen, UNICOM will use a modem init string constructed from the menu selections in the Selected Init String section.

User Entered Init String: An edit box is provided so that you may define your own modem init string. UNICOM appends a terminating carriage return to the end of the string placed here.
Selected Init String: A modem init string is constructed automatically based upon the configurable modem options contained in the Selected Init String section. These options are defined as follows:

Wait for dial tone: (2-255 seconds) DEFAULT = 2 determines the maximum time the modem will wait for a dial tone during dialing operations.

Wait for answer: (1-255 seconds) DEFAULT = 30 determines the time the modem will wait for an answer after dialing has commenced.

Dial Type: Tone or Pulse operation.

Speaker Control: Always OFF, ON for dialing or ON while the phone is off hook.

Auto Answer: ON or OFF.

Answer on ring [x]: If Auto Answer is enabled, the modem will pick up the phone on ring x (if x > 0).

Dialer Speed: Slow, Medium or Fast. This affects the dialing rate for tone operation only.

Call Waiting Protection: ON or OFF. When enabled, this feature will prevent the modem from breaking a phone connection because of a call waiting 'click' associated with incoming calls. The loss of carrier time is extended to 100ms to prevent the modem from hanging up during this type of interruption. This method does not instruct the phone system to block waiting calls.

For more detailed information regarding these (and other) modem settings, refer to your modem reference manual.

Hayes compatible modems may differ in modem responses when attempting a connection or hanging up by dropping the RS-232 data terminal ready signal. A modem-specific setup window has been provided to describe responses and timing behavior that can vary from one Hayes compatible brand of modem to another. To activate the modem-specific setup window, press the MORE pushbutton from the modem setup window.

Connect String: This field should contain your modem's response upon making a successful connection. When dialing, UNICOM examines modem responses to determine the result. The typical default string is uppercase CONNECT for most Hayes compatible modems. Some modems respond with CARRIER [baud].

No Connect Responses: Enter the possible responses produced by your modem that indicate unsuccessful dialing. If UNICOM encounters one of these strings during dialing, the specific response will be reported to the user. Consult your modem reference manual for these response strings.

Hang Up String: Should UNICOM fail to hang up by dropping DTR, it will perform a software hang up procedure. This involves sending the escape to command character sequence '+++' to bring the modem into command mode. Once in command mode, the modem is instructed to hang up using the string defined in this field.

Escape Guard Time: (0.5,1.0,1.5 Sec) This is the amount of time UNICOM will delay before and after sending the

modem attention '+++' sequence to bring the modem into command mode during a software hangup attempt.

Response to DTR drop: Modems typically produce a response string once a connection is dropped for reasons that include loss of DTR. UNICOM drops DTR (RS-232 pin 20) for hang up operations and watches for the response defined here to determine if the attempt was successful. To allow UNICOM to hang up quickly using the DTR drop method, you must provide this hardware signal to your modem using an RS-232 cable that supports pin 20. The modem must also be commanded to drop the line upon loss of DTR. This command is typically provided from the modem init string which is loaded at program initialization. Consult your modem reference for the particular modem command.

Command Speed: (Slow,Med,Fast) Some Hayes compatible modems become confused when commands arrive too quickly to the modem. This option controls the amount of time to delay per character when commands are issued to the modem. A Fast setting means no character delay. Medium introduces a 30 msec delay and Slow introduces a 60 msec delay. For most modems, the Command Speed can be set to Fast.

Keyboard Settings

You may define the meaning of your keyboard by selecting the KEYBOARD option from the Setup menu. The Keyboard Macro Editor window will appear containing edit fields for 12 function keys and the keypad keys. Program Hot Keys or user-defined keystrokes (up to 80 characters in length) may be assigned to individual function keys as displayed in the Macro Editor window below.

To store a keyboard macro, place the keystrokes into the definition editbox for the particular key to be defined. Control characters can be inserted and are denoted with the ^ character prefix. For example: ^C will output a control-C (ASCII 03). Control characters may be mixed with printable ASCII characters. Each macro is limited to a maximum of 80 characters.

Hot Keys are function keys that can be user defined to activate any UNICOM menu pick. For example, I wish to assign Chat Mode activation to function key F6. Use the Hot Key prefix ^^ to prefix the menu column and pulldown row for the item to activate. The Chat Mode option is in the Control menu (menu column 5) and located in the 5th row in the pulldown menu. The constructed Hot Key prefix looks like this ^^55. Spaces are not allowed between digits. For pulldowns that are in positions greater than 9, position 10 or greater must be designated with reference to the characters that follow 9 in the ASCII character set. Position 10 = ':', 11 = ';', 12 = '<' and so on. Please refer to an ASCII table. Hot Keys may also be assigned to user defined application entries within the Utility menu. With one button press, any application may be activated.

Keyboard macros may activated by pressing the corresponding key. A screen button can also be used to activate your macro with a single mouse click. Screen buttons containing user defined labels assigned to each function key are displayed at the bottom of the screen above the status line. To toggle display of these button on or off, select the User Keys item from the Control Menu.

By moving the mouse cursor and clicking on a given screen button, the corresponding Hot Key or keyboard macro will be activated. Each button may be labeled by entering the button name into the corresponding label editbox (within the keyboard macro editor). The buttons contained in the Key Macro Window are updated immediately to reflect changes made.

Host Mode Settings

Host mode allows a remote user to access a specified disk drive for purposes of uploading and downloading files. Before using host mode, it is a good idea to set a System Password, User Login Drive and a Host Identification String. Additional options are available. The Host Setup window is activated by selecting the Host Setup option from the setup menu. The following options will be displayed in the Host Setup window with their current values.

Host Identification String (80 chars max): This field contains the string that identifies your system to a remote user who is attempting to login.

System Password (20 chars max): is the password a remote user must enter to gain access to your system. If this field is not defined, a carriage return should be entered when prompted for the password. The password is case sensitive.

User Login Drive (drive letter): is the drive that a remote user will be confined to when logged in. A remote user may move between any directory within this drive, but cannot reference any other drive.

Greeting File: This file contains text information that will be transmitted to the remote user once a connection has been established. This file may contain embedded escape codes to format the remote terminal screen. At each screenful of text (23 lines), the remote user is prompted: More? (Y/n). A blank entry or invalid filename in this field will disable this option. UNICOM will look for this file to be located in the UNICOM Files Directory as defined in the File Path Setup Window.

Bulletin File: This file is transmitted to the remote user after each successful user login. At each screenful of text, the remote user is prompted: More? (Y/n). A blank entry or invalid filename in this field will disable

this option. UNICOM will look for this file to be located in the UNICOM Files Directory as defined in the File Path Setup Window.

Menu Filename: UNICOM provides a default remote user menu. You may define your own menu and cause UNICOM to display it to the remote user. The menu can be created using a text editor. Special control characters may be embedded in the file. A blank entry or invalid filename in this field will cause UNICOM to display a default menu. UNICOM will look for this file to be located in the UNICOM Files Directory as defined in the File Path Setup Window.

UNICOM File Path

To allow UNICOM to locate its operating files, a pathname must be provided anytime the program is installed or moved to another directory area. Select the FILE PATH option from the Setup menu. A file path setup window will appear. Enter the complete pathname of the location where UNICOM has been installed. By pressing CONFIG-URE, UNICOM will use the path for the current operating session only. TO MAKE THIS CHANGE PERMANENT, select the SAVE SETUP option from the Setup menu. The UNICOM file path is stored in the Windows win.ini file under the 'FilePath=' entry.

Download Directory Path

A Download Directory may also be set by accessing the file path option from the setup menu. UNICOM refers to the pathname you enter when storing files received from file transfers from remote systems. This path is stored in the Windows WIN.INI file under the [UNICOM] 'DownloadPath=' entry. This download path may be overridden for transfers that require a user entered filename. If a drive and directory reference is specified in an XMODEM download filename, the pre-defined download path will be ignored.

Upload Directory Path

The Upload Directory Path determines the default directory for file selection(s) when prompted for a file to be transferred to a remote computer. Shown below is an upload file selection window that contains directory entries from a defined upload directory.

ASCII Transfer Setup

The ASCII transfer setup is divided into operating parameters for uploading and downloading operations. To access the ASCII transfer options, select the ASCII Xfer option from the setup menu. A setup window will appear.

ASCII Upload Parameters

Echo Locally: If enabled, the file data being transferred will be echoed to your screen.

Pace Character: [0-99] The pace character is the numeric value of an ASCII character that is transmitted by the remote host receiving the file. This character is interpreted by UNICOM as 'send the next line'. UNICOM will wait for the remote to sent this character for each line transmitted.

Char Pacing: [0-999] Represents a delay time (in milliseconds) between transmission of each character to the remote host computer. Setting this value to zero, disables any time delay.

Line Pacing: [0-999] Represents the time (in 1/10 seconds) to delay after the transmission of each line or carriage return. A zero value in this field disables line pacing.

CR Translation: [None, Strip or Add LF] Carriage return translation can be used to strip carriage returns or insert linefeeds (after carriage returns) for the file being transmitted. Selecting none disables any translation.

LF Translation: [None, Strip or ADD CR] Linefeed translation will strip linefeeds or add carriage returns after linefeeds to the file being transmitted. Selecting none disables any translation.

ASCII Download Parameters

CR translation and LF translation as described above will filter and control these characters received during ASCII file downloads from remote host computers. The selection and definition (as described above) for downloading is the same as for uploading.

Kermit Transfer Setup

The Kermit is a configurable protocol and you may not want to change these values unless you are an advanced user. Assuming you are, here are the field definitions:

Max Packet Size: This is the maximum length for outbound packets, regardless of what was negotiated with the other Kermit. Normally, you would change this field (from the default) only to send shorter packets than the other Kermit requests, because you know something the other Kermit doesn't know, e.g. there's a device on the communication path with small buffers.

Timeout: This can be used to adjust the normal Kermit timeout parameter for both local and remote systems. Timeout will occur if a packet is not received after the number of seconds specified in this field.

# of pad chars: This value controls the number of pad chars to be requested from the remote Kermit to precede each packet it sends. Padding is not usually required but may be necessary to keep some intervening communication happy.

Padding Char: Use the specified control character for interpacket padding. Some hosts may require padding characters (normally NULL or DEL) before a packet, and certain front ends or other communication equipment may need certain control characters to put them in the right mode. The number is the ASCII decimal value of the padding character (0 - 31, or 127).

EOL Char: This field contains the ASCII value of the packet terminator to put on outbound packets. Normally a carriage return (13). Change this field if the other Kermit requires a nonstandard packet terminator.

Quote Char: This field contains the ASCII value of the character to be used to prefix control and other prefix characters. The only reason to change this would be for sending a very long file that contains many '#' characters (the normal control prefix) as data.

Port: (Switch to N-8-1 or No Switch) This option determines if UNICOM will automatically set the port for binary operation before Kermit is initiated. Selecting N-8-1 (the normal default) will allow Kermit to transfer binary data. No Switch should be used if the remote Kermit does not switch automatically to 8 data bits, No parity and 1 stop bit.

The fixed attribute definitions are not described here. Refer to the Kermit Users Guide from Columbia University.

General Setup Window

The general setup window allows user configuration of the initial UNICOM window style, the editor for creating and modifying script files, the name of the autostart script file, default transfer protocol, default keyboard macro file, default dialing directory and general program behavior. To activate the General Setup window, select General from the setup menu. A window will appear containing the current option settings.

Definitions of General Setup Options

UNICOM Startup Window: Controls the appearance of the UNICOM window upon program activation. **Normal** causes Windows to determine the window size and screen position. **Full Screen**, when set, will ZOOM the UNICOM window to occupy the entire screen. An **Iconic** setting will activate UNICOM without opening a window. Instead, the UNICOM icon will be displayed at the bottom of the screen.

Scroll Bars: When checked, UNICOM will display the user defined function key buttons at the bottom of the screen above the status line upon each program activation.

User Keys: When checked, UNICOM will display both horizontal and vertical scroll bars at each program activation. This allows you to use the 10-page scrollback capability built-in to UNICOM.

General Behavior: These checkboxes determine how UNICOM will behave for operations that include verification, automatic iconization and event logging.

Verification Prompts: When enabled, will cause UNICOM to display a messagebox to prompt for verification during end of transfers, program termination and modem hangup.

Log Events: Events such as dialing, hanging up, executing scripts and other program activities may be recorded to an ASCII for later review. Each event is time-stamped.

Auto Minimize on File Transfers: When checked, UNICOM will automatically iconize itself at the start of every file transfer. This can be useful for clearing the screen quickly so you may resume operating another windows application. UNICOM will pop back up to the screen after the transfer completes.

Auto Minimize on Repeat Dialing: Enable this feature to quickly remove UNICOM from the screen when batch dialing systems that are typically busy. UNICOM will pop back up to the screen when dialing is successful.

Default File Transfer Protocol: Choose the protocol to be selected within the upload and download protocol selection window when transferring files.

Dialing Directory File: Enter the name of the default dialing directory to be loaded each time you activate the Dial option.

Script Editor: The filename of the script language editor of your choice should be entered here. UNICOM activates this editor when the Edit, Edit Last or Create items are selected from the script menu. If this field is empty, UNICOM will activate Notepad by default.

AutoStart Script File: A script filename entered in this edit box will automatically execute upon each initial activation of UNICOM. A blank entry or invalid filename in this field will disable the autostart feature. Script command files must be located in the directory defined by the UNICOM files path.

Keyboard Macro File: The filename of the default keyboard macro file should be entered here. The keyboard macro file defines the meaning of the defined keyboard function keys either as macros or program Hot Keys.

Utility Menu Settings

This setup screen allows configuration of the Utility Menu with application entries of your choice. These applications are then listed by name for quick activation either from a menu selection or with a Hot Key definition. With this configuration screen, you may add many commonly used applications for a quick 'Launch' by UNICOM.

To operate this screen, just use the directory listbox to navigate across drives and directories to make your selections. Selected programs are stored in the right listbox by highlighting the desired application then pressing ADD. This file selection listbox is very similar to the batch upload file selection listbox used for file transfers. Applications names may be removed by highlighting the desired entry in the Selected Applications listbox and pressing delete.

Once you have selected all the desired applications, press OK to instruct UNICOM to configure the Utility Menu. UNICOM stores the complete path for the application in memory. If the application cannot be found (or for any other activation error) when it is selected from the menu, UNICOM will automatically display this setup window. Applications may be 'Launched' with the press of a function key by defining a Hot Key for the particular entry in the Utility Menu. See the previous section on Keyboard Macros.

Zmodem Transfer Setup

UNICOM provides a Zmodem setup window for advanced users of this protocol. If the setup screen seems confusing to you, don't worry, just select the Defaults push button to ensure correct operation. Advanced Zmodem users may wish to use some of the options provided by the design of this protocol. File management options allow examination of an existing file size and length before a transfer will occur. Other options control the amount of feedback during the transfer. Lots of feedback could be useful for determining the source of problem transfers for developers. The default is minimum feedback since the additional reports can be quite confusing if you're not an expert at Zmodem software design.

Saving All Settings

All program settings listed in the Setup menu (including terminal font selections, and keyboard definitions) may be saved to configuration files and loaded automatically for your next UNICOM session. To save all currently defined settings, select SAVE SETUP from the Setup menu. UNICOM will immediately update the file UNICOM.CFG with the current settings. This file will be created if it does not already exist or cannot be found in the defined UNICOM files path. File path settings are written to the Windows WIN.INI file. Keyboard macro definitions are written to the file currently listed in the General Setup Window. UNICOM.KEY is the default containing keyboard definitions.

A special configuration file named UNICOM2.CFG can be used to configure additional UNICOM instances. For example, selecting Spawn UNICOM from the files menu activates another copy of UNICOM. This new copy, or instance will need to be configured for a port different from that of the instance that created it. You may activate additional instances of UNICOM with a configuration file parameter using an external application. Additional UNICOM instances activated from within UNICOM or externally with no parameters will automatically look for a configuration file named UNICOM2.CFG. If this file cannot be found, previously described defaults apply. If these defaults fail, the new UNICOM instance will activate the communication port setup window as a last resort.

Section Three - Operating UNICOM

Connecting to Another Computer

UNICOM is intended for operation between two computers connected by any transport mechanism which utilize the serial port(s) for communication. One of these systems must have Microsoft Windows version 2 or 3 installed with UNICOM up and running. UNICOM supports remote phone connections with the use of a Hayes compatible modem. When UNICOM is activated, it immediately attempts to open a communication channel (port) using information found in the default (or command line specified) configuration file.

If a modem is connected to an open communication channel, it will be initialized with a modem init string defined in the Modem Setup window if the port was configured for modem operation. Modem initialization will be preempted should an AutoStart script file be defined. In which case the AutoStart script file will begin executing. A communication channel defined for a Computer connection (as set by the comm port setup window) will receive no special initialization. In this case, the channel is active once UNICOM opens the communication port. With a Hayes compatible modem, UNICOM can easily establish automatic connections with remote computers. The modem may also be commanded manually to dial the number of a target system (by typing ATD number from the keyboard) or automatically using UNICOM's Directory Assisted Dialing feature.

To take advantage of UNICOM's directory assisted dialing, a dialing directory must be created. The directory contains the name, number and configuration settings for each host system to be listed. These settings are easily entered with the use of a directory editor. To view the dialing directory for editing or dialing, select the DIAL option from the Control menu. The dialing directory window will appear displaying the contents of the designated external directory file. The directory to be used is determined by the directory filename stored in the General Setup Window.

The dialing directory may be edited and saved using the directory maintenance buttons located on the lower right area on the directory window. The system name, phone number and communication parameters can be selected using the directory editor. To activate the directory editor, select the ADD or CHANGE buttons from the directory maintenance area. Other directory files may be opened and displayed from this window by selecting the Open button from the directory maintenance section.

Once the entry information is has been placed into the editor window, select the ADD (or CHANGE) button to update the directory. Once an entry is placed into the directory, the remote host may be automatically dialed by highlighting the listbox entry and selecting the DIAL button. The port is automatically configured to the proper settings before dialing is attempted. For more information about Directory Assisted Dialing, see Section Four.

File Logging

Incoming screen characters may be captured to a log file. Control characters are not filtered during file logging. To activate file logging, select the File Log option from the Files menu or activate the Log File button at the bottom of the display. A window will appear to prompt you for the log filename.

Should you enter a filename of an existing file, UNICOM will ask if you wish to append to this file. A NO response will abort the file log request. File logging is disabled should the program leave terminal mode (enter host mode, for example) and will resume upon return.

Printer Logging

Incoming characters may be echoed directly to a printer. To activate printer logging, select the Printer Logging toggle from the files menu. A checkmark will appear next to the menu item to show that it is active. The printer used by this feature is the current (active) printer defined by configuration settings in your WIN.INI file as set using the Windows Control Panel. Printer logging and file logging may operate simultaneously. UNICOM logs to the printer on a per page basis. The printer will produce output only when logging has exceeded the current printer page size. To disable printer logging, again, select the Printer Logging toggle from the files menu.

Printing the Terminal Screen

A UNICOM screen snapshot may be sent to the printer at any time by selecting PRINT from the File menu. A message box containing a CANCEL button will appear to inform you of the print operation. Press the CANCEL button should you wish to abort printing.

Printing the Screen Buffer

The entire contents of the terminal scroll back buffer can be printed by selecting the PRINT BUFFER option from the files menu. Blank lines are not filtered out when printing. The buffer print is a snapshot in time - what you see at the instant the print was initiated is what you get when printing is finished. Any updates to the terminal or scroll back buffer are ignored during printing.

Configuring the Active Printer

To view or change the current printer settings, activate the Printer Setup option from within UNICOM's file menu. A printer setup window will appear that will allow you to configure specific options for your particular printer.

Configuring Windows

The configuration of your Windows operating environment may be altered by accessing the Windows Control Panel. You may activate this Windows utility from within UNICOM. Select the Control Panel option from the files menu to activate the Windows Control Panel.

Spawning Additional UNICOM Instances

Multiple UNICOM applications may operate concurrently in the Windows multitasking environment. Running additional instances of UNICOM will allow simultaneous communication with multiple remote computers. To 'activate' (Spawn) another UNICOM window, select Spawn UNICOM from within the File menu. The new UNICOM instance will know that it has been cloned and look to open a configuration file named 'UNICOM2.CFG'. If no such configuration file exists, the normal configuration defaults apply.

Running Another Application

UNICOM provides a Run option within the Files menu from which to 'Launch' other applications. When activated, a parameter window will appear to accept a command line to be entered as you would from DOS. The type of window activation may be selected if the application to be launched is a Windows Application. Select Normal to let Windows determine a default window size. Minimize will cause the application to startup iconic. The full screen will be used if the Zoom option is selected.

Clearing the Screen

To clear the terminal screen, select ERASE TERMINAL from the Edit menu. The cursor will move to the first row and column of the active terminal screen. If the cursor should disappear after clearing the screen, the first row of the terminal screen may be located above the top of the window. Should this happen, use the scroll bar to bring the top line into view. This command does not erase the contents of the terminal scroll back buffer. If characters remain on the screen after an erase, they belong to the scroll back buffer.

Erasing the Scroll Buffer

The Scroll Back buffer holds 250 lines of text including the 24 lines of the active terminal screen. By erasing the scroll buffer, all characters are erased from the screen.

Copying Screen Text to the Clipboard

You can copy screen text to the Clipboard, then paste this text into other applications. Select the COPY option from the Edit menu. The entire terminal screen (excluding the scroll back buffer) will be copied, including any rows and columns obscured by a small sized window.

Copying the Scroll Buffer to the Clipboard

The contents of the entire 250 line scroll buffer may be copied to the Clipboard as text. Once on the Clipboard, this text may be saved to a file using the Clipboard's file save option. The text may be copied to any other application supporting a paste option.

Pasting Clipboard Text to the Remote Computer

Clipboard text may be pasted (transmitted) to the remote host computer. This operation is equivalent to uploading an ASCII file. An ASCII file can be copied to the Clipboard using a program such as Notepad. The text can then be pasted (uploaded) to the remote host by selecting PASTE from the Edit menu. The file transfer information window will appear once pasting has begun. A moving bar graph gives a visual readout as to the number of bytes remaining to be transferred at any given time.

Viewing Log Files

Text captured to a log file from file logging can be easily viewed or edited from within UNICOM. Select the Log File option from the Edit menu. A file selection window will appear displaying all files with a '.LOG' extension. You may navigate through drives and directories to make a selection. Highlight the desired file and press Select. UNICOM will 'Launch' the default editor into an edit session with the selected log file.

Viewing Event Files

Event files may be viewed or edited in the same fashion as Log Files. Select the Event File option from the Edit menu. A file selection window will appear displaying all files with a '.EVT' extension. Upon making a selection, UNICOM initiates an editing session with the default text editor.

Signaling the Remote Computer

Some remote systems require the user to set the line to a BREAK state in order to signal an event (such as aborting a display operation). You may send this signal to the remote host by selecting BREAK from the Control menu. The communication line will enter a break condition for a duration of 350 milliseconds.

Terminating a Phone Connection

You may command the modem to hang up the phone by selecting the HANG UP option from the Control menu. UNICOM will attempt to hang up the line by dropping the data terminal ready line (DTR) to cause the modem to drop the line. UNICOM watches for a modem response string to determine if the operation was successful. The specific modem response must have been stored in the modem specific setup window in the Response to DTR drop field. Since UNICOM cannot monitor hardware lines such as DCD, this response method is the only way the program can detect a successful disconnect. Should UNICOM fail to obtain this response string, the Hayes attention sequence ('+++') is transmitted to the modem in order to place it into command mode. Once in command mode, the modem is commanded to hang up using the hang up string defined in the Modem Specific Setup window. The message 'MODEM READY' should appear indicating that the operation completed successfully. Should the message 'MODEM NOT RESPONDING' appear on the status line, invoke the HANG UP command again.

Using Keyboard Macros and Hot Keys

Keyboard macros are activated by pressing the corresponding function key for which a keystroke sequence has been defined. Keystrokes are assigned to a particular function key or keypad key using the Keyboard Macro Editor (activated from the Setup menu). Control characters may be embedded in the macro. The '^' prefix is used to identify the character following as a control character. The maximum macro length is limited to 80 characters. These macros may be activated by a mouse click using a Key Macro window containing user labeled buttons. To activate the Key Macros window, select the User Keys item from the control menu.

Event Logging

UNICOM can record program events such as dialing, hanging up and script execution. This feature is enabled (and disabled) using the General Setup Window. Events may be reviewed with the Edit Event menu option. The Event file is a text file that contains the date and time of each event.

Using Chat Mode

UNICOM provides a Chat capability to support keyboard conversations with a person on the other end of a connection. To activate Chat Mode, select Chat Mode from the control menu. UNICOM will split the screen with two listboxes. The top listbox displays characters received from the remote user. The bottom listbox is used to edit messages for transmission to the remote user. Edit the line of text to be transmitted then press ENTER. The edited line will not be transmitted until a carriage return is entered. This allows each line to be edited (or corrected) before transmission. To exit Chat Mode, select the Chat Mode option from the Control Menu.

Host Mode Operation

Host mode allows remote, password-protected access to the files within all directories on a designated drive. The password and assigned drive are set by selecting the HOST option from the Setup menu. To toggle host mode ON or OFF, select HOST MODE from the Control Menu. Once enabled, UNICOM monitors the port for a remote user login. A remote user receives a login prompt differently depending upon the Connection of your communication port. For a Computer connection, a remote user must enter two consecutive carriage returns to begin the login process. For a Modem connection, the remote login process is initiated after the modem generates a connect string when communication is established after the modem answers the phone.

The login process begins with transmission of a greeting file (if defined in the host setup). The host identification string is then displayed and the user is prompted to enter a name. Once a login name is entered, the user is prompted for a password. Should the password be accepted, the remote user is granted access and a bulletin file is transmitted (if defined). The remote user is then presented with a menu. The menu may be a user defined menu (from an external file if defined in the host setup) or a default menu provided by UNICOM. For more complete information on using Host Mode, see Section Eight.

Journaling

Journaling is a feature used to record a UNICOM session for later playback. Keyboard and mouse interaction with UNICOM can be recorded and played back exactly as it was recorded. This can be useful for demonstrating the use of the program or to completely automate an interaction with a remote computer. Journaling has some built in Microsoft limitations: Some dialog windows will only respond to actual input during a journal playback.

Using the Utility Menu

The Utility Menu is an application starter containing application names configured by the user. Once the menu is configured with application entries (as described in section 2), UNICOM can 'Launch' them quickly and easily. A program parameter line can be constructed using the Set Param entry in the Utility Menu.

Enter the parameter to be passed into the edit box above. It will be passed to the next application to be launched. The Window Activation option controls the startup appearance of the application window. A Normal selection will let Windows determine the size of the window. Zoom causes the application to start up in full screen mode. Minimize will iconize the application upon startup. These Window Activation options are relevant to Windows applications only. Should an error occur in the activation of any application listed in the Utility Menu, UNICOM will display the Utility Menu Setup Window.

Exiting UNICOM

UNICOM may be closed by selecting EXIT from the File menu or CLOSE from the System Menu Box. If verification prompts are enabled in the General Setup window, a message box will appear to verify the request. Otherwise, the program will exit with no questions asked.

Select YES to exit, or NO to continue operating UNICOM. You will also be prompted with this message box should a request be made to shutdown Windows from the Microsoft Executive. If there is a special operation in progress (such as a file transfer), a message box will display a warning and ask if you really want to exit UNICOM.

Should this warning occur, it would be wise to answer NO, then check the operating mode of the program. This warning may be avoided by placing UNICOM into terminal operation mode before exiting the application. Again, these verification Message boxes will not appear if verification prompting is disabled from within the General Setup window.

Section Four - Using the Dialing Directory

The dialing directory is an important tool, useful for automating the task of connecting with remote computers. The directory contains the name, phone number, and

communication settings for each system you define. A script file name may also be included that, if used, contains commands that can automate the login process for a specific remote system. Once the communication link is established, UNICOM will open a script file (if the directory field contains a filename) and begin to execute the script commands. UNICOM will expect script files to be stored in the UNICOM Files directory as defined using the File Paths option from within the Setup window.

To access the dialing directory, select DIAL from the Control menu. The dialing directory will appear. When accessed, the directory is loaded with the information contained in the default directory file or from the last directory file opened.. Once activated, you may select a system to be dialed from the directory or perform directory maintenance.

Adding a Directory Entry

Adding an entry to the directory is fairly simple. Select the ADD button from the dialing directory. A dialog box will appear containing edit fields labeled for the system name, phone number and script file. The communications settings for a system are set by making button selections for baud rate, stop bits, data bits, parity and duplex. Press ADD from within the dialog box to add the entry into the directory and exit. Once added, an entry can be easily changed or removed.

Deleting a Directory Entry

To remove an entry from the dialing directory, scroll the entry into view (if necessary) and highlight your selection with the mouse or keyboard. Press the DELETE button to remove the entry. Multiple entries may be removed in a single delete operation. Just highlight all the desired entries then press DELETE. To restore the directory to its original contents, just exit the dialing directory without saving your changes. The deleted entries will appear the next time the dialing directory is displayed.

Changing a Directory Entry

To edit an existing entry, highlight the desired listbox entry and press CHANGE. A dialog box appears with the system name, phone number and script file displayed in the edit fields. The button selections contain the selected communication settings. Make the necessary changes, then press CHANGE. The directory entry will be updated and positioned by name within the directory.

Saving the Directory

Changes to the directory can be made permanent by selecting SAVE from the dialing directory window. This will update the directory file with the contents of the displayed directory. Should you exit the dialing directory after making unsaved changes, you will be prompted to save them. Be *careful and save your changes before dialing*. Once a connection is made, UNICOM will remove the dialing directory if it is displayed. Any unsaved changes will be lost.

Opening a Directory

Many dialing directories may be maintained and stored on disk for retrieval into the directory display. To load a UNICOM dialing directory, select the OPEN option from within the directory maintenance section. A file selection listbox will appear. Once a valid directory file has been selected, the directory listbox will be updated with the file contents. You may begin dialing or editing operations with any directory file once it has been loaded.

Directory Assisted Dialing

To connect to a system listed in the dialing directory, highlight the target system and press DIAL. Dialing may be also be performed with double mouse click on the listbox entry. UNICOM sets the communication parameters to that of the target system BE**FORE** dialing is attempted. Please note: In order for your modem to receive commands properly, the communication parameters must be as follows:

BAUD	Word Size	Parity	Stop Bits
0 - 300	7 or 8	Even	1 or 2
	7 or 8	Odd	1 or 2
	7 or 8	None	1 or 2
1200 or	7	Even	1 or 2
greater	7	Odd	1 or 2
	8	None	1 or 2

Should you attempt to dial a system with communication settings different from above, the modem may not receive commands properly and a PORT STATE message could appear. The PORT STATE message is displayed on the status line along with an error code any time an error occurs during communication. Parity, Framing and Overrun PORT STATE messages may be user disabled from the Comm Port setup window. For a complete list of these error codes and their meaning, see Appendix A of this manual.

Dialing a Remote Computer

When the DIAL button is pressed after making a directory selection, the communication port is configured using the port parameters of the remote system. The modem is then commanded to dial using the phone number selected from the directory. A dialing message will appear on the status line indicating that UNICOM has entered the dialing state. This message also displays the name of the system being dialed.

Once connected to the remote system, UNICOM checks to see if a script file has been defined in the directory to automate the login process. This script file must be located in the defined UNICOM files directory. If found, UNICOM begins processing the script file until it successfully completes or is aborted by selecting STOP from the Script menu. For more complete information on the use of script files, see Section Seven.

Using the Modem Dialing Prefix and Suffix (Long Distance Services)

UNICOM may be used to dial systems using most long distance services. Long distance services require that you perform the following:

1. **D**ial the local long distance access number & wait for a tone
2. Touch tone the desired long distance number in which to connect.
3. Wait for another tone
4. Touch tone your secret access code
5. Wait for a connection

This procedure may be accomplished with the use of UNICOM's dialing prefix/suffix capability. To setup this special dialing feature, perform the following steps.

- Identify the directory entry to be dialed for special dialing. Enter or edit a system entry in the Dialing Directory and place an asterisk in column one of the name field. UNICOM will recognize the entry for special dialing when it is selected.

- Create the dialing prefix and suffix. In this case, the prefix should contain the local long distance access number to be dialed and some trailing modem pause command characters for an additional connection wait. The suffix will contain some leading modem pause command characters since the phone number is limited in length. The remaining suffix will contain the secret access code to authorize your use of the service.

- To create the dialing prefix and suffix, select the EDIT button from within the dialing directory. A pop up window will appear, displaying the currently defined dialing prefix and suffix. To make changes, place your desired strings into the corresponding edit boxes and press OK. The stored dialing prefix and suffix will be made permanent once the system configuration is saved by selecting Save Setup from the setup menu.

The prefix string contains the local access number for MCI. Trailing commas instruct the modem to wait additional seconds for the connection to be made. UNICOM appends a semicolon to the prefix to command the modem to re-enter command mode. This allows full use of the modems command buffer which typically is limited to 40 characters - not enough to hold the prefix, phone number and suffix for one-shot dialing. In other words, when using special dialing, UNICOM commands the modem to dial up to three times. Once for the prefix, once for the phone number and once for the suffix (if defined). To use this feature, your modem must have the capability to reenter command mode after a dialing command. Most Hayes compatible modems support the semicolon to return to command mode when dialing.

Dialing may be performed with just a prefix, in which case UNICOM will not append a semicolon to the phone number. It is not possible to dial the number and suffix less the prefix.

Automatic Redialing

Some remote systems (such as bulletin boards) may require numerous dialing attempts in order to get through. The automatic redialing feature can be used for this purpose. When enabled, UNICOM will re-dial until a connection is established or until redialing is disabled. To enable or disable this feature, set or clear the checkbox labeled 'Redial.' This checkbox is located below the DIAL button from within the dialing directory. Once set, redialing will occur whenever the modem returns no connect responses as defined in the No Connect fields within the Modem Specific Setup Window.

Aborting a Call In Progress

To ABORT a call initiated from the dialing directory, press the ABORT button from the dialing directory or press the ESC key repeatedly. Since the escape key is also used to exit dialog windows (such as the dialing directory) that may be visible, UNICOM will not recognize the ESC key as an abort until these windows have been closed.

Exiting the Dialing Directory

To exit the dialing directory, press the EXIT button or the ESC key. If any changes were made to the dialing directory, you will be prompted to save them. The dialing directory window is automatically closed upon a successful connection to a remote system. When this occurs, any unsaved directory changes will be lost.

Automatic Batch Dialing

A batch dialing feature has been included for dialing within the dialing directory. This feature is useful when trying to connect with one of any number of typically 'busy' remote systems (such as bulletin boards). Batch dialing will terminate if one of the systems being dialed answers or after the last system has been dialed. The batch operation may be repeated if no connection could be established after dialing all the specified numbers by selecting the redial checkbox. Selecting systems to be dialed in batch can be accomplished as follows:

For Keyboard Users: To make a batch selection, hold down the CTRL key and press the UP or Down Arrow key to move to the system to be selected. Select and highlight the entry by holding down the SHIFT key and pressing the SPACEBAR. Repeat these steps to make more selections.
For Mouse Users: Scroll the listbox entry into view using the scrollbar and position the mouse to the desired entry. Hold down the SHIFT key and press the LEFT mouse button to high-light the entry. Repeat this step to select additional systems to be dialed. When all the systems have been selected, begin dialing by activating the DIAL button with the mouse, or entering ALT D using the keyboard.

Manual Dialing

Should you wish to command the modem to dial without the use of the dialing directory, the Hayes dialing command: 'ATD <number> CR' may be entered directly from the keyboard. When dialing manually, make sure that the communication port is configured properly for the system being dialed. Any Hayes command may be entered from the keyboard. Make sure the commands you send do not interfere with the Modem settings defined in the Setup menu. Should you encounter difficulty in operating the modem after sending a manual Hayes command, instruct UNICOM to reinitialize the modem by selecting the MODEM option from the Setup menu. The modem setup window will appear; press ACCEPT to configure the modem to the settings displayed.

Section Five - Transferring Files

A powerful feature of UNICOM is the ability to exchange information between computers. The protocols provided with this software will allow you to transfer files between many different computers. UNICOM performs file transfer tasks in the background, so you may switch to other running applications at any time.

Downloading Files

To download a file into your computer, start the down-load procedure on the remote system and select the DOWNLOAD FILE option from the Control menu. The PgDn key (if not macro defined) or the DOWNLOAD screen button may also be used. UNICOM will then prompt you to select a protocol from window.

You may choose from XMODEM, YMODEM, ZMODEM, Kermit, CompuServe B, Quick B or ASCII protocols. After a selection has been made, UNICOM will prompt you for a filename in which to store the file. You are not prompted for this information for ZMODEM, YMODEM, CompuServe

B, Quick B and Kermit transfers, since the name is provided by the remote.

Throughout the course of the file transfer, an information window is displayed so that you may easily monitor the transfer operation. This window provides the following information: the name of the file, number of bytes transferred, current block number, error count, estimated transfer time, estimated remaining transfer time, elapsed time, characters per second (CPS), % efficiency and any messages generated from the use of the selected protocol.

A graphical bar display gives a visual report regarding the amount of data transferred at any time. For uploading, the bar moves down on a scale that reflects the bytes remaining to be transferred. Downloading causes the bar to move up on a scale indicating the number of bytes received. To abort a transfer in progress, mouse users may select the ABORT button from the information window. Keyboard users must press the ESC key or hit the space bar.

Uploading Files

To upload a file to the remote system, instruct the remote computer to receive a file from you. Initiate the file upload on your computer by selecting UPLOAD FILE from the transfer menu. A protocol selection window will appear.

The PgUp key (if not macro defined) or the UPLOAD screen button may also be used. After selecting an upload protocol, an upload file selection window will appear, to allow you to search your disk for file(s) to be transferred. The file(s) to be uploaded may be entered by name or selected from the listbox containing directory entries. The file selection window will be displayed for non-batch upload protocols.

The Upload Path determines the default directory for making upload file selections. The upload file directory listbox may be set to display files from a different drive. Just scroll the drive letter into view within the list box and double-click on the entry. To change directories, double-click on the directory entries displayed. For ZMODEM or YMODEM file transfers, a Batch Upload File Selection box will appear containing two listboxes.

The listbox on the left displays the current directory of files from which to select. The listbox on the right contains the selected files for transfer. Batch selections are made by double clicking the mouse on a selected file. Keyboard users must highlight the selection and use the tab key to activate the ADD button. Once this is done, the file is added to the right listbox containing selected files. After making the file selection(s), press GO!. The transfer will begin and an information window will appear for monitoring.

File Transfer Protocols

Seven file transfer protocols have been implemented in UNICOM for full background operation:

XMODEM

XMODEM is a block-oriented error checking protocol introduced to the public domain by Ward Christensen. It is widely used by many electronic bulletin board systems. XMODEM transfers a single file at a time. The protocol uses a checksum or cyclic redundancy check (CRC) for error checking. XMODEM can handle text or binary files with over 99% accuracy. UNICOM provides three common variations of XMODEM: XMODEM Checksum, XMODEM CRC and XMODEM 1K(old YMODEM).

YMODEM BATCH

The YMODEM Batch protocol is an extension to the XMODEM/CRC protocol that permits transmission of full pathnames, file length, file date, and other attribute information. The design approach of the YMODEM Batch protocol is to use the normal routines for sending and receiving XMODEM blocks in a layered fashion similar to packet switching methods.

YMODEM G

Developing technology is providing phone line data transmission at ever higher speeds using very specialized techniques. These high speed modems, as well as session protocols, provide high speed, nearly error-free communications at the expense of considerably increased delay time. This delay time is moderate compared to human interactions, but it cripples the throughput of most error correcting protocols.

YMODEM G has proven effective under these circumstances. YMODEM G is driven by the receiver, which initiates the batch transfer by transmitting a G instead of C. When the sender recognizes the G, it bypasses the usual wait for an ACK to each transmitted block, sending succeeding blocks at full speed, subject to XOFF/XON or other flow control exerted by the medium. The sender expects an initial G to initiate the transmission of a particular file, and also expects an ACK on the EOT sent at the end of each file This synchronization allows the receiver time to open and close files as necessary.

If an error is detected in a YMODEM G transfer, the receiver aborts the transfer with the multiple CAN abort sequence. The ZMODEM protocol should be used in applications that require both streaming throughput and error recovery.

ZMODEM

ZMODEM is a second generation streaming protocol for text and binary file transmission between applications running on microcomputers and mainframes. Zmodem is designed for optimum performance with minimum degradation caused by delays introduced by packed switched networks and timesharing systems.

ZMODEM accommodates network and timesharing system delays by continuously transmitting data unless the receiver interrupts the sender to request retransmission of garbled data. ZMODEM, in effect, uses the entire file as a window. Using the entire file as a window simplifies buffer management, avoiding the window-overrun failure modes that affect other windowing protocols.

Resuming an Aborted Zmodem Transfer

UNICOM supports the ZMODEM Crash Recovery feature so aborted transfers may resume at the point of interruption. When ZMODEM Resume is specified by the receiver on the next transfer attempt, the receiver compares the size of the interrupted file to that of the sender. If the sending file is longer, the receiver instructs the sender to resume transmission at the appropriate offset and appends the incoming data to the existing local file.

Kermit

Kermit is a packet-oriented protocol developed at Columbia University and is available on many computer systems. UNICOM supports only the basic implementation of the Kermit protocol. The following Kermit characters are fixed in this release of UNICOM: No 8 bit Prefixing, One char checksum, No repeat prefix.

CompuServe B

CompuServe B is similar to XMODEM in the send/check/reply design but is a host-controlled protocol. The host (CIS) always tells the remote what to do next, no matter what the direction of transfer. Each packet (block) of the transfer contains a header describing the contents of the packet, either information, data or control.

CompuServe Quick B

UNICOM will automatically step up to QUICK B (QB) when requested to do so by CompuServe. QB is a thoughtful extension of B. The extensions include two new types of packets and acknowledgment windowing for drastically improved bandwidth. QB adds CRC-type checksumming capability to the B arithmetic checksum for improved error detection, and extends packet size to 2K (although the current size used is 1K packets) or reduces packet size to 256 bytes.

ASCII

ASCII is a very basic method of data transfer. No error detection is performed and the file should be free of non-printable characters other than carriage returns or linefeeds. Many systems require XON/XOFF flow control to be used for handshaking purposes during ASCII

transfers. If the remote host computer requires XON/XOFF flow control, set UNICOM for XON/OFF operation.

Using External Protocols

External protocols may be activated by executing a specially constructed UNICOM script file. Though their use is not recommended (or guaranteed), external protocols will require UNICOM to perform the following:

1. Release control of the communications port.
2. Activate the external protocol using specific parameters.
3. Go to sleep.
4. Wake up and re-connect to the communications port when the external protocol has completed.

The script file to accomplish these steps (as described) may resemble the following example:

```
INPUTSTRING FILE
"Enter a Download Filename"

INPUTSTRING EXTERN
"Enter the External Protocol"

PORT N
(UNICOM gives up current port)

RUN COMMAND.COM EXTERN
"download command" FILE "port cfg"

SHOWWINDOW "UNICOM 2.0" HIDE

WHILE NOT FOUND
(Wait till the protocol is done)

FINDWINDOW
"Command"

ENDWHILE

(Re-connect and display UNICOM)

PORT
"LASTDEVICE;LASTBAUD;LASTPARITY;LASTWORD..."

SHOWWINDOW "UNICOM 2.0" SHOW

EXIT
```

The above example is presented as a suggestion for constructing script files to support external protocols. It should not be considered as a fully functional model. External protocols written for DOS may behave poorly in the Windows environment when entering and exiting these applications. Multitasking performance can be drastically reduced when executing DOS (external) applications using Windows versions 2 and 3. Use of external protocols with UNICOM is possible, but not recommended.

Section Six - Transferring the Clipboard

The contents of the Clipboard may be transferred between two computers equipped with UNICOM software. Using this feature, many types of Clipboard formats may be exchanged. Some of these formats include: Bitmaps, Metafile Pictures, Text, User Defined Formats, SYLK, TIFF and more.

A Clipboard format is transferred as a temporary file between two UNICOM systems. This requires sufficient temporary disk and memory space on both computers to hold the format. To send a Clipboard format to a remote UNICOM, the user on each end must agree to the transfer operation by using the keyboard to communicate the request. This transfer must be coordinated by both parties so that both UNICOM's can be commanded at the same time - one to receive, the other to transmit.

Sending a Clipboard Format

Many applications (such as PAINT) allow you to place information onto the Clipboard using a COPY option within an Edit menu. The SEND CLIPBOARD option within the Transfer menu is grayed out when the Clipboard is empty. Once a format is placed on the Clipboard, this option becomes enabled. Place the object to be transferred on the Clipboard using the copy option of the originating Windows application. Select the Send Clipboard option from the UNICOM transfer menu. A listbox will appear containing all formats currently held by the Clipboard.

Select the format you wish to send. Before transmission begins, UNICOM will store the Clipboard format to a temporary file in the default directory or in a directory specified by a TMP environment variable (should it be defined on your system). When this temporary file is successfully written and reopened for reading, an information window will appear for transfer monitoring. At this point the transfer has started and may be aborted at any time by pressing the ABORT button from the transfer information window. The Clipboard transfer may be aborted by either UNICOM.

Receiving a Clipboard Format

To receive a Clipboard format from a remote UNICOM, the sender must inform the receiver when the format is about to be transmitted. The sender may type a message to the receiver using the terminal connection. Once the sender has indicated that the Clipboard is being sent, select the RECEIVE CLIPBOARD option from the Transfer menu. An information window will appear to let you monitor the transfer operation. After this window appears, the sender

has one minute to initiate the transfer at the other end before the receiving UNICOM times out. The receiving UNICOM will store the received Clipboard format to a temporary file located in the current directory or in the directory associated with a TMP environment variable (if defined). Once the transfer is completed, UNICOM will attempt to load the Clipboard with the format contained in the temporary file. The temporary file is deleted after it is read. When the Clipboard is successfully loaded with the received format, UNICOM will activate and display the Clipboard if it is not already running.

Check the format name listed on the Clipboard for the name of the expected format. The previous Clipboard contents should have been removed before the received format was loaded. Should the Clipboard Window disappear after first being displayed, it may have been placed behind the UNICOM Window when UNICOM received screen input. The Clipboard can be easily retrieved by re-sizing or minimizing UNICOM to uncover the window. UNICOM provides no facility to store received Clipboard formats. Should you wish to save the Clipboard contents, use the Clipboard file save capability built into Windows 3.

License

b. Vendors of user-supported or shareware software approved by the ASP may distribute UNICOM, subject to the above conditions, without specific permission. Non approved vendors may distribute UNICOM only after obtaining written permission from Data Graphics. Such permission is usually granted. Please write for details (enclose your catalog). Vendors may charge a disk duplication and handling fee, which, when pro-rated to the UNICOM product, may not exceed eight dollars.

Warranty

Data Graphics guarantees your satisfaction with this product for a period of 30 days from the date of original purchase. If you are unsatisfied with UNICOM within that time period, return the package in saleable condition direct to Data Graphics for a full refund. Data Graphics warrants that all disks provided are free from defects in material and workmanship, assuming normal use, for a period of 30 days from the date of purchase. Data Graphics warrants that the program will perform in substantial compliance with the documentation supplied with the software product. If a significant defect in the product is found, the purchaser may return the product for a refund. In no event will such a refund exceed the purchase price of the product.

EXCEPT AS PROVIDED ABOVE, DATA GRAPHICS DISCLAIMS ALL WARRANTIES, EITHER EXPRESS OR IMPLIED, INCLUD-ING, BUT NOT LIMITED TO IMPLIED WARRANTIES OF MERCHANTABILITY AND FITNESS FOR A PARTICULAR PURPOSE, WITH RESPECT TO

THE PRODUCT. SHOULD THE PROGRAM PROVE DEFECTIVE, THE PURCHASER ASSUMES THE RISK OF PAYING THE ENTIRE COST OF ALL NECESSARY SERVICING, REPAIR, OR CORRECTION AND ANY INCIDENTAL OR CONSEQUENTIAL DAMAGES. IN NO EVENT WILL

DATA GRAPHICS BE LIABLE FOR ANY DAMAGES WHATSO-EVER (INCLUDING WITHOUT LIMITATION DAMAGES FOR LOSS OF BUSINESS PROFITS, BUSINESS INTERRUPTION, LOSS OF BUSINESS INFORMATION AND THE LIKE) ARISING OUT OF THE USE OR THE INABILITY TO USE THIS PRODUCT EVEN IF DATA GRAPHICS HAS BEEN ADVISED OF THE POSSIBILITY OF SUCH DAMAGES.

Use of this product for any period of time constitutes your acceptance of this agreement and subjects you to its contents.

U.S. Government Restricted Rights

Use, duplication, or disclosure by the Government is subject to restrictions as set forth in subdivision (b)(3)(ii) of the Rights in Technical Data and Computer Software clause at 252.227-7013. Contractor/manufacturer is Data Graphics P.O. Box 46354 Seattle, WA 98146. The information in this document is subject to change without notice and does not represent a commitment on the part of Data Graphics.

UNICOM 2.0 Order Form

Quantity	Item / Price		
____	UNICOM 2.0 License / $45.00 ea.	Total	_____
____	UNICOM on 5.25" disk / $5.00 ea.	Total	_____
____	UNICOM on 3.5" disk / $5.00 ea.	Total	_____
____	Illustrated Manual / $10.00 ea.	Total	_____
____	Foreign shipping per disk / $2.00 ea.	Total	_____
____	Foreign shipping per manual / $8.00	Total	_____
____	Washington State Residents Only add 8.2% tax	Total	_____
		TOTAL	_____

Select Method of Payment:

VISA ____ MasterCard ____ *Check ____ **BILL ____

Checks drawn on Non-U.S. banks or in Non U.S funds cannot be accepted.

Checks must be in U.S. Funds drawn from a U.S Bank.

** Purchase orders requiring billing, please add $20

Name: _____

Company: _____

Address 1 _____

Address 2 _____

City_____ State_____ ZIP _____

Phone (____) _____ - _____

For charge purchases, enter your card number and expiration date:

__ __ __ __ - __ __ __ __ - __ __ __ __ - __ __ __ __

Exp.____ /____

Signature:

Send this form with payment to: Data Graphics
P.O. Box 46354
Seattle, WA. 98146

To order by phone using your VISA or MasterCard, call (206)932-8871 Weekdays 9am-6pm Pacific Time

Games

Chess for Windows

Version 1.01
GNUchess Ported to Windows by Daryl K. Baker
Copyright © 1991 by Free Software Foundation, Inc., and John Stanbeck

Description

by Brian Livingston

Chess is a Windows version of the chess game GNUchess, distributed free by the Free Software Foundation, Inc. The foundation's primary work is the distribution of a royalty-free, Unix-compatible operating system called GNU (pronounced new, short for "GNU's Not Unix").

To create the screen shot shown in the figure, showing the computer achieving checkmate in the shortest possible time, I tried to get the program to play with me the famous game of "Fool's Mate," in which Black wins in two moves:

1	f3	....	(King's Bishop Pawn to King's Bishop 3)
1	....	e6	(King's Pawn to King 3)
2	g4	....	(King's Knight Pawn to King's Knight 4)
2	....	Qh4	(Queen to King's Rook 5 — checkmate)

The game's "opening book," however, would not accommodate me, since it is programmed not to assume that any opponent would play so stupidly. Therefore, I had to play a total of five moves to end the game:

1	f3	....	(King's Bishop Pawn to King's Bishop 3)
1	....	Nf6	(King's Knight to King's Bishop 3)
2	g4	....	(King's Knight Pawn to King's Knight 4)
2	....	Nc6	(Queen's Knight to Queen's Bishop 3)
3	Nc3	....	(Queen's Knight to Queen's Bishop 3)
3	....	e6	(King's Pawn to King 3)
4	Ne4	....	(Knight to King 4)
4	....	Nxe4	(Knight takes Knight)
5	x	....	(Pawn takes Knight)
5	....	Qh4	(Queen to King's Rook 5 — checkmate)

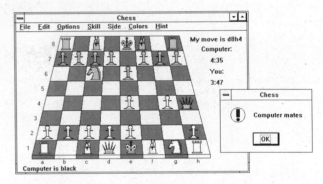

This results in the end position shown in the screen shot. If you want to demonstrate to your friends how good the program is, this little game is the shortest demo possible. If you want to show how good you are, however, you'll have hours of challenging fun.

Since it's a free program, CHESS.EXE does not include documentation or a Help file — it's assumed that you already know how to play chess. Simply pull down each of the menus to see what options are available. One of the first customization steps you'll want to take is changing the program's default time limit from 5 minutes per side to a higher number, using the Time dialog box under its Skill menu. To move the pieces, click with a mouse the piece you want to move, then click the square you want it to move to. To castle, move the King to the position that it should occupy after castling is complete; the program understands that you want to castle, and moves the Rook automatically.

The Free Software Foundation encourages programmers to obtain and examine the Windows source code. This may be obtained on "Chess for Windows" Diskette #2663 for $6 plus $5 shipping and handling (a 5.25" diskette — add 50 cents for 3.5") from PC-SIG, 1030-D East Duane Avenue, Sunnyvale, CA 94086, 800-245-6717 (ask for

Customer Service). It may also be obtained by modem by dialing Channel 1 Communications at 617-354-8873 (1200 or 2400, N, 8, 1). The file to download is CHESSSRC.ZIP, which is located in the Help (5) Conference. This file is over 150 KB in size. For more information on the Free Software Foundation, send a self-addressed, business-size envelope stamped with first-class postage to:

Free Software Foundation, Inc.
675 Massachusetts Ave.
Cambridge, MA 02139

Do not send small contributions. The foundation will send you a catalog, including an order form for a variety of products related to the GNU operating system.

KLOTZ

Version 2.11a
Copyright © 1991 by Wolfgang Strobl

KLOTZ is a game of falling pieces similar to TETRIS for use under Microsoft Windows. Why yet another version of TETRIS? The first reason simply was the wish to have my very own version of this game, as everyone else seems to have. At the CeBit in Hannover here in Germany most booths had some equipment showing falling colored pieces, somehow. In the middle of 1989 a flood of Tetris clones started to show up on Usenet. A second reason to implement it was to have something useful (hah!) to explore the capabilities of Microsoft Windows with. KLOTZ isn't especially well behaved, so please don't take it as a model of a conforming Windows application. It makes too much noise; it grabs the focus or pops up a dialog box when it shouldn't. Its many windows can get confusing. But so what—it's a game!

The program is named KLOTZ.EXE. It stores the scorebook in a file named KLOTZ20.DAT in the current directory or the network directory (see below). This allows you to have more than one scorebook. The position and size of the main window and the position of the dialog boxes can be saved into WIN.INI. These saved positions are used later, automatically. If you want KLOTZ to size and place the windows for you, don't use the Store Desktop function. You will have to edit WIN.INI with an editor and delete the [KLOTZ] section in order to get the automatic positioning back.

Rules of the Game

You get points for every settled piece. How much you get depends on the playing level, i.e., on how fast the pieces move down. If you force a piece down within less than five seconds you can get up to 12 extra points. At level 0 you have 30 seconds before the piece moves down one line, but you get only 3 points per piece placed at the bottom. At level 1 the piece moves every second, and at level 9 it moves over the whole field in one second. At this speed you get 25 points (plus extra points, see above) per piece.

All pieces start at the top of the playing field—same place, same orientation.

The game has a clock. You can hear it ticking, if you have switched Sound to on. At each tick the piece moves down one line. How fast the clock ticks depends on the level; the higher the level, the faster the clock. The level number goes from one to ten. The game normally starts on level five. At level one the piece moves down one line in a second. On level nine it crosses the whole playing field in one second.

If the piece can't be moved at the tick, it will be settled and you get some points for it. Afterwards, you get a new piece. If this isn't possible, the game is finished. In this case your score is compared to the tenth best player. If your score is better, you are asked for your name. If you are already in the Hall Of Fame and your score is better than before, your score is updated. Otherwise you are added. Independent of the clock tick you can move the piece. You can use the numerical keyboard for that purpose. The NumLock key has to be enabled.

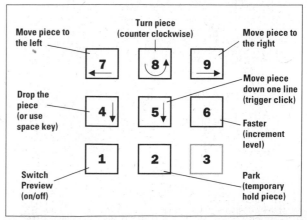

Default keyboard layout

You have five actions (i.e. keystrokes) per line. Any more keystrokes are ignored. Unsuccessful keystrokes count. The ability to turn a piece depends on the target position, not on the possibility to turn it physically into the desired position. So you can turn a stick out of a hole, for example.

The following instructions assume the default keyboard layout.

If you release a piece with key 4, it will not be settled immediately. This will be deferred up to the next beat. You can move the piece in the short time interval between the release and the next beat. Key 5 triggers the next tick. You will find this useful on level 0.

At the tick the following actions occur: Lines which are filled will be removed immediately. All lines above the filled line will be moved down one line. You do not get any points for that, but this is the only way you can get space for new pieces. For every ten lines you get removed your level is increased incrementally, when starting at level one. If you start at a level greater than one, you have that many (ten times the level) more lines before the level is increased. The automatic level increase stops at level 9. You can reach level 10 only with key 6 or the scroll bar in the control box.

If you want to play fast, you can increase your level by using key 6. If you use the scroll bar in the control box of the game to lower the level, your current game is terminated and your score is thrown away. This means, you can't lower your level within a game. Actually, this is not completely true. If KLOTZ cannot move the piece at the intended speed, it decrements the level and freezes it. A frozen level will not be incremented, neither automatically nor manually. Because KLOTZ is not a very large game, there is plenty of space to run other Windows applications concurrently. As long as these other applications don't slow down KLOTZ, this isn't a problem. KLOTZ doesn't try to monopolize the machine, as the commercial AMIGA version of Tetris does, for example. Instead it detects a slowdown and answers with lowering and freezing the level. So you can cheat by dragging around and holding a window to get time, but this will have the effect that you can't get to a higher level anymore. This is visible in the Hall Of Fame.

Key 1 is used to switch the Preview Box on and off. If the Preview Box is shown, you get the points of the next lower level. Key 2 is a bit experimental. It parks the current piece and gives you a new one, which shows up at the usual place at the top of the playing field and starts to move. After this piece is settled, the parked piece starts to move again. You can park more than one piece, if you like. The reactivation policy is LRP (least recently parked). If a full line is removed, the parked pieces above this line will be moved, the pieces below won't. If a parked piece is removed partially as result of a full line removal, it cannot be reactivated anymore.

Operation

There is one main application window for the playing field. All other windows are modeless dialog boxes. You can open and close the dialog boxes at any time. The only required window is the main (playing field) window.

You can resize the playing field at your wish. The game starts with a field which uses the whole screen (without the icon area). The other windows are placed to the right of the playing field. You can resize the playing field and you can move around (and close) the dialog boxes. If you like the layout, you can save it using the menu entry Store Desktop. This saves your window layout into WIN.INI. If Square pieces is checked before resizing, the size of the playing field is adjusted to give square pieces by using the vertical size and adjusting the horizontal size. The menu entry Grid isn't stored into WIN.INI. Sound and Background Color are.

Don't let the Attract Mode of KLOTZ confuse you. What do you have to do to switch KLOTZ into this mode? Nothing particular. Just start KLOTZ and then start another Windows application, i.e. switch to the MSDOS window and start CLOCK, for example. Suddenly KLOTZ starts to play for itself. It does that as long as it isn't the active application. If you go back to KLOTZ (by clicking into the playing field, for example), it will show its normal behavior again.

Background Colors

KLOTZ now uses an optional colored background bitmap. Its generation may take a few seconds and needs a lot of memory. If this isn't available, KLOTZ falls back to the usual gray background. While the bitmap is generated, KLOTZ uses the gray background. This mostly happens under Windows 2.x or Windows 3 in Real Mode. The background color type gets stored when using Store Desktop.

Sound

The handling of sound has been redone; the sound device is opened only if it is really used. Sound doesn't seem to work well under Windows 3 in standard or enhanced mode. I got reports of crashes of Klotz 2.09 under Win3 in standard mode and system clock slowdown (factor five) in enhanced mode. I think I have traced this down to concurrent memory activity and sound usage. **Please don't use sound under Windows 3 in standard or in enhanced mode - it may crash your machine.** Because of these problems I have changed the default to Sound off.

Desktop

The menu entry Store desktop stores more information: sound state, background color, path to the Hall Of Fame file [registered version only]. The new menu entry Square pieces can be checked to restrict the play field resizing to a 1:1 aspect ratio giving square pieces. Use it as follows: select Square pieces, resize the playing field vertically (the horizontal size will be adjusted accordingly), then save it using Store desktop.

Miscellaneous

It is possible to play KLOTZ even if it is minimized and only its icon is visible. Minimize KLOTZ, activate it again by a single click into the icon area, get rid of the system menu by single clicking outside the system menu. Now KLOTZ is active, but minimized. If you use a keyboard layout with numeric keys (the default one, for example), you can play now - if you have good eyes. After placing a piece on top of the playing field, there is one tick without a downward move. This gives a little bit more time when the playing field is nearly full. The keyboard layout is changeable by editing the keys in the Keyboard Help dialog box. So you may use your custom EGAINT keyboard layout, for example.

KLOTZ now has two icons, a monochrome built-in icon, and an external colored icon. An internal colored icon will be added in the next, Windows 3 specific version (if the Windows 3 SDK ever comes to Germany, that is). The Hall Of Fame has been enlarged to fifty entries. Old versions of the Hall Of Fame file will be used and enlarged. Don't use an old (2.09) version of KLOTZ with a new Hall Of Fame file - it will be shortened to ten entries without warning.

The non registered version of Klotz is able to run on a network with a shared Hall Of Fame, but will allow only one player at a time by locking the Hall Of Fame file during the play.

More Information

KLOTZ.EXE is callable from within DOS. If you have Windows and KLOTZ in your path, it starts Windows and then KLOTZ. This is a special KLOTZ feature; it doesn't work with FÜNEF.

KLOTZ20.DAT is protected using a CRC scheme, so please don't mess around with it. This ensures that text and data in the Hall Of Fame aren't hacked.

If your computer is too slow for KLOTZ, you will not be able to play at higher levels.

How to Become a Professional KLOTZPlayer

The following is the result of looking over the shoulders of some of our better players. It takes only a few minutes to learn the game, but it takes months to get the feeling and play it well. But don't play it too much: if you start to dream about colorful pieces, all turning counter clockwise, perhaps you should try something else. Play with borders around the pieces and without the grid on the playing field(default). Learn to use the lookahead box; you will need it on higher levels. Try different positions of the lookahead box; some people prefer it at the top, others at the bottom. If the standard window layout doesn't give you square pieces (it should), adjust the play field and use Store Desktop. Don't give up too early.

Status of KLOTZ and Its Variants (the fine print)

I retain the copyright on all versions of KLOTZ and FÜNEF. You may redistribute KLOTZ version 2.11, if you give it away with all documentation, unmodified, free of charge and without additional restrictions. You may not distribute FÜNEF and NKLOTZ (see below). I have tested and debugged these programs. But there is no explicit or implied warranty. Use them at your own risk.

KLOTZ is the result of a spare time programming activity. Much of it was created during carnival '89, in one week. Later refinements of the implementation were done mostly to explore some hidden corners of Microsoft Windows. So please don't take KLOTZ as the result of a professional programming project. I have other variants of KLOTZ:

FÜNEF, which has a bigger playing field and adds pentominos. Most people here don't play KLOTZ (or TETRIS, for that matter) anymore, because after some training you can play KLOTZ as long as you like, which is boring. After one year of trying only one person here can do that with FÜNEF.

NKLOTZ is nearly identical to KLOTZ, but can use a LAN-wide scorebook.

KLOTZ (D): national language versions of KLOTZ and FÜNEF. I have German versions of KLOTZ and FÜNEF, but would be happy to create others. If you want to get your own NLS variant of KLOTZ and if you are on BITNET, please ask. If I have time, I will send you my resource file of KLOTZ for translation.

So in fact there are six different programs:

English versions:
KLOTZ free of charge, needs no registration
NKLOTZ registered
FÜNEF registered

German versions:
 KLOTZ free of charge, needs no registration
 NKLOTZ registered
 FÜNEF registered

Registered Versions Only

Network: If one of the registered versions of Klotz is played on a PC connected to a LAN, you can put the Hall Of Fame file on a network drive and use it concurrently with other players. If somebody else gets a new score in the Hall Of Fame while you are playing, this is not immediately visible to you, but it will be used if you get a new score into the Hall Of Fame. You can reread the Hall Of Fame while playing using the key 'r', but this isn't necessary. The WIN.INI file may contain an entry like

```
HallOfFame=S:\GAMES\KLOTZ\KLOTZ20.DAT
```

under the heading [KLOTZ] or [FÜNEF] to point Klotz or F̧nef to the Hall Of Fame file. You can enter or modify this

using the menu entry Network... Even if you are not on a network, this may be useful to switch between different players on one machine. ENJOY!

Registration

If you would like to get some or all of the above stuff, please register KLOTZ and send $20 to:

 Wolfgang Strobl
 Argelanderstr. 92
 D-5300 Bonn 1
 FRGermany

I will then send my current versions to you. Because I am living on the other side of the ocean (probably), and because this is not my main job, the delivery may take a few weeks. Please be patient. Thank you.

LANDER v1.1

by George Moromisato
Copyright © 1990 by TMA

Welcome to Lander!

Lander is a real-time simulation of a Lunar Excursion Module on its final approach to the lunar surface. As the pilot of the lander, you must control the vertical and horizontal rockets to guide your craft to a safe landing.

Playing the Game

As a Windows application, Lander attempts to conform to the guidelines set by Microsoft. You may play the game with either the keyboard or the mouse using standard interface conventions. For example, you may make menu selections and interact with dialog boxes as you would in any other Windows program.

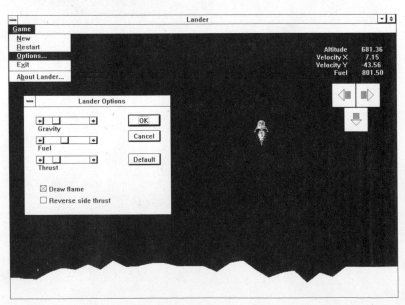

When the game first starts, your lander is at one thousand meters. Press any key or click on the window with the mouse to start the game. The display on the upper-right part of the screen shows your altitude, horizontal velocity, vertical velocity, and remaining fuel. The three buttons below let you apply thrust in three different directions: left, right and down. The object of the game is to land on flat terrain with a horizontal velocity of less than one meter per second and a vertical velocity of less than ten meters per second.

Status Information

The different pieces of information displayed on the screen are described below.

Altitude: The altitude of the lander with respect to the landing pad is displayed in meters. Note that this display is only accurate to within a few meters because of round-off errors.

Velocity X: The horizontal velocity of the lander is displayed in meters per second. If the velocity is negative, the lander is moving to the left; if positive, it is moving to the right. The horizontal velocity must be between -1 and 1 meters per second for a safe landing.

Velocity Y: The vertical velocity of the lander is displayed in meters per second. A negative velocity indicates that the lander is falling towards the ground. The lander must land with a velocity less than ten meters per second.

Fuel: The fuel left in the lander is displayed in kilograms. This contributes to the weight of the lander.

Thrust Controls

The vertical thrust control burns ten kilograms of fuel per second and applies a constant vertical force. The horizontal thrust controls burn two kilograms of fuel per second and apply force horizontally. By default, the right control will thrust to the right, pushing the lander to the left, but you may change this in the Options screen. (See Lander Options.)

New Game and Restart Game

Selecting New from the Game menu will generate a new random terrain and start the lander at one thousand meters. Selecting Restart will restart the lander but use the current terrain.

Lander Options

Several options and parameters can be changed with this screen. The fields available are described below:

Gravity: The acceleration due to gravity may vary from 1.0 to 9.0 meters per second per second in increments of 1.0 meter per second per second. The default is 3.0 meters per second.

Fuel: The initial fuel of the lander may vary from 200 to 2,000 kilograms of fuel in increments of 200 kilograms. The default is 1,000 kilograms.

Thrust: The force applied by the main thruster may vary from 5,000 to 22,500 Newtons in increments of 2,500 Newtons. The default is 10,000 Newtons.

Reverse Thrust: If you prefer the left thrust button to move the lander to the left and the right button to move the lander to the right, select this option. This option is off by default.

Draw Flame: If you want the computer to draw a flame on the lander while it is thrusting, select this option. Because the game is faster if it does not draw the flame, players with slower machines may wish to turn this option off. This option is on by default.

System Requirements

Lander requires Microsoft Windows 3.0 or higher to run; it will not run under Windows 2.*x*.

Source Code

The source code for this program, written in Microsoft C 5.1, is available from TMA for $15. If you would like to see the code, including all resource files and bitmaps, please send a check or money order to:

> TMA
> 15 Whittier Rd.
> Natick, MA 01760
> (508) 655-5823

Name _____

Address _____

_____

_____

Puzzle 1.2

Copyright © 1991 by Paul Beckingham

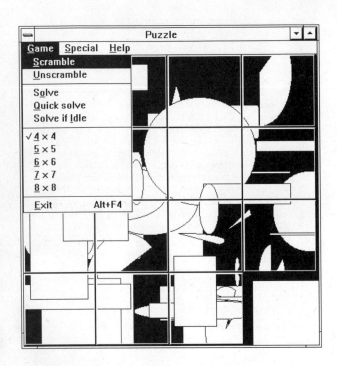

General

How to Play

Puzzle is played by selecting an image to work with, scrambling the tiles, then moving the tiles around by clicking on them with the mouse, or using the arrow keys on your keyboard. Try to reconstruct the original image. Puzzle will let you know when an image has been solved! (See Algorithm for a description of how Puzzle solves itself.)

Using the Keyboard

In order to move a tile using the keyboard, the arrow keys (cursor control keys) are used. In the example, the black tile is moved right, into the space, by hitting the 'left' arrow key.

The tile has moved into the space, leaving a space behind it. The appearance is that the space moves in the direction of the arrow keys. There is an option in the 'Special' menu that will reverse this, so that the right arrow key will move the tile to the left of the space right. See 'Swap key directions' help topic. This option is a preference that is saved when you exit Puzzle. Key usage summary:

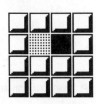

Using the Mouse

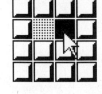

In order to move a tile using the mouse, move the mouse cursor over the tile that you wish to be moved. Note that the tile must be adjacent to the space.

To move the black tile shown into the space to the left, simply click on the tile with the mouse (any mouse button).

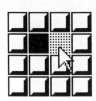

Any tile that is adjacent to the space can be moved into the space by simply clicking on that tile.

Pasting from the Clipboard

To paste an image into Puzzle from the clipboard, select 'Paste' from the 'Special' menu. Puzzle will resize the image to fit the Puzzle window.

Try this: Hit the 'Print Screen' key, then select 'Paste' from the ' Special' menu. The whole screen will have been copied to the clipboard, and then into Puzzle.

Pasting from a Bitmap File

Bitmap files can be loaded into Puzzle by selecting 'Paste from...' from the 'Special' menu. Puzzle will resize the image to fit the Puzzle window. The bitmap file name is saved as a default when you exit Puzzle. There is an option available on the dialog box which forces the image to be Pre-scrambled before it is displayed. This will make solving the puzzle much harder! Try loading some of the wallpaper bitmaps you have.

Problems

If problems or bugs are found in Puzzle, please contact the author, as detailed in the 'About Puzzle...' dialog box. All problems will be addressed. Following are situations where Puzzle does not shine:

- Large, colorful bitmaps consume lots of memory. When memory is low, Puzzle may not function correctly. Tiles may appear blank, and tile numbering may not function. Bitmaps files may not load. Puzzle tries to detect these problems and warn the user.

- When the Puzzle window is large, bitmaps can take a long time to initialize. A smaller window will help.

Game Menu

Scramble

This option will make a series of random tile moves, the result being an image that is mixed up and will require many tile movements to restore. An image may be 'scrambled' several times for greater effect. When an image is loaded from a bitmap file, a Pre-scrambled option is available which will scramble the image before it is seen. Puzzles are very difficult to solve when the original has not been (recently) seen. It will always be possible to restore a scrambled image.

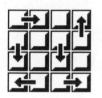

Unscramble

This option restores the image to its original state — unscrambled. This is cheating!

Solve

The puzzle is solved slowly. Solving can be interrupted at any time by clicking with the mouse on the puzzle, or hitting a key. Resume by selecting 'Solve' again, or double-clicking on the puzzle. Try running two instances of Puzzle, and attempting to solve one before the other can solve itself. (**Note:** Puzzle relies on system timers, and if none are available, this option just unscrambles the image.)

Quick Solve

Solves the puzzle as fast as possible. The speed depends largely on the size of the Puzzle window, and how fast bitmaps can be displayed on your system. Quick Solve

can be interrupted at any time by clicking with the mouse on the puzzle, or hitting a key. Resume by selecting 'Quick Solve' again. (**Note:** Puzzle relies on system timers, and if none are available, this option just unscrambles the image.)

Solve If Idle

If Puzzle determines that nothing has happened for a minute or so, it will impatiently solve itself. Turning off this option will prevent this. This option is saved when Puzzle exits.

Number of Tiles

The number of tiles in Puzzle can be changed somewhat to alter the difficulty of solving Puzzle. Grids of tiles in the 4×4, 5×5, 6×6, 7×7 and 8×8 arrangements are available from the Game menu. A larger number of tiles means that it is more difficult to recognize the original location of each tile, and therefore harder to solve. Try numbering tiles to make this easier.

Exit

Exiting Puzzle causes preferred settings to be written to the WIN.INI file. These will be written to a section titled [Puzzle]. Puzzle stores the following information:

- screen location and size of the Puzzle window
- image style (lines, letters ...) and any bitmap file name
- whether tile numbering is in effect
- whether the arrow key directions are swapped
- whether Idle solving is in effect.

Paste

To paste an image into Puzzle from the clipboard, select 'Paste' from the 'Special' menu. Puzzle will resize the image to fit the Puzzle window.

Try this: Hit the 'Print Screen' key, then select 'Paste' from the 'Special' menu. The whole screen will have been copied to the clipboard, and then into Puzzle.

Paste from Bitmap File

Bitmap files can be loaded into Puzzle by selecting 'Paste from...' from the 'Special' menu. Puzzle will resize the image to fit the Puzzle window. The bitmap file name is saved as a default when you exit Puzzle. There is an option available on the dialog box which forces the image to be Pre-scrambled before it is displayed. This will make solving the puzzle much harder! Try loading some of the wallpaper bitmaps you have.

Save to Bitmap File

This option will save a copy of the image currently displayed by Puzzle to a bitmap file (extension 'bmp'). The image is saved as an uncompressed bitmap.

Image Style

There are five different types of image that can be used with Puzzle. Image style can be changed with the 'Special' menu. Where appropriate, Puzzle tries to provide some variation in the appearance and coloring of these patterns.

Lines: Consists of a colored fan of lines, or concentric ellipses. Standard system colors are used to generate this image.
Letters: Presents a more traditional appearance to Puzzle. Standard colors again. Selects a font from any of the installed fonts. This includes the various type faces provided by font management software. **Note:** there are symbol fonts available - don't expect to see just letters.
Shapes: Many colored different shapes, using a color palette. If you have a 256-color display driver, this will be one of the more visually appealing images.
Paste: Will take an image that has been copied to the clipboard, and resize that image to fit the Puzzle window.
Paste from: Will load a bitmap from a file, prompting for the file name. It too will be resized to fit the Puzzle window.

Swap Key Directions

This option reverses the effect of using the arrow keys to move tiles around in Puzzle. The 'up' key will be interpreted as 'down', and 'left' as 'right'. Some prefer to think of the arrow keys moving the space around, and others prefer to think of them moving the tiles around. With this option enabled, the keyboard usage is:

See the help topic 'Keyboard'.

Tile Numbering

Sometimes, when an image is pasted or loaded into Puzzle, two or more tiles may be identical. This option will place a tile identification letter in the lower right corner of each tile. This option can also be switched on, then off to provide a clue to the location of the tiles, which makes some of the more difficult puzzles easier to solve.

Shareware

Puzzle is shareware. This means that Puzzle may be freely distributed, provided this documentation accompanies the program unaltered, and no charge beyond duplication and distribution is made. You may use Puzzle for a trial period. If you use and enjoy Puzzle, you must pay for Puzzle. Please support Shareware. See the 'About Puzzle...' option in the 'Help' menu for details on how to register. Registered users will receive a free copy of the next version when available.

Registration

Registered users will receive a free copy of the next version, when available. To register, please send $7.50 to:

Paul Beckingham 193 Olive St. Ashland, MA 01721

CompuServe: 72230,765 BIX: pbeckingham

Name _____

Address _____

_____

_____

I prefer (check one): 5.25" diskette (   )   3.5" diskette (   )

Utilities

Almanac for Windows

Version 1.04
Copyright © 1990 by Impact Software.

Contents at a Glance

Introduction

Welcome to Almanac!

Almanac for Windows is a full-featured calendar application for the Microsoft Windows operating environment. Version 1.04 of Almanac is compatible with Windows 2.*x* and Windows 3.0 releases. Almanac features include:

- Traditional month calendar display with prior and next month corner calendars.
- Dynamically calculated calendar information for any month, any year.
- Standard Gregorian or Jewish calendar displays. Date conversion maintained when switched.
- Calculation of recurring events including weekly, bi-weekly, monthly, and annual events, religious holidays, birthdays, wedding anniversaries, and span events such as business trips or vacations.
- Special handling of birthdays and wedding anniversaries to include the ordinal year and additionally the traditional and modern anniversary gift themes (i.e., Bob's 24th Birthday, Ted and Sheila's 5th Anniversary Wood, Silverware).
- Desktop mode invoked with a double-click of the mouse or a press of the space bar. The desktop includes scheduler, notepad, alarm clock, day calendar and event viewer. Keep track of notes for each day as well as for each scheduled entry. Alarms may be set with the alarm clock for the current day and can also be selected for schedule entries.
- Configurable world location information is used to calculate sunrise and sunset times and azimuths. Also calculates phases/time of the moon. All times are expressed in local time with the capability of tracking daylight savings time.
- Configure an unlimited amount of calendar environments using auto-load modules and overlays. Auto-load modules specify many parameters including calendar mode, world location, and up to ten overlays, each overlay defining a set of calendar events to display.
- Print support provides for printing of high-quality month calendars, year calendars, notes, and schedule.
- Fonts can be customized for both the video display and print output, allowing selection from all of your Windows and printer fonts.

Installation

Setting Up Your Almanac Environment

Hardware and Software That You Will Need

Almanac requires an IBM Personal Computer or compatible, equipped with the Microsoft Windows operating environment, level 2.0 or higher. A color monitor of at least EGA resolution is recommended, although monochrome and CGA are also supported. Almanac recognizes VGA and several Super VGA resolutions up to 1024×768. The installation will require approximately 300K bytes of file space on your hard disk. More disk space will be required as you use Almanac to create customized calendar environments and keep track of your schedule and notes.

Almanac Files Checklist

Your Almanac release contains multiple files which are used to perform the installation process as well as support your Almanac environment. The following is a list of the files that are required along with a brief description of their use. Please check your installation disk to verify you have received a complete set of Almanac files. Original Almanac files are released by Impact Software in ZIP file format. Extracting an original release file from Impact will produce an authenticity verification if PKUNZIP version 1.1 or higher is used.

Almanac Release Files

ALMANAC.EXE Main program file.
ALMANAC.MST Master configuration file used by ALMANAC.

ALMANAC.ALM Default auto-load module included with this release. Defines default calendar mode, uses USA_HDAY.ALO below.
ALMLOCN.DAT ASCII data base of world locations, their geographic coordinates, and time zone information.
ALMFONTx.FON Custom font files used by Almanac for video display. The lowercase 'x' corresponds to the font suffix used by Windows for font files depending on your monitor type and resolution. In general, the suffix 'A' is used for CGA, 'B' for EGA, and 'E' for VGA monitors. Almanac will load only the fonts required by your display at execution time.
USA_HDAY.ALO Holiday overlay for the United States.
CAN_HDAY.ALO Holiday overlay for Canada.
SWE_HDAY.ALO Holiday overlay for Sweden.
ALMSETUP.EXE Almanac installation utility for setting up Almanac on your system.
ALMANAC.WRI The documentation file that you are reading now.
READ-ME.TXT ASCII text file containing general directions and last-minute updates and changes to this documentation.

Installing Almanac

Almanac comes with an installation utility, ALMSETUP, which must be used to install the Almanac files and properly initialize the ALMANAC.MST parameters. ALMSETUP is a windows application and must be run from a Windows session. The release files should be on a floppy disk or in a 'temporary' directory on your hard disk. DO NOT copy the release files into your Windows sub-directory or any other sub-directory that you want to install the Almanac files to.

1. Windows 2.x users: First change the drive and directory from the Windows MS-DOS Exec window to display the sub-directory containing the release files before starting ALMSETUP. Select 'File' from the main menu of the MS-DOS Exec. Select 'Run...' and enter ALMSETUP. Select 'OK'.
    Windows 3.0 users: Select 'File' from the main menu of the Program Manager (Windows 3.0). Select 'Run...' and enter sub-directory:\ALMSETUP replacing sub-directory with the logical drive and directory containing the Almanac release files.
2. You will be presented with a dialog box allowing selection of the sub-directories for Almanac's files. To accept the default installation paths simply select 'Install'. You may opt to change any of the default selections.

Installation Sub-Directories

Program Directory: Location of the main program, ALMANAC.EXE. This is usually your Windows directory but may be changed to suit individual preferences.

Master Directory: Location of Almanac's support files (i.e., font files, the world location data base) as well as where Almanac will save and retrieve auto load modules. (See 4.1 for a description of auto-load modules)

Overlay Directory: Location to save and retrieve overlay files from. (See 4.2)

Desktop Directory: Location to save and retrieve desktop data files from. (See 3.56)

There is no reason for using four unique sub-directories other than for organizational purposes. You may specify any sub-directory or sub-directories for the different file types. If the sub-directory does not exist it will be created.

3. Select 'Install'. ALMSETUP will copy the release files to their appropriate locations, update the ALMANAC.MST file with your sub-directory selections, and update your Windows WIN.INI configuration file with the master sub-directory for use by Almanac.

4. When the installation has completed, you will be presented with the option to register the Almanac installation if you have not done so already. Registration can also be completed from the shareware splash screen whenever Almanac is started.

Color Icon for Windows 3.0 Program Manager

Version 1.04 of Almanac is compatible with 2.x versions of Microsoft Windows and therefore cannot contain a full-color Windows 3.0 compatible icon. If you are running under Windows 3.0, ALMSETUP will install the file ALMANAC.ICN containing a full-color icon that can be used by Program Manager (Almanac will still display a monochrome icon when minimized). You can tell Program Manager to use this icon for any Group Item that you create by selecting the Change Icon... pushbutton, entering ALMANAC.ICN in the file name edit box, and selecting OK.

Operation

Almanac Basics

Starting Almanac

Almanac can be started in a variety of ways to accommodate your individual preferences and Windows configuration. All standard Windows procedures such as double clicking on the program (and Program Manager icon for Windows 3.0 users) or specifying Almanac to be loaded or displayed by including ALMANAC.EXE on your WIN.INI run= or load= parameter lines can be used.

You may also specify an auto-load module to be used by Almanac on startup by specifying it on the command line or loading Almanac by double clicking on any auto-load module. (Almanac will use the release file auto-load module, ALMANAC.ALM, if one is not specified using

either of these methods). This method can be used with Program Manager (or other commercial Windows' shell packages) by defining multiple Almanac Program Group entries which specify different auto-load modules on their command lines.

The Main Display

Almanac displays the current month's calendar at startup. The status line, located just below the main menu bar, displays the current date and time. The calendar is displayed in traditional wall calendar format with the month and year centered between smaller prior and next month calendars, followed by the main month display. Dates for the main month will display events which have been defined in the current overlays.

Almanac will display different cursor styles for mouse users as the cursor is moved over the components of the display. The cursor will be changed to a pointing hand whenever it is located over a calendar component which will perform an action when clicked or double-clicked. The number of buttons on the cuff of the hand's sleeve indicates whether the area will react to single or double clicks; one button for single and two for double.

For example, if you place the cursor over the last month calendar it will be in the shape of the pointed hand. Double-clicking in this area will switch the main display to the previous month. Likewise the YearView window is activated if you double-click while positioned over the year between the two smaller calendars (press ESC to remove this window from the display). Double-clicking on the status line below the main menu bar will always return the main display to the current date. Almanac makes extensive use of this intuitive 'point-and-shoot' interface wherever possible.

All features accessed by the mouse can also be invoked using the keyboard. Switch to the prior or next month using Page Up and Page Down. Activate the YearView window by pressing Ctrl-Y (a main menu accelerator keystroke).

Almanac's Main Menu

File: The main menu bar is organized into several categories of selections. The first entry, File, contains standard sub-menu selections that can be found in many Windows applications. Open, Save, and Save As... operate upon Almanac's auto-load modules which define the current calendar environment. Almanac uses the 'Master' sub-directory path defined during setup to save and retrieve the auto-load modules. More information regarding these files and their use can be found later in section 4.1. Print... and Change Printer... both invoke dialogs to control the printing of Almanac documents, described in Chapter 5. Save Print Settings can be selected after printing any Almanac document to update the default font faces and sizes and the margin settings.

Settings are saved by document type so that you may select various font and margin sizes for the month, year, notes, and schedule printouts. Choosing Exit will close the Almanac application. Selecting About Almanac... displays the customary icon, release level, copyright, etc.

Overlay: The second main menu selection, Overlay, is used to manage Almanac's overlay files. Add... will prompt you with a list of all overlays (residing in the Overlay sub-directory defined during setup) that can be added to the current calendar environment. Up to ten overlays may be specified in any calendar environment. Remove... allows an overlay to be removed from the environment and Current... will display the names of the active overlays. Clear All removes all active overlays from the environment. New... and Edit... allow you to create or modify overlay files. This procedure is described in detail in Chapter 4.

Select: The next main menu entry, Select, is provided to allow keyboard access to counterpart mouse actions. Today, DayView, and YearView will perform the same functions as double-clicking on the status bar, a date window, or the year respectively. Additionally Date... provides a quick way to skip between distant dates in time.

Config: The Config main menu selection contains sub-menu entries which control many features of Almanac's operation. Moon Phases toggles the calculation of the phases of the moon and their times. When selected, the moon phases are graphically displayed on the video display and printed calendars. The text of the phase and its time and date appear on the brief popup day viewer and the desktop dayviewer. Phases of the moon are calculated a year at a time, and will cause a slight delay when moving from year to year due to the complex calculations involved. Location... invokes a dialog to select a location to be used for the calculation of local sunrise, sunset, and optional moon phase times. For more information describing the location data base see section 7.1.

The Scheduler... selection is used to define parameters used by the desktop scheduler. Christian Holidays and Jewish Holidays toggles the calculation and display of these respective holidays. The next two selections, Gregorian Calendar and Jewish Calendar allow you to toggle the display to either mode. Brief DayView and Desktop DayView toggle the popup action invoked by double-clicking on a date box between these two modes.

The last two selections, Data Paths... and Master Path..., allow you to change the sub-directory paths used by Almanac. Data Paths... can be used to change the sub-directories used for managing overlays and/or desktop data files. Master Path... is used to change where Almanac loads the support files from such as font files and the location data base. Normally this path should be left

alone and is provided only in the event you would like to reorganize your hard disk.

Unlike all other items on the Config menu which are saved in the auto-load module and can vary between calendar environments, the Master Path is saved in the WIN.INI configuration file and does not change.

Preferences: The Preferences menu contains selections which control the initial size and location of the main and popup windows and the fonts used on the display. AutoStart DayView can be toggled to cause Almanac to display the current popup window (either Brief DayView or DeskTop DayView) when Almanac is started. Size DayView Frame will toggle a sizing frame on the Brief DayView window which can be used to change the size and shape of this popup window. Fonts... invokes a dialog which is used to alter the font face and size of the display fonts. When you select Save Display, the current main and Brief DayView popup window sizes and locations are updated in the ALMANAC.MST file in the Master Path sub-directory. The popup window is not required to be on the display when this selection is made.

Selections made from the Preferences menu are stored in the ALMANAC.MST file and are global to your Almanac installation.

Using the Popup Day Viewer

The popup day viewer, or Brief DayView, can be activated by double-clicking on any date in the main month display area. The keyboard may also be used by positioning the highlight rectangle over the desired day of the month using the cursor keys, and then pressing the space bar. (*Note:* To activate the popup day viewer your Almanac configuration must have Brief DayView checked in the Config menu. If you have DeskTop DayView checked, the desktop mode will be activated instead.)

The popup viewer will allow you to view all of the events defined by your active overlays for any given date. It also will display the local time of sunrise and sunset and their azimuths (the direction the sun will be on the horizon). If moon phases have been activated, any moon phase that falls on the viewing date will also be displayed along with the local time of the transition.

Repeating the process of double-clicking on a date will update the popup viewer with the newly selected date's information. The keyboard can be used to perform the same action by pressing the TAB key to toggle the keyboard input focus between the popup viewer and the main window. This will allow the month display to be navigated once again using the keyboard.

The viewer can be removed from the display using the normal Windows procedures to close windows such as double-clicking on the system menu or pressing ALT-F4 when the viewer has the keyboard input focus. (The ESC key can also be used.)

You may toggle between the popup viewer and the desktop mode (section 3.5) by double clicking on the text window of the viewer or by pressing the space bar when the viewer has the keyboard input focus. To return to the popup mode from the desktop you must double-click on the text window of the desktop's day viewer.

The popup window will be displayed in the center of your display when activated for the first time. You may move the window to another desired location of the screen and it will 'remember' the location if removed and reactivated. Select Save Display from the Preferences menu to cause this position to be saved between Almanac sessions.

You may also change the size and shape of the popup viewer as you would like. A sizing frame may be toggled on and off using the Size DayView Frame selection from the Preferences menu. You can drag on the sizing frame to shape the viewer to the size that you desire. The sizing frame can be left on or removed. Use the Save Display selection as described above to save your changes to the frame or size and shape of the viewer.

Using the Desktop Mode

The desktop mode can be activated as described above for the popup viewer. To cause the desktop mode to be entered instead of the popup viewer, select Desktop DayView from the Config menu. The desktop mode is nothing more than another window like the popup viewer, except that it is sized to the maximum display area. The desktop contains several tools which can be used to manage day-to-day information and appointments. You can move the input focus from one object to another by clicking with the mouse or by using the TAB key. As on all of Almanac's windows, remember that a pointing hand cursor indicates a control which will perform an action when clicked with the mouse.

The Day Calendar: The day calendar appears in the upper left corner of the desktop. It will display the date that the other objects on the desktop are currently set to (except the alarm clock) in large, bold characters. A set of controls appears across the top of the day calendar which can be used by the mouse to move the date forward or reverse a day or a month at a time. The keyboard left and right cursor arrows and Page Up/Page Down keys may also be used to perform these actions.

The Day Viewer: The desktop day viewer is located to the right of the day calendar. It functions just like the Brief DayView popup viewer, displaying the overlay information and sun/moon data for the selected date. The input focus is set to the scroll control if one is required, allowing the cursor keys to be used as well as the mouse to scroll the viewing window.

Double-clicking in the text window of the day viewer will toggle the display into desktop mode with the notepad and scheduler.

The Alarm Clock: To the right of the day viewer is the digital alarm clock. Besides displaying the current time, the alarm clock can be used to set visual and audible alarms for today. Double-click on the clock or press the space bar after selecting the clock to activate the alarm setting dialog. Up to five alarms may be set using different audible signals. Enter the message, time, and sound for an alarm and then select Set. You MUST select Set or the alarm will not be activated.

A popup window will appear in the center of your screen accompanied by the audible tone selected when the alarm time is reached. The window will reference the message attached to the alarm and display the current time.

(*Note:* Both Almanac and Windows must be active at the time of the alarm for this to occur. It is not necessary that Almanac be the active window at this time; it may be in the background or iconic. Also, a DOS application running full screen and NOT running in Windows 386 Enhanced Mode will inhibit the alarm from occurring. This is because all other applications are suspended under these circumstances.)

The Notepad: The Notepad is used to include text information attached to a date as well as to any schedule entry. Selecting the notepad will activate the text cursor for creating and modifying notes. The notepad will process most keyboard characters including special ANSI characters. The TAB and DEL keys are not used. The backspace key may be used to erase characters or the Cut function from the desktop Edit menu can be used on selected text.

The notepad will wrap and format text as you type into the notepad. Care should be taken not to attempt to place more characters than will fit on one line without including a space somewhere to allow the line to be wrapped at. Doing so can cause an application error (the next version of Almanac specific for Windows 3.0 will protect against this error).

To save the notepad text, select Save from the Notepad menu. The Restore selection of the Notepad menu will restore any notepad text to that after it was last saved.

Up to eight hundred characters of text can be entered into any notepad entry, depending on the resolution of your monitor display and your Windows display driver.

The Scheduler: The Scheduler is used to track appointments and day-to-day scheduled entries. It is most easily navigated by using the mouse. Double-clicking on the schedule area will invoke the scheduler dialog with a start time nearest the time that was double-clicked upon. From this dialog you may enter a description for your appointment, the start time, and an optional alarm time and audible alert. The start and alarm times have 'loose' links between them. Adjusting the start time will change the alarm time, if selected, by the same amount of time. All times can be entered in abbreviated formats. For example 19 for 19:00 hours if your Windows environment uses military time or 8A for 8:00 AM on a twelve hour clock. Select OK to confirm your schedule information.

Once entries exist on the scheduler, you may double-click on any entry to recall it for modification, or to remove it from the scheduler.

Scheduled entries are given 'pages' in the notepad for notes to be recorded. Clicking on any scheduler entry will recall the notes for the entry on the notepad display. To switch from schedule notes to any general notes for the day, click on the top line of the scheduler labelled General Notes.

Desktop Data Files: Almanac maintains your notepad and schedule information in desktop data files with the filename extension of ALD. The filenames are created using the first three characters of the month and the last two digits of the century (e.g., MAR90.ALD, OCT91.ALD). These files are stored in the sub-directory (desktop data path) that was selected when running ALMSETUP. It is possible to maintain two or more unique desktops of information by changing the desktop data path from the Config menu. All notes, schedules, and alarms are reinitialized using the new desk information when this directory path is changed.

Auto-Load Modules and Overlays

Auto-Load Modules

Auto-Load Modules are used to define different calendar configurations. Almanac comes with a default auto-load module, ALMANAC.ALM. This ALM is loaded by Almanac to define its initial configuration when started. You may make modifications to ALMANAC.ALM by changing your calendar configuration and then selecting Save from the File menu. All parameters that can be changed from the Config menu (except the Master Path) are stored and retrieved from the current ALM. The names of the currently active overlays are also maintained in the auto-load module.

You may select Save As... from the File menu after making changes to your calendar environment to create new auto-load modules. Select Open from the File menu to activate any of your previously stored ALMs. The flexibility provided by using ALM files to control parameters and overlays allows many organizational schemes to be used to meet your calendaring requirements.

Overlays

Overlays are files which contain information about one or more events that allows the dates the events will fall on to be calculated. Each event is identified by a calculation type (i.e., monthly, weekly, etc.) which defines exactly what information is required to perform the calculation.

Overlay files are used by Almanac to dynamically create event information for calendar displays as you navigate through different months and years. This strategy greatly conserves memory and other resources which might otherwise be required to store individual data entries for every occurrence of the event. This does present the limitation of making exceptions to these definitions. We are currently investigating providing the ability to create exception overlay definitions such as 'bumping' events passed holidays or weekends or allowing specific rescheduling to be performed.

You may choose up to ten active overlays at any one time, allowing overlays to be organized by logical categories and then combined on the calendar display to create whatever calendar 'flavor' you are interested in viewing.

Overlays are not intended to be used for displaying appointment schedules or similar information on the calendar. The current lack of an option to display/print your schedule or notes on the main month may prompt you to do so. This is understandable, and we would like to mention that enhancements are being designed to provide these capabilities.

Creating New Overlays: Select New... from the Overlay menu to begin creating a new overlay. An overlay ('untitled') will be created for you to add overlay definitions. A dialog will be displayed for you to use to define the entries. Select New from the dialog listbox to enter a new definition. Another dialog box will prompt you for the type of entry you would like to create. Use the listbox scrollbar to view all of the types that are available for use.

After selecting the type of overlay event, you will be presented with a dialog box which has controls activated for the type of entry you are defining. For example, if you wish to define a recurring fixed annual event, you will be allowed to enter the month and date that the event falls on. If you are defining a monthly event on a particular day of the week, however, you will be required to supply more information. You must select the week of the month and the day of the week. The month and year parameters in this case actually have two values. Selecting the Start/End pushbutton will toggle between the month/year you would like to start the event and end the event. Checking the Red Letter checkbox will display the date numbers in red on the video display.

The Shade... pushbutton can be used to activate colors and patterns to be used when displaying this date on the video display. Select Style to change the pattern of the shade from solid to various cross-hatch patterns or back to 'None'. You may change the color of the fill from the color palette. Note that all standard colors that your video driver will produce are available for selection, although every color may not produce a desirable or readable display. Controls are activated for all required information; be sure that all of these selections are correct for your entry before confirming with OK.

After entering your first overlay entry, several additional pushbuttons will become active in the dialog controlling the build of the overlay. Copy, Edit, and Remove can be selected to act upon existing overlay entries. Copy allows a new entry to be created but initializes all of the parameters to those of the selected event in the listbox. Use Edit to modify the selected entry in the listbox, or Remove to delete it from the overlay. Save and Save As... are also activated, and selecting either one will prompt you for the name to save this file as since it is currently untitled.

Editing Existing Overlays: Select Edit... from the Overlay menu to edit an existing overlay. You will be prompted with a list of all overlays (whether they are currently in the active environment or not) to select one for editing. Selecting an overlay file will invoke the dialog box described in Creating New Overlays, described above. You have access to all of the overlay edit functions to modify the overlay as you wish.

After completing you overlay modifications, select Save to update this overlay file, or select Save As... to save the overlay information into a new overlay file. If the overlay you have updated is currently active in your calendar environment you will be asked if you would like the overlay information refreshed by rereading the overlay files.

The Location Data Base

The location data base file, ALMLOCN.DAT, is located in the sub-directory specified by Almanac's Master Path parameter. This file is read whenever the Location... dialog is activated from the Config menu. The information for a particular location is stored into Almanac's current environment when you make a selection from this dialog, overlaying the previous location data from the current auto-load module.

Many U.S. and world locations have been included with your Almanac release. The data base file can be customized for use using an ASCII text editor such as Windows Notepad. Each location entry is defined on one line. The following is a sample line from the file ALMLOCN.DAT:

Los Angeles, CA: 34 3 15 -118 14 28 -8.0 PST/PDT 4 1 10 25;

The first field for each location is the name (up to twenty-four characters) followed by a colon (:). The next three numbers separated by one or more spaces specifies the

latitude for the location in degrees, minutes, and seconds. This sequence is repeated once again for the longitude. Note that southern latitudes and western longitudes are specified by placing a minus sign (-) in front of the degrees.

The hours offset from GMT (Greenwich Mean Time) follows the latitude/longitude values. This number should include an integer and decimal fraction. The next field specifies the name you would like to use for the location's time zone. If the location observes daylight savings time, you may indicate this by following the standard time zone with a slash and five additional parameters. These parameter values correspond to the daylight name of the time zone, the start month and date of the daylight period, and the end month and date of the daylight period. Each location entry is terminated by a semi-colon (;). Entering the locations in alphabetical order is not required.

Almanac does not perform any error checking of the location file as it is being read into memory. Mistakes made entering new locations could cause Almanac to error or abort. Verify that you can select and use new locations after updating the ALMLOCN.DAT file.

Printing with Almanac

Configuring the Target Printer

Almanac provides a Change Printer... selection on the File menu as do most Windows applications. Use this selection to invoke a dialog which allows you to select a printer for use and optionally to configure the printer. Choose a printer from the listbox and select OK to select the printer for use, or select Setup... to invoke the printer driver's configuration dialog. The configuration dialog will vary from printer to printer. Most drivers allow the selection of portrait or landscape print orientation. If your printer uses optional fonts you may specify the cartridges which are currently available to the printer or the soft fonts you would like to download.

Choosing landscape mode for your printer can provide a larger area to print a month calendar on. Some print drivers print landscape mode better than others. Most laser printers give spectacular results in portrait and landscape, while the HP DeskJet does not support any landscape fonts.

Printing

Almanac can print month calendars, year calendars, notes, or schedule (with or without notes). Select Print from the File menu to invoke the print dialog. Four radio buttons allow the selection of information to be printed. A checkbox to include schedule notes is displayed if scheduler information is selected.

The range in time for the print operation is specified using the From: and To: edit boxes. The format of the from and to times will change depending on the print type requested. Always enter complete year values, not just the digits of the decade.

Selecting the More... pushbutton will expand the print dialog and allow you to change font face names and sizes to be used for printing. Top and left margins and print height and width may also be specified for all print operations except the year calendar. The year calendar is always centered on the printout and its dimensions are dictated by the font sizes which you select. Changes made to fonts or margins may be saved as defaults in the ALMANAC.MST file by selecting Save Print Settings after printing any document.

Almanac Operational Information and Suggestions

Managing Calendar Environments Using Auto-Load Modules

Auto-load modules are used to define many aspects of your calendar environment. They are controlled and managed from the File selection on the main menu. Just as you might open a text document under a word processor or a table in a spreadsheet application, opening an auto-load module controls the information displayed on your screen and the format in which it is displayed. You can create as many auto-load modules as you like by changing your current calendar environment and then selecting Save As.... Subsequent opening of any auto-load module will reset the calendar environment to as it was when that module was last updated (this does not include the date that the calendar was set to when the auto-load module was saved, only the configuration settings).

Auto-load modules contain the overlays to load and calculate from as well as the parameter settings for all of the items found on the Config menu selection except the Master Path. Up to ten overlay files can be included in Almanac and specified in auto-load modules. Only the overlay names are stored in the auto-load modules, NOT the overlay definitions themselves. The overlay files are read and processed when the auto-load module is opened.

You should not delete an overlay file using the File Manager or other application before removing it from all auto-load modules that you will be using. If you forget, Almanac will display a notification message when it tries to open the non-existent file. To stop this from occurring you must select Clear All from the Overlay menu, re-add all other overlay files using Add..., and then select Save from the auto-load module from the File menu.

Managing Overlay Files

Overlay files are used to define recurring events and holidays. Almanac allows up to ten overlays to be active to allow you to organize your overlays according to your

own personal needs. You may then 'mix and match' your overlays in different auto-load modules to add even greater flexibility to your calendar displays. A little bit of forethought about how to best divide your information into overlays will make using Almanac easier and more productive.

For example, you may decide to create one overlay with all of the birthdays of the members of your family, or you may also include wedding anniversaries or birthdays of friends as well. It is much easier to use more overlays and group them into auto-load modules as you desire. This allows for greater flexibility when you want to examine or display certain groups of overlay events, even if only temporarily.

Overlay files were not intended to be used to enter items such as appointments or business dates, although you can do this if you find it useful. The next version of Almanac will attempt to provide for more enhanced month and week displays including schedule information and possibly notes, as well.

Registration

Registration and Licensing

Almanac Registration Options

At Impact Software we recognize the needs and capabilities of different computer users. Two types of registration packages are offered in order to provide you with the level of service that best suits your requirements. Almanac can be registered for use with the package options described below. The Almanac software in each package contains the same features and capabilities. The Basic registration is provided for those users who have easy access to BBS networks using a communications package and modem and who enjoy obtaining quality software at lower shareware prices. The Premium package is targeted for those users who do not have ready access to shareware updates and/or prefer the benefits of a retail software package.

Basic Registration: With the Basic registration you will receive a license number which will prevent the shareware screen from soliciting you for $$$ and also display your name as a registered user at start-up. This registration will be good for all future shareware versions of Almanac. The basic registration does not include update disks or manual. It is up to the user to acquire any future releases of Almanac either directly from our support BBS at Impact Software (telephone 714/590-0500) or through the normal shareware distribution outlets such as electronic bulletin boards, shareware mail order catalogs, etc.

Premium Registration: With Premium registration you will receive the latest version of Almanac on either 5.25 or 3.5 inch floppy disks. This version contains its own license number and will not display a shareware screen upon startup. Along with your new software you will receive a registration card and a bound, professionally printed operation manual for Almanac. As a premium user, you will be notified of new releases of Almanac and their features and will be offered upgrade packages at a discount rate.

Registration Upgrades: A Premium Upgrade option is available for users who have a Basic registration and would like to upgrade to Premium. Shareware users who have registered prior to September 30, 1990 and would like to upgrade to the full-service Premium registration may do so at a 50% discount rate.

Registration Form

License request for Almanac for Windows
Copyright © 1988-1991 by Leonard A. Gray

Almanac is licensed on a per-user basis. The license grants the user the right to install and use the software on one or more computers so long as the total number of users does not exceed the license quantity.

Please include the following information:

Name _____

Street _____

City _____

State/Prov _____ ZIP _____

Type	Qty	Price	Total
Basic Registration	____	x $34.95	_____
Premium Registration	____	x $59.95	_____
Disk Size: __ 5.25 __ 3.5			
Premium Upgrade	____	x $29.95	_____
Disk Size: __ 5.25 __ 3.5			

(If registered prior to 10/1/90 use $14.95)

(Registration number required. See below)

Sub-total_____

California residents add 6.25% sales tax._____

Shipping (Premium only)_____

U.S. and Canada add $4.00 per registration._____

Outside U.S. add $10.00 per registration._____

Grand total:_____

Upgrade requests must include:

Name: _____

Reg #: _____

If you are requesting an upgrade package, please be sure to enter your name requested above exactly as it appears on your current registration. Also include your registration name and number in the space provided. If you do not have your registration information handy, your registered name and number can be found in your Windows configuration file, WIN.INI. The WIN.INI file is located in your Windows directory and can be viewed with the Windows Notepad application. Your registration information will be located under the [Almanac] section in the 'RegName=' and 'Reg#=' fields.

Premium upgrades at reduced rates are only available to users registered before September 30, 1990. You do not have to include proof of the registration date. This information has been recorded during processing of your registration.

License requests from outside the United States: Registrations will be processed upon receipt of U.S. funds in check or money order (cash discouraged, but accepted).

Mail check or money order to:

Impact Software
12140 Central Avenue
Suite 133
Chino, CA 91710
U.S.A.

Thank you for supporting the shareware software concept and encouraging the future development of Almanac for Windows.

Windows is a trademark of Microsoft Corporation

Impact Software
Chino, California
U.S.A.
Voice: (714) 590-8522
BBS: (714) 590-0500

Application Timer

Copyright © 1991 by InfoPerfect, Inc.

The AT.EXE program launches programs at a specified time, or at regular intervals. It can be used to automate backups, asynchronous communications, CPU intensive calculations, etc. It is an easy program to use. Just set the time, date and the program to be launched, and as long as the AT program is running, it will launch your program. It will launch DOS programs as well as Windows programs.

If you plan to use AT.EXE for Daily or Weekly program launching, you should have the program automatically load when you run Windows. To have AT.EXE automatically load as an icon, first associate the .AT extension with the AT.EXE program. Then put your .AT file on the LOAD= line of your WIN.INI file. Example:

```
load= C:\AT\RUNAUTO.AT.
```

The program does not have to be the foreground task to launch applications.

The program is designed to run under Windows 3.0 and use a minimal amount of CPU time. You may set the frequency at which the computer checks for a program to launch. The recommended time is 100 (1 second). With the default setting, you will probably not notice any slowdown on the system. If your computer experiences any slowdown, or your operations are not time critical operations, you may want to increase the number.

To create an .AT file, choose Configure Add, and fill in the time and date that you would like to have the program launched. If you would like the program to be launched at regular intervals, choose one of the intervals, and then set an ending time. For example: If you chose Daily interval, then the program will launch every day at the same time until it passes the Ending Time. You may specify an entire command line in the Run field. Be sure your system clock is correct because the AT program compares the time against your system clock.

To edit an entry in the .AT file, select an entry, and choose Configure Edit, or you may double-click on an entry. This will allow you to make any modifications you would like. The item that you are editing will be inactivated until you have made your modifications and hit OK.

To delete an .AT file entry, select an entry, then choose Configure Delete. You will not be asked for a confirmation.

To use the Application Timer program you must have computer running Windows 3.0. The program works best on a 386 or 486 computer. If you have a 286, be aware that if you launch a DOS program, the DOS program will take control of the machine, and the Application Timer will not be able to launch other programs until the DOS program has been either iconized or exited. For those fortunate enough to have a 386 or 486 computer, the same thing is true for those programs that run in exclusive mode.

The shareware version has been modified to launch programs unattended 90% of the time. For the other 10% it will pop up a confirmation message. This makes the shareware version unacceptable for unattended operation. AT.EXE is a copyrighted program; however, copies of the program may be distributed as long as all documentation and copyright notices are kept with it. The program can be registered for a mere $15.00. For the registration fee you will get a full working version of the program. The fifteen dollar registration fee is a bargain considering a similar program sells for $149.00.

Company names and products are trademarks and registered trademarks of their respective owners.

InfoPerfect Inc. specifically disclaims all warranties, express or implied. Including but not limited to, any implied warranty of merchantability or fitness for a particular purpose. In no event will InfoPerfect's liability for any damages to you or any other person ever exceed the registration cost paid to license the program, regardless of any form of the claim.

Application Timer Registration Form

Name: _____

Address: _____

City: _____

State: _____ Zip: _____

Comments: _____

_____

Disk format : _____ 3.5" _____5.25"

Enclosed is $15.00.

Send to: **InfoPerfect Inc.** **4480 Atherton Drive Suite #22** **Murray, UT 84123**

Mark30

Version 1.50
Copyright © 1990 by Charles E. Kindel, Jr.

Please read this document carefully before attempting to run Mark30 on your system. Mark30 was designed to defeat the mechanism within Windows 3.0 that detects Windows 2.x applications.

Use with EXTREME care! Serious data loss could occur if an ill behaved Windows 2.x application crashes under Windows 3.0! **Use this program at your own risk!** Charles E. Kindel, Jr. IS NOT responsible for any damages caused by the use of this program.

Mark30 DISTRIBUTION FILES

- Mark30.EXE - Mark Three-Oh v1.50 program.
- Mark30.DOC - This Document.

Introduction

Mark30 is a Windows 3.0 utility that marks old Windows applications so that they will run under Windows 3.0 without the Windows 3.0 warning message. This utility does no checking of the application being marked, except to verify that it is a Windows application. There are two flags in the header of a Windows executable file (called the "new executable format"). The memory flag indicates that the application makes clean use of memory, thus enabling it to run under Windows 3.0 in protected mode. The font flag indicates whether the application can handle the proportional system font in Windows 3.0. Mark30 allows you to set and unset both of these flags.

Many Windows 2.x application work fine under Windows 3.0, but many do not. If you have a Windows 2.x application that works under Windows 3.0, and you are tired of the annoying warning message Windows 3.0 gives you each time you run your program, Mark30 will save you. **Important!** Just because a Windows 2.x application APPEARS to work under Windows 3.0 don't assume it is completely compatible, there may be situations where the application will fail!

Usage

To use Mark30, simply start it as you would any Windows application. When it starts up, you are presented with a file selection list box, two check boxes, and several buttons. Select a file either by typing a name in the edit control, or by clicking on a name in the list box. You may also change directories and drives as you normally would in a Windows application. Once you have selected a file, choose the flags you want set. The font flag can only be

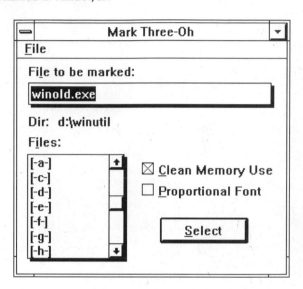

set if the memory flag is set. Press the "Mark File" button to mark the application. If the application you chose is not a Windows application, a message box will appear informing you of this. If the application IS a Windows program, a warning dialog box will appear, asking you to confirm your choice. Once a file is marked, it can be "unmarked" by reversing the check boxes. That's all there is to it!

Copyright Information

Mark30 is a commercial copyrighted program protected by both U.S. and international copyright law. You are authorized to use and distribute it without charge. Mark30 is distributed as freeware. Mark30 may be freely copied and distributed as long as the following three rules are followed:

1. The program and this documentation are not modified in any way, shape, or form.
2. A copy of this documentation (Mark30.DOC) accompanies each copy of the program (Mark30.EXE).
3. No charge, other than a media and handling charge (not to exceed $5.00), is made.

Please send all problem reports, suggestions, and multi-million dollar donations to:

Charles E. Kindel, Jr.
3000 118th Ave, SE, A-203, Bellvue, WΛ 98005
CompuServe: 71551,1455

PKZIP / PKUNZIP

Version 1.1

Contents at a Glance

You will find the complete document on the enclosed disk.

The following 12 files are included in PKWARE Version 1.1:

PKZIP.EXE Main compression program
PKUNZIP.EXE Main extraction program
ADDENDUM.DOC Describes new features of Version 1.1 not in MANUAL.DOC.
ZIP2EXE.EXE Used in creating self-extracting files
README.DOC General Information
DEDICATE.DOC Dedication of file format and extension to the public domain
ORDER.DOC Registration information and order form

LICENSE.DOC Information on Site and Distribution Licenses
OMBDSMAN.ASP Association of Shareware Professionals info
MANUAL.DOC Reference manual for PKWARE File Compression Programs
APPNOTE.TXT Technical background material
PKZIPFIX.EXE Reconstructs corrupted ZIP files

File Compression

The term "compression" means to reduce in size. Computer file compression refers to reducing files in size so that they take up less storage space on disk. PKZIP will perform this reducing process quickly and easily. The compressed files are then stored in a special file called a ZIP file.

ZIP files have three distinct benefits:

1. They use less disk space than normal files. Storing files in compressed form increases the life and storage availability of your expensive hard disk.
2. Many individual files can be compressed into a single ZIP file. This makes file group identification, copying, and transporting faster and easier.
3. Compressed files travel faster via modem which reduces telecommunication transmission and reception. Many BBS (computer bulletin board services) use PKWARE files as their standard. This enables the BBS to store more files and you to have transfer files faster and easier.

Two Related PKWARE Programs —

PKZIP & PKUNZIP

Together, PKZIP and PKUNZIP handle all of your file compression needs. PKZIP is the program that compresses files. This shrinking process is often referred to as data compression. Terms you will see during the compressing process are Storing, Shrinking, and Imploding. PKZIP also handles all file maintenance including adding and deleting files, as well as reporting on technical information from within the compressed file.

PKUNZIP is the program that uncompresses or extracts compressed files. In addition to extracting a complete ZIP file, it can selectively release individual files, show files on the screen for fast viewing, or print them out on a printer.

QUICK START - Extracting a ZIP File

Follow this example to UNZIP your files:

C:>PKUNZIP	A:AnyFile.XYZ	C:
the UNZIP command	Name/ Location of file being extracted	Drive/Path to locate the files on
> The command *must* be located at the prompt **or**	> Use any MS-DOS file notation	
> The program can be located elsewhere through the PATH= setting		

QUICK START — How to Compress Files

Use PKZIP to reduce or compress the size of your files. All compressed files are stored in a ZIP file, while in their compressed state. The benefits of Compressing are:

- Better use of disk storage area
- Faster telecommunication file transfer via a modem
- Collecting numerous files under a single file name

PKZIP uses 4 areas typed at the prompt: PKZIP, ZIPFILE, [options], [files].

1. The actual program name—PKZIP
2. The command options—letter commands, example: -a = add files
3. The name *you* give your ZIP file and its location. If no extension specified, default = .ZIP—NewFile and LOCATION
4. The files that get compressed into the ZIP file—any MS-DOS file notation

Examples:

    C:>PKZIP -a   A:NEWFILE   *.*

This will create a file named NEWFILE.ZIP. The .ZIP extension will be added automatically when the ZIP file has been completed. In this example, all of the files in the current directory will be compressed into NEWFILE.ZIP.

    C:>PKZIP -a   B:BUDGET
    \LOTUS\Checks.Wks \LOTUS\Money.Wks

This will create a ZIP file named BUDGET.ZIP on the B drive. It will contain two files, both currently located in the C:\LOTUS directory.

SnagIt

Version 1.6
Copyright © 1991 by TechSmith Corporation, Inc.

Overview

SnagIt 1.6 is the print utility that Microsoft Windows forgot. Windows changes the meaning of your PrintScreen key from printing the screen, to sending a copy of it to the Clipboard. SnagIt is a screen-print program to regain this function for Windows. With SnagIt 1.6, you can:

- Capture screens and windows and send them to your printer by pressing Ctrl+Shift+P.
- Select different forms of color-to-monochrome conversion for printing to black-and-white printers.
- Scale the printout to any size supported by your printer.

Potential users:

- Developers will want to use SnagIt to print program screens and windows.

- Documentation writers can use SnagIt to print screens and windows for manuals, marketing literature, and other documents.

- Advanced users can use Dynamic Data Exchange (DDE) to control SnagIt's printing functions from other Windows applications.

This free version of SnagIt is a fully-functional Print Screen utility for Windows. Some advanced features, such as writing screens to a file, are not available in the free version, and thus are "grayed out" on the menus. These features are implemented in the Advanced upgrade version. See the "Registration" section of this manual for details on upgrading.

The TechSmith Corporation is a computer consulting and software development company located in Okemos, Michigan. We provide a full range of services to organizations assessing or implementing Windows or OS/2 applications for use in distributed systems. We concentrate our services on those areas that are most likely to complement the capabilities within our customer's organizations. We offer assistance during the assessment and design and development phases. We offer an extensive background in the successful implementation of distributed applications on Windows and OS/2 platforms. Our experience includes projects using all major network topologies, protocols, LAN operating systems, and many LAN-based commercial products.

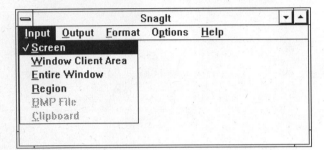

Installation

System Requirements:

- Microsoft Windows 3.0
- A printer that supports bitmaps, such as an HP LaserJet or a Postscript Printer

Installation Steps

1. Copy the file SNAGIT.EXE to your windows directory.
   Example: COPY A:SNAGIT.EXE C:\WINDOWS
2. Start Windows.
3. Select the Accessories Group.
4. Create a new program item for SnagIt with the Program Manager. (Consult your Windows Users Manual if you need help with this operation.)

To load SnagIt automatically each time you start Windows:

1. Edit your WIN.INI file, in the Windows directory
2. Add SNAGIT to the load line.
   Example: Load=CLOCK SNAGIT
   This will load the Clock and SnagIt as icons.

Getting Started

In this section you will:

- Learn how to use some of the basic features of SnagIt
- Create your first screen print

Loading SnagIt

1. Start Windows.
2. If you configured your WIN.INI to load SnagIt automatically, you will see the SnagIt icon displayed at the bottom of your screen.
3. If SnagIt has not been automatically loaded, activate SnagIt by double-clicking on the SnagIt icon in the Accessories Group.

Selecting the Print Area

SnagIt can print the entire screen, a selected region of the screen or a single window. Select the print option, by first double-clicking on the SnagIt icon to restore SnagIt to a window. The SnagIt window will display the current settings. Click on the Input menu item to view the list of options. Select one of the following options:

Screen: Prints the entire screen.
Entire Window: Prints a single window.
Client Area: Prints only the window client area (the text area of Notepad, for example).
Region: Allows you to select a rectangular region anywhere on the screen.

If you selected Entire Window, Window Client Area, or Region from the Input menu, SnagIt will ask you to pick a window or region when you print.

Printing

To print, press Ctrl+Shift+P.

- If you selected the full Screen option from the Input menu, SnagIt immediately sends the entire screen to the printer, and displays a "Printing" dialog box.
- If you selected anything other than the full Screen option from the Input menu, your mouse pointer will change to a pointing finger for selecting a window, or to a crosshair for selecting a region.
- If you selected Entire Window or Window Client Area as the input area, position the pointer on the title bar of the window you wish to print and press the left mouse button.
- If you selected Region as the input area, position the pointer at the upper-left corner of the region you wish to print. Hold down the left mouse button, drag the pointer to the lower-right corner of the region and release the mouse button.

You can cancel the selection process by clicking the right mouse button. To cancel the printing operation, click on the Cancel button in the "Printing" message box that appears. The portion of the image already sent to the printer will still print.

Feature Reference

Mouse Controls

Left Button: The left mouse button is used to select SnagIt menu options and to select screen images.

Right Button: The right mouse button is used to cancel a selection operation.

Keyboard Controls

Ctrl+Shift+P: Activates SnagIt

Input Menu

The Input menu is used to select the image type that SnagIt will print. The currently-selected option is marked by a check mark. The different input options work as follows:

Screen: Select this option to print the entire screen.

Window Client Area: Select this option to print only the client area of a single window. The client area is the area surrounded by the window borders. The client area does not include the borders, title bar, scroll bars or the caption line. After you press Ctrl+Shift+P, select the client area you want to print by positioning pointer anywhere in the client area then clicking the left mouse button.

Entire Window: Select this option to print an entire window. After you press Ctrl+Shift+P, select the window to print by positioning the pointer over the title bar, then clicking the left mouse button. **Note:** Always select the window you want to print by clicking on the title bar. Items within a window, such as OK and Cancel buttons, are actually small windows. Icons are considered windows as well. Clicking on one of these items will result in that item printing, not the entire window.

Region: Select this option to print a rectangular region of the screen. After pressing Ctrl+Shift+P, select a region by positioning the pointer over the upper-left corner of the region. Press and hold the left mouse button. Then drag the pointer to the lower right-hand corner of the region and release the mouse button.

The Advanced version of SnagIt also supports the following Input options:

Bitmap File: Select this option to print an image stored in a bitmap file. When you press Ctrl+Shift+P, SnagIt will display a dialog box requesting the file name. Bitmap files are graphics files generated by some paint programs, SnagIt or other Windows programs. Bitmap files have a file extension of .BMP.

Clipboard: Select the clipboard option to print the contents of the Windows clipboard. Items are placed on the clipboard by using SnagIt or the cut and copy commands in other Windows programs.

Output Menu

The Output menu is used to select the output device for the images captured by SnagIt. SnagIt 1.6 supports the following output devices:

Printer: Select Printer to send the output to the currently-selected Windows printer.

Using the Windows Clipboard: To copy the entire screen to the Clipboard, press the PrintScreen key. To copy just the active window, press Alt+PrintScreen. To save the Clipboard to a bitmap file, open Windows Paintbrush, click Edit Paste, then click File Save.

The Advanced version of SnagIt also supports the following output devices:

Bitmap File: Select BMP File to write the captured image to a BMP file. After you select an input image, SnagIt displays a dialog box asking for a file name.

TIFF File: Select TIF Mono File to write the captured image to a TIFF file. After you select an input image, SnagIt displays a dialog box asking for a file name.

Clipboard: Select Clipboard to send the input image to the Windows Clipboard.

Format Menu

SnagIt 1.6 supports two different format options: Monochrome and Color. Select the format option with the Format Menu. The currently-selected option is identified by a check mark. The format options work as follows:

Monochrome: The input image is converted to monochrome before it is sent to the output device. The Intensity Threshold level (0% to 100%) determines the amount of black and white that will appear in the output image. When you select Monochrome, a dialog box is displayed for setting the Intensity Threshold.

Color: All color information for the selected image is sent to the output device. The Advanced version of SnagIt also supports Gray Scale (dithered) format:

Gray Scale: When Gray Scale is selected, colors are represented by up to 256 shades of gray. **Note:** Gray scaling large images may take a while to complete.

See the Advanced Topics Section for further discussion on formatting options.

Options Menu

Scale: This option allows you to enter an integer scaling factor to be applied to the input image. A scaling factor of 2 will double the size of the input image.

The Advanced version of SnagIt also supports the following options:

Alert: Set the alert options to have SnagIt signal you with a beep(s) when it has completed processing. There is an alert option for both input and output processing. The values entered for these fields determine the number of beeps. This feature is particularly useful when using the Gray Scale option.

Clipboard Chain: Clipboard Chain - Setting the clipboard chain option causes SnagIt to print each time the clipboard changes. Clipboard chaining is useful for doing a Print Screen from a DOS session. When you press the PrintScreen key in a DOS box, Windows copies the screen to the clipboard. If you have the clipboard chain option set, SnagIt automatically copies the image to the printer for you. **Note:** To select Clipboard Chain, the input device must be set to Clipboard, and output device must be set to Printer.

Color Boost: Color boost is used to adjust the color intensities for Red, Green, and Blue. When Color Boost is selected, a dialog box is displayed for color boost values. You may control the intensity for each pixel two ways:

1. Add or subtract intensity levels (hue) for each color range by entering a value from -255 to 255.
2. Increase or decrease intensity levels by a percentage (saturation) by using the slider bar. The default value for each additive range is zero and the percentage bar is 100%. To activate color boost, click on the "Use Color Boost" check box. Color boosting, if enabled, is applied to the input image before it is sent to the output device. For further discussion on the use of color boost, see the Advanced Topics Section.

Save Setup

The Advanced version of SnagIt can save all of the currently selected options. The Save Setup option is located under the system menu. The system menu is accessed by pressing Alt Space or by clicking on the minus sign in the upper left corner of the SnagIt window. When you save the setup, SnagIt writes all of the current settings to your WIN.INI file. SnagIt will read the saved setup each time it is loaded

Advanced Topics

Monochrome Conversion

When Windows converts a color image to monochrome, it converts the background color to white. All other colors are converted to black. This usually results in most of the image getting converted to black. SnagIt uses an Intensity Threshold to control the level of black and white resulting from the conversion process. SnagIt looks at the intensity

level of each pixel and converts higher intensities (lighter colors) to white and lower intensities (darker colors) to black. This conversion process usually results in a more even balance of black and white in the output image. The amounts of black and white are controlled by adjusting the Intensity Threshold value under the Monochrome setting of the Format Menu. You may also use the color boost values to adjust color intensities before conversion to monochrome.

You will get different results converting images to monochrome if you use the Windows Setup program to configure Windows for a monochrome monitor. You may need your Windows diskettes the first time you do this. When configured for a monochrome monitor, Windows creates grays as patterns of black and white dots (dithering), which will print on a monochrome device such as a laser printer. The Advanced version of SnagIt also supports the following options:

Color Boost

Color boost is used to change the intensity of the colors. Increasing the boost value lightens the output. Color boost is performed before gray scaling or monochrome conversion, therefore it can be used to lighten or darken the output with those options as well.

Gray Scaling

Gray scaling is an alternative to monochrome conversion. SnagIt can represent colors with 256 levels of gray. The shades of gray are determined by the intensity level of the colors. You can adjust the color intensity levels with the Color Boost option under the Options Menu. Caution: Gray scaling is a pixel by pixel process and can be very slow. It is a good idea to try a small region before printing the whole screen. You may also want to enable the Alert feature under the Options Menu to let you know when the gray scaling process is completed.

Dynamic Data Exchange Usage

SnagIt supports Windows Dynamic Data Exchange (DDE). You can invoke SnagIt from other Windows programs by sending SnagIt DDE Messages. For Example, you can write an Excel macro that will print a portion of the screen using SnagIt. See Appendix A of this manual for the DDE command reference.

Appendix A - Dynamic Data Exchange Command Reference

Initiating a DDE Session: To initiate a DDE session with SnagIt, send a DDE_INITIATE with the application parameter of "SnagIt" and the topic parameter of "system".

Setting SnagIt Options: All of the SnagIt Menu options can be set using the DDE_EXECUTE command.
    Example [set ("string")]

The parameter string must be one of the following:

- input screen
- input client
- input window
- input region
- input file
- input clipboard
- scale best
- scale screen
- scale n (where n is an integer greater than 0)
- output printer
- output file
- output clipboard
- chain b (where b is 1,True,Yes,0,False, or No)
- boost red,green,blue (integer value 0..1000)
- add red, green, blue (integer value -255..255)
- inalert n (where n is the number of beeps)
- outalert n

Activating SnagIt: SnagIt is activated by sending a DDE_EXECUTE command with the message:
[snag("string")]

The string parameter can be one of the following:

- snag (activates menus selected for input)
- screen
- clipboard
- filename
- x y (where x,y are coordinates within a window)
- client x y
- handle h (where h is a valid window handle)
- client handle h
- tx ty bx by (where tx,ty,bx,by are coordinates defining a region)

Appendix B - Other TechSmith Products

DDEWatch: DDEWatch is a Windows DDE monitoring utility. Each message that DDEWatch displays consists of decoded bit fields, command/data strings and atom names. DDEWatch also supports file logging, allowing DDE conversations to be captured and written to a file.

DDELib: DDELib offers Windows programmers an API that significantly reduces the effort required to write fully functional DDE compliant applications. Client and server demonstration programs are included.

Table Update: Table Update is an end-user Windows front-end for the Microsoft SQL Server and Gupta's SQLBase. It facilitates data entry into a set of hierarchically related tables. Table Update is dynamically driven by the database schema, including primary and foreign keys, so no programming is involved. Table Update features a Basic-style macro language, ad-hoc table queries, Dynamic Data Exchange, Multiple Document Interface and on-line help facilities.

Registration

If you try SnagIt 1.6 and would like the features in version 2.0, please complete your purchase of it by sending payment to TechSmith Corporation at the address below.

Volume discounts and site licenses are also available. Phone us for details.

SnagIt has been tested and performs its functions essentially as documented, without causing any damage to the computer in use or any of its files. However, all users are responsible for backing up their own files, and TechSmith Corporation assumes no responsibility for any damage or losses incurred as a result of its use.

TechSmith Corporation supports SnagIt, by providing technical assistance, bug fixes, and enhancements. If you encounter problems or have suggestions for improvements, please let us know about them.

TechSmith Corporation 1745 Hamilton Road, Suite 300 Okemos, MI 48864

Phone: (517) 347-0800 - Sales only CompuServe: 75226,3136 - Technical support and pre-sales questions

SnagIt 1.6 & SnagIt 2.0: Copyright © 1990, 1991 All Rights Reserved. TechSmith Corporation

---

SnagIt 1.6 Registration and SnagIt 2.0 Order Form

PURCHASER

Name: _____

Company: _____

Address: _____

City: _____

State: _____ Zip code: _____

Country: _____

ORDER	Quantity	Amount
SnagIt 2.0 single user licence at $79 per copy	_____	_____
Telephone support at $50 per half hour		_____
Sales tax for Michigan residents only (4%)		_____
Overseas Shipping at $5 per order		_____
Purchase order processing fee of $5		_____
Total		_____

Media preferred: [ ] 3.5" diskettes [ ] 5.25" diskettes

PAYMENT METHOD

[ ] Check or money order enclosed (U.S. funds only)

[ ] Bill company (enclose purchase order)

NOTES

Payment of $79 per copy of SnagIt entitles the purchaser to:
 * A single user license for SnagIt 2.0. * Printed documentation. * The current release of SnagIt 2.0 without the on-screen reminder. * Three months of technical usage support via CompuServe.

Payment of $50 per half hour of technical support entitles the purchaser to: * A total of one half hour of technical telephone support with a programmer familiar with SnagIt. A minimum of ten minutes per call will be charged.

Utility Pak for Windows

Copyright © 1991 by Moon Valley Software

The Utility Pak includes the following programs: GrabIt, Project Manager, FontView, MemStat, Memory Monitor, and Mem.

GrabIt is a screen-capture and printing utility. With GRABIT.EXE, you can copy the screen or any portion of it to your printer, the Clipboard, or a file. You can also invert or mirror the portion of the screen you select, depending on how you use the mouse to select this area.

The Project Manager (PJM.EXE) allows you to create sets of applications that you can launch, complete with specific files loaded automatically in each window.

FontView (FV.EXE) allows you to see a sample of all the resident screen fonts (including soft fonts) you have installed for use under Windows. This is handy if you want to look at a font before changing the text in your document to a new font.

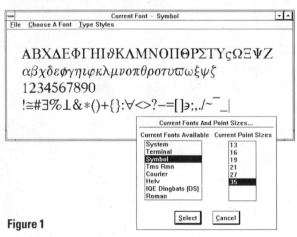

Figure 1

MemStat (MEMSTAT.EXE) displays a window in the lower-right corner of the screen showing the free amount of memory available, and the current operating mode Windows is in: 286/386 protected mode or real mode.

Figure 2

Memory Monitor (MM.EXE) shows in a bar graph the free memory you currently have available. The lines on the graph represent 25% increments. Very useful when

running in standard or real mode, it's not too informative in 386 enhanced mode, due to multitasking.

Figure 3   Memory Monitor

Mem (MEM.COM) is a tiny DOS program that allows you to check on the amount of free memory available for non-Windows applications when running under 386 enhanced mode. CHKMEM.BAT is provided as an example program to run MEM.COM from Windows.

The GrabIt screen capture utility, and the Project Manager start-up launcher, are fully documented here. The other programs are simple, one-function utilities that require only the above information to use.

Figure 4

GrabIt

Introduction

Thank you for taking the time to evaluate GrabIt. You will find a great many uses for this program. It is both a screen capture program and a marvelous utility for working with your favorite graphics program. By using

GrabIt to capture and save the images you have created, you will save many megabytes of hard disk space, since only the crucial information about your bitmap is saved to disk. This results in very small bitmaps that load faster and are much easier to view and store.

If you are a Windows programmer and use Owner Draw or custom controls, GrabIt will become addictive. It will enable you to use high quality bitmaps in your program that use no more space in your programs' resources than an icon! Please keep in mind that GrabIt is being distributed as shareware. This gives you the opportunity to "try before you buy", just like a test drive in that new car you always wanted. But just as the car dealer needs to be paid for his efforts so do we! All we ask is that if you honestly use and find this program of value, please fill out the registration form enclosed with this program, enclose a check and mail it. Doing so will enable us to keep refining this and our other Windows shareware programs; besides, "it's the right thing to do".

Using GrabIt to Enhance a Graphics Program

Using GrabIt in conjunction with the Windows graphics program of your choice will allow you to save large amounts of disk space. In addition, programmers will find it invaluable when creating bitmaps for inclusion in their programs. When you have created and saved a bitmap with your favorite graphics program, Paintbrush for example, you will notice that the resulting file may be more than 300KB in size! It doesn't take very many of these bitmaps to eat up a large quantity of hard disk space. By using GrabIt to capture only that portion of the screen that contains your bitmap you will get a file that is 30 to 40KB in size.

By cutting and pasting images to and from the Clipboard, you can easily create a drawing, capture it, create a mirror image , and then paste the mirror image back into your graphics program to create some very unusual special effects. The variations on this theme are limited only by your imagination. These examples show how much more than just a screen-capture tool GrabIt really is.

GrabIt Procedures

Capturing an Entire Windows Screen

To capture an entire Windows screen follow these steps:

1. Minimize GrabIt by pressing the minimize button on the title bar.
2. Press the Print Screen key on your keyboard. This key is located at the top of your keyboard, next to the Scroll Lock key.

3. Restore GrabIt and press Shift+P to paste the image from the clipboard into GrabIt's client area. You can now save the image to disk, print the image, or edit and clean up the captured image.

Capturing a Screen Area

To capture a portion of the screen follow the steps outlined below:

1. Click on the Mark menu selection, or press Alt+M.
2. The GrabIt window will disappear, and the cursor will change into a crosshair.
3. Move the cursor to the UPPER LEFT-HAND CORNER of the screen you wish to capture.
4. Press and hold down the LEFT mouse button.
5. As you move the mouse, you will see that the area you are marking will be changed to inverse video.
6. When you have marked the area you wish to capture release the mouse button.
7. The image will now be displayed in the GrabIt Client Window. The image attributes in pixel size will be displayed in the title bar. In addition it will show you whether it is an 8-plane 256 color, 4-plane 16 color, or 2-plane monochrome bitmap.

You have successfully captured your screen. See the sections on Saving An Image to Disk, Cleaning Up A Captured Image, or Special Effects for additional information on capturing an area of the screen.

Cleaning Up a Screen Capture

GrabIt allows you to re-cut an image that is in its client area. This is very useful if for example your original capture included an area you didn't intend to capture. To clean up and/or edit a capture, follow the steps below.

1. Move the arrow cursor to the Upper Right Hand point where you wish to begin your edit.
2. Press and hold down the left mouse button.
3. The area you are marking will appear in inverse video.
4. When finished with your edit, release the mouse button and your new image will be displayed in GrabIt's client area. In addition a copy of the image will also be copied to the clipboard. You can also perform any of the Special Effects noted in that section on your edits as well.

Saving a Captured Image to Disk

Once you are satisfied with the image that has been captured you can save it to disk by selecting Save from the File menu, or press Ctrl+S. A dialog box will be displayed, prompting you for the file name you want to use. Optionally, you can enter a drive and path name in addition to the file name, if you so desire. You can use the directory list box to change to the directory into which you wish to save the file, instead of entering it manually.

Copying an Image to the Clipboard

When you capture a screen, a copy of the image is automatically copied to the Clipboard. If you want to use this image in another graphics program, or insert it into a document such as a PageMaker publication, you can do so by simply switching to or starting your application, and then pressing the Shift+Insert keys. To copy the image that is currently in GrabIt's client area to the Clipboard, you can choose clipboard from the menu, and select Copy. Or press the Shift+C keys to copy the image. You can also load a bitmap from disk and then press Shift+C to copy it to the clipboard.

Pasting an Image from the Clipboard

To Paste an image from the clipboard into GrabIt's client area you can choose clipboard from the menu, and select Paste. Or press the Shift+P keys to paste the image. You can then save the bitmap to disk, or print the screen or bitmap.

Printing a Screen or Bitmap

Laser Printers

With GrabIt, you can print a screen or portion of a screen immediately after you have captured it. In addition, you can load from disk and print any Windows bitmap. GrabIt will render to shades of gray all of the colors it can, to give you an accurate representation of your captured screen. This grey scale dithering applies to Postscript and PCL printers.

Image Scaling

GrabIt will size the image currently in its client area to the size of the current page defined in your printer setup. This means that very small bitmaps will be enlarged to 8 1/2" x 11" if that is the current page definition. This is done so that on full screen captures and images loaded from disk you will get a 1:1 aspect ratio printout. If you wish to print images in a smaller format, simply change your printer setup to reflect a smaller page size.

Dot Matrix Printers

GrabIt does not support dot-matrix printers,due to dithering's poor performance on dot-matrix printers. If you wish to print a screen on your dot-matrix printer, follow the directions below:

1. After you have captured a screen with GrabIt, a copy of the image has also been copied to the Clipboard.

2. Start your favorite graphics program or Paintbrush, and then press Shift+Insert to copy your image into the program. You can now print the image you just captured on your dot-matrix printer, provided that your graphics program supports the printer you have installed.

Loading a Bitmap from Disk

To load a bitmap from disk select File from the main menu and choose Open, or press Ctrl+O. You can select a bitmap from the listbox, enter the drive and path to the bitmap you wish to load, or use the directory listbox to change to the directory where your bitmap is located and then select it from the listbox. To open the bitmap, either select it from the listbox and click on OK or press Enter. Alternately, you can just double-click on it to load the image.

Special Effects

GrabIt enables you to create special-effects screen cuts that may be used in conjunction with your graphics program or saved as is.

Creating a Mirror Image

1. Click on the Mark menu selection, or press Alt+M.
2. The GrabIt window will disappear and the cursor will change into a crosshair.
3. Move the cursor to the UPPER RIGHT HAND CORNER of the screen area you wish to capture.
4. Press and hold down the LEFT mouse button.
5. As you move the mouse you will see that the area you are marking will be changed to inverse video.
6. When you have marked the area you wish to capture, release the mouse button.
7. A mirror image of your capture will now be displayed in the GrabIt Client Window.

Creating an Inverted Image

Follow the steps outlined above, except begin your mark in the LOWER LEFT HAND CORNER.

Creating an Inverted Mirror Image

Follow the steps outlined above, except begin your mark in the LOWER RIGHT HAND CORNER. You may want to refer to "Capturing A Screen Area" for additional details.

GrabIt License Agreement

express prior written consent of Moon Valley Software Inc. The use of GrabIt is subject to the following terms and conditions.

Title to the Licensed Software: Title to the licensed software is NOT transferred to the end user. The end user is granted an exclusive license to use the software on a SINGLE computer or computer work station. EACH computer or computer work station must have its own licensed copy of the software.

Copyright Protection: GrabIt is copyrighted material. It is protected by the copyright laws of the United States, the State of Arizona, and other proprietary rights of Moon Valley Software, Inc. You may not make any changes or modifications to GrabIt or this manual. You may not decompile, disassemble, or otherwise reverse-engineer the software in any way. You may make copies of GrabIt only under the terms of the section entitled "Limited License To Copy The Licensed Software". You may use GrabIt on a trial basis provided you do not violate the protection afforded the licensed software by the copyright laws, and you agree to the terms of the license agreement. If you use GrabIt on a regular basis, you are obligated to purchase it.

Limited Warranty: Moon Valley Software does not warrant that the licensed software will meet your requirements or that the operation of the software will be uninterrupted or error free. The warranty does not cover any media or documentation which has been subjected to damage or abuse by you or others. The software warranty does not cover any copy of the licensed software which has been altered or changed in any way. ANY IMPLIED WARRANTIES INCLUDING ANY WARRANTIES OF MERCHANTABILITY OR FITNESS FOR A PARTICULAR PURPOSE ARE LIMITED TO THE TERM OF THE EXPRESS WARRANTIES. Some States do not allow limitations on how long an implied warranty lasts, so the above limitation may not apply to you.

Other Warranties: The warranties set forth above are in lieu of any and all other express or implied warranties, whether oral, written, or implied, and the remedies set forth above are the sole and exclusive remedies.

Limitation of Liability: Moon Valley Software is not responsible for any problems or damage caused by the licensed software that may result from using the licensed software. This includes, but is not limited to, computer hardware, computer software, operating systems, and any computer or computing accessories. End user agrees to hold Moon Valley Software Inc. harmless for any problems arising from the use of the software. Moon Valley Software SHALL NOT IN ANY CASE BE LIABLE FOR ANY SPECIAL, INCIDENTAL, CONSEQUENTIAL, INDIRECT OR OTHER SIMILAR DAMAGES ARISING FROM ANY BREACH OF THESE WARRANTIES EVEN IF Moon Valley Software OR ITS AGENTS OR DISTRIBUTORS HAVE BEEN ADVISED OF THE POSSIBILITY OF SUCH DAMAGES. Some states do not allow the exclusion or limitation of incidental or consequential damages, so the above limitation or exclusion may not apply to you. In no case shall Moon Valley Software's liability exceed the license fees paid for the right to use the licensed software, or a sum no greater than one Dollar ($1.00), whichever is less.

Limited License to Copy the Software: You are granted a limited license to copy GrabIt ONLY FOR THE TRIAL USE OF OTHERS subject to the terms of this software license agreement described herein, and the conditions described below are met: GrabIt MUST

be copied in an unmodified form and ZM301.ZIP MUST contain the following files:

> **GRABIT.EXE** The Windows Executable Program.
> **GRABIT.DOC** The program documentation
> **GRABIT.HLP** The Windows Help File
> **REGISTER.FRM** The shareware registration form.(Please!)
> **README.1ST** Important information not in the documentation.

- No fee, charge or other compensation may be accepted or requested by anyone without the express written permission of Moon Valley Software.

  Public Domain Disk Vendors May NOT CHARGE a fee for GrabIt itself. However, you may include GrabIt on a diskette for which you charge a nominal distribution fee. The purchaser of said diskette must be informed in advance that the fee paid to acquire the diskette does NOT relieve said purchaser from paying the Registration Fee for GrabIt if said purchaser uses GrabIt.

- Operators of electronic bulletin board systems (Sysops) may post GrabIt for downloading by their users without written permission ONLY AS LONG AS THE ABOVE CONDITIONS ARE MET. A fee may be charged for access to the BBS AS LONG AS NO SPECIFIC FEE IS CHARGED FOR DOWNLOADING GrabIt files without first obtaining express written permission from Moon Valley Software to charge such a fee.

The above constitutes the license agreement for GrabIt. It supersedes any and all previous license agreements.

Technical Support

We will provide technical support to unregistered users on their first phone call only if you are calling with the intention of registering your copy of the program once your questions have been answered. Please call us at 602-375-9502 Monday - Friday from 8:00 am - 4:00 pm Mountain Standard Time. Arizona does not go on daylight savings time. (Who wants it to stay light later when its 110 degrees outside!) You can also call our BBS at 602-375-0531, using 1200, 2400, and 9600 bps, N-8-1, and leave us a message in the Moon Valley Shareware Forum. There is lots of other good Windows shareware on the BBS, so feel free to browse around while you're on-line.

Registration Information

To register your copy of GrabIt, please use the file called REGISTER.FRM that is supplied with the program, or cut out the form printed at the end of this chapter. If you wish, you can phone in your order using your Visa or Master Card, Monday - Friday, 8:00 am - 4:00 pm MST. The order phone number is 602-375-9502.

Project Manager

Getting Started

Project Manager allows you to load all of the Windows programs you wish to use when you start Windows, and any time during your Windows session. You can choose to have the programs loaded either as icons or active windows when they are run. You can attach a data file or document to a program when it is loaded. For example, you might wish to start Excel with the worksheet you use most often. Or load two copies of Notepad, each with a different document attached, and immediately be able to cut and paste between them. The combinations available are limited only by your imagination.

Installation and Setup

To install Project Manager copy the following files to your Windows directory:

1. PJM.EXE
2. PJM.HLP
3. The example Project File Scripts. The examples have the file extension of .PRJ.

Technical Support

When you have registered Project Manager you will receive a support ID Number. This number entitles you to unlimited free telephone support.

Menu Commands

The File Menu

Run a Program: This selection displays a list box displaying all of the files in the current directory with the extension of .EXE, It will also allow you to enter any command line arguments you would like to pass to the program at run time.
Start a Project: This selection displays a box listing all of the currently available Project Files.
Exit: This will close the current Project Manager session.

The Edit Menu

Edit/Create a Project File: This selection starts the Windows Notepad program so that you can create or edit an existing Project File.

Procedures

Starting Project Manager.

There are several ways to start Project Manager.

The Project Manager Menu.

To Start A Project from the Project Manager Menu simply double click on the desired project name. This allows you to work with different projects during the day as needed.

The Command Line

From The DOS prompt, type

    WIN PJM {filename.prj}

and press Enter, where {filename.prj} represents the Project File that contains the programs you wish to have loaded when Windows starts. When you define a Project File you can indicate whether you would like to have the program run as an active window or displayed as an icon. If you use the same programs and data files each time you work within Windows you may want to consider writing a simple batch file to start your windows session.

Modifying the WIN.INI File

Modify the LOAD= line in your WIN.INI file so that it looks like the following example:

    load=d:\pathname\pjm.exe

Windows will start and load Project Manager. "d:\" equals the drive letter and "pathname" indicates the directory where Project Manager and your project files are stored. You may also use the RUN= line in the WIN.INI with the same commands as used for the LOAD= line.

Creating a Project File

Creating a Project File is a very simple task. All that is needed is your favorite text editor, or the Windows Notepad. Project Files are simply ASCII text files containing the names of the programs you wish to load and run. You MUST give them an extension of .PRJ. Project Files MUST Contain ONLY Windows Programs. If you wish to run a non-Windows program, create a DOS batch File and execute it from the Run A Program menu selection.

There must not be any blank lines between programs. After you have entered the desired programs BE SURE to press Enter again after the last line you typed. This will indicate to Project Manager that it has found the end of your file. Project Manager interprets the project files and executes them in order until it detects the end of the file, which is indicated by a carriage return. Start Notepad or your favorite text editor. Then enter a list like the one below. If you place the @ symbol before the program name it will become iconic when run.

Example 1

```
notepad memo.txt
calendar
calc
[Enter]
```

In Example 1

Line One will run the Notepad and start it with the file memo.txt.
Line Two will run the Calendar.
Line Three will run the Calculator.

Example 2

```
excel books.xls
excel sales.xls
@word newsltr.doc
notepad
@calendar
@clock
[Enter]
```

In Example 2

Line One will run Excel and start it with the worksheet books.xls.
Line Two will run Excel and start it with the worksheet sales.xls.
Line Three will run Word for Windows and start it with newsltr.doc and force it to become an icon at the bottom of the screen.
Line Four will run the notepad in a normal window.
Line Five will run the Calendar program and force it to become an icon.
Line Six will run the Clock and force it to become an icon.

Editing a Project File

Select Edit from the Project Manager Menu. Click on the Create/Edit menu selection. This will start the Windows Notepad. Select Open from the Notepad Menu, backspace off the *.TXT default extension and enter *.PRJ. The Notepad listbox will show all of the Project Files currently defined. Double-click on the file you wish to edit. When done you can save it to its original file name, or use the "Save As" command to create an entirely new project.

Shareware Registration Form

Return this form along with your remittance to:
Moon Valley Software Inc. 107 East Paradise Lane Phoenix, AZ 85022 USA

Special prices/discounts on quantity orders, Corporate site licenses, and dealer pricing are available. Please call for details.
You can order by phone using your MasterCard or VISA. Call us at (602) 375-9502, Mon. - Fri., 9:00 a.m. - 4:00 p.m., MST ONLY.
On-Line BBS Registration at 602-375-0531, 1200-2400 bps, 24 hrs a day

Please send me (check desired items below):

____ Copy(s) Of Utility Pak 3.0 @ $29.95 ea $ _____
6 Great Utilities (incl. Grablt & Project Manager)
Media Size 3.5 or 5.25: _____

____ Copy(s) Of Zip Manager 3.0 @ $21.95 ea $ _____
Windows Shell For PKZIP and PKUNZIP
Media Size 3.5 or 5.25: _____

____ Copy(s) Of Monitor Saver Version 2.01 @ $21.95 ea $ _____
Screen Saver Now Offers A Line-Drawing Option
Media Size 3.5 or 5.25: _____

Shipping (Per Item) @ 1.50 ea $ _____
(U.S. and Canada, $1.50 Per Item; All Other Countries, $5.00)

Subtotal $ _____

Arizona Residents please add Sales Tax @ 5% $ _____

**Total (U.S.Funds) $ _____
drawn on U.S.Bank**

Payment by: ( )CHECK ( )MC ( )VISA _____

Card #: _____

Exp. Date: _____

Signature of cardholder: _____
(REQUIRED !!)

Prices subject to change without notice. Current prices can be confirmed by calling (602) 375-9502.

Ship To Information -> Please Type Or Print <-

Name: _____

Company: _____

Address: _____

_____

Phone W: _____

 Eve: _____

Please send us any suggestions or problems you have encountered. Your support is greatly appreciated!

Starting a Project File

Select File from the main menu by pressing Alt+F. Press S to select Start a Project from the menu. A dialog box will be displayed listing all currently available Projects. Double-click on the project you wish to use.

Run a Program

Select Run from the File Menu. A dialog box will be displayed that will allow you to enter a program name, or you can double click on a program name displayed in the list box. If you wish to pass command line parameters you may do so by pressing the tab key twice and entering parameters in the box provided.

Sample Project Files

Included with Project Manager are two sample Project Files: samPLE.PRJ and SAMPLE1.PRJ. These are provided to give you some examples on how to create project files.

Registration

Project Manager is being distributed as Shareware. If you use it you are obligated to register it. By registering it you will receive the latest version of the program, and you won't be bothered by the registration box that appears each time you start the program.

Please use the enclosed registration form, or if you wish you can register by phone using your Master Card or Visa. Phone orders are taken 9:00 a.m. - 4:00 p.m., M-F, Mountain Standard Time. Call Moon Valley Software at (602) 375-9502. THANK YOU.

Whiskers

Version 2.6
Copyright © 1991 by Numbers & Co.

Overview

The purpose of Whiskers is to enable the right and middle mouse buttons to act like other keys and keyboard combinations. Whiskers will work with all Windows applications. With Whiskers, working with dialog boxes is very fast. For example, you can re-define the right mouse button to act like the Enter key. Most dialog boxes have a default button and if you press the Enter key of the keyboard that button is activated. With Whiskers, you can press the right mouse button instead of moving the mouse to press the default button or taking your hand off the mouse to press the Enter key of the keyboard. By keeping your hand on the mouse, you save a lot of time as you do your work.

To install Whiskers, copy all the files to the directory where you want Whiskers to be. Then use the File Manager or Program Manager to start Whiskers, using the WHISKERS.EXE file. WHISKERS.EXE uses another file (included with Whiskers) named whiskers.dll. WHISKERS.DLL is a DLL or Dynamic Linked Library. Be sure to keep WHISKERS.EXE and WHISKERS.DLL in the same directory. If you have an older version of Whiskers that used a file named RODENT.EXE, please delete the rodent.exe file. Whiskers no longer needs it.

To run Whiskers, double-click on its icon in the Program Manager or the WHISKERS.EXE file in the File Manager. A Whiskers icon will appear at the bottom of your screen.

At this point, Whiskers is running and the Whiskers icon will have bars showing. The bars indicate that mouse button clicks are being captured and processed, according to the default settings. To view or change the default settings, see the section "Programming the Mouse Buttons" below. Whiskers requires a minimum of 18 KB of memory to run. When using either "hide-it" option, the minimum memory required to run Whiskers is 7 KB.

Load Line

You can put Whiskers on the LOAD= LINE of the win.ini file. Making a Whiskers entry on the LOAD= LINE will run Whiskers when Windows is first started. It is recom-

mended that you make the Whiskers entry on the load=
line and not the run= line.

HideIt Feature

Whiskers has a "Hide Whiskers" checkbox in the Buttons
dialog box, and a "Hide Whiskers" command on the menu.
These options allow you to hide the Whiskers icon. This
reduces screen clutter. The "Hide Whiskers" command on
the menu will hide the Whiskers icon immediately, but
will only stay in effect for the present Windows session.
The "Hide Whiskers" checkbox in the Buttons dialog box
requires that a Whiskers entry is on the load= line of the
win.ini file. This option is permanent until the checkbox is
unselected. With this option, when Windows is started,
the Whiskers icon will be hidden automatically.

When using the "Hide Whiskers" menu command, if you
find that you need to change a button setting or edit the
Exclusion List (see below), start Whiskers by double-
clicking the icon in the Program Manager, and the
Whiskers icon will appear at the bottom of the screen.
Any editing can now be done.

When using the "Hide Whiskers" checkbox option, if you
find that you need to change a button setting or edit the
Exclusion List, you must delete the line in the win.ini file
in the [Whiskers] section that reads hideit=on. Then start
Whiskers again by double-clicking the icon in the Program
Manager, and the Whiskers icon will appear at the bottom
of the screen. Any editing can now be done.

When either of the "Hide Whiskers" options are selected,
the memory required to run Whiskers drops to approximately 7K.

Programming the Mouse Buttons: 2 And 3 Button Mice

Click once on the Whiskers icon at the bottom of your
screen and the system menu will pop up. Select the
Buttons... command, and a dialog box titled "Whiskers'

Whiskers' Mouse College (teach it new tricks)

To program a button activate the desired button(s) by checking the check boxes.
Then select a key from the appropriate list box and press Ok.

shifts+button	☐ middle button		☒ right button	
no shifts	Enter (return)	±	Enter (return)	±
shift	Delete	±	Delete	±
control	Page Up	±	Home	±
shift+control	Page Next	±	End	±

Ok

Cancel

Mouse College" will appear. The Right and Middle button
key combinations have been programmed with default
key values. You may change any of these defaults that you
wish. For example, to program the Right button to be the
DELETE key, turn the checkbox on, then click on the
down arrow of the listbox that is in the "no shifts" row
and in the Right button column. Scroll the listbox until
you find the DELETE entry and then select it. Now press
the OK button.

To program the Shift+Right button combination, follow
the same steps as above, but make your selection in the
listbox in the "shift" row and right button column. Follow
these steps for programming each of the combinations.
Repeat these steps for programming the middle button on
a three (3) button mouse.

Pass Shift States

By default the Pass Shift States checkboxes are
unselected. An example of passing or not passing the Shift
States is as follows:

The Shift+Right button combination has the assignment of
PASTE from the listbox and the Shift State checkbox is
unselected. When the Shift key and the right mouse
button are pressed together, the Paste command will be
executed. Now, with the Shift State checkbox selected,
and the Shift+Right button combination with the
assignment of the Insert key, when the Shift key and the
right mouse button are pressed together, the Paste
command will be executed also.

When the Pass Shift States is selected, the Shift key
message is actually passed on to the active application to
be processed. When the Pass Shift States is unselected,
the Shift key is used to give Whiskers another key
combination;; the Shift message IS NOT passed to the
active application.

Shift+Left Button & Left Double-Click

If you want to use either the Shift+Left Button or the
Shift+Left Double-Click selections, it is recommended that
you program these selections on the shift line of either
button and select the Pass Shift States checkbox.
Otherwise, erratic results may occur, depending on the
applications that you are working with.

Logitech Mice

If you have a Logitech Bus Mouse, you will need to call
Logitech Tech Support at 415-795-8100 to get a new
LMOUSE.DRV file. This new LMOUSE.DRV file will support the
middle button of your mouse.

Middle Button Simulation

To turn on the Middle button simulation, click on the
Whiskers icon at the bottom of the screen and then select
the buttons command. In the buttons dialog box select

the Middle Button Simulation checkbox and then press the OK button. This checkbox will enable the middle button simulation. Whiskers can simulate a Middle button on a two (2) button mouse. To do the middle button simulation press and hold down the right mouse button and then QUICKLY click the left mouse button. The left button will activate whatever key you have assigned to the "no shift middle button". If you find that the click rate is too fast or too slow for you, the click rate can be changed in the Control Panel, Mouse section, Double Click Rate. To do the other middle button key combinations, press and hold down the right button and any of the shift keys and then click the left button. When you let up on the right button, the mouse will revert back to its normal state. To program the simulated Middle button, just follow the steps for programming the middle button of a three (3) button mouse.

The Shift+Left click sequence may be assigned to the right or middle button, but in some applications it will not work. For example, in Excel and Notepad, the Shift+Left click assignment to the right or middle button will produce the appropriate extended selection. However, in the File Manager, which uses Shift+Left click for extended file selection, Whiskers will not work. This problem of Whiskers not working with some applications is caused by the way those applications were written, and there is no way for Whiskers to get around this.

Whiskers Exclusion List

To exclude programs from Whiskers' attention, enter their names exactly as they appear in their title bars (including spaces) separated by commas. Only the base program name need be entered. Document titles, path names, etc do not have to be included in the name.

Example: Micro Zap,Disk Nurse,Flame-Thrower,Chicken Backup

Exclusion list for middle button

Exclusion list for right button

Paintbrush

Ok   Cancel

Exclusion List

Click once on the Whiskers icon at the bottom of your screen, and the system menu will pop up. Select Exclude... and a dialog box will appear. Follow the instructions in the dialog box for excluding certain programs from Whiskers' attention.

You can also turn Whiskers ON and OFF manually by double-clicking on the Whiskers icon at the bottom of the screen — or clicking once on the icon at the bottom of the screen and then selecting Whiskers ON or OFF from the system menu.

To Excel Users

A rodent.exe has been marketed separately in the past as an Excel add-in. If you have purchased the Rodent for Excel, just delete the rodent.exe file and any macros that you may be using. whiskers.dll is a complete replacement for the Rodent.

Registration

Whiskers is being distributed in the shareware market; you are free to make copies to pass along to others who might find Whiskers useful. All files (whiskers.exe, whiskers.dll, invoice.txt and whiskers.txt) must be distributed together. If you find that you like Whiskers and find it useful in your work, you are expected to pay a registration fee of $15.00 per copy. A registration form is included for your convenience at the end of this chapter, along with an invoice file named invoice.txt. Checks, MasterCard and VISA are accepted for payment. To print an invoice, open the invoice.txt file with Notepad, select the File menu, click the Page Setup command and set all margins to 0. Then select the File menu Print command to print the invoice.

Additional mouse functions are available by upgrading to the commercial version of Whiskers 3.01. The commercial version supports additional key combinations. You may upgrade to this version using the order form below.

When your registration fee is received, a registration number and a paid-in-full invoice will be sent to you. When you receive your registration number, it is very important that you enter your registration number exactly as it appears on your invoice. Technical support and site licenses are also available; please call 509-476-2216 for more information. Site licenses are available at the rate of:

$15.00 per copy for 1 - 24

$13.00 per copy for 25 - 99

$10.00 per per copy for 100 - 199

Call for unlimited site license amounts

NUMBERS & CO.
Attn: Windows 3 Secrets
Rt. 1, Box 59A
Oroville, WA 98844
(509) 476-2216

Sold To: _____   Phone: _____

Address: _____   Contact Person: _____

City: _____

State: _____ Zip: _____

Quantity	Title	Unit Price	Total
_____	Whiskers 2.6 registration	$15.00	_____
_____	Whiskers 3.01 commercial version	$24.95 + $2.00 s&h	_____
		TOTAL DUE	_____

[ ] MasterCard _____-_____-_____-_____

[ ] VISA

Expiration Date_____ Signature _____

_____

WinBatch

Copyright © 1988-1991 by Morrie Wilson
All rights reserved.

Contents at a Glance

Abs
AskLine
AskYesNo
Average
Beep
Call
CallExt
Char2Num
ClipAppend
ClipGet
ClipPut
DateTime
Debug
Delay
DirChange
DirGet
DirHome
DirItemize
DirMake
DirRemove
DiskFree
Display
DOSVersion
Drop
EndSession
Environment
ErrorMode
Execute
Exit
Exclusive
FileClose
FileCopy
FileDelete
FileExist
FileExtension
FileItemize
FileLocate
FileMove
FileOpen
FilePath
FileRead
FileRename
FileRoot
FileSize
FileWrite
Goto
If_Then
IgnoreInput
IniRead
IniReadPvt
IniWrite
IniWritePvt
IsDefined
IsKeyDown
IsLicensed
IsNumber
ItemSelect

LastError
LogDisk
Max
Message
Min
Num2Char
ParseData
Pause
Random
Return
Run
RunHide
RunIcon
RunZoom
SendKey
SKDebug
StrCat
StrCmp
StrFill
StrFix
StriCmp
StrIndex
StrLen
StrLower
StrReplace
StrScan
StrSub
StrTrim
StrUpper
TextBox
Version
WinActivate
WinArrange
WinClose
WinCloseNot
WinConfig
WinExist
WinGetActive
WinHide
WinIconize
WinItemize
WinPlace
WinPosition
WinShow
WinTitle
WinVersion
WinWaitClose
WinZoom
Yield
Appendix A: Predefined Constants
Appendix B: Errors
    Minor Errors
    Moderate Errors
    Fatal Errors

No part of this manual may be reproduced or transmitted in any form or by any means, electronic or mechanical, including photocopying and recording, for any purpose without the express written permission of Wilson WindowWare. Information in this document is subject to change without notice and does not represent a commitment by Wilson WindowWare. The software described herein is furnished under a license agreement. It is against the law to copy this software under any circumstances except as provided by the license agreement.

U.S. Government Restricted Rights

Use, duplication, or disclosure by the Government is subject to restrictions as set forth in subdivision (b)(3)(ii) of the Rights in Technical Data and Computer Software clause at 252.227-7013. Contractor/manufacturer is Wilson WindowWare, 2701 California Ave SW Ste. 212, Seattle, WA 98116.

Introduction

WinBatch is a new batch language interpreter which brings the power of batch language programming to the Windows environment. WinBatch files can do pretty much everything the old DOS batch files could do, but WinBatch goes far beyond the capabilities of the DOS batch language. WinBatch files can:

- Run Windows and DOS programs.
- Resize and rearrange windows.
- Send keystrokes directly to applications.
- Display information to the user in various formats.
- Prompt the user for input.
- Present scrollable file and directory lists.
- Copy, move, delete, and rename files.
- Read and write files directly.
- Perform string and arithmetic operations.
- Make branching decisions based upon numerous factors.

And much, much more. Whether you are creating batch files for others, or looking for a way to automate your own work and eliminate the drudgery of repetitive tasks, you will find WinBatch to be a powerful, versatile, and easy-to-use tool.

System Requirements

WinBatch requires an IBM PC or compatible with a minimum of 640K memory running Microsoft Windows version 3.0 or higher.

About This Manual

This manual is divided into four sections: First is Getting Started, where we tell you how to install the program. Then we offer an extensive Tutorial, to get both beginning and advanced users quickly up to speed with creating WinBatch files. Then we describe the different elements of the WinBatch Language (WBL). Finally, there is a comprehensive WBL Function Reference, which contains detailed information on each of the WinBatch functions and statements.

Acknowledgements

WinBatch designed & written by Morrie Wilson. User's Manual designed by Richard Merit. Written by Richard Merit & Morrie Wilson. Our thanks to the many beta-testers for their invaluable comments & suggestions.

Getting Started

WinBatch is quite easy to install. You will find an appropriate diskette in your WinBatch package. Take the diskette and insert it into your floppy drive. The WinBatch installation program is itself a Windows application, so make sure Windows is running.

From the Program Manager, doubleclick on the File Manager icon to run it. When File Manager starts, click on the A: or B: drive icon, depending on which floppy drive you used. A directory tree will appear for the WinBatch diskette. You should see a root directory icon. Doubleclick on this icon and a list of filenames will appear. Find the filename SETUP.EXE and doubleclick on it. Follow whatever instructions Setup gives you. Setup will create the necessary files and place them into a directory it will prompt you for. As the installation program finishes it will display the README.TXT file. You should take the time to read this file as it contains any late-breaking information about your copy of WinBatch.

[**Note:** Because of the column width, code in the following frequently wraps. It is indicated by right-justification. In actual use, place this code all on one line.]

Tutorial

WinBatch Basics

What Is a Batch File?

A batch file, whether a DOS batch file or a WinBatch file, is simply a list of commands for the computer to process. Any task which will be run more than once, or which requires entering many commands or even a single complicated command, is a candidate for a batch file. For

example, suppose you regularly enter the following commands to start Windows:

First:

```
cd\windows
```

then:

```
win
```

and then:

```
cd\
```

Here, you are changing to the Windows directory, running Windows, and then returning to the root directory. Instead of having to type these three commands every time you run Windows, you can create a DOS batch file, called WI.BAT, which contains those exact same commands:

```
cd\windows
win
cd\
```

Now, to start Windows, you merely need to type the single command WI, which starts the WI.BAT batch file, which runs your three commands. WinBatch files work the same way.

Our First WinBatch File

Our first WinBatch file will simply start up our favorite Windows application: Solitaire. First, start up Notepad, or any other editor which is capable of saving text in pure ASCII format (may we suggest WinEdit, from Wilson WindowWare). Next, enter the following line:

```
Run("sol.exe","")
```

Save the file as SOLITARE.WBT. Now, run SOLITARE.WBT by starting or switching to the File Manager, and either moving the cursor to the file name and pressing Enter, or double-clicking on the file name with your mouse. Presto! It's Solitaire. Okay, that wasn't very impressive. But it did serve to illustrate several important WinBatch points. They are:

1. WinBatch files must be edited and saved in ASCII format.
2. WinBatch files should be created with a WBT extension. When WinBatch is first installed, it creates an entry in your WIN.INI file which causes files with a WBT extension to be associated with WinBatch. As long as WINBATCH.EXE is located in your DOS path, you can place WBT files in any directory and run them by simply selecting them.
3. After you have created a WBT file, you run it by cursoring to it and pressing Enter, or double-clicking on it with your mouse (you can also add a WBT file to

a program group and run it using the Program Manager; see your Windows manual for further information). Whatever method you use, we'll use the term Run to refer to selecting and running the file.

Functions and Parameters

Now, let's look more closely at the line we entered:

```
Run("sol.exe", "")
```

The first part, Run, is a WinBatch function. As you might have guessed, its purpose is to run a Windows program. There are over a hundred functions and statements in WinBatch, and each has a certain syntax which must be used. The syntax for all WinBatch functions may be found in the WBL Function Reference. The entry for Run starts off as follows:

Syntax: Run (program-name, parameters)
Parameters: "program-name" = the name of the desired .EXE, .COM, .PIF, .BAT file, or a data file.
"parameters" = optional parameters as required by the application.

Like all WinBatch functions, Run is followed by a number of parameters, enclosed in parentheses. Parameters are simply additional information which are provided when a particular function is used; they made either be required or optional. Optional parameters are indicated by being enclosed in brackets. In this case, Run has two required parameters: the program name, and the parameters which get passed to the application. There are several types of parameters which you can use. Multiple parameters are separated by commas. In the example

```
Run("sol.exe", "")
```

"sol.exe" and "" are both string constants. String constants can be identified by the quote marks which delimit (surround) them (you may use either double ("), single forward (') or single back (`) quote marks as string delimiters; the examples in this manual will use double quotes).

You may have noticed how we said earlier that the two parameters for the Run function are required, and yet the entry for Run in the WBL Function Reference describes the second parameter — "parameters" — as being optional. Which is correct? Well, from a language standpoint, the second parameter is required. That is, if you omit it, you will get a syntax error, and your batch file will not run properly. However, the program that you are running may not need any parameters. Solitaire, for example, does not take any parameters. The way we handle this in our batch file is to specify an empty string — two quote marks with nothing in between — as the second parameter, as we have done in our example

above. To illustrate this further, let's create a WinBatch file called EDIT.WBT, containing the following line:

```
Run("notepad.exe", "")
```

This is just like our previous file, with only the name of the program changed. Save the file, and run it. You should now be in Notepad. Now edit the EDIT.WBT file as follows:

```
Run("notepad.exe", "solitare.wbt")
```

Save the file, exit Notepad, and run EDIT.WBT again. You should now be in Notepad, with SOLITARE.WBT loaded. As we've just demonstrated, Notepad is an example of a program which can be run with or without a file name parameter passed to it by WinBatch. Before you leave Notepad, modify EDIT.WBT as follows:

```
; This is an example of the Run function in
WinBatch
Run("notepad.exe", "solitare.wbt")
```

The semicolon at the beginning of the first line signifies a comment, and causes that line to be ignored. You can place comment lines, and/or blank lines anywhere in your WinBatch files. In addition, you can place a comment on the same line as a function by preceding the comment with a semicolon. For example:

```
Run("sol.exe", "")    ;this is a very useful function
```

Everything to the right of a semicolon is ignored. However, if a semicolon appears in a string delimited by quotes, it is considered part of the string.

Displaying Text

Now, let's modify our SOLITARE.WBT file as follows. You might as well use the EDIT.WBT batch file you created earlier to start up Notepad:

```
; solitare.wbt Display(5, "Good Luck!", "Remember ...
                                  it's only a game.")
Run("sol.exe", "")
```

And run it. Notice the message box which pops up on the screen with words of encouragement. That's done by the Display function in the second line above. Here's the reference for the Display function:

Syntax: Display (seconds, title, text)
Parameters: seconds = integer seconds to display the message (1-15).
"title" = Title of the window to be displayed.
"text" = Text of the window to be displayed.

Note that the Display function has three parameters. The first parameter — in our example, 5 — is the number of seconds which the message box will remain on the screen (you can also make the box disappear by pressing a key or mouse button). This is a numeric constant, and — unlike a string constants — it does not need to be enclosed in quotes (although it can be, if you wish, as WinBatch will automatically try to convert string variables to numeric variables when necessary, and vice versa). The second parameter is the title of the message box, and the third parameter is the actual text displayed in the box. Now, exit Solitaire (if you haven't already done so), and edit SOLITARE.WBT by placing a semicolon at the beginning of the line with the Run function. This is a handy way to disable, or "comment out," lines in your WinBatch files when you want to modify and test only selected segments. Your SOLITARE.WBT file should look like this:

```
; solitare.wbt Display(5, "Good Luck!",
                "Remember ... it's only a game.")
;Run("sol.exe", "")
```

Now, experiment with modifying the parameters in the Display function. Try adjusting the value of the first parameter. If you look up Display in the WBL reference section, you will notice that the acceptable values for this parameter are 1-15. If you try to use a value outside this range, WinBatch will adjust it to "make it fit"; that is, it will treat numbers less than 1 as 1, and numbers greater than 15 as 15. Try it. Also, try giving it a non-integer, such as 2.5, and see what happens. Play around with the text in the two string parameters; try making one, or both, empty strings ("").

Getting Input

Now, let's look at ways of getting input from a user and making decisions based on that input. The most basic form of input is a simple Yes/No response, and, indeed, there is a WinBatch function called AskYesNo:

Syntax: AskYesNo (title, question)
Parameters: "title" = title of the question box.
"question" = question to be put to the user.
Returns: (integer) @YES or @NO, depending on the button pressed.

You should be familiar with the standard syntax format by now; it shows us that AskYesNo has two required parameters. The Parameters section tells us that these parameters both take strings (indicated by the quote marks), and tells us what each of the parameters means.

You will notice that there is also a new section here, titled Returns. This selection shows you the possible values that may be returned by this function. All functions return values. In the case of Run and Display, we weren't concerned with the values that those functions returned.

But with AskYesNo, the returned value is very important, because we will need that information to decide how to proceed. We see that AskYesNo returns an integer value. An integer is simply a non-decimal number, such as 0, 1, or 2. The number 1.5 is not an integer. We see further that the integer value returned by AskYesNo is either @YES or @NO. @YES and @NO are predefined constants in WinBatch. All predefined constants begin with an @ symbol, and we will distinguish them further by typing them in all caps. You will find a list of all predefined constants in Appendix A. Even though the words "Yes" and "No" are strings, it is important to remember that the predefined constants @YES and @NO are not string variables (in fact, they are integers). Now, let's modify our SOLITARE.WBT file as follows:

```
AskYesNo("Really?", "Do you really want to
                    play Solitaire now?")
Run("sol.exe", "")
```

and run it. You should have gotten a nice dialog box which asked if you wanted to play Solitaire, but no matter what you answered, it started Solitaire anyway. This isn't good. We need a way to use the Yes/No response to determine further processing. First, we need to explore the concept and use of variables.

Using Variables

A variable is simply a placeholder for a value. The value that the variable stands for can be either a text string (string variable) or a number (numeric variable). If you remember Algebra 101, you know that if X=3, then X+X=6. X is simply a numeric variable, which stands here for the number 3. If we change the value of X to 4 (X=4), then the expression X+X is now equal to 8. By the same token, we can say that if Y="morning", then "good"+Y="good morning". If we change the value of Y to "afternoon", then the result of our expression is now "good afternoon". Clear so far?

Now, we know that the AskYesNo function returns a value of either @YES or @NO. What we need to do is create a variable to store the value that AskYesNo returns, so that we can use it later on. First, we need to give this variable a name. In WinBatch, variable names must begin with a letter, may contain any combination of letters or numbers, and may be from 1 to 30 characters long. So, let's use a variable called 'response' (we will distinguish variable names in this text by typing them in all lowercase letters; we will type function and statement names starting with a capital letter. However, in WinBatch, the case is irrelevant, so you can use all lowercase, or all uppercase, or whatever combination you prefer). We assign the value returned by the AskYesNo function to the variable called 'response' as follows:

```
response = AskYesNo("Really?", "Do you really
                    want to play Solitaire now?")
```

Notice the syntax. The way that WinBatch process this line is to first evaluate the result of the AskYesNo function. The function returns a value of either @YES or @NO. Then, WinBatch assigns this returned value to 'response'. Therefore, 'response' is now equal to @YES or @NO. Now, all we need is a way to make a decision based upon this variable.

Making Decisions

WinBatch provides a way to conditionally execute a statement. The way this is done is with the If ... Then statement. Actually, there are two parts to this construct: If and Then (naturally). The format is:

```
If condition Then function
```

The use of If ... Then can be illustrated easily by going back to our SOLITARE.WBT file, and making these modifications:

```
response = AskYesNo("Really?", "Do you really
                    want to play Solitaire now?")
If response == @YES Then Run("sol.exe", "")
```

As you can see, we are using If ... Then to test whether the response to the question posed in AskYesNo is @YES. If it is @YES, then we start Solitaire. If it's not @YES, then we don't start Solitaire. The rule is: if the condition following the If keyword is true, then the function following the Then keyword is performed. If the condition following the If keyword is false, then anything following the Then keyword is ignored There is something extremely important that you should note about the condition following the If keyword: the double equal signs (==). In WinBatch, a single equal sign (=) is an assignment operator — it assigns the value on the right of the equal sign to the variable on the left of the equal sign. As in:

```
response = AskYesNo("Really?", "Do you really
                    want to play Solitaire now?")
```

This is saying, in English: "Assign the value returned by the AskYesNo function to the variable called 'response'." But in the statement:

```
If response == @YES Then Run("sol.exe", "")
```

we do not want to assign a new value to response, we merely want to test whether it is equal to @YES. Therefore, we use the double equal sign (==), which is the equality operator in WinBatch. The statement above is saying, in English: "If the value of the variable called 'response' is equal to @YES, then run the program SOL.EXE." What would happen if we used a single equal sign (=) here instead? Well, since the single equal sign (=) is the assignment operator, WinBatch would first assign

the value @YES to the variable 'response'. Then, it would perform the If function by testing the condition following the keyword If. Since an assignment operation always results in a true condition, the condition following the If keyword would always be true, and the function following the Then keyword would always be performed, regardless of the value of AskYesNo.

If you've become confused now, just remember that a single equal sign (=) is an assignment operator, used to assign a value to a variable. A double equal sign (==) is an equality operator, used to test whether the values on both sides of the operator are the same. If you ever have a problem with one of your WinBatch files, the first thing you check should be whether you've used '=' instead of '=='. We cannot emphasize this too strongly! We've seen what happens when the condition following the Then keyword is true. But what happens when it is false? Remember we said that when the If condition is false, the Then function is ignored. There will be times, however when we want to perform an alternate action in this event. For example, suppose we want to display a message if the user decides he or she doesn't want to play Solitaire. We could say:

```
response = AskYesNo("Really?", "Do you really
                    want to play Solitaire now?")
If response == @YES Then Run("sol.exe", "")
If response == @NO Then Display(5, "Game
    Canceled", "Smart move ... I think the boss is
                    standing behind you.")
```

In this case there are two If statements being evaluated, with one and only one of them possibly being true (unless the user selected the Cancel button, which would abort the batch file entirely). However, this is not very efficient from a processing point of view. Furthermore, what would happen if you had several functions you wanted to perform if the user answered 'Yes'? You would end up with something unwieldy, like:

```
response = AskYesNo("Really?", "Do you really
                    want to play Solitaire now?")
If response == @YES Then Display(5, "", "On
                    your mark ...")
If response == @YES Then Display(5, "", "Get
                    set ...")
If response == @YES Then Display(5, "", "Go!")
If response == @YES Then Run("sol.exe", "")
```

Clearly, there must be a better way of handling this.

Branching

Enter the Goto function. Goto, in combination with If ... Then, gives you complete control over the flow of control in your WinBatch files. Goto does exactly what it says — it causes the flow of control to go to another point in the batch file. You must specify where you want the flow of control to be transferred, and you must mark this point with a label. A label is simply a destination address. The form of the Goto function is:

    Goto label

where label is an identifier that you specify. The same rules apply to label names as to variable names (the first character must be a letter, the label name may consist of any combination of letters and numbers, and the label name may be from 1 to 30 characters long). In addition, the label is preceded by a colon at the point where it is being used as a destination address. Here's an example:

    response = AskYesNo("Really?", "Do you really
                    want to play Solitaire now?")
    If response == @NO Then Goto quit
    Display(5, "", "On your mark ...")
    Display(5, "", "Get set ...")
    Display(5, "", "Go!")
    Run("sol.exe", "") :quit

If the If condition is true (that is, the user answered 'No'), then the Goto function is performed. The Goto statement is saying, in English "go to the line marked ':quit' and continue processing from there." Notice how the label 'quit' is preceded by colon on the last line, but not on the line with the Goto function. This is important. Although you can have multiple lines in your batch file which say 'Goto quit', you can have only one line marked ':quit'. Of course, you can use many different labels in a batch file, just as you can use many different variables, as long as each has a unique name. For example:

    response = AskYesNo("Really?", "Do you really
                    want to play Solitaire now?")
    If response == @NO Then Goto quit
    Display(5, "", "On your mark ...")
    Display(5, "", "Get set ...")
    Display(5, "", "Go!")
    Run("sol.exe", "")
    Goto done
    :quit
    Display(5, "Game Canceled", "Smart move ... I
            think the boss is standing behind you.")
    :done

This is a little more complicated. It uses two labels, 'quit' and 'done'. If the user answers 'No', then the If condition

is true, control passes to the line marked ':quit', and a message is displayed. If, on the other hand, the user answers 'Yes', then the If condition is false, and the 'Goto quit' line is ignored. Instead, the next four lines are processed, and then the 'Goto done' line is unconditionally performed. The purpose of this line is to bypass the Display line which follows by transferring control to the end of the batch file. There is another way to keep your batch file processing from "falling through" to unwanted lines at the end of a program, and that is with the Exit function. Exit causes a batch file to end immediately. So, for example, we could rewrite the above batch file as follows:

    response = AskYesNo("Really?", "Do you really
                    want to play Solitaire now?")
    If response == @NO Then Goto quit
    Display(5, "", "On your mark ...")
    Display(5, "", "Get set ...")
    Display(5, "", "Go!")
    Run("sol.exe", "")
    Exit
    :quit
    Display(5, "Game Canceled", "Smart move ... I
            think the boss is standing behind you.")

Since the Run function is the last thing we want to do if the user answers 'Yes', the Exit function simply ends the program at that point. Note that we could put an Exit function at the end of the program as well, but it isn't necessary. An Exit is implied at the end of a WinBatch program.

This concludes the first part of our tutorial. You now have the building blocks you need to create useful WinBatch files. In the second part, which follows, we will look at a some of the WinBatch functions which are available for your use.

Exploring WinBatch

What follows is just a sample of the functions and statements available in WinBatch. These should be sufficient to begin creating versatile and powerful batch files. For complete information on these and all WinBatch functions and statements, refer to the WBL Function Reference.

Running Programs

There are three functions which you can use to start an application, each of which shares a common syntax:

Run (program-name, parameters)

We've already seen the Run function. This function starts a program in a "normal" window. Windows decides where to place the application's window on the screen. Example:

```
Run("Notepad.exe", "myfile.txt")
```

If the program has an EXE extension, its extension may be omitted:

```
Run("Notepad", "myfile.txt")
```

Also, you can "run" data files if they have an extension in WIN.INI which is associated with a program. So, if TXT files are associated with Notepad:

```
Run("myfile.txt", " ")
```

would start Notepad, using the file MYFILE.TXT. When you specify a file to run, WinBatch looks first in the current directory, and then in the directories on your DOS Path. If the file is not found, WinBatch will return an error. You can also specify a full path name for WinBatch to use, as in:

```
Run("c:\windows\apps\winedit.exe", " ")
```

RunZoom (program-name, parameters)

RunZoom is like Run, but it starts a program as a full-screen window. Example:

```
RunZoom("excel", "bigsheet.xls")
```

RunIcon (program-name, parameters)

RunIcon starts a program as an icon at the bottom of the screen. Example:

```
RunIcon("clock", " ")
```

Display and Input

Here we have functions which display information to the user and prompt the user for information, plus a couple of relevant system functions.

Display (seconds, title, text)

Displays a message to the user for a specified time. The message will disappear after the time expires, or after any keypress or mouse click. Example:

```
Display(2, "", "Loading Solitaire now")
```

Message (title, text)

This command displays a message box with a title and text you specify, until the user presses the OK button. Example:

```
Message("Sorry", "That file cannot be found")
```

Pause (title, text)

This command is similar to Message, except an exclamation-point icon appears in the message box, and the user can press OK or Cancel. If the user presses Cancel, the batch file exits. Example:

```
Pause("Delete Backups", "Last chance to stop!")
;if batch file gets this far, the user pressed OK
FileDelete("*.bak")
```

AskYesNo (title, question)

Displays a dialog box with a given title, which presents the user with three buttons: Yes, No, and Cancel. If the user selects the Cancel button, the batch file is terminated. Example:

```
response = AskYesNo("End Session", "Are you
                        sure you want to leave Windows?"
```

AskLine (title, prompt, default)

Displays a dialog box with a given title, which prompts the user for a line of input. Returns the default if the user just presses the OK button. Example:

```
yourfile = AskLine("Edit File", "Filename:",
                                "newfile.txt")
Run("notepad", yourfile)
```

If you specify a default entry (in this case, NEWFILE.TXT), it will appear in the response box, and will be replaced with whatever the user types.

Beep

Beeps once: Beep. And if one beep isn't enough for you: Beep Beep Beep.

Delay (seconds)

Pauses batch file execution. The Delay function lets you suspend batch file processing for 1 to 15 seconds. Again, you can use multiple occurrences for a longer delay:

Delay(15) Delay(15)

Will insert a 30-second pause.

Manipulating Windows

There are a large number of functions which allow you to manage the windows on your desktop. Here are some of them:

WinZoom (partial-windowname)

Maximizes an application window to full-screen.

WinIconize (partial-windowname)

Turns an application window into an icon.

WinShow (partial-windowname)

Shows a window in its "normal" state.

These three functions are used to modify the size of an already- running window. WinZoom is the equivalent of selecting Maximize from a window's control (space-bar) menu, WinIconize is the same as selecting Minimize, and WinShow has the same effect as selecting Restore.

The window that you are performing any of these functions on does not have to be the active window. If the specified window is in the background, and the WinZoom or WinShow function causes the size of the window to change, then the window will be brought to the fore-ground. The WinZoom function has no effect on a window which is already maximized, and WinShow has no effect on an already-"normal" window.

Each of these functions takes a partial windowname as a parameter. The "windowname" is the name which appears in the title bar at the top of the window. You can specify the full name if you wish, but it may often be advantageous not to have to do so. For example, if you are editing the file SOLITARE.WBT in a Notepad window open, the windowname will be

    Notepad - SOLITARE.WBT

You probably don't want to have to hard-code this name into your batch file:

    WinZoom("Notepad - SOLITARE.WBT")

Instead, you can specify the partial windowname 'Notepad':

    WinZoom("Notepad")

If you have more than one Notepad window open, WinBatch will use the first one it finds. Note that WinBatch matches the partial windowname starting with the first character, so that while

    WinZoom("Note")

would be correct,

    WinZoom("pad")

would not result in a match. Also, be aware that the case of the title (upper or lower) is significant, so:

    WinZoom("notepad")

would be invalid.

WinActivate (partial-windowname)

Makes an application window the active window. This function makes a currently-open window the active window. If the specified window is an icon, it will be restored to normal size; otherwise, its size will not be changed.

WinClose (partial-windowname)

Closes an application window.

WinCloseNot (partial-windowname [, partial-windowname]...)

Closes all application windows except those specified. This function lets you close all windows except the one(s) you specify. For example:

    WinCloseNot("Program Man")

would leave only the Program Manager open, and:

    WinCloseNot("Program Man, Solit") 14

would leave the Program Manager and Solitaire windows open.

WinWaitClose (partial-windowname)

Waits until an application window is closed. This function causes your WinBatch file to pause until you have manually closed a specified window. This is a very convenient way to have a WinBatch file open several windows sequentially, without having unnecessary windows open all over your desktop. For example:

    RunZoom("invoices.xls"", "") ;balance the books
    WinWaitClose("Microsoft Ex") ;wait till
                                        Excel closed
    RunZoom("sol", "") ;you deserve a break
    WinWaitClose("Solitaire") ;wait until Sol closed
    Run("winword", "agenda.doc") ;more paperwork
    WinWaitClose("Microsoft Wor") ;wait until
                                        W4W closed
    Run("clock","") ;lunchtime yet?

During the time that the batch file is suspended, the WinBatch icon will remain at the bottom of your screen. You can cancel the batch file at any time by selecting the icon and then selecting "Terminate" from the menu.

WinExist (partial-windowname)

Tells if Window exists. This function returns @TRUE or @FALSE, depending on whether a matching window can be found. This gives you a very handy method of insuring that only one copy of a given window will be open at a time.

If you've been following this tutorial faithfully from the beginning, you probably have several copies of Solitaire running at the moment. You can check by pressing Ctrl-Esc now. You say you've got 5 Solitaire windows open? Okay, close them all. Now, let's modify our SOLITARE.WBT file. First, trim out the excess lines so that it looks like this:

```
Run("sol.exe", "")
```

Now, let's use the WinExist function to make sure that WinBatch only starts Solitaire if it isn't already running:

```
If WinExist("Solitaire") == @FALSE Then
                    Run("sol.exe", "")
```

And this should work fine. Run SOLITARE.WBT twice now, and see what happens. The first time you run it, it should start Solitaire; the second (and subsequent) time, it should not do anything. However, it's quite likely that you want the batch file to do something if Solitaire is already running — namely, bring the Solitaire window to the foreground. This can be accomplished easily by using the WinActivate function, along with a couple of Goto statements, as follows:

```
If WinExist("Solitaire") == @FALSE Then
Goto open
WinActivate("Solitaire")
Goto loaded
:open Run("sol.exe", "")
:loaded
```

Note that we can change this to have WinExist check for a 'True' value instead, by modifying the structure of the batch file, as follows:

```
If WinExist("Solitaire") == @TRUE Then Goto
                                        activate
Run("sol.exe", "")
Goto loaded
:activate
WinActivate("Solitaire")
:loaded
```

Either format is perfectly correct, and the choice of which to use is merely a matter of personal style. The result is exactly the same.

EndSession ( )

Ends the current Windows session. This does exactly what it says. It will not ask any questions, so you may want to build in a little safety net:

```
Sure = AskYesNo("End Session", "Are you sure
                    you want to exit Windows?")
If Sure == @YES Then EndSession()
```

Files and Directories

DirChange (pathname)

Changes the directory to the pathname specified. Use this function when you want to run a program which must be started from its own directory. 'Pathname' may optionally include a drive letter. Example:

```
DirChange("c:\windows\winword")
Run("winword.exe", "")
```

DirGet ( )

Gets the Current Working Directory. This function is especially useful when used in conjunction with DirChange, to save and then return to the current directory. Example:

```
origdir = DirGet()
DirChange("c:\windows\winword")
Run("winword.exe", "")
DirChange(origdir)
```

FileExist (filename)

Determines if a file exists. This function will return @TRUE if the specified file exists, and @FALSE if it doesn't exist. Example:

```
If FileExist("win.bak") == @FALSE Then
                FileCopy("win.ini", "win.bak")
Run("notepad.exe", "win.ini")
```

FileCopy (from-list, to-file, warning)

Copies files. If warning is @TRUE, WinEdit will pop up a dialog box warning you if you are about to overwrite an existing file, and giving you an opportunity to change your mind. If warning is @FALSE, it won't. Example:

```
FileCopy("cmdpost.cpm", "*.sav", @TRUE)
Run("notepad.exe", "cmdpost.cpm")
```

The wildcard (*) will cause cmdpost.cpm to be copied as cmdpost.sav.

FileDelete (file-list)

Deletes files. Example:

```
If FileExist("win.bak") == @TRUE Then
FileDelete("win.bak")
```

FileRename (from-list, to-file)

Renames files to another set of names. We can illustrate the use of the WinBatch file functions with a typical batch file application. Our word processor saves a backup copy of each document with a BAK extension, but we want a larger safety net when editing important files. We want to keep the five most recent versions of the WinBatch manual. Here is our batch file:

```
If FileExist("winbatch.bak") == @TRUE Then
                                  Goto backup
:edit
Run("winword.exe", "winbatch.doc")
Exit
:backup
FileDelete("winbatch.bk5")
FileRename("winbatch.bk4", "winbatch.bk5")
FileRename("winbatch.bk3", "winbatch.bk4")
FileRename("winbatch.bk2", "winbatch.bk3")
FileRename("winbatch.bk1", "winbatch.bk2")
FileRename("winbatch.bak", "winbatch.bk1")
Goto edit
```

If the file WINBATCH.BAK exists, it means that we have made a change to WINBATCH.DOC. So, before we start editing, we delete the oldest backup copy, and perform several FileRename functions, until eventually WINBATCH.BAK becomes WINBATCH.BK1. Notice how the flow of control moves to the line labeled ':backup', and then back to the line labeled ':edit', and how we terminate processing with the Exit statement. If we did not include the Exit statement, the batch file would continue in an endless loop. However, this batch file still isn't quite right. What would happen if the file WINBATCH.BK5 didn't exist? In the DOS batch language, the command would return an error and processing would continue. But in WinBatch, the error would be fatal, and cause the batch file to abort. There are two ways that we can handle this. We could use an If FileExist test before every file operation, and test the returned value for a @TRUE before proceeding. But this would be very clumsy, even with such a small batch file.

Handling Errors

Luckily, there is a WinBatch system function to help us here: ErrorMode. The ErrorMode function determines what happens if an error occurs during batch file processing. Here's the syntax:

ErrorMode (mode): Specifies how to handle errors. **Parameters:** "mode" = @CANCEL, @NOTIFY, or @OFF. **Returns:** (integer) previous error setting.

Use this command to control the effects of runtime errors. The default is @CANCEL, meaning the execution of the batch file will be canceled for any error.

@CANCEL: All runtime errors will cause execution to be canceled. The user will be notified which error occurred.
@NOTIFY: All runtime errors will be reported to the user, and they can choose to continue if it isn't fatal.
@OFF: Minor runtime errors will be suppressed. Moderate and fatal errors will be reported to the user. User has the option of continuing if the error is not fatal.

As you can see, the default mode is @CANCEL, and it's a good idea to leave it like this. However, it is quite reasonable to change the mode for sections of your batch files where you anticipate errors occurring. This is just what we've done in our modified batch file:

```
If FileExist("winbatch.bak") == @TRUE Then
                                  Goto backup
:edit
Run("winword.exe", "winbatch.doc")
Exit
:backup
ErrorMode(@OFF)
FileDelete("winbatch.bk5")
FileRename("winbatch.bk4", "winbatch.bk5)
FileRename("winbatch.bk3", "winbatch.bk4)
FileRename("winbatch.bk2", "winbatch.bk3)
FileRename("winbatch.bk1", "winbatch.bk2)
FileRename("winbatch.bak", "winbatch.bk1)
ErrorMode(@CANCEL)
Goto edit
```

Notice how we've used ErrorMode(@OFF) to prevent errors from aborting the batch file, and then used ErrorMode(@CANCEL) at the end of the backup section to change back to the default mode. This is good practice.

Selection Menus

So far, whenever we have needed to use a file name, we have hard-coded it into our batch files. For example:

```
Run("notepad.exe", "agenda.txt")
```

Naturally, there should be a way to get this information from the user "on the fly", so that we wouldn't have to write hundreds of different batch files. And there is a way. Two ways, actually. Consider, first, a function that we have already seen, the AskLine function:

```
file = AskLine("", "Enter Filename to edit?", "")
Run("notepad.exe", file)
```

This will prompt the user for a filename, and start Notepad using that file. There are only three problems with this approach. First, the user might not remember the name of the file. Second, the user might enter the name incorrectly. And finally, modern software is supposed to be sophisticated enough to handle these things the right way. And WinBatch certainly can.

There are two new functions we need to use for our file selection routine: FileItemize and ItemSelect.

FileItemize (file-list)

Returns a space-delimited list of files. This function compiles a list of filenames and separates the names with spaces. There are several variations we can use:

```
FileItemize("*.doc")
```

would give us a list of all files in the current directory with a DOC extension,

```
FileItemize("*.com *.exe")
```

would give us a list of all files in the current directory with a COM or EXE extension, and

```
FileItemize("*.*")
```

would give us a list of all files in the current directory. Of course, we need to be able to use this file list, and for that we use:

```
ItemSelect (title, list, delimiter)
```

Displays a listbox filled with items from a list you specify in a string. The items are separated in your string by a delimiter character. This function actually displays the list box. Remember that FileItemize returns a file list delimited by spaces, which would look something like this:

```
file1.doc file2.doc file3.doc
```

When we use ItemSelect, we need to tell it that the delimiter is a space. We do this as follows:

```
textfiles = FileItemize("*.doc *.txt")
yourfile = ItemSelect("Select a file to edit",
                                    textfiles, "")
run("notepad.exe", yourfile)
```

First, we use FileItemize to build a list of filenames with DOC and TXT extensions. We assign this list to the variable 'textfiles'. Then, we use the ItemSelect function to build a

list box, passing it the variable 'textfiles' as its second parameter. The third parameter we use for ItemSelect is simply a space with quote marks around it; this tells ItemSelect that the variable 'textfiles' is delimited by spaces. Note that this is different from the empty string that we've spoken about earlier - you must include a space between the quote marks. Finally, we assign the value returned by the ItemSelect function to the variable 'yourfile', and run Notepad using that file.

How does ItemSelect get a file name? As we said, it pops up a list box with all the files returned by the FileSelect function. Then, you highlight a file, using either the cursor keys or a mouse, and select it by pressing Enter, double-clicking on the file, or clicking on the OK button. If you run the above example, you'll see it more easily than we can explain it in words.

If the user presses Enter or clicks on the OK button without a file being highlighted, ItemSelect returns an empty string. If you want, you can test for this condition:

```
textfiles = FileItemize("*.doc *.txt")
:retry
yourfile = ItemSelect("Select a file to edit",
                                    textfiles, "")
if yourfile == "" Then Goto retry
run("notepad.exe", yourfile)
```

DirItemize (dir-list)

Returns a space-delimited list of directories. This function works like FileItemize, but instead of returning a list of files, it returns a list of directories. Remember that we said FileItemize only lists files in the current directory. Often, we want to be able to use files in other directories as well. We can do this by first selecting the appropriate directory, using DirItemize and ItemSelect:

```
DirChange("\")
subdirs = DirItemize("*")
targdir = ItemSelect("Select dir", subdirs, " ")
DirChange(targdir)
files = FileItemize("*.*")
file = ItemSelect("Select file", files, " ")
Run("notepad.exe", file)
```

First we change to the root directory. Then we use the DirItemize function to get a list of all the subdirectories off of root. Next, we use ItemSelect to give us a list box of directories to select from. Finally, we change to the selected directory, and use FileItemize and ItemSelect to pick a file. This batch file works, but needs to be polished up a bit. What happens if the file we want is in the \WIN\BATCH directory? Our batch file doesn't go more than one level deep from root. We want to continue down the directory tree, but we also need a way of telling when we're at the end of a branch. As it happens, there is such a way: DirItemize will return an empty string if there are no directories to process. Given this knowledge, we can set up a loop to test when we are at the lowest level:

```
DirChange("\")
:getdir
subdirs = DirItemize("*")
If subdirs == "" Then Goto getfile
targdir = ItemSelect("Select dir (OK for
                        current)", subdirs, "")
If targdir == "" Then Goto getfile
DirChange(targdir)
Goto getdir
:getfile
files = FileItemize("*.*")
file = ItemSelect("Select file", files, " ")
if file == "" then goto getfile
Run("notepad.exe", file)
```

After we use the DirItemize function, we test the returned value for a blank string. If we have a blank string, then we know that the current directory has no subdirectories, and so we proceed to select the filename from the current directory (Goto getfile) . If, however, DirItemize returns a non-blank list, then we know that there is, in fact, at least one directory. In that case, we use ItemSelect to bring up a list box. Then, we test the value returned by ItemSelect. If the returned value is a blank string, it means that the user did not select a directory from the list, and presumably wants a file in the current directory. We happily oblige (Goto getfile). On the other hand, a non-blank value returned from ItemSelect indicates that the user has selected a subdirectory from the list box. In that case, we change to the selected directory, and loop back to the beginning of the directory selection routine (Goto getdir). We continue this until either (a) the user selects a directory, or (b) there are no directories left to select. Eventually, we get down to the file selection section of the batch file.

Nicer Dialog Boxes

Have you tried displaying long messages, and found that WinBatch didn't wrap the lines quite the way you wanted? Here are a couple of tricks.

Num2Char (integer)

Converts a number to its character equivalent. We want to be able to insert carriage return/line feed combinations in our output, and the Num2Char function will let us do that. A carriage return has an ASCII value of 13, and a line feed has an ASCII value of 10 (don't worry if you don't understand what that means). To be able to use these values, we must convert them to characters, as follows:

```
cr = num2char(13)
lf = num2char(10)
```

Now, we need to be able to place the variables 'cr' and 'lf' in our message. For example, let's say we want to do this:

```
Message("", "This is line one This is line two")
```

If we just inserted the variables into the string, as in:

```
Message("", "This is line one cr lf This is line
                                            two")
```

we would not get the desired effect (try it and see). WinBatch would treat them as ordinary text. However, WinBatch does provide us with a method of performing variable substitution such as this, and that is by enclosing the variables in percentage signs (%%). If we do this:

```
Message("", "This is line one %cr% %lf%This is
                                        line two")
```

we get what we want. Note that there is no space after '%lf%'; this is so the second line will be aligned with the first line (every space inside the quote marks is significant). Now, wouldn't it be convenient if we could combine cr and lf into a single variable? We can.

StrCat (string[, string]...)

Concatenates strings together. The StrCat function lets us combine any number of string constants and/or string variables. Here's how we combine the variables 'cr' and 'lf' into the single variable 'crlf':

```
crlf = StrCat(cr, lf)
```

Note that the strings to be concatenated are separated by commas, within the parentheses. Now, we can rewrite our example, as follows:

```
cr = num2char(13)
lf = num2char(10)
crlf = StrCat(cr, lf)
Message("", "This is line one %crlf%This is line
                                            two")
```

If we wanted to re-use this message a number of times, it would be quite convenient to use the StrCat function to make a single variable out of it:

```
cr = num2char(13)
lf = num2char(10)
crlf = StrCat(cr, lf)
line1 = "This is line one"
line2 = "This is line two"
mytext = StrCat(line1, crlf, line2)
Message("", mytext)
```

Running DOS Programs

WinBatch can run DOS programs, just like it runs Windows programs:

```
dirchange("c:\game")
run("scramble.exe", "")
```

If you want to use an internal DOS command, such as DIR or TYPE, you can do so by running the DOS command interpreter, COMMAND.COM, with the '/c' program parameter, as follows:

```
run("command.com", "/c type readme.txt")
```

Everything that you would normally type on the DOS command line goes after the '/c' in the second parameter. Here's another example:

```
run("command.com", "/c type readme.txt |
                      more")
```

These examples assume that COMMAND.COM is in a directory on your DOS path. If it isn't, you could specify a full path name for it:

```
run("c:\command.com", "/c type readme.txt |
                        more")
```

Or, better still, you could use the WinBatch Environment function.

Environment (env-variable)

Gets a DOS environment variable. Since DOS always stores the full path and filename of the command processor in the environmental variable COMSPEC, it is an easy matter to retrieve this information:

```
coms = environment("comspec")
```

and use it in our batch file:

```
coms = environment("comspec")
run(coms, "/c type readme.txt")
```

To get a DOS window, just run COMMAND.COM with no parameters:

```
coms = environment("comspec")
run(coms, "")
```

Sending Keystrokes to Programs

Here we come to one of the most useful and powerful features of WinBatch: the ability to send keystrokes to Windows programs, just as if you were typing them directly from the keyboard.

SendKey (character-codes)

Sends Keystrokes to the active application. This is an ideal way to automatically program the keys that you enter every time you start a certain program. For example, to start up Notepad and have it prompt you for a file to open, you would use:

```
Run("notepad.exe", "")
SendKey("!FO")
```

The parameter for SendKey is a string to send to the program. This string consists of standard characters, as well as some special characters which you will find listed under the entry for SendKey in the WBL Function Reference. In the example above, the exclamation mark stands for the Alt key, so '!F' is the equivalent of pressing and holding down the Alt key while simultaneously pressing the 'F' key. The 'O' in the example above is simply the letter 'O', and is the same as pressing the 'O' key. As you may know, 'Alt-F' brings up the 'File' menu in Notepad, and 'O' selects 'Open' from the 'File' menu. Here's another example:

```
RunZoom("sol.exe", "")
SendKey("!GC{RIGHT}{SP}~")
```

This starts up Solitaire, brings up the 'Game' menu (!G), selects 'Deck' (C), moves the cursor to the next card back style on the right ({RIGHT}), selects that card back ({SP}), and then selects 'OK' (~). And voila! A different card design every time you play!

Our Completed WinBatch File

Here is the final version of the SOLITARE.WBT file that we've been building throughout this tutorial.

Tutorial

```
; solitare.wbt
mins = AskLine("Solitaire", "How many
                minutes do you want to play?", "")
If WinExist("Solitaire") == @TRUE Then Goto
                                        activate
RunZoom("sol.exe", "")
Goto loaded
:activate
WinActivate("Solitaire")
WinZoom("Solitaire")
:loaded
```

```
SendKey("!GC{RIGHT}{SP}~")
goal = mins * 60
timer = 0
:moretime
remain = goal - timer
WinTitle("Solitaire", "Solitaire (%remain%
                     seconds left)")
delay(10)
timer = timer + 10
If WinExist("Solitaire") == @FALSE Then Exit
If timer < goal Then Goto moretime
```

```
Beep
WinClose("Solitaire")
Message("Time's up", "Get back to work!")
```

It incorporates many of the concepts that we've discussed in this tutorial, as well as using some arithmetic (*, -, +) and relational (<) operators that are covered in the following section on the WinBatch language. If you can understand and follow the structures and processes illustrated in this sample file, and can incorporate them into your own WinBatch files, you are well on your way to becoming a WinBatch guru!

A copy of this program and its complete documentation, including the full language reference, may be found on the disk that came with this book.

Registration Card

I want my *own* copy of WinBatch! Please send it to:

Company: _____

Name: _____

Address: _____

City: _____ State:_____ Zip:_____

Country: _____

Phone:(_____)_____

WinBatch(es) @$69.95 ea. _____

Total _____

Foreign air shipping
(except Canada) @$9.50 _____

Shipping _____

TOTAL _____

Please enclose a check payable to Wilson WindowWare; or you may use VISA, Master Card, or EuroCard. For charge cards, please enter the information below:

Card number: __ __ __ -__ __ __ -__ __ __ -__ __ __

Expiration date: _____/_____

Signature:_____

Send to: Wilson WindowWare
          2701 California Ave SW #212
          Seattle, WA 98116 USA

or call: (800) 762-8383
          (206) 935-7129 (fax)

(Please allow 2 to 4 weeks for delivery)

WinClock

Version 3.04
Copyright © 1991 by David A. Feinleib

Introduction

WinClock is a digital clock for Microsoft Windows 3.0 that has the following features:

- Display of time and date in many different formats
- Ten alarms (which can be set for daily or only a specified date)

- Run Program Timer (ability to run programs at specified times)
- Optional hourly beep
- Allows user to set date and time easily
- Optionally stays in front of other applications

```
☐  12:00 PM  Wed 5/22/91
```

- Remembers its position on the screen
- Two stopwatches
- Two countdown timers
- Colon separating hours and minutes may be set to blink
- Context sensitive help
- Direct Screen saver compatibility (Auto-detects active screen savers)
- Cascade and Tile compatibility

```
┌─────────────────────────────┐
│ Restore                     │
│ Move                        │
│ Size                        │
│ Minimize                    │
│ Maximize                    │
├─────────────────────────────┤
│ Close              Alt+F4   │
├─────────────────────────────┤
│ Switch To...       Ctrl+Esc │
├─────────────────────────────┤
│ Help...                     │
│ Set Time/Date...            │
│ Alarms...                   │
│ Timers...                   │
│ Hourly beep                 │
│ Preferences...              │
│ About...                    │
├─────────────────────────────┤
│ ☐  12:00 PM  Wed 5/22/91    │
└─────────────────────────────┘
```

Requirements for Running WinClock

- Microsoft Windows 3.0
- WinClock (WINCLOCK.EXE, WCHOOK.DLL, WINCLOCK.HLP)

Running/Installing/Upgrading WinClock

Please note that the following directions assume you are using a mouse. If you are not using a mouse, please refer to your Windows documentation for equivalent keystrokes.

Upgrading WinClock

If you are upgrading from a previous version of WinClock, you should copy this version of WinClock to the same directory that the old version is in. Since configuration files of previous versions of WinClock are not compatible with this version, the first time you run WinClock you will see a message which tells you that your configuration file was created by a different version of WinClock and that your preference settings have been reset to the default. You may want to change the settings back to your preferred settings.

1. Copy WINCLOCK.EXE, WCHOOK.DLL, and WINCLOCK.HLP to your Windows directory or another directory of your choice. Note that you must copy WINCLOCK.EXE, WCHOOK.DLL, and WINCLOCK.HLP to the same directory.
2. Do one of the following: **Note:** Option D is highly recommended over A, B, and C.
   a. Click on File then Run... in the Program Manager menu. Type WINCLOCK.EXE (including the path) in the Command line edit box and click OK . If you use this option, you will have to do this every time you want to run WinClock.
   b. Click on one of the program groups in the Program Manager (the Accessories group is suggested). Select File then New... from the program manager menu. Select Program Item and type WINCLOCK.EXE in the Command line edit box. For example, you might type: C:\WINDOWS\WINCLOCK.EXE if that was the directory into which you had copied WinClock. WinClock has several different icons from which you may choose. To see the icons, click on Change icon then click on View next until you find an icon that you like. When you want to run WinClock, double click on the WinClock icon.
   c. On the line that says "load=" in your WIN.INI file, add WINCLOCK.EXE (with the appropriate path). For example, if you copied WINCLOCK.EXE to C:\WINDOWS, the line would say: load=C:\WINDOWS\WINCLOCK.EXE This option will automatically run WinClock each time you run Windows.
   d. Do both B and C, which will automatically run WinClock and allow you to run WinClock easily if you close it.

WinClock Options

To bring up a list of options, click once on the WinClock system box.

Help...

This will bring up help about WinClock and explain how to use context sensitive help. It will also display an index of all help available for WinClock.

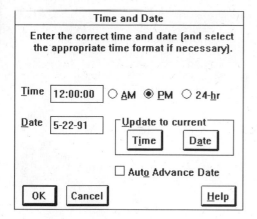

Set Time/Date...

This allows you to easily enter the time and date. When the window pops up, enter the correct time and date. Click AM or PM to set the time in 12-hour format, or click 24-hr and enter the time in 24-hour format. WinClock will automatically convert 24-hour format to 12-hour format if you click PM after 24-hr was selected. WinClock will also convert from PM to 24-hour format.

The current time and date will be shown in the edit boxes when the window originally appears. To update the time and date displayed in the edit boxes to the current time and date, click the Time or Date push-button depending on which you want to update. When you have made all your choices, click OK (or press <Enter>). If you want to leave the old time and date, click Cancel.

Alarms...

This allows you to configure one or both of WinClock's alarms. To set an alarm: Click on the alarm you want to set (Alarm One or Two). When you have made your choices, click OK. If you want to leave the alarms the way they were, click Cancel.

Enabled

If you want the alarm to be on, select Enabled (so that there is an "x" in the box). If you do not want the alarm to be on, but only want to set it for use at a later time, click on Enabled until there is no "x" in the box.

Time

Enter the time for the alarm to go off in the edit box. If you select AM or PM, enter the time in 12-hour format. If you select 24-hr, enter the time in 24-hour format.

Date

One Date: Select One Date to have the alarm go off on a single date. Type the date in the edit box.
Start Date: Select Start Date and enter the start date in the edit box. The start date is the date from which the alarms in the lower portion of the dialog box start. The start date causes the alarm to go off on-Beep To have the alarm beep when it goes off, select Beep so that there is an "x" in the box. Select high or low pitch. Select the duration of the beep. Short is about eight seconds; long is about 30 seconds. Both beeps may be stopped by clicking OK when the box alerting you to the alarm appears.
Week Interval:
Periodic: The periodic section causes alarms to go off on dates such as: Every Thursday, Every other Wednesday, and so on. Select the periods that you want and choose the dates with which they should be combined.
Of Every Month: This section causes alarms to go off on dates such as: The first Thursday of every month, the second Wednesday of every month, and so on.
Day: This section is combined with options you select in the Periodic and Of Every Month sections.
Examples
• *Periodic:* To have an alarm go off Every Other Tuesday, you would

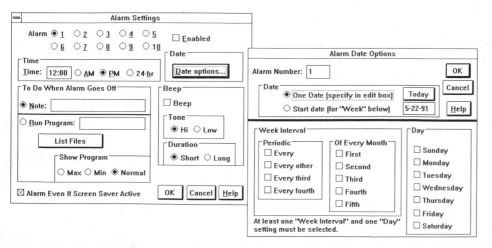

select Every Other in the Periodic Section and Tuesday in the Day section. If you entered 5-15-90 in the Start Date edit box and selected Every and Tuesday, since 5-15-90 is a Tuesday, the alarm would go off on 5-15-90, 5-22-90, 5-29-90, 6-04-90, and so on.

- *Of Every Month:* To have an alarm go off on the Second Wednesday of Every Month, you would select Second in the Of Every Month section and Wednesday in the Day section. If you entered 5-15-90 in the Start Date edit box and selected Third in the Of Every Month Section and Monday in the Day section, the alarm would go off on 6-17-90, since that is the third Monday of the month.

```
┌─────────────────────────────────────────┐
│                 Timers                   │
│ ┌─Timer──────┐ ┌─Display──────┐ ┌──────┐ │
│ │ ◉ Stopwatch 1│ │ ☒ Display Timer│ │  OK  │ │
│ │ ○ Stopwatch 2│ │ ☐ Display Time │ └──────┘ │
│ │ ○ Countdown 1│ │ ☐ Display Date │ ┌──────┐ │
│ │ ○ Countdown 2│ │ ☒ Display Seconds│ │Cancel│ │
│ │            │ └──────────────┘ └──────┘ │
│ │ ┌────────┐ │                  ┌──────┐ │
│ │ │  Start │ │ Countdown From 0:00│ Help │ │
│ │ └────────┘ │                  └──────┘ │
│ │            │ Current Count 00:00:00    │
│ ┌─Countdown Beep─┐┌─Pitch─┐┌─Duration─┐  │
│ │ ☐ When Finished││○Hi ○Low││○Long ○Short│  │
│ └────────────────┘└───────┘└──────────┘  │
└─────────────────────────────────────────┘
```

Note/Run Program

If you want, enter a note to display when the alarm goes off. Select Run Program to run a program at the time for which you have set the alarm. Type the full pathname of the program you want to run. Select Max if you want the program to be maximized when it is run, Min to have it minimized, or Normal to have it shown in its normal size. If you type the name of a program that does not exist on your hard disk, a warning message will appear when you click OK. You may then choose to edit the name of the program to run, or leave it unedited.

Timers...

WinClock has two stopwatches and two countdown timers. By selecting different options you can have WinClock display some or all of the timers as well as the time and date. In order to use a countdown timer, you must type a number from which to countdown in the Countdown from edit box. This number must be in the form HH:MM (hours:minutes). If it is not in this form, any number found (that is before non-numeric numbers, excluding the colon) will be used as the minutes.

Select Display Timer individually for each timer if you want to display it (or to not display it). Select Display Date and/or Display Time if you want to display the date

and/or time while one or more of the timers are running. The display of the date and time are not dependent on the timer that is currently selected. Display seconds is selected by default. If you do not want to display the seconds, click on it so that there is no "x" in the box. You can choose to display the seconds individually for each timer. The seconds will only be displayed if Display Timer has been selected.

The settings that you make in the Timer dialog box only effect the WinClock display while one or more timers are running. The settings will be saved while WinClock is running but will be reset to the default when WinClock is restarted. When you have selected to display a timer, it is displayed as follows:

- The first stopwatch appears as: S1 00:00:00
- The second stopwatch appears as: S2 00:00:00
- The first countdown timer appears as: C1 00:00:00
- The second countdown timer appears as: C2 00:00:00

The current count (time elapsed) of the selected timer will appear in the Current Count box while the Timers dialog box is displayed. When a timer is stopped, its current count will be displayed in the Current Count box until you switch to another timer. The stopped timer will then reset itself to zero. The Start/Stop button will reflect whether the currently selected timer is running. If the current timer is running, the button will display Stop so that you may stop the timer. If the current timer is not running, the button will display Start so that you may start it.

Each countdown timer may be set to beep or not to beep. Select beep so that there is an "x" in the box if you want the countdown timer to beep when it finishes. Select the pitch and the duration of the beep. The short beep lasts about eight seconds; the long beep lasts about thirty seconds. Both beeps may be stopped by clicking OK when the window alerting you that the timer has finished appears.

Hourly Beep

Select this option if you want WinClock to sound a short beep and flash on the hour. A check mark will appear next to Hourly beep if it is selected. To turn off the Hourly beep, click on Hourly beep. The check mark will disappear.

Preferences...

Preferences allows you to change how the date and time are displayed. Select the options you want and click OK.

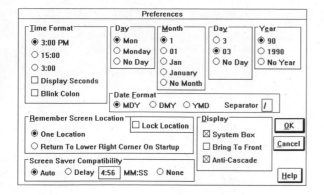

Date Formats

Separator: You may change the character that separates the parts of the date by typing a different character in the Separator edit box. Although it is possible to type more than one character, only the first character you type will be used.

Blinking Colon: If you would like the colon that separates the hours and minutes of the time to blink on the second when the seconds are not displayed, select Blink Colon so that there is an "x" in the box.

Screen Saver Compatibility

WinClock is compatible with most available screen savers. (Note that WinClock itself is not a screen saver.)

Auto Setting: This option will cause WinClock to be hidden when a screen saver saves the screen. This option is compatible with most screen savers; it is recommended that you try this option first if you would like screen saver compatibility.

Delay: Setting this option on will cause WinClock to be hidden (not displayed on the screen) after the amount of time that you specify in the edit box, when the mouse and keyboard have not been activated. You must set the delay in the form MM:SS (minutes:seconds). If it is not in this form, any number found (that is before non-numeric numbers, excluding the colon) will be used as the seconds. It is recommended that you use this option if the auto option (see above) does not work correctly with your screen saver.

None: This turns off screen saver compatibility which means that WinClock will not be hidden if you have a screen saver.

Display

Bring To Front: If you want WinClock to appear over other applications, select Bring To Front.

System Box: If you want WinClock to display a system box, select System Box. Hiding the system box reduces the area that WinClock takes up on the screen. See Displaying/ Hiding the system box for more information.

Anti-Cascade: You should select Anti-Cascade if you do not want WinClock to be cascaded when you cascade the open windows.

Screen Location

One Screen Location: WinClock remembers one screen location by default. This means that when you move WinClock it remembers its position on the screen so that the next time you run WinClock, it will go to the position where it was when it was closed.

Always Return To Default Screen Location: If you want to move WinClock to a certain location for only the current time that WinClock is running but then revert to the default screen position, select Always Return To Default Screen Location. The next time you run WinClock, it will revert to its default location.

Lock Location: This will lock WinClock's location on the screen so that you do not move it accidently.

About...

Select About... to display information about WinClock.

Getting Help

WinClock help may be accessed in three ways:

1. Select help from the WinClock system menu. This will display an index of all help available for WinClock. It will also explain how to use WinClock's context sensitive help.
2. You may access context-sensitive help by clicking on one of the WinClock system menu items, holding down the mouse button, and pressing F1.
3. You may access context-sensitive help from most of WinClock's dialog boxes by clicking on the Help button if one is displayed.

Displaying/Hiding the System Box

You may display/hide the system box in the following ways:

1. Open the Preferences dialog box and select System Box so that there is an "x" in the box. This will display the system box. To hide the system box from the Preferences dialog box, select System Box so that there is no "x" in the box.
2. Double click on the WinClock caption (the caption is the area in which the time and date are displayed). If the system box is hidden, it will appear; if it is displayed, it will be hidden.

The Right Mouse Button

If you want to Tile the open windows, you should click once with the right mouse button on the WinClock client area (the area where the time and date are displayed). This will cause WinClock to be hidden for about seven seconds, during which time you may tile the open windows.

Avoiding Cascading or Tiling WinClock

Cascading

If you want to Cascade the open windows, it is useful to have the Anti-Cascade option selected (in the Preferences dialog box) so that WinClock does not get cascaded. To select Anti-Cascade , select Preferences... from WinClock's system menu. In the Preferences dialog box, select Anti-Cascade so that there is an "x" in the box.

Tiling

If you want to Tile the open windows, you should click once with the right mouse button on the WinClock client area (the are where the time and date are displayed). This will cause WinClock to be hidden for about seven seconds, during which time you may tile the open windows.

Moving WinClock

To move WinClock, click on WinClock and, while holding the mouse button down, move WinClock.

Closing WinClock

To close WinClock, do one of the following:

1. Double click on the WinClock system box.
2. Click once on the WinClock system box and then click on Close.

Error Messages & Solutions

W1000 - No system timers available: WinClock must use one of the Windows Timers to update the time. You should try closing another application, closing WinClock, and running WinClock again.

W1010 - Unable to save WinClock configuration file: WinClock was unable to save the information you entered in the Preferences box.
W1020 - Invalid time entered: You entered an invalid time. Enter a valid time.
W1021 - Invalid date entered: You entered an invalid date. Enter a valid date.

Liability

WinClock is supplied as is. The author disclaims all warranties expressed or implied, including, without limitation, the warranties of merchantability and of fitness for any purpose. The author assumes no liability for damages, direct or consequential, which may result from the use of WinClock.

Thanks!

My thanks to those BIX users who, by downloading WinClock, inspired me to write this version. Credit is due to John Ogren for suggesting the addition of international date formats. Thanks to Guy J. Gallo for his suggestions (most of which were implemented) on the alarms. Thanks to Steve Garcia, Ernest Karhu, Mark Lutton, and William Saito for their suggestions which greatly influenced this version of WinClock and especially to Peter Kaminski for help with the icons and for his numerous comments, suggestions, and support from the beginning and all through the testing stages which resulted in many of the changes in this version. My thanks to Peter W. Meek for testing and making suggestions about the new alarm options. Thanks to Steve Moshier for help with the algorithms used in the new alarm options. Thanks to Bruce Wheelock for his extensive testing. Thanks to Arlan Fuller for his sense of humor and help with various parts of WinClock.

My Other Products for MS Windows 3.0

Utilities

Pos Pos displays the mouse cursor position in relation to the screen (screen coordinates) and in relation to the window which has the input focus. Pos makes a good addition to the Windows Software Development Kit and is also useful when selecting monitor resolutions. It was originally developed to allow the user to move the mouse cursor to screen positions ahead of time. In addition, Pos can display the dimensions of a window.

RunProg RunProg allows you to run a program at a preset size. This means that you could, for example, always run PaintBrush maximized.

ChCursor If you find that you sometimes lose track of the mouse cursor on the screen, ChangeCursor will allow you to press the right mouse button to highlight the cursor. Other features include the ability to position the cursor in the center of the screen with a click of the right mouse button, and the ability to hide the cursor when you start typing and then have it displayed again when the mouse is moved.

Lock Lock is a keyboard lock and screen saver. It will automatically lock the keyboard after a certain time.

SaveSet SaveSet allows you to cause the Save Settings Check Box that appears when you exit Windows to be automatically unchecked or checked.

Click Click will produce a keyboard click . This is especially useful to those users who have used a keyboard click for DOS but have been unable to find one for MS Windows. The duration and pitch of the click may be easily changed by the user.

Games

Hop The only computer Hop-Over puzzle. Hop is a short form of Chinese Checkers. (Hop can undo moves and solve the puzzle automatically, if you want it to.)

Magic Squares The only magic squares game for Windows 3.0. (A magic square is a square array of numbers, in which each row, column, and diagonal adds up to the same number.) Can save and retrieve games, and includes several solutions on disk. Can use different size puzzles, from 3 x 3 to 9 x 9.

Slide Slide is the Classic Sliding Block Puzzle. Features: Saves and retrieves games; can undo moves one at a time; saves last game automatically; 3x3 to 9x9 puzzle size

For DOS

DskNum DskNum estimates the number of disks needed for a DOS Backup. It estimates for 360K, 720K, 1.2MB, and 1.44MB disks.

DlFile (with DirSrch) DlFile goes through your disk directories looking for the filespec you specify. If found, it prompts to delete it. This is very convenient for finding and deleting "*.BAK".

ShowDirs ShowDirs displays directories on your system that match the one specified. It can search a single drive or an entire system.

Mem Mem displays the amount of conventional memory in your computer and the amount free. It displays information about extended memory if you have it in your computer.

These programs are available on BIX, CompuServe, the Boston Computer Society's IBM BBS, and from other ShareWare libraries. If you would like more information, you may contact me as shown below.

How to Contact Me

Comments and suggestions (and reports of problems) would be greatly appreciated. You can contact me in the following ways:

1. Write: David A. Feinleib
   1430 Mass. Ave.
   Suite 306-42
   Cambridge, MA 02138
2. Send BIX mail to: pgm
3. Send CompuServe mail to: 76516,20
4. Send mail on a BBS via FIDONET (IBM UG BBS, Boston MA.) to: David Feinleib

---

Registration for WinClock

WinClock is shareware. You may make copies of this program and give them to others as long as the documentation is provided with the program, both unaltered. Registered versions of WinClock which do not have the shareware reminder message, and include a free update, are available for $15.00 + $3.00 for 5.25", $5.00 for 3.5" disks. (A 5.25" disk would be $18.00; a 3.5" disk would be $20.00.)

Shipping to Canada is an additional $1.50.

Shipping outside of North America is an additional $2.50

Please include your name, address, and current version number. (The version number may be found in the About Box.) See above for the address.

Site licenses, LAN licenses, and substantial quantity discounts are available. Customization of WinClock is available but is not included in the shareware registration fee. The fee charged for customization will depend on the amount and significance of the customization. Please contact me for more information regarding the above two items.

Quantity		Total
_____	WinClock registration(s) @ $15.00	_____
	Add for 5.25" diskettes 3.00	_____
	Add for 3.5" diskettes 5.00	_____
	Add for shipping to Canada 1.50	_____
	Add for shipping outside N. America 2.50	_____
	TOTAL ENCLOSED	_____

Name _____

Address _____

_____

_____

WinExit

Version 2.0
Copyright © 1991 by Howard Silver

Introduction to WinExit

WinExit is one of those simple little programs that can make life a little easier. The purpose of this program is simply to allow you to double-click on an icon and shutdown Windows. You can just simply exit Windows, or configure it to display a dialog box asking you if you really want to exit. This is similar to what you get from Program Manager. You can also configure WinExit to go through Program Manager to exit Windows, so as to allow you to save Program Manager settings. And for total flexibility, you can run WinExit from a folder in Program Manager and exit Windows that way.

But don't worry! This method of closing down Windows is the same way Program Manager does it. So no work will be lost. For example, let's say you have EXCEL running with a spreadsheet you just created or modified, but haven't saved yet. EXCEL (and all running programs) will get notified by Windows that it is closing down, so you have a chance to save your work.

WinExit Installation

There are a number of ways to install WinExit:

* You can just add it to the LOAD= line in your WIN.INI file. The program will load itself as an icon on the bottom of the screen. The program is setup to only allow one instance of itself. There really isn't a point in having two instances running.

* Install it as an entry in a Program Manager folder. WinExit can then be used to exit Windows by being run from that folder. See Running WinExit from a Program Manager folder for details.

Setting Options for WinExit

WinExit options are set by using the SETUP... option from WinExit's System Menu. A dialog box will appear giving you the option to change certain settings that affect the operation of WinExit. Pressing the HELP button on this dialog box will display this page of HELP. WinExit can be used to exit Windows by being run from a folder in Program Manager. See Running WinExit from a Program Manager folder for details. The SETUP dialog box has 3 options that you can set:

Use Program Manager to exit This will shutdown Windows by going through Program Manager. This will allow you to save ProgMan settings.

Quick Exit (no ProgMan save) This will shutdown Windows directly.

Exit dialog box This will display a dialog box asking you if you really want to exit Windows when you initiate the shutdown of Windows. This option is only valid if the QUICK EXIT option is set.

Basic Operations and Commands

Almost all of the basic operation of WinExit is done through the "EXIT" icon system menu. The system menu of WinExit has the following entries:

Exit Windows Choosing this will start the shutdown of Windows.
Setup... This will bring up the SETUP dialog box.
About... This will display the ABOUT dialog box.
Help This will bring up the HELP file.

Double-clicking on the "EXIT" icon of WinExit will also start the shutdown of Windows.

WinExit WIN.INI file entries (format)

The settings for WinExit are stored in the main Windows initialization file WIN.INI, which is located in the WINDOWS directory. They are located under the header [WinExit]. The following are the entries used by WinExit:

    [WinExit] AYSDialogBox=n UseProgMan=n

In the place of "n" is either a zero or one, indicating whether or not that setting is ON or OFF. The entry UseProgMan determines whether or not to go through Program Manager to shutdown Windows. The entry AYSDialogBox is used only if UseProgMan is set OFF. This option, if set ON, will display a dialog box that prompts you to choose if you really want to exit Windows.

Registration

This product is free and requires no registration.

Windows Safe

Version 1.0a
a Windows-aware replacement for CHKDSK.COM
Copyright © 1991 by Michael Maurice

Description

by Brian Livingston

Windows Safe is a replacement DOS program for CHKDSK.COM that prevents accidental corruption of Windows files. If CHKDSK /F (as in Fix) is run in a DOS session under Windows, open files may be mistakenly identified by CHKDSK as "cross-linked" files, broken into sector-sized pieces (approximately 2 KB in size), and renamed FILE0001.CHK, FILE0002.CHK, etc. See Chapter 5 for more information on this and other dangerous DOS commands. A registered version of Windows Safe is also available, which protects Windows from other dangerous DOS commands, as well as from DOS applications that might corrupt open files if run under Windows. See registration information below.

Installation Instructions

After you install WinSafe from the *Windows 3 Secrets* diskette to your hard drive:

1. Rename CHKDSK.COM in your DOS directory to CHKDSK.DOM (DOM as in "Dumb COM program"), using the following commands:

```
c:
cd \dos
REN CHKDSK.COM CHKDSK.DOM
```

2. Copy CHKDSK.EXW from your WinSafe directory to your DOS directory:

```
COPY c:\winsafe\CHKDSK.EXW c:\dos
```

3. Rename CHKDSK.EXW to CHKDSK.EXE:

```
REN CHKDSK.EXW CHKDSK.EXE
```

After you complete these steps, when you issue the command CHKDSK at a DOS prompt, CHKDSK.EXE will run the code in CHKDSK.DOM, *unless* Windows is running and you specified the /F parameter to CHKDSK. In this case, you receive the message, "Can't run in MS Windows," and a CHKDSK.EXE version number. To ascertain the version of CHKDSK.EXE you are running, issue the command CHKDSK !? (an exclamation point followed by a question mark). The program will display a copyright notice and technical support number.

Terms: MasterCard, Visa, Check or Money Order drawn on a U.S.A. bank in U.S. funds. Purchase orders (net 30) accepted for software from larger corporations. All licenses are prepaid only. All orders outside of the continental United States must be prepaid.

Windows Safe Registered U.S. Patent and Trademark Office

Registration

Mom's Software, Box 449, 391 So. Pacific Street, Rockaway, Oregon 97136, 503-355-2281 Voice, 503-355-2281 Fax (request)

Today's date: _____

The registered version of Windows Safe, which protects other DOS commands and DOS applications under Windows, is available by mail, using the order form below, or by Visa or MasterCard, using the order form or telephone.

Name: _____

(Company): _____

(Title): _____

Address: _____

City: _____

State:_____ Zip Code _____

Phone Number: _____

MasterCard: _____ or Visa: _____

Card Number: _____ Exp. Date: _____

Card Holder's Signature REQUIRED _____

WINSAFE (R) for MS-DOS

Current Version: 1.0a

* Diskette with programs and documentation files .... $20. _____

* Site license for the use of Windows Safe.

 (Includes one diskette with program disk & documentation.)

2 to 9 computers at $15 each	# computers ___x	_____
10 to 24 computers at $12 each	# computers ___x	_____
25 to 49 computers at $10 each	# computers ___x	_____
50 to 99 computers at $ 8 each	# computers ___x	_____
100 to 149 computers at $ 7 each	# computers ___x	_____
150 to 199 computers at $ 6 each	# computers ___x	_____
200 or more computers	$1000 one time fee	_____

Diskette format (choose one) 5.25" disk _____ 3.5" disk _____

Please add $2.50 for 2 day shipping and handling. _____

(Please add $5.00 for overseas orders.) _____

Total enclosed _____

* Includes a free upgrade to the next version of the software, when available.

WordBasic Macros

Copyright © 1991 by Brian Livingston

Introduction

The \WRDBASIC directory on the *Windows 3 Secrets* diskettes contains two Word for Windows document templates, which contain all the macros and key assignments described in Chapter 6, and two Word for Windows documents, which print the ANSI character set and Winword shortcut keys described in Chapter 9.

NORMAL.DOT and LETTER.DOT

These Word for Windows document templates (.DOT files) are used to separate "global" macros and key assignments, which are in the file NORMAL.DOT, from template-level typeface and style preferences, which are in LETTER.DOT.

Network administrators will especially benefit from the separation of these functions into two different document templates. You may copy NORMAL.DOT into the template directory of each Word for Windows user. When this NORMAL.DOT file is loaded by Word for Windows, the AutoExec macro in the template directs Word for Windows to automatically open the File Open dialog box, to let you choose a file. If you cancel out of this dialog box, Word for Windows starts a new document based on the LETTER.DOT template, which must be in the same directory. The separation of these two templates allows each Winword user to customize his or her own style preferences in LETTER.DOT (and any other templates in the same directory). When new macros are developed by network administrators, a new copy of NORMAL.DOT is copied to each user's directory — immediately distributing the new macros, but without wiping out any customizations made in LETTER.DOT and other templates. This is explained in more detail in Chapter 12.

Installing NORMAL.DOT and LETTER.DOT

After installing the \WRDBASIC directory from the diskette to your hard drive, add the following line to the [Microsoft Word] section of your WIN.INI file (this section refers to Word for Windows, not Word for DOS):

```
[Microsoft Word]
dotpath=c:\wrdbasic
```

Exit and re-start Windows. When you start Word for Windows, it will use the templates found in the named directory. To use an alternate set of templates in a different directory, change the named directory, re-start Windows, and re-start Word for Windows.

CHARSET.DOC and SHORTCUT.DOC

Important: Before opening these two Word for Windows documents, first open a blank document and set View to Draft mode. These documents otherwise take a very long time to display — CHARSET.DOC requires more than one minute, if Winword is not set to Draft. *Even better:* use File Find to locate these document names, then click Print to print them. This avoids having to open the documents at all. These documents require a PostScript printer to print. Additionally, if you do not have a Dingbats screen font installed, CHARSET.DOC's use of the Dingbats font will show on your screen in the Times screen font — but it will print correctly.

CHARSET.DOC prints the entire ANSI character set, from character 32 to 255 (characters lower than 32 are nonprinting control characters), using the Text, Symbol, and Dingbats type families. This printout can be useful in testing the compatibility or "look" of different PostScript and "PostScript-compatible" printers. The unused characters between 0128 and 0159 are included in the chart as "hidden text." If printed, these characters ordinarily print as blobs, so they were excluded. But you should try printing this file once from Word for Windows using File Print Options Hidden-Text, anyway, to see if these characters produce different results using your particular printer. For example, Adobe Type Manager for Windows produces (on LaserJet printers) a "dotless i" and two accent characters at positions 0157 through 0159, which do not appear when printing to genuine Adobe PostScript printers, such as the Apple LaserWriter and LaserJets with the Adobe PostScript cartridge.

SHORTCUT.DOC prints a two-page chart showing all the key combinations possible under Windows, and which of the combinations are already assigned to a function by Word for Windows. Printing out this chart can be useful in determining which key combinations are available for you to assign your own macros to. Notice that the Ctrl+Shift key combinations are almost always free in Windows applications, and are good choices for your macro key assignments. (The Ctrl+Shift+Alt combinations are not shown on this chart, since few applications or users would want to assign macros to such inconvenient "shortcut" key combinations.)

Once you have determined your key assignments, you can type them into this chart and print as many copies as you like. Again, this requires a printer that can handle the small typefaces involved — such as a PostScript printer. Notice that the "borders" between categories are printed as graphics to your printer. If your printer runs out of memory while printing this chart, you may need to lower the printing resolution in the Control Panel from 300 dpi to 150 dpi (not possible with Microsoft's own Windows PostScript driver, only third-party drivers), or eliminate some of the borders.

Registration

These copyrighted macros are free and require no registration.

W.BAT

W.BAT is a batch program that starts Windows and sets a colorful "banner" prompt that appears in DOS sessions. The use of this batch program is described in the text that accompanies Figure 5-1 in Chapter 5. You must have the line DEVICE=c:\dos\ANSI.SYS in your CONFIG.SYS file before using this batch program.

This is a free, public-domain program and is not copyrighted.

Zip Manager

Version 3.0W
Copyright © 1991 Moon Valley Software, Inc.

Contents at a Glance

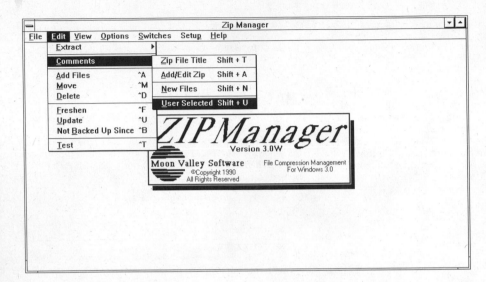

Quick Start

Installing Zip Manager

If you decide to use Zip Manager before reading this documentation, here are the minimum requirements needed to setup Zip Manager:

-> **Please Note:** In addition to the Zip Manager program files, you will also need the following programs in order to use *all* of Zip Manager's features: PKZIP.EXE, PKUNZIP.EXE, ZIP2EXE.EXE, PKZIPFIX.EXE, ARC-E.COM, LHARC.EXE, SCAN.EXE, and LIST.COM. Zip Manager will function with just PKZIP and PKUNZIP, although the other features will not be available. See Appendix B for information on where to obtain these programs.

If you are upgrading from Zip Manager 2.X, read the Upgrading to Zip Manager 3.0 section before proceeding any further!

1. Make a sub-directory where you would like to keep your Zip Manager program files. Copy the contents of the distribution disk to your directory. If you have the shareware version, unzip the ZM30W.zip in your target directory.
2. Check to see that the following files are present:
ZM.EXE -> The MAIN Windows Executable Program.
ZMSCAN.EXE -> The DOS Command Line Interpreter for Zip Manager.
ZMSHELL.EXE -> The DOS Program for Extracting Zip's to a temp directory or ram drive.
ZMSCAN.PIF -> The Program Information File for ZMSCAN.EXE.
ZM.HLP -> The Windows hypertext help file for Zip Manager.
ZM30W.DOC -> The Zip Manager 3.0W Documentation (This File).
REGISTER.FRM -> The shareware registration form.(Please!)
UPDATE.DOC -> Version 3.0W update information.
PRNDOCS.COM -> Program to print the program documentation.
README.1ST -> Important information not in the documentation.
ZMDIAG.TXT -> How to use Zip Manager to test bios compatibility. Included as reference material. Not Applicable to Version 3.0W

Introduction

Zip Manager is a complete Windows 3.0 environment for PKZIP, PKUNZIP, ARC-E, and LHarc file compression utilities. It also supports the virus detection program SCAN, and the popular LIST program. If you do a large amount of file compression work, Zip Manager will increase your productivity significantly. the nature of the Windows GUI (Graphical User Interface) allows you to maintain and create compressed files with a high degree of accuracy and speed. Once you start using Zip Manager you won't want to work any other way!

Zip Manager is being distributed as shareware; it is not free software. After you have evaluated it, you are obligated to register your copy if you continue using it. You are encouraged to make copies of this program and pass them along to your friends, your favorite BBS, etc.

This documentation thoroughly covers the operation of Zip Manager. If you are in a hurry to start, please refer to the Quick Start Section of the documentation. This will ensure that you have installed Zip Manager correctly. If you are upgrading from version 2.X of Zip Manager be sure to read the Upgrading From 2.X section also.

-> Notation Convention <-

Important points throughout the documentation are highlighted by this -> symbol. If you decide to give this document only a cursory read through, please be sure you read the highlighted portions! They contain important information that is crucial for proper program operation.

3. Add the directory into which you have installed Zip Manager to the path statement in your autoexec.bat file.
4. The files ZM.EXE, ZMSCAN.EXE, ZMSHELL.EXE and ZMSCAN.PIF must be kept in the directory you installed Zip Manager in. This will ensure that Zip Manager can locate ZMSCAN.EXE, ZMSHELL.EXE, and Windows will find ZMSCAN.PIF.
5. Add ZM.EXE to a Windows Program Manager group.
   -> Setting the Program Defaults <-
6. Run Zip Manager and select Setup from the menu. You need to tell Zip Manager where it can find the files it needs. the Input Boxes are horizontal scrolling fields which will hold up to a MAXIMUM of 64 characters. for each program file you will need to specify the COMPLETE DRIVE, PATH, AND FILE NAME. See the example below:
   [Setup Example]
   PKZIP Location: c:\utilities\pkzip.exe
   PKUNZIP Location: c:\utilities\pkunzip.exe
   ZIP2EXE Location: c:\utilities\zip2exe.exe
   PKZIPFIX Location: c:\utilities\pkzipfix.exe
   LHARC Location: d:\bin\pgms\lharc.exe
   ARC-E Location: f:\arcs\arc-e.com
   SCAN Location: e:\rx\scan.exe
   LIST Location: c:\utilities\list.com
   TEXT EDITOR Location: d:\path\Editor Name(Your Favorite Text Editor Or Word Processor)
7. The above directions will let get you started using Zip Manager. In order to learn the full potential and correct operation of Zip Manager please read the documentation!

-> Upgrading to Zip Manager 3.0 From Version 2.0

If you have been using Zip Manager 2.X it is vitally important that you follow the instructions below exactly!

1. Delete the following files from your hard drive! ZM.EXE, ZM1.EXE, ZM.HLP, ZM1.PIF, PKZIP.PIF and PKUNZIP.PIF.
2. Zip Manager 3.0 is an entirely new program and shares nothing in common with previous versions.
3. Just to stress again, please be sure that you have deleted all of the files Listed in #1 above.

Using Zip Manager

80386 vs 80286/8088 Operation

-> When you are using a 80386 computer, Zip Manager will open a DOS Window so that you may see the progression of your request. On a 80286/8088 computer, Zip Manager will open a full-screen DOS Window since these processors are not capable of running concurrent virtual machines like the 80386.

Full LAN Compatibility

Zip Manager is fully compatible with all networks currently supported by Windows 3.0. It will provide the user with a "File Currently in Use by Another User" message if two people try to access the same Zip File.

Complete Support of Self-Extracting EXE Files

-> Zip Manager fully supports self-extracting EXE files created with the ZIP2EXE program provided with PKZIP. You can perform exactly the same functions on these files as those described in this manual for Zip files.

A copy of this program and its complete documentation is also on the disk that came with this book.

Appendix C

License Agreement

No part of this manual may be reproduced, transmitted, transcribed, stored in a retrieval system, or translated into any language (natural or binary), in any form or by any means, except as described in the following license agreement or without the express prior written consent of Moon Valley Software Inc. The use of Zip Manager is subject to the following terms and conditions.

Title to the Licensed Software

Title to the licensed software is NOT transferred to the end user. The end user is granted an exclusive license to use the software on a SINGLE computer or computer work station. EACH computer or computer work station must have its own licensed copy of the software.

Copyright Protection

Zip Manager is copyrighted material. It is protected by the copyright laws of the United States, the State of Arizona, and other proprietary rights of Moon Valley Software, Inc. You may not make any changes or modifications to Zip Manager or this manual. You may not decompile, disassemble, or otherwise reverse-engineer the software in any way. You may make copies of Zip Manager only under the terms of the section entitled "Limited License to Copy the Licensed Software". You may use Zip Manager on a trial basis provided you do not violate the protection afforded the licensed software by the copyright laws, and you agree to the terms of the license agreement. If you use Zip Manager on a regular basis you are obligated to purchase it.

Limited Warranty

Moon Valley Software does not warrant that the licensed software will meet your requirements or that the operation of the software will be uninterrupted or error free. The warranty does not cover any media or documentation which has been subjected to damage or abuse by you or others. The software warranty does not cover any copy of the licensed software which has been altered or changed in any way.

ANY IMPLIED WARRANTIES INCLUDING ANY WARRANTIES OF MERCHANTABILITY OR FITNESS FOR A PARTICULAR PURPOSE ARE LIMITED TO THE TERM OF THE EXPRESS

WARRANTIES. Some States do not allow limitations on how long an implied warranty lasts, so the above limitation may not apply to you.

Other Warranties

The warranties set forth above are in lieu of any and all other express or implied warranties, whether oral, written, or implied, and the remedies set forth above are the sole and exclusive remedies.

Limitation of Liability

Moon Valley Software is not responsible for any problems or damage caused by the licensed software that may result from using the licensed software. This includes, but is not limited to, computer hardware, computer software, operating systems, and any computer or computing accessories. End user agrees to hold Moon Valley Software Inc. harmless for any problems arising from the use of the software.

Moon Valley Software SHALL NOT IN ANY CASE BE LIABLE FOR ANY SPECIAL, INCIDENTAL, CONSEQUENTIAL, INDIRECT OR OTHER SIMILAR DAMAGES ARISING FROM ANY BREACH OF THESE WARRANTIES EVEN IF Moon Valley Software OR ITS AGENTS OR DISTRIBUTORS HAVE BEEN ADVISED OF THE POSSIBILITY OF SUCH DAMAGES. Some states do not allow the exclusion or limitation of incidental or consequential damages, so the above limitation or exclusion may not apply to you. In no case shall Moon Valley Software's liability exceed the license fees paid for the right to use the licensed software, or a sum no greater than one Dollar ($1.00), whichever is less.

Limited License to Copy the Software

You are granted a limited license to copy Zip Manager ONLY FOR THE TRIAL USE OF OTHERS subject to the terms of this software license agreement described herein, and the conditions described below are met. Zip Manager MUST be copied in an unmodified form and ZM301.ZIP MUST contain the following files:

ZM.EXE The MAIN Windows Executable Program

ZMSCAN.EXE The DOS Command Line Interpreter for Zip Manager

ZMSHELL.EXE The DOS Program for Extracting Zip's to A temp directory or ram drive

ZMSCAN.PIF The Program Information File for ZMSCAN.EXE

ZM.HLP The Windows hypertext help file for Zip Manager

ZM30W.DOC The Zip Manager 3.0W Documentation (This File).

REGISTER.FRM Thee shareware registration form.(Please!)

UPDATE.DOC -Version 3.0W update information

PRNDOCS.COM Program to print the program documentation

README.1ST Important information not in the documentation

ZMDIAG.TXT How to use Zip Manager to test BIOS compatibility.

-> No fee, charge or other compensation may be accepted or requested by anyone without the express written permission of Moon Valley Software. Public Domain Disk Vendors May NOT CHARGE a fee for Zip Manager itself. However you may include Zip Manager on a diskette for which you charge a nominal distribution fee. The purchaser of said diskette must be informed in advance that the fee paid to acquire the diskette does NOT relieve said purchaser from paying the Registration Fee for Zip Manager if said purchaser uses Zip Manager.

-> Operators of electronic bulletin board systems (Sysops) may post Zip Manager for downloading by their users without written permission ONLY AS LONG AS THE ABOVE CONDITIONS ARE MET. A fee may be charged for access to the BBS AS LONG AS NO SPECIFIC FEE IS CHARGED FOR DOWNLOADING Zip Manager files without first obtaining express written permission from Moon Valley Software to charge such a fee.

The above constitutes the license agreement for Zip Manager. It supersedes any and all previous license agreements.

Registration Information

To register your copy of Zip Manager, please use the order form below, or the file called register.frm that is supplied with the program. The registration fee is $21.95 Return this form along with your remittance to:

> Moon Valley Software Inc.
> 107 East Paradise Lane
> Phoenix, AZ 85022 USA

Special prices/discounts on quantity orders, corporate site licenses, and dealer pricing are available. Please call for details. You can order by phone using your MasterCard or VISA. Call us at (602) 375-9502, Mon. - Fri., 9:00 a.m. - 4:00 p.m., MST ONLY. On-Line BBS Registration at 602-375-0531 12 - 2400 bps 24 hrs a day

Please send me:

_____ Copy(s) of Zip Manager 3.0 @ $21.95 ea. $ _____

Disk Size 3.5 or 5.25 (Circle one)

Shipping (per Item) @ 1.50 ea.   Total $ _____

(U.S.and Canada, $1.50 per Item;
All Other Countries, $5.00)   Subtotal $ _____

Arizona Residents please add Sales Tax @ 5% $ _____

Total (U.S.Funds drawn on U.S.Bank) $ _____

Payment by: ( )Check ( )MC ( )VISA

Card #:

Exp. Date: _____

Signature of cardholder (Required!):

_____

Prices subject to change without notice. Current prices can be confirmed by calling (602) 375-9502.

Ship to Information (Please Type or Print)

Name: _____

Company: _____

Address: _____

_____

_____

Phone W: _____

Eve: _____

Appendix A
Windows Technical Support and CompuServe

Technical support is available for Windows and Windows applications primarily in two distinct forms: telephone support and electronic-mail support via the CompuServe bulletin board system.

The vendors listed below provide technical support through both of these forms. Interestingly, leaving a message on CompuServe regarding a technical-support question often gets you the answer you want faster than using the telephone. Vendors' telephone support lines are frequently busy, and when you do get through, the person you need to speak with may be unavailable and unable to return your call immediately. These same vendors, however, usually have someone check their CompuServe area for messages several times a day, and may respond with more detailed information than they could over the phone.

When you log onto CompuServe, you can immediately change to the area of the vendor to which you want to leave a message by typing GO *forum,* where *forum* is the Forum Name shown in the following chart. You may also need to change to a section number within that forum, if it's used by several vendors. My thanks to Brian Moura, a system operator who compiles this information.

An important forum, which is not listed because it supports *all* Microsoft products, not just Windows, is the Microsoft Knowledge Base, which is reached by typing GO MSKB at a CompuServe prompt. This textbase consists of thousands of tips and anomalies affecting Microsoft software and third-party computers and peripherals. (Microsoft also distributes similar information directly to corporations, in a fee-based program known as On-line Plus.)

For more information on CompuServe, contact CompuServe, Customer Service, P.O. Box 20212, 5000 Arlington Centre Blvd., Columbus, OH 43220; 800-848-8990 or 614-457-8650.

Windows Phone Lines and Forums

Vendor Name	Product Name(s)	Telephone Number(s)	CompuServe Forum Name	Sec.
Microsoft	Windows	206-637-7098	WINNEW	
	Windows Optimization	206-637-7098	WINADV	
	Windows Programming	206-637-7098	MSOPSYS	8
	Excel for Windows	206-637-7099	MSEXCEL	3
	PowerPoint, Project, Winword	206-637-7099	MSAPP	2, 7, 12
Access Softek	Dragnet, Prompt, Take Note	415-654-0116	WINAPA	2
Adobe	Illustrator, Streamline	415-961-0911	ADOBE	5
Adobe	Adobe Type Manager	415-961-0911	ADOBE	14
Aldus	PageMaker	206-628-2320	ALDUS	3
Alien Computing	FaxIt for Windows	805-947-1310	PCEO	5
Aristocad	More Windows	800-338-2629 or 415-426-5355	XEROX	7
Asymetrix	Tool Book	206-637-1500	WINNEW	4
Bell Atlantic	Thinx	800-388-4465 or 304-284-1370	WINAPC	2
CE Software	Calendar Maker PC	515-224-1995	MACAVEN	4
Computer Presentations	Color Lab, Image Prep	513-281-3222	WINAPB	13
Corel Systems	Corel Draw	613-728-8200	WINAPB	2
DaVinci	DaVinci E-Mail	800-328-4624 or 919-881-4320	WINAPA	3
DCA	Crosstalk for Windows	404-442-3210	XTALK	10
Delrina Technology	PerForm Pro, WinFax	716-855-3676	WINAPB	16
Echelon Development	Window Craft	617-272-0999	WINAPB	14
Foresight Resources	Windows Drafix CAD	816-891-8418	PCVENA	13
Future Soft	DynaComm for Windows	713-496-9400	WINAPA	4
Geographix	SeisMap	303-595-0596	WINAPA	5
hDC Computer	File Apps, First Apps, Express	206-885-5550	WINAPA	6
Hewlett-Packard	New Wave	208-323-2551	HP	10
Hi-Q International	APE	904-756-8988	WINAPA	7
ICOM Simulations	Intermission	708-520-4440	WINAPA	16

Vendor Name	Product Name(s)	Telephone Number(s)	CompuServe Forum Name	Sec.
Kidasa	Milestones	800-666-3886 or 512-328-0168	WINAPB	9
Knowledge Garden	Knowledge Pro	518-766-3000	WINAPB	15
Lotus	Notes	617-577-8500	LOTUSB	10
Lotus Samna	Amí and SmarText	800-831-9679 or 404-256-2272	SAMFORUM	2, 6
Matesys	Object View, Simple Win	415-925-2900	WINAPC	1
MCAE	Inertia	317-497-1550	WINAPA	8
Meta Software	Design/IDEF, /OA, MetaDesign	617-576-6920	WINAPA	9
Micrografx	Charisma, Designer, Xport	214-234-2694	WINAPA	10
NBI	Legacy	800-624-1111 or 303-444-5710	WINAPB	3
Olduvai	Read-It OCR	305-665-4665	MACBVEN	6
Owl International	Guide	800-344-9737 or 206-747-3203	WINAPB	4
Polaris	PackRat	619-743-7800	WINAPA	11
Precision	Superbase 2, Superbase 4	214-929-4888	WINAPA	12
Publishing Technologies	BatchWorks, File Organizer	800-782-8324 or 512-682-1700	WINAPA	13
Roykore	ABC Flowcharter, Opus I	415-563-9175	WINAPA	14
Softbridge	Bridge Batch, Tool Kit	617-576-2257	WINAPB	11
SoftCraft	Soft Fonts	608-257-3300	WINAPB	10
SoftView	MacInTax/Windows, TaxView	805-385-5000	WINAPB	5
Software Ventures	Microphone II	415-644-3232	MACBVEN	7
Stirling Group	Dbx/Install/Mem Shield	708-307-9197	WINAPC	3
T/Maker	Windows Clip Art	415-962-0195	MACBVEN	9
Whitewater Group	Actor, Resource Toolkit, et. al.	800-869-1144 or 708-328-3800	WINAPB	6
Wilson WindowWare	WinBatch, WinEdit, et. al.	206-937-9335	WINAPA	15
WUGNET	Windows Journal	215-565-1681	WINAPB	8
Xerox	FormBase, Ventura Publisher	800-822-8221 or 619-673-6000	XEROX	14, 4
Zenographics	Import, Pixie, SuperPrint	714-851-6352	WINAPB	12
ZSoft	SoftType, Type Foundry	404-428-0008	WINAPB	7

Appendix B
Windows Information Resources

The following are some of the best sources of up-to-the-minute information on Windows — newsletters, technical notes, and conferences. This is by no means a complete list, but includes most of the major Windows-specific offerings.

Windows Periodicals

Acknowledge, The Windows Letter
114 Talmadge Road
Mendham, NJ 07945
201-543-6033
A newsletter on technical developments in Windows applications.

Inside Microsoft Windows
The Cobb Group
6420 Bunsen Parkway, Suite 300
800-223-8720 or 502-491-1900
Tutorials on using Windows effectively.

Windows & OS/2 Magazine
1101B Eugenia Place
Carpenteria, CA 93013
805-566-1282
A glossy magazine on Windows and OS/2 applications and news.

Windows Journal
Windows User Group Network (WUGNET)
P.O. Box 1967
Media, PA 19063
215-565-1861
A bimonthly magazine with a diskette of free and shareware programs.

Windows Shopper's Guide
White Fox Communications
1800 NW 169th Ave., Suite 700B
Beaverton, OR 97006
503-629-5612
The best single source for listings of all available Windows applications.

Windows Watcher
Computh!nk, Inc.
15127 NE 24th, Suite 344
Redmond, WA 98052-5530
206-881-7354
An expensive corporate newsletter of Windows industry news.

WPMA View
Windows and Presentation Manager Association (WPMA)
P.O. Box 851385
Richardson, TX 75085-1385
214-234-8857
A newsletter and association for commercial and corporate developers.

Windows Technical Papers

Windows Resource Kit
Microsoft Corp.
1 Microsoft Way
Redmond, WA 98052-6399
800-642-7676 or 206-882-8080
A binder with papers on customizing Setup, PIFs, networks, etc.

Windows Seminars

Windows & OS/2 Conference
CM Ventures
5720 Hollis St.
Emeryville, CA 94608
415-601-5000
A semi-annual conference, Spring in California, Fall in Massachusetts.

Windows Seminar
Mastering Computers, Inc.
11000 N. Scottsdale Rd., Suite 175
Scottsdale, AZ 85254
602-998-7500
A series of one-day seminars in various cities on Windows configuration.

Windows World
The Interface Group
300 First Ave.
Needham, MA 02194-2722
617-449-6600
A conference and show held in conjunction with Comdex/Spring.

Index

Hardware is indexed under the manufacturer's name.

IDG Books Worldwide Registration Card
Windows 3 Secrets

Fill this out—and hear about updates to this book & other IDG Books Worldwide products!

Name _____

Company/Title _____

Address _____

City/State/Zip _____

What is the single most important reason you bought this book? _____

_____

Where did you buy this book?
- ❑ Bookstore (Name _____)
- ❑ Electronics/Software Store (Name _____)
- ❑ Advertisement (If magazine, which? _____)
- ❑ Mail Order (Name of catalog/mail order house _____)
- ❑ Other: _____

How did you hear about this book?
- ❑ Book review in: _____
- ❑ Advertisement in: _____
- ❑ Catalog
- ❑ Found in store
- ❑ Other: _____

How many computer books do you purchase a year?
- ❑ 1
- ❑ 2-5
- ❑ 6-10
- ❑ More than 10

How would you rate the overall content of this book?
- ❑ Very good
- ❑ Good
- ❑ Satisfactory
- ❑ Poor

Why? _____

What chapters did you find most valuable? _____

What did you find least useful? _____

What kind of chapter or topic would you add to future editions of this book? _____

_____

Please give us any additional comments. _____

_____

Thank you for your help!

❑ I liked this book! By checking this box, I give you permission to use my name and quote me in future IDG Books Worldwide promotional materials.

Fold Here

Place
stamp
here

IDG Books Worldwide, Inc.
155 Bovet Road
Suite 730
San Mateo, CA 94402

Attn: Reader Response

DISCLAIMER AND COPYRIGHT NOTICE

NOTE

IDG Books Worldwide Inc. warrants that the physical diskettes that accompany this book are free from defects in materials and workmanship for a period of 60 days from the date of purchase of this book. If your disk(s) are defective, return them to IDG Books Worldwide, Attn: Windows 3 Secrets Disks, c/o IDG Peterborough, 80 Elm St., Peterborough, NH 03458, for replacement (within the warranty period). The remedy for the breach of this warranty will be limited to replacement and will not encompass any other damages, including but not limited to loss of profit, and special, incidental, consequential, or other claims.

3 ½-inch disk format available. The enclosed disks are in 1.2MB 5 ¼-inch format. If you don't have a drive in that size and cannot arrange to transfer the data to the disk size you need, you can obtain the code on 3 ½-inch 1.44MB disks by writing: IDG Books Worldwide, Attn: Windows 3 Secrets Disks, c/o IDG Peterborough, 80 Elm St., Peterborough, NH 03458; or call 800-282-6657. Please allow three to four weeks for delivery.

Complete Installation Instructions for the *Windows 3 Secrets* Diskettes _____

Attention: Before installing any of the shareware on these disks, read the Disclaimer and Copyright Notice on the previous page.

STEPS:

Preparing to Install the Programs

Step 1. First, check your computer for viruses. Place Disk #1 in your floppy drive and, at a DOS prompt, type A: \SCAN C:. Scan each of the hard drives in your system. If the SCAN program reports, "No viruses found," go on to Step 2. If your computer *has* any viruses, read the Viruscan chapter for information on how to remove them before you install any other software.

Step 2. Copy the WinUnzip program. Using Windows' File Manager (or your favorite utility), create a directory called WINUNZIP on your hard drive. Copy the file WINUNZIP.EXE from the WINUNZIP directory on Disk #1 to the WINUNZIP directory on your hard drive. Place this directory on your DOS Path by opening your AUTOEXEC.BAT file in a text editor such as Notepad and adding ;*c:*\WINUNZIP to the end of your PATH= statement (where *c:* is the drive on which you create the directory WINUNZIP). Exit Windows and reboot your PC to make this change take effect. (WinUnzip is a free program for use in installing all the other programs, which are "compressed" in order to get as many as possible on the disks. WinUnzip requires Windows' 286 standard or 386 enhanced mode. In real mode, use the DOS program PKUNZIP—in the PKZIP directory— from Disk #2.)

Installing Specific Programs

(Use steps 3–5 each time you want to install a particular program from the floppy disks.)

Step 3. Create a new directory. Pull down File Manager's File menu and click Create-Directory to make a new directory on the hard drive you wish to install a program to. To install the Magic screen-saver, as an example, create a directory such as C:\MAGIC. Then, open a directory window by double-clicking on that directory.

Step 4. Decompress the program. To install a program (using Magic as an example), first place the correct disk in drive A: (see the file listing on each disk label), pull down File Manager's File menu, click Run, then type

    WINUNZIP A:\MAGIC\MAGIC.ZIP

and click OK. This decompresses and copies Magic's files from the floppy to the current directory on your hard drive. The files expand to about twice their compressed size. (The programs ComReset and W.BAT are not compressed and can simply be copied to your hard disk.)

Step 5. Run the program. At this point, your new program is installed, and you can run it by double-clicking on the .EXE file in the current window. You may first want to read the text file that comes with each program to see how to configure the program the best way for your system; for example, to add it to your Path or to Program Manager.

Note: The following programs require one additional step:

Almanac:	run ALMSETUP.EXE before ALMANAC.EXE.
Magic:	run INSTALL.EXE before MAGIC.EXE.
WinBatch:	run SETUP.EXE before WINBATCH.EXE.
WinSafe:	see the WinSafe chapter.

That's it! Hope you enjoy these programs.

You need to hear both sides of the story, the pros and cons, to make sound decisions.

We're the only *independent* conference and exposition focusing on Windows and OS/2.

And because we are independent, we can give you what you need: unbiased answers and practical solutions.

Take a seat at the Windows & OS/2 Conference.

OVER 40 MUST-ATTEND CONFERENCE SESSIONS

22 FAST TRACKS

DAY-LONG TUTORIALS

250 TOP EXHIBITORS

PLUS NON-STOP EXHIBIT FLOOR ATTRACTIONS

PC Week Lab Shoot-Out ■ The Multimedia Showcase ■ Windows & OS/2 Test Drive Center ■ Hands-on Training Classes, And Much More!

WINDOWS & OS/2 CONFERENCE

August 14-16, 1991
World Trade Center
Boston, Mass.

If you haven't heard the latest news about Windows and OS/2, you'd better sit down.

Yes! Send me complete information on:

❑ Windows & OS/2 Conference, Fall '91, Boston
❑ Other upcoming Windows & OS/2 Conferences

NAME _____ TITLE _____

COMPANY _____

CITY _____ STATE _____ ZIP _____

( ) ( )
PHONE FAX

Please send information to these colleagues:

NAME _____ TITLE _____

NAME _____ TITLE _____

Count on us to deliver the goods.

The Windows & OS/2 Conference offers you a comprehensive conference program and diverse exposition that can give you the objective answers and solutions you need and demand.

You're reading and using this invaluable book because to do your job you must know more; you need real-life answers to every-day questions concerning the implementation and management of Windows.

Clearly, the Windows &

OS/2 Conference is the logical choice for getting the impartial information you can trust and need.

It's the one conference that deserves to be on your "must attend" list.

The Windows & OS/2 Conference program and packed Exhibition floor can open your mind to a new world of possibilities.

Mail this card now for complete information.
It could be the most important computer event you'll attend this year.

NO POSTAGE
NECESSARY
IF MAILED IN
THE UNITED
STATES

BUSINESS REPLY MAIL
FIRST- CLASS MAIL PERMIT NO. 1595 OAKLAND, CA

POSTAGE WILL BE PAID BY ADDRESSEE

CM Ventures, Inc
5720 Hollis Street
Emeryville, Ca 94608